U.S. CIVIL WAR
STORE CARDS

U.S. CIVIL WAR STORE CARDS

Second Edition

George and Melvin Fuld

Quarterman Publications, Inc.
Lawrence, Massachusetts

Copyright 1972, 1973, 1974, and 1975 by The Civil War Token Society.

Copyright © 1975 by Quarterman Publications, Inc.

All rights reserved. This impression may not be
reproduced in any form without written permission.

First Edition published in 1972 by The Civil War Token Society. This Second Edition contains those additions and corrections compiled by The Civil War Token Society which are in the process of being published in the *Journal of The Civil War Token Society,* and which have been placed on the appropriate pages. A publisher's foreword has been added to this Quarterman edition. A final section containing a catalog of the American Numismatic Society's collection of Civil War store cards has been added with the permission of the Civil War Token Society.

International Standard Book Number: 0-88000-135-6
Library of Congress Catalog Card Number: 75-1785

Printed in the United States of America

Quarterman Publications, Inc.
5 South Union Street
Lawrence, Massachusetts 01843

PUBLISHER'S FOREWORD

This republication of George and Melvin Fuld's *U.S. Civil War Store Cards* after a period of only three years since its original 1972 publication will attest to the significance of this work as well as to the current number of its devotees. It is, in the opinion of many, one of the few, new, definitive works on American numismatics to appear in the last decade and represents a standard of comprehensiveness and utility that should be the objective of all references on collecting specialties.

The publishers have reduced the size of the page and illustrations from that of the original 8-1/2 × 11 format in an effort to make this edition more practical to use and transport, as well as to keep production and printing costs within reason. Even so, this is a compromise and its relative success or failure cannot be accurately determined beforehand.

This edition also incorporates a rather lengthy listing of "New Finds and Corrections" which, for the most part, have been published in recent issues of the *Journal of the Civil War Token Society*. These corrections have been typed, reduced and then stripped in on the appropriate pages of text so that they occur in their proper places. Small typographic distinctions will, on inspection, allow the reader to determine in what places these corrections or additions have been made.

The collection and compilation of this material has been diligently and painstakingly accomplished by Jon Harris working together with Clifton A. Temple. Harris acted as major contributor to these corrections through constant comparison between tokens and text for a period of two years, while Temple acted as final compiler of edited corrections, incorporating all contributions and resolving any inconsistencies. The Civil War Token Society, on behalf of all enthusiasts, expresses a sincere debt of gratitude to these gentlemen for so competently achieving such high objectives. Dale Cade, Jack Detwiler and David Gladfelter, also prominent authorities in this field, have made large contributions in this correction activity.

Additionally, the following members of the Civil War Token Society have all contributed in important ways to this new information:

Herman M. Aqua	Glenn H. Firestone
Richard E. Brown	Milton J. Gordon
Lloyd Brumley	Stephen M. Gorman
John W. Canfield	Don E. Grampp
George Fuld	James H. Hall
Melvin Fuld	Harvey L. Hebert

Robert J. Herzog
Byron Johnson
Barbara A. Kelly
David W. Lane
H. Joseph Levine
Robert W. Marvin
Richard McFerran
Roger Merritt
Forest Mintz
Robert G. Mitchell

Helen E. Moore
Michael J. Renner
Niles K. Shultz
Neil Sowards
Kenneth N. Trobaugh
Charles Urquhart
Terry E. Wantz
Millard W. Wasczak
Paul F. White

In addition to these new corrections, this edition includes a few additional photographs not present in the first edition. These have been placed in their proper position in the text. Appreciation is due to Jon Harris, Kenneth N. Trobaugh, Doug Watson, John Canfield and others for providing these illustrations. Other illustrations were reproduced from appropriate issues of the *Journal*.

Certain important changes and additions have been incorporated into the original front matter to the book. A few new metals abbreviations have been defined and a new tabular display of price information has been developed by George and Melvin Fuld.

The original publishing work on this book was accomplished for the Civil War Token Society by Doug Watson. The existence of the original edition, and therefore this republication, owes more than a passing debt to this man. With specialized knowledge and technical skills acquired both before and during his activities with Krause Publications, Inc., of Iola, Wisconsin, he developed the typography and illustrations of the original edition and brought them to a condition that allowed the printing of the original book. An excess of 1,000 hours of personal involvement by Watson represents as major a contribution by a non-author as we have knowledge of in any numismatic publication. The publishers of this edition, as well as the readers, are indebted to Watson for his unique and valuable contributions to the study and understanding of this collecting specialty.

Shortly after the printer had all of the material for this edition, Jon Harris completed his research of the unlisted Civil War storecards in the A.N.S. collection. Published in pamphlet form, the Harris research was felt to be extremely important information which holders of this edition should not be without. A compromise was developed to achieve this end and the Harris Catalog is reprinted here in a separate section at the back of the book.

Lawrence, Massachusetts　　　　　　　　　　　　Quarterman Publications, Inc.
January 1975

Postscript: The price guide on page V of the introduction is obsolete and should be ignored.

THE
CIVIL WAR
TOKEN SOCIETY

The Civil War was the moment of greatest challenge to our Federal system of government. From a numismatic standpoint, the War Between the States also placed the greatest stress upon our circulating medium of exchange. Heavy inflation followed the outbreak of the war; metallic currency was widely hoarded; the Government suspended specie payments and all coins vanished from circulation. Various stopgap measures such as postage stamps, private fractional currency and cardboard checks failed to meet the need for small change, until a variety of metal tokens came on the scene. These became accepted and for three years, 1862, 63, 64, filled merchants' needs for one-cent coins. They also served another purpose: To advertise the merchants and their businesses.

More than 10,000 varieties of Civil War tokens are known. It is estimated that 24-million pieces were issued, the largest outpouring of emergency money in our nation's history. An act of Congress in 1864 stopped their circulation after some merchants refused to redeem them.

QUESTIONS AND ANSWERS:

Q. Does anyone have a complete collection of all the Civil War tokens?

A. No one has ever assembled a complete collection, there are so many different varieties. It is doubtful whether anyone has even assembled a complete set of one token from every town. Some of the ways people collect CWT are as follows: one from every State; one from each town within a particular State; all the merchant tokens in a particular town; a representative sampling of patriotic designs; tokens issued by particular tradesmen such as engravers, doctors, barkeepers, etc.; topics such as Indian heads, historical figures, etc.; metal varieties; merchants with interesting names.

Q. Since many of these tokens are very rare, are they expensive?

A. Prices vary, but most tokens in average VF-EF condition cost $4 to $15 each. Some of the common varieties are fortunately among the most interesting conversation pieces. Occasionally a very rare token, especially in an off-metal, will sell for $100 and more. A price of $1,800 has been reported for a CWT; they have also sold in large lots for $2 each.

The Civil War Token Society

was formed in 1967 as a result of the new interest in Civil War tokens. It quickly attracted several hundred members. Its by-laws state: "The society is organized exclusively for educational purposes and in furtherance of such purposes, to promote, stimulate and advance the study of Civil War tokens along educational, historic and scientific lines." Among the Society's activities are:
* Publication of a quarterly Journal.
* Sponsorship of regular token auctions in which members may both sell and bid.
* Library open to all members.
* Society's own slide program.
* State chapters with such activities as exhibits, other programs.
* Attribution service.

One of the main benefits of the Society is the chance to meet other collectors with similar interest and exchange information. Because there are so many different kinds of Civil War tokens, most collectors specialize in their own areas of interest, and thus each person's collection is different.

The tokens were issued in 23 of the then-existing 35 States, and nearly 400 towns and cities. All sorts of merchants issued them, even undertakers and taxidermists. One token is even inscribed with the name of the City of New York — "I.O.U. One Cent" — although it is doubtful that this was an authorized issue of the city.

Some of the tokens did not have merchant advertising on them, but instead, patriotic inscriptions and designs, such as the Flag, Washington, Lincoln, the head of Liberty, Capitol, U.S. shield, North Star, etc. Those with advertising are called "store cards" and those with patriotic themes "patriotics" by collectors.

A great deal of interest in the tokens developed during the Civil War Centennial, when two guidebooks were published by George and Melvin Fuld, one on storecards and one on patriotics. The Fulds (father and son) published a comprehensive book on Civil War storecards in 1972 which listed over 8,500 different. Their comprehensive patriotic book, edited by Society members, was published in 1980.

Q. What does the term "R-7" mean?
A. The Fuld rarity scale was designed to help collectors estimate the rarity of their tokens. It is a 10-point scale, from R-1 (the most common) to R-10 (unique). "R-7" is quite scarce; the term means only 10 to 20 specimens are known to exist. Obviously, the higher the rarity, the more valuable the token, as a general rule.

MEMBERSHIP APPLICATION

MAIL TO:
Cynthia Grellman, Secretary
670 Korina Street
Vandenberg AFB, CA 93437

Name

Address

Town, State, Zip

ANNUAL DUES $5.00

CIVIL WAR TOKEN SOCIETY

proposed by

INTRODUCTION TO CIVIL WAR STORE CARDS

The present book, is the third and final one of a series by the Authors on Civil War tokens. The initial booklet on patriotic tokens was published in 1960 by Whitman Publishing Co. and is now in its third edition. As a stopgap, a *"Guide to Civil War Store Cards"* was published in 1962 by Whitman (now out of print), and as stated at that time, it was merely a master index to the store card tokens, with some illustrations and an alphabetical index. The present detailed work expands the 96 page, 5" x 7" guide, to the present hopefully complete volume.

As an introduction to the series, the coverage given by Dr. Hetrich over 45 years ago, is still applicable:

"The small coins, known to collectors as tokens, issued during the Civil War, have been neglected in the past, and have not received the attention of the collectors which they deserve. They represent a very important period of the history of our country, and should receive more attention from the American collectors for this reason, if for no other. It seems that the main reason for this neglect has been due to the lack of an adequate list of the different varieties printed in a convenient form, and the compilers trust this want the present volume will fill.

"A little attention given these coins will repay the collector. An interest in these pieces is soon aroused and easily maintained, and it will not be very long before one discovers that the addition of a new variety to his collection will be attended with as much satisfaction as the acquisition of a new variety of the more pretentious series of United States coins.

"Early in 1862 all metallic currency was gradually withdrawn from circulation. Citizens, anticipating the possible increase in value of all metals, commenced hoarding gold, silver and even copper to such an extent that in a short time there were no metallic coins of any denomination in circulation. Tradesmen were thus forced to issue a medium that would supply the place of small coins, and the first of these coins issued on account of the lack of the proper Government currency made their appearance in Cincinnati in the Fall of 1862. In the Spring of 1863 New York followed this example. The first to be made in New York was the Lindenmueller currency, of which a million pieces were struck. William H. Bridgens, the die-cutter, then issued the Knickerbocker currency, which consisted of numerous varieties, and were struck in large quantities.

"The issue of similar pieces became general throughout the Eastern and Middle Western States, until it was estimated that not less than 25,000,000 of these private tokens were in general circulation, which must have included between seven and eight thousand varieties.

"These little coins filled the wants of the trades-people, and were accepted as a means of exchange for the value, which usually was one cent. They undoubtedly were a source of great relief and convenience; but their irresponsible character soon attracted the attention of the Federal Authorities. It is said that the Third Avenue Railroad of New York requested Lindenmueller to redeem a large number of his tokens, which they had accepted in the course of business, but this he laughingly refused to do. The railroad had no redress, and it is not improbably that incidents of this character forced the Government to put a stop to their issue. This was done by the passage of an act of Congress in 1864, forbidding private individuals to issue any form of money."

The listing of Civil War tokens, was first undertaken by Pliny E. Chase in the *Journal of the American Philosophical Society* in 1863. The list is mainly of historical interest, although one piece was recently added to the book from the Chase article. Previously Fox's Casino of Philadelphia was thought to have been struck around 1870, but Chase knew of it in 1863.

The next major listing of Civil War tokens was made by the *Coin Collector's Journal* during 1882 and 1883, and was chiefly based on the Groh collection, now the property of The American Numismatic Society of New York— the Groh collection still ranks as one of the three largest Civil War collections ever assembled. The first illustrated listing of store cards was undertaken by Edgar H. Adams, and was published in the *Coin and Medal Bulletin* from April 1916 to March 1917. The bulletin was discontinued before the series was completed, but Adams made his notes available to Hetrich and Guttag. The reverse dies shown on the H & G plates were made by Adams.

Hetrich and Guttag's book published in 1924, and long out of print (although it has been reprinted twice), listed slightly over 6000 pieces, and at present somewhat over 4,000 additional pieces have been discovered — about 1500 patriotics and 8500 store cards.

Since the publication of the Hetrich & Guttag catalog, various additional pieces have been listed, the major list being published by Joseph Barnett in the *Numismatist* during 1943 and 1944, as well as Stack's *Numismatic Review* of 1944. Additional pieces have been described by the Authors in various articles in the *Numismatist* in the 1950's.

In addition, the D. L. Wing tokens of Albany were described by Howard Kurth in the *Numismatic Scrapbook* of 1943; and various specialized articles on Illinois and Indiana by Raymond Haggenjos; and the most recent booklet *Guide to Wisconsin Civil War Tokens* by Doug Watson.

Various articles on specific issuers have appeared in the *Journal of the Civil War Token Society* since its organization in 1967. The Civil War Token Society will continue to publish additions and corrections to this book. For membership information write: Dale Cade, 26548 Mazur Drive, Rancho Palos Verdes, California 90274.

One of the major problems in compiling this book has been deciding when a piece *is not* a Civil War token. Previous authors have skirted this issue, and we tried to take a more rational approach — an arbitrary one. Any token bearing an actual Civil War die is called Civil War except when obviously of a later date (i.e. when other side bears a later date, etc.). Several pieces listed by Hetrich and Guttag are so obviously of non-Civil War vintage (usually 1870-1880 or even later) that they were "delisted" and placed in the supplement. (Included are such tokens as McLaughlin of London, Ohio; S. C. Martin, Wooster, Ohio; Merchants Exchange, Columbus, Ohio and Columbia Hotel, Johnstown, Pennsylvania. Also tokens listed by Barnett from Defiance, Iowa, Barrett and Colerain, Minnesota have proved to be non-contemporary and are not listed.

One controversial piece, Pfeiffer & Co. of Norfolk has tentatively been listed, although containing a genuine Civil War die, it may be of the 1870 period. The Norfolk papers indicate Pfeifer moved to Norfolk after 1865, but the name is spelled differently, so it may not be the same individual.

One other large group of tokens listed in the supplement, were clearly made in 1858-59. These all bear a common reverse, "Business/Card" in a wreath (Die No. 1368), but most are listed in the booklet "American Store Cards" published by the Numismatic and Antiquarian Society of Philadelphia in 1859. The tokens are mostly from Chicago, with several from Iowa and New York State. However, since so many previous authors have called them Civil Wars, we left them in the main text, but each is marked with an "*" denoting their non-contemporaneous nature.

Several other listed pieces are probably non-Civil War and usually these questionable pieces are noted in the text.

A discussion of Civil War tokens struck in various metals might be helpful. Unfortunately, for the catalogers of this series, while perhaps it is fortunate for collectors, the early collectors of Civil War tokens during and immediately succeeding the War, wanted rare varieties for their collections. Since the pieces were not of an official nature in the first place, various collectors caused to be made many varieties of these tokens in metals other than copper; viz., brass, nickel, German silver, copper-nickel, white metal, silver and lead. However, many of these off-metal variations had to have been struck previous to the striking of the regular copper issues for general circulation as can be shown by die breaks.

Thus, it is difficult at best to decide which of the off-metal belong with the series, and which do not. Thus, one is left with the alternative of not listing any off-metals or listing them all. Naturally, the decision must be made to list them all.

In virtually all cases, the off-metal variations of the Store Card series are rare, only a limited number having been struck. In almost all cases, this was less than 20 full sets, and often many less. It should be pointed out that although most patriotic tokens regularly occur in copper, many of the Tradesmen's Cards regularly were struck in brass (for instance, the Boutwell cards of Troy, New York) or lead (for instance, the Hastings cards of New York). Also, in many cases the tokens are struck over other coins. This may be other Civil War tokens, or in some cases over copper-nickel cents dated from 1857 to 1863 (regular Government issues — there is even a report of an overstrike on an 1856 Flying Eagle cent) or over U.S. dimes generally dated in the 1850's. These overstrikes are recognizable by the original impression showing thru the overstrike, and in the case of the dimes, the piece has a reeded edge. The overstrikes on cents and dimes (as of course; those on high denomination silver coins) are actively sought after by collectors.

The metals in which Civil War cents are struck and the abbreviations used are as follows:

Code	Metal abbrev.	Metal	Code	Metal abbrev.	Metal
a	C	Copper	g	L	Lead
b	BR	Brass	h	R	Rubber
c	N	Nickel	i	Z	Zinc
d	C-N	Copper-nickel	j	G-S	German silver
e	W-M	White metal	k	G-T	Gilt
f	S	Silver	m	T	Tin

(1) There is no distinction, except in a few isolated cases between the various kinds of copper used in these pieces, although a few pieces are listed as bronze, which has a deeper color than copper, similar to uncirculated Indian Head cents.

(2) It is very difficult to distinguish Nickel from German Silver, although both metals were used. In general, the simple way of telling them apart is that nickel will not tarnish, while German Silver does. In almost all cases, these are not differentiated in the text.

(3) Lead includes many of the New York pieces that were struck in a dark composition metal, but there is usually little trouble in distinguishing them. Spectroscopic analysis of these pieces indicates they are mainly zinc with varying quantities of lead and tin.

(4) Zinc as used in the text refers to a particular type of token struck on a plated flan. These were plated before striking either copper or brass, and most often occur with a single die, Die. No. 1042, but occassionally are found with Die No. 1019 or 1037. Any other combination said to be the so-called zinc are probably non-contemporary.

The amateur collector often has great difficulty distinguishing between the various metals. The best solution to this problem is to consult a reputable dealer. However, the following may be of some help. Copper pieces generally look like worn Lincoln or Indian Head cents. Brass pieces have a distinct yellow color resembling a tarnished, dirty doorknob. The nickel pieces resemble in shade the wartime "silver" Jefferson nickel when uncirculated. German silver often has the shade of circulated "silver" Jefferson nickels. Copper-nickel has an entirely different specific gravity than copper and closely resembles the copper-nickel cents of 1857 to 1864. White metal is a soft composition metal that is very light in color and might be said to resemble light colored chrome plating. In addition a white metal piece, when placed on the fingertip, and struck by a copper coin will not give a sharp, lasting "ping." The lead and white metal pieces will not ring — all other metals do! Lead resembles white metal, but is quite dense and is invariably much darker (some lead pieces are found copper-plated). In all cases, the so-called zinc pieces (which invariably occur with two different Indian Head obverses) are copper pieces that are zinc washed. This is an original washing and was not done after the war!

This leads into the subject of silver. In short, we would recommend the inexperienced collector to BEWARE of any tokens which purport to be silver. Many, many of the copper pieces have been silver plated over the years. Silver pieces almost never turn up except in large collections. Original silver pieces are in no case at all common. The plated pieces can be very deceptive — they will tarnish very nicely. The best test is to take the specific gravity of the piece. Another test, though more qualitative in nature is as follows. Take a copper token, preferably of the same variety. The copper piece, when tapped by another coin on the finger tip will give a lower pitched, much longer lasting tone than the silver piece. If the "silver" and copper piece of the same type have almost identical rings, beware. This is not fool-proof, but works most times. Another common test used, though we frown on it, is to scratch the edge of the coin with a sharp knife. If the copper shows through, the piece is plated, although you risk the chance of defacing a potentially valuable coin. Of course in the case of silver pieces over dimes, they can always be identified by the reeded edge. We have never seen a Civil War cent in gold, though one has been reported. Only a very few tokens were originally issued either with silver plating or gold plating. Almost all other pieces are not contemporary — as such we have not priced these prices above 1.50 apiece in the ensuing list.

The rarity of these Civil War coins is at best a guess based on our experience. We have examined numerous collections as well as having inventories on many more and have probably examined at one time or another 100,000 Civil War cents. The rarity scale used is slightly different than the one proposed by Dr. W. H. Sheldon in "Penny Whimsy," but we have found this modification useful in this case. The rarity from R-1 (very common) to R-10 (unique — only one known) is based on the number known as follows:

Rarity Scale	Estimated Number In Existence	Rarity Scale	Estimated Number In Existence
R-1	Greater than 5,000 (very common)	R-6	Between 20 and 75
R-2	Between 2,000 and 5,000	R-7	Between 10 and 20
R-3	Between 500 and 2,000	R-8	Between 5 and 10
R-4	Between 200 and 500	R-9	Between 2 and 4
R-5	Between 75 and 200	R-10	Unique (1 only)

This rarity scale is based on the assumption that about 1,000,000 Civil War cents are still existent, and even if this is not a good guess (which we believe it is), the ratings will still have the same relative meaning. This is especially true for rarities of R-7 or over, which are based on actual surveys of the largest collections still in existence and include most of the off-metals known.

An attempt has been made to price the tokens, based on their rarity and on the metal in which they are struck. This list, shown in Table I, is a tentative one, and of course cannot take into account individual variations of demand. Thus, since many collectors attempt to obtain one token from each town, if there is only one token known from a town, and its rarity is for instance R-6, it will undoubtedly bring more in the open market than a token of R-7 from a town which has many issues known. However, the concept of this rarity table has been well received in the first volume of the series on "Patriotic Civil War Tokens," and its use is extended to this series. Let us mention that the price in this table for the copper and brass tokens are based on a token in fine condition and pieces in unc. condition command a price about double the listed price. For the other metal variations, the price given is already for a token in uncirculated condition, and thus no distinction as to price should be made for these prices. Most of the off-metal variations of these tokens occur only in uncirculated condition as they were usually struck for special purposes.

A comment on pricing is in order. The prices given in the price table for any given rarity does not take into account demand for either that city or state. Certain states command high premiums — and rarity reflects relative availability of any type.

Valuations of Civil War Tokens Based on Rarity and Metal

Rarity	Copper	Brass	Nickel and German Silver	Copper-Nickel	Copper-Nickel over C-N Cent	White Metal	Silver	Silver over U.S. Dime	Silver Plated	Gold Plated	Zinc	Lead	Rubber
R-1	$2.00	$2.00	$—	$—	$—	$—	$—	$—	$—	$—	$—	$2.50	$—
R-2	2.30	2.30	10.00	—	—	—	—	—	—	—	—	3.50	—
R-3	2.70	2.70	12.00	10.00	—	—	—	—	—	—	—	4.50	—
R-4	3.00	3.00	—	12.00	40.00	12.00	20.00	—	—	—	8.00	5.50	25.00
R-5	3.50	3.50	14.00	14.00	45.00	14.00	27.50	—	3.50	3.50	10.00	8.00	30.00
R-6	4.50	4.00	16.00	16.00	50.00	16.00	32.50	—	6.00	6.00	12.00	10.00	35.00
R-7	6.50	6.50	18.00	18.00	55.00	18.00	50.00	80.00	10.00	10.00	15.00	12.00	—
R-8	10.00	10.00	22.50	22.50	60.00	22.50	75.00	100.00	15.00	15.00	17.50	17.50	—
R-9	20.00	20.00	27.50	27.00	75.00	27.50	100.00	125.00	25.00	25.00	22.50	22.50	—
R-10	Values for these prices, when they are sold, are speculative.

NOTE: Prices for copper and brass are for coins in fine condition. When uncirculated, double the basic price. Prices for other metals are already calculated in unc. condition.

The average price for the *commonest* type from any of the following states in given below:

Alabama .... $250.00   Maryland .... 175.00   Virginia 300.00
Iowa .... 80.00   Minnesota .... 35.00   West Virginia .. 15.00
Kansas .... 250.00   Tennessee 90.00

Tokens from other states follow closely the prices in the table, except for those where only one issuer from a city — and they are in demand as type coins. For instance Illinois 920, Indiana 135, 480, 710 or Michigan 865 would be worth a considerable premium over that shown in the price table.

In the main text, all pieces are described in detail, and all punctuation, abbreviations, errors in spelling, etc., are noted. The supplementary lists in the Appendix, list special non-local tokens — those that are clearly Civil War, but whose locale is either highly questionable or completely unknown (listed as SNL).

As in the previous booklet, those Sutler tokens (some 50 plus) which use Civil War token dies only, are shown as non-locals, (NL).

Non-contemporary tokens, often listed as Civil Wars are listed in the third Appendix from NC-1 to NC-35. This list is not complete by any means.

All reverse dies used in the store card series are re-numbered, starting with 1000. Three conversion tables, given equivalence with H & G die numbers and Fuld patriotic numbers.

The key to identification tables should aid in identification of similar dies.

One *final caution,* — for clarity all tokens are shown approximately double size, except those far different from small-cent size — in this case, actual diameter of the coin is given in MM.

The Civil War Token Society would be happy to learn of unlisted varieties, and may be contacted by writing Dale Cade, 26548 Mazur Drive, Rancho Palos Verdes, California 90274.

BIBLIOGRAPHY

1. Baker, W. S. "Metallic Portraits of Washington" Philadelphia, 1885
2. DeWitt, J. D. "A Century of Campaign Buttons 1789-1889" Hartford, 1959
3. Fuld, M. and G. "Medallic Memorials to Franklin" The Numismatist 69:1393 Dec., 1956
4. Ibid. "The Wealth of the South Mulings" The Numismatic Scrapbook Magazine 1785 Sept. 1958
5. Ibid. "The Tokens of Robinson and Ballou" The Numismatist 68:33 Jan., 1955
6. Ibid. "The Tokens of Oliver Boutwell" The Numismatist 65:359 Apr., 1952
7. Ibid. "The Tokens of the Great Central Fair" The Numismatist 65:887 Sept., 1952
8. Haggenjos, R. "Civil War Tokens of Illinois" The Chicago Coin Club Annual Bulletin Vol. IX (1949)
9. Ibid. "The Civil War Tokens of Indiana" Reprinted from The Numismatic Scrapbook Magazine 1958
10. Hetrich, G. and Guttag, J. "Civil War Tokens and Tradesmen's Store Cards" Birdsboro, Pa., 1924
11. King, R. P. "Lincoln in Numismatics" The Numismatist 37:55 Feb., 1924
12. Marvin, W. T. R. "The Medals of the Masonic Fraternity" Boston, 1880
13. Watson, D. "Illustrated Guide to Wisconsin Civil War Tokens" Iola, Wis., 1968

There is also an extensive series of articles that appeared in The Numismatist in the period from 1912 to 1925 on store cards of particular issuers by the late Waldo Moore, as well as a partial revision to Hetrich and Guttag by the late Joseph Barnett, which appeared in The Numismatist in 1943 and 1944, as well as in the Numismatic Review of 1944.

ACKNOWLEDGEMENTS

Any undertaking as complex as this, involving the listing of over 8400 different tokens, is obviously a multi-person effort. In many cases, the authors merely acted as editors, while the routine description of various states were handled by dedicated specialists. However, the final decision whether to list or not list a piece was made by the authors (plus the decisions involving plating, similar metal problems such as German silver vs. nickel, and lead composition vs. zinc — see introduction for details), decisions as to contemporanous of pieces, etc. Thus, any errors, or ommissions are entirely the authors responsibility.

First, we wish to acknowledge major contributions to various sections by the following:

INDIANA: Donald Schramm of Portland, Indiana assisted in proofreading at various stages, and added to the listings from his large collection.

MICHIGAN: The basic section was written by Robert Hailey from notes supplied by the Authors and Clifton Temple. Mr. Hailey wrote the entire section in its entirety, and only editorial changes were made. In addition, Messrs. Temple and John Canfield of Ann Arbor and Edwin Graaf proofread the rough proofs, made numerous corrections and added additional pieces. Many of the photographs are from the Temple collection.

NEW YORK: The complete basic section was written up by Robert Hailey. Kenneth Trobaugh of Front Royal, Va. read manuscript proofs, and made numerous corrections, and supplied most of the tokens for photographing.

OHIO: Although the basic section was written by the Authors, considerable aid in new varieties was supplied by Donald Schramm and Arthur Fritz of Hamilton, Ohio. In addition, Virginia Culver of Thiensville, Wis., spent many hours proofreading and correcting numerous typographical errors.

PENNSYLVANIA: Although this section was written by the Authors, Mrs. Culver read and reread this section making numerous corrections and additions.

WISCONSIN: This entire section was handled capably by Doug Watson of Iola, Wis; based on his illustrated pamphlet published in 1968.

A number of individuals aided in making the list complete and in listing new varieties or supplying tokens for photographs. Special thanks are extended to The American Numismatic Society of New York (and their Assistant Curator Hillel Kaslove); Barney Sipos of Indiana, Pa.; Byron Hoke of Philadelphia; Dr. Leonard Rothstein of Baltimore; and Alfred Hoch of Lincoln, Mass.

A wealth of information was obtained from the notes of Dr. George Hetrich (loaned by Barney Sipos); Joseph Barnett, Otto Kersteiner and Raymond Haggenjos all of whom are deceased. They were pioneers in trying to revise these listings, and their notes made the task possible.

A special mention must be made for the valuable "key to die varieties" tables, prepared by Jack Detwiller of San Diego. These tables, the basic format which he had previously published in the Journal of the Civil War Token Society, are shown on pages XII–XXIV.

Last but not least, the book would never have appeared without the selfless dedication of Doug Watson, while on the staff of the publisher, did all the layout, pasting up, photograph planning, etc., etc in his spare time evening after evening and weekend after weekend. Again, Thanks Doug!!!

DIE CONVERSION TABLE NO. I

NEW NUMBERS — H&G NUMBERS — PATRIOTIC FULD NUMBERS

New No.	H&G No.	Patriotic Fuld No.	New No.	H&G No.	Patriotic Fuld No.	New No.	H&G No.	Patriotic Fuld No.	New No.	H&G No.	Patriotic Fuld No.
1000	1	1	1055	652	—	1121	441	—	1185	473	—
1001	2	3	1056	616	—	1122	442	40	1186	474	—
1002	6	10	1057	665	—	1123	443	—	1187	639	—
1003	6A	9	1058	666	—	1124	30	38	1188	475	—
1004	11	18	1059	669	—	1125	444	—	1189	476	—
1005	16	22	1060	448	—	1126	445	—	1190	476A	—
1006	29	37	1061	449	—	1127	446	39	1191	477	283
1007	400	57B	1062	449A	—	1128	447	—	1192	210	281
1008	401	57A	1063	649	—	1129	447A	—	1193	211	282
1009	402	57	1064	650	—	1130	621	—	1194	482	—
1010	47	58	1065	450	—	1131	340	438	1195	483	—
1011	647	—	1066	451	—	1132	87	105	1196	483A	—
1012	—	—	1067	452	—	1133	88	106	1197	486	286
1013	403	—	1068	453	—	1134	95	116	1198	487	—
1014	646	—	1069	453A	—	1135	658	122	1199	488	—
1015	49	60	1070	595	—	1136	658A	123	1200	121	164
1016	50	61	1071	596	—	1137	99	120	1201	121A	163
1017	56	68	1072	84	101	1138	489	121	1202	121B	165
1018	404	—	1073	46	56	1139	490	—	1203	611	280
	642	—	1074	85	103	1140	491	115	1204	643	—
1019	59	71	1075	85A	—	1141	492	—	1205	209	279
	405	71	1076	85B	—	1142	619	—	1206	484	—
1020	406	72	1077	454	—	1143	648	—	1207	485	—
1021	407	—	1078	455	—	1144	100	124	1208	485A	—
1022	622	—	1079	456	—	1145	102	127	1209	614	—
	663	—	1080	457	—	1146	104	129	1210	614A	—
1023	408	—	1081	458	—	1147	493	134	1211	641	—
	629	—	1082	421	—	1148	494	152	1212	641A	—
1024	409	—	1083	422	—	1149	114	151	1213	654	287
1025	410	—	1084	423	—	1150	114A	153	1214	645	433
1026	617	—	1085	423A	—	1150A	114B	—	1215	336	434
1027	411	—	1086	423B	—	1151	113	144	1216	142	196
1028	60	73	1087	424	—	1152	108	138	1217	142A	197
	412	73	1088	425	—	1153	109	140	1218	143	198
	656	73	1089	426	—	1154	—	—	1219	144	199
1029	413	—	1090	427	—	1155	115	154	1220	157	218
1030	414	74	1091	428	—	1156	115A	154A	1221	128	172
	668	74	1092	429	—	1157	497	145	1222	459	—
1031	634	—	1093	430	—	1158	498	509	1223	460	—
1032	660	—	1094	20	31	1159	496	146	1224	461	192
1033	661	—		632	31	1160	495	148	1225	462	—
1034	415	—	1095	21	32	1161	130A	175	1226	463	193
	659	—		633	32	1162	137	187	1227	464	194
1035	672	—	1096	431	—	1163	137A	—	1228	465	193A
1036	615	—	1097	432	—	1164	190	—	1229	466	—
1037	416	—	1098	433	—	1165	116	155	1230	145	200
1038	58	70	1099	434	31A	1166	117	158	1231	600	—
	417	70	1101	628	30	1167	117A	—	1232	147	202
1039	635	—	1102	644	—	1168	478	—	1233	150	206
1040	—	—	1105	25	33	1169	479	159	1234	152A	211
1041	—	—		620	33	1170	657	156	1235	155	214
1042	418	75	1106	26	34	1171	480	—	1236	165	229
1043	671	70A	1107	27	35	1172	670	157	1237	168	233
1044	662	—	1108	435	—	1173	481	—	1238	169	234
1045	68	84	1110	627	—	1174	118	160	1239	178	244
1046	419	76	1111	436	—	1175	120	162	1240	180	243
1047	420	—	1112	436A	—	1176	467	—	1241	181	248
1048	80	96	1113	437	—	1177	468	—	1242	182	250
1049	69	85	1114	438	—	1178	469	—	1243	185	254
1050	69A	—	1115	612	—	1179	469A	—	1244	217	294
1050A	69B	—	1116	613	—	1180	470	—	1245	218	295
1051	62	78	1117	618	—	1181	471	—	1246	202	271
1052	76	92	1118	439	—	1182	471A	284	1247	259	345
1053	70	86	1119	439A	—	1183	472	285	1248	259A	—
1054	72	88	1120	440	—	1184	640	—	1249	260	346

VIII

DIE CONVERSION TABLE No. I - Continued
NEW NUMBERS — H&G NUMBERS — PATRIOTIC FULD NUMBERS

New No.	H&G No.	Patriotic Fuld No.	New No.	H&G No.	Patriotic Fuld No.	New No.	H&G No.	Patriotic Fuld No.	New No.	H&G No.	Patriotic Fuld No.
1250	263	349	1295	518	—	1340	554	—	1386	183	—
1251	269	355	1296	518A	—	1341	555	448	1387	591	252A
1252	273	359	1297	519	—	1342	556	451	1388	592	—
1253	274	360	1298	520	447A	1343	557	—	1389	593	—
1254	275	361	1299	521	—	1344	558	—	1390	594	—
1255	287	374	1300	521A	—	1345	559	—	1391	664	—
1256	290	377	1301	522	—	1346	560	—	1392	607	—
1257	291	378	1302	523	—	1347	624	—	1393	597	452
1258	292	379	1303	524	—	1348	561	—	1394	598	—
1259	293	380	1304	524A	—	1349	562	—	1395	598A	—
1260	513	—	1305	525	—	1350	563	188A	1396	598B	—
1261	514	—	1306	526	—	1351	564	—	1397	607A	454
1262	515	383	1307	636	—	1352	565	—	1397A	—	—
1263	516	382	1308	636A	—	1353	566	185A	1398	—	—
	653	382	1309	527	—	1354	567	—	1399	608	456A
1264	296A	386	1310	528	—	1355	567A	—	1400	599	455
1265	300	390	1311	623	—	1356	568	—	1401	599A	456
1266	610	—	1312	529	—	1357	206	275	1401A	—	—
1267	301	391	1313	530	470	1358	569	—	1402	—	—
1268	302	392	1314	531	—	1359	570	—	1403	—	—
1269	303	393	1315	531A	—	1360	570A	—	1404	609	—
1270	303A	—	1316	532	—	1361	571	—	1404A	—	—
1271	306	396	1317	533	—	1362	572	—	1405	—	—
1272	324	417	1318	534	—	1363	573	—	1406	601	449
1273	329	424	1319	535	—	1364	574	—	1407	602	450
1274	582	425	1320	536	—	1365	637	—	1408	603	—
1275	335	432	1321	537	—	1366	638	—	1409	604	—
1276	337	435	1322	538	—	1367	655	460	1410	605	—
1277	338	436	1323	539	—	1368	575	461	1411	606	—
1278	339	437	1324	540	—	1369	576	—	1412	606A	—
1279	345	444	1325	541	—	1370	577	459	1413	630	—
1280	499	—	1326	542	—	1371	578	—	1414	631	—
1281	500	—	1327	543	—	1372	579	—	1415	631A	—
1282	501	182		626	—	1373	580	—	1416	667	—
1283	502	183	1328	544	—	1374	581	427	1417	651	—
1284	503	—	1329	675	—	1375	583	—	1417A	—	—
1285	504	184	1330	545	—	1376	583A	—	1418	—	506
1286	505	—	1331	546	—	1377	584	—	1419	—	507
1287	506	—	1332	547	—	1378	584A	—	1420	—	508
1288	507	185	1333	548	—	1379	585	—	1421	—	—
1289	508	—	1334	549	—	1380	585A	—	1422	—	510
1290	509	185B	1335	550	—	1381	586	457	1423	—	511
1291	510	—	1336	551	—	1382	587	—	1424	—	512
1292	511	—	1337	552	—	1383	588	—	1425	—	513
1293	186	—	1338	553	—	1384	589	—	1426	—	514
1294	517	—	1339	553A	—	1385	590	—	1427	—	519

DIE CONVERSION TABLE NO. II

H & G NUMBERS TO NEW NUMBERS

H&G No.	New No.	H&G No.	New No.	H&G No.	New No.	H&G No.	New No.	H&G No.	New No.	H&G No.	New No.
1	1000	186	1293	430	1093	495	1160	561	1348	626	1327
2	1001	190	1164	431	1096	496	1159	562	1349	627	1110
6	1002	202	1246	432	1097	497	1157	563	1350	628	1101
11	1004	206	1357	433	1098	498	1158	564	1351	629	1023
16	1005	209	1205	434	1099	499	1280	565	1352	630	1413
20	1094	210	1192	435	1108	500	1281	566	1353	631	1414
21	1095	211	1193	436	1111	501	1282	567	1354	632	1094
25	1105	217	1244	437	1113	502	1283	568	1356	633	1095
26	1106	218	1245	438	1114	503	1284	569	1358	634	1031
27	1107	259	1247	439	1118	504	1285	570	1359	635	1039
29	1006	260	1249	440	1120	505	1286	571	1361	636	1307
30	1124	263	1250	441	1121	506	1287	572	1362	637	1365
46	1073	269	1251	442	1122	507	1288	573	1363	638	1366
47	1010	273	1252	443	1123	508	1289	574	1364	639	1187
49	1015	274	1253	444	1125	509	1290	575	1368	640	1184
50	1016	275	1254	445	1126	510	1291	576	1369	641	1211
56	1017	287	1255	446	1127	511	1292	577	1370	642	1018
58	1038	290	1256	447	1128	513	1260	578	1371	643	1204
59	1019	291	1257	448	1060	514	1261	579	1372	644	1102
60	1028	292	1258	449	1061	515	1262	580	1373	645	1214
62	1051	293	1259	450	1065	516	1263	581	1374	646	1014
68	1045	300	1265	451	1066	517	1294	582	1274	647	1011
69	1049	301	1267	452	1067	518	1295	583	1375	648	1143
70	1053	302	1268	453	1068	519	1297	584	1377	649	1063
72	1054	303	1269	454	1077	520	1298	585	1379	650	1064
76	1052	306	1271	455	1078	521	1299	586	1381	651	1417
80	1048	324	1272	456	1079	522	1301	587	1382	652	1055
84	1072	329	1273	457	1080	523	1302	588	1383	653	1263
85	1074	335	1275	458	1081	524	1303	589	1384	654	1213
87	1132	336	1215	459	1222	525	1305	590	1385	655	1367
88	1133	337	1276	460	1223	526	1306	591	1387	656	1028
95	1134	338	1277	461	1224	527	1309	592	1388	657	1170
99	1137	339	1278	462	1225	528	1310	593	1389	658	1135
100	1144	340	1131	463	1226	529	1312	594	1390	659	1034
102	1145	345	1279	464	1227	530	1313	595	1070	660	1032
104	1146	400	1007	465	1228	531	1314	596	1071	661	1033
108	1152	401	1008	466	1229	532	1316	597	1393	662	1044
109	1153	402	1009	467	1176	533	1317	598	1394	663	1022
113	1151	403	1013	468	1177	534	1318	599	1400	664	1391
114	1149	404	1018	469	1178	535	1319	600	1231	665	1057
115	1155	405	1019	470	1180	536	1320	601	1406	666	1058
116	1165	406	1020	471	1181	537	1321	602	1407	667	1416
117	1166	407	1021	472	1183	538	1322	603	1408	668	1030
118	1174	408	1023	473	1185	539	1323	604	1409	669	1059
120	1175	409	1024	474	1186	540	1324	605	1410	670	1172
121	1200	410	1025	475	1188	541	1325	606	1411	671	1043
128	1221	411	1027	476	1189	542	1326	607	1392	672	1035
137	1162	412	1028	477	1191	543	1327	608	1399		
142	1216	413	1029	478	1168	544	1328	609	1404		
143	1218	414	1030	479	1169	545	1330	610	1266	DUPLICATE DIES IN H&G	
144	1219	415	1034	480	1171	546	1331	611	1203		
145	1230	416	1037	481	1173	547	1332	612	1115	20	632
147	1232	417	1038	482	1194	548	1333	613	1116	21	633
150	1233	418	1042	483	1195	549	1334	614	1209	25	620
155	1235	419	1046	484	1206	550	1335	615	1036	58	417
157	1220	420	1047	485	1207	551	1336	616	1056	59	405
165	1236	421	1082	486	1197	552	1337	617	1026	60	412
168	1237	422	1083	487	1198	553	1338	618	1117		656
169	1238	423	1084	488	1199	554	1340	619	1142	404	642
178	1239	424	1087	489	1138	555	1341	620	1105	408	629
180	1240	425	1088	490	1139	556	1342	621	1130	414	668
181	1241	426	1089	491	1140	557	1343	622	1022	415	659
182	1242	427	1090	492	1141	558	1344	623	1311	516	653
183	1386	428	1091	493	1147	559	1345	624	1347	543	626
185	1243	429	1092	494	1148	560	1346	625	1329	622	663

X

DIE CONVERSION TABLE NO. III

PATRIOTIC FULD NUMBERS TO NEW NUMBERS

Patriotic Fuld No.	New No.	Patriotic Fuld No.	New No.	Patriotic Fuld No.	New No.	Patriotic Fuld No.	New No.	Patriotic Fuld No.	New No.	Patriotic Fuld No.	New No.
1	1000	74	1030	151	1149	198	1218	345	1247	438	1131
3	1001	75	1042	152	1148	199	1219	346	1249	444	1279
9	1003	76	1046	153	1150	200	1230	349	1250	447A	1298
10	1002	78	1051	154	1155	202	1232	355	1251	448	1341
18	1004	84	1045	154A	1156	206	1233	359	1252	449	1406
22	1005	85	1049	155	1165	211	1234	360	1253	450	1407
30	1101	86	1053	156	1170	214	1235	361	1254	451	1342
31	1094	88	1054	157	1172	218	1220	374	1255	452	1393
31A	1099	92	1052	158	1166	229	1236	377	1256	454	1397
32	1095	96	1048	159	1169	233	1237	378	1257	455	1400
33	1105	101	1072	160	1174	234	1238	379	1258	456	1401
34	1106	103	1074	162	1175	243	1240	380	1259	456A	1399
35	1107	105	1132	163	1201	244	1239	382	1263	457	1381
37	1106	106	1133	164	1200	248	1241	383	1262	459	1370
38	1124	115	1140	165	1202	250	1242	386	1264	460	1367
39	1127	116	1134	172	1221	251	1386	390	1265	461	1368
40	1122	120	1137	175	1161	254	1243	391	1267	470	1313
56	1073	121	1138	182	1282	271	1246	392	1268	506	1418
57	1009	122	1135	183	1283	275	1357	393	1269	507	1419
57A	1008	123	1136	184	1285	279	1205	396	1271	508	1420
57B	1007	124	1144	185	1288	280	1203	417	1272	509	1158
58	1010	127	1145	185A	1353	281	1192	424	1273	510	1422
60	1015	129	1146	185B	1290	282	1193	425	1274	511	1423
61	1016	134	1147	187	1162	283	1191	427	1374	512	1424
68	1017	138	1152	192	1224	284	1182	432	1275	513	1425
70	1038	140	1153	193	1226	285	1183	433	1214	514	1426
70A	1043	144	1151	193A	1228	286	1197	434	1215	519	1427
71	1019	145	1157	194	1227	287	1213	435	1276		
72	1020	146	1159	196	1216	294	1244	436	1277		
73	1028	148	1160	197	1217	295	1245	437	1278		

DIE-A-GRAM NO. S-1   By JACK R. DETWILER
Trademark

GENERAL CLASSIFICATION OF INDIAN HEAD DIES (BY DATES)

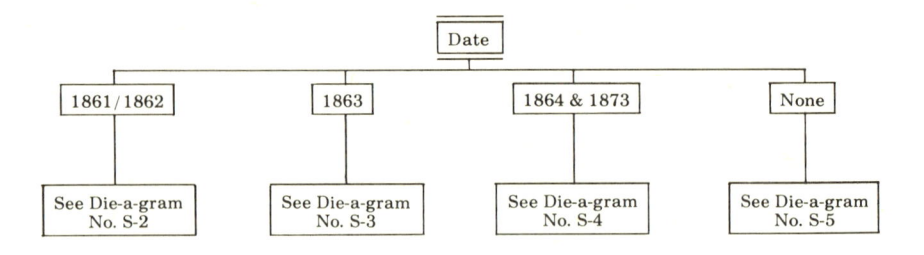

```
                          Date
   ┌───────────────┬───────────────┬───────────────┐
1861/1862        1863        1864 & 1873         None
   │               │               │               │
See Die-a-gram  See Die-a-gram  See Die-a-gram  See Die-a-gram
   No. S-2         No. S-3         No. S-4         No. S-5
```

HOW TO USE DIE-A-GRAMS

1. The purpose of die-a-grams is to provide a quick and easy way of distinguishing between similar dies such as the Indian Heads. The "S" in the die-a-gram number designates the store card series of Civil War tokens (the other classification is the "P" or patriotic series).
2. Compare the date on your token with the classifications of Die-a-gram No. S-1 and refer to the appropriate die-a-gram (S-2, S-3, S-4 or S-5).
3. Check through the identifiers of the appropriate die-a-gram until you reach the photograph which matches the die characteristics of your token. The new die number and the old H&G number are listed below each photograph.

DIE-A-GRAM NO. S-2   INDIAN HEAD DIES
Trademark

1861/1862 INDIAN HEADS

```
   1861 ─────── Date ─────── 1862
    │                         │
    │                  Last Star Is
    │                   Opposite
    │              ┌──────────┼──────────┐
 Legend:       Last (9th)  Next To Last  Between 7th &
BUSINESS CARD   Feather    (8th) Feather  8th Feathers
```

| New 1072 | New 1007 | New 1008 | New 1009 |
| H&G 84 | H&G 400 | H&G 401 | H&G 402 |

XII

DIE-A-GRAM NO. S-3
Trademark

By JACK R. DETWILER

CLASSIFICATION OF 1863 DATES
INDIAN HEAD DIES

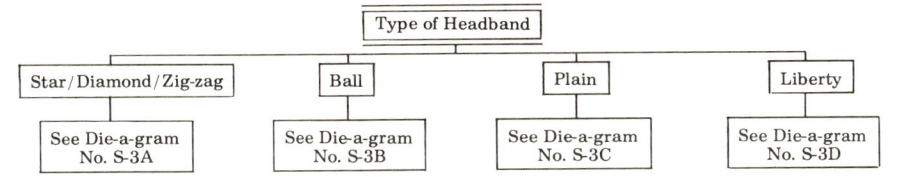

```
                    Type of Headband
    ┌──────────────┬──────────┬──────────┬──────────┐
Star/Diamond/Zig-zag   Ball      Plain     Liberty
See Die-a-gram    See Die-a-gram  See Die-a-gram  See Die-a-gram
  No. S-3A          No. S-3B       No. S-3C       No. S-3D
```

DIE-A-GRAM NO. S-3A
Trademark

INDIAN HEAD DIES

1863 STAR/DIAMOND/ZIG-ZAG HEADBANDS

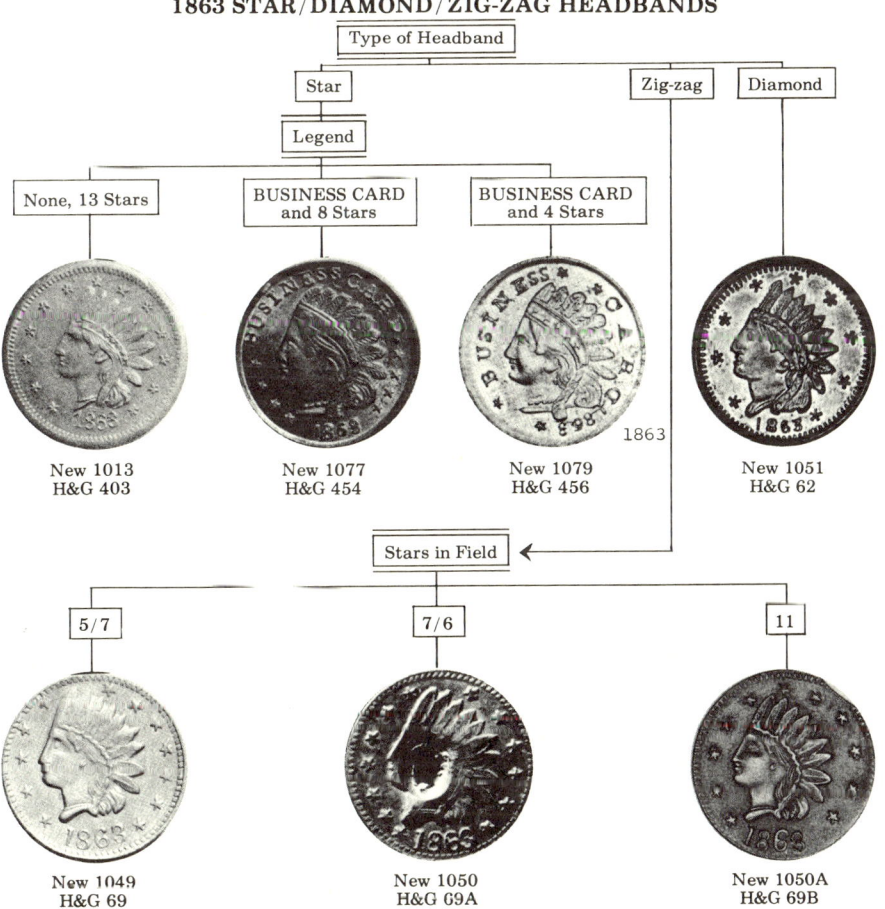

```
                Type of Headband
        ┌─────────┬────────────┬─────────┐
       Star                  Zig-zag   Diamond
      Legend
  ┌──────┬─────────────────┐
None,    BUSINESS CARD    BUSINESS CARD
13 Stars  and 8 Stars       and 4 Stars
```

| New 1013 | New 1077 | New 1079 | New 1051 |
| H&G 403 | H&G 454 | H&G 456 | H&G 62 |

Stars in Field

| 5/7 | 7/6 | 11 |

| New 1049 | New 1050 | New 1050A |
| H&G 69 | H&G 69A | H&G 69B |

XIII

DIE-A-GRAM NO. S-3B
Trademark

By JACK R. DETWILER

1863 BALL HEADBANDS

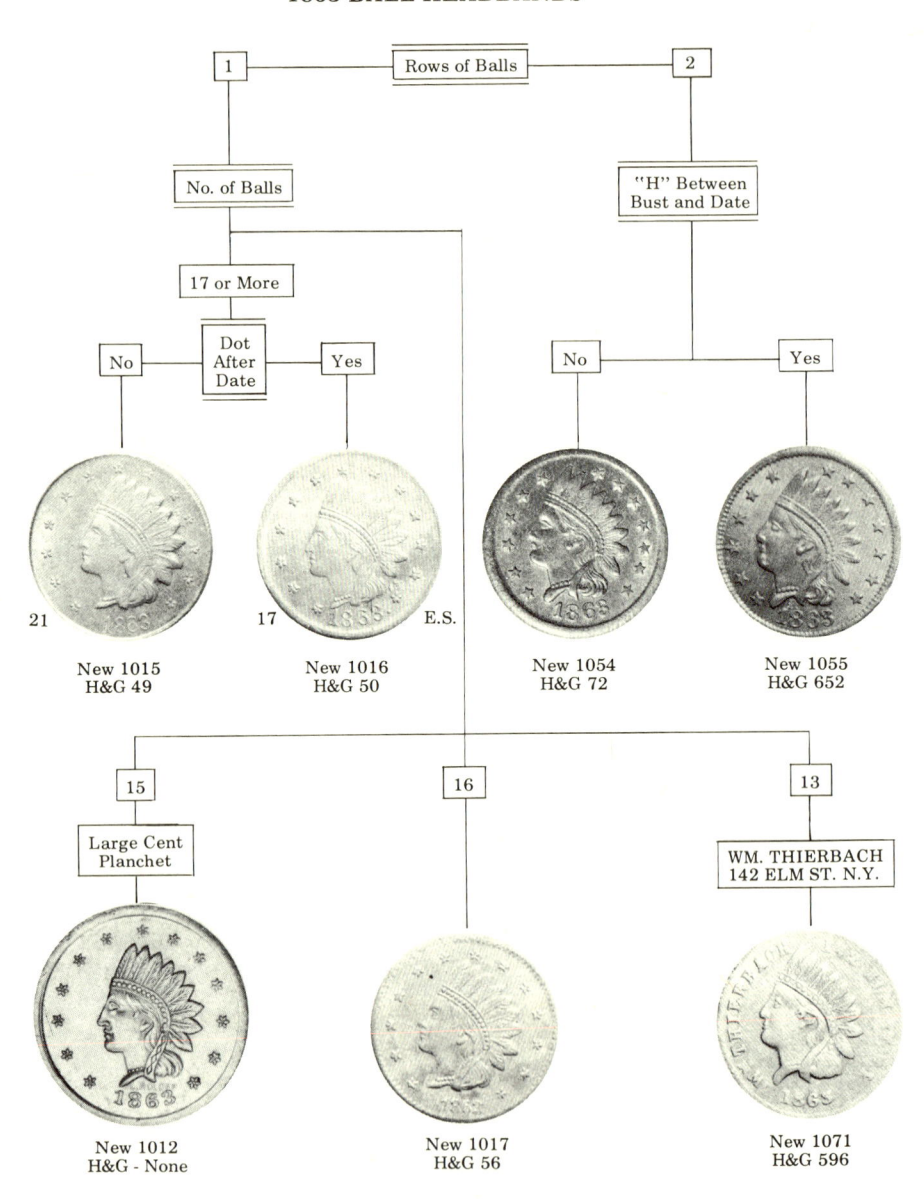

```
                    ┌───┐                          ┌───┐
                    │ 1 │──────Rows of Balls───────│ 2 │
                    └─┬─┘                          └─┬─┘
          ┌───────────┴────┐                ┌────────┴────────┐
          │ No. of Balls   │                │   "H" Between   │
          └───────┬────────┘                │  Bust and Date  │
                  │                         └────────┬────────┘
          ┌───────┴──────┐
          │  17 or More  │
          └───────┬──────┘
                  │
      ┌────┐  ┌───┴────┐  ┌─────┐          ┌────┐               ┌─────┐
      │ No │──│  Dot   │──│ Yes │          │ No │               │ Yes │
      └────┘  │ After  │  └─────┘          └────┘               └─────┘
              │  Date  │
              └────────┘
```

21   17   E.S.

New 1015   New 1016   New 1054   New 1055
H&G 49   H&G 50   H&G 72   H&G 652

```
       ┌────┐              ┌────┐              ┌────┐
       │ 15 │              │ 16 │              │ 13 │
       └─┬──┘              └─┬──┘              └─┬──┘
    ┌────┴─────┐                          ┌──────┴──────┐
    │Large Cent│                          │WM. THIERBACH│
    │ Planchet │                          │142 ELM ST. N.Y.│
    └──────────┘                          └─────────────┘
```

New 1012   New 1017   New 1071
H&G - None   H&G 56   H&G 596

DIE-A-GRAM NO. S-3C
Trademark

By JACK R. DETWILER

1863 PLAIN HEADBANDS
Part 1

- Field
  - Stars (6/7)
    - 7th Star Over
      - 3rd Feather
        - New 1052
        - H&G 76
      - 2nd Feather
        - New 1053
        - H&G 70
  - Legend
  - Stars (13)
    - Nose Opposite
      - Top, 2nd Star
        - New 1057
        - H&G 665
      - 3rd Star
        - New 1058
        - H&G 666

- WM. THIEBACII 142 ELM ST.
  - New 1070
  - H&G 595

- UNITED WE STAND
  - See Part 2 Next Page

- BUSINESS CARD and 12 Stars
  - New 1078
  - H&G 455

xv

DIE-A-GRAM NO. S-3C
Trademark

By JACK R. DETWILER

1863 PLAIN HEADBANDS
Part 2

```
                    ┌─────────────┬─────────────────┬─────────────┐
              Separated         Location of        Continuous
              Left & Right    "UNITED WE STAND"      Above
                    │
            Initials Between
             Bust and Date
          ┌─────────┼─────────┐
          H        None      CDH
```

New 1061
H&G 449

New 1064
H&G 650

New 1065
H&G 450

Position of D
(STAND) to Next
to Last Feather

┌─────────┬─────────┐
Above   Opposite   Below

New 1060
H&G 448

New 1062
H&G 449A

New 1063
H&G 649

XVI

DIE-A-GRAM NO. S-3D
Trademark

By JACK R. DETWILER

1863 LIBERTY HEADBANDS
Part 1

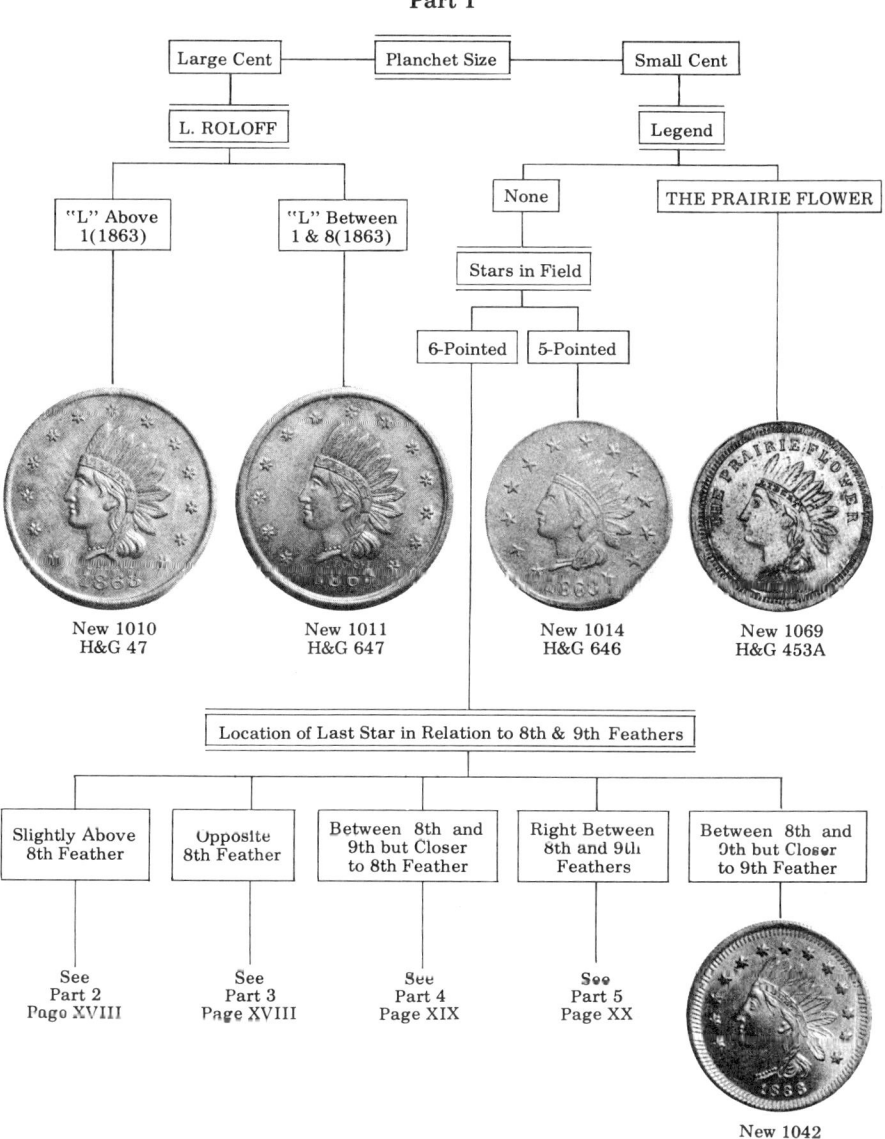

```
                    Large Cent ——— Planchet Size ——— Small Cent
                        |                                 |
                     L. ROLOFF                          Legend
                        |                                 |
              ┌─────────┴─────────┐              ┌────────┴────────┐
         "L" Above            "L" Between      None         THE PRAIRIE FLOWER
         1(1863)              1 & 8(1863)        |
                                           Stars in Field
                                                 |
                                        ┌────────┴────────┐
                                    6-Pointed         5-Pointed
```

New 1010	New 1011	New 1014	New 1069
H&G 47	H&G 647	H&G 646	H&G 453A

Location of Last Star in Relation to 8th & 9th Feathers

Slightly Above 8th Feather	Opposite 8th Feather	Between 8th and 9th but Closer to 8th Feather	Right Between 8th and 9th Feathers	Between 8th and 9th but Closer to 9th Feather
See Part 2 Page XVIII	See Part 3 Page XVIII	See Part 4 Page XIX	See Part 5 Page XX	

New 1042
H&G 418

DIE-A-GRAM NO. S-3D
Trademark

By JACK R. DETWILER

1863 LIBERTY HEADBANDS
Part 2

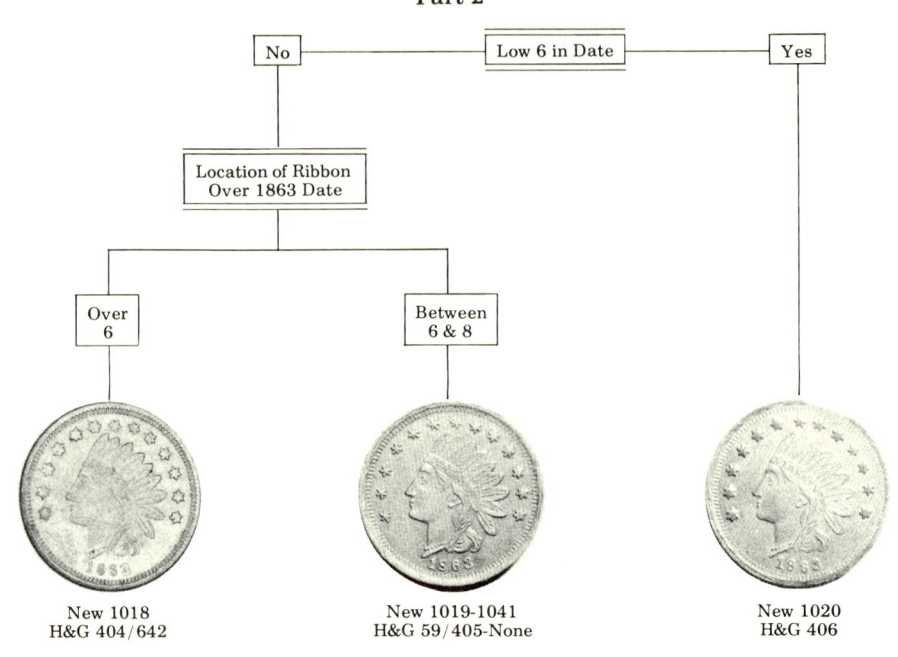

```
         No ——————— Low 6 in Date ——————— Yes
         |                                  |
  Location of Ribbon                        |
   Over 1863 Date                           |
    |         |                             |
  Over     Between                          |
   6        6 & 8                           |
```

New 1018
H&G 404/642

New 1019-1041
H&G 59/405-None

New 1020
H&G 406

Part 3

Location of Ribbon Over Date

| Left Side of 6 | Right Between 8 and 6 | Right Side of 8 | Over 6 |

New 1021
H&G 407

New 1022
H&G 622/663

New 1023
H&G 408/629

New 1024
H&G 409

XVIII

DIE-A-GRAM NO. S-3D
Trademark

By JACK R. DETWILER

1863 LIBERTY HEADBANDS
Part 4

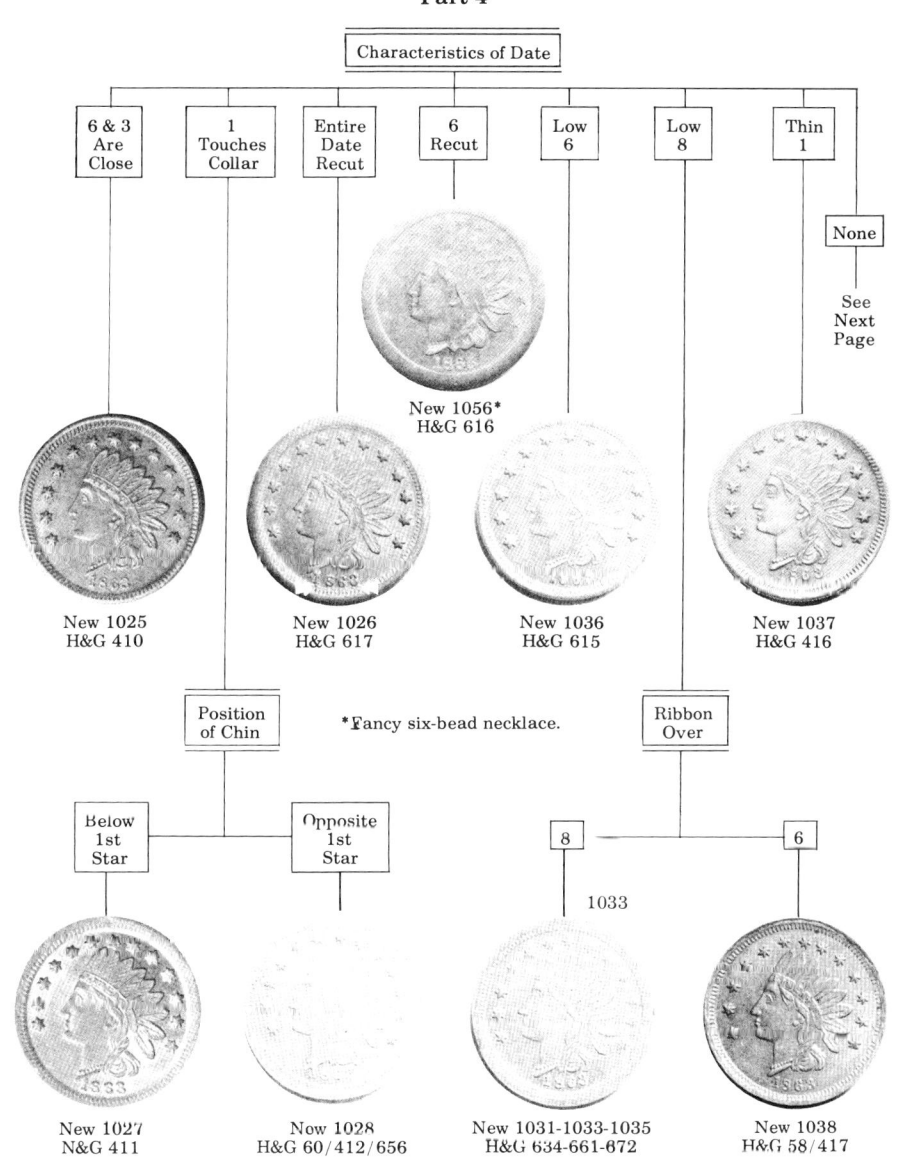

```
                    Characteristics of Date
  ┌──────┬─────────┬────────┬───────┬──────┬──────┬──────┐
 6 & 3    1        Entire    6      Low    Low    Thin
 Are    Touches    Date    Recut    6      8      1
 Close  Collar    Recut
                                                   │
                                                  None
                                                   │
                                                 See Next Page
```

New 1056*
H&G 616

New 1025   New 1026   New 1036   New 1037
H&G 410   H&G 617   H&G 615   H&G 416

Position of Chin   *Fancy six-bead necklace.   Ribbon Over

Below 1st Star   Opposite 1st Star   8   6

                                    1033

New 1027   Now 1028   New 1031-1033-1035   New 1038
N&G 411   H&G 60/412/656   H&G 634-661-672   H&G 58/417

XIX

DIE-A-GRAM NO. S-3D
Trademark

By JACK R. DETWILER

1863 LIBERTY HEADBANDS
Part 4 (Continued)

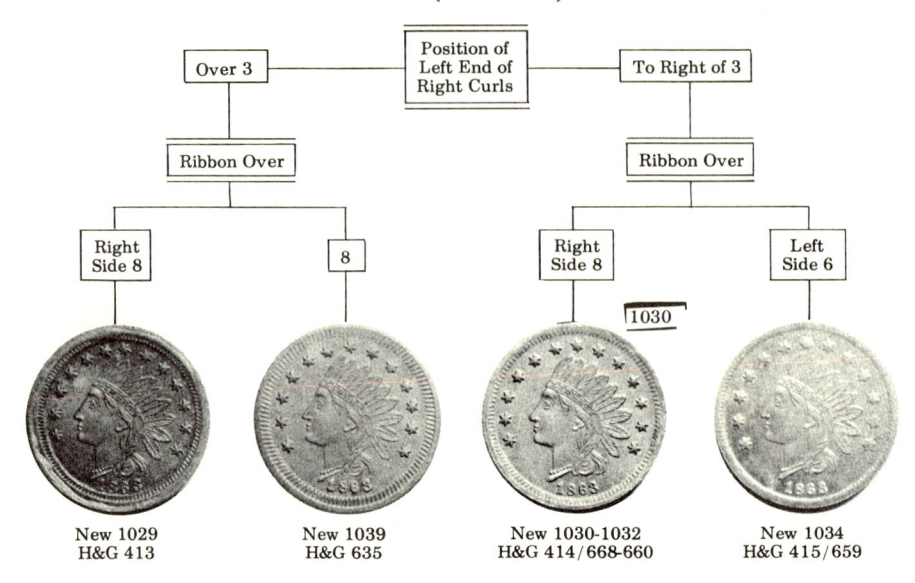

```
                    Position of
                    Left End of
    Over 3          Right Curls        To Right of 3

    Ribbon Over                        Ribbon Over

  Right           8                  Right         Left
  Side 8                             Side 8        Side 6
                                     ┌1030┐
```

New 1029   New 1039   New 1030-1032   New 1034
H&G 413   H&G 635   H&G 414/668-660   H&G 415/659

Part 5

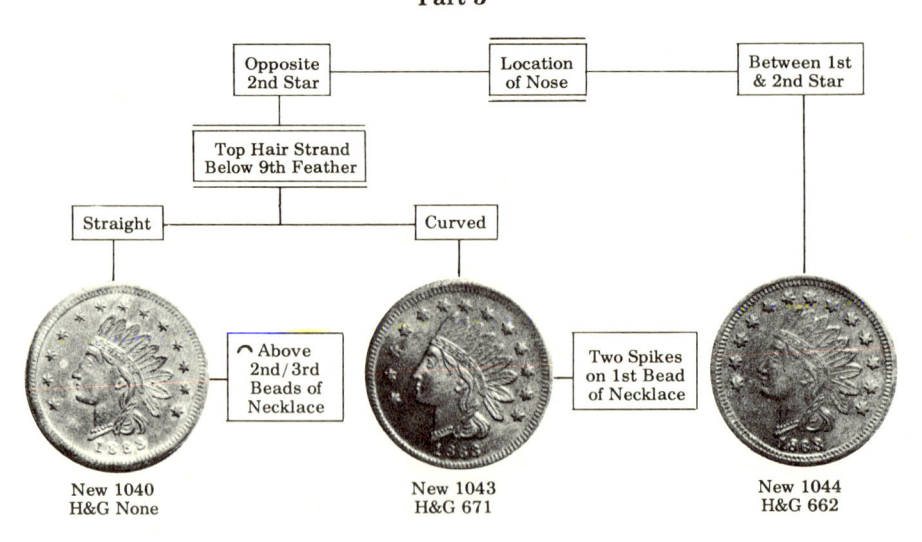

```
              Opposite                Location              Between 1st
              2nd Star                of Nose               & 2nd Star

              Top Hair Strand
              Below 9th Feather

    Straight                Curved
```

	Above	Two Spikes
	2nd/3rd	on 1st Bead
	Beads of	of Necklace
	Necklace	

New 1040   New 1043   New 1044
H&G None   H&G 671   H&G 662

xx

DIE-A-GRAM NO. S-4
Trademark

By JACK R. DETWILER

1864 AND 1873 INDIAN HEADS

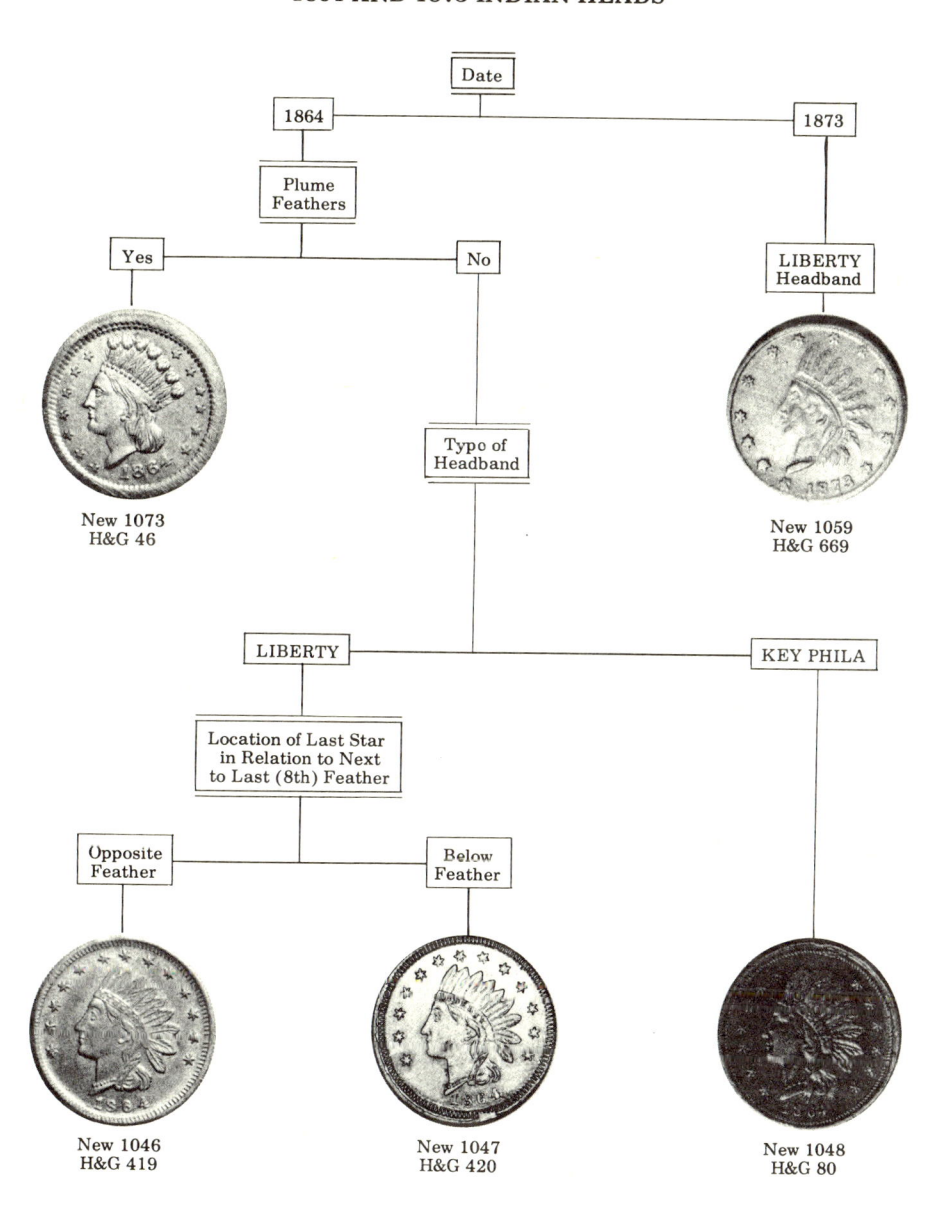

```
                        Date
                    ┌────┴────┐
                  1864       1873
                    │          │
              Plume Feathers   │
              ┌────┴────┐      │
             Yes        No   LIBERTY
              │         │    Headband
              │    Type of
              │    Headband
              │         │
         [coin]         │      [coin]
        New 1073        │     New 1059
         H&G 46         │     H&G 669
                   ┌────┴────┐
                LIBERTY   KEY PHILA
                   │          │
         Location of Last Star
         in Relation to Next
         to Last (8th) Feather
           ┌───────┴───────┐
        Opposite         Below
        Feather          Feather
           │               │           │
        [coin]          [coin]      [coin]
       New 1046        New 1047    New 1048
        H&G 419         H&G 420     H&G 80
```

XXI

DIE-A-GRAM NO. S-5
Trademark

By JACK R. DETWILER

NO-DATE INDIAN HEADS
Part 1

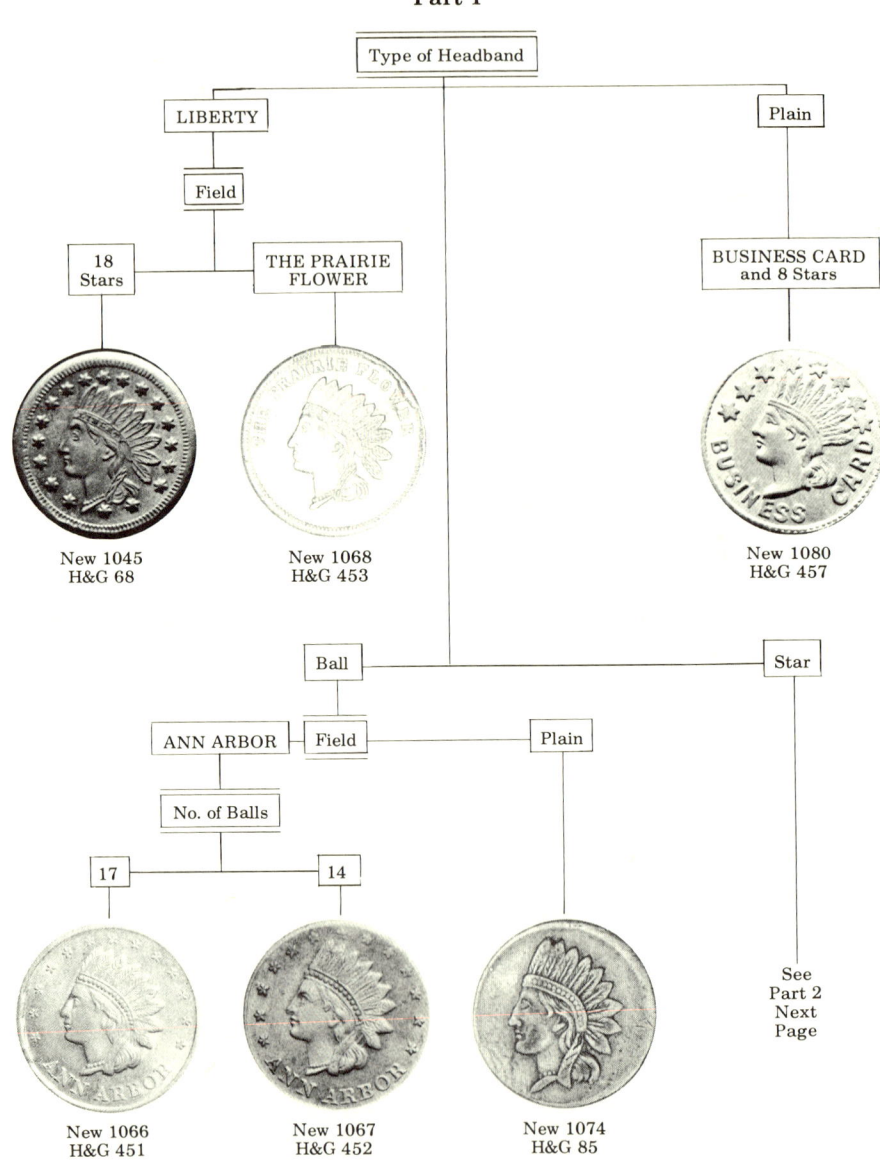

Type of Headband

LIBERTY — Field

Plain

18 Stars

THE PRAIRIE FLOWER

BUSINESS CARD and 8 Stars

New 1045
H&G 68

New 1068
H&G 453

New 1080
H&G 457

Ball — Star

ANN ARBOR — Field — Plain

No. of Balls

17 — 14

New 1066
H&G 451

New 1067
H&G 452

New 1074
H&G 85

See Part 2 Next Page

XXII

DIE-A-GRAM NO. S-5
Trademark

By JACK R. DETWILER

NO-DATE INDIAN HEADS
Part 2

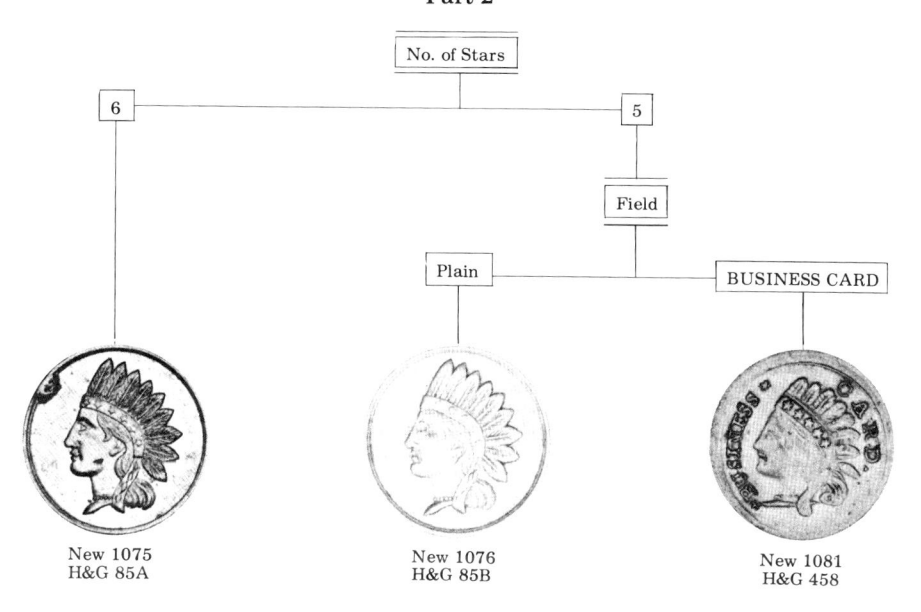

```
                    ┌─────────────┐
                    │ No. of Stars│
                    └──────┬──────┘
       ┌───┐               │                ┌───┐
       │ 6 │───────────────┴────────────────│ 5 │
       └─┬─┘                                └─┬─┘
         │                                    │
         │                            ┌───────┴───────┐
         │                            │     Field     │
         │                            └───────┬───────┘
         │                    ┌───────┐       │       ┌──────────────┐
         │                    │ Plain │───────┴───────│ BUSINESS CARD│
         │                    └───────┘               └──────────────┘
```

New 1075
H&G 85A

New 1076
H&G 85B

New 1081
H&G 458

The store card series of Civil War tokens has other groups of similar dies besides the two groups, Indian Heads and Turban Heads Facing Left, shown in Die-a-grams S-1 through S-6.

Additional die-a-grams such as Turban Heads Facing Right, Not One Cent, Coronet Heads, Spread Eagles, Perched Eagles, Business Cards, and Mercury Heads will appear in the **Journal of the Civil War Token Society** beginning in 1972. These additional die-a-grams should be considered supplemental to the die-a-grams of this catalog.

Mrs. Gail Levine, 5375 Duke Street, Alexandria, Virginia 22304 can supply a membership application for the Civil War Token Society.

DIE-A-GRAM NO. S-6
Trademark

By JACK R. DETWILER

TURBAN HEADS FACING LEFT

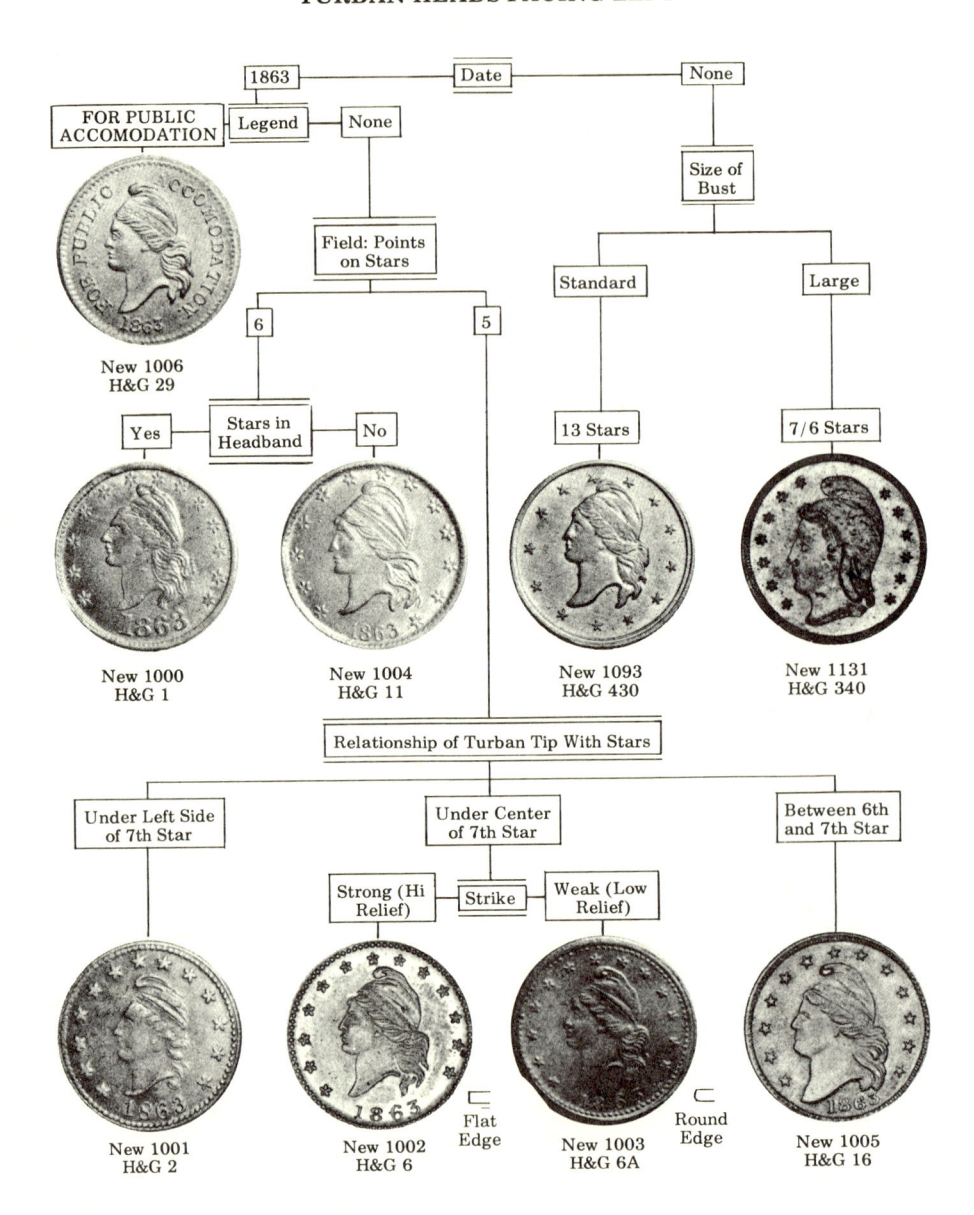

```
                            ┌──────┐         ┌──────┐
                            │ 1863 │──Date───│ None │
                            └──────┘         └──────┘
                               │                │
        ┌─────────────┐  ┌────────┐  ┌──────┐   │
        │ FOR PUBLIC  │──│ Legend │──│ None │   │
        │ACCOMODATION │  └────────┘  └──────┘   │
        └─────────────┘                         │
                                          ┌─────────┐
                                          │ Size of │
                                          │  Bust   │
                                          └─────────┘
                         ┌──────────────┐   │    │
                         │Field: Points │   │    │
                         │  on Stars    │┌──────┐ ┌──────┐
                         └──────────────┘│Stand.│ │Large │
                              │    │     └──────┘ └──────┘
                              6    5
```

New 1006 — H&G 29

| Yes — Stars in Headband — No | 13 Stars | 7/6 Stars |

New 1000 H&G 1   **New 1004** H&G 11   **New 1093** H&G 430   **New 1131** H&G 340

Relationship of Turban Tip With Stars

| Under Left Side of 7th Star | Under Center of 7th Star | Between 6th and 7th Star |

Strong (Hi Relief) — Strike — Weak (Low Relief)

New 1001 H&G 2   **New 1002** H&G 6 — Flat Edge   **New 1003** H&G 6A — Round Edge   **New 1005** H&G 16

REVERSE DIE PHOTOS

1000 1001 1002 1003
1004 1005 1006 1007
1008 1009 1010 1011
1012 1013 1014 1015
1016 1017 1018 1019

XXV

REVERSE DIE PHOTOS

1020	1021	1022	1023
1024	1025	1026	1027
1028	1029	1030	1031
1032	1033	1034	1035
1036	1037	1038	1039

XXVI

REVERSE DIE PHOTOS

1040 1041 1042 1043
1044 1045 1046 1047
1048 1049 1050 1050A
1051 1052 1053 1054
1055 1056 1057 1058

XXVII

REVERSE DIE PHOTOS

1059	1060	1061	1062
1063	1064	1065	1066
1067	1068	1069	1070
1071	1072	1073	1074
1075	1076	1077	1078

XXVIII

REVERSE DIE PHOTOS

1079	1080	1081	1082
1083	1084	1085	1086
1087	1088	1089	1090
1091	1092	1093	1094
1095	1096	1097	1098

XXIX

REVERSE DIE PHOTOS

1099	1101	1102	1105
1106	1107	1108	1110
1111	1112	1113	1114
1115	1116	1117	1118
1119	1120	1121	1122

XXX

REVERSE DIE PHOTOS

1123 1124 1125 1126

1127 1128 1129 1130

1131 1132 1133 1134

1135 1136 1137 1138

1139 1140 1141 1142

XXXI

REVERSE DIE PHOTOS

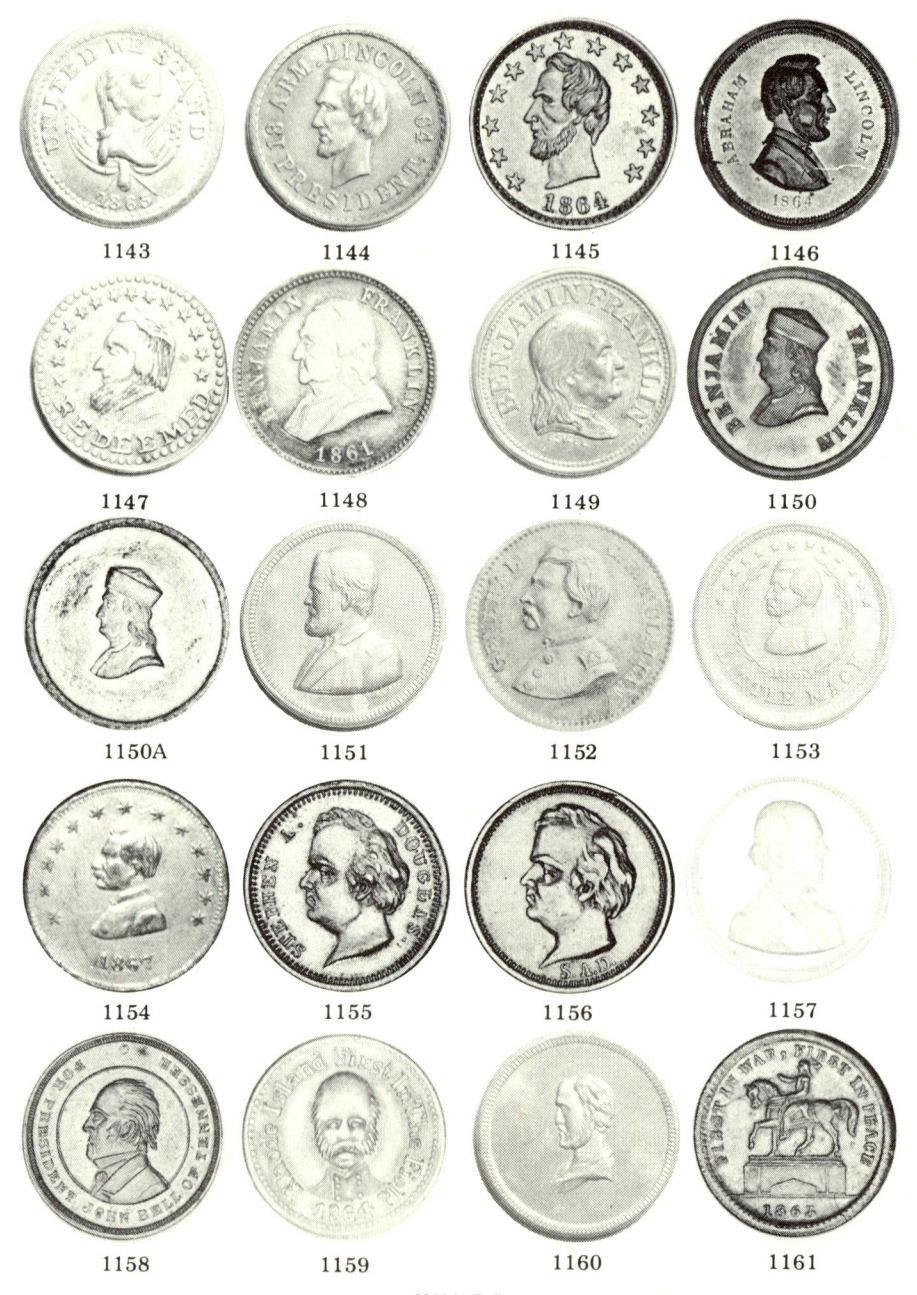

1143	1144	1145	1146
1147	1148	1149	1150
1150A	1151	1152	1153
1154	1155	1156	1157
1158	1159	1160	1161

XXXII

REVERSE DIE PHOTOS

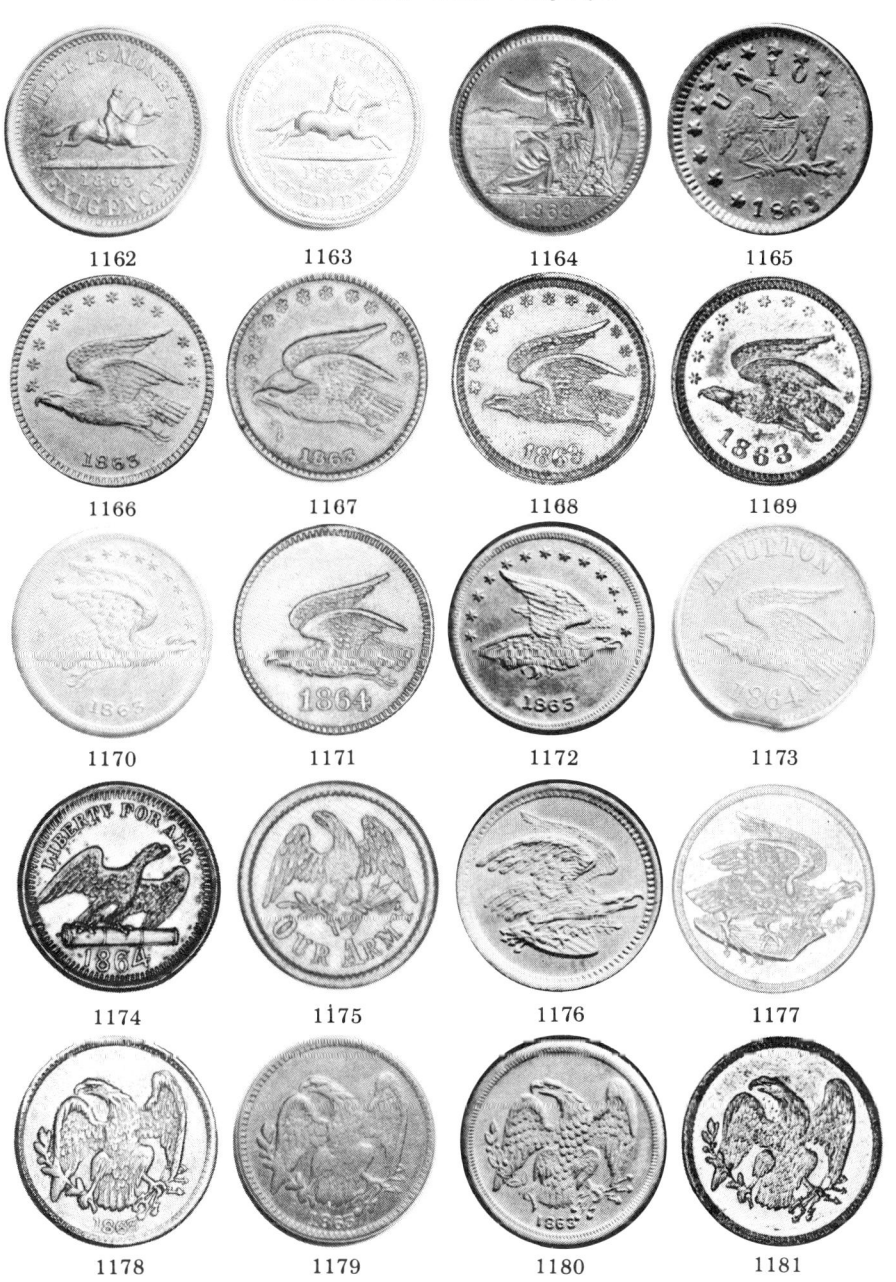

1162	1163	1164	1165
1166	1167	1168	1169
1170	1171	1172	1173
1174	1175	1176	1177
1178	1179	1180	1181

XXXIII

REVERSE DIE PHOTOS

1182 1183 1184 1185

1186 1187 1188 1189

1190 1191 1192 1193

1194 1195 1196 1197

1198 1199 1200 1201

XXXIV

REVERSE DIE PHOTOS

1202	1203	1204	1205
1206	1207	1208	1209
1210	1211	1212	1213
1214	1215	1216	1217
1218	1219	1220	1221

XXXV

REVERSE DIE PHOTOS

1222	1223	1224	1225
1226	1227	1228	1229
1230	1231	1232	1233
1234	1235	1236	1237
1238	1239	1240	1241

XXXVI

REVERSE DIE PHOTOS

1242 1243 1244 1245
1246 1247 1248 1249
1250 1251 1252 1253
1254 1255 1256 1257
1258 1259 1260 1261

XXXVII

REVERSE DIE PHOTOS

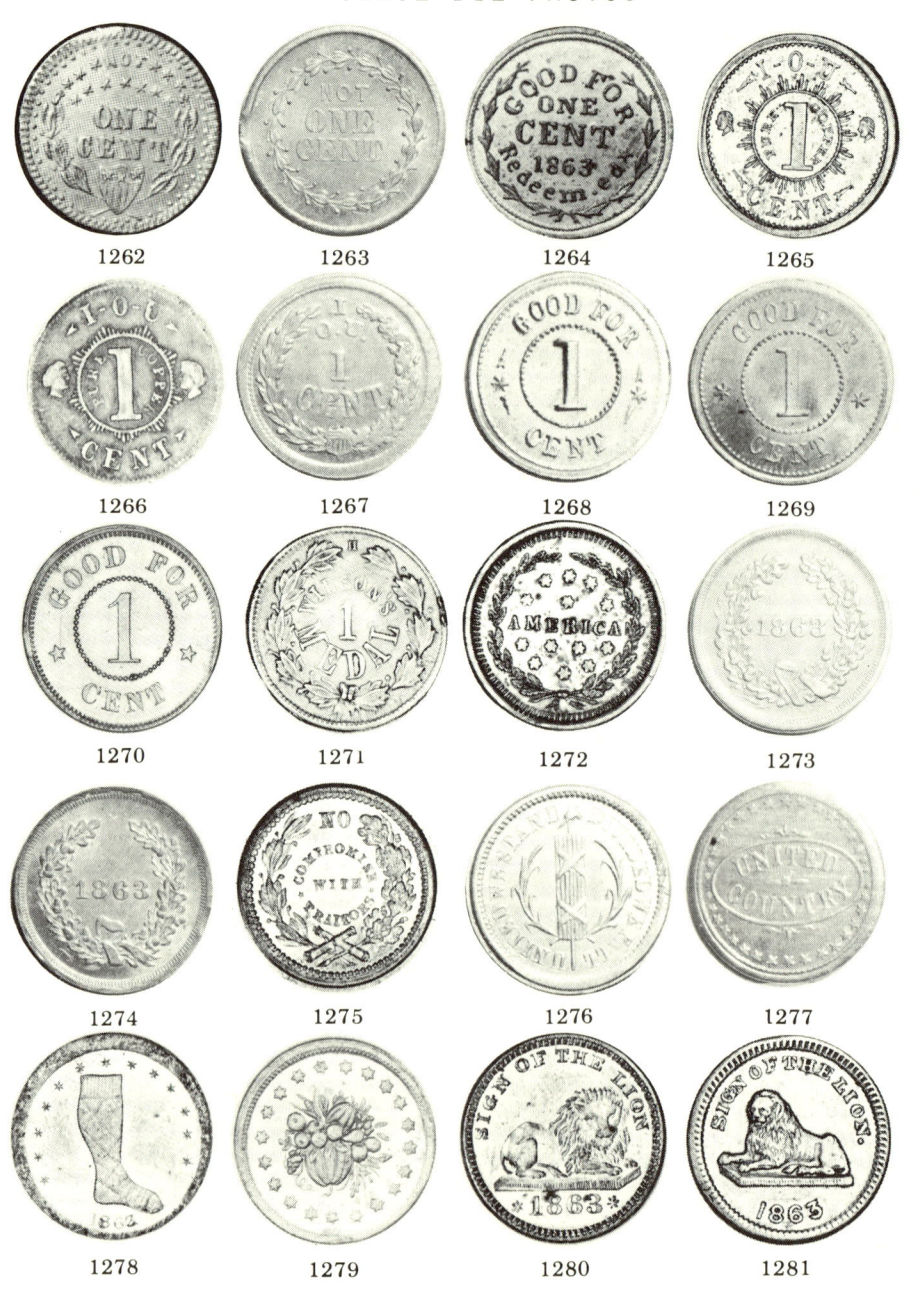

1262 1263 1264 1265
1266 1267 1268 1269
1270 1271 1272 1273
1274 1275 1276 1277
1278 1279 1280 1281

XXXVIII

REVERSE DIE PHOTOS

1282 1283 1284 1285

1286 1287 1288 1289

1290 1291 1292 1293

1294 1295 1296 1297

1298 1299 1300 1301

XXXIX

REVERSE DIE PHOTOS

1302	1303	1304	1305
1306	1307	1308	1309
1310	1311	1312	1313
1314	1315	1316	1317
1318	1319	1320	1321

XL

REVERSE DIE PHOTOS

1322　1323　1324　1325
1326　1327　1328　1329
1330　1331　1332　1333
1334　1335　1336　1337
1338　1339　1340　1341

XLI

REVERSE DIE PHOTOS

1342	1343	1344	1345
1346	1347	1348	1349
1350	1351	1352	1353
1354	1355	1356	1357
1358	1359	1360	1361

XLII

REVERSE DIE PHOTOS

1362 1363 1364 1365
1366 1367 1368 1369
1370 1371 1372 1373
1374 1375 1376 1377
1378 1379 1380 1381

XLIII

REVERSE DIE PHOTOS

1382 1383 1384 1385

1386 1387 1388 1389

1390 1391 1392 1393

1394 1395 1396 1397

1397A 1398 1399 1400

XLIV

REVERSE DIE PHOTOS

1401	1401A	1402	1403
1404	1404A	1405	1406
1407	1408	1409	1410
1411	1412	1413	1414
1415	1416	1417	1417A

REVERSE DIE PHOTOS

1418   1419   1420   1421

1422   1423   1424   1425

1426   1427

XLVI

ALABAMA

NUMBER	OBVERSE	REVERSE	METAL	EDGE	RARITY	H&G

HUNTSVILLE 425

425A-1a	WHITE & SWANN / HUNTSVILLE / ALA.	1047	C	R	R8	
425A-2d	Same	1069	C-N	R	R10	
425A-3a	Same	1392	C	R	R8	2002
425A-3a1	Same	Same	C	PL	R9	2001
425A-3b	Same	Same	BR	R	R8	2004
425A-3b1	Same	Same	BR	PL	R9	2003
425A-3i	Same	Same	Z	R	R8	2006
425A-3i1	Same	Same	Z	PL	R9	2005
425A-4a	Same (See Elder Sale, May 1939, Lot 542)	1394	C	R	R9	
425A-5a	Same	1397	C	R	R8	2010
425A-5a1	Same	Same	C	PL	R9	2009
425A-5b	Same	Same	BR	R	R8	2012
425A-5b1	Same	Same	BR	PL	R9	2011
425A-5i	Same	Same	Z	R	R8	2014
425A-5i1	Same	Same	Z	R	R9	2013
425A-6a	Same	1000	C	R	R9	2018
425A-6a1	Same	Same	C	PL	R9	2017
425A-6b	Same	Same	BR	R	R8	2020
425A-6b1	Same	Same	BR	PL	R9	2019
425A-6i	Same	Same	Z	R	R9	2022
425A-6i1	Same	Same	Z	PL	R9	2021
425A-7a	Same	1399	C	R	R9	2052
425A-8d	Same	1402	C-N	R	R10	2032
425A-9c	Same	1403	N	PL	R9	2039
425A-9e	Same	Same	W-M	PL	R9	2041
425A-10a	Same	1404	C	R	R8	2058
425A-11a	Same	1405	C	R	R9	2044
425A-11a1	Same	Same	C	PL	R9	2043
425A-11b	Same	Same	BR	R	R9	2046
425A-11b1	Same	Same	BR	PL	R9	2045
425A-11i	Same	Same	Z	R	R9	2048
425A-11i1	Same	Same	Z	PL	R9	2047

CONNECTICUT

NUMBER	OBVERSE	REVERSE	METAL	EDGE	RARITY	H&G

BRIDGEPORT 35

35A-1a	E. W. ATWOOD/DEALER/IN/ BOOKS/NEWSPAPER/&C.	1002	C	PL	R3	2103
35A-1b	Same	Same	BR	PL	R9	
35A-2a	Same	1237	C	PL	R3	2104
35A-2b	Same	Same	BR	PL	R8	
35A-2a	Same	Same	N	PL	R9	
35B-1a	A. W. WALLACE above VARIETY/ BAKERY in center BRIDGEPORT, CT. below	1201	C	PL	R3	2100
35B1b	Same	Same	BR	PL	R8	2101

NORWICH 345

345A-1a	WELLER'S/NEWS/DEPOT/ NORWICH	1266	C	PL	R3	2106
345A-1b	Same	Same	BR	PL	R8	
345A-2a	Similar, but no star at right side	Same	C	PL	R8	2107
	(NOTE: The 345A-2a variety might be due to die filling.)					

WATERBURY 560

2

CONNECTICUT - Continued

NUMBER	OBVERSE	REVERSE	METAL	EDGE	RARITY	H&G

WATERBURY 560-Continued

560A-1a	NEW YORK STORE/WATERBURY/CONN/SOUTH MAIN ST.	REDEEMABLE/IN SUMS OF/5 cts/or MORE/IN POSTAL CURRENCY	C	PL	R4	2108
560A-2a	Same	MILLINERY/AND/FANCY GOODS/1863	C	PL	R4	2109
560A2b	Same	Same	BR	PL	R6	

WILLMANTIC 600

600A-1a	DR. O. G. KEITTERIDGE/WILLMANTIC/C. T. /1864/MAIN ST.	1147	C	PL	R9	2111

600B-1b	ARCH SALOON/NO. 10/0.RUDD	1147	BR	PL	R9	2113

(NOTE: Both of the above are unusual tokens, and may be borderline R-8, and at least one specimen of the 600B is known silvered.)

ILLINOIS

| NUMBER | OBVERSE | REVERSE | METAL | EDGE | RARITY | H&G |

ALTON 10

10A-1b   WALTER & SMITH/ALTON/   JOHN STANTON/STAMP/   BR   PL   R8   2115
ILLS./GOOD FOR/10/CENTS   BRAND/CUTTER/CINCINNATI.
(C & S 295)

10A-2b   Similar but 25 instead of 10 (C & S 296)   Same   BR   PL   R9   2116
(NOTE: The two preceding pieces are quite thin, and have been
called sutler tokens, but there is no substantiation of this.)

AURORA 25

25A-1a   IRA H. FITCH/DEALER IN/   1207   C   PL   R3   2118
LEATHER,/HARNESS/&C./
BROADWAY.AURORA.ILL.

ILLINOIS-Continued

NUMBER	OBVERSE	REVERSE	METAL	EDGE	RARITY	H&G

AURORA 25-Continued

| 25B-1a | GATES & TRASK./DEALERS/ IN/WATCHES/JEWELRY/&/ SILVERWARE/AURORA.ILL | 1368 | C | PL | R4 | 2120 |
| 25B-1c | Same | Same | N | PL | R9 | 2121 |

BELVIDERE 45

| 45A-1a | GEORGE B. AMES./DEALER IN/ DRUGS/BOOKS & C./ BELVIDERE,ILL. | Mortar & pestle in center GEORGE B. AMES above with 13 stars--1863 below | C | PL | R5 | 2123 |

45A-1a1	Same, very thick 3mm. (NOTE: see photo of above die trial.)	Same	C	PL	R9	
45A-1b	Same	Same	BR	PL	R2	2124
45A-1e	Same	Same	W-M	PL	R9	
45A-2b	Reverse 111 45A-1a	Same as obverse	BR	PL	R9	

5

ILLINOIS-Continued

NUMBER	OBVERSE	REVERSE	METAL	EDGE	RARITY	H&G

BLOOMINGDALE 65

65A-1a	C.P.SEDGWICK & CO./VARIETY /GOODS,/BLOOMINGDALE/ILL.	1144	C	PL	R9	
65A-2a	Same (Elder May,1938 Lot292)	1145	C	PL	R9	2126
65A-2b	Same (Elder May,1938 Lot293)	Same	BR	PL	R9	2127
65A-2c	Same (Elder May,1938 Lot291)	Same	N	PL	R9	
65A-2d	Same	Same	C-N	PL	R9	2129
65A-2e	Same (Elder May,1938 Lot295)	Same	W-M	PL	R9	2129
65A-2f	Same	Same	S	PL	R9	
65A-2j	Same (H-R 1154)	Same	G-S	PL	R9	
65A-3a	Same	1241	C	PL	R9	2132
65A-4a	Same	1244	C	PL	R9	2135
65A-5a	Same	1245	C	PL	R8	2138
65A-6a	Same	1275	C	PL	R5	2141
65A-6d	Same	Same	C-N	PL	R7	2143

(NOTE: On some of the above pieces, although from the same die, the beads on the obverse border do not appear (see photo).

CAIRO 95

95A   95B

95A-1a	R.C.CULLEY./WATCHMAKER/ &/JEWELER/CAIRO,ILLS.	Blank	C	PL	R9	2145
95A-1b	Same	Same	BR	PL	R8	
95B-1a	D.FORD/WATCHMAKER/AND/ JEWELER,/CAIRO./ILLS.	1122	C	PL	R6	2147
95B-1b	Same	Same	BR	PL	R9	2148
95B-2a	Same	1348	C	PL	R9	2149
95B-2b	Same	Same	BR	PL	R9	2150
95B-3a	Same	Blank	C	PL	R9	2151
95B-3b	Same	Same	BR	PL	R7	2152

(NOTE: Ill.95B-3b is reported to come with numbers stamped on the reverse and was obviously used as a watchcheck.)

| 95B-3d | Same (Kreisberg 10/66 Lot 585) | Blank | C-N | PL | R9 | |

ILLINOIS-Continued

NUMBER	OBVERSE	REVERSE	METAL	EDGE	RARITY	H&G

CHEMUNG 140

| 140A-1a | WM.MOORE/DEALER/IN/DRY/ GOODS./GROCERIES,/DRUGS/ &C./CHEMUNG.ILL. | 1099 | C | PL | R8 | 2155 |
| 140A-2a | Same | 1105 | C | PL | R6 | 2154 |

140B-1a	B.A.WADE & CO./DEALERS/ IN/DRY GOODS/GROCERIES/ &C&C./CHEMUNG.ILL.	1099	C	PL	R9	
140B-2a	Same	1357	C	PL	R5	2157
140B-3a	Same	1390	C	PL	R9	2158

CHICAGO 150

150A-1b	BAIERLE'S/SALOON/CHICAGO	GOOD FOR ONE Beer mug in center, surrounded by a wreath.	BR	PL	R9	2160
	(NOTE: A small token measuring 14mm.)					
150aA-1b	GOOD FOR/1 (over 4)/CENTS/G A	1352A	BR	PL	R9	

7

ILLINOIS-Continued

NUMBER	OBVERSE	REVERSE	METAL	EDGE	RARITY	H&G

CHICAGO 150-Continued

150B

150C

*150B-1a	BARKER & ILLSLEY/ HARDWARE/NAILS/&/STOVES /77 STATE ST/CHICAGO	1368	C	PL	R3	2162
*150B-1c	Same	Same	N	PL	R8	2163
150C-1b	GOOD FOR/4/CENTS/G. BAUERNSCHMIDT (Note: slightly smaller, 18mm.)	1296	BR	PL	R9	2165

150D

150E

150D-1b	GOOD FOR/1/CENTS/AB (NOTE: The 1 is stamped over a '4' and AB is incused with a Q in the background--18mm.)	1296	BR	PL	R9	
150E-1b	GOOD FOR/1/CENTS/FB (NOTE: same comment as Ill. 150D-1b)	1296	BR	PL	R9	

150F

150F-1b	GOOD FOR/CENT./I.B. (NOTE: I.B incuse--18mm.)	1296	BR	PL	R9	

ILLINOIS-Continued

NUMBER　　OBVERSE　　REVERSE　　METAL　EDGE　RARITY　H&G

CHICAGO 150-Continued

(NOTE: City Brewery H&G 2197, is identical to H&G 10112, and both should be under Grand Rapids, Mich. See article by D. Watson, Journal of Civil Token Society, Summer, 1970)

Number	Obverse	Reverse	Metal	Edge	Rarity	H&G
*150M-1a	R.H.COUNTISS/GROCER/&/ TEA DEALER/CLARK ST.COR/ VAN BUREN/CHICAGO.ILL	1368	C	PL	R3	2200
*150M-2a	R.H.COUNTISS/GROCER/COR/ OF/STATE & NORTH/& COR CLARK &/VAN BUREN/STS./ CHICAGO.ILL.	1368	C	PL	R3	2202
*150M-2c	Same	Same	N	PL	R9	2203
150N-1a	DODD'S ELGIN DAIRY/PURE/ MILK/57/WEST/MADISON/ST.	1105	C	PL	R7	2205
150N-2a	Same	1111	C	PL	R4	2206
	(NOTE: This piece comes with a heavy reverse die break.)					
150N-3a	Same	1206	C	PL	R6	2207
150N-4a	Same	1208	C	PL	R6	2208
150 O-1a	D.DRYER & CO./GROCERIES/ PROVISIONS/35 S.CLARK ST.	1080	C	PL	R6	2211

ILLINOIS-Continued

NUMBER	OBVERSE	REVERSE	METAL	EDGE	RARITY	H&G

CHICAGO 150-Continued

*150P-1a	F.N.DUBOIS/SILVER WARE/ BADGE & MEDAL/ MANUFACTURY/P.O.BOX. 1899/CHICAGO.ILL (NOTE: It is possible that the above die combination does not exist)	1271	C	PL	R10	2213
*150P-2a	Same	1368	C	PL	R6	2214
*150Q-1a	EDWARDS/FINE/WATCHES/ JEWELRY/101/CLARK.ST/ CHICAGO ILL	1368	C	PL	R4	2216
150R-1a	A.W.ESCHERICH.404 ST,CLARK ST, around CHICAGO/ILLINOIS. /1861 in center.	1080	C	PL	R4	2218
150R-2a	Same	1369	C	PL	R7	
150R-3a	A.W.ESCHERICH.1861 ENGRAVER around 404/S.CLARK /C.ILL. in center.	1188	C	PL	R8	2219

ILLINOIS-Continued

NUMBER	OBVERSE	REVERSE	METAL	EDGE	RARITY	H&G

CHICAGO 150-Continued

150G 150H 150I

150G-1a	IRA BROWN/BOOK DEALER/ 611 WEST KINZIE/ST/ CHICAGO	1096	C	PL	R5	2169
150G-2a	Same	1105	C	PL	R9	2167
150G-3a	Same	1107	C	PL	R7	2168
*150H-1a	J.J.BROWN'S/GROCERY/171/ WEST/HARRISON.ST/ CHICAGO.ILL	1368	C	PL	R4	2171
150I-1a	WATCHES CLOCKS & JEWELRY /A CANDLER/393/STATE ST/ CHICAGO	1105	C	PL	R8	2173
150I-2a	Same	1203	C	PL	R9	2176
150I-3a	Same	1207	C	PL	R6	2174
150I-4a	Same	1356	C	PL	R3	2175

150J-1 thru 7 150J-8 thru 14

150J-1a	CHILDS DIE SINKER & ENGRAVER around. 117½/ RANDOLPH/ST./CHICAGO in center. Single ornament below.	1097	C	PL	R5	2177
150J-1a1	Same, thick 2½ mm.	Same	C	PL	R9	
150J-1b	Same	Same	BR	PL	R8	
150J-1b1	Same, thick 2½ mm.	Same	BR	PL	R9	
150J-2a	Same	1099	C	PL	R8	
150J-3a	Same	1111	C	PL	R3	2178
150J-4a	Same	1113	C	PL	R8	
150J-5a	Same	1206	C	PL	R2	2179
150J-6a	Same	1208	C	PL	R8	
150J-7a	Same	1356	C	PL	R9	2180
150J-8a	Similar, but two ornaments below. (NOTE: This piece comes with heavy obverse die break)	1111	C	PL	R2	2181

ILLINOIS-Continued

NUMBER	OBVERSE	REVERSE	METAL	EDGE	RARITY	H&G

CHICAGO 150-Continued

NUMBER	OBVERSE	REVERSE	METAL	EDGE	RARITY	H&G
150J-8b	Same	Same	BR	PL	R9	
150J-9a	Same	1113	C	PL	R5	2182
150J-10a	Same	1114	C	PL	R9	
150J-11a	Same	1115	C	PL	R7	
	(NOTE: This piece comes with heavy reverse die break)					
150J-11b	Same	Same	BR	PL	R7	
150J-12a	Same	1116	C	PL	R5	2184
150J-12b	Same	Same	BR	PL	R5	2185
150J-12c	Same	Same	N	PL	R9	2186
150J-13a	Same	1118	C	PL	R8	2183
150J-14a	Same	1356	C	PL	R8	
150J-14b	Same (Adams Ill. 11)	Same	BR	PL	R8	
150J-14c	Same	Same	N	PL	R10	

NUMBER	OBVERSE	REVERSE	METAL	EDGE	RARITY	H&G
150K-1a	CHILDS'/MANUFACTURER/ OF/ADVERTISING/COIN/ CHICAGO,ILLS.	1094	C	PL	R9	
150K-2a	Same	1098	C	PL	R3	2190
150K-3a	Same	1102	C	PL	R8	
150K-4a	Same	1203	C	PL	R2	2191
150K-4c	Same	Same	N	PL	R6	2192
150K-4c1	Same, thick 2mm.	Same	N	PL	R8	
150K-5d	Same (H-R 1155)	1204	C-N	PL	R9	
150K-5j	Same (H-R 1156)	Same	G-S	PL	R9	
150K-6a	Same	1205	C	PL	R5	2189
150K-7a	Same	1357	C	PL	R6	2188
150K-8a	1111	1338	C	PL	R8	2195
150K-9a	1111	1339	C	PL	R8	
150K-4d	Same	1203	C-N	PL	R9	

150K-10   150K-11

| 150K-10a | 1111 | DRY GOODS, CLOTHING, BOOTS & SHOES/HATS/& CAPS/ GROCERIES/&C./AT/LOW PRICES | C | PL | R9 | |
| 150K-11a | 1390 | DEALER IN/NAILS/STOVES/ CROCKERY/&/PAINTS | C | PL | R8 | 2194 |

ILLINOIS-Continued

NUMBER   OBVERSE   REVERSE   METAL   EDGE   RARITY   H&G

CHICAGO 150-Continued

Number	Obverse	Reverse	Metal	Edge	Rarity	H&G
150R-4a	A.W.ESCHERICH, WIRE WORKERS,1861 around 404/ S.CLARK/CHICAGO/ILL. in center.	1369	C	PL	R6	2220
*150S-1a	FLAGGS. CHEAP.STORE/BOOTS /&/SHOES/189/LAKE.ST/ CHICAGO	1368	C	PL	R3	2222
*150T-1a	FLAGG & MACDONALD/ BOOTS/&/SHOES/181/LAKE. ST/CHICAGO.ILL	1368	C	PL	R3	2224
*150T-2a	Very similar--wider space between FLAGG and CHICAGO and between ILL and MACDONALD	Same	C	PL	R5	2225
150U-1d	JAMES FOSTER JR. & CO OPTICIANS around 46 CLARK ST./CHICAGO/ILL. in center.	1046	C-N	R	R10	2227

13

ILLINOIS-Continued

NUMBER	OBVERSE	REVERSE	METAL	EDGE	RARITY	H&G

CHICAGO 150-Continued

150U-2a	Same	1047	C	R	R9	
150U-2d	Same	Same	C-N	R	R10	
150U-3b	Same	Blank (edge is not raised)	BR	PL	R10	

(NOTE: It is doubtful if this series was regularly issued due to its extreme rarity.)

　　　　　　　　150V　　　　　　　　150W-1　　　　　　　　150W-2

*150V-1a	FREEDMAN & GOODKIND/ DRY/GOODS/&/MILLINERY/ 171/LAKE ST./CHICAGO	1111	C	PL	R8	2230
*150V-2a	Same	1118	C	PL	R3	2231
*150V-3a	Same	1207	C	PL	R8	2232
*150V-4a	Same	1357	C	PL	R9	2229
*150W-1a	FREEDMAN.GOODKIND & CO/ DRY/GOODS/ 171/LAKE.ST/ CHICAGO.ILL	1368	C	PL	R2	2235
*150W-1c	Same	Same	N	PL	R9	
*150W-2a	FREEDMAN.GOODKIND & .CO/ DRY/GOODS/135/LAKE.ST/ CHICAGO.ILL	Same	C	PL	R2	2234
150Wa-1b	GOOD FOR/5/CENT./F.G. (size 18mm)	1296	BR	PL	R9	

　　　　　　　　150X　　　　　　　　150Y

*150X-1a	P.GAFFNEY/GROCER/&/TEA/ DEALER/150 N.HALSTEAD.ST/ CHICAGO	1368	C	PL	R3	2237
*150X-1c	Same	Same	N	PL	R9	
150Y-1a	NEW YORK/MEAT/MARKET/ F.GALL/CHICAGO/N.92 MILWAUKEE AV.	1286	C	PL	R2	2239
150Y-1b	Same	Same	BR	PL	R9	2240

ILLINOIS-Continued

NUMBER	OBVERSE	REVERSE	METAL	EDGE	RARITY	H&G

CHICAGO 150-Continued

150Z

150AA

*150Z-1a	C.E.GERTS & CO / BRUSH / FACTORY / & STORE / 204 / RANDOLPH.ST / CHICAGO	1368	C	PL	R3	2243
*150Z-1c	Same	Same	N	PL	R9	2244
150AA-1a	HAAS & POWELL / BUTCHERS / NORTH MARKET	1111	C	PL	R4	2247
150AA-2a	Same	1205	C	PL	R9	2246
150AA-3a	Same	1207	C	PL	R8	2248

150AB-1

150AB-2

150AB-1a	WM. HARLEV, / TRUNKS / & / VALISES / 94 / MIL / AVE. / CHICAGO.	Trunk in center WM. HARLEV, / ONE PRICE above, CLOTHING / 94 MILWAUKEE AVE. below.	C	PL	R2	2252
150AB-2a	WM HARLEV / TRUNKS / & / VALISES / 94 / MIL / AVE. / CHICAGO. (letter is also smaller than on 150BA-1a)	Same	C	PL	R8	2253

150AC-1a	HARLEV & JOHNSON / TRUNKS / & / VALISES / 94 / MIL AVE. / CHICAGO.	Trunk in center. HARLEV & JOHNSON / ONE PRICE above. CLOTHING / 94 MILWAUKEE AVE. below.	C	PL	R2	2250

15

ILLINOIS-Continued

NUMBER	OBVERSE	REVERSE	METAL	EDGE	RARITY	H&G

CHICAGO 150-Continued

150AC-2a	HARLEV & JOHNSON/TRUNKS/&/VALISES/WHOLESALE & RETAIL/94/MIL'AVE./CHICAGO.ILL	Same	C	PL	R2	2251
* 150AD-1a	R.HEILBRONER/FANCY/DRY/GOODS/217/S.CLARK.ST/CHICAGO.ILL	1368	C	PL	R2	2255
*150AD-1c	Same	Same	N	PL	R9	2256
* 150AE-1a	W.A.HENDRIE/WATCHES./CLOCKS/&/JEWELRY/35 CLARK.ST/CHICAGO.ILL	1368	C	PL	R4	2258
150AF-1b	GOOD FOR/5/CENTS/W.HILD (NOTE: The 5 is stamped over '4' and W. Hild incuse--18mm.)	1296	BR	PL	R9	
150AG-1a	S.A.INGRAM,/WATCHES/AND/CLOCKS/CHICAGO,ILL.	1007	C	PL	R9	2261

16

ILLINOIS-Continued

NUMBER	OBVERSE	REVERSE	METAL	EDGE	RARITY	H&G

CHICAGO 150-Continued

NUMBER	OBVERSE	REVERSE	METAL	EDGE	RARITY	H&G
150AG-2a	Same	1172	C	PL	R9	
150AG-2f	Same	Same	S	PL	R9	
150AG-3a	Same	1274	C	PL	R9	2260
150AG-3f	Same	Same	S	PL	R9	
150AG-4f	Same	J.A.HUGHES above--CINCINNATI below. METALLIC/CARDS in a wreath (Obv.Ohio 165BZ-1)	S	PL	R9	2262

(NOTE: Due to the great rarity and use of silver, undoubtedly these pieces were never placed in circulation.)

NUMBER	OBVERSE	REVERSE	METAL	EDGE	RARITY	H&G
150AG-5a	Same (Kreisberg 10/66 Lot 587)	1131	C	PL	R9	
150AG-5f	Same (Kreisberg 10/66 Lot 587)	1131	S	PL	R9	

150AH

150AI

NUMBER	OBVERSE	REVERSE	METAL	EDGE	RARITY	H&G
150AG-6a	Same (Kreisberg 10/66 Lot 587)	Obv. of Ohio 165H	C	PL	R9	
*150AH-1a	JUDD & CORTHELL./BOOTS/ &/SHOES/106/LAKE.ST/ CHICAGO.ILL	1368	C	PL	R3	2264
*150AH-1c	Same	Same	N	PL	R9	2265
150AI-1a	O.KENDALL'S SONS & CO/ BREAD/GOOD FOR/ONE/LOAF	1094	C	PL	R7	2267
150AI-1b	Same	Same	BR	PL	R8	2268
150AI-2a	Same	1098	C	PL	R6	2269
150AI-3a	Same	1390	C	PL	R8	2270
150AI-3b	Same	Same	BR	PL	R7	2271
150AI-3bi	Same, thin 3/4 mm.	Same	BR	PL	R9	

150AJ-1

150AJ-2

NUMBER	OBVERSE	REVERSE	METAL	EDGE	RARITY	H&G
*150AJ-1a	F.A.LEAVITT/FAMILY/ GROCERY/355 STATE.ST/ CHICAGO.ILL	1368	C	PL	R3	2273
*150AJ-2a	F.A.LEAVITT/FAMILY/ GROCERIES/CROCKERY & C/WHOLESALE/&RETAIL/ 355 STATE.ST/CHICAGO.ILL	1368	C	PL	R3	2274

ILLINOIS-Continued

NUMBER	OBVERSE	REVERSE	METAL	EDGE	RARITY	H&G

CHICAGO 150-Continued

150AK-1a	MARSH & MINER/MILITARY/ CLOTHIERS/33&35/LAKE.ST. /CHICAGO	1023	C	PL	R6	2276
150AK-2a	Same	1030	C	PL	R4	2277
150AK-3a	Same	1042	C	R	R7	2278
150AK-3b	Same	Same	BR	R	R8	
150AK-3i	Same	Same	Z	R	R9	
150AK-4a	Same	1047	C	R	R9	
150AK-4d	Same	Same	C-N	R	R10	
150AK-5a	Same	1069	C	R	R9	2280
150AK-5a1	Same	Same	C	PL	R9	2279
150AK-5b	Same	Same	BR	R	R9	2281
150AK-5d	Same	Same	C-N	R	R10	2282

| 150AL-1a | A,MEYER. S. CLARK, ST 377 around. In center RAG,STOR/ CHICAGO/ILL (NOTE: Error in spelling of STORE) | 1080 | C | PL | R6 | 2284 |

| 150AM-1b | C.E.MEYER/196 RANDOLPH. ST. Beer mug in center (H-R 1158) | GOOD FOR/ONE GLASS/BEER | BR | PL | R7 | 2286 |

18

ILLINOIS-Continued

NUMBER	OBVERSE	REVERSE	METAL	EDGE	RARITY	H&G

CHICAGO 150-Continued

| 150AN-1a | GOOD FOR/5 CTS/G.R.MEYER. | House, flagpole and flag flying, surrounded by trees. | C | PL | R9 | 2288 |

(NOTE: The reverse of this piece is most unusual and attractive.)

150AO-1a	BOARDING HOUSE 33.CANAL ST. around. J.U./MUNGERS (in script)/SALOON in center	1080				2290
150AP-1b	GOOD FOR/4/CENTS/PH./ODENWALD (18mm.)	1296	BR	PL	R9	
*150AQ-1a	OPPENHEIMER & METZGER/JEWELRY/&/WATCH/MATERIALS/104/LAKE.ST/CHICAGO/ILL	1368	C	PL	R3	2292
*150AQ-1c	Same	Same	N	PL	R9	
150AR-1b	WM.OSTENDORF/210/RANDOLPH/STREET/CHICAGO.	GOOD FOR/ONE GLASS/BEER (Same as Rev.ILL 150-AM)	BR	PL	R8	2294

19

ILLINOIS-Continued

NUMBER	OBVERSE	REVERSE	METAL	EDGE	RARITY	H&G

CHICAGO 150-Continued

| 150AS-1a | PASSAGE CERTIFICATE/FROM/ LIVERPOOL/TO/CHICAGO/NO. 6./CLARK ST. | BANK DRAFTS/FOR/1 AND/ UPWARDS/ONTHE/ROYAL BANK OF/IRELAND/1861 | C | PL | R5 | 2296 |
| 150AS-2a | Rev. of ILL 150AS-1a | 1111 | C | PL | R9 | 2298 |

150AT-1a	W.G.PECK/GROCER/92 STATE ST./CHICAGO	1105	C	PL	R8	2300
150AT-2a	Same	1111	C	PL	R7	2301
150AT-3a	Same	1113	C	PL	R8	
150AT-4a	Same	1114	C	PL	R4	2302
150AT-5a	Same	1115	C	PL	R9	2305
150AT-6a	Same	1116	C	PL	R5	2306
150AT-7a	Same	1207	C	PL	R5	2303
150AT-8a	Same	1356	C	PL	R3	2304

150AU　　　　　　　　　　　　　　150AV

| *150AU-1a | W.R.PRENTICE/FAMILY/ GROCER/75/CANAL.ST/ CHICAGO.ILL | 1368 | C | PL | R3 | 2307 |
| 150AV-1b | GOOD FOR/4/CENTS/F.W.R. (NOTE: F.W.R. incuse--18mm.) | 1296 | BR | PL | R8 | |

20

ILLINOIS-Continued

NUMBER	OBVERSE	REVERSE	METAL	EDGE	RARITY	H&G

CHICAGO 150-Continued

150AW

150AX

150AW-1b	GOOD FOR/5/CENT./L S R (NOTE: 5 and L S R incuse--18mm.)	1296	BR	PL	R8	
150AX-1a	H. REGENSBURG/GROCERY/&/BAKERY/NO.30/N.WELLS.ST. CHICAGO.	1080	C	PL	R3	2309
150AY-1b	Same (NOTE: Comes with heavy die break on obverse.)	1286	BR	PL	R9	

| 150AY-1a | GREAT WEST MARKET/FRESH & SALT MEAT,/WM./REINHARDT/158/RANDOLPH/W./CHICAGO (NOTE: comes with heavy die break on the obverse) | 1286 | C | PL | R2 | 2311 |

150AZ

150BA

150AZ-1a	WALL PAPERS/81/RANDOLPH ST./CHICAGO/F.E.RIGBY	1111	C	PL	R9	
150AZ-2a	Same	1206	C	PL	R3	2315
150AZ-3a	Same	1208	C	PL	R2	2316
150AZ-4a	Same	1256	C	PL	R2	2317
150AZ-5a	Same	1357	C	PL	R9	2313
150BA-1b	GOOD FOR/4/CENTS/J S (NOTE: J S incuse--18mm)	1352A	BR	PL	R8	

ILLINOIS-Continued

NUMBER	OBVERSE	REVERSE	METAL	EDGE	RARITY	H&G

CHICAGO 150-Continued

150BB-1   150BB-4

150BB-1a	DEUTSCHES GAST & BOARDING HAUS around. J.F.SIEHLER/ LARABEE/AT./NEAR CLYDBOURNE AVE./CHICAGO in center.	1072	C	PL	R5	2319
150BB-2a	Same	1080	C	PL	R9	
150BB-3a	Same	1354 (name reads BIER on shield)	C	PL	R4	2320
150BB-4a	Similar die, but comma after SIEHLER	1355 (name reads BEER on shield)	C	PL	R8	

150BC-1a	C.&S. STEIN/DRY GOODS/STORE /177/LAKE ST./CHICAGO./ILL.	1111	C	PL	R8	
150BC-2a	Same	1116	C	PL	R3	2326
150BC-3a	Same	1118	C	PL	R5	2323
150BC-4a	Same	1205	C	PL	R9	2322
150BC-5a	Same	1207	C	PL	R5	2324
150BC-6a	Same	1356	C	PL	R5	2325

150BD-1a	P.STUMPS/M'F'R/& DEALER IN/ FIREMANS HATS/& BELTS/312 COTTAGE AVE.	Fireman's cap in center made to order around Chicago below cap.	C	PL	R8	
	(NOTE: This piece is entirely different from the pieces listed as Adams Ill.40)					
150BD-1b	Same (Kreisberg 10/66 Lot 591) Fireman's Cap		BR	PL	R9	

22

ILLINOIS-Continued

NUMBER	OBVERSE	REVERSE	METAL	EDGE	RARITY	H&G

CHICAGO 150-Continued

*150BE-1a	W.TRELEAVEN/GOLD.PEN/ MAKER/&/JEWELER/150 LAKE. ST/UP.STAIRS/CHICAGO.ILL	1368	C	PL	R5	2328
150BF	S.WILSONS, listed under non-local					
150BG-1a	C.WINSAUER/GUNSMITH/N.111 S.WELLS/ST.CHICAGO. Crossed swords & guns in center.	1345	C	PL	R4	2330
150BG-1J	Same	Same	GS	PL	R10	

ILLINOIS-Continued

NUMBER　　OBVERSE　　　　　　　REVERSE　　　　　　　　METAL　EDGE　RARITY　H&G

DE KALB 200

200A-1　　　　　　　　　　　　　　　　200A-2

200A-1a	I.L.ELLWOOD/HARDWARE/TIN, STOVES/DE KALB ILL. (Baker 533)	1137	C	PL	R5	2332
200A-1b	Same	Same	BR	PL	R9	2333
200A-2a	I.L.ELLWOOD./HARDWARE/DE KALB.ILL.	1105	C	PL	R9	2335
200A-3a	Same	1207	C	PL	R8	2336
200A-4a	Same	1356	C	PL	R7	2337

DIXON 210

210A-1a	ED.WEIBEZAHN/DEALER/IN/GROCERIES/&DRY/GOODS/DIXON.ILL.	1105	C	PL	R7	2339
210A-2a	Same	1390	C	PL	R9	2340

DURAND 225

24

ILLINOIS-Continued

NUMBER	OBVERSE	REVERSE	METAL	EDGE	RARITY	H&G

DURAND 225-Continued

225A-1a	H.L.MOSLEY,/DURAND,ILLS.	GROCERIES,/HARDWARE,/GROCKERY, NOTIONS.	C	PL	R3	2342
	(NOTE: Spelling error in word CROCKERY.)					
225A-1b	Same	Same	BR	PL	R5	

ELGIN 270

| 270A-1a | M.MC.NEIL/DEALER/IN/DRY GOODS/GROCERIES/BOOTS&/SHOES/ELGIN,ILL. | 1209 | C | PL | R5 | 2344 |

EL PASO 275

275A-1a	P. H. THOMPKINS/DEALER/IN/DRY GOODS./GROCERIES/&C./EL PASO. ILL.	1108	C	PL	R7	2347
275A-1b	Same	Same	BR	PL	R9	
275A-2a	Same	1390	C	PL	R8	2348

FAIRVIEW 300

| 300A-1a | C.VANDORN/LARGEST & CHEAPEST/STORE/FAIRVIEW. ILL. | I.O.U. CENT around, 5 in center. | C | PL | R8 | |
| | (NOTE: Although of consistant Civil War fabric, the die work suggests this piece may be post-Civil War.) | | | | | |

25

ILLINOIS-Continued

NUMBER	OBVERSE	REVERSE	METAL	EDGE	RARITY	H&G

FREEPORT 320

320A-1a	D.S.BOGAR/FARMERS STORE/DRY/GOODS&/GROCERIES/FREEPORT/ILLS.	1095	C	PL	R8	
320A-2a	Same	1098	C	PL	R9	2351
320A-3a	Same	1105	C	PL	R9	2350
320A-4a	Same	1209	C	PL	R8	2352

| 320B-1a | D.S.BREWSTER/DEALER/IN/BUTTER.EGGS & C./FREEPORT,ILL. | 1209 | C | PL | R4 | 2355 |
| 320B-2a | Same | 1390 | C | PL | R8 | 2354 |

| 320C-1a | J.D.DIFFENFAUGH/CONFECTIONIER/AND/DEALE IN/FRUIT/FREEPORT/ILL. (NOTE: Error in spelling DEALER.) | 1095 | C | PL | R3 | 2356 |
| 320C-2a | Same | 1357 | C | PL | R7 | 2357 |

26

ILLINOIS-Continued

NUMBER	OBVERSE	REVERSE	METAL	EDGE	RARITY	H&G

FREEPORT 320-Continued

320D-1a	W.P.EMMERT./HARDWARE/ STOVES.IRON/&/TIN WARE./ FREEPORT.ILLS.	1205	C	PL	R9	2360
320D-2a	Same	1357	C	PL	R8	2359
320E-1a	FREEPORT BREWERY/BY/ HELENA/HERTRICH./ADAMS/ ST./FREEPORT,ILL.	1106	C	PL	R6	9369
320E-1b	Same	Same	BR	PL	R9	
320E-2a	Same	1220	C	PL	R7	2361
320E-2a1	Same, thick 2½ mm.	Same	C	PL	R9	

LACON 472

472A-1a	ELLSWORTH & HALSEY/ GENERAL/MERCHANDISE/ &/GOODS/FOR/LADIES/ WEAR/LACON,ILL'S	1046	C	R	R8	2365
472A-1a1	Same	Same	C	PL	R8	2364
472A-1b	Same	Same	BR	R	R9	
472A-1d	Same	Same	C-N	R	R9	2366
472A-1i	Same	Same	Z	R	R9	
472A-2a	Same	1047	C	R	R9	

ILLINOIS-Continued

NUMBER	OBVERSE	REVERSE	METAL	EDGE	RARITY	H&G

LA SALLE 495

| 495A-1a | ADAMS & HATCH/DRY/GOODS./CARPETS./BOOTS &/SHOES/LA SALLE.ILL. | 1105 | C | PL | R4 | 2371 |
| 495A-2a | Same | 1205 | C | PL | R9 | 2372 |

LENA 500

500A-1a	W.J.BOLLINGER/DEALER/IN/HARDWARE/IRON&STEEL/LENA,ILLINOIS. Lock in lower field.	1357	C	PL	R5	2374
500A-2a	Similar, but lock under left center of "D" of hardware.	Same	C	PL	R9	
500B-1a	M.WEAVER/DEALER IN/DRY GOODS/& GROCERIES/LENA.ILL.	1106	C	PL	R2	2377
500B-2a	Same	1107	C	PL	R3	2378
500B-3a	Same	1205	C	PL	R6	2380
500B-4a	Same	1357	C	PL	R9	2379
500B-5a	Similar to 500B-1a, but different spacing	1205	C	PL	R9	

ILLINOIS-Continued

NUMBER	OBVERSE	REVERSE	METAL	EDGE	RARITY	H&G

LODI 520

520A-1a	C.H.TAYLOR/STOVES/FINE/ TABLE &/POCKET/CUTLERY/ LODI, ILL.	1107	C	PL	R9	
520A-2a	Same	1205	C	PL	R9	2382
520A-2b	Same	Same	BR	PL	R9	2383

MARENGO 540

| 540A-1a | H.G.SKINNER/AGT./DEALER IN/GROCERIES/& PROVISIONS /MARENGO/ILL. | 1357 | C | PL | R4 | 2384 |

MENDOTA 560

| 560A-1a | A. ERLENBORN/DEALER/IN/ GROCERIES & C./MAIN STREET/MENDOTA./ILLS. | 1205 | C | PL | R5 | 2386 |

29

ILLINOIS-Continued

NUMBER	OBVERSE	REVERSE	METAL	EDGE	RARITY	H&G

NAPERVILLE 615

615A-1a	ROBERT NAPER/DRY/GOODS/ GROCERIES/& C./NAPERVILLE, ILLS.	1046	C	R	R7	2388
615A-1b	Same	Same	BR	R	R9	2389
615A-1d	Same	Same	C-N	R	R10	2390
615A-1i	Same	Same	Z	R	R9	2391
615A-2a	Same	1047	C	R	R9	

OTTAWA 660

| 660A-1a | A & H.ALSCHULER/OTTAWA Large rossette in center | 1205 | C | PL | R8 | 2392 |
| 660A-2a | Same | 1338 | C | PL | R3 | 2393 |

PALATINE 680

| 680A-1a | DEAN & SLADE/DRY GOODS/ HARDWARE/&C./PALATINE, ILL. | 1195 | C | PL | R4 | 2395 |
| 680A-1a1 | Same, large 21mm., thick 3 mm. | Same | C | PL | R8 | |

ILLINOIS-Continued

NUMBER	OBVERSE	REVERSE	METAL	EDGE	RARITY	H&G

PARIS 690

690A

690B

690A-1a	COLLINS BRO'S/DRUGGISTS/PARIS,ILLS	1036	C	PL	R5	2401
690A-2a	Same	1042	C	R	R7	2398
690A-2a1	Same	Same	C	PL	R9	
690A-2b	Same	Same	BR	R	R8	2399
690A-2i	Same	Same	Z	R	R9	
690A-3a	Same	1045	C	PL	R6	2397
690A-4a	Same	1046	C	R	R9	2403
690A-5a	Same	1047	C	R	R9	
690A-5d	Same	Same	C-N	R	R10	
690B-1a	A.C.CONNELY'S/DRY/GOODS/STORE/PARIS,ILL.	1026	C	PL	R4	2410
690B-2a	Same	1042	C	R	R7	2406
690B-2b	Same	Same	BR	R	R7	
690B-2i	Same	Same	Z	R	R9	
690B-3a	Same	1045	C	PL	R0	2405
690B-4a	Same	1047	C	R	R9	
690B-4d	Same	Same	C-N	R	R9	
690B-5d	Same	1069	C-N	R	R10	
690B-6d	Same	1341	C-N	R	R10	2409

690C

690C-1a	JAMES MILLER/DRY/GOODS/STORE/PARIS,ILL.	1026	C	PL	R9	
690C-2a	Same	1029	C	PL	R5	2411
690C-2a	Same	1042	C	R	R6	2412
690C-3b	Same	Same	BR	R	R7	2413
690C-3i	Same	Same	Z	R	R9	
690C-4a	Same	1047	C	R	R9	
690C-5d	Same	1069	C-N	R	R10	2415

31

ILLINOIS-Continued

NUMBER	OBVERSE	REVERSE	METAL	EDGE	RARITY	H&G

PARIS 690-Continued

690D 690E

690D-1a	PENOYER & LARKIN/ GROCERS/&/PROVISION/ DEALERS/PARIS,ILL	1028	C	PL	R6	2417
690D-2a	Same	1029	C	PL	R9	
690D-3a	Same	1042	C	R	R7	2418
690D-3b	Same	Same	BR	R	R7	2419
690D-3b1	Same	Same	BR	PL	R9	
690D-4a	Same	1045	C	PL	R9	
690D-5a	Same	1047	C	R	R9	
690D-6d	Same	1069	C-N	R	R10	2421
690D-3i	Same	Same	Z	R	R8	
690E-1a	SISK & WHALEN/RESTAURANT /E. SIDE PUB. SQ./PARIS,ILLS. Running dog in center.	1026	C	PL	R6	
690E-2a	Same	1042	C	R	R6	2423
690E-2b	Same	Same	BR	R	R7	2424
690E-2i	Same	Same	Z	R	R9	2425
690E-3a	Same	1047	C	R	R9	
690E-4d	Same	1069	C-N	R	R10	2426

PERU 695

| 695A-1a | LININGER & BRO./DEALERS/ IN/DRY GOODS/NOTIONS, /BOOTS & SHOES/PERU,ILL. | 1357 | C | PL | R4 | 2428 |
| 695A-2a | Same | 1390 | C | PL | R8 | 2429 |

ILLINOIS-Continued

NUMBER	OBVERSE	REVERSE	METAL	EDGE	RARITY	H&G

PONTIAC 700

| 700A-1a | DEHNER & MAPLES / DRY / GOODS / GROCERIES / &C. / PONTIAC, ILL. | 1105 | C | PL | R5 | 2431 |

ROCKFORD 755

755A-1a	A.J. DAVIS / GROCER / ROCKFORD.ILLS.	1095	C	PL	R6	2433
755A-2a	Same	1105	C	PL	R3	2434
755A-3a	Same	1106	C	PL	R8	
755A-4a	Same	1205	C	PL	R7	2435

| 755B-1a | HOLMES & NORTON / (Mortar & pestle) / DRUGGISTS / ROCKFORD / ILL. | 1209 | C | PL | R4 | 2438 |
| 755B-2a | Same | 1357 | C | PL | R8 | 2437 |

ILLINOIS-Continued

NUMBER	OBVERSE	REVERSE	METAL	EDGE	RARITY	H&G

ROCKFORD 755-Continued

755C-1a	HOPE & CLOW/STOVES/ HARDWARE/IRON &C./ (Padlock)/ROCKFORD,ILL.	1094	C	PL	R3	2440
755C-2a	Same	1098	C	PL	R8	2442
755C-3a	Same	1205	C	PL	R6	2441

(NOTE: The comma after Rockford is almost horizontal.)

| 755D-1a | WILLIAM KNAPP/ARTESIAN/ WELL/DRILLER/ ROCKFORD,ILL. | 1107 | C | PL | R3 | 2444 |

ROCKTON 762

762A-1a	V.A.LAKE/GRAIN/DEALER/ ROCKTON,ILL.	1018	C	R	R8	2446
762A-2a	Same	1047	C	R	R9	
762A-2d	Same	Same	C-N	R	R10	
762A-3d	Same	1069	C-N	R	R10	

34

ILLINOIS-Continued

NUMBER	OBVERSE	REVERSE	METAL	EDGE	RARITY	H&G

SANDWICH 775

| 775A-1a | SANDWICH/BANK/M.B. CASTLE/SANDWICH/ ILLINOIS. | DEPOSIT/EXCHANGE/&/ LOAN/OFFICE | C | PL | R5 | |

(NOTE: The M is apparently recut over a W, so it is uncertain whether this is the correct spelling, or whether the 775B-W.B.Castle is the correct spelling. H-R1162.)

775A-1b	Same	Same	BR	PL	R8	
775B-1a	W.B.CASTLE/DRUGGIST/ SANDWICH/ILLS.	1316	C	PL	R2	2448
775B-2a	SANDWICH/BANK/W.B. CASTLE,/SANDWICH,/ ILINOIS.	DEPOSITE/EXCHANGE/AND/ LOAN/OFFICE	C	PL	R2	2450

(NOTE: Error in spelling ILLINOIS AND DEPOSIT)

775B-2d	Same	Same	C-N	PL	R10	
775C-1a	A.G.GREENMAN/(mortar & pestle)/DRUGGIST/SANDWICH/ ILL.	1316	C	PL	R4	2453
775C-1b	Same	Same	BR	PL	R9	

35

ILLINOIS-Continued

NUMBER	OBVERSE	REVERSE	METAL	EDGE	RARITY	H&G

SPRINGFIELD 795

795A-1a	J.C.YAGER,/TRUNK/MAKER/ SPRINGFIELD ILL (H-R-1164)	1172	C	PL	R8	
795A-2a	Same	1274	C	PL	R2	2456
795A-2d	Same	Same	C-N	PL	R10	

795A-3
795A-4

| 795A-3a | Same | HENRY JENKENS/WHOLESALE /&/RETAIL/CLOTHIER/ST. LOUIS,MO. (Obv. MO.910C) | C | PL | R10 | 2457 |
| 795A-4a | Same | JOS.ZANONE/ICE/CREAM/ SALOON/285/CENTRAL AV. (Obv. OHIO 165GX) | C | PL | R8 | 2458 |

SYCAMORE 825

825A-1a	LOTT & WARNER/DRY GOODS/ GROCERIES/&C./SYCAMORE, ILLS.	1111	C	PL	R9	2463
825A-2a	Same	1117	C	PL	R5	2462
825A-3a	Same	1205	C	PL	R8	2460
825A-4a	Same	1207	C	PL	R7	2461

ILLINOIS-Continued

NUMBER	OBVERSE	REVERSE	METAL	EDGE	RARITY	H&G

WAUKEGAN 890

| 890A-1a | KINGSLEY/&/WHIPPLE/ GROCERIES &/ PROVISIONS/ WAUKEGAN/ILL. | 1105 | C | PL | R8 | |
| 890A-1b | Same | Same | BR | PL | R9 | |

890B-1b	J.L. LOVEDAY & CO./DRY GOODS/AND/GROCERIES/ WAUKEGAN ILL. (NOTE: All pieces reported to be copper have been found to be brass-- the copper piece is assumed to be non-existant.)	1106	BR	PL	R4	2464
890B-2a	J.L. LOVEDAY & CO./ 63 WASHINGTON ST./ WAUKEGAN/ILL.	1142	C	PL	R5	2466
890B-2b	Same	Same	BR	PL	R8	2467
890B-2e	Same	Same	W-M	PL	R9	2468

| 890C-1a | D.P. MILLEN/DEALER/IN/ BOOTS/& SHOES/WAUKEGAN/ LAKE CO./ILL. | 1105 | C | PL | R9 | 2471 |
| 890C-2a | Same | 1107 | C | PL | R8 | 2470 |

37

ILLINOIS-Continued

NUMBER   OBVERSE   REVERSE   METAL EDGE RARITY H&G

WOODSTOCK 920

920A-1a   M.D.STEVERS/GRAIN/DEALER   1195   C   PL   R7   2473
          /WOODSTOCK,ILL.

INDIANA

NUMBER	OBVERSE	REVERSE	METAL	EDGE	RARITY	H&G

ALBANY 5

| 5A-1a | ALLEGRE & WROUGHTON/ DEALERS/IN/DRY GOODS/ &/GROCERIES/ALBANY IND. | 1122 | C | PL | R5 | 2501 |

ALEXANDRIA 10

10A-1a	WOLFE & SHERMAN/STAPLE & FANCY/DRY GOODS/ ALEXANDRIA, IND.	1037	C	R	R4	2503
10A-1a1	Same	Same	C	PL	R8	2504
10A-1b	Same	Same	BR	R	R8	
10A-1i	Same	Same	Z	R	R8	
10A-2a	Same	1046	C	R	R9	2505
10A-2d	Same	Same	C-N	R	R10	2506
10A-3a	Same	1047	C	R	R9	
10A-3D	Same	Same	C-N	R	R10	

ANDERSON 20

20A    20B

39

INDIANA-Continued

NUMBER	OBVERSE	REVERSE	METAL	EDGE	RARITY	H&G

ANDERSON 20-Continued

20A-1a	J. P. BARNES/DEALER/IN/ STOVES/&/TINWARE/ ANDERSON/IND.	1299	C	PL	R4	2510
20A-2a	Same	1346	C	PL	R4	2511
20B-1a	T. & N. C. Mc CULLOUGH/ DEALERS/IN/HARDWARE/ ANDERSON/*IND*	1326	C	PL	R5	2513
20B-1b	Same	Same	BR	PL	R9	

AVILLA 70

70A-1a	BAUM WALTER & CO./ DEALERS IN/DRY/GOODS/ GROCERIES & C./AVILLA,IND.	1037	C	R	R6	2516
70A-1b	Same	Same	BR	R	R9	2517
70A-1i	Same	Same	Z	R	R9	2518
70A-2d	Same	1046	C-N	R	R10	
70A-3a	Same	1047	C	R	R9	
70A-3d	Same	Same	C-N	R	R10	2519

BETHEL 100

100A-1a	THOMPSON & WILEY/ DEALERS/IN/DRY GOODS/ AND/GROCERIES/BETHEL, IND.	1124	C	PL	R5	2527
100A-1b	Same	Same	BR	PL	R9	
100A-2a	Same	1180	C	PL	R4	2526

INDIANA-Continued

NUMBER　　OBVERSE　　　　　　　　REVERSE　　　　　　　　　METAL　EDGE　RARITY　H&G

BOWLING GREEN 120

NUMBER	OBVERSE	REVERSE	METAL	EDGE	RARITY	H&G
120A-1a	O.H.P. ASH'S/CHEAP/CASH/STORE/BOWLING GREEN, IND.	1021	C	PL	R9	2529
120A-2a	Same	1038	C	PL	R7	2530
120A-3a	Same	1042	C	R	R5	2531
120A-3b	Same	Same	BR	R	R6	2532
120A-3i	Same	Same	Z	R	R8	2533
120A-4d	Same	1046	C-N	R	R10	2534
120A-5a	Same	1047	C	R	R9	
120A-5d	Same	Same	C-N	R	R10	
120A-6d	Same	1069	C-N	R	R10	
120B-1a	ASH & BLACK/CASH/STORE/BOWLING GREEN	1030	C	PL	R3	2536
120B-2a	Same	1042	C	R	R5	2537
120B-2b	Same	Same	BR	R	R5	2538
120B-2i	Same	Same	Z	R	R8	
120B-3a	Same	1046	C	R	R9	2540
120B-4a	Same	1047	C	R	R9	
120B-4d	Same	Same	C-N	R	R10	

BRAZIL 130

NUMBER	OBVERSE	REVERSE	METAL	EDGE	RARITY	H&G
130A-1b	CONNELY'S/NEW/YORK/STORE/BRAZIL, IND.	1018	C	R	R8	
130A-1b	Same	Same	BR	R	R9	
130A-1c	Same	Same	Z	R	R9	
130A-2a	Same	1022	C	PL	R4	2541
130A-3a	Same	1026	C	PL	R6	
130A-4a	Same	1036	C	PL	R8	

41

INDIANA-Continued

NUMBER	OBVERSE	REVERSE	METAL	EDGE	RARITY	H&G

BRAZIL 130-Continued

130A-5a	Same	1042	C	R	R5	2542
130A-5b	Same	Same	BR	R	R6	2543
130A-5i	Same	Same	Z	R	R8	
130A-6a	Same	1047	C	R	R8	
130A-6d	Same	Same	C-N	R	R10	
130A-7d	Same	1069	C-N	R	R10	
130A-8a	Same	CARL HASS/493VINE ST. (Obverse of Ohio 165AM-1)	C	R	R10	

BROOKLYN 135

135A-1a	COX & LANDERS/DRY/GOODS/ CLOTHING/BOOTS/&/SHOES/ BROOKLYN, IND.	1046	C	R	R8	
135A-1a1	Same	Same	C	PL	R9	
135A-1d	Same	Same	C-N	R	R10	
135A-2a	Same	1047	C	R	R9	
135A-2a1	Same	Same	C	PL	R9	
135A-2d	Same	Same	C-N	R	R10	2547

BROOKVILLE 140

140A-1a	H. LINCK/DRY/GOODS/ GROCERIES/&/HARDWARE/ BROOKVILLE. IND.	1019	C	PL	R6	2550
140A-1a1	Same	Same	C	PL	R9	
140A-2a	Same	1026	C	PL	R8	
140A-3a	Same	1042	C	R	R6	2551
140A-3b	Same	Same	BR	R	R7	2552
140A-3i	Same	Same	Z	R	R8	
140A-4a	Same	1045	C	PL	R6	2549
140A-4i	Same	Same	Z	PL	R7	
140A-5a	Same	1047	C	R	R7	
140A-5d	Same	Same	C-N	R	R10	
140A-6d	Same	1069	C-N	R	R10	2554

INDIANA-Continued

NUMBER	OBVERSE	REVERSE	METAL	EDGE	RARITY	H&G

BROWNSBURG 145

145A-1a	G. W. NASH/DRUGS/ MEDICINES/WINES/LIQUORS/ NOTIONS & C./ BROWNSBURG, IND.	1311	C	R	R7	2556
145A-1b	Same	Same	BR	R	R9	
145A-1i	Same	Same	Z	R	R9	2558

BROWNSTOWN 150

| 150A-1a | S. S. EARLY & CO./DEALERS/ IN/DRY GOODS &./GROCERIES /BROWNSTOWN,/IND. | 1088 | C | PL | R6 | 2559 |
| 150A-1d | Same | Same | C-N | PL | R9 | |

BUTLER 155

| 155A-1a | J.LUTES/DEALER IN/DRY GOODS/AND/GROCERIES/ BUTLER,/IND. | 1122 | C | PL | R5 | 2561 |
| 155A-1d | Same | Same | C-N | PL | R9 | |

INDIANA-Continued

NUMBER	OBVERSE	REVERSE	METAL	EDGE	RARITY	H&G

CADIZ 160

160A / 160B

160A-1a	C. BOND above, crossed square and compasses in center DRUGGIST/CADIZ, IND. below	1037	C	R	R4	2563
160A-1b	Same	Same	BR	R	R9	
160A-1i	Same	Same	Z	R	R9	2565
160A-2d	Same	1046	C-N	R	R10	
160A-3a	Same	1047	C	R	R8	
160A-3d	Same	Same	C-N	R	R9	
160B-1a	HIATT & SHOWALTER/DRY/ GOODS/GROCERIES/&C./ CADIZ, IND.	1037	C	PL	R7	2567
160B-1a1	Same	Same	C	R	R8	2568
160B-1b	Same	Same	BR	R	R9	2569
160B-1i	Same	Same	Z	R	R9	2570
160B-2d	Same	1046	C-N	R	R10	2571
160B-3a	Same	1047	C	R	R8	
160B-3d	Same	Same	C-N	R	R10	

CENTERVILLE 165

165A-1a	GENTRYS/GROCERS/ CENTERVILLE/IND.	1046	C	R	R8	2574
165A-1b	Same	Same	BR	R	R9	2575
165A-1d	Same	Same	C-N	R	R10	
165A-1i	Same	Same	Z	R	R9	
165A-2a	Same	1047	C	R	R9	
165A-2d	Same	Same	C-N	R	R10	

44

INDIANA-Continued

NUMBER	OBVERSE	REVERSE	METAL	EDGE	RARITY	H&G

COLUMBIA CITY 175

| 175A-1a | GAFFNEY AND McDOWELL/ GROCERIES/LIQUORS/ CIGARS & C/COLUMBIA CITY/IND. | 1226 | C | PL | R7 | 2576 |
| 175A-1b | Same | Same | BR | PL | R9 | |

175B-1a	HARLEY & LINVILL/ HARDWARE,/STOVES/&/ TIN WARE,/COLUMBIA CITY/IND.	1088	C	PL	R4	2578
175B-1b	Same	Same	BR	PL	R8	
175B-2a	Same	1299	C	PL	R6	2579
175B-3a	Same	1302	C	PL	R9	

| 175C-1a | W. W. KEPNER & SON/DRY GOODS/&.GROCERIES,/ COLUMBIA CITY/*IND.* | 1088 | C | PL | R6 | 2581 |

INDIANA-Continued

NUMBER	OBVERSE	REVERSE	METAL	EDGE	RARITY	H&G

COLUMBIA CITY 175-Continued

175D-1a	DR. C. KINDERMAN/DRUGGIST/&/BOOK/SELLER/COLUMBIA CITY, IND.	1047	C	R	R8	
175D-1d	Same	Same	C-N	R	R10	2584
175D-2a	Same	1373	C	R	R3	2583
175D-2a1	Same	Same	C	PL	R9	

175E-1a	S. S. LAVEY/WATCHMAKER/&/JEWELRY/COLUMBIA CITY, IND.	DEALER/IN/CLOCKS/WATCHES/&/JEWELRY	C	R	R7	
175E-1a1	Same	Same	C	PL	R9	2587
175E-1i	Same	Same	Z	R	R7	
175E-2a	Same	1047	C	R	R8	
175E-2d	Same	Same	C-N	R	R10	2588

| 175F-1a | JOHN C. WASHBURN/DRY GOODS/&/GROCERIES/COLUMBIA CITY/*IND.* | 1169 | C | PL | R6 | 2590 |

INDIANA-Continued

NUMBER	OBVERSE	REVERSE	METAL	EDGE	RARITY	H&G

COMO 185

185A-1a	JACOB GROYER/GROCER/ MAIN ST./COMO, IND.	1176	C	PL	R4	2592
185A-1d	Same	Same	C-N	PL	R10	
185A-1e	Same	Same	W-M	PL	R10	2593
185A-2a	Same	1295	C	PL	R8	2594
185A-3a	Same	1331	C	PL	R9	
185A-3d	Same	Same	C-N	PL	R9	

CORUNNA 190

190A

190B

190A-1a	SAM'L BECK/DEALER/IN/ BUTTER, EGGS/HIDES, AND/ PELTS,/CORUNNA,/IND.	1127	C	PL	R5	2596
190A-1b	Same	Same	BR	PL	R5	2597
190A-2a	Same	1130	C	PL	R8	2598
190B-1a	IRA W. BOWEN,/DEALER/IN/ DRUGS,/MEDICINES,/ GROCERIES/&/HARDWARE,/ CORUNNA, IND.	1084	C	PL	R8	
190B-2b	Same	1085	BR	PL	R8	
190B-3a	Same	1181	C	PL	R6	2600
190B-4a	Same	1316	C	PL	R6	2601
190B-4b	Same	Same	BR	PL	R8	

47

INDIANA-Continued

NUMBER	OBVERSE	REVERSE	METAL	EDGE	RARITY	H&G

CORUNNA 190-Continued

190C

190D

190C-1a	JOHN CHILDS/DEALER/IN/ DRY GOODS,/GROCERIES,/ &C./CORUNNA,/*IND.*	1089	C	PL	R5	2603
190D-1a	J. L. & G. F. ROWE/DEALERS/ IN/DRY GOODS/GROCERIES & C./CORUNNA/IND.	1088	C	PL	R5	2605
190D-2a	Same	1089	C	PL	R6	2606
190D-3a	Same	1090	C	PL	R6	2607
190D-4a	Same	1128	C	PL	R6	2608
190D-5a	Same	1168	C	PL	R8	
190D-5b	Same	Same	BR	PL	R8	

DANVILLE 230

230A

230B

230A-1a	R. K. CARTER/DRY/GOODS/ GROCERIES BOOTS/&/SHOES/ DANVILLE, IND.	1046	C	R	R8	
230A-1d	Same	Same	C-N	R	R10	
230A-2a	Same	1047	C	R	R9	
230A-2d	Same	Same	C-N	R	R10	
230B-1a	CRADDICK & HOMAN/DEALERS IN/BOOKS/STATIONERY/ TOBACCO/&/CIGARS/ DANVILLE, IND.	1046	C	R	R6	2610
230B-1d	Same	Same	C-N	R	R10	
230B-1i	Same	Same	Z	R	R8	
230B-2a	Same	1047	C	R	R9	
230B-2d	Same	Same	C-N	R	R10	

INDIANA-Continued

NUMBER	OBVERSE	REVERSE	METAL	EDGE	RARITY	H&G

DANVILLE 230-Continued

230C-1a	S. A. RUSSELL/MERCHANT/ DANVILLE/IND.	1046	C	R	R8	2612
230C-1a1	Same	Same	C	PL	R9	
230C-1b	Same	Same	BR	R	R9	2613
230C-1d	Same	Same	C-N	R	R10	2614
230C-1i	Same	Same	Z	R	R9	2615
230C-2	Same	1047	C	R	R9	2616

DUBLIN 250

250A-1a	A. JENKS/DEALER IN/DRY/ GOODS/&/GROCERIES/ DUBLIN, IND.	1037	C	R	R7	2619
250A-1b	Same	Same	BR	R	R9	
250A-1i	Same	Same	Z	R	R9	
250A-2d	Same	1046	C-N	R	R10	2622
250A-3a	Same	1047	C	R	R9	
250A-3d	Same	Same	C-N	R	R10	

ELKHART 260

260A-1    260A-3

INDIANA-Continued

NUMBER	OBVERSE	REVERSE	METAL	EDGE	RARITY	H&G

ELKHART 260-Continued

NUMBER	OBVERSE	REVERSE	METAL	EDGE	RARITY	H&G
260A-1a	WM. BROOKS/HARDWARE/ AND/STOVES/BATTLE CREEK/&/ELKHART	1003	C	PL	R9	
260A-2a	Same	1202	C	PL	R8	2521
260A-3a	Similar to above, but the inside border shows beading all around	1206	C	PL	R5	2522
260A-4a	Same	1207	C	PL	R6	2523
260A-5a	Same	1208	C	PL	R8	

NOTE: This card is a joint token of Battle Creek, Mich and Elkhart, Ind., and was mistakenly listed by Hetrich and Guttag under Battle Creek, Ind which does not exist.

260B   260C-1a

NUMBER	OBVERSE	REVERSE	METAL	EDGE	RARITY	H&G
260B-1a	J. DAVENPORT & SON/ DEALERS/IN/DRY GOODS/ IND/ELKHART	1003	C	PL	R8	2624
260B-2a	Same	1161	C	PL	R9	
260C-1a	C. T. GREENE. & CO./ GROCERIES/& PROVISION./ DEALERS/ELKHART IND.	1003	C	PL	R8	2626
260C-2a	Same, but different die	1161	C	PL	R9	
260C-3a	Same	1161	C	PL	R9	

NUMBER	OBVERSE	REVERSE	METAL	EDGE	RARITY	H&G
260D-1a	Boot and shoe in center; JOHN GUIPE above. DEALER/ ELKHART, IND. below.	1114	C	PL	R5	2629
260D-2a	Same	1205	C	PL	R8	2628
260D-3a	Same	1207	C	PL	R5	2630

INDIANA-Continued

NUMBER	OBVERSE	REVERSE	METAL	EDGE	RARITY	H&G

EVANSVILLE 280

| 280A-1a | BITTROLFF & GEISLER./ JEWELERS/EVANSVILLE/ IND Small eagle below | Blank | C | PL | R9 | |
| 280B-1bo | P. L. GEISSLER/WATCH/ MAKER/4 (cstp)/ EVANSVILLE, IND | Blank struck over McClellan token | BR | PL | R9 | |

FORTVILLE 285

285A-1a	J. H. THOMAS/DEALER/ IN/DRY GOODS/GROCERIES & C/FORTVILLE,/IND.	1088	C	PL	R4	2632
285A-2a	Same	1122	C	PL	R5	2633
285A-3a	Same	1168	C	PL	R6	2634
285A-4a	Same	1350	C	PL	R5	2635

FORT WAYNE 290

| 290A-1a | C. ANDERSON/DEALER/IN/ GROCERIES/&/PROVISIONS/ FT. WAYNE, IND. NOTE: This piece comes with a badly broken reverse die. | 1228 | C | PL | R4 | 2637 |

INDIANA-Continued

NUMBER	OBVERSE	REVERSE	METAL	EDGE	RARITY	H&G

FORT WAYNE 290-Continued

290B

290C

290B-1a	ANDERSON & EVANS/ GROCERS/FT. WAYNE/IND.	1226	C	PL	R5	
290C-1d	PHOENIX GROCERY/T. K. BRACKENRIDGE/GROCERIES /&/PROVISIONS,/FT. WAYNE/ *IND.*	1222	C-N	PL	R9	
290C-2a	Same	1226	C	PL	R4	2647

290D

290E

290D-1a	A. D. BRANDIFF & CO./ HARDWARE/&/STOVES/ FT. WAYNE/*IND.*	1299	C	PL	R6	2639
290D-1d	Same	Same	C-N	PL	R9	
290E-1a	W. H. BROOKS JR./ WHOLESALE/DEALER IN/ WALL &/WINDOW PAPER,/ FT. WAYNE,/IND.	1089	C	PL	R9	
290E-2a	Same	1171	C	PL	R7	2643
290E-3a	Same	1226	C	PL	R9	
290E-4a	Same	1229	C	PL	R6	2642
290E-5a	Same	1323	C	PL	R6	2644
290E-5d	Same	Same	C-N	PL	R9	
290E-6a	Same	1350	C	PL	R6	2645
290E-7a	W.H. BROOKS, JR./WHOLESALE/ DEALER IN/WALL AND WINDOW/ PAPER/FT. WAYNE,/IND.	1350	C	PL	R7	

52

INDIANA-Continued

NUMBER	OBVERSE	REVERSE	METAL	EDGE	RARITY	H&G

FORT WAYNE 290-Continued

| 290F-1a | I. LAUFERTY/91/COLUMBIA/ST/FT. WAYNE,/IND. | 1337 | C | PL | R5 | 2650 |

| 290G-1a | P.PIERR/DRY GOODS/&/GROCERIES/FT. WAYNE,/IND. | 1088 | C | PL | R5 | 2652 |

| 290H-1a | C. SCHOERPF & CO./WHOLESALE/DRUGGISTS/FT. WAYNE/IND. | 1316 | C | PL | R3 | 2654 |

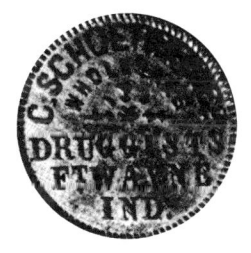

INDIANA-Continued

NUMBER	OBVERSE	REVERSE	METAL	EDGE	RARITY	H&G

FRANKLIN 295

305A

295A-1a	HULSMAN & ALEXANDER/ SALOON/SALE/&/LIVERY/ STABLE/FRANKLIN, IND.	1046	C	R	R5	2657
295A-1d	Same	Same	C-N	R	R10	2659
295A-2a	Same	1047	C	R	R9	
295A-2d	Same	Same	C-N	R	R10	

FREMONT 305

295A

305A-1a	G. W. FOLLETT/DRY/GOODS/ GROCERIES/BOOTS & SHOES/ &/HARDWARE/FREMONT, IND.	1037	C	R	R5	2661
305A-2a	Same	1046	C	R	R8	2663
305A-2b	Same	Same	BR	R	R8	2664
305A-2d	Same	Same	C-N	R	R10	
305A-2i	Same	Same	Z	R	R8	
305A-3a	Same	1047	C	R	R9	
305A-3d	Same	Same	C-N	R	R10	

INDIANA-Continued

NUMBER	OBVERSE	REVERSE	METAL	EDGE	RARITY	H&G

GALVESTON 320

320A-1

320A-2

320A-1b	R. S. McKEEN & CO./40/ DRAYAGE/GALVESTON	MURDOCK & SPENCER/139 W' FIFTH/STREET/CINCINNATI (Same as obv. Ohio 165DZ)	BR	R	R9	
320A-2b	R. S. McKEEN & CO./75/ DRAYAGE/GALVESTON	Same	BR	R	R9	

GOSHEN 350

350A-1a	DEMOCRAT JOB PRINTING OFFICE around border. W. A. BEANE/GOSHEN/IND. in center	1111	C	PL	R7	2667

350B-1a	HASCALL, ALDERMAN & BROWN around border. DRY/ GOODS/GROCERIES/&C./ GOSHEN/*IND.* in center.	1111	C	PL	R5	2675
350B-2a	Same	1114	C	PL	R7	

55

INDIANA-Continued

NUMBER	OBVERSE	REVERSE	METAL	EDGE	RARITY	H&G

GOSHEN 350-Continued

350C-1a	J. L. KINDIG/DRY/GOODS/ MERCHANT/GOSHEN, IND.	1037	C	R	R7	
350C-1i	Same	Same	Z	R	R8	
350C-2a	Same	1046	C	R	R5	2670
350C-2b	Same	Same	BR	R	R9	2671
350C-2d	Same	Same	C-N	R	R10	2672
350C-2i	Same	Same	Z	R	R9	2673
350C-3a	Same	1047	C	R	R8	
350C-3d	Same	Same	C-N	R	R10	

| 350D-1a | WM. H. LASH & CO./DRY/ GOODS,/GROCERIES/&C./ GOSHEN, IND. | 1111 | C | PL | R6 | 2677 |
| 350D-1b | Same | Same | BR | PL | R7 | |

350E-1a	JOSEPH LAUFERTY/ CLOTHIER/CHEAPSIDE/ BL'K/GOSHEN, IND.	1111	C	PL	R9	
350E-2a	Same	1339	C	PL	R6	
350E-2b	Same	Same	BR	PL	R5	2679

56

INDIANA-Continued

NUMBER	OBVERSE	REVERSE	METAL	EDGE	RARITY	H&G

GOSHEN 350-Continued

| 350F-1a | LAWRENCE & NOBLE/STOVES/&/HARDWARE/GOSHEN. IND. Padlock below | 1114 | C | PL | R4 | 2680 |
| 350F-1b | Same | Same | BR | PL | R4 | 2681 |

| 350G-1a | C.G.MARCH/WHOLESALE/GROCER &/DRUGGIST/IMPR. OF/LIQUORS & CIGARS/GOSHEN, IND. | 1111 | C | PL | R5 | 2683 |

GRANVILLE 355

355A-1a	C. CROOKS & CO./DRY/GOODS/HARDWARE/BOOTS/& SHOES/GRANVILLE,IND.	1037	C	R	R5	2685
355A-1b	Same	Same	BR	R	R9	2686
355A-1i	Same	Same	Z	R	R9	2688
355A-2d	Same	1046	C-N	R	R10	
355A-3a	Same	1047	C	R	R8	
355A-3d	Same	Same	C-N	R	R10	

INDIANA-Continued

NUMBER	OBVERSE	REVERSE	METAL	EDGE	RARITY	H&G

GREENFIELD 360

360A-1a	CARR RYON & CO/DRY/ GOODS/GREENFIELD, IND.	1046	C	R	R6	2691
360A-1b	Same	Same	BR	R	R8	2692
360A-1d	Same	Same	C-N	R	R10	
360A-1i	Same	Same	Z	R	R9	
360A-2a	Same	1047	C	R	R8	
360A-2d	Same	Same	C-N	R	R10	

GREENSBORO 365

| 365A-1a | BALDWIN & SWEET/DEALERS/ ALL KINDS/OF/GROCERIES/ GREENSBORO IND | 1387 | C | PL | R8 | 2695 |

HAGERSTOWN 370

| 370A-1a | E. & L. SMALL/DEALER/IN/ DRY GOODS/BOOTS/&/SHOES/ HARTFORD CITY,IND. | 1007 | C | PL | R6 | 2697 |
| 370A-2b | Same | 1018 | BR | R | R9 | |

58

INDIANA-Continued

NUMBER	OBVERSE	REVERSE	METAL	EDGE	RARITY	H&G

HAGERSTOWN 370-Continued

370A-2d	Same	Same	C-N	R	R9	
370A-3a	Same	1028	C	PL	R8	2698
370A-4a	Same	1042	C	R	R7	2700
370A-4b	Same	Same	BR	R	R7	2701
370A-4i	Same	Same	Z	R	R9	2702
370A-5a	Same	1047	C	R	R8	
370A-6a	Same	1069	C	R	R9	2703
370A-6d	Same	Same	C-N	R	R10	2704

HARTFORD CITY 395

395A-1a	JAS. LYON/DRY/GOODS/ GROCERIES/BOOTS/& SHOES/ HARTFORD CITY, IND.	1037	C	R	R7	2706
395A-1b	Same	Same	BR	R	R9	2707
395A-1i	Same	Same	Z	R	R9	
395A-2a	Same	1046	C	R	R7	2709
395A-3a	Same	1047	C	R	R8	2710
395A-3d	Same	Same	C-N	R	R10	

HUNTINGTON 430

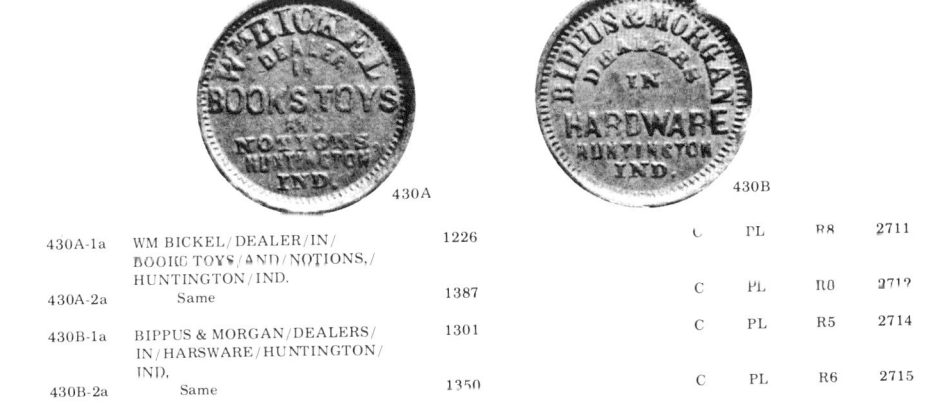

430A

430B

430A-1a	WM BICKEL/DEALER/IN/ BOOKS TOYS/AND/NOTIONS,/ HUNTINGTON/IND.	1226	C	PL	R8	2711
430A-2a	Same	1387	C	PL	R8	2712
430B-1a	BIPPUS & MORGAN/DEALERS/ IN/HARSWARE/HUNTINGTON/ IND.	1301	C	PL	R5	2714
430B-2a	Same	1350	C	PL	R6	2715

59

INDIANA-Continued

NUMBER	OBVERSE	REVERSE	METAL	EDGE	RARITY	H&G

HUNTINGTON 430-Continued

| 430C-1a | SAM BUCHANAN/DEALER/IN/AGRICULTURAL/IMPLEMENTS/HUNTINGTON/IND. | 1169 | C | PL | R6 | 2717 |

430D

430E

430D-1a	JESSE DAVIS/DEALER/IN/DRUGS/AND/MEDICINES/HUNTINGTON/IND.	1166	C	PL	R9	
430D-2a	Same	1316	C	PL	R4	2719
430D-3a	Same	1323	C	PL	R9	2720
430E-1a	J. W. GRIFFITH/DEALER/IN/DRUGS/AND/MEDICINES/HUNTINGTON/IND	1316	C	PL	R8	

| 430F-1a | J. H. INSWORTH & CO/DEALERS/IN/DRY GOODS/&/GROCERIES/HUNTINGTON/IND. | 1169 | C | PL | R5 | 2721 |

60

INDIANA-Continued

NUMBER	OBVERSE	REVERSE	METAL	EDGE	RARITY	H&G

HUNTINGTON 430-Continued

430G-1a	J. S. REAM/DEALER/IN/ GROCERIES/AND/PROVISIONS, /HUNTINGTON/IND.	1171	C	PL	R9	
430H-1a	SCHAFER & BRO./DRUGGISTS/ &/APOTHECARIES,/ HUNTINGTON,/IND.	1316	C	PL	R8	2723

INDIANAPOLIS 460

460A-1a	ALVORD, CALDWELL & ALVORD./WHOLESALE/ GROCERS/68/E. WASH.ST./ INDIANAPOLIS	1037	C	R	R5	2725
460A-1b	Same	Same	BR	R	R6	2726
460A-1i	Same	Same	Z	R	R9	
460A-2a	Same	1042	C	R	R9	
460A-3a	Same	1043	C	R	R9	

61

INDIANA-Continued

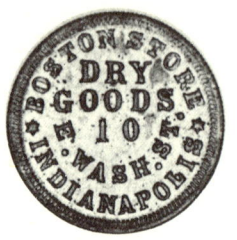

NUMBER	OBVERSE	REVERSE	METAL	EDGE	RARITY	H&G

INDIANAPOLIS 460-Continued

460B-1a	BOSTON STORE/DRY/GOODS/ 10/E.WASH. ST./INDIANAPOLIS	1037	C	R	R4	2727
460B-1b	Same	Same	BR	R	R7	2728
460B-1i	Same	Same	Z	R	R9	
460B-2a	Same	1042	C	R	R9	
460B-3d	Same	1046	C-N	R	R10	
460B-4a	Same	1047	C	R	R8	

| 460C-1a | C. E. GEISENDORFF & CO./ WOOL/DEALERS/&/MAN'FRS. | HOOSIER WOOLEN/FACTORY/ INDIANAPOLIS, IND. | C | PL | R5 | 2730 |
| 460C-2a | Same inscription, but name of firm in small letters | Same | C | PL | R5 | 2731 |

| 460D-1a | Same inscription, but G. W. instead of C. E. | Same | C | PL | R3 | 2733 |
| 460D-2a | G. W. GEISENDORFF & CO./ DOMESTIC/STAPLE/AND/ FANCY. GOODS/61 & 63 WEST/WASHINGTON/ INDIANAPOLIS/*IND.* | HOOSIER JEANS/AND/ HOME MADE/WOOLEN GOODS/OF EVERY/VARIETY/ ALWAYS/ON HAND. | C | PL | R6 | 2734 |

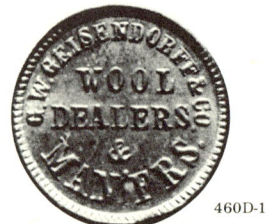

62

INDIANA-Continued

NUMBER　　OBVERSE　　　　　　REVERSE　　　　　　　　METAL　EDGE　RARITY　H&G

INDIANAPOLIS 460-Continued

460E

460F

460E-1a	M. H. GOOD/WHOLESALE/ &/RETAIL/DRY GOODS/ INDIANAPOLIS.	1028	C	R	R9	2736
460E-2a	Same	1037	C	R	R6	2737
460E-2b	Same	Same	BR	R	R6	2738
460E-2i	Same	Same	Z	R	R9	
460E-3a	Same	1043	C	R	R8	
460E-4d	Same	1046	C-N	R	R10	2739
460E-5a	Same	1047	C	R	R8	
460F-1a	CITY/SHOE/STORE/J. B. GROUT/3 & 5/W.WASH.ST. /INDIANAPOLIS	1028	C	R	R8	2741
460F-2a	Same	1037	C	R	R4	2742
460F-2b	Same	Same	BR	R	R6	2743
460F-2i	Same	Same	Z	R	R7	2744
460F-3d	Same	1046	C-N	R	R10	
460F-4a	Same	1047	C	R	R8	
460F-4d	Same	Same	C-N	R	R10	

460G

460H

460G-1a	J. C. HERETH/SADDLER/ 89/E.WASH.ST./INDIANAPOLIS	1037	C	R	R3	2746
460G-1b	Same	Same	BR	R	R5	2747
460G-1i	Same	Same	Z	R	R9	
460G-2a	Same	1017	C	R	R8	
460G-2d	Same	Same	C-N	R	R10	2749
460H-1a	CITY/GROCERY/C. L. HOLMES/ INDIANAPOLIS	1037	C	R	R5	2751
460H-1b	Same	Same	BR	R	R6	2752
460H-1i	Same	Same	Z	R	R8	2753
460H-2a	Same	1043	C	R	R9	

63

INDIANA-Continued

NUMBER	OBVERSE	REVERSE	METAL	EDGE	RARITY	H&G

INDIANAPOLIS 460-Continued

460H-3d	Same	1046	C-N	R	R10	2754
460H-4a	Same	1047	C	R	R8	
460H-4d	Same	Same	C-N	R	R9	

460I

460J

460I-1a	J. B. JOHNSON/GROCER/&/ PRODUCE/DEALER/ INDIANAPOLIS	1037	C	R	R3	2756
460I-1b	Same	Same	BR	R	R5	2757
460I-1i	Same	Same	Z	R	R8	
460I-2a	Same	1043	C	R	R9	
460I-3d	Same	1046	C-N	R	R10	2759
460I-4d	Same	1047	C-N	R	R10	
460J-1a	CHARLES KUHN/BUTCHER/ 107/MICH./ST. INDIANAPOLIS	1037	C	R	R4	2761
460J-1b	Same	Same	BR	R	R5	2762
460J-1i	Same	Same	Z	R	R8	2763
460J-2a	Same	1047	C	R	R8	
460J-2d	Same	Same	C-N	R	R10	2764

460K-1a	J. F. LENOUR/DRUGGIST/ NO 5/BATES/HOUSE. INDIANAPOLIS	1047	C	R	R8	2766
460K-1d	Same	Same	C-N	R	R10	
460K-2a	Same	1311	C	R	R6	2768
460K-2b	Same	Same	BR	R	R7	2769
460K-2i	Same	Same	Z	R	R8	2770

NOTE: The Lenour cards are a die error intended for Senour. See Ind. 460R

64

INDIANA-Continued

NUMBER　　OBVERSE　　　　　　　REVERSE　　　　　　　　　METAL　EDGE　RARITY　H&G

INDIANAPOLIS 460-Continued

460L-1a	JOSEPH McCREERY/NO. 85/ EAST/WASHINGTON ST./ IND'PLS./IND.	STOVES/CUTLERY/GLASS &/ QUEENSWARE/WHOLESALE/ &/RETAIL	C	PL	R3	2771
460M-1a	MORITZ, BRO.&CO./ CLOTHIERS/CLOTHS/ CASSIMERES/&VESTINGS/ INDIANAPOLIS	1037	C	R	R5	2773
460M-1b	Same	Same	BR	R	R6	2774
460M-1i	Same	Same	Z	R	R9	
460M-2a	Same	1043	C	R	R9	
460M-3a	Same	1047	C	R	R8	
460M-3d	Same	Same	C-N	R	R10	2776
460N-1a	R.R.PARKER/SELLS/ LADIES/AND GENTS/ FURNISHING/GOODS/30 W./ WASINGTON, ST./ INDIANAPOLIS/IND.	Half length figure in center shows shirt labeled PARKER/ SHIRTS/WILL FIT Above H.H. Parker and INDIANAPOLIS, IND. below	C	PL	R5	2778

65

INDIANA-Continued

NUMBER	OBVERSE	REVERSE	METAL	EDGE	RARITY	H&G

INDIANAPOLIS 460-Continued

460O

460P

460O-1a	POMEROY, FRY & CO. / IRON / MERCHANTS / INDIANAPOLIS	1037	C	R	R6	2780
460O-1b	Same	Same	BR	R	R6	2781
460O-1i	Same	Same	Z	R	R8	2782
460O-2d	Same	1046	C-N	R	R10	2783
460O-3a	Same	1047	C	R	R9	
460O-3d	Same	Same	C-N	R	R10	
460P-1a	ROLL & SMITH / CARPETS / & / WALL PAPER / 16 ILL.ST. / INDIANAPOLIS	1037	C	R	R4	2785
460P-1b	Same	Same	BR	R	R6	2786
460P-1i	Same	Same	Z	R	R8	
460P-2d	Same	1046	C-N	R	R10	2788
460P-3a	Same	1047	C	R	R8	
460P-3d	Same	Same	C-N	R	R10	

460Q

460R

460Q-1a	ROOS & SCHMALZRIED / BUTCHERS / INDIANAPOLIS	1037	C	R	R4	2790
460Q-1b	Same	Same	BR	R	R6	2791
460Q-1i	Same	Same	Z	R	R8	2792
460Q-2a	Same	1043	C	R	R9	
460Q-3a	Same	1047	C	R	R8	
460Q-3d	Same	Same	C-N	R	R10	2793
460R-1a	J. F. SENOUR / DRUGGIST / NO 5 / BATES / HOUSE / INDIANAPOLIS	1037	C	R	R6	2795
460R-1b	Same	Same	BR	R	R6	2796
460R-1i	Same	Same	Z	R	R8	
460R-2d	Same	1047	C-N	R	R10	
460R-3a	Same	1311	C	R	R5	2799

INDIANA-Continued

NUMBER	OBVERSE	REVERSE	METAL	EDGE	RARITY	H&G

INDIANAPOLIS 460-Continued

| 460R-4a | ONE GLASS/SODA/WATER/AT/J. F. SENOUR'S/DRUG STORE | 1316 | C | PL | R5 | 2801 |

| 460S-1a | SMITH & TAYLOR/NO/20/TOY/STORE/NO. 20./WASHINGTON ST. INDIANAPOLIS | 1084 | C | PL | R5 | 2803 |

460T-1a	M. SPENCER/GROCER/202/E.WASH.ST./INDIANAPOLIS	1037	C	R	R6	2805
460T-1a1	Same	Same	C	PL	R9	
460T-1b	Same	Same	BR	R	R7	2806
460T-1i	Same	Same	Z	R	R8	2807
460T-2a	Same	1043	C	R	R9	
460T-3d	Same	1046	C-N	R	R10	2808
460T-4a	Same	1047	C	R	R9	2809
460T-4d	Same	Same	C N	R	R10	

67

INDIANA-Continued

NUMBER	OBVERSE	REVERSE	METAL	EDGE	RARITY	H&G

INDIANAPOLIS 460-Continued

460U-1a	MRS.A.THOMSON & SON/ STATIONERS/NO 7/PENN /ST./INDIANAPOLIS	1037	C	R	R7	2810
460U-1b	Same	Same	BR	R	R7	2811
460U-1i	Same	Same	Z	R	R9	2812
460U-2a	Same	1042	C	R	R9	
460U-3a	Same	1043	C	R	R8	
460U-4a	Same	1047	C	R	R8	
460U-4d	Same	Same	C-N	R	R10	2814

| 460V-1a | TYLER'S/BEE HIVE/DRY GOODS/2 WEST/WASHINGTON. ST./INDIANAPOLIS | 1351 | C | PL | R6 | 2816 |

| 460W-1a | VOEGLE & METZGER,/NO. 83/ EAST/WASHINGTON/STREET./ IND'PLS./IND. | MANUFACTURERS/OF/STOVES/ TINWARE/STAMPED WARE/ &/JAPANERS. | C | PL | R6 | 2818 |

68

INDIANA-Continued

NUMBER　　OBVERSE　　　　　　REVERSE　　　　　　　METAL　EDGE　RARITY　H&G

INDIANAPOLIS 460-Continued

NUMBER	OBVERSE	REVERSE	METAL	EDGE	RARITY	H&G
460X-1a	WEAVER & MAGUIRE/ GROCERS/COR./ILLS.ST. & IND/AVE./INDIANAPOLIS	1037	C	R	R6	2820
460X-1b	Same	Same	BR	R	R6	2821
460X-1i	Same	Same	Z	R	R8	2822
460X-2d	Same	1046	C-N	R	R10	
460X-3a	Same	1047	C	R	R8	
460X-3d	Same	Same	C-N	R	R10	

460Y-1a	J. B. WILSON/DEALER/IN/ HARDWARE/&/CUTLERY/ INDIANAPOLIS.	1037	C	R	R4	2826
460Y-1b	Same	Same	BR	R	R5	2827
460Y-1i	Same	Same	Z	R	R8	2828
460Y-2a	Same	1047	C	R	R9	
460Y-2d	Same	Same	C-N	R	R10	2830

| 460Y-3e | GOOD AT J. B. WILSON'S/ FOR outside wreath. Inside wreath ONE/DIME (size 18mm) | BREAD in center of wreath 2 large and 4 small stars surrounding word. | W-M | PL | R8 | |

INDIANA-Continued

NUMBER	OBVERSE	REVERSE	METAL	EDGE	RARITY	H&G

INDIANAPOLIS 460-Continued

460Y-4e	Similar to above, but HALF/DIME within wreath (Size 14mm)	Similar to preceding, but only two stars in wreath	W-M	PL	R8	
460Z-1a	A.D.WOOD/HARDWARE/MERCHANT/INDIANAPOLIS In center is small square and compasses	1037	C	R	R7	2832
460Z-1b	Same	Same	BR	R	R7	2833
460Z-1i	Same	Same	Z	R	R9	
460Z-2a	Same	1043	C	R	R9	
460Z-3a	Same	1047	C	R	R8	
460Z-3d	Same	Same	C-N	R	R10	

70

INDIANA-Continued

NUMBER	OBVERSE	REVERSE	METAL	EDGE	RARITY	H&G

JAMESTOWN 470

470A-1a	G. W. WAYLAND/GOODS/ DRUGS/MEDICINES NOTIONS/ & C./JAMESTOWN, IND.	1046	C	R	R9	
470A-2a	Same	1047	C	R	R9	
470A-2d	Same	Same	C-N	R	R10	

JONESBORO 495

495A-1a	ROBT. COODER/DRY/GOODS/ &/GROCERIES/JONESBORO, IND. (NOTE: Also struck on very thin flan)	1046	C	R	R6	2808
495A-1b	Same	Same	BR	R	R9	2839
495A-1d	Same	Same	C-N	R	R10	2840
495A-1i	Same	Same	Z	R	R9	2841
495A-2a	Same	1047	C	R	R8	
495A-2d	Same	Same	C-N	R	R10	

71

INDIANA-Continued

NUMBER	OBVERSE	REVERSE	METAL	EDGE	RARITY	H&G

KENDALLVILLE 500

| 500A-1a | BEYER, MEYER & BRO./ WHOLESALE/&/RETAIL/ DRUGGIST/KENDALLVILLE/ IND. | 1316 | C | PL | R9 | 2843 |

500B-1a	BOSWORTH & WHITFORD/ DEALERS/IN/GROCERIES/ &/PROVISIONS/KENDALLVILLE /IND.	1091	C	PL	R8	2847
500B-1b	Same	Same	BR	PL	R9	2848
500B-2a	Same	1227	C	PL	R9	

| 500C-1a | M.M. BOWEN/DEALER IN/ GROCERIES/PROVISIONS/&/ CEGARS/KENDALLVILLE, IND. | 1127 | C | PL | R8 | 2845 |

INDIANA-Continued

NUMBER　OBVERSE　REVERSE　METAL　EDGE　RARITY　H&G

KENDALLVILLE 500-Continued

NUMBER	OBVERSE	REVERSE	METAL	EDGE	RARITY	H&G
500D-1a	W. & J. R. BUNYAN/DEALERS IN/DRUGS/MEDICINES/ PAINTS, OILS/&C./ KENDALLVILLE,IND.	1130	C	PL	R8	2851
500D-2a	Same	1226	C	PL	R7	2850
500E-1a	J.F.CORLE/DEALER IN/DRY GOODS &/GROCERIES/ KENDALLVILLE,IND.	1171	C	PL	R6	2853
500E-2a	Same	1181	C	PL	R5	2852
500F-1a	S.C.EVANS & CO./DEALERS/ IN/DRY GOODS/GROCERIES & C./KENDALLVILLE,/IND.	1082	C	PL	R7	2855
500F-1b	Same	Same	BR	PL	R8	2856
500F-2a	Same	1089	C	PL	R6	2857
500F-2b	Same	Same	BR	PL	R8	
500F-3a	Same	1226	C	PL	R7	2858

INDIANA-Continued

NUMBER	OBVERSE	REVERSE	METAL	EDGE	RARITY	H&G

KENDALLVILLE 500-Continued

| 500G-1a | G.C. GLATTE/DEALER/IN/ GROCERIES/PROVISIONS/ &C./KENDALLVILLE,IND. | 1122 | C | PL | R7 | |
| 500G-2a | Same | 1181 | C | PL | R5 | 2860 |

500H 500I

500H-1a	J. H. GOTSCH/DEALER/IN/ CLOCKS,/WATCHES/&/ JEWELRY,/KENDALLVILLE, IND.	1321	C	PL	R9	2862
500H-1b	Same	Same	BR	PL	R9	2863
500I-1a	E. GRADEN/LIVERY &/SALE/ STABLE/KENDALLVILLE,IND.	1127	C	PL	R3	2865

| 500J-1a | JACOBS & CO./DEALERS/IN/ DRY GOODS/& CLOTHING/ KENDALLVILLE, IND. | 1083 | C | PL | R8 | 2867 |
| 500J-2a | Same | 1181 | C | PL | R8 | 2868 |

74

INDIANA-Continued

NUMBER	OBVERSE	REVERSE	METAL	EDGE	RARITY	H&G

KENDALLVILLE 500-Continued

500K-1a	JONES & MOSHER'S/BAKERY/ &/PROVISION/STORE,/ KENDALLVILLE,/IND.	1229	C	PL	R7	2870
500K-1b	Same	Same	BR	PL	R7	2871
500K-1d	Same	Same	C-N	PL	R9	

| 500L-1a | J. J. JOYCE/DEALER/IN/ GROCERIES/&/PROVISIONS/ KENDALLVILLE/IND. | 1335 | C | PL | R5 | 2873 |

| 500M-1a | J.LANTS/DEALER/IN/BOOTS &/SHOES,/KENDALLVILLE,/ IND. | 1318 | C | PL | R5 | 2875 |

75

INDIANA-Continued

NUMBER	OBVERSE	REVERSE	METAL	EDGE	RARITY	H&G

KENDALLVILLE 500-Continued

500N-1a	S.J.M.LOOMIS/DEALER/IN/DRY GOODS/AND/GROCERIES/KENDALLVILLE/IND.	1083	C	PL	R8	2877
500N-1b	Same	Same	BR	PL	R9	2878
500N-2a	Same	1089	C	PL	R6	2879
500N-2b	Same	Same	BR	PL	R7	2880
500N-3a	Same	1127	C	PL	R6	2881
500-N4a	Same	1128	C	PL	R8	2882

| 500O-1a | F.W. MESSING/DEALER/IN/GROCERIES/&/LIQUORS/KENDALLVILLE/IND. | 1335 | C | PL | R4 | 2884 |

| 500P-1a | MILLER & CROW/DEALERS/IN/GROCERIES/&/PROVISIONS/KENDALLVILLE/IND. | 1350 | C | PL | R5 | 2886 |
| 500P-1d | Same | Same | C-N | PL | R9 | |

76

INDIANA-Continued

NUMBER | OBVERSE | REVERSE | METAL | EDGE | RARITY | H&G

KENDALLVILLE 500-Continued

500Q-1a	G.S.ROWELL & SON / PRODUCE / DEALERS / KENDALLVILLE, IND.	1091	C	PL	R5	2888
500Q-1b	Same	Same	BR	PL	R9	
500Q-2a	Same	1130	C	PL	R5	2889

500R   500S

500R-1a	STEER & BOWEN / DEALERS / IN / HARDWARE / KENDALLVILLE / IND.	1326	C	PL	R6	2892
500R-1b	Same	Same	BR	PL	R9	2893
500S-1a	JOSEPH THEW / MANUFR. / DEALER IN / BOOTS / & / SHOES, / KENDALLVILLE, IND.	1318	C	PL	R8	2895

| 500T-1a | W.S.THOMAS / DEALER / IN / DRY GOODS / & / GROCERIES / KENDALLVILLE, IND. | 1122 | C | PL | R8 | |
| 500T-2a | Same | 1181 | C | PL | R7 | 2897 |

77

INDIANA-Continued

NUMBER	OBVERSE	REVERSE	METAL	EDGE	RARITY	H&G

KENDALLVILLE 500-Continued

500U-1a	D.S.WELCH/DRY GOODS/ AND/GROCERIES,/ KENDALLVILLE,/IND.	1127	C	PL	R6	2902
500U-2a	Same	1168	C	PL	R6	
500U-2b	Same	Same	BR	PL	R6	
500U-3a	Same	1181	C	PL	R9	2900
500U-3b	Same	Same	BR	PL	R9	2901
500U-4a	Same	1226	C	PL	R5	2899

KOKOMO 510

| 510A-1a | J.V.CULLEN/DEALER/IN/ GROCERIES/KOKOMO,/IND. | 1122 | C | PL | R6 | 2903 |

| 510B-1a | HASKETT & CO/NEXT/DOOR TO/JAY & DOLLMAN,/ KOKOMO,/IND. | GO TO THE/PRAIRIE/STORE/ FOR/DRY GOODS | C | PL | R5 | 2905 |

INDIANA-Continued

NUMBER	OBVERSE	REVERSE	METAL	EDGE	RARITY	H&G

KOKOMO 530-Continued

510C-1a	I.N.PATTISON/DRUGGIST/ DRUGGIST/KOKOMO/IND Mortar and pestle in center.	1316	C	PL	R7	2907

LA PORTE 530

530A-1a	L.ELIEL/CLOTHIER/NO 1./ TEEGARDEN BL'K/LA PORTE, IND.	1114	C	PL	R6	2909

530B-1a	J. FALLER & SON/ WATCHMAKERS./AND/ JEWELERS/LA PORTE, IND	1003	C	PL	R6	2911
530B-2a	Same	1165	C	PL	R7	2912
530B-2b	Same	Same	BR	PL	R7	2913
530B-3a	Same	1202	C	PL	R6	2914

INDIANA-Continued

NUMBER	OBVERSE	REVERSE	METAL	EDGE	RARITY	H&G

LAPORTE 530-Continued

530C-1a	JAS.LEWIS & CO. above, beehive in center LA PORTE, IND. below	1112	C	PL	R6	
530C-2a	Same	1114	C	PL	R3	2916
530C-3a	Same	1116	C	PL	R6	

530D 530E

| 530D-1a | J.M.NEUBURGER/CLOTHIER/BALL'S CORNER/LA PORTE, IND. | 1357 | C | PL | R6 | 2918 |
| 530E-1a | NEUBURGER & HAMBURGER/CLOTHIERS/NO. 1/UNION BL'K/LA PORTE/IND. | 1119 | C | PL | R7 | 2920 |

| 530F-1a | W.W.WALLACE/WHOLESALE/&/RETAIL/GROCER/LA PORTE, /IND. | 1115 | C | PL | R5 | |
| 530F-2a | Same | 1119 | C | PL | R6 | 2922 |

INDIANA-Continued

NUMBER	OBVERSE	REVERSE	METAL	EDGE	RARITY	H&G

LAPORTE 530-Continued

530G-1a	L.D.WEBBER./STOVES/&/ HARDWARE/LA PORTE, IND.	1112	C	PL	R9	
530G-2a	Same	1118	C	PL	R3	2924
530G-3a	Same	1119	C	PL	R5	

LIGONIER 550

| 550A-1a | O.ARNOLD/DRUGGIST/AND/ GROCER/LIGONIER,/IND. | 1316 | C | PL | R3 | 2925 |

550B-1a	BARNEY BRO./GENERAL/ DRY GOODS/LIGONIER,/IND/	1001	C	PL	R5	2927
550B-2a	Same	1222	C	PL	R6	2928
550B-3a	Same	1224	C	PL	R5	2929
550B-3b	Same	Same	BR	PL	R6	2930
550B-4a	Same	1225	C	PL	R7	
550B-1b	Same	Same	BR	PL	R9	

81

INDIANA-Continued

NUMBER　　OBVERSE　　　　　　　　REVERSE　　　　　　　METAL　EDGE　RARITY　H&G

LIGONIER 550-Continued

| 550C-1a | J.C.BEST/HARDWARE/STOVES /TINWARE/&C./LIGONIER, IND. | 1299 | C | PL | R6 | 2932 |
| 550C-2a | Same | 1326 | C | PL | R8 | 2933 |

550D-1a	J DECKER/GROCERIES/AND/ PROVISIONS/LIGONIER,/IND.	1084	C	PL	R4	2935
550D-1b	Same	Same	BR	PL	R4	2936
550D-2a	Same	1088	C	PL	R7	
550D-3a	Same	1223	C	PL	R7	

550E-1a	S.MIER & CO./DRY GOODS/ CLOTHING &/PRODUCE/ DEALERS,/LIGONIER,/IND.	1083	C	PL	R4	2939
550E-2a	Same	1089	C	PL	R5	2940
550E-2b	Same	Same	BR	PL	R6	2941
550E-3a	Same	1091	C	PL	R5	2942
550E-3b	Same	Same	BR	PL	R9	

INDIANA-Continued

NUMBER	OBVERSE	REVERSE	METAL	EDGE	RARITY	H&G

LIGONIER 550-Continued

550F-1a	GEO.C.NILL/DRUGS/ GROCERIES/STATIONARY & C/LIGONIER,/IND.	1169	C	PL	R8	
550F-2a	Same	1310	C	PL	R5	2944
550F-2b	Same	Same	BR	PL	R8	2945

550G-1a	J. PEARCE,/DRUGS,/ GROCERIES/& NOTIONS,/ LIGONIER/IND.	1169	C	PL	R5	
550G-1b	Same	Same	BR	PL	R8	
550G-2a	Same	1310	C	PL	R5	

| 550G-3a | J. PEARCE/DRUGS,/ GROCERIES,/& NOTIONS,/ LIGONIER/MICH | 1310 | C | PL | R6 | 4469 |
| 550G-3b | Same | Same | BR | PL | R8 | 4470 |

NOTE: The above piece, originally listed as Michigan, is a die error.

83

INDIANA-Continued

NUMBER	OBVERSE	REVERSE	METAL	EDGE	RARITY	H&G

LIGONIER 550-Continued

| 550H-1a | E.REEVE/GROCERIES,/CROCKERY,/GLASSWARE/&C./LIGONIER,/IND. | 1088 | C | PL | R4 | 2947 |
| 550H-1b | Same | Same | BR | PL | R5 | |

550I-1a	STRAUS BROTHERS/GENERAL/DRY GOODS/CLOTHING &/PRODUCE/DEALERS/LIGONIER,IND.	1084	C	PL	R4	2949
550I-1b	Same	Same	BR	PL	R6	2950
550I-2a	Same	1088	C	PL	R4	2951
550I-3a	Same	1171	C	PL	R5	2952
550I-3b	Same	Same	BR	PL	R9	

| 550J-1a | C.G.VAIL/DRY GOODS/GROCERIES/&C./LIGONIER,IND. | 1088 | C | PL | R7 | 2954 |

84

INDIANA-Continued

NUMBER	OBVERSE	REVERSE	METAL	EDGE	RARITY	H&G

LIGONIER 550-Continued

550K-1a	J.C.ZIMMERMAN/DRY GOODS/ CLOTHING & C./LIGONIER, /IND.	1088	C	PL	R6	2957
550K-2a	Same	1224	C	PL	R5	2958
550K-2b	Same	Same	BR	PL	R5	2959

LISBON 560

560A-1a	C.D.BAUGHMAN & BRO./ DEALERS/IN/DRY GOODS/ AND/GROCERIES/LISBON, /IN	1318	C	PL	R6	2961
560A-1d	Same	Same	C-N	PL	R9	

LOGANSPORT 570

570A-1a	BOOTH & STURGES/DEALERS/ IN/BOOTS/AND/SHOES/ LOGANSPORT,/IND.	1318	C	PL	R6	2963

INDIANA-Continued

NUMBER	OBVERSE	REVERSE	METAL	EDGE	RARITY	H&G

LOGANSPORT 570-Continued

570B-1b	H.C.EVERSOLE/BROADWAY/ LOGANSPORT,IND.	DEALER/IN/CLOCKS/ WATCHES/-&-/JEWELRY (Same as Rev Ind. 175E-1)	BR	PL	R9	
570C-1a	M.H.GRIDLEY/LOGANSPORT,/ IND. Eagle in glory in center	1326	C	PL	R6	2965
570D-1a	A.KENDALL/DEALERS/IN/ GROCERIES/&/FLOUR./ LOGANSPORT.IND	1171	C	PL	R7	2967
570E-1a	KING & REED/DEALERS/IN/ STOVES/&/TINWARE/ LOGANSPORT.IND.	1171	C	PL	R7	
570E-2a	Same	1304	C	PL	R5	2969

INDIANA-Continued

NUMBER	OBVERSE	REVERSE	METAL	EDGE	RARITY	H&G

LOGANSPORT 570-Continued

| 570F-1a | KRUG & REED/DEALERS/IN/ STOVES/&/TINWARE,/ LOGANSPORT,/IND. | 1304 | C | PL | R8 | 2970 |

NOTE: The above piece spelled KRUG is probably an error intended to read KING.

| 570G-1a | MCDONALD & CO./DEALERS/ IN/DRY GOODS/AND/CARPETS, /LOGANSPORT,/IND. | 1122 | C | PL | R7 | 2971 |
| 570G-2a | Same | 1349 | C | PL | R9 | |

| 570H-1a | A.J.MURDOCK/DEALER/IN/DRY GOODS/&/GROCERIES/ LOGANSPORT IND. | 1171 | C | PL | R9 | 2973 |

87

INDIANA-Continued

NUMBER	OBVERSE	REVERSE	METAL	EDGE	RARITY	H&G

LYNN 580

580A

580B

NUMBER	OBVERSE	REVERSE	METAL	EDGE	RARITY	H&G
580A-1a	ELLIOT & HINSHAW/DRY/ GOODS/&/GROCERIES/ LYNN,IND.	1046	C	R	R8	2976
580A-1a1	Same	Same	C	PL	R7	2975
580A-1b	Same	Same	BR	R	R9	
580A-1d	Same	Same	C-N	R	R10	
580A-1i	Same	Same	Z	R	R9	
580A-2a	Same	1047	C	R	R8	
580A-2d	Same	Same	C-N	R	R10	2979
580B-1a	J.A.HINSHAW/DRY/GOODS/ &/GROCERIES/LYNN,IND.	1026	C	PL	R8	2985
580B-2a	Same	1027	C	R	R6	2981
580B-3a	Same	1042	C	R	R6	2982
580B-3b	Same	Same	BR	R	R7	2983
580B-3i	Same	Same	Z	R	R8	
580B-4a	Same	1045	C	PL	R7	
580B-5d	Same	1046	C-N	R	R10	2984
580B-6a	Same	1047	C	R	R8	
580B-6d	Same	Same	C-N	R	R10	

MECHANICSBURG 600

NUMBER	OBVERSE	REVERSE	METAL	EDGE	RARITY	H&G
600A-1a	ELLIOT & SWAIN/DRY GOODS,/ GROCERIES/HARDWARE &C/ MECHANICSVILLE INDIANA.	1124	C	PL	R9	
600A-2a	Same	1127	C	PL	R9	2988

INDIANA-Continued

NUMBER	OBVERSE	REVERSE	METAL	EDGE	RARITY	H&G

MECHANICSBURG 600-Continued

| 600B-1a | EZRA SWAIN/DRY GOODS/ GROCERIES/HARDWARE &C/ MECHANICSBURG/INDIANA | 1124 | C | PL | R6 | 2992 |
| 600B-2a | Same | 1180 | C | PL | R8 | 2991 |

MIDDLEBURY 615

615A-1a	C.STUTZ/DRY/GOODS/ CLOTHING/BOOTS & SHOES/ MIDDLEBURY, IND.	1037	C	R	R5	2994
615A-1b	Same	Same	BR	R	R8	
615A-1i	Same	Same	Z	R	R8	
615A-2a	Same	1047	C	R	R8	
615A-2d	Same	Same	C-N	R	R10	2996

MIDDLETOWN 620

INDIANA-Continued

NUMBER	OBVERSE	REVERSE	METAL	EDGE	RARITY	H&G

MIDDLETOWN 620-Continued

620A-1a	Large square and compasses in center W.W.COTTERAL,P.M. above MIDDLETOWN, IND. below	1037	C	R	R8	
620A-2a	Same	1046	C	R	R5	2998
620A-2b	Same	Same	BR	R	R9	2999
620A-2i	Same	Same	Z	R	R9	
620A-3a	Same	1047	C	R	R9	
620A-3d	Same	Same	C-N	R	R10	
620A-4a	Same	BLANK	C	R	R9	3000

MISHAWAKA 630

630A-1

630A-3

630A-1a	H.D.HIGGINS/JEWELRY/ OPTICIAN/& MFR OF/ BAROMETERS/MISHAWAKA	1003	C	PL	R5	3002
630A-2a	Same	1327	C	PL	R4	3003
630A-3a	H.D.HIGGINS./JEWELER/ OPTICIAN/MFR OF/ BAROMETERS/MISHAWAKA.IND.	1003	C	PL	R6	3005

630A-4

630A-6

630A-4a	H.D.HIGGINS./JEWELER/ OPTICIAN/&/MF'R OF/ BAROMETERS/MISHAWAKA	1003	C	PL	R8	
630A-4b	Same	Same	BR	PL	R9	
630A-5a	Same	1328	C	PL	R3	3007
630A-5b	Same	Same	BR	PL	R4	
630A-6a	H.D.HIGGINS/JEWELER/&/ OPTICIAN/MISHAWAKA,IND.	1049	C	PL	R3	3009
630A-6b	Same	Same	BR	PL	R6	3010
630A-7a	Same	1050A	C	PL	R9	
630A-8b	Same	1050	BR	PL	R9	

(NOTE: The only specimen known of the reverse 1050 has a large hole in the center, and may have been a rejected die trial)

630A-9a	Same	1329	C	PL	R9	

INDIANA-Continued

NUMBER	OBVERSE	REVERSE	METAL	EDGE	RARITY	H&G

MISHAWAKA 630-Continued

NUMBER	OBVERSE	REVERSE	METAL	EDGE	RARITY	H&G
630A-10a	H.D.HIGGINS/JEWELER/&/ OPTICIAN/MISHAWAKA,IND (No period after Ind)	1097	C	PL	R8	
630A-10b	Same	Same	BR	PL	R8	
630A-11a	Same	1111	C	PL	R6	3012
630A-12a	Same	1383	C	PL	R7	3013
630A-12b	Same	Same	BR	PL	R9	
630A-13a	H.D.HIGGINS/JEWELER/&/ OPTICIAN/MISHAWAKA,IND. The N on line with D.	1329	C	PL	R5	3014
630A-13b	Same	Same	BR	PL	R7	3015
630B-1a	B. HOLCOMB/DEALER/IN/ GROCERIES/STONE WARE/ OILS & C./MISHAWAKA.	1049	C	PL	R4	3018
630B-2b	Same	Rev. of Obv 630A-6a (A mule)	BR	PL	R8	

INDIANA-Continued

NUMBER	OBVERSE	REVERSE	METAL	EDGE	RARITY	H&G

MISHAWAKA 630-Continued

| 630B-3a | Similar to preceding, but comma after GROCERIES, | 1077 | C | PL | R8 | |
| 630B-3b | Same | Same | BR | PL | R8 | |

| 630C-1a | S.H.JUDKINS/GROCERIES/ &/PROVISIONS/MISHAWAKA, IND. | 1114 | C | PL | R5 | 3020 |

MOORESVILLE 640

640A-1a	W.H.P.WOODWARD/DRY/ GOODS/&C./MOORESCILLE, IND.	1046	C	R	R6	3022
640A-2a	Same	1047	C	R	R8	
640A-2d	Same	Same	C-N	R	R10	

92

INDIANA-Continued

NUMBER	OBVERSE	REVERSE	METAL	EDGE	RARITY	H&G

NEW CASTLE 690

690A-1a	M.L.POWELL/DEALER IN/ STOVES/&/TINWARE./ NEW CASTLE, IND.	1125	C	PL	R8	3024
690A-2a	Same	1180	C	PL	R7	3025
690A-3a	Same	1299	C	PL	R6	3027
690A-4a	Same	1304	C	PL	R6	3026

NEW PARIS 710

710A-1a	A.M.DAVIS/DRY/GOODS/ GROCERIES/CROCKERY/ DRUGS/&C./NEW PARIS, IND.	1003	C	PL	R9	
710A-2a	Same	1161	C	PL	R9	
710A-3a	Same	1234	C	PL	R9	

NORTH VERNON 715

INDIANA-Continued

NUMBER	OBVERSE	REVERSE	METAL	EDGE	RARITY	H&G
NORTH VERNON 715-Continued						
715A-1a	JOHN WENTZEL/DEALER/IN/ STOVES/&/TIN WARE./ NORTH VERNON, IND.	1299	C	PL	R5	3031
715A-1b	Same	Same	BR	PL	R9	

OLDENBURG 730

730A-1b	J. HOLKER/GOOD FOR/ DRINK/AT THE/BAR/ OLDENBURG,IND.	1391	BR	R	R9	3032

PERU 740

740A-1a	J.KREUTZER/DEALER/IN/ GLASS/QJEENSWARE/&/ CROCKERY/PERU/IND (NOTE: the spelling of Queensware)	1346	C	PL	R5	3033

94

INDIANA-Continued

NUMBER	OBVERSE	REVERSE	METAL	EDGE	RARITY	H&G

PERU 740-Continued

740B-1a	J.S.QUEEBY/DEALER/IN/DRY GOODS/&/NOTIONS,/PERU, IND.	1176	C	PL	R5	3035
740B-2a	Same	1290	C	PL	R3	3036
740B-3a	Same	1295	C	PL	R6	3037
740B-4a	Same	1331	C	PL	R8	3038
740B-5a	Same	1352	C	PL	R4	3039
740B-6a	Same	1384	C	PL	R2	3040

| 740B-7a | Same | PITTSBURGH/GAZETTE/84/FIFTH/ST. A mule with obv. of PA. 765S | C | PL | R9 | |
| 740B-8a | Same | REYMERS & BROS./CONFECTIONERS/PITTSBURG PA. A mule with the Obv of Pa 765T | C | PL | R9 | 9494 |

| 740C-1a | SAINE & MILLER/GROCERIES/NOTIONS/BOOTS & SHOES/PERU,IND. | 1318 | C | PL | R6 | 3042 |

95

INDIANA-Continued

NUMBER	OBVERSE	REVERSE	METAL	EDGE	RARITY	H&G

PIERCETON 760

760A-1  760A-2

| 760A-1a | MURRAY & BRO/DRY GOODS/ &/GROCERIES,/PIERCETON,/ IND. | 1088 | C | PL | R6 | 3044 |
| 760B-1a | REED & SPAYDE/DEALERS IN/ DRY GOODS/&/GROCERIES/ PEIRCETON...IND. (NOTE: Error in spelling Pierceton) | 1183 | C | PL | R5 | 3046 |

PLAINFIELD 770

770A-1  770A-4

770A-1a	DRY GOODS/&/CLOTHING/ JOHNSON/&/OURSLER/ PLAINFIELD,IND.	1037	C	R	R8	3047
770A-1b	Same	Same	BR	R	R8	
770A-1i	Same	Same	Z	R	R8	
770A-2a	Same	1047	C	R	R9	
770A-2d	Same	Same	C-N	R	R10	3050
770A-3a	Same	Obverse of IND 770A-4	C	R	R8	
770A-4a	JOHNSON & OURSLER/ DEALERS/IN/DRY/GOODS/ BOOTS & SHOES/PLAINFIELD, IND.	1018	C	R	R8	3053
770A-4b	Same	Same	BR	R	R8	3054
770A-4i	Same	Same	Z	R	R8	
770A-5a	Same	1047	C	R	R8	
770A-5d	Same	Same	C-N	R	R10	3052

96

INDIANA-Continued

NUMBER	OBVERSE	REVERSE	METAL	EDGE	RARITY	H&G

PLAINFIELD 770-Continued

770B-1

770B-2

770B-1a	M.OSBORN/GROCERIES/ NOTIONS/TOYS/&/FANCY ARTICLES/PLAINFIELD,IND.	1047	C	R	R8	
770B-1d	Same	Same	C-N	R	R10	3059
770B-2a	Same	QUEENSWARE/WILLOW/&/ WOODEN/WARE/AT/M.OSBORN'S	C	R	R7	3056
770B-2b	Same	Same	BR	R	R7	3057
770B-2i	Same	Same	Z	R	R8	3058
770B-3d	Same as the Rev. of IND. 770B-2a	1046	C-N	R	R10	3061
770B-4a	Same	1047	C	R	R8	3062

770C

770D

770C-1a	DRY GOODS/&/CLOTHING/ AT/I.M.SHIDLERS/POST OFFICE/BUILDING/ PLAINFIELD,IND.	Hat and cap in center. ISAAC M SHIDLER/DEALER/ IN above. BOOTS & SHOES/ AND NOTIONS. below.	C	R	R6	3064
770C-1b	Same	Same	BR	R	R7	3065
770C-1d	Same	Same	C-N	R	R9	
770C-1i	Same	Same	Z	R	R9	
770C-2d	Same	1047	C-N	R	R10	3067
770C-3d	Same	1069	C-N	R	R10	3068
770D-1d	TAMSEY & BALLARD/DEALERS /IN/DRUGS/&/MEDICINES/ PLAINFIELD,IND.	1019	C-N	R	R10	
770D-2a	Same	1047	C	R	R8	
770D-3d	Same	1069	C-N	R	R10	3073
770D-4a	Same	1311	C	R	R9	
770D-5a	Same	1312	C	R	R5	3070
770D-5b	Same	Same	BR	R	R7	3071
770D-5i	Same	Same	Z	R	R8	3072

INDIANA-Continued

NUMBER	OBVERSE	REVERSE	METAL	EDGE	RARITY	H&G

PLYMOUTH 780

780A-1a	J.M.DALE/DRY GOODS/ GROCERIES,/CROCKERY,/ BOOTS SHOES &C./ PLYMOUTH,/IND.	1342	C	PL	R7	3074
780B-1a	H.B.DICKSON & CO/HARDWARE /STOVES,/AND/TINWARE, PLYMOUTH,/IND.	1299	C	PL	R4	3077
780C-1a	H.HUMRICHOUSER/GRAIN/ &/PRODUCE/DEALER,/ PLYMOUTH,/IND.	1222	C	PL	R5	3080

98

INDIANA-Continued

NUMBER	OBVERSE	REVERSE	METAL	EDGE	RARITY	H&G

RICHMOND 800

800A-1a	C.C.BUHL/DEALER/IN/ STOVES AND/TIN WARE,/ 51/MIN ST./RICHMOND,IND.	1168	C	PL	R6	3082
800A-2a	Same	1299	C	PL	R5	3083
800B-1a	G.P.EMSWILER & CO./FANCY GOODS/&/TOYS/49 MAIN,ST./ RICHMOND,IND.	1023	C	R	R8	
800B-1a1	Same	Same	C	PL	R9	
800B-2a	Same	1030	C	PL		
800B-3a	Same	1042	C	R	R7	3086
800B-3a1	Same	Same	C	PL	R9	3085
800B-3b	Same	Same	BR	R	R8	3087
800B-3i	Same	Same	Z	R	R8	
800B-4d	Same	1046	C-N	R	R10	3089
800B-5a	Same	1047	C	R	R9	
800B-6d	Same	1069	C-N	R	R10	
800B-7a	Same	1192	C	PL	R9	

800C-1a	E.F.HIRST/WATCH/MAKER/ &/JEWELER/38 MAIN ST/ RICHMOND IND.	1008	C	PL	R7	3091
800C-1i	Same	Same	Z	PL	R9	
800C-2a	Same	1028	C	R	R8	
800C-3a	Same	1042	C	R	R7	3092
800C-3b	Same	Same	BR	R	R8	3093
800C-3i	Same	Same	Z	R	R8	3094
800C-4d	Same	1046	C-N	R	R10	3095
800C-5a	Same	1047	C	R	R8	
800C-5d	Same	Same	C-N	R	R10	

INDIANA-Continued

NUMBER	OBVERSE	REVERSE	METAL	EDGE	RARITY	H&G

ROCHESTER 810

810A-1a	D.S.GOULD/DRY/GOODS/&/ GROCERIES/OPP./COURTHOUSE /SQR./ROCHESTER,IND.	1046	C	R	R6	3097
810A-1b	Same	Same	BR	R	R7	3098
810A-1d	Same	Same	C-N	R	R10	3099
810A-1i	Same	Same	Z	R	R9	3100
810A-2a	Same	1047	C	R	R9	
810A-2d	Same	Same	C-N	R	R10	

SEYMOUR 830

830A-1a	J.F.JOHNSON/NEWS/DEALER,/ SEYMOUR,/IND.	1091	C	PL	R8	3102
830A-2a	Same	1223	C	PL	R7	3103
830A-2b	Same	Same	BR	PL	R8	3104

INDIANA-Continued

| NUMBER | OBVERSE | REVERSE | METAL | EDGE | RARITY | H&G |

SOUTH BEND 860

| 860A-1a | W.W.BEMENT/EDGE/TOOL/ MANF'R/SOUTH BEND.IND. | Obverse of IND 630A-13a H.D.HIGGINS of Mishawaka, Ind. | C | PL | R9 | 3105 |

860B-1a	BLOWNEY & JOHNSON/MFR'S/ COMPOSITION/ROOFING/ SOUTH BEND IND.	1161	C	PL	R8	
860B-1b	Same	Same	BR	PL	R9	
860B-2a	Same	1202	C	PL	R8	3106

| 860C-1a | S.M.CHORD/DEALER IN/ DRY GOODS/GROCERIES/ CROCKERY/CARPETS &C / SOUTH BEND IND. | 1233A | C | PL | R3 | 3107 |

101

INDIANA-Continued

| NUMBER | OBVERSE | REVERSE | METAL | EDGE | RARITY | H&G |

SOUTH BEND 860-Continued

860D-1   860D-2

| 860D-1a | HAMMONDS/SHOE/STORE/ SOUTH BEND,IND. | 1106 | C | PL | R5 | 3109 |
| 860D-2a | HAMMONDS/STOVE/STORE/ SOUTH BEND,IND. | 1106 | C | PL | R9 | |

(NOTE: Apparently the word STOVE is an error on the 800D-2 piece, as apparently the correct usage is SHOE)

860E-1a	J.C.KNOBLOCK/AGT./BAKER/ &/GROCER/SOUTH BEND.IND.	1099	C	PL	R4	3111
860E-2a	Same	1114	C	PL	R4	3112
860E-3a	Same	1207	C	PL	R5	3113

| 860F-1a | A.M.PURDY/NURSEYMAN/ &/FRUIT/GROWER/SOUTH BEND,IND | 1110 | C | PL | R4 | 3116 |
| 860F-2a | Same | 1357 | C | PL | R6 | 3115 |

102

INDIANA-Continued

NUMBER	OBVERSE	REVERSE	METAL	EDGE	RARITY	H&G

SOUTH BEND 860-Continued

860G-1a	GEORGE WYMAN/FANCY/DRY GOODS/SOUTH BEND/IND.	1097	C	PL	R8	
860G-2a	Same	1098	C	PL	R8	
860G-3a	Same	1101	C	PL	R6	3118
860G-4a	Same	1102	C	PL	R8	
860G-5a	Same	1205	C	PL	R6	3119
860G-6a	Same	Blank	C	PL	R10	

SULLIVAN 870

870A-1a	PRICE BROTHERS/DRY/GOODS/ CLOTHING/BOOTS & SHOES/ &C./SULLIVAN,IND.	1030	C	PL	R9	
870A-2a	Same	1042	C	R	R6	3122
870A-2b	Same	Same	BR	R	R7	3123
870A-2i	Same	Same	Z	R	R8	3124
870A-3a	Same	1047	C	R	R8	
870A-4d	Same	1060	C-N	R	R10	3126

INDIANA-Continued

NUMBER	OBVERSE	REVERSE	METAL	EDGE	RARITY	H&G

SWAN 880

| 880A-1a | D.H.HAINES & BRO./DEALERS /IN/DRY GOODS/GROCERIES/ &C/SWAN,IND. | 1223 | C | PL | R6 | 3129 |
| 880A-1b | Same | Same | BR | PL | R7 | 3130 |

TERRE HAUTE 890

| 890A-1a | FRANK HEINIG & BRO/ Large eagle in center | UNION STEAM BAKERY/ GOOD/FOR ONE/FIVE/CENT/ LOAF OF BREAD. | C | PL | R8 | |

(NOTE: This piece may possibly be post-Civil War vintage)

INDIANA-Continued

NUMBER	OBVERSE	REVERSE	METAL	EDGE	RARITY	H&G

VALPARAISO 915

915A-1

| 915A-1a | BARTHOLOMEW & McCLELLAND. around edge DRY GOODS/BOOTS SHOES/&C/IND./VALPARAISO in center | 1234 | C | PL | R7 | 3133 |
| 915A-2a | Similar, with city name spelled VALPARISO | 1238 | C | PL | R5 | 3134 |

VINCENNES 930

| 930A-1b | CHAS.F.RAKER/DEALER/IN/ DRY GOODS/&/GROCERIES/ VINCENNES,IND. | 1394 | BR | R | R9 | 3135 |
| 930A-2b | Same | 1399 | BR | R | R9 | |

INDIANA-Continued

NUMBER	OBVERSE	REVERSE	METAL	EDGE	RARITY	H&G

WABASH 940

| 940A-1a | GORDON & THURSTON/ DEALERS/IN/DRUGS,/BOOKS/ &/JEWELRY,/WABASH,IND. | DRUGS & MEDICINES 1863 around edge. Motar and pestle in a circle of 13 stars in center | C | PL | R6 | 3136 |
| 940A-2b | Same | Blank | BR | PL | R9 | |

WARSAW 950

950A-1b	D CARLILE/DEALER/IN/ OYSTERS/CONFECTIONARY/ CIGARS/&C./WARSAW,IND.	1008	BR	PL	R9	
950A-2a	Same	1047	C	R	R9	
950A-2d	Same	Same	C-N	R	R10	3140
950A-3d	Same	1069	C-N	R	R10	
950A-4a	Same	1400	C	PL	R9	
950A-4b	Same	Same	BR	PL	R8	3139

| 950B-1a | JOHN LANE/WATCHMAKER/ &/JEWELER,/WARSAW,/IND. | Blank | C | PL | R9 | 3141 |
| 950B-1b | Same | Same | BR | PL | R9 | |

106

INDIANA-Continued

NUMBER	OBVERSE	REVERSE	METAL	EDGE	RARITY	H&G

WARSAW 950-Continued

| 950C-1a | D.R.POTTENGER & CO./ DURGGISTS,/above, small mortar and pestle in center. WARSAW,/IND. below | 1316 | C | PL | R7 | |
| 950C-1b | Same | Same | BR | PL | R9 | |

WHEELING 970

970A-1a	J.G.WILLIAMS & CO./DRY /GOODS/HARWARE/BOOTS/ &/SHOES/WHEELING,IND.	1046	C	R	R9	
970A-2a	Same	1047	C	R	R9	
970A-2d	Same	Same	C-N	R	R10	
970A-2i	Same	Same	Z	R	R9	

107

INDIANA-Continued

NUMBER	OBVERSE	REVERSE	METAL	EDGE	RARITY	H&G

WOLF CREEK 995

995A-1a	WOLF/CREEK/PIKE/G. HAINES	1046	C	R	R6	3144
995A-1b	Same	Same	BR	R	R9	
995A-1d	Same	Same	C-N	R	R10	3145
995A-1i	Same	Same	Z	R	R9	
995A-2d	Same	1047	C-N	R	R10	

IOWA

| NUMBER | OBVERSE | REVERSE | METAL | EDGE | RARITY | H&G |

CEDAR RAPIDS 150

150A-1a	YOU CAN BUY/GOODS CHEAP/AT/THE/NEW YORK/STORE/CEDAR RAPIDS, IOWA.	Female head to left. REYNOLDS & CO above. NEW YORK STORE below.	C	PL	R6	3146
150A-2a	Same	1105	C	PL	R9	3147
150A-3a	Same as rev. of 150A-1a	1205	C	PL	R8	3148

DEFIANCE - See listing under non-contemporary tokens.

LANSING 560

560A-1a	WM. FLEMMING & BRO./LUMBER/LATH/&/SHINGLES/LANSING, IOWA	1037	C	R	R7	3149
560A-1b	Same	Same	BR	R	R8	3150
560A-1i	Same	Same	Z	R	R9	
560A-2a	Same	1047	C	R	R9	
560A-3a	Same	1043	C	R	R9	

IOWA - Continued

NUMBER	OBVERSE	REVERSE	METAL	EDGE	RARITY	H&G

LYONS 570

| • 570A-1a | GAGE. LYALL & KEELER./ GROCERS/MAIN. ST/LYONS/ IOWA. | 1368 | C | PL | R6 | 3155 |

WATERLOO 930

930A-1a	H. & C. GOODHUE/LATH SHINGLES/&/LUMBER/SASH/ BLIND/& DOOR/FACTORY/ WATERLOO, IOWA	1046	C	R	R9	3157
930A-1b	Same	Same	BR	R	R9	3158
930A-1d	Same	Same	C-N	R	R10	3159
930A-1i	Same	Same	Z	R	R10	
930A-2a	Same	1047	C	R	R9	
930A-2d	Same	Same	C-N	R	R10	

KANSAS

NUMBER	OBVERSE	REVERSE	METAL	EDGE	RARITY	H&G

LEAVENWORTH 550

| 550A-1a | A. COHEN/CLOTHING/AND GENTS/FURNISHING GOODS/ 21 DELAWARE ST./LEAVENWORTH,/ KANSAS | 1085 | C | PL | R7 | 3165 |
| 550A-1b | Same | Same | BR | PL | R8 | 3166 |

111

KENTUCKY

NUMBER	OBVERSE	REVERSE	METAL	EDGE	RARITY	H&G

COVINGTON 150

150A

150B

150A-1a	ARBEITER/HALLE/PIKE/ST./COVINGTON, KY.	1023	C	PL	R5	3181
150A-2a	Same	1028	C	R	R9	3175
150A-2b	Same	Same	BR	R	R9	3176
150A-3a	Same	1030	C	R	R9	
150A-3a1	Same	Same	C	PL	R9	
150A-4a	Same	1042	C	R	R2	3178
150A-4b	Same	Same	BR	R	R8	3179
150A-4i	Same	Same	Z	R	R9	
150A-5a	Same	1047	C	R	R9	
150A-5d	Same	Same	C-N	R	R10	
150B-1a	COV. & CIN./FERRY/COMPANY (Atwood Ohio 165-F)	1042	C	R	R7	3184
150B-1b	Same (Atwood Ohio 165-G)	Same	BR	R	R8	3185
150B-2d	Same	1046	C-N	R	R10	3187
150B-3a	Same (Atwood Ohio 165-H)	1047	C	R	R9	
150B-4d	Same	1069	C-N	R	R10	

150C

150D

150C-1a	J.DOLMAN/STOCKING/MANUFACTURER/COV,KY.	1278	C	PL	R4	3189
150D-1a	V.C.ENGERT/GERMANIA/SALOON/6' ST./COVINGTON,KY.	1019	C	PL	R9	3195
150D-2a	Same	1026	C	PL	R5	3192
150D-3a	Same	1028	C	PL	R6	3191
150D-4a	Same	1042	C	R	R8	3197
150D-4b	Same	Same	BR	R	R9	3198
150D-5a	Same	1047	C	R	R9	3200
150D-5d	Same	Same	C-N	R	R10	

KENTUCKY-Continued

NUMBER	OBVERSE	REVERSE	METAL	EDGE	RARITY	H&G

HENDERSON 370

| 370A-1a | W. S. JOHNSON & BRO / DRUGGISTS / HENDERSON / KY. | SODA CHECK / 1 (in circular design) GLASS | C | PL | R9 | |
| 370A-1e | Same | Same | W-M | PL | R9 | 3201 |

| 370A-2e | Similar, different spacing | Similar, different spacing | W-M | PL | R9 | |

LEXINGTON 480

480A-1a	J. N. KEININGHAM / GROCER / LEXINGTON / KY.	1047	C	R	R8	
480B-1a	JOHN W. LEE / BAKER / & / CONFECTIONER / 10 MAIN ST. / LEXINGTON, KY	1047	C	R	R9	3202
480B-2a	Same	1068	C	R	R9	3204
480B-2b	Same	Same	BR	R	R9	3205
480B-2d	Same	Same	C-N	R	R9	3206
480B-3a	Same	ONE / HALF / PINT / OF / MILK	C	R	R7	3208
480B-3b	Same	Same	BR	R	R8	3209

113

KENTUCKY-Continued

| NUMBER | OBVERSE | REVERSE | METAL | EDGE | RARITY | H&G |

LEXINGTON 480-Continued

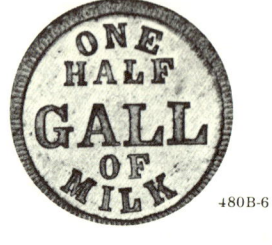

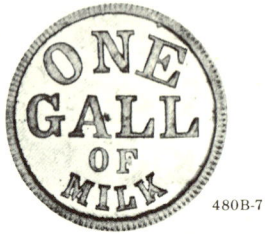

480B
480B-3
480B-4
480B-5
480B-6
480B-7

480B-3i	Same	Same	Z	R	R9	3210
480B-4a	Same	1/PINT/OF/MILK	C	R	R8	3211
480B-4b	Same	Same	BR	R	R9	3212
480B-4i	Same	Same	Z	R	R9	3213
480B-5a	Same	ONE/QUART/OF/MILK	C	R	R8	3214
480B-5b	Same	Same	BR	R	R9	3215
480B-5i	Same	Same	Z	R	R9	3216
480B-6a	Same	ONE/HALF/GALL/OF/MILK	C	R	R8	3217
480B-6b	Same	Same	BR	R	R9	3218
480B-6i	Same	Same	Z	R	R9	3219
480B-7a	Same	ONE/GALL/OF/MILK	C	R	R8	3220
480B-7b	Same	Same	BR	R	R9	3221
480B-7i	Same	Same	Z	R	R9	3222

LOUISVILLE 510

510A-1
510A-2

510A-1a	MADE BY H. MILLER & CO./1/PINT/LOUISVILLE	A.WEBER	C	PL	R9

114

KENTUCKY-Continued

NUMBER　　OBVERSE　　　　　　REVERSE　　　　　　　　METAL　EDGE　RARITY　H&G

LOUISVILLE 510-Continued

510A-2

510A-3

510A-4

510A-5

510A-6

510A-7

510A-8

510A-9

510A-10

510A-1b	Same	Same	BR	PL	R7	3224
510A-1fo	Same, over U. S. Dime	Same	S	R	R9	3225
510A-2a	Hand holding a beer mug with 5 enclosed by capitol C in center — H.MILLER & CO. to left — LOUISVILLE to right.	GEORGE/BRUCKLACHER	C	PL	R9	3233
510A-2b	Same	Same	BR	PL	R8	3234
510A-2fo	Same, over U.S. Dime	Same	S	R	R9	3235
510A-2b	Same	S.S. CLARKE/WHISKEY/ WHOLESALE/&/RETAIL	BR	PL	R9	
510A-3d	Same	Same	C-N	PL	R9	
510A-4b	Same	M.EGELHOFF	BR	PL	R9	
510A-5a	Same	J.KUNTZ	C	PL	R9	
510A-5b	Same	Same	BR	PL	R9	3237
510A-6b	Same	ROEHRS & BRYANT	BR	PL	R9	
510A-7b	Same (Typo 9/68 Lot 23)	SCHONE AUSICHT	BR	PL	R9	
510A-8b	Same (Elder 9/38 Lot 371)	T.T.S./F. C. STUMP	BR	PL	R9	
510A-9a	Same	GARRETT/TOWNSEND in circle of stars	C	PL	R9	

115

KENTUCKY-Continued

NUMBER	OBVERSE	REVERSE	METAL	EDGE	RARITY	H&G

LOUISVILLE 510-Continued

510A-9fo	Same, over U.S. Dime	Same	S	R	R9	3230
510A-10b	Same	A. WEBER (Rev Key 510A-1)	BR	PL	R9	3227

510B-1a	H. PREISSLER/LOUISVILLE,KY	2 crossed arrows on snake. In center, SODA above, WATER below. All enclosed in a circle of 13 stars. Below in exergue H. MILLER & CO. LOUISVILLE KY.	C	PL	R5
510B-1ap	Same	Same	C-pl	PL	R7
510B-lf	Same	Same	S	PL	R9

NEWPORT 640

640A  640B

640A-1a	J.BUTCHER'S/DRY/GOODS STORE/NEWPORT KY.	1026	C	PL	R9	3240
640A-2a	Same	1030	C	PL	R6	3239
640A-3a	Same	1042	C	R	R7	3242
640A-3b	Same	Same	BR	R	R8	3243
640A-3i	Same	Same	Z	R	R9	
640A-4a	Same	1047	C	R	R9	
640A-4d	Same	Same	C-N	R	R10	
640B-1a	N'PT & COV/BRIDGE/COMPANY	1029	C	PL	R9	
640B-2a	Same (Atwood Ky 640A)	1034	C	PL	R9	3245
640B-2b	Same (Atwood Ky 640C)	Same	BR	PL	R9	
640B-3a	Same (Atwood KY 640B)	1042	C	R	R7	3247
640B-3b	Same (Atwood KY 640D)	Same	BR	R	R8	3248
640B-4a	Same (Atwood KY 640E)	1047	C	R	R9	
640B-4d	Same	Same	C-N	R	R10	3250

116

MAINE

NUMBER	OBVERSE	REVERSE	METAL	EDGE	RARITY	H&G

BANGOR 100

| 100A-1a | R. S. TORREY/INVENTOR/OF THE/MAINE STATE/BEE HIVE/ 5TH ST./BANGOR, ME. | 1105 | C | PL | R6 | 3255 |

| 100A-2a | INVENTOR/OF THE/MAINE STATE/BEE HIVE/1864 in center. R. S. TORRY above, BANGOR, ME. below | 1200 | C | PL | R4 | 3257 |
| 100A-2b | Same | Same | BR | PL | R9 | |

117

MARYLAND

NUMBER	OBVERSE	REVERSE	METAL	EDGE	RARITY H&G

BALTIMORE 60

| 60A-1b | MT. VERNON/5/CLUB | 1001 | BR | PL | R7 |
| 60A-2b | MT. VERNON/25/CLUB (25mm) | Liberty head surrounded by 13 stars | BR | PL | R8 |

| 60B-1b | SHAKESPEARE CLUB/5/ BALTO. | 1001 | BR | PL | R6 |
| 60B-2b | SHAKESPEARE CLUB/10/ BALTO. | 1001 | BR | PL | R8 |

| 60B-3b | SHAKESPEARE CLUB/25/ (25mm) | Liberty head surrounded by 13 stars | BR | PL | R9 |

MARYLAND-Continued

NUMBER	OBVERSE	REVERSE	METAL	EDGE	RARITY	H&G

HAGERSTOWN 560

560A-1b	G. R.BOWMAN/CONFECTIONER/ 1862/HAGERSTOWN, MD,	TO OBSERVATORY/ (telescope)/ AND/TELESCOPES.	BR	PL	R8	3259
750A-5a	SNOW HILL/5/CENTS	1046	C	R	R9	
750A-6d	SNOW HILL/10/CENTS	1046	C-N	R	R10	
750A-7d	SNOW HILL/25/CENTS	1046	C-N	R	R10	
750A-8d	SNOW HILL/50/CENTS	1046	C-N	R	R10	
750A-9d	SNOW HILL/2/DOLLARS	1046	C-N	R	R10	
750A-10d	SNOW HILL/5/DOLLARS	1046	C-N	R	R10	

NOTE: Some consider these to be Indiana pieces.

SNOW HILL 750

750A-1a	SNOW HILL/5/CENTS	PAYABLE/IN/MERCHANDISE	C	R	R9
750A-2a	SNOW HILL/10/CENTS	Same	C	R	R9
750A-3a	SNOW HILL/2/DOLLARS	Same	C	R	R9
750A-4a	SNOW HILL/5/DOLLARS	Same	C	R	R9
750A-4b	Same, thin ½mm.	Same	BR	R	R9

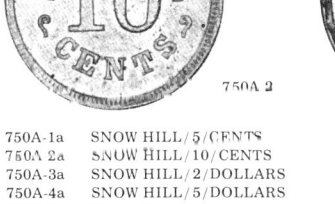

119

MASSACHUSETTS

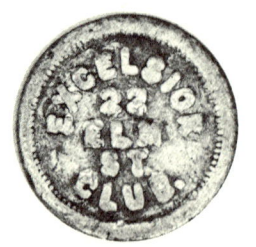

NUMBER	OBVERSE	REVERSE	METAL	EDGE	RARITY	H&G

BOSTON 115

| 115A-1e | COMERS/COMMERCIAL COLLEGE/BOSTON. (NOTE: This may well be post-Civil War) | COLLEGE above, BANK below, 1 in center | W-M | PL | R7 | |

115B-1    115B-3    115B-4

115B-1a	DUNN & CO'S above — OYSTER HOUSE below. 1864 within wreath of 24 leaves.	1413	C	PL	R6	3260
115B-1b	Same	Same	BR	PL	R8	
115B-2a	Same	1414	C	PL	R5	3262
115B-3a	Similar, but wreath contains only 22 leaves.	1414	C	PL	R9	3264
115B-4a	DUNN & CO/OYSTER/HOUSE/ 1864	1415	C	PL	R8	3266
115B-4b	Same	Same	BR	PL	R9	

| 115C-1e | EXCELSIOR/22/ELM/ST./ CLUB. | 1284 | W-M | PL | R9 | |

120

MASSACHUSETTS - Continued

NUMBER	OBVERSE	REVERSE	METAL	EDGE	RARITY	H&G

BOSTON 115-Continued

115D-1   115D-2   115D-3

115D-1e	MERRIAM & CO/19/BRATTLE/ SQR/BOSTON	1284	W-M	PL	R8	
115D-2a	Salamander press in center, MERRIAM & CO./BOSTON above, 19 BRATTLE/SQR' below.	1284	C	PL	R9	3271
115D-2b	Same	Same	BR	PL	R8	3272
115D-3b	MERRIAM & CO/SEALS/19/ BRATTLE/SQUARE/BOSTON	1284	BR	PL	R9	
115D-3ep	Same, copper plated	Same	W-M	PL	R9	

115E-1   115E-2

115E-1a	JOS. H. MERRIAM/MEDALIST/ DIE SINKER/AND/LETTER CUTTER/ESTABLISHED 1850/ NO.18/BRATTLE SQUARE.BOSTON.	1284	C	PL	R5	3268
115E-1b	Same	Same	BR	PL	R8	
115E-1d	Same	Same	C-N	PL	R9	
115E-1i	Same	Same	Z	PL	R8	
115E-2a	Same	NOT/ONE/CENT in center of wreath. JOS. H. MERRIAM, BOSTON. above—1863 below.	C	PL	R5	3269
115E-2b	Same	Same	BR	PL	R7	3270
115F-1e	SAM'S/10/INN	1284	W-M	PL	R9	
115G-1a	Steer's head in center C. F. TUTTLE'S above—RESTAURANT below.	130WASHINGTON STREET/ GOOD FOR/5/CENTS IN/ REFRESHMENTS	C	PL	R6	3275
115G-2a	Same	Similar, but for 10 CENTS	C	PL	R6	3276
115G-3a	Same	Similar, but for 25 CENTS	C	PL	R6	3277
115G-4a	Same	Similar, but for 50 CENTS	C	PL	R6	3278
115EA-1a	Pulmonales/For/Coughs/ and/Colds	1371	C	PL	R5	
115EA-1b	Same	Same	BR	PL	R8	

NOTE: Formerly listed as NY 10E-1a & 1b.

MASSACHUSETTS - Continued

NUMBER   OBVERSE   REVERSE   METAL EDGE RARITY H&G

BOSTON 115-Continued

115F

115G-1

115G-2

115G-3

115G-4

FALL RIVER 260

260A-1a   E. P. FRANCIS/CITY/HOTEL/   NO/27-31/PLEASANT STREET   C   PL   R5   3281
           FALL RIVER/MASS./1864   in center — BILLIARD ROOM &
                                         RESTAURANT around border.

122

MASSACHUSETTS - Continued

NUMBER	OBVERSE	REVERSE	METAL	EDGE	RARITY	H&G

FALL RIVER 260-Continued

260A-1b	Same	Same	BR	PL	R5	3282
260A-1c	Same	Same	N	PL	R7	3283
260A-1d	Same	Same	C-N	PL	R9	
260A-1e	Same	Same	W-M	PL	R9	3284
260A-1f	Same	Same	S	PL	R9	
260A-1g	Same	Same	G-S	PL	R9	
260A-1j	Same	Same	L	PL	R9	
260A-1fp	Same	Same	S-P	PL	R8	

HARVARD 320

| 320A-1a | BAY STATE/HORSE POWER/ SEND FOR/CIRCULAR/A. & C. F. WRIGHT/HARVARD,/MASS. | 1120 | C | PL | R5 | 3286 |

NANTUCKET 530

530A-1a	GOD LOVETH A CHEERFUL GIVER/GREAT FAIR/IN AID OF THE/U. S./SANITARY/ COMMISSION,/NANTUCKET,/ MASS./AUGUST, 1864. (Baker 364)	1138	C	PL	R5	
530A-1b	Same	Same	BR	PL	R7	
530A-1c	Same	Same	N	PL	R9	
530A-1e	Same	Same	W-M	PL	R8	
530A-1f	Same	Same	S	PL	R9	

MASSACHUSETTS-Continued

NUMBER	OBVERSE	REVERSE	METAL	EDGE	RARITY	H&G

WORCESTER 970

| 970A-1a | Head to left in center — above, CHARLES LANG — below 1863 | DIE SINKER /&/ GEN'L / ENGRAVER / WORCESTER, MS. | C | PL | R4 | 3287 |
| 970A-1b | Same | Same | BR | PL | R6 | 3288 |

MICHIGAN

| NUMBER | OBVERSE | REVERSE | METAL | EDGE | RARITY | H&G |

ADDISON 3

3A-1a	SMITH BROTHERS,/sheaf of wheat/ADDISON, MICH	DEALERS IN/DRY GOODS/ GROCERIES/& HARDWARE/ 1863	C	PL	R4	3300
3A-1b	Same	Same	BR	PL	R8	3301
3A-1c	Same	Same	N	PL	R9	

ADRIAN 5

| 5A-1a | BLACKMAN & DIBBLE/ DRUGGISTS/ADRIAN....MICH. | 1183 | C | PL | R4 | 3303 |

5B-1a	BUCK & FARRAR/DEALERS/IN/ HARDWARE,/STOVES,/& TIN./ ADRIAN, MICH	1096	C	PL	R8	
5B-2a	Same	1099	C	PL	R4	3304
5B-3a	Same	1390	C	PL	R8	3305
5B-4a	Same	Obverse of Mich. 920D-1a	C	PL	R9	

125

MICHIGAN-Continued

NUMBER	OBVERSE	REVERSE	METAL	EDGE	RARITY	H&G

ADRIAN 5-Continued

5C-1a	J. A. CASTLE/GROCER/ MAUMEE/ST. /ADRIAN. MICH.	1205	C	PL	R6	3307
5C-2a	Same	1097	C	PL	R4	3308
5C-3a	Same	1098	C	PL	R3	
5C-4a	Same	1099	C	PL	R3	3309
5D-1a	REMINGTON & BENNET/ DRUGGISTS/&GROCERS. / MAUMEE ST. /ADRIAN (G of Grocers under D of Druggists)	1097	C	PL	R8	3312
5D-2a	Same	1098	C	PL	R6	3313
5D-3a	Same	1105	C	PL	R5	3311
5D-4a	Same inscription as above but GR of Grocers under D of Druggists	1097	C	PL	R6	

5E-1a	S. SAMMONS/INN/KEEPER/ MANSION/HOUSE/MAUMEE ST. ADRIAN	1098	C	PL	R6	3316
5E-2a	Same	1099	C	PL	R6	3317
5E-3a	Same	1390	C	PL	R9	3318
5F-1a	WM. S. WILCOX/DEALER/IN/ HARDWARE/ADRIAN. MICH.	1094	C	PL	R9	
5F-2a	Same	1097	C	PL	R4	
5F-3a	Same	1098	C	PL	R6	
5F-4a	Same	1102	C	PL	R9	

MICHIGAN-Continued

| NUMBER | OBVERSE | REVERSE | METAL | EDGE | RARITY | H&G |

ALBION 25

| 25A-1a | ALBION COMMERCIAL COLLEGE. / IRA MAYHEW, / PRES'T, / ALBION / MICH. | MAYHEW'S PRACTICAL BOOK-KEEPING / THE / CHEAPEST / AND THE / BEST. / 1863 | C | PL | R3 | 3320 |
| 25A-1b | Same | Same | BR | PL | R4 | 3321 |

25B-1a	COMSTOCK & BRO. / Mortar and pestle / DRUGGISTS, / ALBION, / MICH.	1094	C	PL	R6	3325
25B-2a	Same	1203	C	PL	R5	3324
25B-3a	Same	1205	C	PL	R6	3323

ALMONT 35

| 35A-1a | D. W. RICHARDSON / DRUGS / AND / BOOKS / ALMONT, MICH. | 1205 | C | PL | R8 | 3327 |
| 35A-2a | Same | 1099 | C | PL | R4 | 3326 |

MICHIGAN-Continued

NUMBER   OBVERSE   REVERSE   METAL   EDGE   RARITY   H&G

ANN ARBOR 40

Number	Obverse	Reverse	Metal	Edge	Rarity	H&G
40A-1a	PHILIP BACH/DRY/GOODS/ 1863.	1015	C	PL	R3	3330
40A-1b	Same	Same	BR	PL	R6	3331
40A-1c	Same	Same	N	PL	R7	3332
40A-1d	Same	Same	C-N	PL	R7	3333
40A-1do	Same, over U. S. C-N cent	Same	C-N	PL	R7	
40A-1e	Same	Same	W-M	PL	R8	3334
40A-1fo	Same, over U. S. dime	Same	S	R	R9	
40A-2a	Same	1066	C	PL	R3	3336
40A-2b	Same	Same	BR	PL	R6	3337
40A-2c	Same	Same	N	PL	R7	3338
40A-2d	Same	Same	C-N	PL	R7	3339
40A-2do	Same, over U. S. C-N cent	Same	C-N	PL	R8	
40A-2e	Same	Same	W-M	PL	R7	3340
40A-2fo	Same, over U. S. dime	Same	S	R	R9	
40B-1a	DEAN & CO. /HOUSE/ FURNISHING/GOODS. /1863.	1015	C	PL	R3	3343
40B-1b	Same	Same	BR	PL	R6	3344
40B-1c	Same	Same	N	PL	R7	3345
40B-1d	Same	Same	C-N	PL	R7	3346
40B-1do	Same, over U. S. C-N cent	Same	C-N	PL	R8	
40B-1e	Same	Same	W-M	PL	R8	3347
40B-1fo	Same, over U. S. dime	Same	S	R	R9	
40B-2a	Same	1066	C	PL	R3	3349
40B-2b	Same	Same	BR	PL	R7	3350
40B-2c	Same	Same	N	PL	R8	3351
40B-2d	Same	Same	C-N	PL	R9	
40B-2do	Same, over U. S. C-N Cent	Same	C-N	PL	R9	
40B-2e	Same	Same	W-M	PL	R7	3353
40B-2f	Same	Same	S	PL	R9	
40B-3a	Same	1067	C	PL	R9	
40B-3b	Same	Same	BR	PL	R9	
40B-3c	Same	Same	N	PL	R9	
40B-3do	Same, over U. S. C-N cent	Same	C-N	PL	R9	

MICHIGAN-Continued

NUMBER	OBVERSE	REVERSE	METAL	EDGE	RARITY	H&G

ANN ARBOR 40-Continued

| 40C-1a | C. H. MILLEN/DEALER/IN/ DRY GOODS/& GROCERIES/ ANN ARBOR/MICH. | 1095 | C | PL | R4 | 3356 |
| 40C-2a | Same | 1205 | C | PL | R6 | 3355 |

40D-1a	STEBBINS & WILSON/DRY GOODS/AND/GROCERIES/ BUSINESS CARD (D of Dry close to T)	1314	C	PL	R2	3358
40D-2a	Same	1315	C	PL	R9	
40D-3a	Same inscription, but D of Dry close to S of Stebbins.	1314	C	PL	R2	3359

40E-1a	WM. WAGNER/MERCHANT/ TAILOR./DEALER IN/ CLOTHING/ANN ARBOR,MICH. (L of Dealer under I)	1095	C	PL	R4	
40E-2a	Same inscription, but L of Dealer under IL of Tailor.	Same	C	PL	R3	3362
40E-3a	Same	1390	C	PL	R7	3361

129

MICHIGAN-Continued

NUMBER	OBVERSE	REVERSE	METAL	EDGE	RARITY	H&G

ATLAS 45

45A-1a	F. J. & J. PALMER'S/WOOLEN/ FACTORY,/ATLAS,/GENESEE• CO. MICH.	1024	C	R	R8	
45A-2a	Same	1031	C	R	R3	3367
45A-3a	Same	1042	C	R	R3	3365
45A-3b	Same	Same	BR	R	R8	3366
45A-3i	Same	Same	Z	R	R9	
45A-4a	Same	1047	C	R	R9	
45A-4d	Same	Same	C-N	R	R9	3369

BATTLE CREEK 60

60A   60B   60C

60A-1a	V. P. COLLIER/GENERAL/ HARDWARE/NO: 40/BATTLE CREEK. MICH.	1184	C	PL	R9	
60A-2a	Same	1187	C	PL	R7	
60B-1a	J. B. LEONARD/BOOT/&/ SHOE/MAKER,/BATTLE CREEK, MIC	1186	C	PL	R7	3372
60C-1a	J. STUART & SON/STOVES/ HARDWARE/IRON &/NAILS/ BATTLE CREEK.	1098	C	PL	R5	3374
60C-2a	Same	1390	C	PL	R9	3375

NOTE: Cards of Wm. Brooks are listed under IND. 260A.

MICHIGAN-Continued

NUMBER	OBVERSE	REVERSE	METAL	EDGE	RARITY	H&G

BAY CITY 65

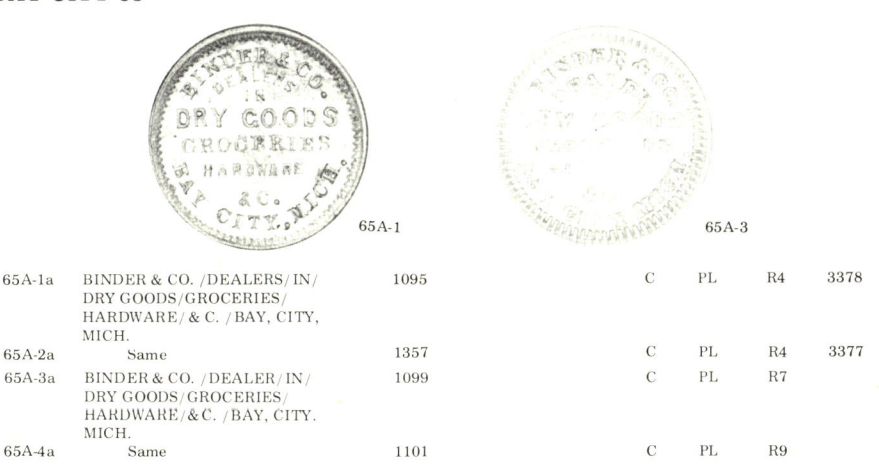

65A-1a	BINDER & CO. /DEALERS/IN/ DRY GOODS/GROCERIES/ HARDWARE/ & C. /BAY, CITY, MICH.	1095	C	PL	R4	3378
65A-2a	Same	1357	C	PL	R4	3377
65A-3a	BINDER & CO. /DEALER/IN/ DRY GOODS/GROCERIES/ HARDWARE/&C. /BAY, CITY. MICH.	1099	C	PL	R7	
65A-4a	Same	1101	C	PL	R9	

BRIGHTON 85

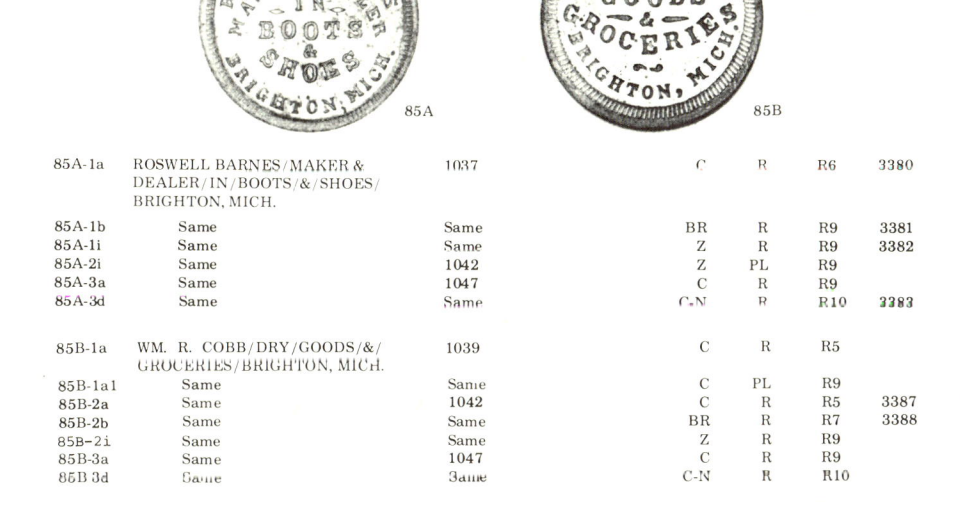

85A-1a	ROSWELL BARNES/MAKER & DEALER/IN/BOOTS/&/SHOES/ BRIGHTON, MICH.	1037	C	R	R6	3380
85A-1b	Same	Same	BR	R	R9	3381
85A-1i	Same	Same	Z	R	R9	3382
85A-2i	Same	1042	Z	PL	R9	
85A-3a	Same	1047	C	R	R9	
85A-3d	Same	Same	C-N	R	R10	3383
85B-1a	WM. R. COBB/DRY/GOODS/&/ GROCERIES/BRIGHTON, MICH.	1039	C	R	R5	
85B-1a1	Same	Same	C	PL	R9	
85B-2a	Same	1042	C	R	R5	3387
85B-2b	Same	Same	BR	R	R7	3388
85B-2i	Same	Same	Z	R	R9	
85B-3a	Same	1047	C	R	R9	
85B 3d	Same	Same	C-N	R	R10	

MICHIGAN-Continued

NUMBER	OBVERSE	REVERSE	METAL	EDGE	RARITY	H&G

BRIGHTON 85-Continued

85C-1a	W. H. NAYLOR/DEALER IN/ HARDWARE/&/CUTLERY/ BRIGHTON, MICH.	1039	C	R	R5	
85C-2a	Same	1042	C	R	R5	3394
85C-2b	Same	Same	BR	R	R7	3395
85C-2i	Same	Same	Z	R	R9	
85C-3a	Same	1047	C	R	R9	
85C-3d	Same	Same	C-N	R	R9	3397

BUCHANAN 90

| 90A-1a | WEAVER & FOX/STOVES/TIN./ HARDWARE/& C/BUCHANAN/ MICH. | 1105 | C | PL | R6 | 3399 |
| 90A-2a | Same | 1110 | C | PL | R3 | 3400 |

CASSOPOLIS 135

| 135A-1a | BOYD & BRADLY/WHOLESALE/ &/RETAIL/GROCERIES/MICH/ CASSOPOLIS | 1003 | C | PL | R9 | |

MICHIGAN-Continued

NUMBER	OBVERSE	REVERSE	METAL	EDGE	RARITY	H&G

CHARLOTTE-160

160A-1a	C. CUMMINGS, /DRY GOODS/ GROCERIES/BOOTS SHOES & C. /CHARLOTTE/MICH.	1168	C	PL	R6	3407
160A-1b	Same	Same	BR	PL	R7	3408
160A-2a	Same	1225	C	PL	R6	3404
160A-2b	Same	Same	BR	PL	R7	3405

160 B-1a	HIGBY & BROTHER/GENERAL/ MERCHANTS/CHARLOTTE,/MICH.	1225	C	PL	R3	3410
160B-1b	Same	Same	BR	PL	R7	3411
160C-1a	J. MIKESELL & BRO. /DEALERS /IN/GROCERIES, AND/PROVISIONS,/ CHARLOTTE, MICH.	1225	C	PL	R5	3413
160C-1b	Same	Same	BR	PL	R7	3414

| 160D-1a | C. J. PIPER/GROCERIES,/ BOOTS, SHOES & C/ CHARLOTTE,/MICH. | 1317 | C | PL | R5 | 3416 |
| 160D-1b | Same | Same | BR | PL | R7 | 3417 |

MICHIGAN-Continued

NUMBER	OBVERSE	REVERSE	METAL	EDGE	RARITY	H&G

CHELSEA 175

| 175A-1a | CONGDON BROTHERS/DRY /GOODS,/GROCERIS/ HARDWARE/CHELSEA ... MICH. | 1183A | C | PL | R9 | |
| 175A2a | Same | 1186 | C | PL | R6 | 3419 |

CLARKSTON 180

180A   180B

180A-1a	M. H. CLARK/DRY/GOODS/ HARDWARE/BOOTS/&/SHOES/ CLARKSTON, MICH.	1042	C	R	R5	3423
180A-1b	Same	Same	BR	R	R7	3424
180A-1i	Same	Same	Z	R	R9	
180A-2d		1046	C-N	R	R10	
180A-3a	Same	1047	C	R	R9	
180A-3d	Same	Same	C-N	R	R9	3425
180A-4a	Same	1039	C	R	R6	
180A-4a1	Same	Same	C	PL	R10	
180B-1a	R & J. T. PETER/DRUGGISTS/ CLARKSTON	1024	C	R	R9	
180B-1a1	Same	Same	C	PL	R9	
180B-2a	Same	1042	C	R	R5	3427
180B-2b	Same	Same	BR	R	R8	3428
180B-3a	Same	1047	C	R	R9	
180B-3d	Same	Same	C-N	R	R9	

MICHIGAN-Continued

NUMBER	OBVERSE	REVERSE	METAL	EDGE	RARITY	H&G

COLDWATER 185

| 185A-1a | N. T. WATERMAN/BOOKS/&/ JEWELRY/COLDWATER. MICH. (J of Jewelry almost touches the O of Coldwater) | 1111 | C | PL | R8 | |
| 185A-2a | Same inscription, except the J of Jewelry almost touches the C of Coldwater | Same | C | PL | R8 | |

CONSTANTINE 190

190A-1a	BUY YOUR HARDWARE/OF/ E. H SHELDON/CONSTANTINE /MICH	E. H. SHELDON/shield with ribbon/1863	C	PL	R2	3432
190A-1b	Same	Same	BR	PL	R8	
190A-2a	Same	Incuse of the obverse	C	PL	R9	
190A-3a	Reverse of 190A-1a	Incuse of the obverse	C	PL	R9	

MICHIGAN-Continued

NUMBER	OBVERSE	REVERSE	METAL	EDGE	RARITY	H&G

CORUNNA 200

200A-1a	H. A. CRANE/STOVES/&/ HARDWARE./CORUNNA, MICH.	1094	C	PL	R5	3434
200A-2a	Same	1205	C	PL	R6	3435
200A-3a	Same	1099	C	PL	R5	3436
200A-4a	Same	1207	C	PL	R5	

200B-1a	G. W. GOODELL/DRUGS,/ MEDICINES/& C./CORUNNA, MICH.	1094	C	PL	R4	3438
200B-2a	Same	1357	C	PL	R6	3439
200B-3a	Same	1097	C	PL	R4	3440
200B-4a	Same	1099	C	PL	R4	3441

MICHIGAN-Continued

NUMBER	OBVERSE	REVERSE	METAL	EDGE	RARITY	H&G

DETROIT 225

225A-1d	W. J. ADDERLEY/GROCER/ 157/GRATOIT/ST./DETROIT	1046	C-N	R	R9	3445
225A-2a	Same	1068	C	R	R9	3444
225A-3a	Same	1069	C	R	R3	3443
225A-4a	W. J. ADDERLY/GROCER/ 157/GRATOIT/ST/DETROIT	1028	C	PL	R9	3447
225A-5a	Same	1039	C	R	R3	
225A-5a1	Same	Same	C	PL	R9	
225A-6a	Same	1042	C	R	R3	3449
225A-6b	Same	Same	BR	R	R9	3450
225A-6i	Same	Same	Z	R	R9	3451
225A-7d	Same	1046	C-N	R	R9	
225A-8a	Same	1047	C	R	R9	
225A-8d	Same	Same	C-N	PL	R9	

225B-1a	AMERICAN/COFFEE/MILLS/ 25 JEFF. AVE/DETROIT	1037	C	R	R9	3457
225B-2a	Same	1039	C	R	R8	
225B-2a1	Same	Same	C	PL	R9	
225B-3a	Same	1042	C	R	R6	3454
225B-3b	Same	Same	BR	R	R9	3455
225B-3i	Same	Same	Z	R	R9	3456
225B-4d	Same	1046	C-N	R	R9	
225B-5a	Same	1047	C	R	R9	
225B-5d	Same	Same	C-N	R	R9	3458

225C-1a	T. H. ARMSTRONG/DEALER/ IN/HATS/CAPS AND FURS/ DETROIT	1005	C	R	R7	
225C-1d	Same	Same	C-N	R	R10	3460
225C-2a	Same	1042	C	R	R5	3461
225C-2b	Same	Same	BR	R	R8	3462
225C-2i	Same	Same	Z	R	R9	3463

MICHIGAN-Continued

NUMBER	OBVERSE	REVERSE	METAL	EDGE	RARITY	H&G
DETROIT 225-Continued						
225C-3d	Same	1046	C-N	R	R9	
225C-4a	Same	1047	C	R	R9	
225C-4d	Same	Same	C-N	R	R9	3464

225D

225E

225D-1a	BLINDBURY'S/HOTEL/ ANTISDEL/&/HILLS/DETROIT, MICH.	1018	C	R	R2	3466
225D-2a	Same (H-R-1184)	1027	C	R	R9	
225D-2a1	Same	Same	C	PL	R10	
225D-3a	Same	1042	C	R	R2	3467
225D-3b	Same	Same	BR	R	R8	3468
225D-3i	Same	Same	Z	R	R9	3469
225D-4a	Same	1047	C	R	R9	3471
225D-5d	Same	1069	C-N	R	R9	
225E-1a	G. BAMLET/GROCER/&/ PRODUCE/DEALER/17 GR. RIV. ST/DETROIT	1039	C	R	R6	
225E-1a1	Same	Same	C	PL	R9	
225E-2a	Same	1042	C	R	R6	3473
225E-2b	Same	Same	BR	R	R9	3474
225E-2i	Same	Same	Z	R	R9	
225E-3d	Same	1046	C-N	R	R10	
225E-4a	Same	1047	C	R	R9	
225E-4d	Same	Same	C-N	R	R9	3476

225F-1a	L. W. BARIE/BAKER/114/ FORT/ST/DETROIT	1019	C	R	R5	3479
225F-1a1	Same	Same	C	PL	R9	
225F-2a	Same	1024	C	R	R8	
225F-2a1	Same	Same	C	PL	R9	
225F-3a	Same	1037	C	R	R5	

138

MICHIGAN-Continued

NUMBER	OBVERSE	REVERSE	METAL	EDGE	RARITY	H&G

DETROIT 225-Continued

225F-4a	Same	1042	C	R	R5	3481
225F-4b	Same	Same	BR	R	R8	3482
225F-4i	Same	Same	Z	R	R9	3483
225F-5d	Same	1046	C-N	R	R9	
225F-6a	Same	1047	C	R	R9	

225G

225H

225G-1a	GEO. BEARD & SON/OYSTER/ FRUIT/FISH & GAME/DEPOT/ DETROIT	1025	C	R	R5	3487
225G-2a	Same	1042	C	R	R5	3489
225G-2b	Same	Same	BR	R	R9	3490
225G-2i	Same	Same	Z	R	R9	3491
225G-3d	Same	1046	C-N	R	R10	
225G-4a	Same	1047	C	R	R9	
225G-4d	Same	Same	C-N	R	R9	3493
225H-1a	H. W. BEESON/GROCERIES/ &/SHIP/STORES/22 WOODWARD AVE/DETROIT	1025	C	R	R4	3495
225H-2a	Same	1039	C	R	R4	3503
225H-3a	Same	1042	C	R	R4	3497
225H-3b	Same	Same	BR	R	R9	3498
225H-3i	Same	Same	Z	R	R9	3499
225H-4a	Same	1046	C	R	R9	
225H-5a	Same	1047	C	R	R9	
225H-5d	Same	Same	C-N	R	R9	3501

225I-1a	FR. BEHR/Bear standing up and holding a mug in right paw	EIN GLAS BIER/Wreath with ten pin and ball	C	PL	R9	

MICHIGAN-Continued

NUMBER	OBVERSE	REVERSE	METAL	EDGE	RARITY	H&G

DETROIT 225-Continued

225J

225K

225J-1a	FRED'K C. BLOME/DRY/GOODS /61 WOOD. AVE/DETROIT	1042	C	R	R4	3505
225J-1b	Same	Same	BR	R	R8	3506
225J-1i	Same	Same	Z	R	R9	3507
225J-2a	Same	1047	C	R	R9	3509
225J-3d	Same	1069	C-N	R	R10	
225J-4a	Same	1370	C	R	R4	3511
225K-1a	BROEG & GERBER/ BUTCHERS/35/MICH./ AVE./DETROIT	1025	C	R	R3	3513
225K-2a	Same	1027	C	R	R9	
225K-3a	Same	1042	C	R	R4	3514
225K-3b	Same	Same	BR	R	R8	3515
225K-3i	Same	Same	Z	R	R9	3516
225K-4a	Same	1046	C	R	R9	
225K-5a	Same	1047	C	R	R9	3517
225K-5d	Same	Same	C-N	R	R9	

225L

225M

225L-1a	F. A. BURKHART/BUTCHER/ COR./HASTING/&GRATOIT/ STS./DETROIT	1037	C	R	R9	3518
225L-2a	Same	1039	C	R	R7	
225L-3a	Same	1042	C	R	R7	3520
225L-3b	Same	Same	BR	R	R9	3521
225L-3i	Same	Same	Z	R	R9	3522
225L-4a	Same	1046	C	R	R9	
225L-5a	Same	1047	C	R	R9	
225L-5d	Same	Same	C-N	R	R9	3524
225M-1a	CHARLES BUSCH/HARDWARE/ STOVES/&/GRATES/201 JEFF. AVE./DETROIT	1018	C	R	R3	3528
225M-2a	Same	1027	C	R	R7	3530

MICHIGAN-Continued

NUMBER	OBVERSE	REVERSE	METAL	EDGE	RARITY	H&G

DETROIT 225-Continued

NUMBER	OBVERSE	REVERSE	METAL	EDGE	RARITY	H&G
225M-3a	Same	1042	C	R	R6	3532
225M-3b	Same	Same	BR	R	R8	3533
225M-3i	Same	Same	Z	R	R9	3534
225M-4a	Same	1047	C	R	R9	3537
225M-4d	Same	Same	C-N	R	R9	
225M-5d	Same	1069	C-N	R	R10	

NUMBER	OBVERSE	REVERSE	METAL	EDGE	RARITY	H&G
225MA-1a	CAMPBELL & CALNON/GROCERS/MICH./GRAND AVE./DETROIT	1037	C	R	R9	
225MA-2a	Same	1009	C	R	R7	3545
225MA-3a	Same	1042	C	R	R6	3539
225MA-3b	Same	Same	BR	R	R8	3540
225MA-3i	Same	Same	Z	R	R9	3541
225MA-4a	Same	1047	C	R	R9	
225MA-4d	Same	Same	C-N	R	R9	3543

225N

225N-2

NUMBER	OBVERSE	REVERSE	METAL	EDGE	RARITY	H&G
225N-1a	CAMPBELL. LINN & CO./Thistle/.BUSINESS CARD	SCOTCH STORE/DRY GOODS/AND/MILLINERY/DETROIT MICH	C	PL	R2	3547
225N-2a	CAMPBELL LINN & CO./Thistle/BUSINESS CARD	Same	C	PL	R2	3548

MICHIGAN-Continued

NUMBER	OBVERSE	REVERSE	METAL	EDGE	RARITY	H&G

DETROIT 225-Continued

225N-3

225N-4

| 225N-3a | Same | SCOTCH STORE/DRY GOODS/ AND MILLINERY/DETROIT MICH. | C | PL | R2 | 3550 |
| 225N-4a | Same | Same inscription, but the letters are smaller, and ornaments have been added. | C | PL | R2 | 3549 |

(NOTE: Above pieces are very brassy-copper.)

225O

225P

225 O-1a	H. A. CHRISTIANSEN/ GROCERIES/&/PROVISIONS/ 259 JEFF. AVE/DETROIT	1018	C	R	R3	3552
225 O-1a1	Same	Same	C	PL	R9	
225 O-2a	Same	1027	C	R	R8	
225 O-2a1	Same	Same	C	PL	R9	
225 O-3a	Same	1037	C	R	R9	3554
225 O-4a	Same	1042	C	R	R3	3556
225 O-4b	Same	Same	BR	R	R8	3557
225 O-4i	Same	Same	Z	R	R9	3558
225 O-5a	Same	1047	C	R	R9	
225 O-5d	Same	Same	C-N	R	R9	3560
225 O-6d	Same	1069	C-N	R	R10	
225P-1a1	G & W. CLARK/BUTCHERS/ COR./LARNED & 1'ST/DETROIT	1037	C	PL	R10	3562
225P-2a	Same	1039	C	R	R5	
225P-2a1	Same	Same	C	PL	R9	
225P-3a	Same	1042	C	R	R5	3563
225P-3b	Same	Same	BR	R	R8	3564
225P-3i	Same	Same	Z	R	R9	3565
225P-4d	Same	1046	C-N	R	R10	
225P-5a	Same	1047	C	R	R9	
225P-5d	Same	Same	C-N	R	R9	3567

MICHIGAN-Continued

NUMBER	OBVERSE	REVERSE	METAL	EDGE	RARITY	H&G

DETROIT 225-Continued

225Q-1a	S. COHEN/CLOTHING/ DEALER/155 JEFF. AVE./ DETROIT	1027	C	R	R5	3569
225Q-1a1	Same	Same	C	PL	R9	
225Q-2a	Same	1042	C	R	R8	3571
225Q-2b	Same	Same	BR	R	R9	3572
225Q-2i	Same	Same	Z	R	R9	3573
225Q-3a	Same	1047	C	R	R9	
225Q-3d	Same	1047	C-N	R	R9	3575
225Q-4d	Same (H-R-1186)	1069	C-N	R	R10	

225R 225S

225R-1a	A. W. COPLAND'S/STEAM/ BAKERY/20 MONROE, AVE/ DETROIT	1039	C	R	R6	3583
225R-1a1	Same	Same	C	PL	R9	
225R-2a	Same	1042	C	R	R6	3577
225R-2b	Same	Same	BR	R	R8	3578
225R-2i	Same	Same	Z	R	R9	3579
225R-3d	Same	1046	C-N	R	R10	
225R-4a	Same	1047	C	R	R9	
225R-4d	Same	Same	C-N	R	R9	3581
225S-1a	C. L. CROSBY/FRUIT/&/ PRODUCE/DEALER/ DETROIT	1039	C	R	R7	3590
225S-1a1	Same	Same	C	PL	R9	
225S-2b	Same	1042	BR	R	R8	3586
225S-2i	Same	1042	Z	R	R9	
225S-2a	Same	1042	C	R	R6	
225S-4d	Same	1047	C-N	R	R9	3588

143

MICHIGAN-Continued

NUMBER	OBVERSE	REVERSE	METAL	EDGE	RARITY	H&G

DETROIT 225-Continued

225T-1a	GEO. E. CURTIS/LEATHER/ &/FINDINGS/215 JEFF. AVE./ DETROIT	1027	C	R	R4	3591
225T-2a	Same	1042	C	R	R7	3593
225T-2b	Same	Same	BR	R	R8	3594
225T-2i	Same	Same	Z	R	R9	3595
225T-3a	Same	1047	C	R	R9	3597
225T-3d	Same	Same	C-N	R	R9	3598
225T-4d	Same	1069	C-N	R	R10	

225U   225V

225U-1a	GODFREY DEAN & CO/ PAINTERS/&/PICTURE FRAME/MAKERS/DETROIT	1037	C	R	R3	3599
225U-1a1	Same	Same	C	PL	R9	
225U-1b	Same	Same	BR	R	R9	
225U-2a	Same	1039	C	R	R6	
225U-3a	Same	1042	C	R	R3	3601
225U-3b	Same	Same	BR	R	R8	3602
225U-3i	Same	Same	Z	R	R9	3603
225U-4a	Same	1047	C	R	R9	3605
225U-4b	Same	Same	BR	PL	R10	
225U-4d	Same	Same	C-N	R	R10	3606
225V-1a	DETROIT/CITY/FLOUR/MILLS /COR. LARNED & 2' STS.	1037	C	R	R6	3607
225V-2a1	Same	1038	C	PL	R10	
225V-3a	Same	1039	C	R	R4	
225V-4a	Same	1042	C	R	R4	3609
225V-4b	Same	Same	BR	R	R8	3610
225V-4i	Same	Same	Z	R	R9	3611
225V-5d	Same	1046	C-N	R	R10	
225V-6a	Same	1047	C	R	R10	
225V-6d	Same	Same	C-N	R	R10	3613

MICHIGAN-Continued

NUMBER	OBVERSE	REVERSE	METAL	EDGE	RARITY	H&G

DETROIT 225-Continued

225W-1a	D. DICKSON/GROCER/&/ PROVISION/DEALER/1' & LARNED, STS/DETROIT	1037	C	R	R10	3615
225W-2a	Same	1040	C	R	R5	
225W-3a	Same	1042	C	R	R5	3617
225W-3b	Same	Same	BR	R	R8	3618
225W-3i	Same	Same	Z	R	R9	3619
225W-4d	Same	1046	C-N	R	R10	
225W-5a	Same	1047	C	R	R9	3621
225W-5d	Same	Same	C-N	R	R10	3622

225X

225Y

225X-1a	E. A. DRURY/GROCER/150/ WOODWARD/AVENUE/ DETROIT	1025	C	R	R4	3624
225X-2a	Same	1042	C	R	R6	3626
225X-2b	Same	Same	BR	R	R8	3627
225X-2i	Same	Same	Z	R	R9	3628
225X-3d	Same	1046	C-N	R	R9	
225X-4a	Same	1047	C	R	R9	
225X-4d	Same (H-R 1187)	Same	C-N	R	R9	3630
225Y-1a	FRANCIS ECCARD/ TOBACCONIST/DETROIT	1024	C	R	R3	3632
225Y-2a	Same	1037	C	R	R10	3634
225Y-3a	Same	1042	C	R	R4	3636
225Y-3b	Same	Same	BR	R	R8	3637
225Y-3i	Same	Same	Z	R	R9	3638
225Y-4a	Same	1039	C	R	R4	
225Y-4a1	Same	Same	C	PL	R9	
225Y-5d	Same	1046	C-N	R	R10	
225Y-6a	Same	1047	C	R	R10	3640
225Y-6d	Same	Same	C-N	R	R10	3641

MICHIGAN-Continued

NUMBER	OBVERSE	REVERSE	METAL	EDGE	RARITY	H&G

DETROIT 225-Continued

225Z-1a	PENINSULAR/HOTEL/ DETROIT/WM. EISENLORD	1037	C	R	R9	3643
225Z-2a	Same	1039	C	R	R9	
225Z-2a1	Same	Same	C	PL	R9	
225Z-3a	Same	1042	C	R	R6	3645
225Z-3b	Same	Same	BR	R	R7	3646
225Z-4a	Same	1047	C	R	R10	3648
225Z-4d	Same	Same	C-N	R	R10	3649

225AA

225AB

225AA-1a	FARMERS/CLOTHING/STORE/ 251 & 253/GRATOIT, ST./ DETROIT	1042	C	R	R6	3650
225AA-1b	Same	Same	BR	R	R9	3651
225AA-1i	Same	Same	Z	R	R10	3652
225AA-2d	Same	1046	C-N	R	R10	
225AA-3a	Same	1047	C	R	R10	
225AA-3d	Same	Same	C-N	R	R10	3653
225AB-1a	C. FITZSIMONS & CO./ GROCER/7 & 9/WOODWARD/ AVE/DETROIT	1039	C	R	R5	3660
225AB-2a	Same	1042	C	R	R5	3655
225AB-2a1	Same	Same	C	PL	R9	
225AB-2b	Same	Same	BR	R	R9	3656
225AB-3d	Same	1046	C-N	R	R10	
225AB-4a	Same	1047	C	R	R9	
225AB-4d	Same (H-R-1188)	Same	C-N	R	R10	3658

146

MICHIGAN-Continued

NUMBER	OBVERSE	REVERSE	METAL	EDGE	RARITY	H&G

DETROIT 225-Continued

225AC-1a	L. S. FREEMAN/NEWS/DEALER /OPPOSITE/BIDDLE/HOUSE/ DETROIT, MICH.	1024	C	R	R9	
225AC-1a1	Same	Same	C	PL	R10	
225AC-2a	Same	1025	C	R	R6	
225AC-3a	Same	1042	C	R	R6	3662
225AC-3b	Same	Same	BR	R	R8	3663
225AC-3i	Same	Same	Z	R	R9	3664
225AC-4a	Same	1036	C	R	R9	3668
225AC-5d	Same	1016	C-N	R	R10	
225AC-6d	Same	1047	C-N	R	R10	3666

| 225AD-1b | FRISBIE'S CARD | 53 WOODWARD & 167 JEFFERSON AV'S/WHOLESALE/&/RETAIL/ DRY GOODS/DETROIT MICH. | BR | PL | R2 | 3670 |
| 225AD-2b | Similar But Word "FRISBIES" Low | Same | BR | PL | R3 | |

| 225AE-1a | F. GEIS & BRO'S/FIRE & /WATER/PROOF/ROOFING/ COR./CONG & BRUSH/STS./ DETROIT | 1037 | C | R | R5 | 3672 |

147

MICHIGAN-Continued

NUMBER	OBVERSE	REVERSE	METAL	EDGE	RARITY	H&G

DETROIT 225-Continued

NUMBER	OBVERSE	REVERSE	METAL	EDGE	RARITY	H&G
225AE-2a	Same	1042	C	R	R5	3674
225AE-2b	Same	Same	BR	R	R8	3675
225AE-2i	Same	Same	Z	R	R9	
225AE-3a	Same	1043	C	R	R9	
225AE-4d	Same	1047	C-N	R	R10	3677

225AF-1　　　　　225AF-2

NUMBER	OBVERSE	REVERSE	METAL	EDGE	RARITY	H&G
225AF-1a	F. GEISS & BRO'S/FIRE &/WATER/PROOF/ROOFING/COR./CONG &BRUSH/STS./DETROIT	1042	C	R	R8	3679
225AF-1b	Same	Same	BR	R	R9	3680
225AF-2a	F. GEISS/DEALER IN/GROCERIES/&/PROVISIONS/HAY &/STRAW/BOOTS & SHOES (H-R 1190)	1037	C	R	R9	3684
225AF-3a	Same	1042	C	R	R7	3685
225AF-3a1	Same	Same	C	PL	R10	
225AF-3b	Same	Same	BR	R	R8	3686
225AF-3i	Same	Same	Z	R	R9	3687
225AF-4d	Same	1046	C-N	R	R10	
225AF-5a	Same	1047	C	R	R9	
225AF-5d	Same	Same	C-N	R	R9	3689
225AF-6a	Same	Obverse of 225AF-1a	C	R	R4	3682
225AF-6a1	Same	Same	C	PL	R9	
225AF-6b	Same	Same	BR	R	R9	3683

NUMBER	OBVERSE	REVERSE	METAL	EDGE	RARITY	H&G
225AG-1a	F. GIES & BRO'S/FIRE &/WATER/PROOF/ROOFING/COR./CONG & BRUSH/STS./DETROIT	1037	C	R	R7	3684
225AG-1a1	Same	Same	C	PL	R9	
225AG-2d	Same	1047	C-N	R	R10	

148

MICHIGAN-Continued

NUMBER	OBVERSE	REVERSE	METAL	EDGE	RARITY	H&G

DETROIT 225-Continued

225AG-3a	F. GIES/DEALER IN/ GROCERIES/&/PROVISIONS/ HAY &/STRAW/BOOTS & SHOES	1018	C	R	R8	3691
225AG-4a	Same	1042	C	R	R9	3692
225AG-4b	Same	Same	BR	R	R9	3693
225AG-5a	Same	1047	C	R	R8	
225AG-3a1	Same	Same	C	PL	R9	

225AH

225AI

225AH-1a	C. B. GOODRICH/DEALER IN/ BOOTS & SHOES/OPP./ PERKINS/HOTEL/DETROIT	1037	C	R	R9	3695
225AH-2a	Same	1040	C	R	R9	
225AH-2a1	Same	Same	C	PL	R10	
225AH-3a	Same	1042	C	R	R6	3697
225AH-3b	Same	Same	BR	R	R8	3698
225AH-3i	Same	Same	Z	R	R9	3699
225AH-4d	Same	1046	C-N	R	R10	
225AH-5a	Same	1047	C	R	R9	
225AH-5d	Same	Same	C-N	R	R10	3701

225AI-1a	F. HAMMAN & CO/LIQUOR/ STORE/COR. MACOMB AVE/ & GR. RIV. ST./DETROIT	1039	C	R	R5	3708
225AI-1a1	Same	Same	C	PL	R9	
225AI-2a	Same	1042	C	R	R5	3703
225AI-2b	Same	Same	BR	R	R8	3704
225AI-2i	Same	Same	Z	R	R9	
225AI-3a	Same	1047	C	R	R9	
225AI-3d	Same	Same	C-N	R	R10	3706

149

MICHIGAN-Continued

NUMBER	OBVERSE	REVERSE	METAL	EDGE	RARITY	H&G

DETROIT 225-Continued

225AJ-1a	HANNA & CO./WHOLESALE/ TOBACCONISTS/112/ WOODWARD/AVE./DETROIT	1025	C	R	R8	
225AJ-1a1	Same	Same	C	PL	R9	
225AJ-2a	Same	1037	C	R	R9	3710
225AJ-3a	Same	1042	C	R	R7	3712
225AJ-3b	Same	Same	BR	R	R8	3713
225AJ-4a	Same	1047	C	R	R9	
225AJ-4d	Same	Same	C-N	R	R10	3715

225AJa-1a	BUY/CLOTHING/AT/ HEINMAN'S/UNDER THE/ RUSSELL/HOUSE/&/SAVE 25 PER.CT.	1025	C	R	R5	7151
225AJa-2a	Same	1042	C	R	R8	7152
225AJa-2b	Same	Same	BR	R	R9	7153
225AJa-2i	Same	Same	Z	R	R9	
225AJa-3a	Same	1047	C	R	R9	7154

(This token was formerly listed as Ohio 165BQ)

| 225AK-1a | HERINTONS/DOUBLE THREAD/$15/SEWING/ MACHINE/DETROIT, MICH. | 1106 | C | PL | R4 | 3717 |

150

MICHIGAN-Continued

NUMBER	OBVERSE	REVERSE	METAL	EDGE	RARITY	H&G

DETROIT 225-Continued

225AL-1a	HIGBY & STEARNS/ DRUGGISTS/DETROIT	1025	C	R	R4	3719
225AL-1a1	Same	Same	C	PL	R10	
225AL-2a	Same	1042	C	R	R4	3721
225AL-2b	Same	Same	BR	R	R8	3722
225AL-2i	Same	Same	Z	R	R9	3723
225AL-3a	Same	1047	C	R	R9	
225AL-3d	Same	Same	C-N	R	R10	3725

225AM   225AN

225AM-1a	HILTERSCHEID BRO'S/ MEAT/MARKET/COR. FORT &/RUSSELL,ST/ DETROIT	1039	C	R	R5	3733
225AM-1a1	Same	Same	C	PL	R10	
225AM-2a	Same	1042	C	R	R5	3727
225AM-2b	Same	Same	BR	R	R8	3728
225AM-2i	Same	Same	Z	R	R9	3729
225AM-3a	Same	1047	C	R	R9	
225AM-3d	Same	Same	C-N	R	R9	3731
225AN-1a	JACOB HOCHSTADT/ BUTCHER/COR./2ND. &/ MICH. AVE./DETROIT	1040	C	R	R9	
225AN-2a	Same	1042	C	R	R6	3737
225AN-2b	Same	Same	BR	R	R8	3738
225AN-2i	Same	Same	Z	R	R9	3739
225AN-3a	Same	1047	C	R	R9	
225AN-3d	Same	Same	C-N	R	R10	3741

MICHIGAN-Continued

NUMBER	OBVERSE	REVERSE	METAL	EDGE	RARITY	H&G

DETROIT 225-Continued

225AO-1a	C. J. HOLTHOFER/DEALER IN/ DRY/GOODS/DETROIT	1024	C	R	R5	3743
225AO-1a1	Same	Same	C	PL	R10	
225AO-2a	Same	1037	C	R	R5	3745
225AO-3a	Same	1039	C	R	R7	
225AO-4a	Same	1042	C	R	R6	3747
225AO-4b	Same	Same	BR	R	R8	3748
225AO-4i	Same	Same	Z	R	R9	3749
225AO-5d	Same	1047	C-N	R	R9	3751
225AO-6a	C. I. HOLTHOFER DEALER DRY GOODS DETROIT	1039	C	R	R9	
225AO-6a1	Same	1039	C	PL	R10	
225AO-7a	Same	1042	C	PL	R9	

225AP

225AQ

225AP-1a	WM. B. HOWE/BOOK/ SELLER/192 JEFF. AVE/ DETROIT	1027	C	R	R5	3753
225AP-2a	Same	1042	C	R	R6	3755
225AP-2b	Same	Same	BR	R	R8	3756
225AP-2i	Same	Same	Z	R	R9	3757
225AP-3a	Same	1047	C	R	R9	
225AP-3d	Same	Same	C-N	R	R10	3759
225AQ-1a	EDWARD KANTER/GROCERIES /PRODUCE/&/SHIP/ CHANDLERY/DETROIT	1025	C	R	R9	
225AQ-1a1	Same	Same	C	PL	R10	
225AQ-2a	Same	1042	C	R	R7	3761
225AQ-2b	Same	Same	BR	R	R8	3762
225AQ-2i	Same	Same	Z	R	R9	3763
225AQ-3a	Same	1047	C	R	R9	
225AQ-3d	Same	Same	C-N	R	R9	3765

MICHIGAN-Continued

NUMBER	OBVERSE	REVERSE	METAL	EDGE	RARITY	H&G

DETROIT 225-Continued

225AR-1a	P. N. KNEELAND/DEALER/ IN/STOEVS/&/TINWARE/ COR. GRAND RIVER/& GRISWOLD ST/DETROIT	1037	C	R	R9	
225AR-2a	Same	1040	C	R	R7	3773
225AR-2a1	Same	Same	C	PL	R10	
225AR-3a	Same	1042	C	R	R6	3767
225AR-3b	Same	Same	BR	R	R9	3768
225AR-3i	Same	Same	Z	R	R9	3760
225AR-4a	Same	1047	C	R	R10	
225AR-4d	Same	Same	C-N	R	R10	3771
225AS-1a	LAPHAM & THAYER/NEW/&/ SECOND HAND/FURNITURE/ 14/MCIH. AVE/DETROIT	1040	C	R	R5	
225AS-1a1	Same	Same	C	PL	R9	
225AS-2a	Same	1042	C	R	R5	3775
225AS-2b	Same (H-R 1193)	Same	BR	R	R8	3776
225AS-2i	Same	Same	Z	R	R9	3777
225AS-3a	Same	1047	C	R	R10	
225AS-3d	Same (H-R 1192)	Same	C-N	R	R10	3779

(NOTE: Michigan Ave. spelled MCIH. on this token)

225AT-1a	LEWIS & MOSES/DEALERS/ IN/CROCKERY/&/GLASSWARE /221 JEFF. AVE./DETROIT	1018	C	R	R8	
225AT-2a	Same	1024	C	R	R9	
225AT-3a	Same	1025	C	R	R3	3781
225AT-4a1	Same	1027	C	PL	R10	
225AT-5a	Same	1042	C	R	R6	3784
225AT-5b	Same	Same	BR	R	R8	3785
225AT-5i	Same	Same	Z	R	R9	3786
225AT-6a	Same	1047	C	R	R9	3788
225AT-6d	Same (H-R 1194)	Same	C-N	R	R10	

MICHIGAN-Continued

NUMBER	OBVERSE	REVERSE	METAL	EDGE	RARITY	H&G

DETROIT 225-Continued

225AU-1a	C. LOTZ/GROCER/COR./ HASTINGS/&/CATHERINE, STS./DETROIT	1037	C	R	R8	
225AU-2a	Same	1040	C	R	R9	
225AU-3a	Same	1042	C	R	R7	3793
225AU-3b	Same	Same	BR	R	R8	3794
225AU-3i	Same	Same	Z	R	R9	3795
225AU-4a	Same	1047	C	R	R10	
225AU-4d	Same	Same	C-N	R	R9	3797

225AV

225AW

225AV-1a	MARTIN BRO'S/CHEAP/BOOT/ &/SHOE/STORE/154 WOODWARD AVE.	1042	C	R	R7	3799
225AV-1b	Same	Same	BR	R	R8	3800
225AV-2a	Same	1047	C	R	R9	
225AV-2d	Same	Same	C-N	R	R10	3802
225AV-3d	Same	1069	C-N	R	R10	
225AW-1a	M. MARX/GROCER/&/ LIQUOR/DEALER/94 GRATOIT, ST./DETROIT	1037	C	R	R8	3804
225AW-2a	Same	1039	C	R	R7	
225AW-2b	Same	Same	BR	R	R9	
225AW-3a	Same	1042	C	R	R7	3806
225AW-3b	Same	Same	BR	R	R8	3807
225AW-3i	Same	Same	Z	R	R9	3808
225AW-4a	Same	1047	C	R	R10	
225AW-4d	Same	Same	C-N	R	R10	3810

MICHIGAN-Continued

NUMBER	OBVERSE	REVERSE	METAL	EDGE	RARITY	H&G

DETROIT 225-Continued

225AX-1a	MATHER & SHEFFERLY / CROCKERY / STORE / 138 & 140 / WOODWARD / AVE. / DETROIT	1025	C	R	R3	3812
225AX-2a	Same	1037	C	R	R3	3814
225AX-3a	Same	1040	C	R	R4	
225AX-4a	Same	1042	C	R	R5	3816
225AX-4b	Same	Same	BR	R	R8	3817
225AX-4i	Same	Same	Z	R	R9	3818
225AX-5a	Same	1047	C	R	R10	
225AX-5d	Same	Same	C-N	R	R10	3820

225AY

225AZ

225AY-1a	MESSMORE & LUCKING / BUTCHERS / 209 / WOODWARD / AVE. / DETROIT	1039	C	R	R7	3828
225AY-1a1	Same	Same	C	PL	R10	
225AY-2a	Same	1042	C	R	R6	3822
225AY-2b	Same	Same	BR	R	R8	3823
225AY-2i	Same	Same	Z	R	R9	3824
225AY-3a	Same	1047	C	R	R10	
225AY-3d	Same	Same	C-N	R	R9	3826
225AZ-1a	ROBT. MILLAR / GROCER / & / LIQUOR / DEALER / 200 WOODWARD AVE. / DETROIT	1025	C	R	R3	3830
225AZ-1a1	Same	Same	C	PL	R10	
225AZ-2a	Same	1042	C	R	R6	3832
225AZ-2b	Same	Same	BR	R	R8	3833
225AZ-2i	Same	Same	Z	R	R9	3834
225AZ-3a	Same	1047	C	R	R9	
225AZ-3d	Same (H-R 1196)	Same	C-N	R	R10	3836

MICHIGAN-Continued

NUMBER	OBVERSE	REVERSE	METAL	EDGE	RARITY	H&G

DETROIT 225-Continued

225BA

225BB

225BA-1a	GEO. MOE/GROCER/&/ LIQUOR/DEALER/DETROIT	1037	C	R	R7	3838
225BA-2a	Same	1039	C	R	R6	
225BA-3a	Same	1042	C	R	R4	3840
225BA-3b	Same	Same	BR	R	R8	3841
225BA-3i	Same	Same	Z	R	R9	3842
225BA-4a	Same	1047	C	R	R9	
225BA-4d	Same (H-R 1197)	Same	C-N	R	R10	3844
225BB-1a	GEO. H. PARKER/DEALER IN/ HIDES/LEATHER/&/WOOL/ COR. STATE &/FARMER STS/ DETROIT	1037	C	R	R10	3846
225BB-2a	Same	1040	C	R	R7	
225BB-3a	Same	1042	C	R	R7	3848
225BB-3b	Same	Same	BR	R	R9	3849
225BB-3i	Same	Same	Z	R	R9	3850
225BB-4a	Same	1047	C	R	R10	
225BB-4d	Same	Same	C-N	R	R10	3852

225BC

225BD

225BC-1a	PERKINS/HOTEL/COR. GR. RIVER &/MIDDLE/STS/ DETROIT	1042	C	R	R7	3854
225BC-1b	Same	Same	BR	R	R9	3855
225BC-1i	Same	Same	Z	R	R9	3856
225BC-2a	Same	1047	C	R	R9	
225BC-3d	Same	1069	C-N	R	R10	
225BC-2d	Same	1047	C-N	R	R10	
225BD-1a	W. PERKINS, JR/GROCER/&/ PROVISION/DEALER/DETROIT	1037	C	R	R9	3862
225BD-2a	Same	1042	C	R	R7	3864
225BD-2b	Same	Same	BR	R	R8	3865
225BD-2i	Same	Same	Z	R	R9	3866

MICHIGAN-Continued

NUMBER	OBVERSE	REVERSE	METAL	EDGE	RARITY	H&G

DETROIT 225-Continued

225BD-3a	Same	1047	C	R	R9	
225BD-3d	Same	Same	C-N	R	R9	3868
225BD-4a	Same	Obverse of 225BC-1a	C	R	R6	3870
225BD-4a1	Same	Same	C	PL	R9	3871

225BE-1a	G. C. POND/GROCER/&/ PROVISION/DEALER/DETROIT	1024	C	R	R9	
225BE-2a	Same	1025	C	R	R9	
225BE-2a1	Same	Same	C	PL	R9	
225BE-3a	Same	1030	C	R	R9	
225BE-4a	Same	1037	C	R	R9	3874
225BE-5a	Same	1039	C	R	R7	
225BE-5a1	Same	Same	C	PL	R9	
225BE-6a	Same	1042	C	R	R5	3876
225BE-6b	Same	Same	BR	R	R8	3877
225BE-6i	Same	Same	Z	R	R9	3078
225BE-7a	Same	1047	C	R	R9	
225BE-7d	Same	Same	C-N	R	R9	3879

225BF

225BG

225BF-1a	F. PROUTY/GROCER/&/ PROVISION/DEALER/GR RIVER ST/DETROIT	1040	C	R	R7	
225BF-1a1	Same	Same	C	PL	R9	
225BF-2a	Same	1042	C	R	R7	3883
225BF-2b	Same	Same	BR	R	R9	3884
225BF-2i	Same	Same	Z	R	R9	3885
225BF-3a	Same	1047	C	R	R0	
225BF-3d	Same	Same	C-N	R	R9	3887

| 225BG-1a | RANDAL'S/PHOTOGRAPHIC /GALLERY/FISHERS/BLOCK /DETROIT | 1037 | C | R | R9 | 3889 |
| 225BG-1a1 | Same | Same | C | PL | R9 | |

157

MICHIGAN-Continued

NUMBER	OBVERSE	REVERSE	METAL	EDGE	RARITY	H&G

DETROIT 225-Continued

NUMBER	OBVERSE	REVERSE	METAL	EDGE	RARITY	H&G
225BG-2a	Same	1040	C	R	R7	
225BG-2a1	Same	Same	C	PL	R9	
225BG-2b	Same	Same	BR	R	R9	
225BG-3a	Same	1042	C	R	R7	3891
225BG-3b	Same	Same	BR	R	R9	3892
225BG-3i	Same	Same	Z	R	R9	3893
225BG-4a	Same	1047	C	R	R9	
225BG-4d	Same	Same	C-N	R	R9	3895

225BH

225BI

225BH-1a	RAYMOND'S/PHOTOGRAPH/GALLERY/205/JEFF. AVE/DETROIT	1040	C	R	R9	
225BH-2a	Same	1042	C	R	R5	3897
225BH-2b	Same	Same	BR	R	R8	3898
225BH-2i	Same	Same	Z	R	R9	3899
225BH-3d	Same (H-R 1199)	1047	C-N	R	R9	3901
225BI-1a	JOSEPH RIGGS/GROCERIES/PROVISIONS/&/FLOUR/DETROIT	1039	C	R	R3	3909
225BI-1a1	Same	Same	C	PL	R9	
225BI-2a	Same	1042	C	R	R5	3903
225BI-2b	Same	Same	BR	R	R9	3904
225BI-2i	Same	Same	Z	R	R9	3905
225BI-3a	Same	1047	C	R	R9	
225BI-3b	Same	Same	BR	R	R9	
225BI-3d	Same	Same	C-N	R	R9	3907

225BJ-1a	J. A. RODIER/BOOT/&/SHOE/DEALER/DETROIT	1037	C	R	R10	3911
225BJ-2a	Same	1039	C	R	R8	

MICHIGAN-Continued

NUMBER	OBVERSE	REVERSE	METAL	EDGE	RARITY	H&G

DETROIT 225-Continued

225BJ-3a	Same	1042	C	R	R6	3913
225BJ-3b	Same	Same	BR	R	R8	3914
225BJ-3i	Same	Same	Z	R	R9	3915
225BJ-4a	Same	1047	C	R	R9	
225BJ-4d	Same	Same	C-N	R	R9	3917

225BK

225BL

225BK-1a	ALONZO ROLFE/PRODUCE/ FRUIT/&/COMMISSION/ MERCHANT/DETROIT	1039	C	R	R8	
225BK-2a	Same	1042	C	R	R5	3919
225BK-2b	Same	Same	BR	R	R9	3920
225BK-2i	Same	Same	Z	R	R9	3921
225BK-3a	Same	1047	C	R	R9	
225BK-3d	Same	Same	C-N	R	R9	3923
225BL-1a	DR. L. C. ROSE/TREATS ALL /CHRONIC/FEMALE/& VENEREAL/DISEASES/ DETROIT	1037	C	R	R9	3925
225BL-2a	Same	1039	C	R	R8	
225BL-3a	Same	1042	C	R	R5	3927
225BL-3b	Same	Same	BR	R	R8	3928
225BL-3i	Same	Same	Z	R	R9	
225BL-4d	Same	1047	C-N	R	R9	3930

225BM

225BM-1a	M. ROSENBERGER/DEALER IN/ READY MADE/CLOTHING/ 140 GR. RIV. ST. /DETROIT	1037	C	R	R9	3932
225BM-2a	Same	1039	C	R	R10	
225BM-3a	Same	1042	C	R	R5	3934
225BM-3b	Same	Same	BR	R	R8	3935
225BM-3i	Same	Same	Z	R	R9	3936
225BM-4d	Same (H-R 1201)	1047	C-N	R	R10	3030

MICHIGAN-Continued

NUMBER	OBVERSE	REVERSE	METAL	EDGE	RARITY	H&G

DETROIT 225-Continued

225BN

225BO

225BN-1a	J. SCHMIDT/GROCER/COR. MICH. AVE. /&/BATES,STS. / DETROIT	1025	C	R	R3	3940
225BN-2a	Same	1042	C	R	R5	3942
225BN-2b	Same	Same	BR	R	R8	3943
225BN-2i	Same	Same	Z	R	R9	3944
225BN-3a	Same	1047	C	R	R10	
225BN-3d	Same	Same	C-N	R	R10	3946
225BO-1a	JOHN SCHRODER & CO. / /CLOTHING/HATS/&/CAPS /BOOTS & SHOES	1042	C	R	R5	3948
225BO-1b	Same	1042	BR	R	R8	
225BO-1i	Same	1042	Z	R	R9	
225BO-2a	Same	1047	C	R	R9	
225BO-3d	Same	1069	C-N	R	R10	3951
225BO-4a	Same	Obverse of 225AA-1a	C	R	R4	3953
225BO-5d	Same	1018	C-N	R	R10	

225BP

225BQ

225BP-1a	H. A. SEALY/BUTCHER/65/ GR. RIVER ST. /DETROIT	1037	C	R	R10	3955
225BP-2a	Same	1040	C	R	R6	
225BP-2a1	Same	Same	C	PL	R10	
225BP-3a	Same	1042	C	R	R6	3957
225BP-3b	Same	Same	BR	R	R8	
225BP-3i	Same	Same	Z	R	R9	3959
225BP-4a	Same	1047	C	R	R9	3961
225BP-4d	Same	Same	C-N	R	R10	
225BQ-1a	CHEAP/JOHN/SEELEY/ DETROIT	1037	C	R	R9	3963
225BQ-2a	Same	1039	C	R	R6	
225BQ-2a1	Same	Same	C	PL	R10	

160

MICHIGAN-Continued

NUMBER	OBVERSE	REVERSE	METAL	EDGE	RARITY	H&G

DETROIT 225-Continued

225BQ-3a	Same	1042	C	R	R6	3965
225BQ-3b	Same	Same	BR	R	R8	3966
225BQ-3i	Same	Same	Z	R	R9	3967
225BQ-4a	Same	1047	C	R	R9	
225BQ-4d	Same	Same	C-N	R	R10	3969

225BR

225BS

225BR-1a	J. B. SHAGNON/GROCER/&/ PROVISION /DEALER/DETROIT	1040	C	R	R9	
225BR-1a1	Same	Same	C	PL	R9	
225BR-2a	Same	1042	C	R	R7	3971
225BR-2a1	Same	Same	C	PL	R10	3974
225BR-2b	Same	Same	BR	R	R8	3972
225BR-2b1	Same	Same	BR	PL	R10	3975
225BR-2i	Same	Same	Z	R	R9	3973
225BR-3a	Same	1047	C	R	R9	
225BR-3d	Same	Same	C-N	R	R10	3077
225BS-1a	E. B. SMITH/BOOK SELLER/&/ STATIONER/116/WOODWARD/ AVE/DETROIT	1025	C	R	R9	
225BS-1a1	Same	Same	C	PL	R9	
225BS-2a	Same	1042	C	R	R6	3981
225BS-2b	Same	Same	BR	R	R9	3982
225BS-2i	Same	Same	Z	R	R10	3983
225BS-3a	Same	1047	C	R	R10	
225BS-3d	Same	Same	C-N	R	R9	

225BT-1a	SETH SMITH & SON/BARREL/&/ TEA BOXES/DETROIT MICH	GENERAL DEALER/IN/FAMILY GROCERY/FLOUR & FEED/ GLASSWARE/ETC ETC/390/ GRAND RIVER AVE	C	PL	R9

161

MICHIGAN-Continued

| NUMBER | OBVERSE | REVERSE | METAL | EDGE | RARITY | H&G |

DETROIT 225-Continued

225BU

225BV

225BU-1a	WM. B. SMITH/BUTCHER/129 & 131/WOODBRIDGE/ST/DETROIT	1040	C	R	R5	
225BU-2a	Same	1042	C	R	R6	3987
225BU-2b	Same	Same	BR	R	R8	3988
225BU-2i	Same	Same	Z	R	R9	3989
225BU-3a	Same	1046	C	R	R9	
225BU-4a	Same	1047	C	R	R9	
225BU-4d	Same	Same	C-N	R	R9	3991
225BV-1a	YANKEE/SMITH'S/SALOON/ NO. 1 MICH. AVE. /DETROIT	1025	C	R	R4	3993
225BV-1a1	Same	Same	C	PL	R9	
225BV-2a	Same	1039	C	R	R4	4001
225BV-3a	Same	1042	C	R	R6	3995
225BV-3b	Same (H-R 1203)	Same	BR	R	R9	
225BV-3i	Same	Same	Z	R	R9	3997
225BV-4a	Same	1047	C	R	R9	
225BV-4d	Same (H-R 1204)	Same	C-N	R	R9	3999

225BW

225BX

225BW-1a1	Same	Same	C	PL	R9	
225BW-1a	GEO. SNOOKS/FISH/DEPOT/ COR. /1' & LARNED STS/ DETROIT	1040	C	R	R7	
225BW-1b	Same	Same	BR	R	R9	
225BW-2a	Same	1042	C	R	R5	4005
225BW-2b	Same	Same	BR	R	R8	4006
225BW-2i	Same	Same	Z	R	R9	4007
225BW-3a	Same	1047	C	R	R9	
225BW-3d	Same	Same	C-N	R	R9	4008
225BX-1a	WM. SNOW/WIRE/CLOTH/ HARDWARE/&/CUTLERY/ DETROIT	1039	C	R	R4	4014
225BX-1a1	Same	Same	C	PL	R10	
225BW-4a	Same	1037	C	R	R7	4003
225BW-4b	Same	Same	BR	R	R9	

MICHIGAN-Continued

NUMBER	OBVERSE	REVERSE	METAL	EDGE	RARITY	H&G

DETROIT 225-Continued

225BX-2a	Same	1042	C	R	R4	4009
225BX-2b	Same	Same	BR	R	R8	4010
225BX-3a	Same	1047	C	R	R9	
225BX-3d	Same (H-R 1206)	Same	C-N	R	R9	4012

225BY-1a	J. D. & C. B. STANDISH'S/ PORK/&/WOOL/DEALERS,/ DETROIT. /CARD.	Shield with 13 stars within a large circle of 24 stars	C	PL	R2	4016
225BY-1b	Same	Same	BR	PL	R8	

225BZ 225CA

225BZ-1a	L. J. STAPLES/WHOLESALE/ GROCER/&/CONFECTIONER/ WOODWARD/185 DETROIT. AVE	1024	C	R	R7	
225BZ-1a1	Same	Same	C	PL	R9	
225BZ-2a	Same	1025	C	R	R6	4018
225BZ-2a1	Same	Same	C	PL	R9	
225BZ-3a	Same	1037	C	R	R9	4020
225BZ-4a	Same	1042	C	R	R5	4022
225BZ-4b	Same	Same	BR	R	R8	4023
225BZ-5a	Same	1047	C	R	R9	
225BZ-5d	Same (H-R1208)	Same	C-N	R	R9	4025
225CA-1a	GOFF STENTON/MEAT /MARKET/COR./RIVARD & JEFF/AVE./DETROIT	1039	C	R	R5	4032
225CA-2a	Same	1042	C	R	R5	4027
225CA-2b	Same	Same	BR	R	R8	4028
225CA-3d	Same	1046	C-N	R	R10	
225CA-4a	Same	1047	C	R	R9	
225CA-4d	Same (H-R1210)	Same	C-N	R	R10	4030

MICHIGAN-Continued

NUMBER	OBVERSE	REVERSE	METAL	EDGE	RARITY	H&G

DETROIT 225-Continued

225CB

225CC

225CB-1a	MRS. A. STRINGER/DRY /GOODS/MILLINERY/&/DRESS MAKING/MICH. AVE/DETROIT	1039	C	R	R7	4039
225CB-2a	Same	1042	C	R	R7	4034
225CB-2b	Same	Same	BR	R	R8	4035
225CB-2i	Same	Same	Z	R	R9	4036
225CB-3a	Same	1046	C	R	R9	
225CB-4a	Same	1047	C	R	R9	
225CB-4d	Same	Same	C-N	R	R9	4037
225CC-1a	G. W. SUTHERLAND/GROCER/ MARKET/SQUARE/DETROIT	1024	C	R	R6	4041
225CC-2a	Same	1025	C	R	R6	4043
225CC-3a	Same	1042	C	R	R6	4045
225CC-3b	Same	Same	BR	R	R8	4046
225CC-3i	Same	Same	Z	R	R9	4047
225CC-4a	Same	1047	C	R	R9	
225CC-4d	Same	Same	C-N	R	R9	4049

225CD

225CE

225CD-1a	I. & C. TAYLOR/GROCERS/&/ PROVISION/DEALERS/DETROIT	1039	C	R	R8	4058
225CD-1a1	Same	Same	C	PL	R9	
225CD-2a	Same	1042	C	R	R6	4052
225CD-2b	Same	Same	BR	R	R8	4053
225CD-2i	Same	Same	Z	R	R9	4054
225CD-3a	Same	1047	C	R	R9	4056
225CD-3d	Same	Same	C-N	R	R9	
225CE-1a	THE/TEA/STORE/146/ WOODWARD/AVE/DETROIT	1039	C	R	R7	
225CE-2a	Same	1042	C	R	R7	4062
225CE-2b	Same	Same	BR	R	R8	4063
225CE-2i	Same	Same	Z	R	R9	4064
225CE-3a	Same	1047	C	R	R8	4066
225CE-3d	Same	Same	C-N	R	R10	

MICHIGAN-Continued

NUMBER	OBVERSE	REVERSE	METAL	EDGE	RARITY	H&G

DETROIT 225-Continued

225CF

225CG

225CF-1a	W. E. TUNIS/GENERAL/NEWS/ DEALER/DETROIT/CLIFTON, C. W. / & MILWAUKEE	1040	C	R	R6	
225CF-1a1	Same	Same	C	PL	R9	
225CF-2a	Same	1042	C	R	R6	4070
225CF-2b	Same	Same	BR	R	R8	4071
225CF-2i	Same	Same	Z	R	R9	4072
225CF-3a	Same	1047	C	R	R9	4074
225CF-3d	Same	Same	C-N	R	R9	
225CG-1d	TURNER HUBBELL & CO/ WHOLESALE/BOOT & SHOE/ MANUFACTURERS/195 JEFF. AVE/DETROIT	1024	C-N	R	R9	
225CG-2a	Same	1027	C	R	R6	4076
225CG-2a1	Same	Same	C	PL	R9	
225CG-3a	Same	1042	C	R	R5	4078
225CG-3b	Same	Same	BR	R	R9	4079
225CG-3i	Same	Same	Z	R	R9	4080
225CG-4a	Same	1047	C	R	R10	4082

| 225CH-1a | C. C. TYLER & CO/WILL PAY/ ONE/CENT/IN GOODS | DETROIT,/BOOTS/&/SHOES/ MICHIGAN | C | PL | R6 | |
| 225CH-1b | Same | Same | BR | PL | R8 | |

165

MICHIGAN-Continued

NUMBER	OBVERSE	REVERSE	METAL	EDGE	RARITY	H&G

DETROIT 225-Continued

225CI-1   225CI-2

225CI-1a	R. G. TYLER/WHOLESALE/ GROCER/DETROIT MICH.	1367	C	PL	R3	
225CI-1b	Same	Same	BRZ	PL	R3	4084
225CI-2a	R. G. TYLER/WHOLESALE/ GROCER/DETROIT MICH	Same	C	PL	R3	
225CI-2b	Same	Same	BRZ	PL	R3	4086

225CK-6

225CJ   225CK-1

225CJ-1a	VENN & WREFORD/BUTCHERS/ 271/JEFF. /AVE. /DETROIT	1037	C	R	R5	4094
225CJ-2a	Same	1042	C	R	R6	4088
225CJ-2b	Same	Same	BR	R	R9	
225CJ-2i	Same	Same	Z	R	R9	4090
225CJ-3a	Same	1047	C	R	R9	4092
225CJ-3d	Same (H-R 1211)	1047	C-N	R	R10	

NOTE: For Ward's Lake Superior Line, See Cleveland, Ohio

225CK-1a	HENRY WEBER/FURNITURE/ DEALER/129/WOODWARD, A./ DETROIT	1018	C	R	R9	
225CK-2a	Same	1024	C	R	R9	
225CK-3a	Same	1037	C	R	R9	
225CK-4a	Same	1042	C	R	R5	4104
225CK-4b	Same	Same	BR	R	R8	4105
225CK-4l	Same	Same	Z	R	R9	4106
225CK-5a	Same	1047	C	R	R9	4108
225CK-5d	Same	Same	C-N	R	R9	
225CK-6a	HENRY WEBER/FURNITURE/ DEALER/140/WOODWARD, A./ DETROIT	1040	C	R	R9	
225CK-7a	Same	1042	C	R	R9	4110
225CK-7b	Same	Same	BR	R	R9	4111
225CK-8a	Same	1047	C	R	R9	4113

MICHIGAN-Continued

NUMBER	OBVERSE	REVERSE	METAL	EDGE	RARITY	H&G

DETROIT 225-Continued

225CL-1a	B. WEBSTER/WHOLESALE/& RETAIL/FISH/DEALER/DETROIT	1039	C	R	R8	4121
225CL2a	Same	1042	C	R	R7	4115
225CL-2b	Same	Same	BR	R	R8	4116
225CL-2i	Same	Same	Z	R	R9	4117
225CL-3a	Same	1047	C	R	R9	4119
225CL-3d	Same	Same	C-N	R	R9	

225CM

225CN

225CM-1a	W. W. WHITLARK/WITH/GROVER/& BAKER/S. M. CO./FISHERS BLOCK/DETROIT	1039	C	R	R7	
225CM-1a1	Same	Same	C	PL	R9	
225CM-2a	Same	1040	C	R	R9	
225CM-3a	Same	1042	C	R	R6	4123
224CM-3b	Same	Same	BR	R	R8	4124
225CM-3i	Same	Same	Z	R	R9	4125
225CM-4a	Same	1047	C	R	R9	4127
225CM-4d	Same	Same	C-N	R	R9	
225CN-1a	WILKINS & MARTINS/CELEBRATED/INK/&/BLACKING/DEPOT/DETROIT	1042	C	R	R6	4131
225CN-1b	Same	Same	BR	R	R8	4132
225CN-1i	Same	Same	Z	R	R9	4133
225CN-2a	Same	1047	C	R	R9	4134
225CN-2d	Same (H-R 1212)	Same	C-N	R	R10	
225CN-3a	Same	Obverse of 225AV-1a	C	R	R3	4129
225CN-3a1	Same	Same	C	PL	R9	

167

MICHIGAN-Continued

NUMBER	OBVERSE	REVERSE	METAL	EDGE	RARITY	H&G

DETROIT 225-Continued

225CO-1a	J. W. WINCKLER/BAKER/81/ LARNED/ST./DETROIT	1037	C	R	R9	4136
225CO-2a	Same	1039	C	R	R6	
225CO-3a	Same	1042	C	R	R7	4138
225CO-3b	Same	Same	BR	R	R9	
225CO-3i	Same	Same	Z	R	R9	
225CO-4a	Same	1047	C	R	R9	
225CO-4d	Same	Same	C-N	R	R9	

225CP

225CQ

225CP-1a	F. M. WING/GROCER/&/ COMMISSION/MERCHANT/ 83 CONG. ST./DETROIT	1037	C	R	R9	4139
225CP-2a	Same	1039	C	R	R7	
225CP-3a	Same	1042	C	R	R6	4141
225CP-3b	Same	Same	BR	R	R8	4142
225CP-3i	Same	Same	Z	R	R9	4143
225CP-4a	Same	1047	C	R	R9	4145
225CP-4d	Same (H-R 1213)	Same	C-N	R	R9	
225CQ-1a	G. WINTER/HATTER/250/ BIDDLE HOUSE/DETROIT	1025	C	R	R8	
225CQ-1a1	Same	Same	C	PL	R9	
225CQ-2a	Same	1042	C	R	R7	4147
225CQ-2b	Same	Same	BR	R	R8	4148
225CQ-2i	Same	Same	Z	R	R9	4149
225CQ-3a	Same	1047	C	R	R9	4151
225CQ-3d	Same	Same	C-N	R	R9	

MICHIGAN-Continued

NUMBER	OBVERSE	REVERSE	METAL	EDGE	RARITY	H&G

DETROIT 225-Continued

225CR-1a	A. WITGEN/GROCERIES/MEAT/ MARKET/DETROIT	1037	C	PL	R9	
225CR-2a	Same	1039	C	PL	R4	4159
225CR-3a	Same	1042	C	R	R6	4153
225CR-3b	Same	Same	BR	R	R8	4154
225CR-3i	Same	Same	Z	R	R9	4155
225CR-4a	Same	1047	C	R	R0	4157
225CR-4d	Same (H-R 1214)	Same	C-N	R	R9	

225CS-1a	HENRY WOLFF/TRUNK/ MANUFACTORY/211/JEFF. AVE. /DETROIT, MICH.	1018	C	R	R2	4162
225CS-2a	Same	1019	C	R	R8	4162
225CS-3d	Same	1024	C-N	R	R9	
225CS-4a	Same	1027	C	R	R2	4163
225CS-4a1	Same	Same	C	PL	R9	
225CS-5a	Same	1042	C	R	R5	4164
225CS-5b	Same	Same	BR	R	R8	4165
225CS-5i	Same	Same	Z	R	R9	4166
225CS-6a	Same	1047	C	R	R9	4167
225CS-7d	Same	1069	C-N	R	R10	4169

169

MICHIGAN-Continued

NUMBER	OBVERSE	REVERSE	METAL	EDGE	RARITY	H&G

DOWAGIAC 250

250A 250B 250C

250A-1a	A. N. ALWARD/BOOKS,/STATIONERY/& WALL/PAPERS/DOWAGIAC. MICH.	1094	C	PL	R8	4172
250A-2a	Same	1357	C	PL	R8	4174
250B-1a	ANDREWS & COOPER/FAMILY/GROCERIES/&/PROVISIONS/FRONT/ST./DOWAGIAC. MICH.	1105	C	PL	R9	4176
250B-2a	Same	1106	C	PL	R8	4177
250B-3a	Same	1107	C	PL	R8	4178
250B-4a	Same	1205	C	PL	R9	4180
250C-1a	A. M. DICKSON & CO./DRY/GOODS./CLOTHING/BOOTS/& SHOES/DOWAGIAC, MICH	1099	C	PL	R7	
250C-2a	Same	1101	C	PL	R9	
250C-3a	Same	1107	C	PL	R9	4182
250C-4a	Same	1205	C	PL	R9	4183
250C-5a	Same	1046	C	PL	R9	

250D 250E 250F

250D-1a	D. LARZELERE & CO./DRY/GOODS,/GROCERIES,/&/CLOTHING/DOWAGIAC, MICH.	1094	C	PL	R6	4186
250D-2a	Same	1105	C	PL	R8	4187
250E-1a	C. POND/GROCER./AND/CONFECTIONER/DOWAGIAC,/MICH.	1094	C	PL	R9	4189
250E-2a	Same	1105	C	PL	R8	4190
250F-1a	G. A. WHEELOCK/DEALER/IN/GROCERIES/& PROVISIONS/DOWAGIAC/MICH.	1094	C	PL	R9	
250F-2a	Same	1205	C	PL	R8	4192

MICHIGAN-Continued

NUMBER	OBVERSE	REVERSE	METAL	EDGE	RARITY	H&G

EAST SAGINAW 280

		280A		280B		

280A-1a	CHARLES W. BERNACKI/ DRUGGIST/Mortar and pestle/ EAST/SAGINAW/MICH.	1099	C	PL	R9	
280A-2a	Same	1101	C	PL	R8	4196
280A-3a	Same	1390	C	PL	R9	4195
280B-1a	N. W. CLARK & CO/ MERCHANTS/COMMERCIAL/ BLOCK/EAST SAGINAW, MICH.	1039	C	R	R7	4203
280B-1a1	Same	Same	C	PL	R9	
280B-2a	Same	1042	C	R	R7	4198
250B-2b	Same	Same	BR	R	R9	4199
280B-3d	Same	1046	C-N	R	R9	
280B-4a	Same	1047	C	R	R9	4201
280B-4d	Same	Same	C-N	R	R-9	

	280C		280D		

280C-1a	S. T. LEGGETT/PRACTICAL/ WATCHMAKER/&/JEWELER/ EAST/SAGINAW/MICH.	1211	C	PL	R6	4205
280C-1a1	Same	Same	C	R	R9	
280D-1a	JOHN MC KAY/OYSTER/FRUIT/ &/FISH/DEPOT/EAST SAGINAW	1039	C	R	R9	4213
280D-2a	Same	1042	C	R	R8	4207
280D-2b	Same	Same	BR	R	R8	4208
280D-2i	Same	Same	Z	R	R9	
280D-3a	Same	1047	C	R	R9	4211
280D-3d	Same	Same	C-N	R	R9	

MICHIGAN-Continued

NUMBER	OBVERSE	REVERSE	METAL	EDGE	RARITY	H&G

EAST SAGINAW 280-Continued

280E-1a	A. SCHMITZ/picture of plow/ EAST/SAGINAW/MICH.	DEALER IN/IRON./NAILS./STOVES./CROCKERY/&/PAINTS. (Period after Paints to the left of the Y of Crockery)	C	PL	R5	4215
280E-2a	Same	Same inscription, but Period after Y of Crockery. Crockery	C	PL	R9	
280E-3a	Same	1390	C	PL	R9	4216

280F-1a	TOWN BRANCH/STORE/REDEEMABLE/IN/GOODS	1047	C	R	R8	4217
280F-2d	Same	1069	C-N	R	R10	
280F-3a	Same	1391	C	R	R8	
280F-4a	Same	1394	C	R	R8	
280F-5b	Same	1399	BR	R	R9	

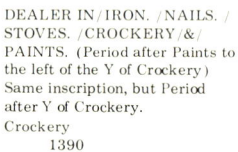

(NOTE: No concrete evidence has been found of the existence of this store having been located in the Saginaw area, attributed here by Barnett.)

| 280G-1a | CHARLES TURNER/DEALER/IN/FURS/& SKINS./EAST SAGINAW/MICH. | 1101 | C | PL | R9 | 4218 |

172

MICHIGAN-Continued

NUMBER	OBVERSE	REVERSE	METAL	EDGE	RARITY	H&G

EATON RAPIDS 300

300A-1a	A. C. DUTTON M. D/BOOKS,/STATIONERY,/GROCERIES & C./EATON RAPIDS/MICH.	1310	C	PL	R5	4219
300A-1b	Same	Same	BR	PL	R8	4220
300B-1a	H. M. FROST/DRUGGIST/AND/GROCER,/EATON RAPIDS/MICH.	1310	C	PL	R5	4222
300B-1b	Same	Same	BR	PL	R8	4223
300C-1a	FROST & DANIELS/DRY GOODS,/GROCERIES,/BOOTS, SHOES & C/EATON RAPIDS/MICH.	1225	C	PL	R4	4225
300C-1b	Same	Same	BR	PL	R7	4226
300D-1a	P. LEONARD/DRY GOODS/GROCERIES/BOOTS SHOES & C/EATON RAPIDS,/MICH.	1168	C	PL	R6	4228
300D-1b	Same	Same	BR	PL	R8	4229
300E-1a	A. MESTER & CO./MARBLE/WORKS,/EATON RAPIDS,/MICH	1340	C	PL	R5	4231
300E-1b	Same	Same	BR	PL	R8	4232
300E-1d	Same	Same	C-N	PL	R10	

MICHIGAN-Continued

NUMBER	OBVERSE	REVERSE	METAL	EDGE	RARITY	H&G

EATON RAPIDS 300-Contined

| 300F-1a | WM. F. STIRLING,/DRY GOODS,/UNION BLOCK,/ EATON RAPIDS,/MICH. | THE CELEBRATED/TEA/ ESTABLISHMENT. | C | PL | R3 | 4234 |
| 300F-1b | Same | Same | BR | PL | R8 | 4235 |

FLINT 320

| 320A-1a | GILES BISHOP/GROCERIES/ AND/LIQUORS/BUSINESS CARD | DRUGGIST/mortar and pestle/ FLINT MICH. | C | PL | R9 | |
| 320A-1b | Same | Same | BRZ | PL | R2 | 4238 |

| 320B-1a | CLARK'S/DRUGS,/MEDICINES,/ GROCERIES. /& C. /FLINT, MICH | 1101 | C | PL | R5 | 4242 |
| 320B-2a | Same | 1205 | C | PL | R5 | 4240 |

174

MICHIGAN-Continued

NUMBER	OBVERSE	REVERSE	METAL	EDGE	RARITY	H&G

GRAND HAVEN 360

360A-1a	H. BROUWER/& BRO. /DRY GOODS,/GROCERIES,/BOOTS &/SHOES. /GRAND HAVEN, MICH	1094	C	PL	R6	4244
360A-2a	Same	1205	C	PL	R8	4245
360A-3a	Same	1209	C	PL	R6	4246
360A-4a	Same	1210	C	PL	R9	

| 360B-1a | GEO. E. HUBBARD/DEALER/ IN/STOVES/AND/HARDWARE/ GRAND HAVEN/MICH. | 1226 | C | PL | R5 | 4247 |
| 360B-2a | GEO. E. HUBBARD/STOVES/ HARDWARE/IRON & C/GRAND HAVEN/MICH. | 1212 | C | PL | R5 | |

| 360C-1a | G. V. SCHELVEN/DEALER/ IN/GROCERIES/AND/CANDIES/ GRAND HAVEN MICH | 1108 | C | PL | R7 | |
| 360C-1f | Same | Same | S | PL | R9 | |

MICHIGAN-Continued

NUMBER	OBVERSE	REVERSE	METAL	EDGE	RARITY	H&G

GRAND RAPIDS 370

370A-1a	GEO. P. BARNARD/BOOK/SELLER/&/STATIONER/GRAND/RAPIDS/MICH.	1101	C	PL	R5	4253
370A-2a	Same	1390	C	PL	R9	4252
370B-1a	RUSIAN CLOTHING/STORE,/COURLANDER/&/PRESSGOOD,/GRAND RAPIDS,/MICH.	1337	C	PL	R7	4255
370B-1b	Same (NOTE: Spelling error Rusian)	Same	BR	PL	R9	4256
370B-2a	Russian clthing/STORE,/COURLANDER/&/PRESSGOOD,/GRAND RAPIDS/MICH.	Same	C	PL	R7	4257
370B-2b	Same (NOTE: Spelling error Clthing)	Same	BR	PL	R8	4258
370C-1a	FOSTER & METCALF/cook stove/GRAND RAPIDS, MICH.	1861/WORKERS IN/COPPER, TIN, BRASS,/AND/HEAVY SHEET IRON,/PLUMBING,/GAS FITTING/ETC. ETC. ETC.	C	PL	R8	
370C-1b	Same	Same	BR	PL	R4	4260

176

MICHIGAN-Continued

NUMBER	OBVERSE	REVERSE	METAL	EDGE	RARITY	H&G

GRAND RAPIDS 370-Continued

370C-2a	FOSTER & METCALF/cook stove GRAND RAPIDS MICH	Same	C	PL	R8	
370C-2a1	Same	Same	BRZ	PL	R4	
370C-2b	Same	Same	BR	PL	R9	
370C-2e	Same	Same	W-M	PL	R8	4261
370C-2fp	Same	Same	Sptd	PL	R9	
370D-1a	GOODRICH & GAY/DEALERS/IN/HARDWARE/IRON,STEEL,/NAILS & GLASS,/GRAND RAPIDS, MICH (N of Nails over A of Grand)	1305	C	PL	R9	
370D-1b	Same	Same	BR	PL	R2	4263
370D-1c	Same	Same	N	PL	R9	
370D-1fp	Same	Same	Sptd	PL	R9	
370D-2a	Same inscription, but N of Nails over N of Grand)	1307	C	PL	R2	1964
370D-2b	Same	Same	BR	PL	R2	4265
370D-3a	Same	1308	C	PL	R9	
370D-3b	Same	Same	BR	PL	R9	

370E-1a	KRUGER & BOOTH/DEALERS IN/SADDLES/HARNESS/TRUNKS/GRAND RAPIDS/MICH.	1101	C	PL	R6	4268
370E-2a	Same	1357	C	PL	R6	4267
370F-1a	C. KUSTERER/horse and wagon/GRAND RAPIDS/MICH	CITY BREWERY/MANF'R/OF/LAGER BEER/STOCK/& CREAM/ALE	C	PL	R3	1270
370F-2a	Same	1205	C	PL	R9	4271
370F-3a	Same	1211	C	PL	R9	
370F-4a	Same as reverse of 370F-1a	1105	C	PL	R9	10112

(Note: This token was formerly listed under Milwaukee, Wis.)

MICHIGAN-Continued

NUMBER	OBVERSE	REVERSE	METAL	EDGE	RARITY	H&G

GRAND RAPIDS 370-Continued

370G   370H-1   370H-4

370G-1a	L. A. MERRILL/ PHOTOGRAPHIC/ARTIST. / GRAND/RAPIDS/MICH	1101	C	PL	R6	4274
370G-2a	Same	1105	C	PL	R6	4273
370H-1a	J. W. PEIRCE/DRY GOODS/ AND/GROCERIES/GRAND RAPIDS MICH (G of Groceries opposite the N of And)	1358	C	PL	R9	
370H-1b	Same	Same	BRZ	PL	R2	4276
370H-2b	Same	1359	BRZ	PL	R2	4277
370H-3a	Same	1360	C	PL	R9	
370H-4a	Same inscription, but G of Groceries opposite the AN of And.	1361	C	PL	R2	4278
370H-4b	Same	Same	BRZ	PL	R2	4279
370H-5a	Same	1362	C	PL	R8	4280
370H-5b	Same	Same	BR	PL	R2	4281
370H-6a	Same	1363	C	PL	R7	4282
370H-6b	Same	Same	BR	PL	R2	4283
370H-7a	Same	1365	C	PL	R2	4284

370I-1   370I-2

370I-1a	E. K. POWERS/ CONFECTIONER/& DEALER IN /SODA WATER/GRAND/RAPIDS /MICH.	1101	C	PL	R6	4288
370I-2a	Same	1205	C	PL	R9	4287
370I-3a	Same inscription, but the S of Powers is over the NE of Confectioner.	1101	C	PL	R9	

178

MICHIGAN-Continued

NUMBER	OBVERSE	REVERSE	METAL	EDGE	RARITY	H&G

GRAND RAPIDS 370-Continued

370J-1a	L. H. RANDALL/WHOLESALE/ &/RETAIL/GROCER/GRAND RAPIDS. MICH.	L. H. RANDALL. /Tea chest with large letter T on it/1862	C	PL	R3	4290
370J-1b	Same	Same	BR	PL	R3	4291
370J-1fp	Same	Same	Sptd	PL	R9	

370K-1a	A. ROBERTS & SON/DRY GOODS/GROCERIES/ CROCKERY/& C/GRAND RAPIDS	1362	C	PL	R8	
370K-1b	Same	Same	BR	PL	R4	4292
370K-2a	Same	1365	C	PL	R8	
370K-2b	Same	Same	BR	PL	R4	4293
370K-3a	Same	1366	C	PL	R8	
370K-3b	Same	Same	BR	PL	R4	4294

370L-1a	TOMPKINS/PHOTOGRAPH/ AND/AMBROTYPE/GALLERY. / GRAND/RAPIDS/MICH	1105	C	PL	R6	4296
370L-2a	Same	1205	C	PL	R9	4297
370L-3a	Same	1211	C	PL	R6	

179

MICHIGAN-Continued

NUMBER	OBVERSE	REVERSE	METAL	EDGE	RARITY	H&G

HASTINGS 440

440A-1a	D. C. HAWLEY/GROCERIES/&/ PROVISIONS/HASTINGS. / MICH.	1101	C	PL	R6	4304
440A-2a	Same	1094	C	PL	R6	4300
440A-3a	Same	1105	C	PL	R6	4301
440A-4a	Same	1107	C	PL	R9	4302
440A-5a	Same	1205	C	PL	R9	4303

HILLSDALE 450

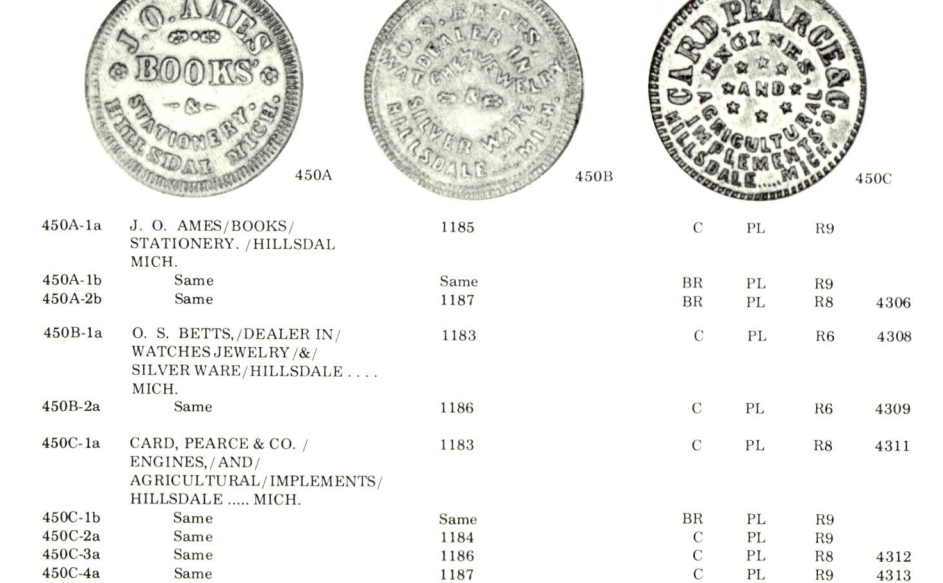

450A   450B   450C

450A-1a	J. O. AMES/BOOKS/ STATIONERY. /HILLSDAL MICH.	1185	C	PL	R9	
450A-1b	Same	Same	BR	PL	R9	
450A-2b	Same	1187	BR	PL	R8	4306
450B-1a	O. S. BETTS,/DEALER IN/ WATCHES JEWELRY /&/ SILVER WARE/HILLSDALE .... MICH.	1183	C	PL	R6	4308
450B-2a	Same	1186	C	PL	R6	4309
450C-1a	CARD, PEARCE & CO. / ENGINES,/AND/ AGRICULTURAL/IMPLEMENTS/ HILLSDALE ..... MICH.	1183	C	PL	R8	4311
450C-1b	Same	Same	BR	PL	R9	
450C-2a	Same	1184	C	PL	R9	
450C-3a	Same	1186	C	PL	R8	4312
450C-4a	Same	1187	C	PL	R9	4313

MICHIGAN-Continued

NUMBER	OBVERSE	REVERSE	METAL	EDGE	RARITY	H&G

HILLSDALE 450-Continued

| 450D-1a | FARNAM'S/BRONCHIAL/TABLETS | 1185 | C | PL | R8 | 4314 |
| 450D-2b | Same | 1187 | BR | PL | R9 | |

450E-1a	FRENCH & PARSONS/DRUGGISTS/&/GROCERS/HILLSDALE, MICH.	1111	C	PL	R7	4315
450E-1b	Same	Same	BR	PL	R8	
450F-1a	J. GOTTLIEB/CLOTHIER/HILLSDALE, MICH.	1184	C	PL	R9	
450F-2a	Same	1185	C	PL	R10	4316
450F-3a	Same	1187	C	PL	R9	
450F-3b	Same	Same	BR	PL	R8	4317

450G-1a	A. GLEASON,/DIE-SINKER/&/ENGRAVER/HILLSDALE MICH.	1183	C	PL	R4	4319
450G-2a	Same	1184	C	PL	R4	4322
450G-3a	Same	1186	C	PL	R4	4320
450G-4a	Same	1187	C	PL	R9	4321

MICHIGAN-Continued

NUMBER	OBVERSE	REVERSE	METAL	EDGE	RARITY	H&G

HILLSDALE 450-Continued

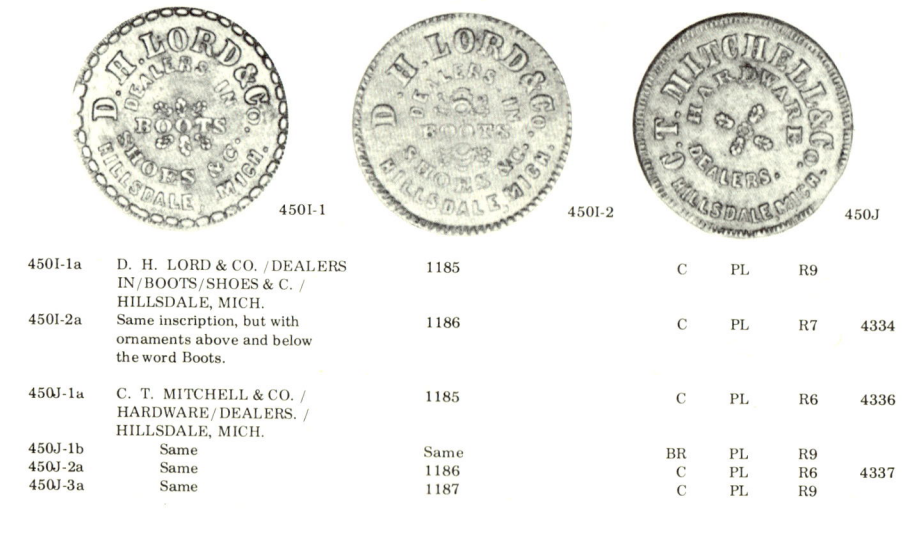

450G-5a	Same	1221	C	PL	R4	4318
450G-6a	1185	1262	C	PL	R4	4324
450G-7a	1186	Same	C	PL	R4	4326
450G-7b	Same	Same	BR	PL	R6	4327
450G-7d	Same	Same	C-N	PL	R9	
450G-8a	1187	Same	C	PL	R6	4328
450G-8b	Same	Same	BR	PL	R10	

450H-1a	E. C. KEATING/GROCER. / AND/PRODUCE DEALER/ HILLSDALE ..... MICH.	1183	C	PL	R9	
450H-2a	Same	1185	C	PL	R8	4331
450H-2b	Same	Same	BR	PL	R9	
450H-3a	Same	1186	C	PL	R7	4332

450I-1   450I-2   450J

450I-1a	D. H. LORD & CO. /DEALERS IN/BOOTS/SHOES & C. / HILLSDALE, MICH.	1185	C	PL	R9	
450I-2a	Same inscription, but with ornaments above and below the word Boots.	1186	C	PL	R7	4334
450J-1a	C. T. MITCHELL & CO. / HARDWARE/DEALERS. / HILLSDALE, MICH.	1185	C	PL	R6	4336
450J-1b	Same	Same	BR	PL	R9	
450J-2a	Same	1186	C	PL	R6	4337
450J-3a	Same	1187	C	PL	R9	

MICHIGAN-Continued

NUMBER	OBVERSE	REVERSE	METAL	EDGE	RARITY	H&G

HILLSDALE 450-Continued

450K-1

450K-2

| 450K-1a | C. E. MOTT & CO. /DRY/ GOODS/CARPETING/& C. / HILLSDALE, MICH. (D of Dry under M of Mott) | 1111 | C | PL | R4 | 4338 |
| 450K-2a | C. E. MOTT & CO. /DRY/ GOODS/CARPETING/& C. / HILLSDALE. MICH. (D of Dry under Mo of Mott) | 1117 | C | PL | R5 | 4339 |

450L-1a	MOTT & BRO. /DRUGGISTS/ AND/GROCERS/HILLSDALE. MICH.	1111	C	PL	R5	
450L-2a	Same	1115	C	PL	R9	
450L-3a	Same	1117	C	PL	R4	4342
450L-4a	Same	1185	C	PL	R9	4341

| 450M-1a | SAMM & KUHLKE,/GROCERS/ HILLSDALE....M. | 1185 | C | PL | R7 | 4344 |
| 450M-2a | Same | 1186 | C | PL | R5 | 4345 |

183

MICHIGAN-Continued

NUMBER	OBVERSE	REVERSE	METAL	EDGE	RARITY	H&G

HILLSDALE 450 -Continued

| 450N-1a | UNION PLANING & STAVE MILL,/R. ROWE,/HILLSDALE/ MICH. | 1183 | C | PL | R9 | 4346 |
| 450N-2a | Same | 1186 | C | PL | R7 | 4347 |

| 450O-1a | GEO. W. UNDERWOOD/ DRUGGIST/&/GROCER/ HILLSDALE, MICH.. | 1115 | C | PL | R9 | |
| 450O-2a | Same | 1117 | C | PL | R5 | 4349 |

HUDSON 480

| 480A-1a | BAKER & BROWN/DRY/ GOODS/AND/GROCERIES/ HUDSON...MICH. | 1184 | C | PL | R9 | |
| 480A-2a | Same | 1186 | C | PL | R6 | 4351 |

MICHIGAN-Continued

NUMBER	OBVERSE	REVERSE	METAL	EDGE	RARITY	H&G

HUDSON 480-Continued

      480B   480C   480D

480B-1a	A. H. BOWEN/BAKER/&/ GROCER/HUDSON...MICH	1183	C	PL	R7	
480C-1a	GILLETT & NILES/Mortar and pestle/DRUGGISTS/HUDSON,/ MICH.	1099	C	PL	R8	
480C-2a	Same	1101	C	PL	R9	4354
480C-3a	Same	1204	C	PL	R0	
480C-4a	Same	1390	C	PL	R8	4353
480D-1a	GREEN & WARDSWORTH. / LIVERY/HUDSON..MICH.	1183	C	PL	R7	
480D-2a	Same	1184	C	PL	R9	4356

      480E   480F   480G

480E-1a	H. HOWE & CO. /DEALERS IN/ GENERAL, /HARDWARE/ HUDSON..MICH.	1183	C	PL	R8	4357
480E-2a	Same	1184	C	PL	R9	
480E-3a	Same	1186	C	PL	R8	5358
480F-1a	PALMER & GOODSALL/ HARDWARE/DEALERS,/ HUDSON, MICH.	1183	C	PL	R7	4360
480F-2a	Same	1186	C	PL	R7	4361
480G-1a	TUBBS & SPEAR/GROCERS/ HUDSON...MICH.	1183	C	PL	R5	
480G-2a	Same	1186	C	PL	R9	4362
480G-2b	Same	Same	BR	PL	R9	

185

MICHIGAN-Continued

NUMBER	OBVERSE	REVERSE	METAL	EDGE	RARITY	H&G

IONIA 495

495A-1a	JAMES. KENNEDY. /Indian head to left/1863	EXCHANGE INSURANCE/ COLLECTION/& U. S. /WAR CLAIM/OFFICE/IONIA MICH	C	PL	R2	4363
495A-1b	Same	Same	BR	PL	R9	
495A-1c	Same	Same	N	PL	R10	
495A-2a	JAMES KENNEDY,/Shield/1863	Same	C	PL	R4	4364
495A-2b	Same	Same	BR	PL	R10	

495B-1a	F. SLOAN/STOVES,/ HARDWARE,/IRON, STEEL/& NAILS/IONIA, MICH.	1101	C	PL	R4	4367
495B-2a	Same	1211	C	PL	R8	4368
495B-3a	Same	1212	C	PL	R4	
495B-4a	Same	1357	C	PL	R4	4366

JACKSON 525

| 525A-1a | S. HOLLAND & SON/Mortar and pestle/DRUGGISTS/JACKSON,/ MICH. | 1098 | C | PL | R8 | 4370 |
| 525A-2a | Same | 1390 | C | PL | R8 | 4371 |

186

MICHIGAN-Continued

NUMBER	OBVERSE	REVERSE	METAL	EDGE	RARITY	H&G

JACKSON 525-Continued

| 525B-1a | H. S. ISMON/DEALER/IN STAPLE/& FANCY/DRY GOODS/ JACKSON, MICH | 1098 | C | PL | R5 | 4373 |

525C-1a	WM JACKSON/X/*CLUSIVE*/ TRADE/IN/GROCERIES. (Two dots under M of WM)	JACKSON HALL/BLOCK/ JACKSON,/MICH.	C	PL	R3	4375
525C-2a	Same	JACKSON HALL/JACKSON/ MICH./1863/*	C	PL	R3	4376
525C-2b	Same	Same	BR	PL	R9	4377
525C-3a	WM JACKSON,/X/*CLUSIVE*/ TRADE/IN/GROCERIES.	Same	C	PL	R9	
525C-3b	Same	Same	BR	PL	R9	
525C-4a	Same	JACKSON HALL/JACKSON MICH./1863/*******	C	PL	R10	
525C-5a	Same	JACKSON HALL/JACKSON,/ MICH./1863	C	PL	R5	

187

MICHIGAN-Continued

| NUMBER | OBVERSE | REVERSE | METAL | EDGE | RARITY | H&G |

JACKSON 525-Continued

525C-6a	WM JACKSON,/X/CLUSIVE/ TRADE/IN/GROCERIES.	Same	C	PL	R3	4378
525C-7a	WM JACKSON/X/*CLUSIVE*/ TRADE/IN/GROCERIES. (One dot under M of WM)	JACKSON HALL/Eagle in glory/JACKSON/MICH./1863	C	PL	R5	4384
525C-7d	Same	Same	C-N	PL	R10	4385
525C-8a	Reverse of 525C-2a	1130	C	PL	R6	4386
525C-9a	WM. JACKSON/DEALER/IN/ GROCERIES/JACKSON./MICH.	1094	C	PL	R6	4387
525C-10a	WM. JACKSON/DEALER/IN/ GROCERIES JACKSON, MICH.	1099	C	PL	R8	4389
525C-11a	Same	1105	C	PL	R8	4388

525D-1a	W. JAXON/GROCER,/ JACKSON HALL/JACKSON,/ MICH./1863	1168	C	PL	R9	4391
525D-2a	Same	1348	C	PL	R3	4393
525D-2b	Same	Same	BR	PL	R8	4394
525D-2d	Same	Same	C-N	PL	R10	
525D-3a	Same	1387	C	PL	R9	4396
525D-3b	Same	Same	BR	PL	R8	

MICHIGAN-Continued

NUMBER	OBVERSE	REVERSE	METAL	EDGE	RARITY	H&G

JACKSON 525-Continued

| 525D-4a | W. JAXON/GROCER,/ JACKSON HALL/JACKSON,/ MICH. /1864 | 1349 | C | PL | R3 | 4398 |
| 525D-4b | Same | Same | BR | PL | R9 | |

JONESVILLE 527

527A-1a	C. C. BLAKESLEE/Mortar and pestle/DRUGGIST./ JONESVILLE, MICH	1187	C	PL	R8	4400
527A-1b	Same	1187	BR	PL	R9	
527B-1a	A. & H. GALE/MANFRS/OF/ AGRICULT. RL. IMPLEMENTS/ JONESVILLE, M.	1187	C	PL	R9	4402
527C-1a	H. R. GARDNER & CO. WOOLEN/MANUF'RS./ JONESVILLE, MICH	1185	C	PL	R7	4404
527C-2a	Same	1186	C	PL	R9	4405
527C-2b	Same	Same	BR	PL	R9	

MICHIGAN-Continued

NUMBER	OBVERSE	REVERSE	METAL	EDGE	RARITY	H&G

JONESVILLE 527-Continued

527D-1a	J. S. LEWIS,/HARDWARE/IRON & NAILS,/JONESVILLE.....MICH.	1185	C	PL	R9	4407
527D-1b	Same	Same	BR	PL	R9	
527D-2a	Same	1186	C	PL	R9	

| 527E-1a | VAN NES & TURNER/DRY GOODS/AND/GROCERIES/ JONESVILLE.....MICH. | 1185 | C | PL | R5 | 4409 |
| 527E-1b | Same | Same | BR | PL | R9 | |

| 527F-1a | D. A. WISNER & SON/DRY/ GOODS/AND/GROCERIES/ JONESVILLE...MICH. | 1185 | C | PL | R6 | 4411 |
| 527F-1b | Same | Same | BR | PL | R9 | |

190

MICHIGAN-Continued

| NUMBER | OBVERSE | REVERSE | METAL | EDGE | RARITY | H&G |

JUNEAU See Wisconsin 320A

KALAMAZOO 530

530A

530B-1

530B-2

530A-1a	BABCOCK & COBB/DRY/ GOODS/CARPETS/&/CLOTHING /KALAMAZOO.	1108	C	PL	R7	4417
530A-2a	Same	1203	C	PL	R6	4418
530A-3a	Same	1357	C	PL	R8	4416
530B-1a	COBB & FISHER/DEALERS/IN/ CROCKERY/KALAMAZOO.	1094	C	PL	R9	4419
530B-2a	COBB & FISHER/DEALERS/IN/ CROCKERY/KALAMAZOO	1094	C	PL	R4	4420
530B-3a	Same	1205	C	PL	R9	4421

530C-1

530C-2

530D

530C-1a	DAVIS & BATES/ONE/PRICE/ CASH/STORE/KALAMAZOO.	1094	C	PL	R9	
530C-2a	DAVIS & BATES/ONE/PRICE/ CASH/STORE/KALAMAZOO	1094	C	PL	R5	4423
530C-3a	Same	1095	C	PL	R7	4425
530C-4a	Same	1390	C	PL	R9	4424
530D-1a	R. R. HOWARD/HARDWARE/ CUTLERY & C. /KALAMAZOO/ MICH.	1094	C	PL	R4	4426
530D-2a	Same	1357	C	PL	R9	4427

MICHIGAN-Continued

NUMBER	OBVERSE	REVERSE	METAL	EDGE	RARITY	H&G

KALAMAZOO 530-Continued

530E-1a	KELLOGG & CO. /MANFR'S/OF/ LUMBER/DOORS/BLINDS & SASH/KALAMAZOO/MICH.	1094	C	PL	R5	4429
530E-2a	Same	1095	C	PL	R5	4430
530E-3a	Same	1105	C	PL	R5	4431
530E-4a	Same	1357	C	PL	R9	4432

530F-1a	H. S. PARKER & CO. /HATS/ CAPS/BOOTS/& SHOES/ KALAMAZOO	1094	C	PL	R7	4434
530F-2a	Same	1108	C	PL	R5	4435
530F-3a	Same	1390	C	PL	R9	4436

530G-1   530G-2

530G-1a	L. W. PERRIN/DRY/GOODS/ GROCERIES/& CARPETS/ KALAMAZOO	1037	C	R	R4	4438
530G-2a	L. W. PERRIN/DRY/GOODS/ CROCKERY/&/CARPETS/ KALAMAZOO	1037	C	R	R9	
530G-3a	Same	1047	C	R	R9	4440
530G-3d	Same	Same	C-N	R	R9	

MICHIGAN-Continued

NUMBER	OBVERSE	REVERSE	METAL	EDGE	RARITY	H&G

KALAMAZOO 530-Continued

| 530H-1a | ROBERTS & / HILLHOUSE / DRUGGISTS. / SIGN / OF / EAGLE & MORTAR / KALAMAZOO, MICH. | 1357 | C | PL | R9 | 4442 |
| 530H-2a | Same | 1203 | C | PL | R3 | 4444 |

LANSING 560

560A-1   560B

560A-1a	DAVID EKSTEIN / DEALER / IN / GROCERIES / AND / PROVISIONS / LANSING, / MICH.	1123	C	PL	R8	
560A-2a	Same	1126	C	PL	R5	4448
560A-3a	Same	1166	C	PL	R5	4447
560A-4a	Same	Obverse of Ohio 165CY	C	PL	R9	4449
560B-1a	A. J. VIELE, / BOOKS, / STATIONERY, / PIANOS & / SEWING / MACHINES, / LANSING, / MICH.	1123	C	PL	R9	
560B-2a	Same	1168	C	PL	R4	4450
560B-2b	Same	Same	BR	PL	R7	
560B-3a	Same	1321	C	PL	R7	4452
560B-3b	Same	Same	BR	PL	R9	4453
560B-4a	Same	1322	C	PL	R4	4454
560B-4b	Same	Same	BR	PL	R8	4455

MICHIGAN-Continued

NUMBER	OBVERSE	REVERSE	METAL	EDGE	RARITY	H&G

LAPEER 565

565A-1a	H. GRISWOLD & CO. /DEALERS/ IN/DRY/GOODS/GROCERIES/ & C. /LAPEER, MICH.	1024	C	R	R5	4457
565A-2a	Same	1042	C	R	R6	4459
565A-2b	Same	Same	BR	R	R8	
565A-2i	Same	Same	Z	R	R8	
565A-3a	Same	1047	C	R	R9	4461
565A-3d	Same	Same	C-N	R	R9	

LAWTON 570

570A-1a	FAIRBANK & SCRIVER/ STOVES. /HARDWARE/&/ CUTLERY/LAWTON,MIC.	1094	C	PL	R8	4467
570A-2a	Same	1098	C	PL	R6	
570A-3a	Same	1099	C	PL	R6	4465
570A-4a	Same	1205	C	PL	R7	4463

194

MICHIGAN-Continued

NUMBER	OBVERSE	REVERSE	METAL	EDGE	RARITY	H&G

LIGONIER See Indiana 550G

LITCHFIELD 577

| 577A-1a | A. BURLESON/DRY/GOODS,/ GROCERIES,/BOOTS & SHOES./ LITCHFIELD, MICH. | 1187 | C | PL | R9 | 4472 |
| 577A-1b | Same | Same | BR | PL | R8 | 4473 |

LOWELL 580

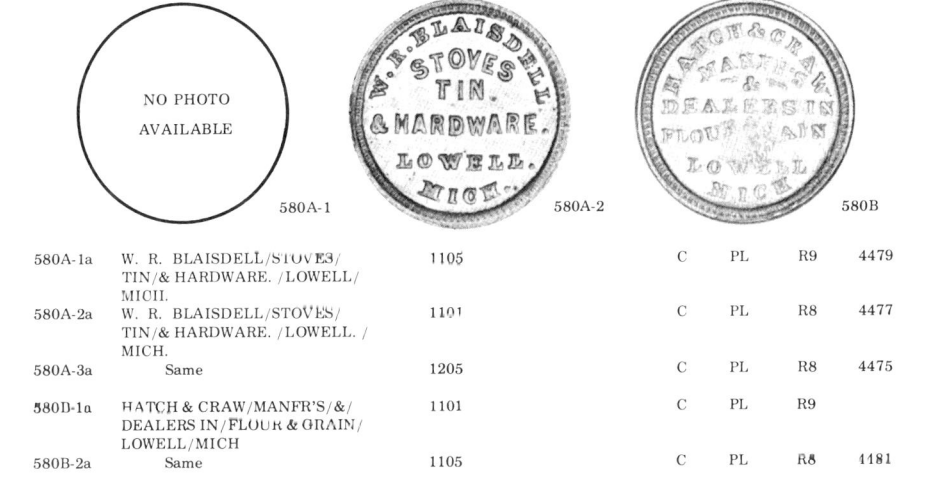

580A-1   580A-2   580B

580A-1a	W. R. BLAISDELL/STOVES/ TIN/& HARDWARE./LOWELL/ MICH.	1105	C	PL	R9	4479
580A-2a	W. R. BLAISDELL/STOVES/ TIN/& HARDWARE./LOWELL./ MICH.	1101	C	PL	R8	4477
580A-3a	Same	1205	C	PL	R8	4475
580D-1a	HATCH & CRAW/MANFR'S/&/ DEALERS IN/FLOUR & GRAIN/ LOWELL/MICH	1101	C	PL	R9	
580B-2a	Same	1105	C	PL	R8	4481

195

MICHIGAN-Continued

NUMBER	OBVERSE	REVERSE	METAL	EDGE	RARITY	H&G

LOWELL 580-Continued

| 580B-3a | HATCH & CRAW/MANFR'S/&/ DEALERS IN/FLOUR & GRAIN/ LOWELL,/MICH. | 1101 | C | PL | R7 | 4483 |
| 580B-4a | Same | 1108 | C | PL | R7 | 4482 |

LYONS 587

587A-1a	BAUDER & BUTTON/WAR/ CLAIM/AGENTS/ATTORNEYS/ AT LAW/LYONS, MICH	1101	C	PL	R8	
587A-1b	Same	Same	BR	PL	R9	
587A-2a	Same	1105	C	PL	R8	4485
587B-1a	A. BUTTON/WAR/CLAIM ATTORNEY/AND GENERAL/ GENERAL COLECTING/AGENT. /LYONS, MICH.	1169	C	PL	R7	4488
587B-1b	Same	Same	BR	PL	R9	4489
587B-2a	A. BUTTON/WAR/CLAIM ATTORNEY/GENERAL COLLECTING/AND/INSURANCE /AGENT. /LYONS MICH.	1173	C	PL	R7	4490
587B-2b	Same	Same	BR	PL	R8	4491
587B-2d	Same	Same	C-N	PL	R10	

MICHIGAN-Continued

NUMBER	OBVERSE	REVERSE	METAL	EDGE	RARITY	H&G

LYONS 587

| 587C-1a | L. F. HEATH,/WATCH/ MAKER/AND/PHOTOGRAPHER, /LYONS,/MICH. | 1321 | C | PL | R7 | 4493 |
| 587C-1b | Same | Same | BR | PL | R7 | 4494 |

MANCHESTER 588

588A-1a	VAN DUYN & LYNCH/ DRUGGISTS/AND/GROCERS,/ MANCHESTER/MICH.	1310	C	PL	R9	4496
588A-1b	Same	Same	BR	PL	R7	4497
588A-2a	Same	1316	C	PL	R8	4498
588A-2b	Same	Same	BR	PL	R9	4499

MAPLE RAPIDS 595

| 595A-1a | ISAAC HEWITT/DRY GOODS/&/ GROCERIES./MAPLE/RAPIDS/ MICH. | 1101 | C | PL | R9 | 4502 |
| 595A-2a | Same | 1105 | C | PL | R8 | 4501 |

MICHIGAN-Continued

NUMBER	OBVERSE	REVERSE	METAL	EDGE	RARITY	H&G

MARSHALL 610

610A 610B-1 610B-5

610A-1a	ISAAC BEERS. /STOVES/ HARDWARE/TOOLS &/TINWARE /MARSHALL, MICH.	1098	C	PL	R9	
610A-2a	Same	1390	C	PL	R9	4503
610B-1a	C. M. BREWER/DEALER/IN/ DRY GOODS/GROCERIES &/ HARDWARE/MARSHALL,/ MICH.	1095	C	PL	R6	4504
610B-2a	Same	1098	C	PL	R6	4506
610B-3a	Same	1106	C	PL	R8	
610B-4a	Same	1205	C	PL	R6	4505
610B-5a	C. M. BREWER/DEALER/IN/ DRY GOODS/GROCERIES &/ HARDWARE/MARSHALL/ MICH.	1106	C	PL	R8	

610C-1  610C-3

610C-1a	L. H. ROBINSON/DEALER/IN/ GROCERIES/&/NOTIONS/ MARSHLL,/MICH.	1025	C	R	R8	
610C-1a1	Same	Same	C	PL	R9	
610C-2a	Same	1034	C	R	R8	
610C-3a	L. H. ROBINSON/DEALER/IN/ GROCERIES/&/NOTIONS/ MARSHALL,/MICH.	1018	C	R	R7	4514
610C-3d	Same	Same	C-N	R	R9	
610C-4a	Same	1025	C	R	R7	4508
610C-5a	Same	1042	C	R	R7	4510
610C-5b	Same	Same	BR	R	R8	4511
610C-5i	Same	Same	Z	R	R9	
610C-6a	Same	1047	C	R	R9	
610C-7d	Same	1069	C-N	R	R10	4513

MICHIGAN-Continued

NUMBER	OBVERSE	REVERSE	METAL	EDGE	RARITY	H&G

MASON 615

615A-1a	J. W. PHELPS & CO/ HARDWARE/TIN & COPPER/ WARE/DRUGS/&/MEDICINES/ MASON, MICH.	1024	C	R	R9	4516
615A-2a	Same	1042	C	R	R5	4518
615A-2b	Same	Same	BR	R	R8	4519
615A-2i	Same	Same	Z	R	R9	4521
615A-3a	Same	1047	C	R	R9	4520
615A-3d	Same	Same	C-N	R	R9	

MORENCI 660

660A    660B

660A-1a	J. M. PAGE & CO. /DEALERS IN/GENERAL/HARDWARE/ MORENCI,MICH.	1186	C	PL	R6	4522
660A-1b	Same	Same	BR	PL	R9	
660B-1a	RICHARDS & CO. /DEALERS/ IN/DRY GOODS. /HARDWARE/ &C./MORENCI,/MICH.	1098	C	PL	R6	4525
660B-2a	Same	1099	C	PL	R3	4526
660B-3a	Same	1205	C	PL	R6	4524

199

MICHIGAN-Continued

NUMBER	OBVERSE	REVERSE	METAL	EDGE	RARITY	H&G

MUSSEY 680

680A-1a	E. C. MORSE/DRY/GOODS/ GROCERIES/& C. /MUSSEY	1037	C	R	R5	8650
680A-1i	Same	Same	Z	R	R9	
680A-2a	Same	1042	C	R	R8	8651
680A-2b	Same	Same	BR	R	R8	8652
680A-3a	Same	1047	C	R	R9	8653
680A-3d	Same	Same	C-N	R	R9	8654

NOTE: Formerly listed as Ohio by H & G, which was in error:

NILES 700

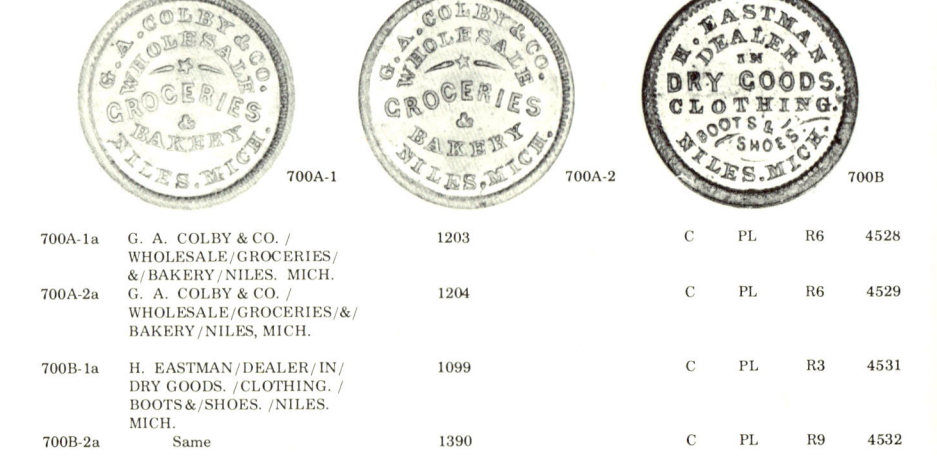

700A-1   700A-2   700B

700A-1a	G. A. COLBY & CO. / WHOLESALE/GROCERIES/ &/BAKERY/NILES. MICH.	1203	C	PL	R6	4528
700A-2a	G. A. COLBY & CO. / WHOLESALE/GROCERIES/&/ BAKERY/NILES, MICH.	1204	C	PL	R6	4529
700B-1a	H. EASTMAN/DEALER/IN/ DRY GOODS. /CLOTHING. / BOOTS&/SHOES. /NILES. MICH.	1099	C	PL	R3	4531
700B-2a	Same	1390	C	PL	R9	4532

MICHIGAN-Continued

NUMBER	OBVERSE	REVERSE	METAL	EDGE	RARITY	H&G

NILES 700-Continued

700C-1

700C-3

700C-1a	E. S. PARKER/DEALER/IN /HATS. CAPS/& FURS/NILES, MICH.	1105	C	PL	R9	4534
700C-2a	Same	1098	C	PL	R6	4535
700C-3a	E. S. PARKER/DEALER/IN/ HATS CAPS/&/FURS/NILES, MICH.	1046	C	R	R7	4537
700C-3b	Same	Same	BR	R	R9	4538
700C-3d	Same	Same	C-N	R	R9	5439
700C-3i	Same	Same	Z	R	R9	4540
700C-4a	Same	1047	C	R	R9	4541A
700C-4d	Same	Same	C-N	R	R9	

700D

700E

700D-1a	G. W. & H. C. PLATT/STOVES. /AND/HARDWARE/NILES./ MICH.	1095	C	PL	R9	
700D-2a	Same	1101	C	PL	R5	4542
700D-3a	Same	1108	C	PL	R4	
700E-1a	H. G. SLEIGHT/DEALER/IN/ GROCERIES. /SEEDS/& C. / NILES, MICH.	1095	C	PL	R6	4547
700E-2a	Same	1098	C	PL	R6	4545
700E-3a	Same	1099	C	PL	R8	
700E-4a	Same	1101	C	PL	R4	4546
700E-5a	Same	1357	C	PL	R6	4544

MICHIGAN-Continued

NUMBER	OBVERSE	REVERSE	METAL	EDGE	RARITY	H&G

OWOSSO 735

| 735A-1a | C. E. SHATTUCK/DEALER IN/ BRICK/&/DRAIN TILE/ OWASSO,/MICH. | 1122 | C | PL | R5 | 4549 |
| 735A-1b | Same | Same | BR | PL | R8 | 4550 |

735B-1a	M. L. STEWART,/WHOLESALE/ AND/RETAIL/GROCER,/ OWOSSO,/MICH.	1127	C	PL	R5	4552
735B-2a	Same	1128	C	PL	R5	4554
735B-2b	Same	Same	BR	PL	R8	4555

PARMA 740

| 740A-1a | GLAZIER'S PHARMACY/Mortar and pestle/PARMA MIC. | BUY YOUR MEDICINES/AND/ OILS/AT/PAINTS | C | PL | R3 | 4557 |
| 740A-1b | Same | Same | BR | PL | R8 | 4558 |

202

MICHIGAN-Continued

NUMBER	OBVERSE	REVERSE	METAL	EDGE	RARITY	H&G

PAW PAW 745

745A-1a	J. R. FOOTE/CROCKERY/ GLASSWARE/&/GROCERIES/ PAW PAW,/MICH.	1099	C	PL	R7	4561
745A-2a	Same	1101	C	PL	R8	
745A-3a	Same	1205	C	PL	R7	4560

745B-1a	G. W. LONGWELL/DRUGS/&/ GROCERIES. /MAIN ST/ PAW PAW. MICH	1102	C	PL	R8	4564
745B-2a	Same	1105	C	PL	R8	4563
745B-2b	Same	Same	BR	PL	R9	
745C-1a	A. SHERMAN & CO. /GENERAL MERCHANTS/&/PROPR'S OF/ PAW PAW/FLOURING MILLS/ PAW PAW MICH	1003	C	PL	R7	4566

| 745D-1a | J. D. SHERMAN/WHOLESALE/ GROCERIES/&/PROVISIONS/ PAW PAW,/MICH. | 1105 | C | PL | R6 | 4568 |
| 745D-2a | Same | 1203 | C | PL | R6 | 4569 |

203

MICHIGAN-Continued

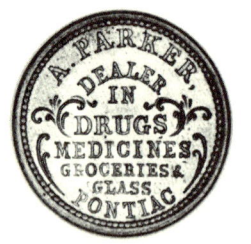

NUMBER	OBVERSE	REVERSE	METAL	EDGE	RARITY	H&G

PONTIAC 770

770A-1a	FOX & SMITH/PRODUCE &/ COMMISSION/MERCHANTS/ & DEALERS IN/PLASTER /PONTIAC, MICH.	1105	C	PL	R7	4571
770A-2a	Same	1210	C	PL	R3	4572
770A-3a	Same	1211	C	PL	R3	4573
770B-1a	MORRIS & MESSINGER/ DEALERS/IN/HARDWARE/ IRON, STEEL/NAILS & GLASS./ PONTIAC	1305	C	PL	R8	
770B-1b	Same	Same	BR	PL	R4	4575
770B-2a	MORRIS & MESSINGER/ DEALERS/NI/HARDWARE/ IRON, STEEL,/NAILS & GLASS. /PONTIAC	Same	C	PL	R8	
770B-2b	Same	Same	BR	PL	R8	
770C-1a	A. PARKER,/DEALER/IN/ DRUGS/MEDICINES/ GROCERIES &/GLASS/ PONTIAC	FRENCH'S HAIR RESTORATIVE/ FOR RESTORING GRAY HAIR/ Bottle with "FRENCH'S on it	C	PL	R8	
770C-1ep	Same	Same	W-M plated copper	PL	R9	
770C-1b	Same	Same	BR	PL	R3	4577

204

MICHIGAN-Continued

NUMBER	OBVERSE	REVERSE	METAL	EDGE	RARITY	H&G

SAGINAW CITY 845

| 845A-1a | WM. BINDER/DRY/GOODS/ GROCERIES. /SAGINAW/CITY/ MICH | 1101 | C | PL | R8 | 4580 |
| 845A-2a | Same | 1205 | C | PL | R9 | 4579 |

| 845B-1a | EPTING & EATON/DEALERS/ IN/DRUGS &/MEDICINES. / SAGINAW CITY/MICH. | 1095 | C | PL | R8 | 4582 |
| 845B-2a | Same | 1357 | C | PL | R9 | 4583 |

SALINA 855

855A-1a	GALLAGHER & HESS/Mortar and pestle/DRUGGISTS. / SALINA,/MICH.	1095	C	PL	R5	4585
855A-2a	Same	1105	C	PL	R9	4586
855A-3a	Same	1211	C	PL	R5	4587

205

MICHIGAN-Continued

| NUMBER | OBVERSE | REVERSE | METAL | EDGE | RARITY | H&G |

SARANAC 865

865A-1

865A-2

| 865A-1a | W. DARLING/SARANAC/MICH/ 1864 (Thirteen stars around) | Wreath enclosing a boot and seven stars | C | PL | R8 | 4589 |
| 865A-2a | Same inscription, but with fifteen stars around. | Same | C | PL | R9 | |

SCHOOLCRAFT 900

900A-1a	I. ALLEN & SON/STOVES/&/ HARDWARE/SCHOOLCRAFT/ MICH.	1094	C	PL	R8	4593
900A-2a	Same	1095	C	PL	R8	4591
900A-3a	Same	1105	C	PL	R8	4592

900B-1

900B-3

900B-1a	I. W. PRUSEL & CO/DRY/ GOODS/GROCERIES/BOOTS/ &/SHOES/SCHOOLCRAFT	1110	C	PL	R8	4596
900B-2a	Same	1390	C	PL	R9	4595
900B-3a	I. W. PURSEL & CO/DRY/ GOODS/GROCERIES/BOOTS/&/ SHOES/SCHOOLCRAFT	1357	C	PL	R8	4598

(NOTE: PURSEL is apparently the correct spelling!)

MICHIGAN-Continued

NUMBER	OBVERSE	REVERSE	METAL	EDGE	RARITY	H&G

ST. JOHNS 915

		915-A1		915A-2		
915A-1a	G. W. STEPHENSON/ GENERAL/MERCHANT/ ST. JOHNS/MICH.	1310	C	PL	R5	4600
915A-1b	Same	Same	BR	PL	R8	4601
915A-2a	G. W. STEPHENSON/& SON/ DRY GOODE/CLOTHING/ BOOTS/SHOES/ST. JOHNS. MICH.	1101	C	PL	R5	4602

TECUMSEH 920

		920A		920B		920C
920A-1a	FISHER & HENDRYX,/ DRUGGISTS/AND/GROCERS/ CHICAGO ST. /TECUMSEH,/ MICH.	1310	C	PL	R6	4604
920A1b	Same	Same	BR	PL	R9	4605
920B-1a	DR. E. HAUSE/DENTIST/ TECUMSEH/MICH.	1094	C	PL	R6	4607
920B-2a	Same	1095	C	PL	R6	4608
920B-3a	Same	1099	C	PL	R5	
920B-4a	Same	1101	C	PL	R9	
920B-5a	Same	1357	C	PL	R7	4609
920C-1a	G. T. KETCHAM/NEWSDEALER /&/BOOK/SELLER/TECUMSEH, MICH	1099	C	PL	R4	4612
920C-2a	Same	1357	C	PL	R6	4611

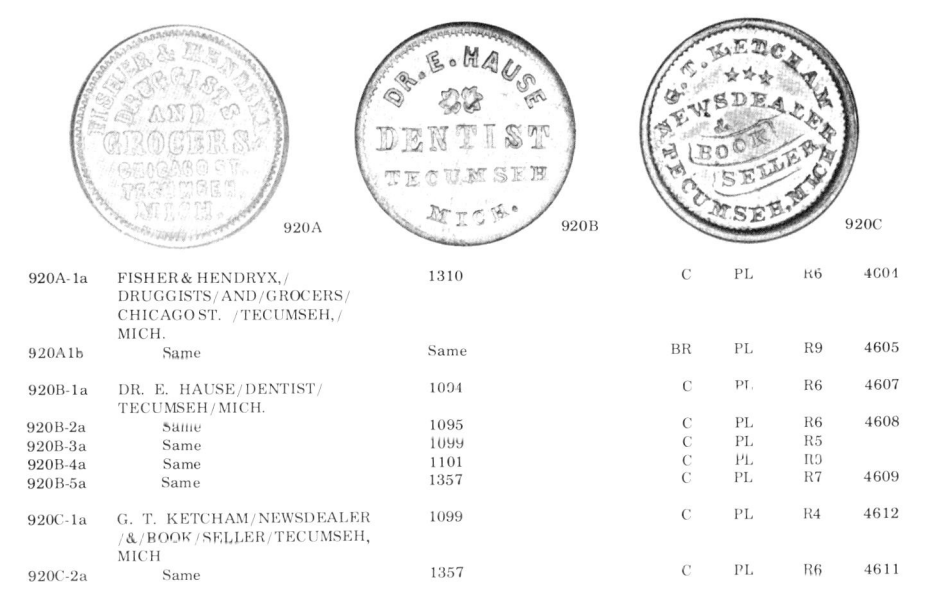

207

MICHIGAN-Continued

NUMBER	OBVERSE	REVERSE	METAL	EDGE	RARITY	H&G

TECUMSEH 920-Continued

920D-1a	C. S. PATTERSON/Mortar and pestle/DRUGGIST./TECUMSEH/MICH.	1099	C	PL	R4	4615
920D-2a	Same	1105	C	PL	R8	4614
920D-3a	Same	1316	C	PL	R9	

YPSILANTI 960

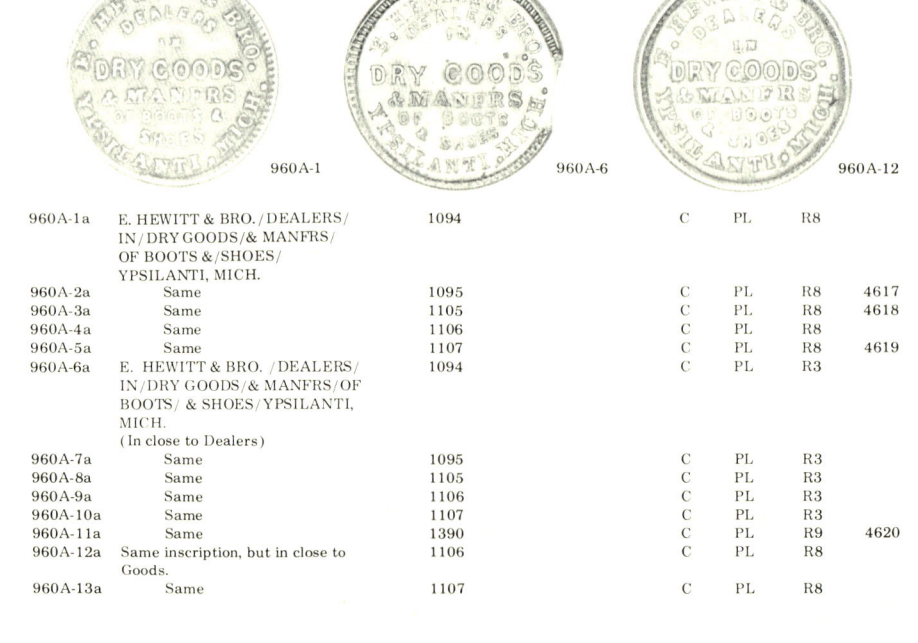

960A-1a	E. HEWITT & BRO./DEALERS/IN/DRY GOODS/& MANFRS/OF BOOTS &/SHOES/YPSILANTI, MICH.	1094	C	PL	R8	
960A-2a	Same	1095	C	PL	R8	4617
960A-3a	Same	1105	C	PL	R8	4618
960A-4a	Same	1106	C	PL	R8	
960A-5a	Same	1107	C	PL	R8	4619
960A-6a	E. HEWITT & BRO. /DEALERS/IN/DRY GOODS/& MANFRS/OF BOOTS/ & SHOES/YPSILANTI, MICH. (In close to Dealers)	1094	C	PL	R3	
960A-7a	Same	1095	C	PL	R3	
960A-8a	Same	1105	C	PL	R3	
960A-9a	Same	1106	C	PL	R3	
960A-10a	Same	1107	C	PL	R3	
960A-11a	Same	1390	C	PL	R9	4620
960A-12a	Same inscription, but in close to Goods.	1106	C	PL	R8	
960A-13a	Same	1107	C	PL	R8	

MICHIGAN-Continued

NUMBER　　OBVERSE　　　　　　REVERSE　　　　　　　METAL　EDGE　RARITY　H&G

YPSILANTI 960-Continued

Number	Obverse	Reverse	Metal	Edge	Rarity	H&G
960B-1a	SHOWERMAN & BRO. /DEALERS/ IN /DRY GOODS/CLOTHING/ HATS & CAPS/BOOTS/& SHOES/ YPSILANTI, MICH. (G of Goods over TH of Clothing)	1105	C	PL	R4	4622
960B-2a	Same	1209	C	PL	R8	4623
960B-3a	Same	1210	C	PL	R4	4624
960B-4a	Same inscription, but G of Goods over T of Clothing.	1105	C	PL	R8	

MINNESOTA

NUMBER	OBVERSE	REVERSE	METAL	EDGE	RARITY	H&G

BARRETT and COLERAIN - See listing under non-contemporary tokens.

RED WING 680

680A-1a	A. W. E. /RED WING,/MINN.	1220	C	PL	R9	4650
680A-1b	Same	Same	BR	PL	R9	4651
680A-1d	Same	Same	C-N	PL	R9	4653
680A-1e	Same	Same	W-M	PL	R9	4654
680A-2a	Same	1272	C	PL	R7	4656
680A-2b	Same	Same	BR	PL	R8	4657
680A-2d	Same	Same	C-N	PL	R8	4659
680A-2e	Same	Same	W-M	PL	R9	4660
680A-3b	Same	Blank	BR	PL	R10	

ROCHESTER 720

720A-1a	F. W. ANDREWS/DRY GOODS/&C./ROCHESTER,/MINN. Eagle in glory	1089	C	PL	R9	4663
720A-2a	Same	1128	C	PL	R9	4664
720A-3a	Same	1168	C	PL	R7	4666
720A-3b	Same	Same	BR	PL	R9	
720A-3d	Same	Same	C-N	PL	R10	
720A-4a	Same	1224	C	PL	R8	4665
720A-5a	Same	1284	C	PL	R9	4667

MINNESOTA - Continued

NUMBER	OBVERSE	REVERSE	METAL	EDGE	RARITY	H&G

ST. PAUL 760

760A-1

760A-2

760A-3

| 760A-1a | D. C. GREENLEAF/WATCH/ MAKER./ST.PAUL,/MIN. | Blank | C | PL | R8 | 4669 |

NOTE: These pieces are known with numbers stamped on the reverse from 1 to 102 inclusively. All numbers are known **except** Nos. 9,11,15,24,26,28,35,46,47,50,59,60,65,67,81,86,93,and 94.

It may be assumed that the missing numbers exist. The two pieces stamped 101 and 102 have additional incuse markings as follows:

| 760A-2a | Same | 101/SENOUR | C | PL | R10 | |
| 760A-3a | Same | 102/LANPHEAR/CINCINNATI.O. (the lettering is upside down on the above piece) | C | PL | R10 | |

No more than two of any number has been reported, and most are known in single examples.

| 760B-1a | WHEELER & WILSONS/SEWING/ MACHINES/F. M. JOHNSON/ AGT./3RD ST/ST PAUL, MINN. | 1298 | C | PL | R6 | 4671 |
| 760B-1d | Same | Same | C N | PL | R10 | |

MINNESOTA - Continued

NUMBER	OBVERSE	REVERSE	METAL	EDGE	RARITY	H&G

WINONA 980

| 980A-1a | C. BENSON,/DRUGGIST/WINONA,/MINN. | 1310 | C | PL | R7 | 4674 |
| 980A-1b | Same | Same | BR | PL | R7 | 4675 |

| 980B-1a | COE & HAYDEN/DRY GOODS,/CROCKERY,/BOOTS,SHOES,/AND/GROCERIES./THE REGULATOR | THE REGULATOR/NO. 2, SIMPSON/BLOCK,/SECOND ST./WINONA,/MINN./1863 | C | PL | R6 | 4677 |
| 980B-1b | Same | Same | BR | PL | R7 | 4678 |

MISSOURI

NUMBER	OBVERSE	REVERSE	METAL	EDGE	RARITY	H&G

IRONTON 400

400A-1a	D. PECK & CO./DEALERS/IN/ GROCERIES/DRUGS/&/ MEDICINES/IRONTON,MO.	1046	C	R	R7	4700
400A-1b	Same	Same	BR	R	R8	4701
400A-1i	Same	Same	Z	R	R9	4702
400A-2d	Same	1047	C-N	R	R10	

ST. JOSEPH 880

| 880A-1b | JOHN KENMUIR/MFG. JEWELER/ST JOSEPH MO | JOHN KENMUIR/WATCH/ MAKER/FELIX ST/ ST. JOSEPH, MO. | BR | PL | R9 | |

ST. LOUIS 910

| 910A-1a | DROVER/HOTEL/125 NORTH 4'ST./ST. LOUIS,MO. Steers head in center. | 1008 | C | PL | R6 | 4704 |

213

MISSOURI-Continued

NUMBER	OBVERSE	REVERSE	METAL	EDGE	RARITY	H&G

ST. LOUIS 910-Continued

NUMBER	OBVERSE	REVERSE	METAL	EDGE	RARITY	H&G
910A-1i	Same	Same	Z	PL	R9	
910A-2a	Same	1009	C	PL	R7	4705
910A-3a	Same	1038	C	PL	R7	4706
910A-3b	Same	Same	BR	PL	R9	
910A-4a	Same	1042	C	R	R6	4707
910A-4b	Same	Same	BR	R	R8	4708
910A-5a	Same	1047	C	R	R9	
910A-6a	Same	1288	C	PL	R8	4710
910A-6b	Same	Same	BR	PL	R9	

910B-1a	USE/LALLEMAND'S/SPECIFIC/ SOLD/BY/DRUGGISTS/JNO.H. BLOOD AGT./24FIFTH ST./ ST. LOUIS.	LALLEMAND'S/RHEUMATISM/ GOUT/&/NEURALGIA/SPECIFIC	C	R	R8	4716
910B-1b	Same	Same	BR	R	R9	4717
910B1i	Same	Same	Z	R	R9	
910B-2a	Same	1047	C	R	R9	
910B-3a	Reverse of MO.910B-1a	1018	C	R	R9	
910B-4a	Same	1047	C	R	R8	
910B-5d	Same	1069	C-N	R	R10	4718

910C-1 910C-2

910C-1a	HENRY JENKENS/WHOLESALE/ &/RETAIL/CLOTHIER/ST. LOUIS, MO.	1274	C	PL	R4	4712
910C-2a	Same	Same as the obverse, but from a slightly different die	C	PL	R9	4713
910C-3a	Same	Obverse incused	C	PL	R9	4714

214

NEW HAMPSHIRE

| NUMBER | OBVERSE | REVERSE | METAL | EDGE | RARITY | H&G |

CONCORD 120

| 120A-1a | A. W. GALE/RESTORATOR/AT/DEPOT/CONCORD,N. H. | GOOD FOR/ONE/CENT/IN GOODS | C | PL | R5 | 4721 |

NEW JERSEY

| NUMBER | OBVERSE | REVERSE | METAL | EDGE | RARITY | H&G |

ATLANTIC CITY 20

20A-1a	NEPTUNE/HOUSE/ATLANTIC/ CITY/1863 within circle of thirteen large stars. (NOTE: Comes with extensive obverse die breaks)	SMICK'S within an oak wreath	C	PL	R2	4725
20A-1a1	Same (thin planchet)	Same	C	PL	R3	4726
20A-2a	NEPTUNE/HOUSE/ATLANTIC/ CITY within circle of thirteen small stars	SMICK'S within oak wreath Small date 1863 below.	C	PL	R3	4727

ELIZABETH PORT 220

220A-1a	JOHN ENGEL/MERCHANT/ tailor/52/FIRST ST./ELIZABETH PT NJ.	1152	C	PL	R4	4729
220A-2a	Same	1214	C	PL	R3	4736
220A-2e	Same	Same	W-M	PL	R9	4739
220A-3a	Same (Baker 534)	1265	C	PL	R3	4733
220A-2fp	Same	Same	S.Pl.	PL	R9	

216

NEW JERSEY - Continued

NUMBER	OBVERSE	REVERSE	METAL	EDGE	RARITY	H&G

JERSEY CITY 350

| 350A-1a | TERHUNE BROTHERS/71&73/ NEWARK AV/JERSEY CITY/ N J/HARDWARE | 1215 | C | PL | R2 | 4742 |

NEWARK 555

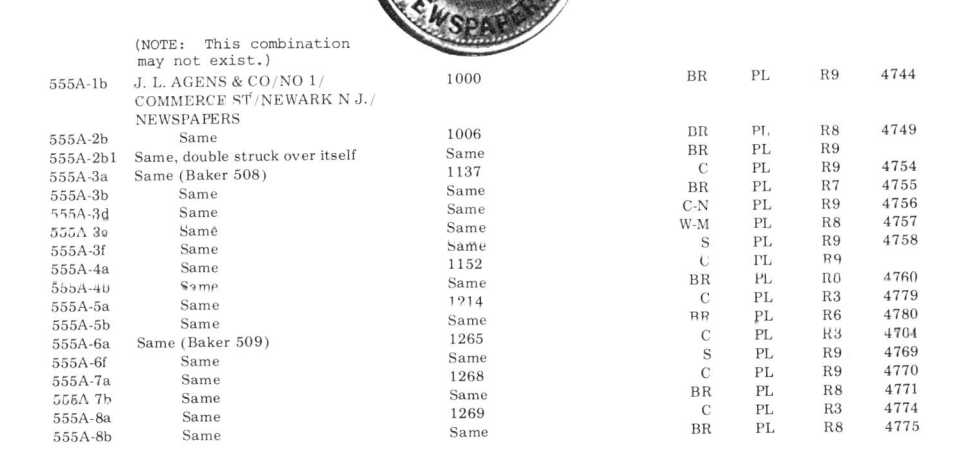

	(NOTE: This combination may not exist.)					
555A-1b	J. L. AGENS & CO/NO 1/ COMMERCE ST/NEWARK N J./ NEWSPAPERS	1000	BR	PL	R9	4744
555A-2b	Same	1006	BR	PL	R8	4749
555A-2b1	Same, double struck over itself	Same	BR	PL	R9	
555A-3a	Same (Baker 508)	1137	C	PL	R9	4754
555A-3b	Same	Same	BR	PL	R7	4755
555A-3d	Same	Same	C-N	PL	R9	4756
555A-3e	Same	Same	W-M	PL	R8	4757
555A-3f	Same	Same	S	PL	R9	4758
555A-4a	Same	1152	C	PL	R9	
555A-4b	Same	Same	BR	PL	R0	4760
555A-5a	Same	1214	C	PL	R3	4779
555A-5b	Same	Same	BR	PL	R6	4780
555A-6a	Same (Baker 509)	1265	C	PL	R3	4704
555A-6f	Same	Same	S	PL	R9	4769
555A-7a	Same	1268	C	PL	R9	4770
555A-7b	Same	Same	BR	PL	R8	4771
555A-8a	Same	1269	C	PL	R3	4774
555A-8b	Same	Same	BR	PL	R8	4775

NEW JERSEY - Continued

NUMBER	OBVERSE	REVERSE	METAL	EDGE	RARITY	H&G

NEWARK 555-Continued

555B-1a	CHARLES KOLB/102/MARKET ST./RESTAURANT.	1014	C	PL	R3	4784
555B-1a1	Same, thick 2mm.	Same	C	PL	R7	
555B-1b	Same	Same	BR	PL	R3	4785
555B-1b1	Same, thin 3/4mm.	Same	BR	PL	R7	
555B-1c	Same	Same	N	PL	R9	4786
555B-1do	Same, over C-N cent	Same	C-N	PL	R6	4787
	(NOTE: all specimens seen of this piece in C-N have been struck over a C-N cent.)					
555B-1e	Same	Same	W-M	PL	R8	4788
555B-1f	Same	Same	S	PL	R9	
555B-2a	Same	Incuse of Obv.	C	PL	R9	
555C-1a	J. WIGHTMAN/188 WASHINGTON/ST./NEWARK,N.J.	1000	C	PL	R8	4790
555C-1b	Same	Same	BR	PL	R8	4791
555C-1c	Same	Same	N	PL	R8	4792
555C-1d	Same	Same	C-N	PL	R9	
555C-1e	Same	Same	W-M	PL	R8	4794
555C-2a	Same	1016	C	PL	R3	4796
555C-3a	Same (H-R 1232)	1017	C	PL	R9	4798
555C-3b	Same	Same	BR	PL	R7	4799
555C-3c	Same	Same	N	PL	R8	4800
555C-3d	Same	Same	C-N	PL	R9	
555C-3e	Same	Same	W-M	PL	R8	
555C-4a	Same	1052	C	PL	R8	4804
555C-4b	Same	Same	BR	PL	R9	4805
555C-4c	Same	Same	N	PL	R8	4806
555C-4d	Same	Same	C-N	PL	R9	
555C-4e	Same	Same	W-M	PL	R8	4808
555C-5a	Same (Baker 585)	1132	C	PL	R9	4810
555C-5b	Same	Same	BR	PL	R9	4811
555C-5c	Same	Same	N	PL	R9	4812
555C-5d	Same	Same	C-N	PL	R9	4813
555C-5e	Same	Same	W-M	PL	R8	4814

NEW JERSEY - Continued

NUMBER	OBVERSE	REVERSE	METAL	EDGE	RARITY	H&G

NEWARK 555-Continued

NUMBER	OBVERSE	REVERSE	METAL	EDGE	RARITY	H&G
555C-6b	Same (H-R 1233)	1218	BR	PL	R8	4816
555C-6c	Same	Same	N	PL	R8	4817
555C-6d	Same	Same	C-N	PL	R9	4818
555C-6e	Same	Same	W-M	PL	R8	4819
555C-7a	Same	1219	C	PL	R8	4821
555C-7b	Same	Same	BR	PL	R8	4822
555C-7c	Same	Same	N	PL	R8	4823
555C-7e	Same	Same	W-M	PL	R8	4824
555C-8a	Same	1236	C	PL	R9	4826
555C-8b	Same	Same	BR	PL	R9	
555C-8c	Same	Same	N	PL	R9	4828
555C-8d	Same	Same	C-N	PL	R9	
555C-8e	Same	Same	W-M	PL	R9	4830
555C-9a	Same	1252	C	PL	R8	4832
555C-9b	Same	Same	BR	PL	R9	4833
555C-9c	Same	Same	N	PL	R9	4834
555C-9d	Same	Same	C-N	PL	R9	4835
555C-9e	Same	Same	W-M	PL	R9	4836
555C-10a	Same	1253	C	PL	R8	4838
555C-10b	Same	Same	BR	PL	R8	4839
555C-10c	Same	Same	N	PL	R9	4840
555C-10d	Same	Same	C-N	PL	R9	
555C-10e	Same	Same	W-M	PL	R8	4842
555C-11a	Same	1267	C	PL	R9	4844
555C-11b	Same	Same	BR	PL	R9	
555C-11c	Same	Same	N	PL	R9	4846
555C-11d	Same	Same	C-N	PL	R9	
555C-11e	Same	Same	W-M	PL	R9	
555C-12a	Same	1277	C	PL	R8	4849
555C-12b	Same	Same	BR	PL	R8	1850
555C-12c	Same	Same	N	PL	R8	4851
555C-12d	Same (H-R 1234)	Same	C-N	PL	R9	
555C-12e	Same	Same	W-M	PL	R8	4853

PERTH AMBOY 690

NUMBER	OBVERSE	REVERSE	METAL	EDGE	RARITY	H&G
690A-1a	COUTTS & BRO./DRY GOODS/ &/GROCERIES/P. AMBOY,N J. (Baker 528)	1265	C	PL	R4	4855
690A-2a	Same	1269	C	PL	R4	4857

NEW JERSEY - Continued

| NUMBER | OBVERSE | REVERSE | METAL | EDGE | RARITY | H&G |

TRENTON 885

885A-1b	E. W. TITUS/20/E..STATE ST./ TRENTON N. J.	DRY GOODS/OIL CLOTHS/ CARPETS/&C.	BR	PL	R3	4859
	(NOTE: comes with obverse die breaks.)					
885A-1cp	Same	Same	N-pl	PL	R8	4860
885A-2b	Same	Similar, ornaments further away from CARPETS	BR	PL	R3	4861

WILLIAMSTOWN 925

| 925A-1b | ONE CENT/BODINE &/ BROTHERS/1863 in center. DUE BEARER IN MDZE AT COUNTER OF OUR STORE/around. (Adams N.J. 11-27mm.) | Incuse of obverse | BR | PL | R8 |

220

NEW YORK

NUMBER   OBVERSE   REVERSE   METAL EDGE RARITY H&G

ALBANY 10

10A-1

10A-2

10A-3

10A-4

10A-5

10A-1a	BENJAMIN & HERRICK / FRUIT / DEALERS / ALBANY, N.Y. F of FRUIT touches first N of BENJAMIN	REDEEMED AT / 427 / BROADWAY / 1863 Top of 7 is curved	C	PL	R2	4900
10A-1b	Same	Same	BR	PL	R8	
10A-2a	Same inscription, but F of FRUIT is opposite left leg of A in BENJAMIN	Same inscription, but top of 7 is straight	C	PL	R2	4901
10A-3a	Same inscription, but F of FRUIT is opposite J of BENJAMIN, and T of FRUIT is opposite second R in HERRICK	Same	C	PL	R8	
10A-4a	Same, but F of FRUIT almost touches the J, and T of FRUIT does touch the second R	Same inscription, top of 7 is curved, and bottom right of 2 has a die break	C	PL	R2	4904
10A-4b	Same	Same	BR	PL	R8	4905
10A-4e	Same	Same	W-M	PL	R8	
10A-5a	Same inscription, but F between N and J	Same	C	PL	R2	4906
10A-5b	Same	Same	BR	PL	R7	4907
10A-5e	Same	Same	W-M	PL	R9	

221

NEW YORK-Continued

NUMBER	OBVERSE	REVERSE	METAL	EDGE	RARITY	H&G

ALBANY 10-Continued

10A-6a	Very similar to 10A-4a, but point of F is in line with the vertical part of the J	Same	C	PL	R2	4909
10A-6b	Same	Same	BR	PL	R8	
10A-7b	Similar to 10A-1a, but F is closer to the J than the N, and often has a cracked die	Similar inscription, with top of 7 straight	BR	PL	R7	4911
10A-7f	Same	Same	S	PL	R10	
10A-8a	Reverse of 10A-2a	1153	C	PL	R9	4912
10A-9a	Obverse of 10A-4a	1276	C	PL	R8	4915
10A-9b	Same	Same	BR	PL	R8	4916
10A-9c	Same (H-R 1240)	Same	N	PL	R8	4917
10A-9d	Same	Same	C-N	PL	R8	4918
10A-9e	Same	Same	W-M	PL	R8	4919
10A-9f	Same	Same	S	PL	R9	
10A-10b	Obverse of 10A-4a	Reverse of 10A-2a	BR	PL	R7	4922

10B-1a	P.V. FORT & CO./DEALERS/IN/FRUIT/AND/NUTS/ALBANY N.Y. Flourish ends over L of ALBANY	REDEEMED/AT/NO. 427/BROADWAY/1864	C	PL	R3	4924
10B-1c	Same	Same	N	PL	R9	
10B-2a	Same inscription, but flourish ends over first A of ALBANY	Same	C	PL	R3	4925

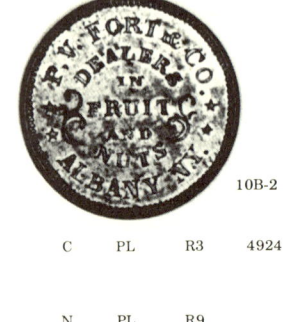

222

NEW YORK-Continued

| NUMBER | OBVERSE | REVERSE | METAL | EDGE | RARITY | H&G |

ALBANY 10-Continued

| 10C-1a | JOS. MC. BURNEY/CIGAR BOX MANUF'R/MULBERRY ST./ ALBANY N.Y. | REDEEMED/AT/26/MULBERRY ST./ALBANY N.Y. | C | PL | R3 | 4927 |

| 10D-1a | N.Y.C.R.R.EX.TRAIN/LEAVE/ ALBANY/7-30 & 9/A.M./ 12-20 & 6/P.M. | N.Y.C.R.R.EX.TRAINS/LEAVE BUFFALO/5 & 8/A.M./ 5-45 & 10-55/P.M. | C | PL | R4 | 4929 |
| 10D-2a | Reverse 10D-1a | Obverse incused | C | PL | R10 | |

10F-1a	STRAIGHT'S ELEPHANTINE/ SHOE STORE/elephant in boots to right with rug on its back marked 398/BROADWAY/1863	REDEEMED AT MY SHOE STORE/398/BROADWAY/ ALBANY/N.Y.	C	PL	R3	4932
10F-1b	Same	Same	BR	PL	R8	
10F-1c	Same	Same	N	PL	R10	

223

NEW YORK-Continued

NUMBER　　OBVERSE　　　　　　REVERSE　　　　　　　METAL　EDGE　RARITY　H&G

ALBANY 10-Continued

10G-1a	JOHN THOMAS JR./PREMIUM/	REDEEMED/EXCHANGE/&/	C	PL	R3	4934
	MILLS/COFFEE & SPICES	DEAN ST'S/1863/ALBANY N.Y.				
10G1b	Same	Same	BR	PL	R9	4935

D. L. WING - Obverse Photos

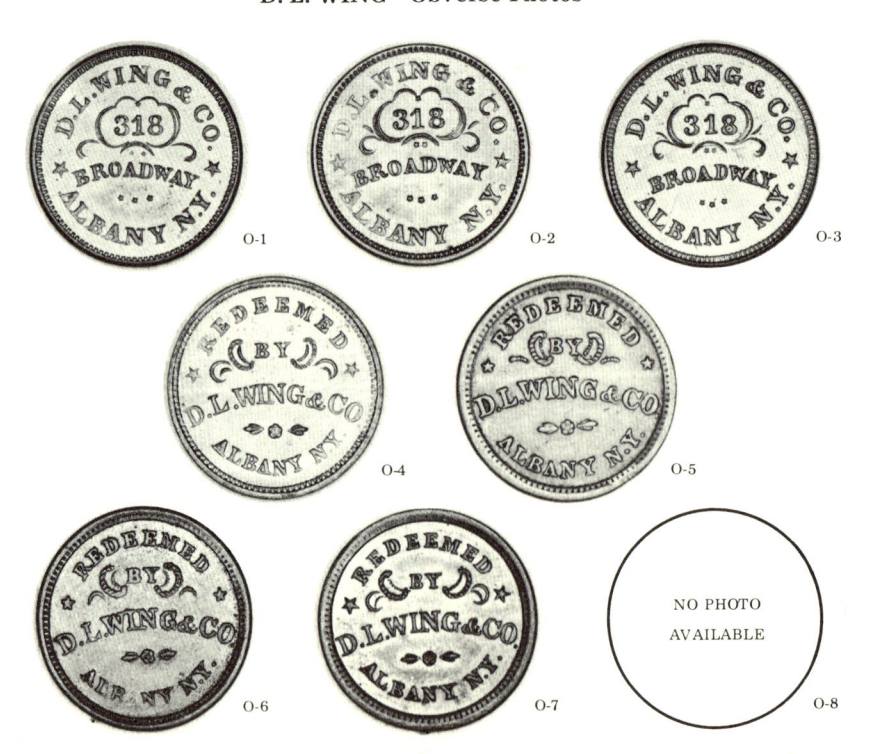

O-1　　　　O-2　　　　O-3

O-4　　　　O-5

O-6　　　　O-7　　　　NO PHOTO AVAILABLE　O-8

224

NEW YORK-Continued

NUMBER   OBVERSE   REVERSE   METAL EDGE RARITY H&G

ALBANY 10-Continued

D. L. WING - Reverse Photos

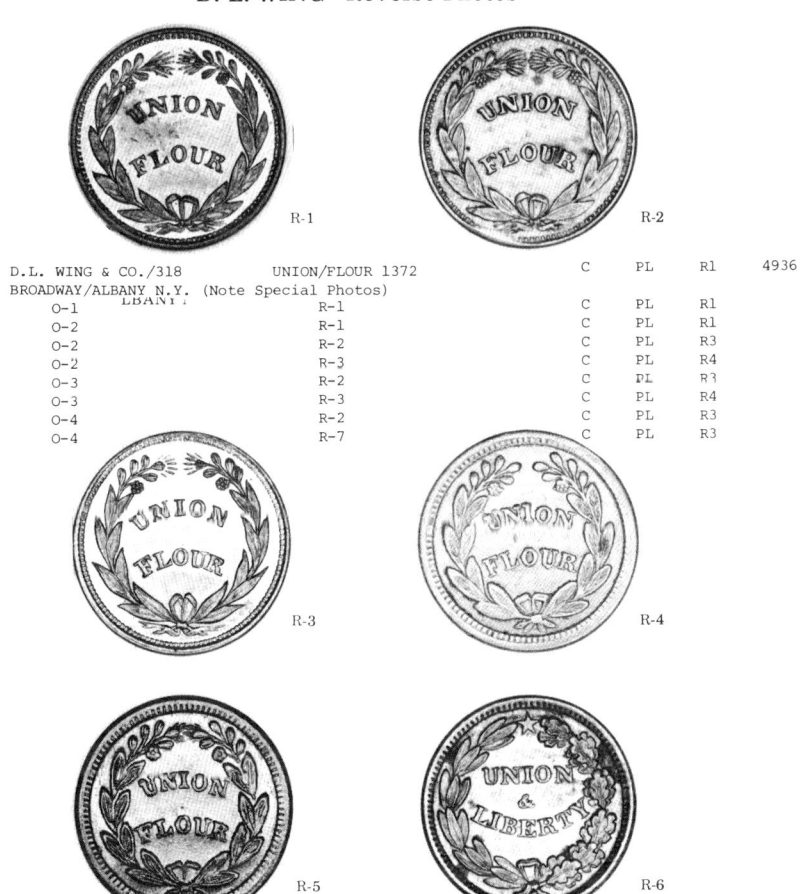

R-1

R-2

10H-	D.L. WING & CO./318 BROADWAY/ALBANY N.Y. (Note Special Photos)	UNION/FLOUR 1372	C	PL	R1	4936
10H-1a	O-1	R-1	C	PL	R1	
10H-2a	O-2	R-1	C	PL	R1	
10H-3a	O-2	R-2	C	PL	R3	
10H-3aa	O-2	R-3	C	PL	R4	
10H-4a	O-3	R-2	C	PL	R3	
10H-4aa	O-3	R-3	C	PL	R4	
10H-5a	O-4	R-2	C	PL	R3	
10H-5aa	O-4	R-7	C	PL	R3	

R-3

R-4

R-5

R-6

10H-	REDEEMED/BY/D.L. WING & CO./ALBANY N.Y.	UNION/FLOUR	C	PL	R2	4937
10H-6a	O-5	R-4	C	PL	R2	
10H-7a	O-6	R-5	C	PL	R3	
10H-8a	O-7	R-5	C	PL	R3	
10H-	REDEEMED/BY/D.L. WING & CO./ALBANY N.Y.	1371				
10H-9a	O-7	R-6	C	PL	R3	
10H-9b	O-7	R-6	BR	PL	R7	

NEW YORK-Continued

NUMBER	OBVERSE	REVERSE	METAL	EDGE	RARITY	H&G

ALMOND 15

| 15A-1a | H. DARTT/DRY GOODS GROCERIES/&/EXCHANGE/ OFFICE/ALMOND.N.Y. | 1090 | C | PL | R4 | 4940 |

BELMONT 77

| 77A-1a | LANGDONS. HARDWARE STORE /&/EXCHANGE/OFFICE/ BELMONT/N.Y. | 1096 | C | PL | R5 | 4943 |
| 77A-2a | Same | 1107 | C | PL | R5 | 4942 |

| 77A-3a | LANGDON'S/HARDWARE/ STORE/& EXCHANGE/ OFFICE/BELMONT, N.Y. | 1228 | C | PL | R5 | 4944 |

NEW YORK-Continued

NUMBER	OBVERSE	REVERSE	METAL	EDGE	RARITY	H&G

BINGHAMPTON 80

*80A-1a	EVANS & ALLEN / WATCHES / & / JEWELRY / BINGHAMTON / NY	1368	C	PL	R3	4946
*80A-1c	Same	Same	N	PL	R8	4947
*80B-1a	HERSCHMAN. BROS & CO / DRY / GOODS / 20 / COURT. ST / BINGHAMTON / NY	1368	C	PL	R3	4949
*80B-1c	Same	Same	N	PL	R8	4950

BROOKLYN 95

95A-1a	BRAUN & SCHELLWORTH'S / 132, 134, 136 / COURT ST / BROOKLYN / PAVILION	1243	C	PL	R2	4951
95A-1b	Same	Same	BR	PL	R0	1052
95A-2a	Same	1265	C	PL	R2	4953
95A-2f	Same	Same	S	PL	R9	
95B-1a	C.J. HAUCK / 108 / LEONARD ST / BROOKLYN, E.D / N.Y.	1256	C	PL	R2	4954
95B-1ao	Same, over U.S. large cent	Same	C	PL	R10	

227

NEW YORK-Continued

NUMBER	OBVERSE	REVERSE	METAL	EDGE	RARITY	H&G

BROOKLYN 95-Continued

95C-1g	M IBERT/COR/MONTROSE &/ GRAHAM/AVE/BROOKLYN ED	GOOD FOR/.1/CENT	L	PL	R9	4955
95D-1a	T. IVORY./COR./FULTON & ORANGE/STS/BROOKLYN/ BILLIARD SALOON	1006	C	PL	R5	4956
95D-1b	Same	Same	BR	PL	R3	4957
95D-1c	Same	Same	N	PL	R8	4958
95D-2a	Same	1137	C	PL	R3	4963
95D-2b	Same (H-R 1251)	Same	BR	PL	R7	4964
95D-2bo	Same, obverse struck over reverse	Same	BR	PL	R9	
95D-2c	Same	Same	N	PL	R8	4965
95D-2d	Same	Same	C-N	PL	R9	4966
95D-2e	Same	Same	W-M	PL	R8	4967
95D-2f	Same	Same	S	PL	R9	
95D-2fo	Same, over U.S. dime	Same	S	R	R9	
95D-3a	Same	1152	C	PL	R4	4969
95D-3b	Same	Same	BR	PL	R3	4970
95D-3bo	Same, over NY630BG	Same	BR	PL	R9	
95D-3c	Same	Same	N	PL	R8	4971
95D-4a	Same	1214	C	PL	R8	4998
95D-4b	Same (H-R 1255)	Same	BR	PL	R8	4999
95D-4bo	Same, over NY95O 2b	Same	BR	PL	R9	
95D-4c	Same (H-R 1256)	Same	N	PL	R8	5000
95D-5a	Same	1243	C	PL	R8	4975
95D-5b	Same	Same	BR	PL	R7	4976
95D-5c	Same	Same	N	PL	R8	4977
95D6a	Same	1265	C	PL	R3	4981
95D-7a	Same	1268	C	PL	R10	4986
95D-7b	Same	Same	BR	PL	R8	4987
95D-7c	Same	Same	N	PL	R8	4988
95D-8a	Same	1269	C	PL	R3	4992
95D-8b	Same (H-R 1254)	Same	BR	PL	R9	4993
95D-8do	Same, Over U.S. C-N cent	Same	C-N	PL	R9	4993

NEW YORK-Continued

NUMBER	OBVERSE	REVERSE	METAL	EDGE	RARITY	H&G

BROOKLYN 95-Continued

95E-1a	JOHN JOERGERS/NORTH 2ND ST/BROOKLYN, E.D./L.I.	1256	C	PL	R2	5002
95F-1a	DANIEL WILLIAMS/GROCER/CORNER/COURT & WARREN/STS/BROOKLYN.	1006	C	PL	R2	5004
95F-1c	Same	Same	N	PL	R10	5006
95F-2a	Same	1137	C	PL	R2	5009
95F-2b	Same	Same	BR	PL	R10	5010
95F-2d	Same	Same	C-N	PL	R10	5012
95F-2e	Same	Same	W-M	PL	R9	5013
95F-2f	Same	Same	S	PL	R9	
95F-3a	Same	1265	C	PL	R2	5015
95F-4a	Same	1268	C	PL	R2	5020
95F-4b	Same	Same	BR	PL	R9	5021
95F-4c	Same	Same	N	PL	R9	5022
95F-4e	Same	Same	W-M	PL	R10	5024
95F-5a	Same	1269	C	PL	R2	5025
95F-5do	Same, over U.S. C-N cent	Same	C-N	PL	R10	

BUFFALO 105

| 105A-1a | JAMES ADAMS & CO./TOBACCO/&/CIGARS./207/WASHINGTON/ST/BUFFALO | 1077 | C | PL | R4 | 5028 |

NEW YORK-Continued

| NUMBER | OBVERSE | REVERSE | METAL | EDGE | RARITY | H&G |

BUFFALO 105-Continued

105B-1a	ALBERGER'S/MEAT/STORE/ BUFFALO	1039	C	R	R3	5033
105B-1a1	Same	Same	C	PL	R9	
105B-1b	Same	Same	BR	R	R9	5034
105B-2a	Same	1042	C	R	R3	5030
105B-2b	Same	Same	BR	R	R8	5031
105B-3a	Same	1047	C	R	R9	5032
105B-3d	Same	Same	C-N	R	R10	
105C-1a	E.G. BARROWS/BRANDIES/ WINES & CIGARS/NO. 6/EAST SWAN/ST./BUFFALO	1024	C	R	R3	5035
105C-2a	Same	1042	C	R	R5	5037
105C-2b	Same	Same	BR	R	R8	5038
105C-3d	Same	Same	C-N	R	R10	
105C-4a	Same	1047	C	R	R7	5040
105C-4d	Same	Same	C-N	R	R10	
105D-1a	F.J. BIELER./157/MAIN ST./ BUFFALO.	1077	C	PL	R3	5042
105D-1a1	Same	Same	C	R	R8	
105D-1ao	Same, struck over itself	Same, struck over itself	C	PL	R10	5043
105D-2a	Same	1079	C	PL	R3	5044
105D-3a	Same	1081	C	PL	R6	5045

| 105E-1a | T J CONRY/PICTURE/FRAMES./ NEWSPAPERS & C/19/SENECA ST/BUFFALO | 1077 | C | PL | R3 | 5046 |
| 105E-1a1 | Same | Same | C | R | R8 | |

230

NEW YORK-Continued

NUMBER	OBVERSE	REVERSE	METAL	EDGE	RARITY	H&G

BUFFALO 105-Continued

105E-2a	T J CONRY,/PICTURE FRAMES &C:/SENECA ST/BUFFALO	1077	C	PL	R9	5047
105E-3a	Same	1078	C	PL	R5	5048
105E-4a	Same	1079	C	PL	R9	5049
105E-5a	T J CONRY,/PICTURE FRAMES &C:/SENECA S.T./BUFFALO	1078	C	PL	R10	

105F-1a	A.M. DUBURN/CANAL/TIN SHOP/NO 29/COMMERCIAL/ST./BUFFALO	1024	C	R	R2	5051
105F-2a	Same	1042	C	R	R7	5052
105F-2b	Same	Same	BR	R	R8	5053
105F-2i	Same	Same	Z	R	R9	
105F-3a	Same	1047	C	R	R9	5054
105F-3d	Same	Same	C-N	R	R10	

105G

105H

105G-1a	HOWES/SCALES/L. DANFORTH/AGT./93 MAIN, ST./BUFFALO.	1037	C	R	R5	5055
105G-2a	Same	1042	C	R	R7	5056
105G-2b	Same	Same	BR	R	R7	5057
105G-3a	Same	1043	C	R	R9	
105G-4a	Same	1047	C	R	R8	5058
105G-4d	Same	Same	C-N	R	R9	

105H-1a	W.G. FOX/OYSTERS/FRUITS/&/LIQUORS/195 MAIN ST./BUFFALO	1024	C	R	R3	5060
105H-2a	Same	1042	C	R	R7	5061
105H-2b	Same	Same	BR	R	R9	5062
105H-3d	Same	1046	C-N	R	R10	5063
105H-4a	Same	1047	C	R	R8	5064

231

NEW YORK-Continued

NUMBER	OBVERSE	REVERSE	METAL	EDGE	RARITY	H&G

BUFFALO 105-Continued

105I-1a	GEO. GAGE/GROCER/334/MAIN/ST./BUFFALO	1027	C	R	R8	5065
105I-2a	Same	1030	C	R	R8	
105I-3a	Same	1037	C	R	R2	5066
105I-4a	Same	1042	C	R	R2	5067
105I-4b	Same	Same	BR	R	R8	5068
105I-4i	Same	Same	Z	R	R8	
105I-5a	Same	1043	C	R	R9	
105I-5a1	Same	Same	C	PL	R9	
105I-6d	Same	1046	C-N	R	R10	
105I-7a	Same	1047	C	R	R7	5070
105I-7d	Same	Same	C-N	R	R10	

105J   105K

105J-1a	HOCHSTETTER & STRAUSS/DRY/GOODS/280/MAIN/ST./BUFFALO	1024	C	R	R3	5072
105J-1a1	Same	Same	C	PL	R9	
105J-2a	Same	1039	C	R	R8	
105J-3a	Same	1042	C	R	R5	5073
105J-3b	Same	Same	BR	R	R8	5074
105J-3i	Same	Same	Z	R	R9	
105J-4a	Same	1046	C	R	R9	5075
105J-5d	Same	1047	C-N	R	R10	
105K-1a	A.M. JOHNSTON/GROCER/52/MAIN/ST/BUFFALO	1039	C	R	R2	5080
105K-2a	Same	1042	C	R	R6	5077
105K-2b	Same	Same	BR	R	R8	5078
105K-2i	Same	Same	Z	R	R10	5079
105K-3a	Same	1047	C	R	R8	5081
105K-3d	Same	Same	C-N	R	R0	

232

NEW YORK-Continued

| NUMBER | OBVERSE | REVERSE | METAL | EDGE | RARITY | H&G |

BUFFALO 105-Continued

105L-1a	JOHN C. POST / PAINTS / OILS / & / GLASS / NO. 8 SWAN, ST. / BUFFALO	1024	C	R	R3	5082
105L-1a1	Same	Same	C	PL	R9	
105L-2a	Same	1042	C	R	R8	5083
105L-2b	Same	Same	BR	R	R9	5084
105L-2i	Same	Same	Z	R	R9	
105L-3a	Same	1047	C	R	R9	
105L-3d	Same	Same	C-N	R	R9	5085
*105M-1a	REILLY'S / BAZAAR / 228 / MAIN. ST / BUFFALO. NY	1368	C	PL	R5	5086

105N-1a	ROBINSON & BALL / GENTS / FURNISHING / GOODS / 275 MAIN ST / BUFFALO	1037	C	R	R4	5088
105N-2a	Same	1042	C	R	R5	5090
105N-2b	Same	Same	BR	R	R8	5091
105N-2i	Same	Same	Z	R	R9	
105N-3a	Same	1047	C	R	R9	5093
105N-3d	Same	Same	C-N	R	R10	
105O-1a	ROWE & CO / OYSTER / & FOREIGN FRUIT / DEPOT / 197 MAIN, ST. / BUFFALO	1024	C	R	R3	5094
105O-2a	Same	1042	C	R	R3	5095
105O-2b	Same	Same	BR	R	R8	5096
105O-2i	Same	Same	Z	R	R9	
105O-3a	Same	1047	C	R	R9	5097
105O-3d	Same	Same	C-N	R	R10	

NEW YORK-Continued

NUMBER　　OBVERSE　　　　　　REVERSE　　　　　　　METAL　EDGE　RARITY　H&G

BUFFALO 105-Continued

105P-1a	USE/SEWARD'S/COUGH/CURE/ S.B. SEWARD/DRUGGIST/ BUFFALO	1040	C	R	R5	5098
105P-1a1	Same	Same	C	PL	R9	
105P-2a	Same	1042	C	R	R7	5099
105P-2b	Same	Same	BR	R	R7	5100
105P-2i	Same	Same	Z	R	R10	
105P-3a	Same	1046	C	R	R5	5101
105P-4a	Same	1047	C	R	R7	5102
105P-4d	Same	Same	C-N	R	R9	5103
105Q-1a	SOHM & ROHMANN/BUTCHERS /BUFFALO	1037	C	R	R9	
105Q-2a	Same	1042	C	R	R4	5104
105Q-2b	Same	Same	BR	R	R8	5105
105Q-2i	Same	Same	Z	R	R9	
105Q-3a	Same	1043	C	R	R8	
105Q-4d	Same	1046	C-N	R	R10	
105Q-5a	Same	1047	C	R	R8	5106
105Q-5d	Same	Same	C-N	R	R10	
105R-1a	WATSONS NEURALGIA KING:/ C.R. WALKER/255/MAIN ST./ BUFFALO	1077	C	PL	R5	5107
105R-1do	Same, over U.S. C-N cent	Same	C-N	PL	R8	5108
105S-1a	WEBSTER & CO./GROCERS/NO. 1/ SENECA/ST./BUFFALO.N.Y.	1077	C	PL	R3	5109

234

NEW YORK-Continued

NUMBER	OBVERSE	REVERSE	METAL	EDGE	RARITY	H&G

COHOES 140

140A-1

140A-2

140A-1a	ALDEN & FRINK / above an Indian head to left in center / 1863	MERCHANTS / 40 / MOHAWK ST / COHOES N-Y.	C	PL	R1	5111
140A-1b	Same	Same	BR	PL	R9	5112
140A-1c	Same	Same	N	PL	R10	
140A-2a	ALDEN & FRINK / above a U.S. shield in center / 1863	Same	C	PL	R1	5113
140A-2a1	Same	Same	BRNZ	PL	R2	5114
140A-2b	Same	Same	BR	PL	R9	
140A-2e	Same	Same	W-M	PL	R10	
140A-3a	MERCHANTS / 40 / MOHAWK ST / COHOES N-Y. (Rev. NY 140A-1a)	Blank	C	PL	R10	

COOPERSTOWN 145

145A-1a	BINGHAM / & / JARVIS / DRUGS, / MEDICINES, PAINTS, OILS &C.	1175 Thick planchet	C	PL	F5	5116
145A-1a1	Same, thin planchet	Same	C	PL	R5	5117
145A-1b	Same	Same	BR	PL	R6	5118
145A-1c	Same	Same	N	PL	R7	5119
145A-1d	Same	Same	C-N	PL	R8	5120
145A-1do	Same, over U.S. C-N cent	Same	C-N	PL	R0	
145A-1e	Same	Same	W-M	PL	R7	5121
145A-1f	Same	Same	S	PL	R9	5122
145A-1g	Same	Same	L	PL	R9	
145A-2a	Same, thick planchet	1236	C	PL	R5	5123
145A-2a1	Same, thin planchet	Same	C	PL	R5	5124
145A-2b	Same	Same	BR	PL	R6	5125
145A-2c	Same	Same	N	PL	R7	5126
145A-2d	Same	Same	C-N	PL	R8	5127
145A-2e	Same (H-R 1268)	Same	W-M	PL	R7	5128
145A-2f	Same	Same	S	PL	R9	5129

NEW YORK-Continued

NUMBER	OBVERSE	REVERSE	METAL	EDGE	RARITY	H&G

COOPERSTOWN 145-Continued

NUMBER	OBVERSE	REVERSE	METAL	EDGE	RARITY	H&G
145A-3a	Same, thick planchet	1277	C	PL	R7	5130
145A-3a1	Same, thin planchet	Same	C	PL	R7	5131
145A-3b	Same	Same	BR	PL	R8	5132
145A-3c	Same	Same	N	PL	R7	5133
145A-3d	Same	Same	C-N	PL	R8	5134
145A-3do	Same, over U.S. C-N cent	Same	C-N	PL	R9	
145A-3e	Same	Same	W-M	PL	R8	5135
145A-3f	Same	Same	S	PL	R9	5136

145B-1

145B-3

145B-1a	G.L. BOWNE / WILL / REDEEM / AT THE / IRON CLAD / COOPERSTOWN, N.Y. Thick planchet.	BINGHAM / & / JARVIS / DRUGS, / MEDICINES / PAINTS, OILS & C.	C	PL	R2	5137
145B-1a1	Same, thin planchet	Same	C	PL	R4	
145B-1a2	Same, small planchet	Same	C	PL	R4	
145B-1b	Same	Same	BR	PL	R4	5138
145B-1b1	Same, thin planchet	Same	BR	PL	R4	
145B-1c	Same	Same	N	PL	R6	5139
145B-1d	Same (H-R 1270)	Same	C-N	PL	R7	5140
145B-1e	Same	Same	W-M	PL	R8	5141
145B-1g	Same	Same	L	PL	R9	
145B-2a	Same, thick planchet	1073	C	PL	R7	5143
145B-2a1	Same, thin planchet	Same	C	PL	R7	5144
145B-2b	Same	Same	BR	PL	R8	5145
145B-2c	Same	Same	N	PL	R8	5146
145B-2d	Same	Same	C-N	PL	R8	5147
145B-2e	Same (H-R 1269)	Same	W-M	PL	R8	5148
145B-2f	Same	Same	S	PL	R9	5149
145B-3a	Same	Incuse of obverse	C	PL	R9	

NEW YORK-Continued

NUMBER	OBVERSE	REVERSE	METAL	EDGE	RARITY	H&G

ELMIRA 230

230A-1a	LOUIS STRAUSS & CO./DRY/ GOODS/NO. 3/UNION/BLOCK/ ELMIRA,N.Y.	1024	C	R	R4	5153
230A-1a1	Same	Same	C	PL	R8	
230A-2a	Same	1042	C	R	R7	5155
230A-2b	Same	Same	BR	R	R7	5156
230A-3a	Same	1047	C	R	R8	
230A-3d	Same	Same	C-N	R	R9	

FORT EDWARDS 270

270A-1a	HARVEY & CO./above an Indian head to left in center/1863	GENERAL/STORE/FORT EDWARD N-Y.	C	PL	R2	5150
270A-1b	Same	Same	BR	PL	R7	5151
270A-1c	Same	Same	N	PL	R9	5152

270A

330-A

GREENPOINT 330

330A-1a	A. KILLEEN/NO 1 & 16/FERRY/ ST/GREENPOINT.	1006	C	PL	R5	5158
330A-2a	Same	1137	C	PL	R6	5160
330A-3a	Same	1152	C	PL	R5	5162
330A-4a	Same	1214	C	PL	R6	5170
330A-5a	Same	1232	C	PL	R3	5164
330A-5e	Same	Same	W-M	PL	R8	5166
330A-6a	Same	1265	C	PL	R5	5168
330A-7a	Same	1269	C	PL	R3	5170
330A-7c	Same	Same	N	PL	R9	5172
330A-7do	Same, over U.S. C-N cent	Same	C-N	PL	R8	5173
330A-7e	Same	Same	W-M	PL	R8	5174

NEW YORK-Continued

NUMBER	OBVERSE	REVERSE	METAL	EDGE	RARITY	H&G

NEW YORK CITY 630

630A-1a	ATLANTIC GARDEN/50/ BOWERY,/NEW YORK./1863.	GRAND CONCERT/EVERY NIGHT./lyre with oak branches at side/ADMISSION/FREE.	C	PL	R2	5178
630A-1a1	Same, thin planchet	Same	C	PL	R2	5179
630A-1b	Same	Same	BR	PL	R4	5180
630A-1b1	Same, thin planchet	Same	BR	PL	R4	
630A-1c	Same (H-R 1277)	Same	N	PL	R7	5181
630A-1d	Same	Same	C-N	PL	R9	5182
630A-1e	Same (H-R 1278)	Same	W-M	PL	R8	5183
630A-1f	Same	Same	S	PL	R9	
630A-1do	Same, over C-N cent	Same	C-N	PL	R9	

630B-1    630B-5

630B-1a	CAFE AUTENRIETH/85/ CHATHAM ST./N.Y./1863.	1075	C	PL	R1	5185
630B-1do	Same, over U.S. C-N cent	Same	C-N	PL	R10	
630B-2a	Same	1256	C	PL	R1	5186
630B-3a	Same	1257	C	PL	R1	5187
630B-4a	Same	1259	C	PL	R1	5188
630B-5a	CAGE AUTENRIETH/85/ CHATHAM/ST./N.Y./1863	1260	C	PL	R3	5189
630B-6a	Same	1261	C	PL	R3	5190

630C-1    630C-9

238

NEW YORK-Continued

NUMBER	OBVERSE	REVERSE	METAL	EDGE	RARITY	H&G

NEW YORK CITY 630-Continued

NUMBER	OBVERSE	REVERSE	METAL	EDGE	RARITY	H&G
630C-1a	C. BAHR/COR CLIFF/AND/ FRANKFORT ST./NEW YORK.	1075	C	PL	R2	5192
630C-2a	Same	1076	C	PL	R7	
630C-3a	Same	1216	C	PL	R2	5193
630C-4a	Same	1240	C	PL	R2	5194
630C-4do	Same, over U.S. C-N Cent	Same	C-N	PL	R10	
630C-5a	Same	1256	C	PL	R9	5195
630C-6a	Same	1257	C	PL	R2	5196
630C-7a	Same	1259	C	PL	R4	5197
630C-8a	Same	1261	C	PL	R2	5198
630C-9a	Same	TOM CULLEN/LIQUORS/609/ GRAND ST. N.Y. (NY 630-S obv)	C	PL	R8	5199

NUMBER	OBVERSE	REVERSE	METAL	EDGE	RARITY	H&G
630C 10a	Same					
630C-11a	Same (H-R 1284)	J. A. C. GRUBE/SEGARS/AND/ TOBACCO./ BOWERY /NEW YORK. (NY 630AF obv.)	C	PL	R10	
630C-12a	Same (H-R 1286)	KNOOPS SEGARS & TOBACCO/ 131/BOWERY/N.Y./ 1863(NY 630-AO obv)	C	PL	R6	5200
		H.M. LANE/LAMPS/KEROSENE OIL&C/18/SPRING ST N.Y. (NY 630-AP obv.)	C	PL	R8	5201

NUMBER	OBVERSE	REVERSE	METAL	EDGE	RARITY	H&G
630D-1a	H. J. BANG,/RESTAURANT/231/ BROADWAY.	IMPORTER OF/bunch of grapes with the name GLAUBRECHT under them/RHINE WINES.	C	PL	R2	5203
630D-1b	Same	Same	BR	PL	R5	5204
630D-1e	Same	Same	W-M	PL	R8	5206

239

NEW YORK-Continued

NUMBER	OBVERSE	REVERSE	METAL	EDGE	RARITY	H&G

NEW YORK CITY 630-Continued

| 630E-1a | THOS. BENNETT/N.Y. in wreath 213 FULTON ST./ in very small letters, A.L. HENNING N.Y. | J. C. BAILEY/JERSEY/CITY/ CITY HOTEL | C | PL | R1 | 5208 |
| 630E-1f | Same | Same | S | PL | R9 | |

630F-1a	V. BENNER & CH. BENDINGER/ Indian head to left with the name L. ROLOFF under it/1863 Eighth feather is below the level of the R in BENDINGER	IMPORTERS OF WINES & LIQUORS wine bottle in wreath NO 1 AVE A.	C	PL	R2	5210
630F-1f	Same	Same	S	PL	R9	
630F-2a	Same, except that eighth feather is on the level of the R	Same	C	PL	R2	5212
630F-2b	Same	Same	BR	PL	R8	5213
630F-2bo	Same, over political token	Same	BR	PL	R10	
630F-2bol	Same, over Mitao token	Same	BR	PL	R10	
630F-2d	Same	Same	C-N	PL	R9	
630F-2e	Same	Same	W-M	PL	R8	5216
630F-2f	Same	Same	S	PL	R9	
630F-2fo	Same, over U.S. quarter	Same	S	R	R9	

| 630G-1b | I.W. BLAIN/10cts/16 & 18'/ FULTON MARKET N.Y./1862 | Blank | BR | PL | R9 | 5217 |

240

NEW YORK-Continued

NEW YORK CITY 630-Continued

NUMBER	OBVERSE	REVERSE	METAL	EDGE	RARITY	H&G
630H-1a	J.L. BODE/Mounted stag's head to left/BIRDSTUFFER/1863	BOHEMIAN/FANCY/GLASSWORK/16/N. WILLIAM ST N.Y.	C	PL	R1	5218
630H-1b	Same	Same	BR	PL	R9	5219
630H-1c	Same	Same	N	PL	R9	5220
630H-1do	Same, over U.S. C-N cent	Same	C-N	PL	R10	5221
630H-1e	Same	Same	W-M	PL	R9	5222
630H-1f	Same	Same	S	PL	R9	5223
630H-2a	Same	1010	C	PL	R7	5225
630H-2b	Same	Same	BR	PL	R9	5226
630H-3a	Same	1011	C	PL	R2	5229
630H-4a	Same	Blank	C	PL	R10	

630I-1a	JAS. BRENNAN/37/NASSAU ST/FOREIGN/&/U.S. POSTAGE STAMPS.	1152	C	PL	R3	5232
630I-1b	Same	Same	BR	PL	R5	5233
630I-2a	Same	1214	C	PL	R5	5240
630I-2b	Same	Same	BR	PL	R7	5241
630I-2c	Same	Same	N	PL	R8	5242
630I-2e	Same	Same	W-M	PL	R8	5243
630I-3a	Same	1243	C	PL	R9	5236
630I-3b	Same	Same	BR	PL	R7	5237

630J-1a	BRIDGENS./METAL TOKENS/&/STORE CARDS/189/WILLIAM ST. N-Y,	1006	C	PL	R5	5246
630J-1b	Same	Same	BR	PL	R6	5247
630J-2a	Same	1137	C	PL	R3	5250
630J-2b	Same	Same	BR	PL	R5	5251
630J-2b1	Same, thick planchet	Same	BR	PL	R5	
630J-2c	Same	Same	N	PL	R10	5252
630J-2d	Same	Same	C-N	PL	R10	5253
630J-2e	Same	Same	W-M	PL	R7	5254
630J-2f	Same	Same	S	PL	R9	

241

NEW YORK-Continued

NEW YORK CITY 630-Continued

NUMBER	OBVERSE	REVERSE	METAL	EDGE	RARITY	H&G
630J-3a	Same	1152	C	PL	R4	5256
630J-3b	Same	Same	BR	PL	R6	5257
630J-4a	Same	1243	C	PL	R6	5260
630J-4b	Same	Same	BR	PL	R7	5261

630K-1   630K-3   630K-5

NUMBER	OBVERSE	REVERSE	METAL	EDGE	RARITY	H&G
630K-1a	T. BRIMELOW, DRUGGIST,/ figure 1 in wreath, surrounding a mortar and pestle which divides the date, 1863/432 THIRD AVENUE N.Y.	1138	C	PL	R3	5264
630K-1b	Same	Same	BR	PL	R8	5265
630K-1c	Same	Same	N	PL	R8	5266
630K-1e	Same	Same	W-M	PL	R9	5268
630K-1f	Same	Same	S	PL	R9	5269
630K-2a	Same	1139	C	PL	R3	5270
630K-2b	Same	Same	BR	PL	R8	5271
630K-2c	Same	Same	N	PL	R9	5272
630K-2e	Same	Same	W-M	PL	R9	5273
630K-2f	Same	Same	S	PL	R9	5274
630K-3a	Same (H-R 1299)	GOOD FOR/ONE GLASS OF SODA/ 31 stars around border	C	PL	R8	5275
630K-3b	Same	Same	BR	PL	R8	5276
630K-3c	Same (H-R 1300)	Same	N	PL	R7	5277
630K-3e	Same	Same	W-M	PL	R9	5278
630K-3f	Same	Same	S	PL	R8	5279
630K-4a	Reverse of 630K-3a (H-R 1298)	1138	C	PL	R9	
630K-4b	Same	Same	BR	PL	R9	
630K-4c	Same	Same	N	PL	R9	
630K-4e	Same	Same	W-M	PL	R9	
630K-4f	Same	Same	S	PL	R9	
630K-5a	T. BRIMELOW, DRUGGIST,/ wreath around bust of Franklin to left/432 THIRD AVENUE, N.Y.	1138	C	PL	R5	5280
630K-5b	Same	Same	BR	PL	R5	5281
630K-5c	Same	Same	N	PL	R7	5282
630K-5do	Same, over U.S. C-N Cent	Same	C-N	PL	R10	
630K-5e	Same	Same	W-M	PL	R8	5283
630K-5f	Same	Same	S	PL	R8	5284
630K-6a	Same	Obverse of 630K-1a	C	PL	R8	5285
630K-6b	Same	Same	BR	PL	R8	5286
630K-6c	Same	Same	N	PL	R8	5287
630K-6e	Same	Same	W-M	PL	R9	5288
630K-6f	Same	Same	S	PL	R9	5289
630K-7a	Same	Reverse of 630K-3a	C	PL	R8	5291
630K-7b	Same	Same	BR	PL	R8	5292
630K-7c	Same	Same	N	PL	R9	5293
630K-7e	Same	Same	W-M	PL	R9	5294
630K-7f	Same	Same	S	PL	R9	5295

NEW YORK-Continued

NUMBER	OBVERSE	REVERSE	METAL	EDGE	RARITY	H&G

NEW YORK CITY 630-Continued

630K-8a	T. BRIMELOW, DRUGGIST,/figure 2 in wreath/432 THIRD AVENUE, N.Y.	1139	C	PL	R8	5297
630K-8b	Same	Same	BR	PL	R7	5298
630K-8c	Same	Same	N	PL	R9	5299
630K-8e	Same	Same	W-M	PL	R8	5300
630K-8f	Same	Same	S	PL	R9	5301
630K-9a	T. BRIMELOW, DRUGGIST,/ mortar and pestle dividing the date 1864/432 THIRD AV.N.Y.	1133	C	PL	R7	5303
630K-9b	Same	Same	BR	PL	R7	5304
630K-9c	Same	Same	N	PL	R8	5305
630K-9d	Same	Same	C-N	PL	R8	5306
630K-9e	Same	Same	W-M	PL	R9	5307
630K-9f	Same	Same	S	PL	R8	5308
630K-10e	obverse of 630K-5a	Blank	W-M	PL	R10	
630K-11c	reverse of 630K-3a	Blank	W-M	PL	R10	
630K-11f	Same	Same	S	PL	R10	
630L-1a	BROAS BROS/wreath around ARMY/AND/NAVY/NEW-YORK.	1004	C	PL	R2	5310
630L-1b	Same	Same	BR	PL	R4	5211
630L-1d	Same	Same	C-N	PL	R8	5312
630L-1e	Same	Same	W-M	PL	R8	5313
630L-1f	Same	Same	S	PL	R9	5314
630L-2a	Same	1121 (without die break)	C	PL	R2	5316
630L-2a1	Same, large planchet	Same	C	PL	R8	
630L-2b	Same	Same	BR	PL	R5	5319
630L-2d	Same	Same	C-N	PL	R8	5321
630L-2e	Same	Same	W-M	PL	R8	5323
630L-2e1	Same, large planchet	Same	W-M	PL	R5	
630L-2f	Same	Same	S	PL	R8	5325
630L-3a	Same	1121 (with die break)	C	PL	R2	5317
630L-3a1	Same, large planchet	Same	C	PL	R5	5318
630L-3b	Same	Same	BR	PL	R7	5320

243

NEW YORK-Continued

NUMBER	OBVERSE	REVERSE	METAL	EDGE	RARITY	H&G

NEW YORK CITY 630-Continued

630L-3d	Same (H-R 1302)	Same	C-N	PL	R8	5322
630L-3e	Same	Same	W-M	PL	R8	5324
630L-3f	Same	Same	S	PL	R9	5326
630L-3j	Same	Same	G-S	PL	R9	
630L-4a	Same	1149	C	PL	R2	5327
630L-4a1	Same, large planchet	Same	C	PL	R2	5328
630L-4b	Same (H-R 1303)	Same	BR	PL	R8	5329
630L-4c	Same	Same	N	PL	R8	
630L-4d	Same	Same	C-N	PL	R8	5330
630L-4do	Same, over U.S.C-N cent	Same	C-N	PL	R9	
630L-4e	Same (H-R 1304)	Same	W-M	PL	R7	5331
630L-4f	Same (H-R 1305)	Same	S	PL	R8	5332
630L-4fo	Same, over U.S. Dime	Same	S	R	R9	
630L-4ao	Same, struck over Patriotic 178/267	Same	C	PL	R10	

630L-5a	BROAS BROS/wreath around ARMY/AND/NAVY/NEW YORK (Similar to 630L-1a, but ARMY AND NAVY is in larger letters and there is no hyphen in NEW YORK)	1063	C	PL	R2	5333
630L-5b	Same	Same	BR	PL	R2	5334
630L-5e	Same	Same	W-M	PL	R7	
630L-5f	Same	Same	S	PL	R9	

630M-1a	BROAS PIE BAKER/ONE/COUNTRY/H under a 5 pointed star/131 41ST ST N.Y. (T of 41ST directly under the H)	1060	C	PL	R2	5337
630M-1b	Same	Same	BR	PL	R2	5338
630M-1d	Same	Same	C-N	PL	R10	
630M-1do	Same, over U.S.C-N cent	Same	C-N	PL	R10	
630M-1e	Same (H-R 1311)	Same	W-M	PL	R8	5339
630M-1g	Same	Same	L	PL	R5	5340

NEW YORK-Continued

NUMBER　　OBVERSE　　　　　　　REVERSE　　　　　　　　METAL　EDGE　RARITY　H&G

NEW YORK CITY 630-Continued

NUMBER	OBVERSE	REVERSE	METAL	EDGE	RARITY	H&G
630M-2a	Identical inscription, but different die. (T of 41ST slightly to left of the H)	1061	C	PL	R6	5341
630M-2g	Same	Same	L	PL	R5	
630M-3a	Obverse of 630M-1a	1063	C	PL	R5	5342
630M-3g	Same	Same	L	PL	R8	5344
630M-4a	Same	1062	C	PL	R5	
630M-4b	Same	Same	BR	PL	R9	
630M-4g	Same	Same	L	PL	R9	
630M-5a	Same	1063A	C	PL	R9	
630M-6ao	Obverse of 630M-2a, but overstruck	1061	C	PL	R3	5346
630M-6bo	Same	Same	BR	PL	R5	5347
630M-6eo	Same	Same	W-M	PL	R9	5348
630M-6go	Same	Same	L	PL	R5	5349
630M-7go	Same	Incuse of obverse	L	PL	R9	

630M-8b	Identical inscription of 630M-1a, but B of BROAS and R of BAKER farther from C and Y of COUNTRY.	1065	BR	PL	R3	5351
630M-9a	Same, but no H under the star	1061	C	PL	R5	5354
630M-9b	Same	Same	BR	PL	R9	5355
630M-9c	Same	Same	N	PL	R9	
630M-9d	Same	Same	C-N	PL	R9	5356
630M-9e	Same	Same	W-M	PL	R9	5357
630M-9fo	Same, (over 12 SOLS)	Same	S	PL	R10	
630M-9g	Same	Same	L	PL	R5	5358
630M-9i	Same	Same	Z	PL	R6	5359
630M-10a	Same	1062A	C	PL	R9	
630M-11ao	Obverse of 630M-6ao	1064	C	PL	R5	5360
630M-11eo	Same	Same	W-M	PL	R8	5361
630M-11go	Same	Same	L	PL	R8	
630M-12ao	Obv of 630M-6a	Obverse of 630M-8b	C	PL	R6	5363
630M-12bo	Same	Same	BR	PL	R6	5364

NOTE: 630M-11a, 630M-11e, 630M-11g, and 630M-12a have clashed die impressions.

NEW YORK-Continued

NUMBER	OBVERSE	REVERSE	METAL	EDGE	RARITY	H&G

NEW YORK CITY 630-Continued

630M-12do	Same	Same	C-N	PL	R9	
630M-12dol	Same, over U.S. C-N cent	Same	C-N	PL	R9	
630M-12eo	Same	Same	W-M	PL	R9	5365
630M-12go	Same	Same	L	PL	R6	5366

630M-13a	BROAS BROTHERS/in wreath, OUR/COUNTRY/PIE BAKERS	1143	C	PL	R3	5368
630M-13b	Same	Same	BR	PL	R4	5369
630M-13c	Same	Same	N	PL	R9	5370
630M-13f	Same	Same	S	PL	R9	
630M-13g	Same	Same	L	PL	R9	

630N-1b	M.S. BROWN in double row of stars and dots, E PLURIBUS UNUM on band above	In German letters, EUREKA/2/WARREN ST./NEW YORK	BR	PL	R9	5373

630N-2a	M.S. BROWN/1863 in open wreath with shield. B of BROWN under point of shield.	EUREKA/2/WARREN ST./NEW YORK	C	PL	R2	5375
630N-2b	Same	Same	BR	PL	R8	
630N-2c	Same	Same	N	PL	R8	
630N-2f	Same	Same	S	PL	R9	

246

NEW YORK-Continued

NUMBER	OBVERSE	REVERSE	METAL	EDGE	RARITY	H&G

NEW YORK CITY 630-Continued

630N-3   630N-4   630O-1

630N-3a	Same inscription, name less curve. R of BROWN under point of shield.	Same	C	PL	R4	5376
630N-4a	Same inscription, but ROWN of BROWN in smaller letters than the B	Same	C	PL	R2	5377
630N-4b	Same	Same	BR	PL	R8	
630N-4do	Same, over U.S. C-N cent	Same	C-N	PL	R9	
630N-4e	Same	Same	W-M	PL	R9	
630O-1a	W.S. BROWN / 1863 in wreath with shield.	Same	C	PL	R3	5381
630O-1b	Same	Same	BR	PL	R6	5382
630O-1do	Same, over U.S.C-N cent (H R 1315)	Same	C-N	PL	R8	5383
630O-1e	Same	Same	W-M	PL	R9	
630O-2b	Same	1011	BR	PL	R9	

630P-1   630P-2

630P-1a	CARLAND'S / 95 / BOWERY / COR. OF / HESTER ST. N.Y. (F of OF under right side of R of BOWERY)	FINE ALE / DRAWN / FROM WOOD.	C	PL	R2	5384
630P-2a	Same inscription, F of OF under left side of R of BOWERY	Same	C	PL	R7	

247

NEW YORK-Continued

NUMBER　　OBVERSE　　　　　　　　REVERSE　　　　　　　　　　METAL　EDGE　RARITY　H&G

NEW YORK CITY 630-Continued

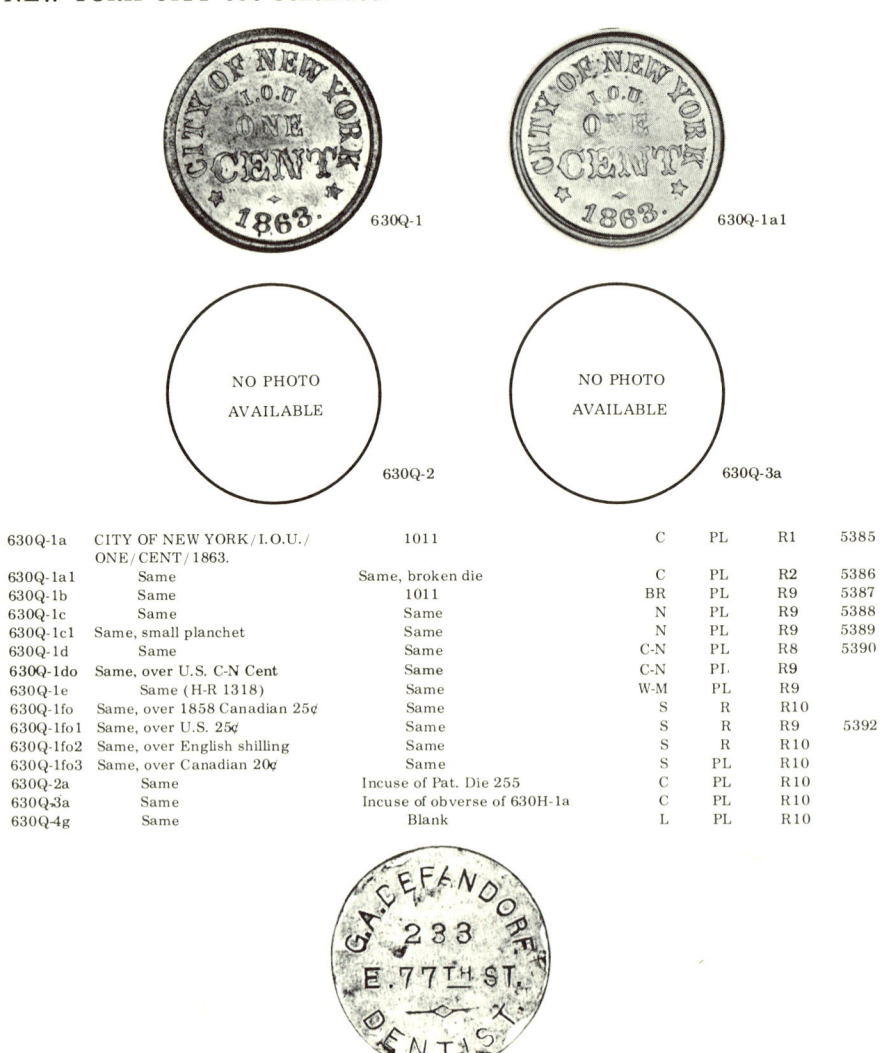

630Q-1

630Q-1a1

630Q-2 — NO PHOTO AVAILABLE

630Q-3a — NO PHOTO AVAILABLE

630Q-1a	CITY OF NEW YORK/I.O.U./ONE/CENT/1863.	1011	C	PL	R1	5385
630Q-1a1	Same	Same, broken die	C	PL	R2	5386
630Q-1b	Same	1011	BR	PL	R9	5387
630Q-1c	Same	Same	N	PL	R9	5388
630Q-1c1	Same, small planchet	Same	N	PL	R9	5389
630Q-1d	Same	Same	C-N	PL	R8	5390
630Q-1do	Same, over U.S. C-N Cent	Same	C-N	PL	R9	
630Q-1e	Same (H-R 1318)	Same	W-M	PL	R9	
630Q-1fo	Same, over 1858 Canadian 25¢	Same	S	R	R10	
630Q-1fo1	Same, over U.S. 25¢	Same	S	R	R9	5392
630Q-1fo2	Same, over English shilling	Same	S	R	R10	
630Q-1fo3	Same, over Canadian 20¢	Same	S	PL	R10	
630Q-2a	Same	Incuse of Pat. Die 255	C	PL	R10	
630Q-3a	Same	Incuse of obverse of 630H-1a	C	PL	R10	
630Q-4g	Same	Blank	L	PL	R10	

630R-1j

630R-1j	G.A. CEFANDORF/233/E 77TH. ST/DENTIST	Same as obverse	G-S	PL	R9	5393

NOTE: The first letter of the last name is probably a "D" that wasn't stamped with enough pressure.

NEW YORK-Continued

NUMBER	OBVERSE	REVERSE	METAL	EDGE	RARITY	H&G

NEW YORK CITY 630-Continued

630S-1a	TOM CULLEN/LIQUORS/609/ GRAND ST N.Y.	1240	C	PL	R8	5394
630S-2a	Same	1255	C	PL	R2	5395
630S-3a	Same	1256	C	PL	R2	5396
630S-4a	Same	1257	C	PL	R2	5397
630S-5a	Same	Obverse of 630AP-1a H.M. LANE)	C	PL	R8	
630T-1a	J.J. DIEHL UNDERTAKER/133/coffin in open wreath/ESSEX ST/ NEW YORK.	1011	C	PL	R2	5399
630T-1a1	Same, badly broken die	Same	C	PL	R5	
630T-1ao	Same, over U.S. large cent	Same	C	PL	R10	5400
630T-1b	Same	Same	BR	PL	R8	5401
630T-1c	Same	Same	N	PL	R9	5402
630T-1e	Same	Same	W-M	PL	R9	5403
630T-1f	Same	Same	S	PL	R9	5404
630T-1fo	Same, over U.S. quarter	Same	S	R	R9	
630U-1a	CARL DIEM./CONSTANZER/ BRAUEREI/565 & 567/4TH ST./ NEW YORK.	1417	C	PL	R7	5406
630U-1a1	Same, large planchet	Same	C	PL	R3	5407
630U-1b	Same	Same	BR	PL	R7	5408
630U-1b1	Same, small planchet	Same (see photo 1417A)	BR	PL	R9	
630U1o	Same, large planchet	Same	W-M	PL	R8	5409
630U-1fo	Same, over U.S. quarter	Same	S	R	R9	
630U-1j	Same, large planchet	Same	G-S	PL	R8	5410
630U-1j1	Same, double struck	Same	G-S	PL	R10	
630V-1a	C. DOSCHER/wreath around NOT/ONE/CENT/H/241 WASHINTON ST. N.Y.	1005	C	PL	R7	5413
630V-2a	Same, large planchet	1053	C	PL	R7	5414
630V-2a1	Same, small planchet	Same	C	PL	R2	5415
630V-3a	Same	1054	C	PL	R2	5416
630V-4a	Same	1055	C	PL	R2	5417
630V-5a	Same	Blank	C	PL	R10	5418

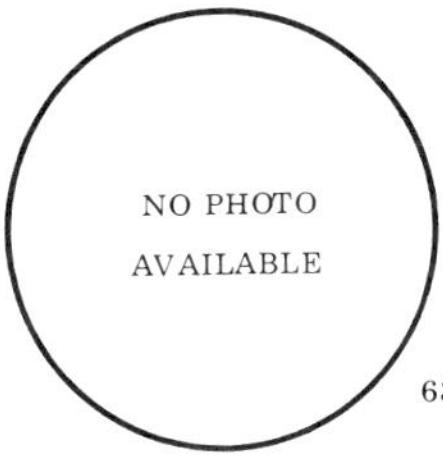

249

NEW YORK-Continued

NUMBER	OBVERSE	REVERSE	METAL	EDGE	RARITY	H&G

NEW YORK CITY 630-Continued

630V-6a	C. DOSCHER 241 WASHN ST. N.Y./bust of Washington to right/ 1863. (One dot under T of ST.)	1254	C	PL	R2	5420
630V-7a	Same inscription and bust, but date in smaller figures. (Two dots under T of ST.)	1254	C	PL	R2	5421
630V-7a1	Same, broken die	Same	C	PL	R4	5422
630V-7g	Same	Same	L	PL	R10	5423
630V-8a	Same	1254A	C	PL	R9	

630W-1a	FELIX/Hebrew letters for "Kosher"/DINING/SALOON/ 256/BROADWAY,/NEW YORK.	1015	C	PL	R3	5425
630W-1b	Same	Same	BR	PL	R5	5426
630W-1c	Same (H-R 1327)	Same	N	PL	R8	5427
630W-1do	Same, over U.S. C-N cent (H-R 1326)	Same	C-N	PL	R8	5428
630W-1e	Same	Same	W-M	PL	R8	5429
630W-1f	Same	Same	S	PL	R9	5430
630W-2a	Same	1249	C	PL	R5	5432
630W-2b	Same	Same	BR	PL	R6	5433
630W-2c	Same	Same	N	PL	R8	5434
630W-2do	Same, over U.S. C-N cent (H-R 1325)	Same	C-N	PL	R8	5435
630W-2e	Same	Same	W-M	PL	R8	5436
630W-2f	Same	Same	S	PL	R9	5437
630W-2fo	Same, over U.S. dime	Same	S	R	R9	
630X-1j	FEUCHTWANGER COMPOSITION /in wreath THREE CENTS	Large eagle with date 1864	G-S	R	R7	

250

NEW YORK-Continued

NUMBER	OBVERSE	REVERSE	METAL	EDGE	RARITY	H&G

NEW YORK CITY 630-Continued

| 630Y-1a | J. FISHER./254/SEVENTH/AV./ SEGAR STORE. | 1214 | C | PL | R2 | 5439 |
| 630Y-1e | Same | Same | W-M | PL | R10 | 5443 |

| 630Z-1a | FR. FREISE, LEICHENBESORGER /Indian Head to left/12 AVE.A,/NEW YORK. | FR. FREISE, UNDERTAKER/ wreath enclosing casket with 12 above wreath and AVE. A. below/ NEW 1863 YORK. | C | PL | R3 | 5445 |
| 630Z-1ao | Same, struck over a 630BM-1a | Same | C | PL | R10 | |

630AA-1a	J.F. GARDNER/55/HENRY/ST./ N.Y.	1019	C	PL	R4	5447
630AA-1b	Same	Same	BR	PL	R7	5448
630AA-1c	Same	Same	N	PL	R9	
630AA-1d	Same	Same	C-N	PL	R9	5450
630AA-1do	Same, over C-N cent	Same	C-N	PL	R9	
630AA-1fo	Same, over U.S. dime (H-R 1330)	Same	S	R	R9	5452

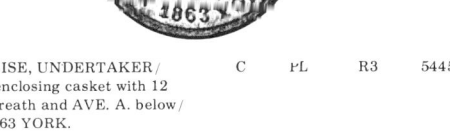

251

NEW YORK-Continued

NUMBER	OBVERSE	REVERSE	METAL	EDGE	RARITY	H&G

NEW YORK CITY 630-Continued

630AB-1a	A. GAVRON./213/BOWERY/&/ 102 PITT ST./N-Y/SAUSAGES.	1006	C	PL	R2	5456
630AB-1b	Same	Same	BR	PL	R7	5457
630AB-1c	Same (H-R 1333)	Same	N	PL	R7	5458
630AB-1d	Same	Same	C-N	PL	R8	5459
630AB-1e	Same	Same	W-M	PL	R9	
630AB-1f	Same	Same	S	R	R9	5461
630AB-2a	Same (H-R 1334)	1137	C	PL	R9	5463
630AB-2b	Same	Same	BR	PL	R7	5464
630AB-2c	Same (H-R 1336)	Same	N	PL	R7	5465
630AB-2d	Same (H-R 1337)	Same	C-N	PL	R8	5466
630AB-2e	Same (H-R 1335)	Same	W-M	PL	R9	5467
630AB-2f	Same	Same	S	PL	R9	
630AB-3a	Same	1152	C	PL	R4	5469
630AB-3b	Same (H-R 1339)	Same	BR	PL	R7	5470
630AB-3c	Same (H-R 1340)	Same	N	PL	R7	5471
630AB-3d	Same (H-R 1341)	Same	C-N	PL	R8	5472
630AB-3e	Same	Same	W-M	PL	R9	5473
630AB-3f	Same	Same	S	PL	R9	5474
630AB-4a	Same	1214	C	PL	R9	5498
630AB-4b	Same	Same	BR	PL	R8	5499
630AB-4c	Same	Same	N	PL	R8	5500
630AB-4d	Same (H-R 1351)	Same	C-N	PL	R8	5501
630AB-4e	Same (H-R 1352)	Same	W-M	PL	R9	
630AB-4f	Same	Same	S	PL	R9	5503
630AB-5a	Same	1243	C	PL	R2	5476
630AB-5b	Same	Same	BR	PL	R4	5477
630AB-5c	Same (H-R 1343)	Same	N	PL	R7	5478
630AB-5d	Same (H-R 1344)	Same	C-N	PL	R8	5479
630AB-5e	Same (H-R 1345)	Same	W-M	PL	R8	5480
630AB-5f	Same	Same	S	PL	R10	5481
630AB-6a	Same	1265	C	PL	R2	5483
630AB-7a	Same	1268	C	PL	R2	5486
630AB-7b	Same	Same	BR	PL	R7	5487
630AB-7c	Same	Same	N	PL	R8	5488
630AB-7d	Same	Same	C-N	PL	R8	5489
630AB-7e	Same	Same	W-M	PL	R8	5490
630AB-7f	Same	Same	S	PL	R9	
630AB-8a	Same	1269	C	PL	R2	5492
630AB-8b	Same (H-R 1347)	Same	BR	PL	R9	5493
630AB-8d	Same (H-R 1349)	Same	C-N	PL	R9	
630AB-8e	Same (H-R 1348)	Same	W-M	PL	R9	5496
630AC-1a	CHARLES GENTSCH/Indian Head to left/1863	CAFE/RESTAURANT/DU COMMERCE/NO 426/BROADWAY N-Y.	C	PL	R2	5505
630AC-1c	Same	Same	N pl	PL	R7	5506

252

NEW YORK-Continued

NUMBER	OBVERSE	REVERSE	METAL	EDGE	RARITY	H&G

NEW YORK CITY 630-Continued

630AD-1a	H.D. GERDTS / BROKER / & / COIN DEALER / 240 / GREENWICH ST. N.Y.	1137	C	PL	R3	5508
630AD-1b	Same	Same	BR	PL	R7	5509
630AD-1c	Same	Same	N	PL	R9	5510
630AD-1do	Same, over U.S. C-N cent	Same	C-N	PL	R9	
630AD-1e	Same	Same	W-M	PL	R9	5512
630AD-1fo	Same, over U.S. dime	Same	S	R	R9	
630AD-2a	Same	1243	C	PL	R3	5514
630AD-2b	Same	Same	BR	PL	R8	5515
630AE-1a	G. GRAHAM, / COR. / HENRY / & MONTGOMERY ST. / COR. BLEECKER & / TENTH / ST. / LIQUORS	1263	C	PL	R2	5517
630AE-1b	Same	Same	BR	PL	R7	5518
630AE-1i	Same, Obverse struck over reverse	Same	BR	PL	R8	
630AE-1c	Same (H-R 1356)	Same	N	PL	R8	5519
630AE-1do	Same, over U.S. C-N cent	Same	C-N	PL	R8	5520
630AE-1e	Same	Same	W-M	PL	R8	5521
630AE-1fo	Same, over U.S. dime	Same	S	R	R8	5522
630AE-1i	Same	Same	Z	PL	R9	

630AF-1a	J.A.C. GRUBE, / SEGARS / AND / TOBACCO. / 7 BOWERY 7 / NEW YORK.	1240	C	PL	R3	5524
630AF-2a	Same	1257	C	PL	R2	5525
630AF-3a	Same	1258	C	PL	R2	5526
630AF-4a	Same	1259	C	PL	R9	
630AF-5a	Same	Obverse of 630AO-1a (Knoops)	C	PL	R9	5527

253

NEW YORK-Continued

NUMBER	OBVERSE	REVERSE	METAL	EDGE	RARITY	H&G

NEW YORK CITY 630-Continued

630AG-1

630AG-2

630AG-1a	JOHN P. GRUBER/Set of balances/NEW YORK. One with broken die.	1197	C	PL	R2	5529
630AG-1b	Same	Same	BR	PL	R7	5530
630AG-1c	Same	Same	N	PL	R10	5531
630AG-1do	Same, over U.S. cent	Same	C-N	PL	R8	5532
630AG-1e	Same (H-R 1361)	Same	W-M	PL	R8	5533
630AG-1f	Same (H-R 1362)	Same	S	PL	R9	5534
630AG-2a	Same	ESTABLISHED/Two story house with the name WARMKESSEL on it. A. to left of house, D. to right/ HORTER/1850.	C	PL	R8	5536
630AG-2b	Same	Same	BR	PL	R8	5537
630AG-2c	Same (H-R 1372)	Same	N	PL	R8	5538
630AG-2e	Same	Same	W-M	PL	R10	5540
630AG-2f	Same	Same	S	PL	R10	5541

630AG-3

630AG-3a	JOHN P. GRUBER/set of balances/178 CHATHAM SQ.	1015	C	PL	R2	5547
630AG-3ao	Same, struck over a 630W-1a (H-R 1363)		C	PL	R9	
630AG-3b	Same	Same	BR	PL	R7	5549
630AG-3c	Same	Same	N	PL	R8	5550
630AG-3do	Same, over U.S. C-N cent	Same	C-N	PL	R9	5551
630AG-3e	Same (H-R 1364)	Same	W-M	PL	R8	5552
630AG-4a	Same	1230	C	PL	R7	5554
630AG-4ao	Same, struck over a 630W-1a (H-R 1365)	Same	C	PL	R9	
630AG-4c	Same	Same	N	PL	R9	5556
630AG-4do	Same, over U.S. C-N cent (H-R 1366)	Same	C-N	PL	R8	5557
630AG-4e	Same	Same	W-M	PL	R8	5558
630AG-5a	Same	1249	C	PL	R3	5560
630AG-5b	Same (Also thick planchet)	Same	BR	PL	R7	5561
630AG-5c	Same	Same	N	PL	R8	5562
630AG-5do	Same, over U.S. C-N cent	Same	C-N	PL	R8	5563
630AG-5e	Same (H-R 1369)	Same	W-M	PL	R8	5564

NEW YORK-Continued

NUMBER	OBVERSE	REVERSE	METAL	EDGE	RARITY	H&G

NEW YORK CITY 630-Continued

NUMBER	OBVERSE	REVERSE	METAL	EDGE	RARITY	H&G
630AG-5fo	Same, over English Sixpence	Same	S	PL	R10	5565
630AG-5fo1	Same, over U.S. dime	Same	S	R	R9	
630AG-6a	Same	1198	C	PL	R3	5567
630AG-6b	Same	Same	BR	PL	R7	5568
630AG-6c	Same	Same	N	PL	R8	5569
630AG-6f	Same	Same	S	PL	R9	5572
630AG-6fo	Same, over U.S. dime	Same	S	R	R9	
630AG-7a	Same	1199	C	PL	R7	5574
630AG-7b	Same	Same	BR	PL	R7	5575
630AG-7c	Same	Same	N	PL	R9	5576
630AG-7d	Same (H-R 1371)	Same	C-N	PL	R8	5577
630AG-7f	Same	Same	S	PL	R10	5579
630AG-8a	1199	1213	C	PL	R9	5585
630AG-8b	Same	Same	BR	PL	R9	5586
630AG-8c	Same	Same	N	PL	R9	5587
630AG-8d	Same	Same	C-N	PL	R9	5588
630AG-8e	Same	Same	W-M	PL	R10	5589

NUMBER	OBVERSE	REVERSE	METAL	EDGE	RARITY	H&G
630AH-1a	A.J. HENNING/DIE/ SINKER/&/ENGRAVER	Wreath, enclosing 87/FULTON ST./N-Y.	C	PL	R4	5595
630AH-1b	Same	Same	BR	PL	R9	5596
630AH-1e	Same (H-R 1375)	Same	W-M	PL	R9	5597
630AH-1f	Same	Same	S	PL	R10	5598
630AH-1f1	Same	Same	S	R	R10	

NUMBER	OBVERSE	REVERSE	METAL	EDGE	RARITY	H&G
630AI-1a	WILLIAM HASTINGS/Indian head to left/1863	Wreath, enclosing IM-/PORTED/ LIQUORS	C	PL	R9	5601
630AI-1e	Same	Same	W-M	PL	R9	
630AI-1g	Same	Same	L	PL	R2	5602
630AI-1g1	Same	Same	L-Cpl	PL	R9	

255

NEW YORK-Continued

NUMBER	OBVERSE	REVERSE	METAL	EDGE	RARITY	H&G

NEW YORK-Continued

630AJ-1   630AK-1   630AK-2

630AJ-1a	CHR. F. HETZEL/ROOFER/ NEW-YORK	1330	C	PL	R3	5604
630AK-1a	HUSSEY'S SPECIAL MESSAGE POST/50/WILLIAM ST/ NEW YORK	1162	C	PL	R2	5606
630AK-1b	Same	Same	BR	PL	R8	5607
630AK-1d	Same	Same	C-N	PL	R9	
630AK-1f	Same	Same	S	PL	R9	
630AK-1g	Same	Same	L	PL	R10	
630AK-2a	HUSSEY'S/small locomotive/ 50 WM ST/N. YORK/SPECIAL MESSAGE POST	1163	C	PL	R3	5608
630AK-2b	Same	Same	BR	PL	R9	
630AK-2c	Same	Same	N	PL	R10	
630AK-2f	Same	Same	S	PL	R9	

630AL   630AM

630AL-1a	GEORGE HYENLEIN/23/ CHRYSTIE ST/N.Y.	1016	C	PL	R2	5612
630AL-2a	Same	1017	C	PL	R2	5613
630AL-3a	Same	1132	C	PL	R2	5614
630AL-4a	Same	1253	C	PL	R7	5615
630AL-5a	Same	1257	C	PL	R2	5616
630AL-6a	Same (H-R 1382 if correctly attributed)	1258	C	PL	R9	
630AL-7a	Same	1259	C	PL	R2	5617
630AM-1a	CHRISTOPH KARL/lyre in wreath/42 AVENUE A, NEW YORK.	1164	C	PL	R1	5619
630AM-1a1	Same, thick planchet	Same	C	PL	R1	5620
630AM-1b	Same	Same	BR	PL	R6	5621
630AM-1b1	Same, thick planchet	Same	BR	PL	R6	

NEW YORK-Continued

NUMBER	OBVERSE	REVERSE	METAL	EDGE	RARITY	H&G

NEW YORK CITY 630-Continued

630AM-1c	Same (Also thick planchet)	Same	N	PL	R7	5622
630AM-1do	Same, over U.S. C-N cent (H-R 1385)	Same	C-N	PL	R8	5623
630AM-1e	Same (Also thick planchet)	Same	W-M	PL	R8	5624
630AM-1fo	Same, over U.S. quarter	Same	S	R	R9	5625
630AM-1h	Same	Same	IRON	PL	R10	
630AM-1j	Same (H-R 1384)	Same	G-S	PL	R8	
630AM-2c	Same	Blank	N	PL	R10	

630AMa   630AN

630AMa-1a	H&M. KAYSER & CO. / IMPORTERS / OF / FANCY / GOODS / NEW YORK	1190	C	PL	R7	
630AMa-1b	Same	Same	BR	PL	R9	
630AMa-1g	Same	Same	L	PL	R9	

630AN-1a	R.T. KELLY, / high hat dividing the date 1863 / 1319 THIRD AVE. / NEW YORK	1249	C	PL	R3	5627
630AN-1b	Same	Same	BR	PL	R5	5628
630AN-1c	Same	Same	N	PL	R7	5629
630AN-1do	Same, over U.S. C-N cent (H-R 1388)	Same	C-N	PL	R8	5630
630AN-1e	Same	Same	W-M	PL	R8	5631
630AN-1f	Same	Same	S	PL	R9	5632
630AN-2a	Same	1230	C	PL	R7	5634
630AN-2ao	Same, struck over N.Y. 630W-1 (H-R 1386)	Same	C	PL	R9	

630AO-1a   630AO-6a

630AO-1a	KNOOPS SEGARS & TOBACCO / 131 / BOWERY / N.-Y. / 1863	1075	C	PL	R2	5636
630AO-2a	Same	1210	C	PL	R4	5637
630AO-3a	Same	1257	C	PL	R2	5638
630AO-4a	Same	1258	C	PL	R2	5639
630AO-5a	Same	1261	C	PL	R4	5640
630AO-6a	Same inscription and spacing as 630AO-1a, but has two incused stars, one above 131 and one below N-Y.	1075	C	PL	R8	
630AO-7a	Similar to 630AO-a but obverse bottom star points to left of dash	1075	C	PL		

NEW YORK-Continued

NUMBER	OBVERSE	REVERSE	METAL	EDGE	RARITY	H&G

NEW YORK CITY 630-Continued

NUMBER	OBVERSE	REVERSE	METAL	EDGE	RARITY	H&G
630AP-1a	H.M. LANE/LAMPS/KEROSENE OIL & C/18/SPRING ST N.Y.	1000	C	PL	R6	5642
630AP-1b	Same	Same	BR	PL	R7	5643
630AP-1c	Same	Same	N	PL	R8	5644
630AP-1d	Same	Same	C-N	PL	R9	
630AP-1e	Same	Same	W-M	PL	R7	5646
630AP-2a	Same	1016	C	PL	R2	5648
630AP-3a	Same	1017	C	PL	R8	5650
630AP-3b	Same	Same	BR	PL	R8	5651
630AP-3c	Same	Same	N	PL	R8	5652
630AP-3d	Same	Same	C-N	PL	R9	
630AP-3e	Same (H-R 1395)	Same	W-M	PL	R9	
630AP-3j	Same	Same	G-S	PL	R9	
630AP-4a	Same	1052	C	PL	R8	5655
630AP-4b	Same	Same	BR	PL	R9	5656
630AP-4c	Same	Same	N	PL	R8	5657
630AP-4d	Same (H-R 1397)	Same	C-N	PL	R9	
630AP-4e	Same	Same	W-M	PL	R9	5659
630AP-5a	Same	1132	C	PL	R1	5661
630AP-5b	Same	Same	BR	PL	R7	5662
630AP-5c	Same	Same	N	PL	R8	5663
630AP-5d	Same	Same	C-N	PL	R9	5664
630AP-5e	Same (H-R 1401)	Same	W-M	PL	R9	5665
630AP-5j	Same (H-R 1400)	Same	G-S	PL	R9	
630AP-6a	Same	1216	C	PL	R1	5667
630AP-6b	Same	Same	BR	PL	R9	5668
630AP-6c	Same	Same	N	PL	R9	5669
630AP-6do	Same, over U.S. C-N cent	Same	C-N	PL	R9	5670
630AP-6j	Same (H-R 1403)	Same	G-S	PL	R9	
630AP-7a	Same	1218	C	PL	R9	5674
630AP-7b	Same	Same	BR	PL	R8	5675
630AP-7c	Same	Same	N	PL	R9	5676
630AP-7do	Same, over U.S. C-N cent	Same	C-N	PL	R9	
630AP-7e	Same	Same	W-M	PL	R9	
630AP-8a	Same	1219	C	PL	R8	5679
630AP-8ao	Same, Obverse struck over reverse	Same	C	PL	R9	
630AP-8b	Same	Same	BR	PL	R9	5680
630AP-8c	Same	Same	N	PL	R9	5681
630AP-8d	Same (H-R 1404)	Same	C-N	PL	R9	
630AP-8e	Same	Same	W-M	PL	R9	5683
630AP-9a	Same	1236	C	PL	R7	5685
630AP-9b	Same	Same	BR	PL	R8	5686
630AP-9c	Same	Same	N	PL	R9	5687
630AP-9e	Same (H-R 1405)	Same	W-M	PL	R9	5689
630AP-10a	Same	1240	C	PL	R2	5691
630AP-11a	Same	1251	C	PL	R4	5693
630AP-11b	Same	Same	BR	PL	R9	5694

NEW YORK-Continued

NUMBER	OBVERSE	REVERSE	METAL	EDGE	RARITY	H&G

NEW YORK CITY 630-Continued

NUMBER	OBVERSE	REVERSE	METAL	EDGE	RARITY	H&G
630AP-11c	Same	Same	N	PL	R9	5695
630AP-11do	Same, over U.S. C-N cent	Same	C-N	PL	R9	5696
630AP-11e	Same	Same	W-M	PL	R8	5697
630AP-12a	Same	1252	C	PL	R8	5699
630AP-12b	Same	Same	BR	PL	R8	5700
630AP-12c	Same	Same	N	PL	R8	5701
630AP-12e	Same	Same	W-M	PL	R8	5703
630AP-12j	Same (H-R 1407)	Same	G-S	PL	R9	
630AP-13a	Same	1253	C	PL	R7	5705
630AP-13b	Same	Same	BR	PL	R7	5706
630AP-13c	Same	Same	N	PL	R7	5707
630AP-13d	Same	Same	C-N	PL	R10	
630AP-13e	Same	Same	W-M	PL	R8	5709
630AP-14a	Same	1257	C	PL	R1	5711
630AP-15a	Same	1258	C	PL	R8	5713
630AP-16a	Same	1259	C	PL	R1	5715
630AP-17a	Same	1277	C	PL	R4	5717
630AP-17b	Same	Same	BR	PL	R9	5718
630AP-17c	Same	Same	N	PL	R9	5719
630AP-17d	Same	Same	C-N	PL	R9	
630AP-17e	Same	Same	W-M	PL	R9	5721
630AP-17j	Same (H-R 1408)	Same	G-S	PL	R9	

630AQ-1

630AQ-2   630AQ-3

630AQ-1a	GUSTAVUS LINDENMUELLER/ wreath enclosing beer mug/ NEW-YORK (26 berries in the wreath) (Also thick planchet)	Bust of bearded man to left with name L. ROLOFF below bust. 13 stars and date 1863 around.	C	PL	R1	5723
630AQ-1b	Same	Same	BR	PL	R7	5724
630AQ-1c	Same (H-R 1411)	Same	N	PL	R7	5725
630AQ-1d	Same	Same	C-N	PL	R9	
630AQ-1e	Same	Same	W-M	PL	R8	5726
630AQ-1g	Same	Same	L	PL	R9	5727
630AQ-2a	Same	Incuse of obverse	C	PL	R9	
630AQ-3a	Same	Same as reverse of 630AQ-1a without the name L. ROLOFF	C	PL	R1	5729

259

NEW YORK-Continued

NUMBER	OBVERSE	REVERSE	METAL	EDGE	RARITY	H&G

NEW YORK CITY 630-Continued

NUMBER	OBVERSE	REVERSE	METAL	EDGE	RARITY	H&G
630AQ-3b	Same	Same	BR	PL	R9	5730
630AQ-3c	Same	Same	N	PL	R8	5731
630AQ-3d	Same	Same	C-N	PL	R9	
630AQ-3e	Same	Same	W-M	PL	R9	5732

630AQ-4 630AQ-6

630AQ-4a	Same inscription and design as 630AQ-1a, but less space between NEW and YORK, and 28 berries in the wreath.	Reverse of 630AQ-1a	C	PL	R1	5734
630AQ-4b	Same (Also very thin planchet)	Same	BR	PL	R7	5735
630AQ-4c	Same	Same	N	PL	R7	5736
630AQ-4d	Same	Same	C-N	PL	R9	
630AQ-4e	Same	Same	W-M	PL	R7	5737
630AQ-4f	Same	Same	S	PL	R9	5738
630AQ-4fo	Same, over silver coin of Equador	Same	S	R	R10	
630AQ-4fob	Same, over 1857 25¢ (H-R 1412)	Same	S	R	R10	
630AQ-5a	Same	Reverse of 630AQ-3a	C	PL	R7	
630AQ-5b	Same (H-R 1413)	Same	BR	PL	R7	5741
630AQ-5c	Same	Same	N	PL	R8	5742
630AQ-5d	Same (H-R 1414)	Same	C-N	PL	R9	
630AQ-5e	Same (H-R 1415)	Same	W-M	PL	R8	5743
630AQ-5g	Same	Same	L	PL	R9	
630AQ-6a	GUSTAVUS LINDENMUELLER/ wreath enclosing the word ODEON/NEW-YORK	Same as reverse of 630AQ-3a except the date is in smaller figures	C	PL	R3	5746
630AQ-6b	Same, Very thin planchet	Same	BR	PL	R9	5747
630AQ-6c	Same	Same	N	PL	R9	5748
630AQ-6d	Same	Same	C-N	PL	R9	
630AQ-6do	Same, over U.S. C-N cent (H-R 1416)	Same	C-N	PL	R9	
630AQ-6e	Same (H-R 1418)	Same	W-M	PL	R8	5749
630AQ-6f	Same	Same	S	PL	R9	5750
630AQ-6fo	Same, over U.S. quarter (H-R 1419)	Same	S	R	R9	
630AQ-6j	Same (H-R 1417)	Same	G-S	PL	R9	
630AQ-7a	Obverse of 630AQ-1a (H-R 1421)	Obverse of 630AQ-4a	C	PL	R9	
630AQ-7b	Same	Same	BR	PL	R9	
630AQ-7d	Same	Same	C-N	PL	R9	
630AQ-7e	Same	Same	W-M	PL	R9	
630AQ-8a	Reverse of 630AQ-1a (H-R 1420)	Reverse of 630AQ-3a	C	PL	R8	5752
630AQ-8b	Same	Same	BR	PL	R9	
630AQ-8d	Same	Same	C-N	PL	R9	
630AQ-8e	Same	Same	W-M	PL	R9	
630AQ-9a	Obverse of 630AQ-1a	Similar to reverse of 630AQ-1a, but more space between bust and L of ROLOFF	C	PL	R8	

NEW YORK-Continued

NUMBER OBVERSE REVERSE METAL EDGE RARITY H&G

NEW YORK CITY 630-Continued

630AQ-9

630AR

630AR-1a	CHARLES A. LUHRS / 77 / PIKE SLIP / COR. WATER ST. / NEW YORK. (Also thick planchet)	PIKE SLIP SHAKES / Wreath enclosing beer glass / 1863.	C	PL	R2	5755
630AR-1b	Same	Same	BR	PL	R6	5756
630AR-1c	Same	Same	N	PL	R8	5757
630AR-1d	Same	Same	C-N	PL	R8	5758
630AR-1do	Same, over U.S. C-N cent (H-R 1424)	Same	C-N	PL	R8	
630AR-1e	Same (H-R 1425)	Same	W-M	PL	R9	5759
630AR-1fo	Same, over U.S. dime (H-R 1426)	Same	S	R	R9	5761
630AR-1j	Same	Same	G-S	PL	R9	5760
630AR-2d	Same	1293	C-N	PL	R9	

630AS

630AT

630AS-1a	C. MAGNUS' NATIONAL PRINTING ESTABLISHMENT. around border, eagle on shield in center, with NEW YORK above eagle	Small bust of Washington to right in center, with 100 ENTITLE TO A $2.00 VIEW / OF NEW YORK CITY. around the bust	C	PL	R7	5763
630AS-1b	Same	Same	BR	PL	R9	5764
630AS-1e	Same	Same	W-M	PL	R9	5765
630AS-2a	Same	1141	C	PL	R9	5768
630AT-1a	J. MAHNKEN / 19&22 / WEST ST. / N-Y / LIQUORS & SEGARS	1006	C	PL	R2	5770
630AT-2a	Same	1152	C	PL	R2	5771
630AT-3a	Same	1214	C	PL	R2	5774
630AT-4a	Same	1205	C	PL	R3	5772
630AT-5a	Same	1269	C	PL	R3	5773

NEW YORK-Continued

NUMBER	OBVERSE	REVERSE	METAL	EDGE	RARITY	H&G

NEW YORK CITY 630-Continued

| 630AU-1a | B. MALONEY/ Indian head to left/PROPRIETOR. | NATIONAL/499/THIRD AVENUE/1863 | C | PL | R2 | 5776 |
| 630AU-1b | Same | Same | BR | PL | R4 | 5777 |

| 630AV-1a | JOHN MATTHEWS/ MANUFACTURER/OF SODA WATER/APPARATUS/NO. 437 FIRST AVE./NEW-YORK. | Laureated female head to left with MATTHEWS MEDAL around, 1863 at bottom | C | PL | R4 | |

630AW-1a	H.B. MELVILLE,/Bust of man to left/AGT. 1863.	JEWELER./GOOD FOR/ONE/ CENT/76 BLEECKER ST. N.Y.	C	PL	R4	5779
630AW-1b	Same	Same	BR	PL	R8	5780
630AW-1c	Same	Same	N	PL	R10	5781
630AW-1d	Same	Same	C-N	PL	R9	5782
630AW-1do	Same, over C-N cent (H-R 1433)	Same	C-N	PL	R9	
630AW-1e	Same (H-R 1435)	Same	W-M	PL	R9	5783
630AW-1f	Same (H-R 1434)	Same	S	PL	R9	5784

NEW YORK-Continued

NUMBER	OBVERSE	REVERSE	METAL	EDGE	RARITY	H&G

NEW YORK CITY 630-Continued

630AX-1a	EDWARD MIEHLING'S/85/AVE. B./N-Y./MEAT MARKET	1010	C	PL	R1	5786
630AX-2a	Same	1011	C	PL	R1	5787
630AX-2b	Same	Same	BR	PL	R9	
630AX-2c	Same	Same	N	PL	R9	
630AX-2e	Same	Same	W-M	PL	R9	
630AX-3a	Same	1012	C	PL	R1	5788

| 630AY-1a | USE MILLER'S /50/CENTS/ N,Y,/HAIR DYE | USE/MILLER'S/25/CENTS/ HAIR/INVIGORATOR | C | PL | R2 | 5790 |
| 630AY-2a | USE MILLER'S/50/CENT/HAIR DYE All lettering incused | Same incused lettering as obverse die | C | PL | R4 | 5791 |

NEW YORK-Continued

| NUMBER | OBVERSE | REVERSE | METAL | EDGE | RARITY | H&G |

NEW YORK CITY 630-Continued

| 630AZ-1a | USE/L. MILLER'S/HAIR/ INVIGORATOR/N.Y. All lettering incused | Same incused lettering as obverse die | C | PL | R4 | 5792 |
| 630AZ-1d | Same | Same | C-N | PL | R9 | |

630BA-1

630BA-2

630BA-1a	G.M. MITTNACHT'S EAGLE SAFE around border with safe in center	23 SPRING ST./large chopping block/NEW YORK	C	PL	R4	5794
630BA-2a	Same inscription and safe, but three small stars above safe.	Same	C	PL	R3	5795
630BA-2c	Same	Same	N-PL	PL	R9	5796
630BA-1b	Same	Same	BR	PL	R7	

630BB-1a	MONK'S/METAL/SIGNS. in a circle of 34 stars with a small eagle below (Also thick plan.)	1000	C	PL	R3	5798
630BB-1b	Same (Also thick plan.)	Same	BR	PL	R4	5799
630BB-1c	Same (H-R 1442)	Same	N	PL	R8	5800
630BB-1d	Same	Same	C-N	PL	R8	5801
630BB-1e	Same	Same	W-M	PL	R8	5802
630BB-1f	Same	Same	S	PL	R9	5803
630BB-1g	Same (H-R 1443)	Same	L	PL	R7	5804

264

NEW YORK-Continued

NUMBER	OBVERSE	REVERSE	METAL	EDGE	RARITY	H&G

NEW YORK CITY 630-Continued

NUMBER	OBVERSE	REVERSE	METAL	EDGE	RARITY	H&G
630BB-2a	Same	1218	C	PL	R9	
630BB-3a	Same	1236	C	PL	R5	
630BB-3b	Same	Same	BR	PL	R7	
630BB-3c	Same	Same	N	PL	R8	5808
630BB-3d	Same	Same	C-N	PL	R8	
630BB-3e	Same	Same	W-M	PL	R9	5810
630BB-3f	Same	Same	S	PL	R9	
630BB-4a	Same	1252	C	PL	R7	5812
630BB-4b	Same	Same	BR	PL	R8	5813
630BB-4c	Same	Same	N	PL	R8	5814
630BB-4e	Same	Same	W-M	PL	R9	
630BB-5a	Same (H-R 1444)	1253	C	PL	R8	5817
630BB-5b	Same (H-R 1445)	Same	BR	PL	R9	5818
630BB-5c	Same	Same	N	PL	R9	5819
630BB-5d	Same	Same	C-N	PL	R9	5820
630BB-5e	Same	Same	W-M	PL	R9	5821
630BB-5i	Same (H-R 1446)	Same	G-S		R8	
630BB-6a	Same	1267	C	PL	R6	5823
630BB-6c	Same	Same	N	PL	R9	
630BB-6e	Same	Same	W-M	PL	R9	
630BB-7a	Same (Also thick flan)	Small bust of Washington to right enclosed in wreath, with 399 B'WAY, N.Y. above, 1863 below.	C	PL	R3	5827
630BB-7b	Same (Also thick flan)	Same	BR	PL	R4	5828
630BB-7c	Same	Same	N	PL	R8	5829
630BB-7d	Same	Same	C-N	PL	R8	5830
630BB-7do	Same, over U.S.C-N cent	Same	C-N	PL	R9	
630BB-7e	Same	Same	W-M	PL	R9	5831
630BB-7f	Same	Same	S	PL	R9	5832
630BB-8a	Same as the reverse of 630BB-7a	1000	C	PL	R9	5834
630BB-8b	Same	Same	BR	PL	R9	5835
630BB-8c	Same	Same	N	PL	R8	5836
630BB-8d	Same	Same	C-N	PL	R9	5837
630BB-8e	Same	Same	W-M	PL	R9	5838
630BB-8f	Same	Same	S	PL	R9	5839
630BB-9a	Same	1218	C	PL	R8	
630BB-9b	Same	Same	BR	PL	R9	
630BB-9c	Same	Same	N	PL	R9	
630BB-9d	Same	Same	C-N	PL	R9	
630BB-9e	Same	Same	W-M	PL	R9	
630BB-10a	Same (H-R 1451?)	1219	C	PL	R0	
630BB-10b	Same (H-R 1452?)	Same	BR	PL	R9	
630BB-10c	Same (H-R 1453?)	Same	N	PL	R9	
630BB-10e	Same	Same	W-M	PL	R9	
630BB-11a	Same (Also thick flan)	1236	C	PL	R7	5841
630BB-11b	Same (H-R 1454)	Same	BR	PL	R8	5842
630BB-11c	Same	Same	N	PL	R8	5843

NEW YORK-Continued

NUMBER	OBVERSE	REVERSE	METAL	EDGE	RARITY	H&G

NEW YORK CITY 630-Continued

NUMBER	OBVERSE	REVERSE	METAL	EDGE	RARITY	H&G
630BB-11d	Same	Same	C-N	PL	R8	5844
630BB-11e	Same	Same	W-M	PL	R9	5845
630BB-11f	Same	Same	S	PL	R9	5846
630BB-12a	Same (Also thick flan)	1252	C	PL	R7	5848
630BB-12b	Same	Same	BR	PL	R8	5849
630BB-12c	Same	Same	N	PL	R8	
630BB-12d	Same	Same	C-N	PL	R9	
630BB-12e	Same	Same	W-M	PL	R9	
630BB-12f	Same	Same	S	PL	R9	
630BB-13a	Same (Also thick flan)	1253	C	PL	R7	5853
630BB-13b	Same (H-R 1457)	Same	BR	PL	R7	5854
630BB-13c	Same	Same	N	PL	R8	5855
630BB-13d	Same	Same	C-N	PL	R8	
630BB-13e	Same (H-R 1458)	Same	W-M	PL	R9	
630BB-13j	Same (H-R 1455)	Same	G-S	PL	R8	
630BB-14a	Same (Also thick flan)	1267	C	PL	R4	5858
630BB-14b	Same	Same	BR	PL	R7	5859
630BB-14c	Same (H-R 1462)	Same	N	PL	R9	5860
630BB-14d	Same	Same	C-N	PL	R8	5861
630BB-14e	Same	Same	W-M	PL	R9	5862
630BB-14f	Same	Same	S	PL	R9	5863
630BB-15a	Same	1277	C	PL	R4	5865
630BB-15b	Same (H-R 1459)	Same	BR	PL	R6	5866
630BB-15c	Same	Same	N	PL	R8	5867
630BB-15d	Same	Same	C-N	PL	R8	5868
630BB-15do	Same, over U.S.C-N cent	Same	C-N	PL	R9	
630BB-15e	Same (H-R 1460)	Same	W-M	PL	R8	5869
630BB-15f	Same	Same	S	PL	R9	5870
630BB-15g	Same	Same	L	PL	R9	

NUMBER	OBVERSE	REVERSE	METAL	EDGE	RARITY	H&G
630BC-1a	HENRY C. MONTZ /bust of man to left/ORPHEUS HALL	A TOKEN /OF/THE WAR/FOR THE/UNION./1863	C	PL	R3	5872
630BC-1a1	Same, thin planchet	Same	C	PL	R5	5873
630BC-1b	Same	Same	BR	PL	R6	5874
630BC-1b1	Same, thin planchet	Same	BR	R	R7	
630BC-1c	Same	Same	N	PL	R7	5875
630BC-1e	Same (H-R 1465)	Same	W-M	PL	R7	5876
630BC-1f	Same	Same	S	PL	R10	5877
630BC-1g	Same	Same	L	PL	R10	
630BC-1j	Same	Same	G-S	PL	R9	
630BC-2a	Reverse 630BC-1	Incused	C	PL	R10	

NEW YORK-Continued

NUMBER OBVERSE REVERSE METAL EDGE RARITY H&G

NEW YORK CITY 630-Continued

630BD-1a	NEW-YORK AND ALBANY / PEOPLES / LINE / OF / STEAM BOATS	TIME TABLE / LEAVE N.Y. 6 P.M. / LEAVE ALBANY / 7½ P.M.	C	PL	R2	5879
630BD-1b	Same	Same	BR	PL	R9	

630BE-1a	G. PARSONS / 24 / JOHN ST. / N.Y. / FIREWORKS	1000	C	PL	R7	5881
630BE-1b	Same (H-R 1467)	Same	BR	PL	R8	5882
630BE-1c	Same	Same	N	PL	R8	5883
630BE-1d	Same (H-R 1468)	Same	C-N	PL	R9	
630BE-1e	Same (H-R 1470)	Same	W-M	PL	R8	5885
630BE-1j	Same (H-R 1469)	Same	G-S	PL	R9	
630BE-2a	Same	1017	C	PL	R3	5887
630BE-2b	Same	Same	BR	PL	R7	5888
630BE-2c	Same	Same	N	PL	R8	5889
630BE-2d	Same	Same	C-N	PL	R9	
630BE-2e	Same	Same	W-M	PL	R9	
630BE-2j	Same	Same	G-S	PL	R9	
630BE-3a	Same	1052	C	PL	R8	5893
630BE-3b	Same (H-R 1471)	Same	BR	PL	R8	5894
630BE-3c	Same	Same	N	PL	R9	5895
630BE-3d	Same	Same	C-N	PL	R9	
630BE-3e	Same (H-R 1473)	Same	W-M	PL	R8	5897
630BE-3j	Same (H-R 1472)	Same	G-S	PL	R9	
630BE-4a	Same	1132	C	PL	R9	5899
630BE-4b	Same (H-R 1475)	Same	BR	PL	R7	5900
630BE-4c	Same	Same	N	PL	R9	5901
630BE-4e	Same (H-R 1476)	Same	W-M	PL	R8	5903
630BE-5a	Same	1137	C	PL	R9	5905
630BE-6a	Same	1218	C	PL	R4	5911
630BE-6b	Same (H-R 1477)	Same	BR	PL	R7	5912
630BE-6c	Same	Same	N	PL	R9	5913
630BE-6e	Same	Same	W-M	PL	R8	5915

NEW YORK-Continued

NUMBER	OBVERSE	REVERSE	METAL	EDGE	RARITY	H&G

NEW YORK CITY 630-Continued

NUMBER	OBVERSE	REVERSE	METAL	EDGE	RARITY	H&G
630BE-7a	Same (H-R 1478)	1219	C	PL	R9	5917
630BE-7b	Same	Same	BR	PL	R8	5918
630BE-7c	Same (H-R 1479)	Same	N	PL	R8	5919
630BE-7d	Same	Same	C-N	PL	R9	
630BE-7e	Same	Same	W-M	PL	R9	5921
630BE-8a	Same	1236	C	PL	R9	5923
630BE-8b	Same (H-R 1480)	Same	BR	PL	R9	5924
630BE-8c	Same (H-R 1481)	Same	N	PL	R9	5925
630BE-8d	Same	Same	C-N	PL	R9	
630BE-8e	Same	Same	W-M	PL	R9	5927
630BE-9a	Same	1252	C	PL	R8	5929
630BE-9b	Same	Same	BR	PL	R8	5930
630BE-9d	Same	Same	C-N	PL	R9	
630BE-9e	Same	Same	W-M	PL	R9	
630BE-10a	Same (H-R 1482)	1253	C	PL	R9	5935
630BE-10b	Same	Same	BR	PL	R8	5936
630BE-10c	Same (H-R 1483)	Same	N	PL	R8	5937
630BE-10e	Same (H-R 1484)	Same	W-M	PL	R9	
630BE-11a	Same	1267	C	PL	R9	5941
630BE-11b	Same (H-R 1485)	Same	BR	PL	R9	
630BE-11c	Same	Same	N	PL	R9	5943
630BE-11d	Same	Same	C-N	PL	R9	
630BE-11e	Same	Same	W-M	PL	R9	5945
630BE-12a	Same (H-R 1486)	1277	C	PL	R8	5947
630BE-12b	Same	Same	BR	PL	R9	5948
630BE-12c	Same	Same	N	PL	R9	5949
630BE-12d	Same	Same	C-N	PL	R9	
630BE-12e	Same (H-R 1487)	Same	W-M	PL	R9	5951

NUMBER	OBVERSE	REVERSE	METAL	EDGE	RARITY	H&G
630BF-1a	CHES PFAFF,/RESTAURANT/ 647/BROADWAY,N.Y.	Full length figure of a monk standing to left.	C	PL	R2	5953
630BF-1ao	Same, Obverse struck over reverse	Same	C	PL	R8	

NUMBER	OBVERSE	REVERSE	METAL	EDGE	RARITY	H&G
630BG-1a	JOHN QUINN/GROCER/COR 26 STS/LEXINGTON AV.	1006	C	PL	R9	5958

268

NEW YORK-Continued

NUMBER	OBVERSE	REVERSE	METAL	EDGE	RARITY	H&G

NEW YORK CITY 630-Continued

NUMBER	OBVERSE	REVERSE	METAL	EDGE	RARITY	H&G
630BG-1b	Same	Same	BR	PL	R9	5959
630BG-1c	Same	Same	N	PL	R9	5960
630BG-1d	Same	Same	C-N	PL	R9	5962
630BG-1e	Same (H-R 1489)	Same	W-M	PL	R9	
630BG-2a	Same	1137	C	PL	R9	5964
630BG-2b	Same	Same	BR	PL	R8	5965
630BG-2b1	Same, thin planchet (H-R 1490)	Same	BR	PL	R8	5966
630BG-2c	Same	Same	N	PL	R9	5967
630BG-2d	Same	Same	C-N	PL	R9	5968
630BG-2e	Same (H-R 1491)	Same	W-M	PL	R8	5969
630BG-2f	Same	Same	S	PL	R9	5970
630BG-3b	Same	1152	BR	PL	R8	5973
630BG-3c	Same	Same	N	PL	R9	5974
630BG-3d	Same	Same	C-N	PL	R8	5975
630BG-3e	Same	Same	W-M	PL	R8	5976
630BG-4a	Same	1214	C	PL	R9	5992
630BG-4b	Same	Same	BR	PL	R8	5993
630BG-4c	Same	Same	N	PL	R9	5994
630BG-4d	Same	Same	C-N	PL	R8	5995
630BG-4e	Same	Same	W-M	PL	R9	5996
630BG-5a	Same	1243	C	PL	R2	5978
630BG-5b	Same	Same	BR	PL	R4	5979
630BG-5c	Same	Same	N	PL	R10	5980
630BG-5d	Same	Same	C-N	PL	R9	5981
630BG-5e	Same	Same	W-M	PL	R10	5982
630BG-6a	Same	1265	C	PL	R2	5983
630BG-7b	Same (H-R 1495)	1268	BR	PL	R8	5987
630BG-7c	Same	Same	N	PL	R10	5988
630BG-7d	Same	Same	C-N	PL	R9	5989
630BG-7e	Same	Same	W-M	PL	R8	5990

630BH-1

630BH-2

NUMBER	OBVERSE	REVERSE	METAL	EDGE	RARITY	H&G
630BH-1a	CHRISTIAN RAUH / large basket of flowers / 48 AVE A. N.Y. / CONFECTIONER	1293	C	PL	R2	5998
630BH-1b	Same	Same	BR	PL	R8	5999
630BH-1d	Same	Same	C-N	PL	R9	6001
630BH-1e	Same (H-R 1499)	Same	W-M	PL	R8	6002
630BH-2a	CHRISTIAN RAUH / small basket of flowers / N.Y. / CONFECTIONER	1293	C	PL	R2	6004
630BH-2b	Same	Same	BR	PL	R8	6005
630BH-2c	Same	Same	N	PL	R9	6006
630BH-2d	Same (H-R 1497)	Same	C-N	PL	R9	6007
630BH-2do	Same, over U.S.C-N cent	Same	C-N	PL	R9	
630BH-2e	Same	Same	W-M	PL	R9	6008

NEW YORK-Continued

NUMBER	OBVERSE	REVERSE	METAL	EDGE	RARITY	H&G

NEW YORK CITY 630-Continued

630BI-1a	FREDERICK FOLLWAGEN.JR./ Indian head to left/1863	587/THIRD AVENUE,/AND/ 20 & 21/CENTRE MARKET,/N.Y.	C	PL	R2	6010
630BI-1f	Same	Same	S	PL	R9	
630BI-1g	Same	Same	L	PL	R9	
630BI-2a	FREDERICK ROLLWAGEN,JR/ Indian head to left/1863	Same	C	PL	R2	6011

630BJ-1a	BLESSED IS THE GIVER/GREAT FAIR/FOR THE/SANITARY COMMISSION/NEW YORK/MAY 1864	1138	C	PL	R4	
630BJ-1b	Same	Same	BR	PL	R8	
630BJ-1c	Same	Same	N	PL	R8	
630BJ-1e	Same	Same	W-M	PL	R8	
630BJ-1fo	Same, over 1 franc	Same	S	PL	R9	

| 630BK-1a | ED. SCHAAF/14 & 16/DIVISION ST. | 1230 | C | PL | R1 | 6013 |
| 630BK-1b | Same | Same | BR | PL | R7 | 6014 |

270

NEW YORK-Continued

NUMBER	OBVERSE	REVERSE	METAL	EDGE	RARITY	H&G

NEW YORK CITY 630-Continued

NUMBER	OBVERSE	REVERSE	METAL	EDGE	RARITY	H&G
630BK-1c	Same (H-R 1503)	Same	N	PL	R8	6015
630BK-1do	Same, over U.S.C-N cent (H-R 1504)	Same	C-N	PL	R8	6016
630BK-1e	Same (H-R 1505)	Same	W-M	PL	R8	6017
630BK-1f	Same	Same	S	PL	R9	6018
630BK-1fo	Same, over U.S. dime	Same	S	R	R9	
630BK-1j	Same	Same	G-S	PL	R9	
630BK-2a	EDW. SCHAFF / 14 & 16 / DIVISION ST.	Same	C	PL	R1	6020
630BK-2b	Same	Same	BR	PL	R7	6021
630BK-2c	Same	Same	N	PL	R8	6022
630BK-2d	Same	Same	C-N	PL	R9	6023
630BK-2do	Same, over U.S.C-N cent	Same	C-N	PL	R9	
630BK-2e	Same	Same	W-M	PL	R9	6024
630BK-2f	Same	Same	S	PL	R10	6025
630BK-3a	Same	1231	C	PL	R5	6027
630BK-4a	Same	Incuse of obverse	C	PL	R10	

630BL-1g	J SCHORK / 1863 CH-R 1507)	Clock dial showing 3 o'clock	L	PL	R8	6029

630BM-1a	JOHN SCHUH'S / 88 / FIRST AVE. / N-Y / SALOON	1010	C	PL	R1	6031
630BM-2a	Same, but on smaller planchet	Same	C	PL	R9	6032
630BM-3a	Same	Obverse of 630Q-1a (City of NEW YORK)	C	PL	R7	6035

NEW YORK-Continued

NUMBER	OBVERSE	REVERSE	METAL	EDGE	RARITY	H&G

NEW YORK CITY 630-Continued

630BN

630BO

630BN-1a	FIRST AVE. HALL/96/ BETWEEN/ 5TH & 6TH/STS./ GEO. D. SCHMIDT.	1015	C	PL	R4	6038
630BN-1ao	Same, struck over N.Y. 630W-1a (H-R 1509)	Same	C	PL	R9	6039
630BN-1b	Same	Same	BR	PL	R7	6040
630BN-1do	Same, over U.S.C-N cent	Same	C-N	PL	R9	6042
630BN-1e	Same	Same	W-M	PL	R9	6043
630BN-1fo	Same, over U.S. dime	Same	S	PL	R10	6044
630BO-1a	EDWD. SCHULZE'S/24 WILLIAM/STREET/RESTAURANT.	1291	C	PL	R1	6052
630BO-1b	Same	Same	BR	PL	R7	6053
630BO-2a	Same	1292	C	PL	R1	6045
630BO-2a1	Same, but very small planchet	Same	C	PL	R7	6046
630BO-2b	Same	Same	BR	PL	R7	6047
630BO-2c	Same (H-R 1513)	Same	N	PL	R9	6048
630BO-2d	Same	Same	C-N	PL	R8	6049
630BO-2e	Same	Same	W-M	PL	R8	6050
630BO-2fo	Same, over 1 reale	Same	S	PL	R9	

630BP-1

630BP-2

| 630BP-1h | REDEEMABLE/S.H. SCRIPTURE/ IN CURRENCY Flourish ends under first C of CURRENCY | GOOD FOR/4/CENTS. | Hard rubber | PL | R5 | |
| 630BP-2h | Same inscription and spacing, but flourish ends under first R of CURRENCY | Same | Hard rubber | PL | R5 | |

NOTE: 1863 NYC directories indicate that this may be a Brooklyn card

272

NEW YORK-Continued

NUMBER	OBVERSE	REVERSE	METAL	EDGE	RARITY	H&G

NEW YORK CITY 630-Continued

630BQ-1

630BQ-2

630BQ-1a	PH. J. SEITER'S / Bull's head to left / MARKET Left ear of bull points to R OF SEITER'S (Also thick planchet)	REDEEMED / AT / MY MARKET / 102 THIRD AVE. / N.Y.	C	PL	R7	6056
630BQ-1b	Same	Same	BR	PL	R1	6057
630BQ-1c	Same	Same	N	PL	R8	6058
630BQ-1d	Same (H-R 1516)	Same	C-N	PL	R9	6059
630BQ-1e	Same	Same	W-M	PL	R8	6060
630BQ-1f	Same	Same	S	PL	R9	6061
630BQ-2a	Same inscription and spacing, but left ear of bull points to last S in SEITER'S (Also thick planchet)	Same	C	PL	R4	6063
630BQ-2b	Same	Same	BR	PL	R9	6064
630BQ-2c	Same	Same	W-M	PL	R10	6067
630BQ-3a	(Obverse of 630BQ-1a) Also thick planchet)	1219	C	PL	R8	6069
630BQ-3c	Same	Same	N	PL	R9	6070
630BQ-3d	Same	Same	C-N	PL	R9	6071
630BQ-3e	Same	Same	W-M	PL	R9	
630BQ-4a	Reverse of 630BQ-1a	1052	C	PL	R8	6072
630BQ-4c	Same (H-R 1517)	Same	N	PL	R9	
630BQ-4e	Same	Same	W-M	PL	R9	
630BQ-5e	Same	1219	W-M	PL	R9	

630BR

630BS-1

630BS-2

630BR-1a	JONES WOOD / HOTEL / N.Y. / I. SOMMERS	1382	C	PL	R2	6075
630BR-1b	Same	Same	BR	PL	R8	6076
630BR-1c	Same	Same	N	PL	R10	6077
630BR-1e	Same	Same	W-M	PL	R8	6078
630BR-1f	Same	Same	S	PL	R9	6079
630BS-1a	STAUDINGER'S / 116 / BROADWAY N-Y.	1375	C	PL	R2	6081
630BS-2a	STAUDINGER'S / 116 / BROADWAY, N.Y.	1376	C	PL	R2	6082
630BS-2c	Same	Same	N	PL	R9	

NEW YORK-Continued

NUMBER	OBVERSE	REVERSE	METAL	EDGE	RARITY	H&G

NEW YORK CITY 630-Continued

630BT-1a	ST. CHARLES BILLIARD ROOMS / 584 & 586, / 8TH. AVE. / N Y	1075	C	PL	R3	6085
630BT-2a	Same	1257	C	PL	R3	6086
630BT-3a	Same	1258	C	PL	R9	6087
630BT-4a	Same	1259	C	PL	R3	

630BU-1a	S. STEINFELD / coat of arms, with sceptre pointing to G of AGENT / SOLE AGENT FOR THE U.S.	PRINCIPAL DEPOT / 1863 / OF THE / FRENCH / COGNAC / BITTERS / 70 / NASSAU ST. N.Y.	C	PL	R1	6089
630BU-1e	Same	Same	W-M	PL	R10	
630BU-2a	Same inscription and similar coat of arms, but sceptre points to E of AGENT	PRINCIPAL DEPOT / OF THE / FRENCH / COGNAC / BITTERS / 70 / NASSAU ST.	C	PL	R1	6090
630BU-2e	Same (H-R 1523)	Same	W-M	PL	R9	
630BU-3a	Same	Reverse of 630BU-1a	C	PL	R1	6091
630BU-4e	Obv of 630BU-1a	1010	W-M	PL	R10	

NEW YORK-Continued

NUMBER	OBVERSE	REVERSE	METAL	EDGE	RARITY	H&G

NEW YORK CITY 630-Continued

630BV-1

630BV-2

630BV-1a	STORY & SOUTHWORTH / GROCERS / 53 / VESEY ST. / NEW YORK.	1330	C	PL	R1	6093
630BV-2a	STORY & SOUTHWORTH / GROCERS / 53 / VESEY / ST. / N.Y. First S and last H above the word VESEY	1016	C	PL	R1	6095
630BV-3a	Same	1017	C	PL	R8	6097
630BV-3b	Same	Same	BR	PL	R8	6098
630BV-3c	Same	Same	N	PL	R8	6099
630BV-3d	Same	Same	C-N	PL	R9	
630BV-3e	Same	Same	W-M	PL	R8	6101
630BV-4a	Same (H-R 1548)	1052	C	PL	R8	6103
630BV-4b	Same	Same	BR	PL	R8	6104
630BV-4c	Same	Same	N	PL	R8	6105
630BV-4d	Same	Same	C-N	PL	R9	6106
630BV-4e	Same (H-R 1549)	Same	W-M	PL	R9	6107
630BV-5b	Same	1132	B	PL	R8	6110
630BV-5c	Same	Same	N	PL	R9	
630BV-5d	Same	Same	C-N	PL	R9	6112
630BV-5e	Same	Same	W-M	PL	R8	6113
630BV-5f	Same	Same	S	PL	R9	6114
630BV-6a	Same	1216	C	PL	R1	6115
630BV-6b	Same	Same	BR	PL	R9	6116
630BV-6c	Same	Same	N	PL	R9	6117
630BV-6d	Same	Same	C-N	PL	R9	6118
630BV-6e	Same	Same	W-M	PL	R10	6119
630BV-7a	Same	1217	C	PL	R6	
630BV-7b	Same	Same	BR	PL	R9	
630BV-8a	Same	1218	C	PL	R6	
630BV-8b	Same	Same	BR	PL	R6	6122
630BV-8c	Same	Same	N	PL	R9	
630BV-8d	Same	Same	C-N	PL	R9	6124
630BV-8e	Same	Same	W-M	PL	R8	6125
630BV-9a	Same	1219	C	PL	R6	6127
630BV-9b	Same (H-R 1551)	Same	BR	PL	R8	6128
630BV-9c	Same (H-R 1553)	Same	N	PL	R8	6129
630BV-9d	Same	Same	C-N	PL	R9	6130
630BV-9e	Same	Same	W-M	PL	R9	6131
630BV-9f	Same (H-R 1552)	Same	S	PL	R9	
630BV-10a	Same	1236	C	PL	R0	
630BV-10c	Same	Same	N	PL	R10	
630BV-10d	Same	Same	C-N	PL	R9	
630BV-10e	Same	Same	W-M	PL	R9	
630BV-11a	Same	1251	C	PL	R4	6133
630BV-11do	Same, over U.S. C-N cent	Same	C-N	PL	R9	
630BV-12a	Same (Also thick flan)	1252	C	PL	R7	6135

NEW YORK-Continued

NUMBER	OBVERSE	REVERSE	METAL	EDGE	RARITY	H&G

NEW YORK CITY 630-Continued

NUMBER	OBVERSE	REVERSE	METAL	EDGE	RARITY	H&G
630BV-12b	Same	Same	BR	PL	R8	6136
630BV-12c	Same	Same	N	PL	R9	
630BV-12d	Same	Same	C-N	PL	R9	
630BV-12e	Same	Same	W-M	PL	R8	6139
630BV-13a	Same (Also thick flan)	1253	C	PL	R7	6141
630BV-13b	Same (H-R 1554)	Same	BR	PL	R8	6142
630BV-13c	Same	Same	N	PL	R8	6143
630BV-13d	Same	Same	C-N	PL	R10	
630BV-13e	Same	Same	W-M	PL	R9	6145
630BV-14a	Same	1257	C	PL	R9	
630BV-15a	Same (Also thick flan)	1267	C	PL	R7	6147
630BV-15c	Same	Same	N	PL	R8	6149
630BV-15d	Same	Same	C-N	PL	R10	
630BV-15e	Same	Same	W-M	PL	R9	6151
630BV-16a	Same (H-R 1555)	1277	C	PL	R7	6153
630BV-16b	Same	Same	BR	PL	R8	6154
630BV-16c	Same	Same	N	PL	R8	6155
630BV-16d	Same	Same	C-N	PL	R10	
630BV-16e	Same	Same	W-M	PL	R9	6157

NUMBER	OBVERSE	REVERSE	METAL	EDGE	RARITY	H&G
630BV-17a	STORY & SOUTHWORTH / GROCERS / 53 / VESEY / ST. / N.Y. First S and last H below the word VESEY	1006	C	PL	R7	6159
630BV-17b	Same (H-R 1527)	Same	BR	PL	R8	6160
630BV-17c	Same (H-R 1529)	Same	N	PL	R8	6161
630BV-17d	Same (H-R 1528)	Same	C-N	PL	R9	
630BV-17e	Same	Same	W-M	PL	R8	6163
630BV-18a	Same	1017	C	PL	R8	6165
630BV-18b	Same	Same	BR	PL	R8	6166
630BV-18c	Same (H-R 1530)	Same	N	PL	R8	6167
630BV-18d	Same	Same	C-N	PL	R10	6168
630BV-18e	Same	Same	W-M	PL	R8	6169
630BV-19a	Same	1052	C	PL	R9	6171
630BV-19b	Same (H-R 1532)	Same	BR	PL	R8	6172
630BV-19c	Same	Same	N	PL	R9	6173
630BV-19d	Same	Same	C-N	PL	R9	6174
630BV-19e	Same	Same	W-M	PL	R8	6175
630BV-20a	Same	1132	C	PL	R10	6177
630BV-20b	Same (H-R 1533)	Same	BR	PL	R8	6178
630BV-20c	Same (H-R 1534)	Same	N	PL	R9	
630BV-20d	Same (H-R 1535)	Same	C-N	PL	R10	6180
630BV-20e	Same (H-R 1536)	Same	W-M	PL	R8	6181
630BV-21b	Same	1218	BR	PL	R7	6184
630BV-21c	Same	Same	N	PL	R8	6185
630BV-21d	Same (H-R 1537)	Same	C-N	PL	R9	
630BV-21e	Same (H-R 1538)	Same	W-M	PL	R8	6187

NEW YORK-Continued

NUMBER	OBVERSE	REVERSE	METAL	EDGE	RARITY	H&G

NEW YORK CITY 630-Continued

NUMBER	OBVERSE	REVERSE	METAL	EDGE	RARITY	H&G
630BV-22a	Same	1219	C	PL	R9	6189
630BV-22b	Same	Same	BR	PL	R9	6190
630BV-22c	Same	Same	N	PL	R9	6191
630BV-22e	Same	Same	W-M	PL	R9	6193
630BV-23a	Same	1252	C	PL	R8	6195
630BV-23b	Same	Same	BR	PL	R8	6196
630BV-23c	Same	Same	N	PL	R8	6197
630BV-23d	Same	Same	C-N	PL	R9	
630BV-23e	Same	Same	W-M	PL	R8	6199
630BV-23j	Same	Same	G-S	PL	R10	
630BV-24a	Same	1253	C	PL	R8	6201
630BV-24b	Same	Same	BR	PL	R8	6202
630BV-24c	Same (H-R 1539)	Same	N	PL	R8	6203
630BV-24d	Same	Same	C-N	PL	R9	
630BV-24e	Same (H-R 1541)	Same	W-M	PL	R8	6205
630BV-25a	Same	1257	C	PL	R1	6207
630BV-26a	Same	1259	C	PL	R2	6209
630BV-27a	Same	1267	C	PL	R8	6211
630BV-27b	Same (H-R 1543)	Same	BR	PL	R9	
630BV-27c	Same	Same	N	PL	R9	
630BV-27d	Same (H-R 1544)	Same	C-N	PL	R9	
630BV-27e	Same	Same	W-M	PL	R9	6215
630BV-28c	Same	1268	N	PL	R9	
630BV-29a	Same (Also thick flan)	1277	C	PL	R8	6217
630BV-29b	Same (H-R 1545)	Same	BR	PL	R8	6218
630BV-29c	Same (H-R 1546)	Same	N	PL	R8	6219
630BV-29d	Same	Same	C-N	PL	R9	
630BV-29e	Same (H-R 1547)	Same	W-M	PL	R9	6221
630BV-30a	Same	1330	C	PL	R10	
	(it is questionable whether this place exists)		C	PL	R9	
630BV-31a	Same	1236				

630BW-1b	STRASBURGER & NUHN / IMPORTERS / 65 / MAIDENLANE / NEW YORK	1189	BR	PL	R5	6223
630BX-1e	WM THIERBACH 142 ELM ST. / Indian head to left / 1863 Die 1070)	Wreath enclosing the word GROCER	W-M	PL	R9	
630BX-1g	Same	Same	L	PL	R2	6226
630BX-1g1	Same, copper plated	Same	L-Cpl	PL	R8	

277

NEW YORK-Continued

NUMBER	OBVERSE	REVERSE	METAL	EDGE	RARITY	H&G

NEW YORK CITY 630-Continued

630BX-2a	WM. THIERBACH 142 ELM ST. N.Y./Indian head to left/1863 (Die 1071)	GRO/CER enclosed in a wreath	C	PL	R8	
630BX-2b	Same	Same	BR	PL	R8	6229
630BX-2e	Same	Same	W-M	PL	R8	6230
630BX-2g	Same	Same	L	PL	R2	6228
630BX-2g1	Same, copper plated	Same	L-Cpl	PL	R7	

| 630BY-1a | C. TOLLNER & HAMMACHER/ HARDWARE/209/BOWERY,/ NEW YORK | 1256 | C | PL | R3 | 6231 |
| 630BY-1a1 | Same, nickel plated | Same | C-Npl | PL | R9 | 6232 |

630BZ-1a	PETER WARMKESSEL/ 8/DUANE ST./ NEW YORK.	ESTABLISHED/House with A on left, D on right, and the name WARMKESSEL across it/1850.	C	PL	R2	6234
630BZ-1ao	Same, struck over N.Y. 630AE-1a	Same	C	PL	R8	
630BZ-1b	Same	Same	BR	PL	R7	6235
630BZ-1c	Same (H-R 1561	Same	N	PL	R8	6236
630BZ-1d	Same	Same	C-N	PL	R8	6237
630BZ-1do	Same, over U.S. C-N cent (H-R 1562)	Same	C-N	PL	R9	

278

NEW YORK-Continued

NUMBER	OBVERSE	REVERSE	METAL	EDGE	RARITY	H&G

NEW YORK CITY 630-Continued

NUMBER	OBVERSE	REVERSE	METAL	EDGE	RARITY	H&G
630BZ-1e	Same	Same	W-M	PL	R8	6238
630BZ-1fo	Same, over 6 pence	Same	S	PL	R10	
630BZ-2a	Same	1197	C	PL	R8	6240
630BZ-2b	Same (Also thick flan)	Same	BR	PL	R8	6241
630BZ-3a	Same	1263	C	PL	R7	6244
630BZ-3ao	Same, over N.Y. 630AE-1 (H-R 1567)	Same	C	PL	R8	
630BZ-4a	Reverse of 630BZ-1a	1197	C	PL	R6	6246
630BZ-4ao	Same, struck over N.Y. 630AE-1	Same	C	PL	R8	
630BZ-4b	Same	Same	BR	PL	R7	6247
630BZ-4c	Same	Same	N	PL	R9	
630BZ-4j	Same	Same	G-S	PL	R9	
630BZ-5a	Same	1263	C	PL	R7	6249
630BZ-5ao	Same, over (N.Y. 630AE-1a) (H-R 1565)	Same	C	PL	R9	
630BZ-5b	Same	Same	BR	PL	R7	6250
630BZ-5c	Same	Same	N	PL	R9	
630BZ-5e	Same	Same	W-M	PL	R9	
630BZ-5f	Same	Same	S	PL	R9	
630BZ-5j	Same	Same	G-S	PL	R9	

630CA

630CB

630CC

NUMBER	OBVERSE	REVERSE	METAL	EDGE	RARITY	H&G
630CA-1a	J.H. WARNER/104/BARCLAY/ST/NEW-YORK	1385	C	PL	R3	6254
630CA-1b	Same	Same	BR	PL	R8	6255
630CA-1c	Same	Same	N	PL	R9	6256
630CA-1d	Same	Same	C-N	PL	R8	6257
630CA-1e	Same	Same	W-M	PL	R8	6258
630CA-1f	Same	Same	S	PL	R8	6259
630CA-1fo1	Same, over U.S. dime	Same	S	PL	R10	
630CA-1fo2	Same, over 6 pence	Same	S	PL	R10	
630CA-1g	Same	Same	L	PL	R10	6260
630CB-1a	WM. F. WARNER/NO 1/CATHERINE MARKET.	1006	C	PL	R3	6262
630CB-1b	Same	Same	BR	PL	R9	6263
630CB-1c	Same	Same	N	PL	R9	6264
630CB-2a	Same	1265	C	PL	R3	6266
630CC-1a	WASHINGTON MARKET/large turkey to left/EXCHANGE	1144	C	PL	R10	
630CC-2a	Same	1245	C	PL	R10	
630CC-2f	Same	Same	S	PL	R10	6275
630CC-3e	Same	1275	W-M	PL	R10	
630CC-4a	Same	1353	C	PL	R2	6268
630CC-4b	Same	Same	BR	PL	R8	
630CC-4e	Same	Same	W-M	PL	R9	6272
630CC-4f	Same	Same	S	PL	R9	6273

NEW YORK-Continued

NUMBER	OBVERSE	REVERSE	METAL	EDGE	RARITY	H&G

NEW YORK CITY 630-Continued

| 630CD-1a | WASHINGTON/NO 1/ BROADWAY,/N-Y/RESTAURANT. | 1265 | C | PL | R3 | 6277 |
| 630CD-1e | Same | Same | W-M | PL | R9 | |

630CE-1a	JOHN WATSON 381 BOWERY, N.Y/Indian head to left/1863	UNION/TEA/STORE enclosed in a wreath	C	PL	R3	6280
630CE-1b	Same (H-R 1572)	Same	BR	PL	R9	6281
630CE-1c	Same	Same	N	PL	R9	6282
630CE-1d	Same (H-R 1573)	Same	C-N	PL	R8	6283
630CE-1do	Same, over C-N cent	Same	C-N	PL	R9	
630CE-1e	Same	Same	W-M	PL	R8	6284
630CE-1f	Same	Same	S	PL	R10	6285
630CE-1g	Same	Same	L	PL	R10	
630CE-2a	Same	1219	C	PL	R8	6287
630CE-2b	Same (H-R 1574)	Same	BR	PL	R8	6288
630CE-2c	Same	Same	N	PL	R10	6289
630CE-2d	Same (H-R 1575)	Same	C-N	PL	R8	6290
630CE-2e	Same	Same	W-M	PL	R9	6291
630CE-2f	Same (H-R 1576)	Same	S	PL	R9	6292

| 630CF-1g | WATSON'S/T/STORE (H-R 1577) | GOOD FOR/1/CENT | L | PL | R7 | |

280

NEW YORK-Continued

NUMBER	OBVERSE	REVERSE	METAL	EDGE	RARITY	H&G

NEW YORK CITY 630-Continued

| 630CG-1a | WHITE/HATTER/216/BROADWAY. | 1051 | C | PL | R3 | 6294 |

630CH-1a	THOMAS WHITE/Indian head to left/1863	BUTCHER/NO/13 & 14,/ABATTOIR/PLACE /WEST 39TH ST N-Y.	C	PL	R1	6296
630CH-1a1	Same, nickel plated	Same	C-Npl	PL	R9	
630CH-2a	Same	BUTCHER/WEST 39TH ST N-Y.	C	PL	R9	6298
630CH-3a	THOMAS WHITE/Pig to left/1863	13 & 14/ABATTOIR/PLACE/WEST 39TH ST N-Y.	C	PL	R7	6300
630CH-3b	Same	Same	BR	PL	R9	
630CH-4a	Same	Obverse of N.Y. 695A-2a	C	PL	R9	6302

281

NEW YORK-Continued

| NUMBER | OBVERSE | REVERSE | METAL | EDGE | RARITY | H&G |

NEW YORK CITY 630-Continued

630CI-1

630CI-3

630CI-4

630CI-1a	WILLARD & JACKSONS/eagle on shield/OYSTER HOUSE/ 532 BROADWAY, N-Y.	Flag and staff on building in open wreath. 1863 on shield below building.	C	PL	R2	6304
630CI-2a	Same	Same, except no flag and staff	C	PL	R9	6305
630CI-3a	Same (H-R 1582)	incused	C	PL	R9	
630CI-4a	Same, except flag and cap behind and above eagle	Reverse of 630CI-1a	C	PL	R7	
630CI-4a1	Same, nickel plated	Same	C-Npl	PL	R9	
630CI-4b	Same (H-R 1581)	Same	BR	PL	R9	

282

NEW YORK-Continued

NUMBER	OBVERSE	REVERSE	METAL	EDGE	RARITY	H&G

NIAGARA FALLS 640

640A-1a	M. WALSH & SONS/STAPLES & FANCE/DRY/GOODS/ NIAGRA, FALLS, N.Y.	1042	C	R	R4	6309
640A-1b	Same	Same	BR	R	R8	6310
640A-1i	Same	Same	Z-PL	R	R9	
640A-2a	Same	1043	C	R	R8	6307
640A-3a	Same	1047	C	R	R9	
640A-3d	Same	Same	CN	R	R10	

OGDENSBURG 665

665A   665B

665A1a	G. IDLER'S/MEAT/MARKET OGDENSBURGH, N.Y.	1042	C	R	R4	6317
665A-1b	Same	Same	BR	R	R8	6318
665A-1i	Same	Same	Z-PL	R	R9	
665A-2a	Same	1043	C	R	R6	6315
665A-2a1	Same	Same	C	PL	R9	6316
665A-3a	Same	1047	C	R	R9	
665A-3d	Same	Same	CN	R	R10	
665B-1a	JOHNSON/HOUSE/A.M. SHERMAN/PRO./ OGDENSBURGH, N.Y.	1042	C	R	R4	6324
665B-1b	Same	Same	BR	R	R8	6325
665B1i	Same	Same	Z-PL	R	R9	
665B-2a	Same	1043	C	R	R4	6322
665B-2a1	Same	Same	C	PL	R9	
665B-3a	Same	1047	C	R	R9	
665B-3d	Same	Same	CN	R	R10	

NEW YORK-Continued

NUMBER	OBVERSE	REVERSE	METAL	EDGE	RARITY	H&G

OSWEGO 695

| 695A-1a | M.L. MARSHALL'S VARIETY STORE/man fishing/OSWEGO, N.Y. | DEALER/IN/BERLIN WOOLS/ EMBROIDERY GOODS/FISHING TACKLE/& FANCY GOODS | C | PL | R6 | 6330 |
| 695A-1b | Same | Same | BR | PL | R8 | |

695A-2a	M.L. MARSHALL/fish to left /1863/OSWEGO, N.Y.	TOYS, FANCY GOODS,/FISHING/ TACKLE/AND/RARE COIN.	C	PL	R1	6332
695A-2b	Same	Same	BR	PL	R9	
695A-2e	Same	Same	W-M	PL	R9	
695A-2f	Same	Same	S	PL	R9	

POUGHKEEPSIE 760

| 760A-1d | EASTMAN/NATIONAL/ BUSINESS/COLLEGE/ POUGHKEEPSIE, N.Y. (H-R 1586) | ACTUAL BUSINESS/open book with 1 on left, C on right/ DEPARTMENT | C-N | PL | R7 | 6335 |

284

NEW YORK-Continued

| NUMBER | OBVERSE | REVERSE | METAL | EDGE | RARITY | H&G |

SENECA FALLS 845

845A-1a

845A-2

845A-1a	D. SKIDMORE/GOOD FOR ONE/ eagle with cigar in beak/ SENECA FALLS, N.Y.	SKIDMORE'S/HEAD/ QUARTERS/95 FALL ST./HOTEL.	C	PL	R4	6338
845A-1b	Same	Same	BR	PL	R7	6339
845A-1e	Same	Same	W-M	PL	R9	6342
845A-1f	Same	Same	S	PL	R9	6343
845A-2b	Same	Incuse of obverse	BR	PL	R10	

TROY 890

890A-1

890A-2

890A-3

890A-1a	CHARLES BABCOCK, JEWELER/72/CONG./ST/ TROY, N.Y.	1013	C	PL	R3	6345
890A-1b	Same	Same	BR	PL	R9	
890A-2a	CHARLES BABCOCK/JEWELER/ TROY. N.Y.	REDEEMED AT MY STORE/72/ CONG.ST./1863.	C	PL	R4	6347
890A-3a	C. BABCOCK/small arm and hammer/JEWELER/TROY N.Y.	ONE CENT TOKEN/1/.1863.	C	PL	R9	
890A-3e	Same	Same	W-M	PL	R8	6349
890A-3g	Same	Same	L	PL	R9	

285

NEW YORK-Continued

OLIVER BOUTWELL-Obverse Dies

O-1   O-1-1   O-2

O-3   O-4

O-5   O-6   O-7

O-8   O-9

O-10   O-11   O-12

NEW YORK-Continued

OLIVER BOUTWELL-Obverse Dies

O-13 O-14

O-15 O-16 O-17

O-18 O-18-1

OLIVER BOUTWELL-Reverse Dies

R-1  R-1-1  R-2

287

NEW YORK-Continued

OLIVER BOUTWELL-Reverse Dies

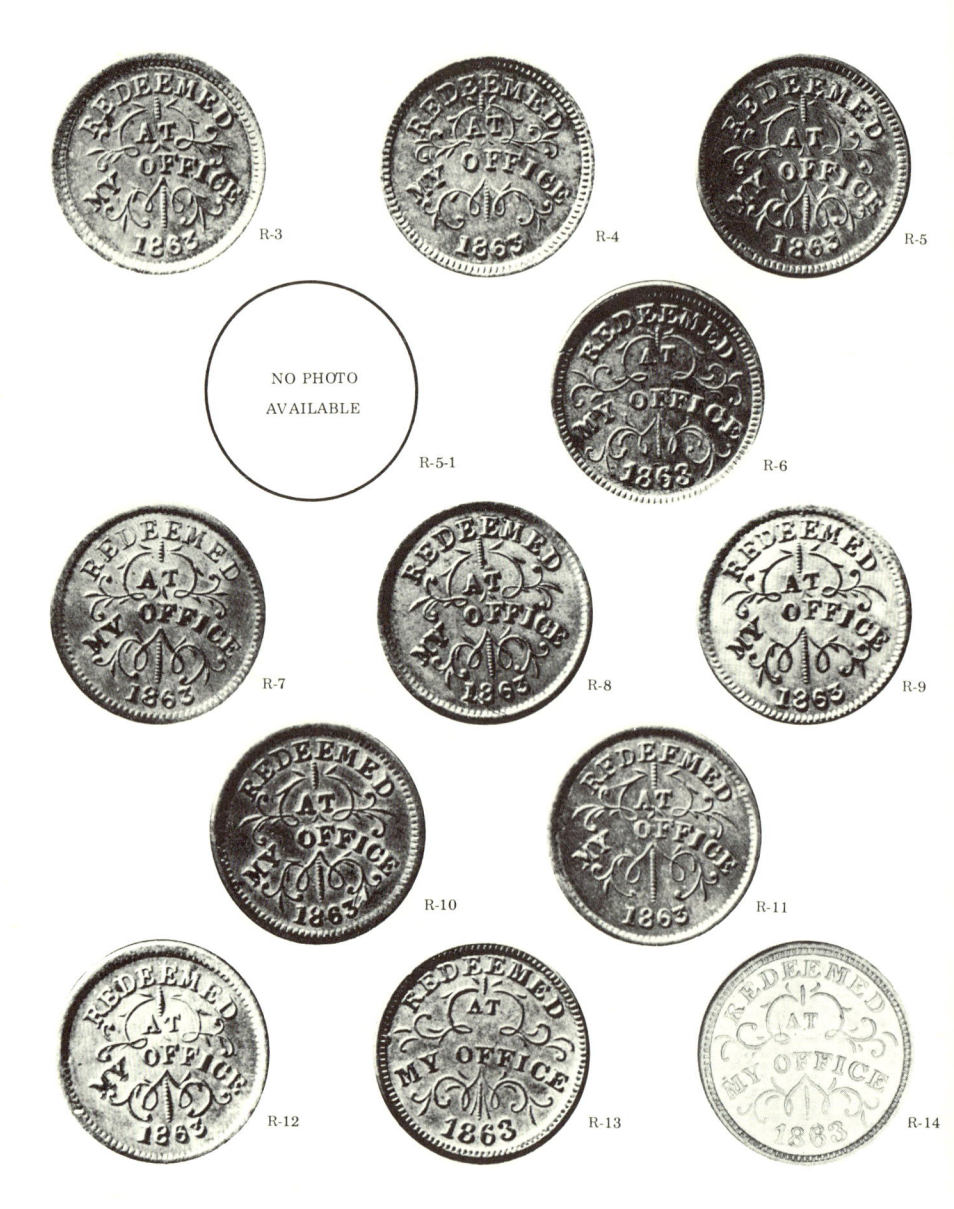

R-3 R-4 R-5

R-5-1 (NO PHOTO AVAILABLE) R-6

R-7 R-8 R-9

R-10 R-11

R-12 R-13 R-14

NEW YORK-Continued

OLIVER BOUTWELL-Reverse Dies

R-15 R-16

R-17 R-18 R-19

R-20 R-21

NUMBER	OBVERSE	REVERSE	METAL	EDGE	RARITY	H&G
890B-	OLIVER BOUTWELL/MILLER/ TROY N.Y.	REDEEMED/AT/MY OFFICE /1863	BR	PL		6351
	The following die numbers refer to the numbers used in the article in the April 1952 *Numismatist* by M and G Fuld					
890B-1b	O-1	R-1	BR	PL	R1	a
890B-2b	O-1	R-1-1	BR	PL	R6	a-1
890B-3b	O-1-1	R-1	BR	PL	R8	a-2
890B-4b	O-1	R-2	BR	PL	R1	b
890B-5b	O-2	R-3	BR	PL	R1	c
890B-6b	O-3	R-4	BR	PL	R1	d
890B-7b	O-3	R-5	BR	PL	R6	e
890B-8b	O-3	R-5-1	BR	PL	R8	e-1
890B-9b	O-4	R-6	BR	PL	R1	f
890B-9bo	Same, obverse struck over reverse	Same	BR	PL	R9	
890B-10b	O-5	R-7	BR	PL	R4	g
890B-11b	O-5	R-9	BR	PL	R7	h
890B-12b	O-6	R-8	BR	PL	R7	i
890B-13b	O-7	R-8	BR	PL	R5	j
890B-14b	O-7	R-10	BR	PL	R5	k
890B-15b	O-7	R-11	BR	PL	R5	l
890B-16b	O-7	R-12	BR	PL	R6	m
890B-10a	O-5	R-7	C	PL		g-1

NEW YORK-Continued

NUMBER	OBVERSE	REVERSE	METAL	EDGE	RARITY	H&G

TROY 890-Continued

NUMBER	OBVERSE	REVERSE	METAL	EDGE	RARITY	H&G
890B-17b	O-8	R-6	BR	PL	R5	n
890B-18b	O-8	R-13	BR	PL	R1	o
890B-19b	O-9	R-1	BR	PL	R4	p
890B-20b	O-9	R-2	BR	PL	R2	q
890B-21b	O-9	R-14	BR	PL	R6	r
890B-22b	O-9	R-15	BR	PL	R6	s
890B-23b	O-10	R-16	BR	PL	R3	t
890B-24b	O-11	R-17	BR	PL	R7	u
890B-25b	O-12	R-18	BR	PL	R6	v
890B-26b	O-13	R-5-1	BR	PL	R6	w
890B-27b	O-14	R-19	BR	PL	R7	x
890B-28b	O-15	R-6	BR	PL	R8	y
890B-29b	O-15	R-14	BR	PL	R8	z
890B	OLIVER BOUTWELL/MILLER/TROY N.Y.	REDEEMED/IN/BILLS/AT MY OFFICE	BR	PL		6352
890B-30b	O-16	R-20	BR	PL	R2	a
890B-31b	O-5	R-21	BR	PL	R1	b
890B-32b	O-13	R-21	BR	PL	R8	c
890B-33b	O-17	R-21	BR	PL	R6	d
890B-34b	O-18	R-21	BR	PL	R9	e
890B-35b	O-18-1	R-21	BR	PL	R6	e-1
890B-36b	Reverse of 890B	Incuse of obverse	BR	PL	R10	
890B-37b	O-3 (See Photo)	Incuse of Patriotic D6 #307	BR	PL	R10	

890C-1h	FRED. A. PLUM./1/CENT	GOODYEAR/INDIA RUBBER/DEPOT/190/RIVER ST./TROY. N.Y.	Hard Rubber	PL	R6
890C-2h	Same	Similar, "Y" of N.Y. further from "T" of ST.	Hard Rubber	PL	R6

890D-1h	W. E. HAGAN/NO. 1/FIRST ST./TROY, N.Y.	SODA WATER/5/CENTS	Hard Rubber	PL	R6

NEW YORK-Continued

ROBINSON BALLOU-Obverse & Reverse Dies

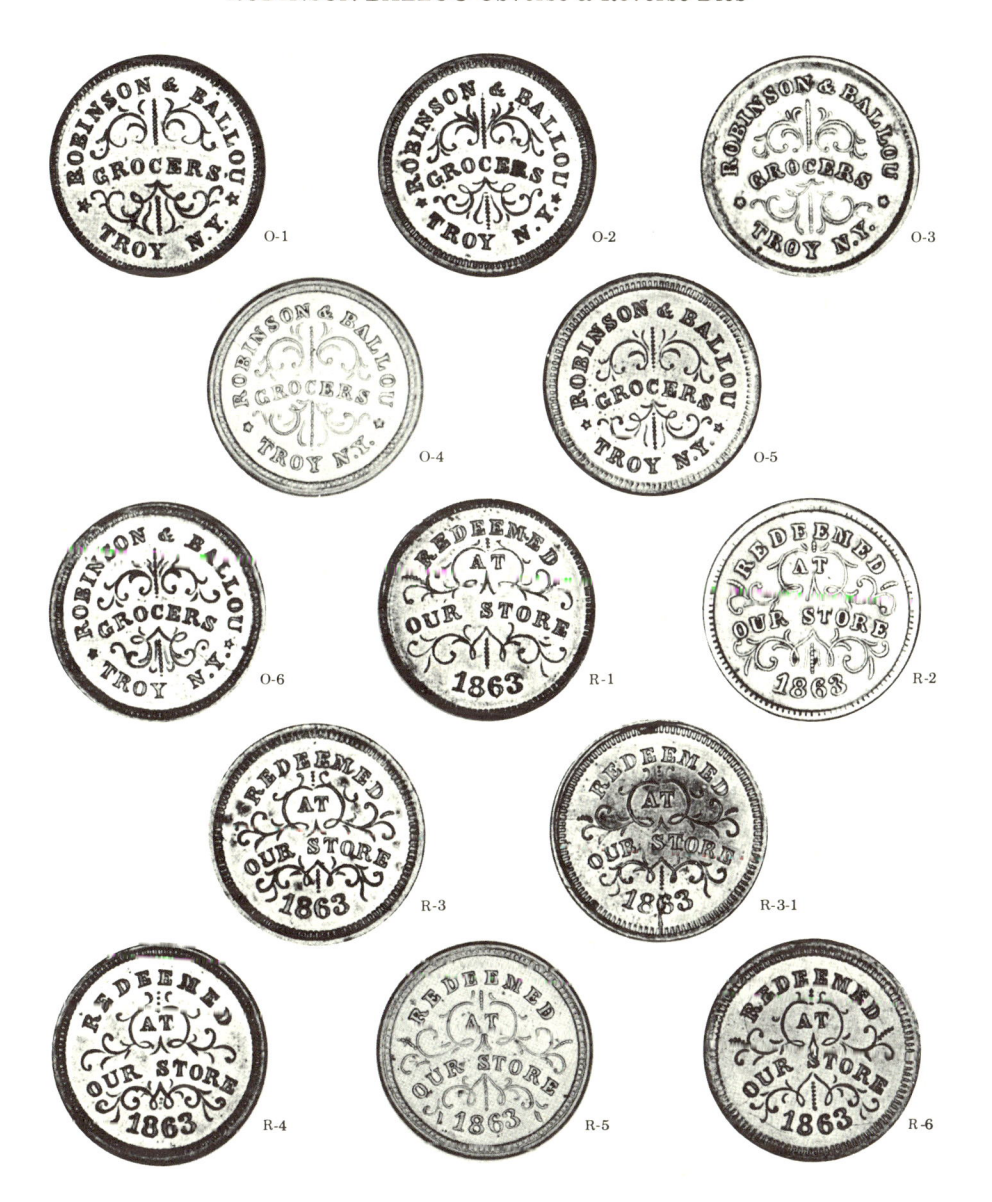

O-1 O-2 O-3

O-4 O-5

O-6 R-1 R-2

R-3 R-3-1

R-4 R-5 R-6

291

NEW YORK-Continued

NUMBER	OBVERSE	REVERSE	METAL	EDGE	RARITY	H&G
890E-	ROBINSON & BALLOU / GROCERS / TROY N.Y.	REDEEMED / AT / OUR STORE / 1863		PL		6354
	The following die numbers refer to the numbers used in the article in the January 1955 *Numismatist* by M and G Fuld					
890E-1b	O-1	R-1	BR	PL	R1	a
890E-2a	O-1	R-1	C	PL	R8	b
890E-3b	O-1	R-2	BR	PL	R5	c
890E-4b	O-2	R-3	BR	PL	R2	d
890E-5b	O-2	R-3-1	BR	PL	R3	d-1
890E-6b	O-2	R-4	BR	PL	R7	e
890E-7b	O-3	R-2	BR	PL	R4	f
890E-8b	O-4	R-5	BR	PL	R6	g
890E-9b	O-5	R-6	BR	PL	R2	h
890E-10b	O-5	R-3-1	BR	PL	R3	i
890E-11j	O-5	R-3-1	G-S	PL	R9	j
890E-12b	O-6	R-4	BR	PL	R4	k
890E-13b	Reverse of 890E	Incused of obverse	BR	PL	R10	

UTICA 905

905A

905B

905A-1a	DICKENSON COMSTOCK & CO. / DRUGGISTS / & / GROCERS / UTICA N.Y.	1266	C	PL	R5	6356
905A-1c	Same	Same	N	PL	R10	

905B-1a	I.J. KNAPP / NO 8 / LIBERTY ST / N-Y / WINES & LIQUORS.	1265	C	PL	R4	6358
905B-2a	Same	1266	C	PL	R2	6359

905C-1a	SHERWOOD & HOPSON / CHINA / EMPORIUM / UTICA N.Y.	1233	C	PL	R3	6361
905C-1b	Same	Same	BR	PL	R7	6362

NEW YORK-Continued

NUMBER	OBVERSE	REVERSE	METAL	EDGE	RARITY	H&G

WATERLOO 940

940A-1

940A-3

940A-1a	HENRY C. WELLES/DRUGGIST &/BOOK/SELLER/WATERLOO N.Y. B of BOOK opposite A of WATERLOO	1358	C	PL	R3	6364
940A-2a	Same	1367	C	PL	R5	6366
940A-3a	Same inscription, but B of BOOK opposite W of WATERLOO	Same	C	PL	R7	6367

| 940A-4a | HENRY C. WELLES/WATERLOO N.Y. | 1358 | C | PL | R9 | |

WATERTOWN 945

| 945A-1a | WATERTOWN N.Y./HART'S/ ARCADE/GALLERY/FOR BEST PICTURES | 1407 | C | PL | R3 | 6369 |
| 945A-2a | Same | 1408 | C | PL | R4 | 6370 |

NEW YORK-Continued

| NUMBER | OBVERSE | REVERSE | METAL | EDGE | RARITY | H&G |

WHITEHALL 985

985A-1a	TO PURIFY THE BLOOD, / E.W. HALL / WHITEHALL, / N.Y. / USE ATHERTON'S PILLS	TRY ATHERTON'S / WILD / CHERRY / SYRUP / FOR / COUGHS & COLDS	C	PL	R1	6372
985A-1b	Same	Same	BR	PL	R8	6373
985A-1c	Same	Same	N	PL	R9	6374

WILLIAMSVILLE 990

| 990A-1a | WILLIAMSVILLE / LEAVES / 8.A.M. / WILLIAMSVILLE / EXPRESS | WILLIAMSVILLE / LEAVES / BUFFALO / 3.P.M. / EXPRESS | C | R | R6 | 6375 |

YONKERS 995

995A-1a	E.E. HASSE / YONKERS / N.Y.	1075	C	PL	R2	6377
995A-2a	Same	1240	C	PL	R2	6378
995A-3a	Same	1257	C	PL	R4	6379

294

OHIO

NUMBER　　OBVERSE　　　　　　　　REVERSE　　　　　　　　METAL　EDGE　RARITY　H&G

ADAMSVILLE 5

5A-1a	STONER & SHROYER/DRY GOODS/ADAMSVILLE/OHIO	1048	C	PL	R3	6400

(NOTE: For a detailed discussion of these tokens, see article by W.C. MOORE 'The Stoner and Shroyer Tokens', **The Numismatist 56** No. 1 pg 1 - 10 (1943 and M.M. Schwartz 'A New View of the Stoner and Shroyer Tokens' **The Numismatist 56** No. 5, pp 337 - 339 (1943).

5A-1a1	Same, thick 2 mm.	Same	C	PL	R5	
5A-1b	Same	Same	BR	PL	R7	6401
5A-1c	Same	Same	N	PL	R7	6402
5A-1d	Same	Same	C-N	PL	R8	6403
5A-1e	Same	Same	W-M	PL	R8	6404
5A-1f	Same	Same	S	PL	R9	6405
5A-2a	Same (Baker 574)	1134	C	PL	R7	6406
5A-2a1	Same thick 2 mm.	Same	C	PL	R8	
5A-2b	Same	Same	BR	PL	R6	6407
5A-2b1	Same, thick 2mm.	Same	BR	PL	R7	
5A-2c	Same	Same	N	PL	R8	
5A-2d	Same	Same	C-N	PL	R9	
5A-2e	Same	Same	W-M	PL	R8	
5A-2f	Same	Same	S	PL	R9	6411
5A-3a	Same	1146	C	PL	R8	6413
5A-3b	Same	Same	BR	PL	R9	6414
5A-3e	Same	Same	W-M	PL	R8	6417
5A-3f	Same	Same	S	PL	R9	6418
5A-4a	Same	1150	C	PL	R9	6440
5A-4b	Same	Same	BR	PL	R9	
5A-4c	Same	Same	N	PL	R9	
5A-4e	Same	Same	W-M	PL	R9	6444
5A-4f	Same	Same	S	PL	R9	6445
5A-5a	Same	1151	C	PL	R8	6420
5A-5b	Same	Same	BR	PL	R9	6421
5A-5e	Same	Same	W-M	PL	R8	6424
5A-5f	Same	Same	S	PL	R9	6425
5A-6a	Same	1157	C	PL	R9	6452
5A-6b	Same	Same	BR	PL	R9	6453
5A-6d	Same	Same	C-N	PL	R9	
5A-6e	Same	Same	W-M	PL	R9	6456
5A-6f	Same	Same	S	PL	R9	6457
5A-7a	Same	1193	C	PL	R9	
5A-7b	Same	Same	BR	PL	R9	
5A-7c	Same	Same	N	PL	R9	6429
5A-7e	Same	Same	W-M	PL	R9	6431
5A-7f	Same	Same	S	PL	R9	
5A-8a	Same	1250	C	PL	R8	6433
5A-8b	Same	Same	BR	PL	R9	6434
5A-8d	Same	Same	C-N	PL	R9	6436
5A-8e	Same	Same	W-M	PL	R9	6437
5A-8f	Same	Same	S	PL	R9	6438

OHIO-Continued

| NUMBER | OBVERSE | REVERSE | METAL | EDGE | RARITY | H&G |

ADELPHI 10

| 10A-1a | D.H.STROUS/FLOUR/&/WOOLEN/ MANUF'RS/ADELPHI.O. | 1091 | C | PL | R7 | 6459 |
| 10A-2a | Same | 1171 | C | PL | R4 | 6460 |

ASHLAND 25

25A-1bo Same, over political token   Same   BR   R9
(NOTE: Known over Lincoln political token DeW. AL 1864-37, and also over McClellan political token DeW. GMcC 1864-27 (A.N.S.)

BARNESVILLE 50-Continued

| 50A-1a | N. PATTERSON/SADDLERY/ HARDWARE/BARNESVILLE/ OHIO. | LEATHER/AND/SHOE FINDINGS/WOOL,/SHEEP/ PELTS,/SHIPPING/FURRS,/ &C.&C. | C | PL | R5 | 6462 |

(NOTE: FURS spelled with two R's on reverse)

50B

| 50B-1a | W.A. TALBOT & SON/DRY GOODS/ BARNESVILLE/OHIO. | 1091 | C | PL | R5 | 6464 |

296

OHIO-Continued

NUMBER	OBVERSE	REVERSE	Metal	Edge	Rarity	H&G

BARNESVILLE 50-Continued

50B-2a	Same	1126	C	PL	R3	6465
50B-3a	Same	1127	C	PL	R5	6466
50B-4a	Same	1128	C	PL	R5	6467
50B-5a	Same	1229	C	PL	R7	6468
50B-6a	Same	1332	C	PL	R9	6469

BELLAIRE 60

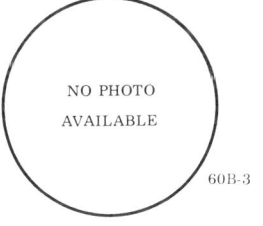

| 60A-1a | BELLAIRE/FERRY/TICKET. | 1168 | C | PL | R7 | 6471 |

(Listed as transportation token, Atwood Ohio 60A)

60B-1a	J.S.BONBRIGHT/HARDWARE/AND/STOVE/DEALER/BELLAIRE/OHIO.	1084	C	PL	R5	6473
60B-2a	Same	1123	C	PL	R4	6474
60B-3a	Same	Obverse incused	C	PL	R10	

| 60C-1a | RICHARDSON & BRO. DRY GOODS NOTIONS DRUGS AND MEDICINES BELLAIRE OHIO | 1178 | C | PL | R9 | |
| 60C-2a | Same | 1180 | C | PL | R6 | |

OHIO-Continued

NUMBER	OBVERSE	REVERSE	METAL	EDGE	RARITY	H&G

BELLAIRE 60-Continued

NUMBER	OBVERSE	REVERSE	METAL	EDGE	RARITY	H&G
60C-3a	RICHARDSON & BRO./DRY GOODS/&/GROCERIES/ BELLAIRE, O.	1180	C	PL	R9	6477
60D-1a	E.B.WINANS& CO./DRY GOODS,/ NOTIONS,/DRUGS AND/ MEDICINES,/BELLAIRE/OHIO.	1091	C	PL	R5	6480
60D-1b	Same	Same	BR	PL	R8	6481
60D-2a	Same	1166	C	PL	R6	6479
60D-3a	Same	1168	C	PL	R7	6483
60D-4a	Same	1180	C	PL	R8	6482
60D-5a	Same	1181	C	PL	R9	
60D-6b	Same	1224	BR	PL	R9	
60D-7a	Same	1310	C	PL	R8	6484

BELLEVUE 65

NUMBER	OBVERSE	REVERSE	METAL	EDGE	RARITY	H&G
65A-1a	CHEAP CASH STORE/ APPLEGATE/& CO/BELLEVUE, O.	1181	C	PL	R5	6487
65B-1a	P. BRADY,/DEALER/IN/ STOVES, TIN/AND HOUSE/ FURNISHING/GOODS,/ BELLEVUE, OHIO.	1122	C	PL	R7	6489
65B-1d	Same	Same	C-N	PL	R10	
65B-2a	Same	1300	C	PL	R8	6490
65B-3a	P. BRADY/DEALER/IN /STOVES/TINWARE/&C./ BELLEVUE,O.	1297	C	PL	R7	6492
65B-3b	Same	Same	BR	PL	R8	6493
65B-3c	Same	Same	N	PL	R9	6494
65B-3d	Same	Same	C-N	PL	R9	6495
65B-3e	Same	Same	W-M	PL	R9	6496
65B-3do	Same, over C-N cent (A.N.S.)	Same	C-N	PL	R10	
65B-3g	Same (A.N.S.)	Same	L	PL	R10	
65B-4g	Same (A.N.S.)	Blank	L	PL	R10	

OHIO-Continued

NUMBER	OBVERSE	REVERSE	METAL	EDGE	RARITY	H&G

BELLEVUE 65-Continued

| 65C-1a | C.A.WILLARD / DRY GOODS / BELLEVUE,O. | 1127 | C | PL | R6 | 6498 |

BELMONT 70

| 70A-1a | O.C.METCALF / DRY GOODS / BELMONT / OHIO | 1090 | C | PL | R8 | 6501 |

BEREA 74

74A-1a	D.E.STEARNS,BEREA, O above. Grindstone in center, 1863 below.	GRINDSTONES / MOUNTED / WITH PATENT / ADJUSTABLE REST FOR / GRINDING / ALL SIZES / HARVESTER KNIVES	C	R	R9	6503
74A-1a1	Same	Same	C	PL	R3	6502
74A-1b	Same	Same	BR	R	R9	6505
74A-1b1	Same	Same	BR	PL	R8	6504
74A-1d	Same	Same	C-N	R	R10	

299

OHIO-Continued

NUMBER	OBVERSE	REVERSE	METAL	EDGE	RARITY	H&G

BEREA 74-Continued

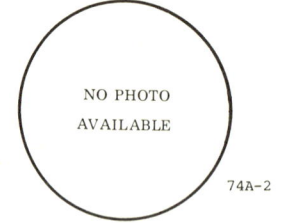

74A-2,  74A-3,  74A-11

74A-2a	Same	FAMILY/&/SHOP/REAPER/ &MOWER/MOUNTED/ GRINDSTONES	C	R	R9	6506
74A-3a	Same	Similar, but SHOP reads SHIP	C	R	R7	
74A-3a1	Same	Same	C	PL	R9	6507
74A-4a	Same	1018	C	R	R9	
74A-4d	Same	Same	C-N	R	R10	
74A-5a	Same	1019	C	R	R9	6509
74A-6a	Same	1037	C	R	R9	
74A-7a	Same	1042	C	R	R8	6511
74A-7b	Same	Same	BR	R	R9	6512
74A-8a	Same	1047	C	R	R9	
74A-9d	Same	1069	C-N	R	R10	6508
74A-10a	Same	1203	C	PL	—	6510

(NOTE: There is considerable doubt that this piece (74A-10a) exists.)

74A-11a	D.E.STEARN BEREA,OHIO above Grindstone in center, 1863 below.	Same as rev Ohio 74A-1a	C	PL	R7	6513
74A-12a	Same	Same as obv. Ohio 74A-1a	C	PL	R9	6514
74A-13a	Same	1046	C	R	R9	
74A-14a	Rev. Ohio 74A-3a	Same	C	R	R8	

(NOTE: Also to be listed as Patriotic Civil War Token.)

| 74A-15a | Same | 1047 | C | R | R10 | |

(NOTE: Also to be listed as Patriotic Civil War Token.)

| 74A-16a | STEARNS BEREA, O above grindstone in center, 1863 below | Rev of Ohio 74A-1a | C | PL | R9 | |

BEVERLY 76

| 76A-1a | P.BURKHOLTER/DEALER/IN /GROCERIES/PROVISIONS/ CONFECTIONARY/AND/ PRODUCE,/BEVERLY,/OHIO. | 1082 | C | PL | R5 | 6516 |

(NOTE: T in BURKHOLTER reengraved over a D. The uncorrected piece may exist.)

OHIO-Continued

NUMBER	OBVERSE	REVERSE	METAL	EDGE	RARITY	H&G

BIRMINGHAM 79

| 79A-1a | CRAIG & FOY/DRY GOODS/ BIRMINGHAM/OHIO | 1082 | C | PL | R6 | 6518 |
| 79A-2a | Same | 1089 | C | PL | R4 | 6519 |

BRYAN 100

| 100A-1a | JEFF MILLER/DEALER/IN/ HARDWARE,/BRYAN,/OHIO. | 1326 | C | PL | R3 | 6521 |
| 100A-1d | Same | Same | C-N | PL | R9 | |

100B-1a	E.G.SELBY & CO./DEALERS/IN/ HARDWARE/BRYAN,/OHIO.	STEREOSCOPIC/PICTURES/ AND/INSTRUMENTS/FOR/SALE/ P.O.BOX 2566	C	PL	R9	6523
100B-2a	Same	1334	C	PL	R4	6524
100B-3a	Rev. Ohio 100B-1a	W.K.LANPHEAR above, CINCINNATI below. MANU'FR/ OF/METALIC/CARDS in wreath. Obv. Ohio 165CY-1)	C	PL	R7	7405
100B-3b	Same	Same	BR	PL	R7	7406
100B-4a	Same	1346	C	PL	R8	
100B-3d	Same (H-R 1715)	Same	C-N	PL	R10	

OHIO-Continued

NUMBER	OBVERSE	REVERSE	METAL	EDGE	RARITY	H&G

BRYAN 100-Continued

| 100B-5a | GOOD FOR ONE/CENT/IN GOODS/AT/E.G.SELBY S/STORE | 1122 | C | PL | R6 | 6526 |
| 100B-6a | Same | 1228 | C | PL | R5 | 6527 |

CADIZ 110A

110A   110B

110A-1a	G B BARRETT/DEALER/IN/ WATCHES/CLOCKS/JEWELRY/ FANCY GOODS/CADIZ,O.	1018	C	R	R8	
100A-1a1	Same	Same	C	PL	R9	
110A-2a	Same	1019	C	R	R9	6529
110A-3a	Same	1025	C	R	R7	6530
110A-3a1	Same	Same	C	PL	R9	
110A-4a	Same	1028	C	PL	R9	
110A-5a	Same	1042	C	R	R6	6531
110A-5b	Same	Same	BR	R	R7	6532
110A-5i	Same	Same	Z	R	R9	
110A-6a	Same	1046	C	R	R9	6533
110A-7a	Same	1047	C	R	R9	
110A-7d	Same	Same	C-N	R	R10	
110A-8d	Same	1069	C-N	R	R10	

(NOTE: Pieces listed as H&G 6534 thru 6536 with rev. 1178, 1180 and 1181 resp. are apparently non-existant and will not be listed.)

110B-1a	J.M.ROBINSON/DEALER/IN/ HARDWARE/STOVES/FIRE FRONTS&C./CADIZ,O.	1018	C	R	R6	6539
110B-1a1	Same	Same	C	PL	R9	
110B-1d	Same	Same	C-N	R	R10	
110B-2a	Same	1025	C	R	R6	6540
110B-3a	Same	1042	C	R	R7	6542
110B-3b	Same	Same	BR	R	R7	6543
110B-3i	Same	Same	Z	R	R9	
110B-4a	Same	1047	C	R	R9	
110B-5d	Same	1069	C-N	R	R10	6545

302

OHIO-Continued

NUMBER	OBVERSE	REVERSE	METAL	EDGE	RARITY	H&G

CAMBRIDGE 115

115A-1 · 115A-7 · 115A-8

115A-1a	A.C.COCHRAN above. HARDWARE/DEALER on lock in center. CAMBRIDGE,O. below	1166	C	PL	R8	6547
115A-2a	Same	1178	C	PL	R4	6548
115A-3a	Same	1179	C	PL	R7	
115A-4a	Same	1180	C	PL	R7	6549
115A-5a	Same	1303	C	PL	R7	6550
	(NOTE: This piece also known double struck.)					
115A-6a	Same (Elder 9/38, Lot 326)	Blank	C	PL	R9	
115A-7a	Same	Obv. incused	C	PL	R9	
115A-8a	Same	Rev is incused Ohio 975F-1a	C	PL	R9	

115B-1a	J.J.SQUIER/DRY GOODS/ CAMBRIDGE,O.	1084	C	PL	R6	6553
115B-2a	Same	1085	C	PL	R7	
115B-3a	Same	1087	C	PL	R9	6554
115B-4a	Same	1088	C	PL	R8	6555
115B-5a	Same	1122	C	PL	R6	6556
115B-6a	Same	1126	C	PL	R3	6557
115B-7a	Same	1130	C	PL	R8	
115B-8a	Same	1166	C	PL	R9	6552
115B-9a	Same	1168	C	PL	R5	6560
115B-9b	Same	Same	BR	PL	R9	
115B-10a	Same	1179	C	PL	R7	6559
115B-11a	Same	1228	C	PL	R6	6558

OHIO-Continued

NUMBER	OBVERSE	REVERSE	METAL	EDGE	RARITY	H&G

CAMDEN 120

120A-1a	C.CHADWICK/DEALER/IN/DRY GOODS/(eagle)/CAMDEN,O.	1171	C	PL	R9	6563
120A-2a	Same	1229	C	PL	R6	6562
120B-1a	J.P.FORNSHELL/GROCER/&/OYSTER/DEALER/CAMDEN,O.	1038	C	PL	R6	6565
120B-2a	Same	1042	C	R	R6	6566
120B-2b	Same	Same	BR	R	R9	6567
120B-2i	Same	Same	Z	R	R9	
120B-3d	Same	1047	C-N	R	R10	
120B-4d	Same	1069	C-N	R	R10	

CANAAN 122

| 122A-1a | GRIMES & GRINER/DEALERS/IN/DRY GOODS/NOTIONS &C./CANAAN,/OHIO. | 1123 | C | PL | R5 | 6571 |

304

OHIO-Continued

NUMBER	OBVERSE	REVERSE	METAL	EDGE	RARITY	H&G

CANTON 125

125A-1a	J.A.MEYER/WATCHES/CLOCKS/ -&-/JEWELRY/CANTON,O.	1028	C	R	R9	
125A-1a1	Same	Same	C	PL	R5	6574
125A-2a	Same	1042	C	R	R5	6575
125A-2b	Same	Same	BR	R	R8	6576
125A-2i	Same	Same	Z	R	R9	
125A-3a	Same	1045	C	PL	R9	6573
125A-4a	Same	1046	C	R	R9	6577
125A-5a	Same	1047	C	R	R8	
125A-5d	Same	Same	C-N	R	R10	
125A-6d	Same	1069	C-N	R	R10	6578
125B-1a	C.OBERLY,/DEALER/IN/ GROCERIES,/PROVISIONS,/ CONFECTIONERY,/WOODEN &WILLOW/WARE,/CANTON, OHIO	1122	C	PL	R6	6580
125B-2a	Same	1346	C	PL	R7	6581
125B-2b	Same	Same	BR	PL	R9	6582
125B-2d	Same	Same	C-N	PL	R10	

CENTERVILLE 135

135A-1a	JAMES MATHEWS/DEALER/IN/ DRY GOODS,/GROCERIES/&C./ CENTERVILLE,O.	1085	C	PL	R6	6584
135A-1b	Same	Same	BR	PL	R7	6585
135A-2a	Same	1227	C	PL	R6	6586
135A-2b	Same	Same	BR	PL	R8	

305

OHIO-Continued

NUMBER	OBVERSE	REVERSE	METAL	EDGE	RARITY	H&G

CHESTERVILLE 150

150A 150B

150A-1a	BARTLETT GOBLE & CO/ STAPLE & FANCY/DRY/ GOODS/GROCERIES/&C./ CHESTERVILLE,O.	1046	C	R	R6	6588
150A-1b	Same	Same	BR	R	R9	6589
150A-1d	Same	Same	C-N	R	R10	
150A-1i	Same	Same	Z	R	R9	
150A-2a	Same	1047	C	R	R9	6592
150A-2d	Same	Same	C-N	R	R10	
150B-1a	MILES & SPERRY/DEALERS IN/ DRY/GOODS/GROCERIES/&C./ CHESTERVILLE,O.	1046	C	R	R7	6594
150B-1a1	Same	Same	C	PL	R9	
150B-1b	Same	Same	BR	R	R9	6595
150B-1i	Same	Same	Z	R	R9	
150B-2a	Same	1047	C	R	R9	
150B-2d	Same	Same	C-N	R	R10	

CHILLICOTHE 160

160A 160B

160A-1a	JOHN BOHM/CHILLICOTHE,O. (Elder Sale 9/38 Lot 361)	1391	C	PL	R9	
160A-1b	Same	Same	BR	R	R8	
160A-1b1	Same	Same	BR	PL	R9	6597
160B-1a	JNO.F.BIER & BRO./DEALERS/ IN/GROCERIES/BOOTS & SHOES/ 101 PAINT STREET/CHILLICOTHE, O.	1084	C	PL	R7	6600
160B-2a	Same	1123	C	PL	R4	6601
160B-3a	Same	1166	C	PL	R9	6599
160B-4a	Same	1178	C	PL	R9	6602

OHIO-Continued

NUMBER	OBVERSE	REVERSE	METAL	EDGE	RARITY	H&G

CHILLICOTHE 160-Continued

| 160C-1b | JAS.DRISCOLL/CHILLICOTHE, O. | 1391 | BR | R | R8 | |
| 160D-1a | H.KEIM/GROCER/COR./ FOURTH & HICKORY/STS./ CHILLICOTHE. O. | 1171 | C | PL | R8 | 6604 |

| 160E-1b | PHOENIX HOUSE/NO.135/ SECOND ST./M.KIRSCH/ PROP./CHILLICOTHE,O. | GOOD FOR/5/CENTS/AT/M KIRSCH'S/BAR | BR | R | R9 | |

(NOTE: This piece is quite questionable, and is probably after 1870).

160F-1a	A.S.KRAMER/DEALER/IN/ CONFECTIONERY,/TOYS/ NOTIONS & C/ALLEN/BLOCK/ PAINT ST./CHILLICOTHE,O.	1126	C	PL	R9	6607
160F-2a	Same	1166	C	PL	R8	6606
160F-3a	Same	1227	C	PL	R6	6608

OHIO-Continued

NUMBER	OBVERSE	REVERSE	METAL	EDGE	RARITY	H&G

CHILLICOTHE 160-Continued

160G-1a	RUFUS MOTTER,/BOOK,/ PERIODICAL,/NEWS,CIGAR,/ TOBACCO/-AND-/-NOTION-/ DEALER,/CHILLICOTHE,O.	1125	C	PL	R5	6610
160G-2a	Same	1176	C	PL	R9	6611
160G-3a	Same	1177	C	PL	R7	6612
160G-4a	Same	1180	C	PL	R7	6613
160G-5a	Same	1322	C	PL	R3	6614
160G-5b	Same	Same	BR	PL	R9	6615
160G-6a	Same	1323	C	PL	R9	6617
160G-7a	Same	1324	C	PL	R4	6619
160G-7d	Same	Same	C-N	PL	R10	6621
160H-1a	T.RUPEL & CO/GROCERS/NO.52/ 4TH ST/CHILLICOTHE O.	1125	C	PL	R5	6623
160H-2a	Same	1178	C	PL	R9	6624
160H-3a	Same	1180	C	PL	R9	6625
160H-4a	Same	1181	C	PL	R4	6626
160H-5a	Same	1337	C	PL	R9	6627
160I-1a	W M.SOSMAN/BAKER/&/ GROCER/CHILLICOTHE/ OHIO.	1125	C	PL	R4	6630
160I-2a	Same	1126	C	PL	R9	6631
160I-2d	Same	Same	C-N	PL	R9	6632
160I-3a	Same	1166	C	PL	R9	
160J-1a	A.WALLACE,/NEWS/DEPOT,/ TOBACCO,/CIGARS/&/NOTIONS,/ CHILLICOTHE,O.	1168	C	PL	R5	6636
160J-2a	Same	1229	C	PL	R6	6635
160J-3a	Same	1323	C	PL	R5	6637
160J-4a	Same	1324	C	PL	R9	6638

OHIO-Continued

NUMBER	OBVERSE	REVERSE	METAL	EDGE	RARITY	H&G

CINCINNATI 165

| | | 165A | | 165B | | 165C |

165A-1a	M.ADELTA/570 CEN/AVENUE/ CINCINNATI	1026	C	PL	R4	
165A-2a	Same	1029	C	PL	R7	
165A-3a	Same	1033	C	PL	R7	
165A-4a	Same	1036	C	PL	R3	6645
165A-5a	Same	1039	C	PL	R4	6646
165A-6a	Same	1042	C	R	R6	6641
165A-6b	Same	Same	BR	R	R7	6642
165A-6i	Same	Same	Z	R	R9	6643
165A-7a	Same	1047	C	R	R9	6644
165A-7d	Same	Same	C-N	R	R10	
165B-1a	W.ALENBURG,/NO 622/ CENTRAL/AVENUE/MEAT STORE (Marvin 726i)	1386	C	PL	R7	6649
165C-1a	B.B.ARMSTRONG/BLACK/BEAR/ HOTEL/9'& SYCAMORE/STS./ CINCINNATI	1018	C	PL	R8	
165C-2a	Same	1019	C	PL	R7	
165C-3a	Same	1022	C	PL	R6	6656
165C-4a	Same	1042	C	R	R6	6651
165C-4b	Same	Same	BR	R	R8	6652
165C-4i	Same	Same	Z	R	R9	
165C-5d	Same	1046	C-N	R	R10	6654
165C-6d	Same	1069	C-N	R	R10	
165C-7a	Same (H-R 1602)	Rev. of 165FN-1a	C	R	R10	

| 165D-1b | F.M.ASHTON/WATCHCHECK | MURDOCK & SPENCER/139/W' FIFTH/STREET/CINCINNATI (Obv. Ohio 165DZ-1) | BR | PL | R8 | |

309

OHIO-Continued

NUMBER　　OBVERSE　　　　　　　REVERSE　　　　　　　　METAL　EDGE　RARITY　H&G

CINCINNATI 165-Continued

Number	Obverse	Reverse	Metal	Edge	Rarity	H&G
165E-1i	GRUHLERS/GARDEN/CONCERT/ SALOON/470 VINE ST./F.ARNOLD	1019	Z	PL	R9	
165E-2a	Same	1021	C	PL	R5	6660
165E-3a	Same	1038	C	PL	R3	6662
165E-4a	Same	1042	C	R	R5	6663
165E-4b	Same	Same	BR	R	R6	6664
165E-4i	Same	Same	Z	R	R8	6665
165E-5a	Same	1047	C	R	R9	6667
165E-5d	Same	Same	C-N	R	R10	6668
165E-6a	Same	1192	C	PL	R7	6658
165E-7d	Same (H-R 1603)	1069	C-N	R	R10	
165F-1a	J.S.AUSTIN/DEALER/IN/ STAPLE & FANCY/GROCERIES/ 5TH & ELM/STS./CINCINNATI	1009	C	PL	R3	6670
165F-1i	Same	Same	Z	R	R9	
165F-2a	Same	1019	C	PL	R8	
165F-2b	Same	Same	BR	PL	R9	
165F-3a	Same	1042	C	R	R7	6672
165F-3b	Same	Same	BR	R	R7	6673
165F-3i	Same	Same	Z	R	R8	6674
165F-4a	Same	1047	C	R	R9	
165F-4d	Same	Same	C-N	R	R10	6676
165G-1a	H.AVERMAAT/DEALER/IN/ BUTTER/&/EGGS/315 FINDLAY ST/CINCINNATI	1008	C	PL	R2	6678
165G-2a	Same	1019	C	PL	R8	6680
165G-2b	Same	Same	BR	PL	R9	
165G-3a	Same	1020	C	PL	R3	6681
	(NOTE: Also comes with broken reverse die.)					
165G-4a	Same	1038	C	PL	R7	
165G-5a	Same	1042	C	R	R7	6683
165G-5b	Same	Same	BR	R	R7	6684
165G-5i	Same	Same	Z	R	R9	
165G-6a	Same	1047	C	R	R9	6685
165G-6d	Same	Same	C-N	R	R10	6686

OHIO-Continued

NUMBER	OBVERSE	REVERSE	METAL	EDGE	RARITY	H&G

CINCINNATI 165-Continued

165H-1a	S.BACCIOCCO/CONFECTIONARY/ AND/ICE/CREAM/SALOON/176 FIFTH ST.	1131	C	PL	R7	6689
165H-1f	Same (H-R 1610)	Same	S	PL	R10	
165H-2a	Same (H-R 1608)	1172	C	PL	R8	6688
165H-3a	Same	1274	C	PL	R5	6690

165I-1a	E.BACHER in script on plain planchet	GOOD/FOR/FIVE CENTS/IN/ REFRESHMENTS/UNION SALOON	C	PL	R6	6692
165I-1b	Same	Same	BR	PL	R7	6693
165I-2a	Same	1348	C	PL	R9	6694
165I-2b	Same	Same	BR	PL	R9	6695
165I-1d	Same (Kreisberg 10/66 Lot 770)	Same	C-N	PL	R10	

165J-1a	R.BATHGATE/DEALER/IN/ BOOTS,SHOES/&/GROCERIES/ 198 W.6'ST./CINCINNATI	1008	C	PL	R5	6696
165J-2a	Same	1019	C	PL	R8	
165J-3a	Same	1042	C	R	R7	6698
165J-3b	Same	Same	BR	R	R8	6699
165J-3i	Same	Same	Z	R	R9	
165J-4a	Same	1047	C	R	R9	
165J-4d	Same	Same	C-N	R	R10	6701
165J-1a1	Same	Same	C	R	R10	

311

OHIO-Continued

NUMBER	OBVERSE	REVERSE	METAL	EDGE	RARITY	H&G

CINCINNATI 165-Continued

165K-1a	JOHN BAUER/29/FRONT/ST. CINCINNATI	1022	C	PL	R6	6704
165K-2a	Same	1026	C	PL	R4	
165K-3a	Same	1029	C	PL	R6	
165K-4a	Same	1030	C	PL	R4	6703
165K-5a	Same	1031	C	PL	R4	6705
165K-6a	Same	1033	C	PL	R5	
165K-7a	Same	1035	C	PL	R5	
165K-8a	Same	1042	C	R	R7	6707
165K-8b	Same	Same	BR	R	R7	6708
165K-8i	Same	Same	Z	R	R8	
165K-9a	Same	1043	C	PL	R6	
165K-10a	Same	1047	C	R	R9	
165K-10d	Same	Same	C-N	R	R10	6710

165L-1a	C.H.BEER'S/SALOON/55/BROADWAY/CINT'I.O. (Three stars on sides)	ALSO/CUTLERY,/NOTIONS/& C	C	PL	R2	6712
165L-1e	Same (thick 3mm.)	Same	W-M	PL	R9	
165L-2a	Same	1124	C	PL	R8	6713
165L-2d	Same (H-R 1616)	Same	C-N	PL	R9	6714
165L-3a	Same	1170	C	PL	R8	6721
165L-3a1	Same, thick 2½mm.	Same	C	PL	R9	
165L-4a	Same	1176	C	PL	R5	6715
165L-5a	Same	1177	C	PL	R5	6717
165L-5d	Same	Same	C-N	PL	R9	6718
165L-6a	Same	1295	C	PL	R9	6719
165L-7a	Same	1331	C	PL	R9	6720
165L-8b	C.H.BEERS/REVOLVERS/CUTLERY & NOTIONS/55/BROADWAY/CINCINNATI, OHIO.	Blank	BR	PL	R7	
165L-1d	Same (H-R 1615)	Same	C-N	PL	R10	
165L-9b	Same	Obv of 165DZ-1	BR	PL	R9	

OHIO-Continued

NUMBER	OBVERSE	REVERSE	METAL	EDGE	RARITY	H&G

CINCINNATI 165-Continued

165M-1a	TEETH/EXTRACTED/WITHOUT/PAIN,/BY/B.P.BELKNP.	1346	C	PL	R6	6723

(NOTE: Probable error in spelling, as believe should be BELKNAP.)

165N-1a	DR. BENNETT'S/MEDICINES/CURE/SICKNESS/& PAIN	1124	C	PL	R7	6725
165N-1d	Same (H-R 1619)	Same	C-N	PL	R9	6726
165N-2a	Same	1176	C	PL	R5	6727
165N-2g	Same	Same	L	PL	R10	
165N-3a	Same	1295	C	PL	R8	6728
165N-4a	Same	1331	C	PL	R9	6729
165N-5a	Same	Obv. incused	C	PL	R9	6730
165N-6a	Same	J.W.FITZGOOD/COR/FIFTH/AND/BROADWAY/CINCINNATI (Obv. Ohio 165AV)	C	PL	R10	
165N-7a	Same	200,000/FAMILIES/NOW/USE/DR. BENNETTS/MEDICINES	C	PL	R5	6732
165N-7d	Same (H-R 1622)	Same	C-N	PL	R9	6733

313

OHIO-Continued

NUMBER	OBVERSE	REVERSE	METAL	EDGE	RARITY	H&G

CINCINNATI 165-Continued

165N-8
165N-8aa 
165N-9 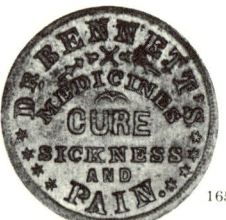
165N-10 
165N-20 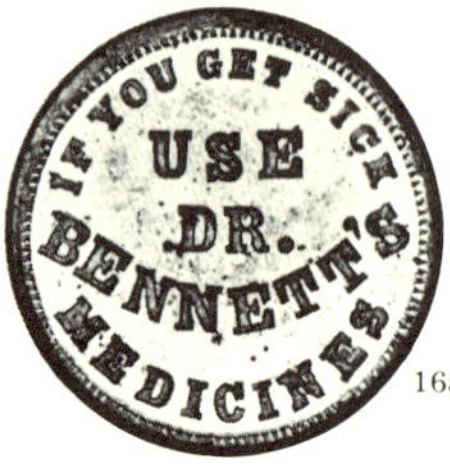

165 N-8a	200,000/FAMILIES/NOW/ USE/DR. BENNETTS/MEDICINES (Same as Rev. Ohio 165N-7a)	1290	C	PL	R4	6734
165 N8aa	Same	Same as obv. Ohio 165CY-103	C	PL	R10	
165N-9a	DR BENNETT'S/MEDICINES/ CURE/SICKNESS/AND/PAIN.	1352	C	PL	R1	6735
165N-9aa	Same	Obv incused	C	PL	R9	
165N-10a	500000/PERSONS/ANNUALLY/ CURED/BY/DR BENNETT'S/MEDICINES	1018	C	R	R8	
165N-11a	Same	1023	C	PL	R4	
165N-12a	Same	1028	C	PL	R2	6738
165N-13a	Same	1034	C	PL	R2	6739
165N-14a	Same	1038	C	PL	R5	
165N-15a	Same	1042	C	R	R7	6743
165N-15b	Same	Same	BR	R	R8	6744
165N-15i	Same	Same	Z	R	R9	6745
165N-16a	Same	1044	C	PL	R5	6741
165N-17a	Same	1045	C	PL	R8	6736
165N-18a	Same	1047	C	R	R8	
165N-19a	Same	IF YOU GET SICK/USE/DR. BENNETT'S/MEDICINES	C	R	R8	6748
165N-19a1	Same	Same	C	PL	R2	6747
165N-19d	Same (H-R 1625)	Same	C-N	R	R10	
165-N20a	IF YOU GET SICK/USE/DR./ BENNETT'S/MEDICINES (Rev. Ohio 165N-19)	1026	C	PL	R3	6751
165-N-21a	Same	1033	C	PL	R6	
165-N-22a	Same	1034	C	PL	R4	6753
165-N-23a	Same	1039	C	PL	R6	6752
165N-24a	Same	1042	C	R	R6	6755
165N-24b	Same	Same	BR	R	R6	6756
165N-24i	Same	Same	Z	PL	R9	
165N-25a	Same	1045	C	PL	R4	6750
165N-26a	Same	1047	C	R	R9	6758
165N-26d	Same	Same	C-N	R	R10	6759
165N-18d	Same	Same	C-N	R	R10	

OHIO-Continued

| NUMBER | OBVERSE | REVERSE | METAL | EDGE | RARITY | H&G |

CINCINNATI 165-Continued

165O-1a	C.H.BENNETT above — sheaf of wheat in center STEAM to left — BAKERY to right — 89 COURT ST below.	1024	C	PL	R9	
165O-2a	Same	1029	C	PL	R2	6761
165O-3a	Same	1030	C	PL	R8	6762
165O-4a	Same	1033	C	PL	R6	
165O-5a	Same	1034	C	PL	R8	
165O-6a	Same	1035	C	PL	R7	
165O-7a	Same	1036	C	PL	R3	6764
165O-8a	Same	1037	C	PL	R9	6763
165O-9a	Same	1042	C	R	R7	6766
165O-9b	Same	Same	BR	R	R7	6767
165O-9i	Same	Same	Z	R	R9	6768
165O-10a	Same	1047	C	R	R9	
165O-10d	Same	Same	C-N	R	R9	
165O-11d	Same (H-R 1627)	1069	C-N	R	R10	
165O-12a	Same (Dorge 3/74 Lot 530)	1022	G	PL	R9	

165P-1a	FRANK BERESFORD above — square and compass in center CINCINATI below. (Marvin 728)	BUY YOUR/MEAT/OF/ FRANK/BERESFORD/IN/ MARKET	C	R	R9	6771
165P-1a1	Same	Same	C	PL	R2	6770
165P-2a	Same	1018	C	R	R9	
165P-3a	Same (Marvin 729)	1042	C	R	R5	6772
165P-3b	Same	Same	BR	R	R7	6773
165P-3i	Same	Same	Z	R	R8	6774
165P-4a	Same	1047	C	R	R8	
165P-5a	Same	BLANK	C	PL	R9	
165P-6a	Rev. Ohio 165P-1	1019	C	R	R9	
165P-7a	Same	1042	C	R	R7	6776
165P-7b	Same	Same	BR	R	R8	6777
165P-7i	Same	Same	Z	R	R9	6778
165P-8a	Same	1047	C	R	R9	
165P-8d	Same	Same	C-N	R	R10	6780

315

OHIO-Continued

NUMBER	OBVERSE	REVERSE	METAL	EDGE	RARITY	H&G

CINCINNATI 165-Continued

165Q-1b DUE THE BEARER/25/CENTS/ JOHN STANTON/STAMP/BRAND/ BR PL R7
IN/BEER/F.Billiods/BREWER CUTTER/CINCINNATI

165R-1

165R-8

165R-1a	LEW.BOMAN/SETS A/LUNCH/ AT THE/BRIGHTON/HOTEL/AT 10 O'CLOCK/SUNDAY	1009	C	PL	R6	6784
165R-1b	Same	Same	BR	PL	R7	
165R-1i	Same	Same	Z	PL	R9	
165R-2a	Same	1019	C	PL	R8	
165R-2b	Same	Same	BR	PL	R8	
165R-3a	Same	1036	C	PL	R6	6786
165R-4a	Same	1042	C	R	R7	6788
165R-4b	Same	Same	BR	R	R8	6789
165R-4i	Same	Same	Z	R	R9	6790
167R-5a	Same	1045	C	PL	R8	6783
165R-6a	Same	1047	C	R	R9	
165R-6d	Same	Same	C-N	R	R10	6791
165R-7a	Same	1288	C	PL	R6	6785
165R-7b	Same	Same	BR	PL	R8	
165R-7i	Same	Same	Z	PL	R8	
165R-8a	I PROMISE/TO PAY/5/CENTS/ LEW.BOMAN	1009	C	PL	R9	
165R-9b	Same	1018	BR	PL	R9	
165R-10d	Same	1046	C-N	R	R10	
165R-11a	Same	1192	C	R	R7	6795
165R-11a1	Same (very thick planchet 3mm)	Same	C	R	R8	
165R-11a2	Same	Same	C	PL	R9	6798
165R-11b	Same	Same	BR	R	R8	6796
165R-11i	Same	Same	Z	R	R9	6797
165R-11i1	Same	Same	Z	PL	R9	6800
165R-12a	Same	1289	C	R	R9	6794
165R-12a1	Same	Same	C	PL	R6	6793
165R-12Ad	Same	1069	C-N	PL	R10	

316

OHIO-Continued

NUMBER	OBVERSE	REVERSE	METAL	EDGE	RARITY	H&G

CINCINNATI 165-Continued

165R-13a	I PROMISE/TO PAY/10/CENTS/LEW.BOMAN	1009	C	PL	R9	
165R-14a	Same	1019	C	PL	R9	
165R-14b	Same	Same	BR	PL	R9	
165R-15a	Same	1030	C	PL	R9	
165R-16d	Same	1047	C-N	R	R10	6810
165R-17a	Same	1289	C	R	R8	6808
165R-17a1	Same	Same	C	PL	R9	6807
165R-17b	Same	Same	BR	R	R9	
165R-17b1	Same	Same	BR	PL	R9	
165R-18a	Same	1393	C	R	R8	6802
165R-18a1	Same	Same	C	PL	R9	6805
165R-18b	Same	Same	BR	R	R8	6803
165R-18i	Same	Same	Z	R	R9	6804
165R-19a	1289	1018	C	R	R9	6814
165R-19a1	Same	Same	C	PL	R9	6813
165R-20a	Same	1042	C	R	R7	6816
165R-20b	Same	Same	BR	R	R8	6817
165R-20i	Same	Same	Z	R	R9	6818
165R-21a	Same	1047	C	R	R9	6819
165R-21d	Same	Same	C-N	R	R10	6820
165R-22d	Same	1069	C-N	R	R10	

165S-1a	A.BRUGGEMANN/GROCER/COR.LIBERTY/&WALNUT.	1056	C	PL	R9	
165S-2a	Same (Marvin 726b)	1386	C	PL	R4	6824
165T-1a	J.CAMPBELL/GROCER/&/PROVISION/DEALER/481 JOHN.ST.	1023	C	PL	R5	6827
165T-2a	Same	1028	C	PL	R8	6828
165T-3a	Same	1030	C	PL	R9	
165T-4a	Same	1034	C	PL	R5	6829

317

OHIO-Continued

NUMBER	OBVERSE	REVERSE	METAL	EDGE	RARITY	H&G

CINCINNATI 165-Continued

165T-5a	Same	1042	C	R	R7	6831
165T-5b	Same	Same	BR	R	R8	6832
165T-5i	Same	Same	Z	R	R9	
165T-6a	Same	1047	C	R	R9	
165T-6d	Same	Same	C-N	R	R10	6834
165T-7d	Same (H-R 1629)	1069	C-N	R	R10	
165T-8a	Same	C.G.BRUCE/AUTHORIZED/ WAR/CLAIM/AGENT/1863/ CLEVELAND O. (Obv. Ohio 175C)	C	PL	R9	6836

| 165U-1a | BUY YOUR COAL NOW/AT/ CENTRAL/COAL OFFICE/ 56/W.FOURTH ST. CIN'T. | Around, GOOD FOR/ONE CENTS WORTH OF COAL. Portrait in center, facing left. | C | PL | R8 | 6838 |

165V-1d	CHAMBERLAIN BROS around border 1/GLASS/SODA/WATER in center.	1046	C-N	R	R10	
165V-2a	Same	1047	C	R	R9	
165V-2d	Same	Same	C-N	R	R10	6843

318

OHIO-Continued

NUMBER	OBVERSE	REVERSE	METAL	EDGE	RARITY	H&G

CINCINNATI 165-Continued

NUMBER	OBVERSE	REVERSE	METAL	EDGE	RARITY	H&G
165V-3a	Same	1311	C	R	R9	6842
165V-4a	Same	1312	C	R	R8	6840
165V-4b	Same	Same	BR	R	R7	6841
165V-4i	Same	Same	Z	R	R9	
165V-5a	Same	ARTIC GOOD FOR 1 GLASS SODA WATER	C	R	R9	

165W

165W-9

NUMBER	OBVERSE	REVERSE	METAL	EDGE	RARITY	H&G
165W-1a	CIN. & COV. FERRY COMPANY (Atwood Ohio 165A)	1022	C	PL	R3	
165W-2a	Same	1026	C	PL	R4	6852
165W-3a	Same	1033	C	PL	R8	
165W-4a	Same	1036	C	PL	R3	6850
165W-5a	Same	1039	C	PL	R5	
165W-6a	Same (Atwood Ohio 165B)	1042	C	R	R7	6845
165W-6b	Same (Atwood Ohio 165C)	Same	BR	R	R8	6846
165W-6i	Same	Same	Z	R	R9	
165W-7a	Same (Atwood Ohio 165D)	1047	C	R	R9	
165W-7d	Same (Atwood Ohio 165E)	Same	C-N	R	R10	6848
165W-9a	Same	ROBERT WRIGHT DRY GOODS 397 CEN AVENUE (obv Ohio 165GS-1)	C	PL	R10	

NUMBER	OBVERSE	REVERSE	METAL	EDGE	RARITY	H&G
165X-1a	CITY HOISERY STORE/LADIES/ &/ GENTS/FURNISHING/&/ FANCY GOODS/NO.12 W.5'ST	1021	C	PL	R5	6854
165X-2a	Same	1042	C	R	R6	6856
165X-2b	Same	Same	BR	R	R7	6857
165X-2i	Same	Same	Z	R	R8	
165X-3a	Same	1046	C	R	R9	6859
165X-4a	Same	1047	C	R	R8	6860
165X-4d	Same (A.N.S.)	1047	C-N	R	R10	

OHIO-Continued

NUMBER	OBVERSE	REVERSE	METAL	EDGE	RARITY	H&G

CINCINNATI 165-Continued

165Y-1b	GOOD FOR/ONE/SHAVE/AT C.E. CLARK'S/LIGHTNING/ HAIR DYEING ROOM/NO.4/ BURNET HOUSE	1019	BR	PL	R9	6862
165Y-1i	Same	Same	Z	PL	R9	
165Y-2a	Same	1042	C	R	R6	6864
165Y-2b	Same	Same	BR	R	R7	6865
165Y-2i	Same	Same	Z	R	R9	
165Y-3a	Same	1047	C	R	R9	6868
165Y-4a	Same	1068	C	R	R9	6870
165Y-4a1	Same	Same	C	PL	R6	6872
165Y-4b	Same	Same	BR	R	R9	6871
165Y-4b1	Same	Same	BR	PL	R7	6873
165Y-5a	Same	1393	C	PL	R9	
165Y-5c	Same	Same	N	PL	R9	6875
165Y-6d	Same (Kreisberg 10/66 Lot 774)	1069	C-N	R	R10	

165Z-1a	GOOD FOR/ONE/CENT/AT/ COLE'S BAKERY	1009	C	PL	R6	6877
165Z-2a	Same	1022	C	PL	R8	
165Z-3a	Same	1026	C	PL	R8	6886
165Z-4a	Same	1031	C	PL	R9	
165Z-5a	Same	1038	C	PL	R8	6879
165Z-6a	Same	1042	C	R	R6	6880
165Z-6b	Same	1042	BR	R	R7	6881
165Z-7a	Same	1046	C	R	R9	6883
165Z-8a	Same	1047	C	R	R8	
165Z-8d	Same	Same	C-N	R	R10	6884
165Z-9a	Same	REDEEMED/IN/PAR FUNDS/ IN SUMS/OF/ONE/DOLLAR (Fuld Pat Die 473)	C	R	R9	
165Z-9a1	Same	Same	C	PL	R7	6887
165Z-9d	Same (Kreisberg 10/66 Lot 775)	Same	C-N	R	R10	
165Z-10d	Same (Kreisberg 10/66 Lot 775)	Same	C-N	R	R10	

OHIO-Continued

NUMBER	OBVERSE	REVERSE	METAL	EDGE	RARITY	H&G

CINCINNATI 165-Continued

165AA-1a	COMMISSION/BOOTS/&/SHOES/154/MAIN ST./CINCINNATI	1008	C	PL	R5	6894
165AA-2a	Same	1019	C	PL	R9	
165AA-2b	Same	Same	BR	PL	R9	
165AA-3a	Same	1042	C	R	R6	6896
165AA-3b	Same	Same	BR	R	R7	6897
165AA-3i	Same	Same	Z	R	R9	6898
165AA-4a	Same	1047	C	R	R8	
165AA-4d	Same	Same	C-N	R	R10	6999

| 165AB-1a | CONN.MUT.LIFE INS.CO./CAPITAL/OVER 6000000/DOLLARS/1864 | 1047 | C | R | R8 | 6892 |
| 165AB-1d | Same (Elder 5/39 Lot 581 | Same | C-N | R | R10 | |

321

OHIO-Continued

NUMBER	OBVERSE	REVERSE	METAL	EDGE	RARITY	H&G

CINCINNATI 165-Continued

165AC-1a	CHAS. CONROY/GROCER/&/LIQUOR/DEALER/3 & CEN. AVENUE	1026	C	PL	R4	6906
165AC-2a	Same	1039	C	PL	R7	
165AC-3a	Same	1042	C	R	R7	6901
165AC-3b	Same	Same	BR	R	R8	6902
165AC-3i	Same	Same	Z	R	R9	6903
165AC-4d	Same	1046	C-N	R	R10	6904
165AC-5a	Same	1047	C	R	R9	6905
165AC-5d	Same	Same	C-N	R	R10	

| 165AD-1a | CONSULERE/GENERI/HOMINUM/HO HI/WHANG/B.C./129374 3 stars on each side in circles | 1046 | C | R | R8 | |
| 165AD-2a | Same | MAGI GENII/QUBO/DAIRI/WHANG | C | R | R7 | |

(NOTE: The two above pieces are assumed to be magician's satrical pieces).

| 165ADa-1b | GOOD FOR/10/CENTS/IN DRINKS AT/THE/CONTINENTAL Ohio | JOHN STANTON/STAMP/BRAND/CUTTER/CINCINNATI | BR | PL | R9 | |
| 165ADb-1b | Continental/Hotel/Money/Check (same as Rev of Ohio 165FM-6) | Blank | BR | PL | R9 | |

322

OHIO-Continued

NUMBER	OBVERSE	REVERSE	METAL	EDGE	RARITY	H&G

CINCINNATI 165-Continued

165AE-1a	COSTELLO'S/TRIMMINGS/&/ FANCY GOODS/138/FIFTH ST/ CINCINNATI	1007	C	R	R9	6909
165AE-1a1	Same	Same	C	PL	R4	6908
165AE-1b	Same	Same	BR	R	R9	6910
165AE-2a	Same	1008	C	PL	R9	6911
165AE-3a	Same	1019	C	PL	R9	6912
165AE-4a	Same	1020	C	PL	R6	6913
165AE-5a	Same	1021	C	PL	R4	6914
165AE-6a	Same	1023	C	PL	R4	6915
165AE-7a	Same	1026	C	PL	R6	6924
165AE-8a	Same	1029	C	PL	R5	6916
165AE-9a	Same	1030	C	PL	R6	6917
	(NOTE: Comes with broken reverse die.)					
165AE-9b	Same	Same	BR	PL	R9	
165AE-10a	Same	1032	C	PL	R7	
165AE-11a	Same	1034	C	PL	R7	
165AE-12a	Same	1042	C	R	R7	6919
	(NOTE: Comes with broken die.)					
165AE-12a1	Same	Same	C	PL	R8	6918
165AE-12b	Same	Same	BR	R	R7	6920
165AE-12i	Same	Same	Z	R	R9	6922
165AE-13d	Same	1047	C-N	R	R10	6923
165AE-3b	Same (A.N.S.)	1019	BR	PL	R9	

165AF

165AG

| 165AF-1a | CRITTENDEN/SHADES, Star above & below | 1056 | C | PL | R6 | 6927 |
| | (NOTE: The piece listed as H&G 6926 could not exist as shown.) | | | | | |

165AG-1a	BATES/HOUSE/ONE/MEAL/ J.M. DAGGERT & CO.	1046	C	R	R9	6929
165AG-1b	Same	Same	BR	R	R9	
165AG-1d	Same	Same	C-N	R	R10	6930
	(NOTE: The reverse die has a sharp break from tip of bust to border.)					
165AG-2a	Same	1047	C	R	R9	

323

OHIO-Continued

NUMBER	OBVERSE	REVERSE	METAL	EDGE	RARITY	H&G

CINCINNATI 165-Continued

165AH-1a	GEO. R. DIXON & CO./SPICE/MILLS/SYCAMORE/BET.7 &8' STS./CINCINNATI	1007	C	PL	R3	6933
165AH-2a	Same	1008	C	PL	R3	6934
165AH-2b	Same	Same	BR	PL	R6	6935
165AH-2i	Same (H-R 1634)	Same	Z	PL	R9	
165AH-3a	Same	1009	C	PL	R4	6936
165AH-3b	Same	Same	BR	PL	R8	
165AH-3i	Same	Same	Z	PL	R8	
165AH-4a	Same	1019	C	PL	R5	
165AH-4b	Same	Same	BR	PL	R6	
165AH-4i	Same	Same	Z	PL	R8	
165AH-5a	Same	1021	C	PL	R3	6937
165AH-6a	Same	1042	C	R	R7	6938
165AH-6b	Same	Same	BR	R	R7	6939
165AH-6i	Same	Same	Z	R	R9	6940
165AH 7a	Same	1047	C	R	R9	
165AH-7d	Same	Same	C-N	R	R10	6941
165AH-8b	Same	1068	BR	PL	R9	6942
165AH-9d	Same (H-R 1636)	1069	C-N	R	R10	
165AH-10a	Same	1192	C	PL	R9	6932

165AI-1a	J.N.DONIPHAN/188/EAST/PEARL/ST./CINCINNATI.	1032	C	PL	R5	6949
165AI-2a	Same	1042	C	R	R7	6944
165AI-2b	Same	Same	BR	R	R8	6945
165AI-2i	Same	Same	Z	R	R8	
165AI-3a	Same	1044	C	PL	R9	
165AI-4a	Same	1047	C	R	R8	
165AI-4d	Same	Same	C-N	R	R10	6947
165AI-5d	Same(H-R 1639)	1069	C-N	R	R10	
165AI-6a	Same	BLANK	C	PL	R10	

324

OHIO-Continued

NUMBER	OBVERSE	REVERSE	METAL	EDGE	RARITY	H&G

CINCINNATI 165-Continued

165AJ

165AK

165AJ-1a	GARRET T. DORLAND/IMPORTER/OF/WATCHES/AND/JEWELRY/N.W. COR. MAIN & PEARL/STS./CINCINNATI	1008	C	PL	R3	6951
165AJ-2a	Same	1019	C	PL	R7	
165AJ-3a	Same	1029	C	PL	R4	6952
165AJ-4a	Same	1042	C	R	R6	6953
165AJ-4b	Same	Same	BR	R	R7	6954
165AJ-4i	Same	Same	Z	R	R9	6955
165AJ-5a	Same (H-R 1641)	1047	C	R	R9	
165AJ-5d	Same	Same	C-N	R	R10	6956
165AJ-6a	Same	1068	C	PL	R9	
165AJ-7a	Same	1069	C	PL	R9	6957
165AJ-7d	Same (H-R 1640)	1069	C-N	R	R10	
165AJ-1a1	Same	Same	C	R	R10	
165AK-1d	R DOWNING/PUBLISHER/OF/SHEET SONGS/& DEALER IN/OLD/COINS/CINCINNATI	1046	C-N	R	R10	6960
165AK-2a	Same	1047	C	R	R8	
165AK-3b	Same	1069	BR	PL	R9	6962
165AK-4b	Same	1192	BR	PL	R9	
165AK-5e	Same	1270	W-M	PL	R9	6959
165AK-6b	Same	1283	BR	PL	R9	
165AK-7a	Same	1370	C	R	R9	6963
165AK-7b	Same	Same	BR	R	R9	6964

165AL-1a	L.ECKERT/BOOKBINDER/STATIONER/&/FANCY GOODS/N.W.COR./WALNUT & 13'STS/CINCINNATI	1007	C	PL	R7	6972
165AL-2a	Same	1019	C	PL	R5	6973
165AL-2b	Same	Same	BR	PL	R9	6974
165AL-3a	Same	1020	C	PL	R6	

OHIO-Continued

NUMBER	OBVERSE	REVERSE	METAL	EDGE	RARITY	H&G

CINCINNATI 165-Continued

165AL-4a	Same	1026	C	PL	R5	6977
165AL-5a	Same	1030	C	PL	R5	6975
165AL-6a	Same	1036	C	PL	R6	
165AL-7a	Same	1038	C	PL	R6	6976
165AL-8a	Same	1039	C	PL	R8	

165AM-1a	C.W.ELLIS/GEN. AGT./35 W. 3D ST./CIN,O/DAYTON AGENCY/44 JEFF,ST.	CONN.MUT.LIFE INS.CO./ CAPITAL/OVER/60000000/ DOLLARS/1864 (Obv Ohio 165AB)	C	R	R7	6979
165AM-1a1	Same	Same	C	PL	R9	
165AM-2a	Same	1047	C	R	R9	6980
165AM-2d	Same	Same	C-N	R	R10	

165AMa   165AMa-2   165AMb

165AMa-1b	EVEN'S/ALL KINDS OF/ SEWING/MACHINES/ REPAIRED/164 W.4TH.ST. (Thin planchet, Adams Ohio 15)	Blank	BR	PL	R6	
165AMa-1bp	Same	Same	BR-pl	PL	R6	
165AMa-2b	Same	JOHN STANTON/STAMP/ BRAND/CUTTER/CINCINNATI	BR	PL	R6	
165AMa-2bp	Same	Same	BR-pl	PL	R6	
165AMb-1a	EXCELSIOR/TOBACCO/ WORKS/210 & 212/ELM ST. CIN.O/ESTABLISHED/1835 (King 624)	1418	C	PL	R8	
165AMb-2bp	Same	1426	BR-pl	PL	R8	

326

OHIO-Continued

NUMBER	OBVERSE	REVERSE	METAL	EDGE	RARITY	H&G

CINCINNATI 165-Continued

165AN

165AO

165AN-1a	FENTON & BECK/DAILY/ MARKET/N.W.COR 6' & PLUM	1030	C	PL	R4	6982
165AN-2a	Same	1034	C	PL	R9	
165AN-3a	Same	1042	C	R	R6	6983
165AN-3b	Same	Same	BR	R	R7	6984
165AN-3i	Same	Same	Z	R	R9	
165AN-4a	Same	1047	C	R	R9	
165AO-1a	J. FERGUSON/GROCER/COR. 9' & VINE STS/CINCINNATI/ GOODS DELIVERED/FREE OF CHARGE (NOTE: Comes with broken reverse die.)	1008	C	PL	R4	6986
165AO-2a	Same	1019	C	PL	R9	
165AO-2b	Same	Same	BR	PL	R9	
165AO-3a	Same	1021	C	PL	R5	6987
165AO-4a	Same	1012	C	R	R7	6988
165AO-4b	Same	Same	BR	R	R7	6989
165AO-4i	Same	Same	Z	R	R9	6990
165AO-5a	Same (H-R 1648)	1047	C	R	R9	
165AO-5d	Same	Same	C-N	R	R10	
165AO-6a	Same	1068	C	PL	R6	6993
165AO-7d	Same (H-R 1647)	1069	C-N	R	R10	
165AO-6a1	Same (H-R 1646)	1068	C	R	R9	

165AP-1a	E.FIEDLER'S/BEER/HALL/ 206/VINE,ST.	1022	C	PL	R3	7000
165AP-2a	Same	1026	C	PL	R4	6999
165AP-3a	Same	1029	C	PL	R6	
165AP-4a	Same	1030	C	PL	R7	
165AP-5a	Same	1033	C	PL	R4	7002
165AP-6a	Same	1035	C	PL	R4	
165AP-7a	Same	1036	C	PL	R5	6998

327

OHIO-Continued

NUMBER	OBVERSE	REVERSE	METAL	EDGE	RARITY	H&G

CINCINNATI 165-Continued

165AP-8a	Same	1042	C	R	R6	6995
165AP-8b	Same	Same	BR	R	R7	6996
165AP-8i	Same	Same	Z	R	R8	6997
165AP-9a	Same	1044	C	PL	R4	7002
165AP-10a	Same	1047	C	R	R9	

165AQ-1e	EMIL FIEDLER	C3 in a circle of stars	W-M	PL	R9	7004

*165AR-1b FIFTH STREET/5/GARDEN   JAS MURDOCK JR./165 RACE ST/CIN'TI   BR   R   R8

165AS

165AS-5

165AS-1a	F.FISCHER/214/VINE/ST./CINCINNATI	1036	C	PL	R5	7009
165AS-2a	Same	1042	C	R	R6	7005
165AS-2b	Same	Same	BR	R	R6	7006
165AS-2i	Same	Same	Z	R	R8	7007
165AS-3a	Same	1047	C	R	R9	
165AS-3d	Same	Same	C-N	R	R10	7008
165AS-4d	Same (H-R 1651)	1069	C-N	R	R10	
165AS-5a	Same (H-R 1655)	CHAS.FLACH/DEALER/IN/PROVISIONS/COR./MADISON & CANAL/CINCINNATI. (Obv. Ohio 165A W-2)	C	PL	R10	

328

OHIO-Continued

NUMBER	OBVERSE	REVERSE	METAL	EDGE	RARITY	H&G

CINCINNATI 165-Continued

165AT-1a	FISLER & CHANCE above — POLAR Below 1/GLASS/SODA/WATER in center.	1047	C	R	R8	7011
165AT-1d	Same	Same	C-N	R	R10	7012
165AT-2b	Same	1312	BR	R	R9	7013

| 165AU-1b | W.C.FITHIAN/PAINTER & GRAINER/420 EIGHTH ST/CINCINNATI | MURDOCK & SPENCER/139/W" FIFTH/STREET/CINCINNATI (Obv Ohio 165DZ) | BR | PL | R9 | |

165AV-1a	J.W.FITZGERALD/GROCER/COR/FIFTH/AND/BROADWAY/CINCINNATI.	1127	C	PL	R5	7015
165AV-2a	Same	1384	C	PL	R5	7016
165AV-3a	Same	BLANK	C	PL	R10	7017

OHIO-Continued

NUMBER	OBVERSE	REVERSE	METAL	EDGE	RARITY	H&G

CINCINNATI 165-Continued

165AW-1a	CHAS.FLACH/DEALER/IN/ PROVISIONS/COR./MADISON & COURT/CINCINNATI. (NOTE: Apparently COURT was an error & was intended to be CANAL — see next variety.)	1036	C	PL	R6	7023
165AW-2a	Same as preceding, but die corrected to CANAL (Overcutting shows clearly.)	1026	C	PL	R5	7024
165AW-3a	Same	1033	C	PL	R5	7025
165AW-4a	Same	1035	C	PL	R8	
165AW-5a	Same	1039	C	PL	R8	
165AW-6a	Same	1042	C	R	R7	7019
165AW-6b	Same	Same	BR	R	R8	7020
165AW-6i	Same	Same	Z	R	R9	7021
165AW-7a	Same	1047	C	R	R9	
165AW-7d	Same	Same	C-N	R	R10	7022
165AW-8d	Same (H-R 1654)	1069	C-N	R	R10	
165AW-9a	Same (H-R 1656)	D.E.STEARNS BEREA OHIO Grindstone in center. (Obv. Ohio 74A-10)	C	R	R10	

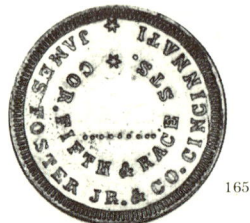

165AX-1a	JAMES FOSTER JR. & CO. CINCINNATI around border COR. FIFTH & RACE STS. in circle in center - 2 stars.	1047	C	R	R8	7027
165AX-2b	Same, cstp. (NOTE: The only specimen seen is cstp 22.)	Blank	BR	R	R9	
165AX-1d	Same (Kreisberg 10/66 Lot 780)	1047	C-N	R	R10	

330

OHIO-Continued

NUMBER　　OBVERSE　　　　　　REVERSE　　　　　　　　METAL　EDGE　RARITY　H&G

CINCINNATI 165-Continued

Number	Obverse	Reverse	Metal	Edge	Rarity	H&G
165AX-3b	J.FOSTER JR & CO/CHECK/ S.W.COR.5' & RACE (listed as Adams Ohio 14)	MURDOCK & SPENCER/139/ W' FIFTH/STREET/CINCINNATI (Obv. Ohio 165DZ)	BR	PL	R8	
165AX-4m	Same NOTE: Extremely thin planchet.	Obv incused	T	PL	R10	

Number	Obverse	Reverse	Metal	Edge	Rarity	H&G
165AY-1a	JOHN FRANK above — eight small circles around ornament in center — 5 stars below (NOTE: The series of reverse dies used here are identical to those used on KY-480B)	ONE/HALF/PINT/OF/MILK	C	R	R7	7030
165AY-1b	Same	Same	BR	R	R8	7031
165AY-1i	Same	Same	Z	R	R8	7033
165AY-2a	Same	1/PINT/OF/MILK	C	R	R7	7035
165AY-2b	Same	Same	BR	R	R8	7036
165AY-2i	Same	Same	Z	R	R8	7037
165AY-3a	Same	ONE/QUART/OF/MILK	C	R	R7	7000
165AY-3b	Same	Same	BR	R	R8	7040
165AY-3i	Same	Same	Z	R	R7	7041
165AY-4a	Same	ONE/HALF/GALL/OF/MILK	C	R	R9	
165AY-5a	Same	ONE/GALL/OF/MILK	C	R	R9	7043
165AY-6d	Same	1047	C-N	R	R10	7047
165AY-2d	Same (Kreisberg 10/66 Lot 781)	Same	C-N	R	R10	
165AY-3f	Same	Same	S	R	R10	
165AY-4d	Same (Kreisberg 10/66 Lot 781)	Same	C-N	R	R10	

OHIO-Continued

NUMBER　　OBVERSE　　　　　　　REVERSE　　　　　　　METAL　EDGE　RARITY　H&G

CINCINNATI 165-Continued

165AZ-1a	USE/FROST'S/MEDICINE/SOLD/BY/DRUGGISTS	1037	C	R	R7	7049
165AZ-1b	Same	Same	BR	R	R8	7050
165AZ-1i	Same	Same	Z	R	R9	7051
165AZ-2a	Same	1042	C	R	R8	7052
165AZ-2b	Same	Same	BR	R	R9	
165AZ-3a	Same	1046	C	R	R5	7053
165AZ-4a	Same	1047	C	R	R9	
165AZ-4d	Same (H-R 1658)	Same	C-N	R	R10	
165BA-1a	JOHN GALVAGNI/FANCY/GOODS/&/TOYS/513/VINE BET.14' & 15'/STS./CINCINNATI	1007	C	PL	R4	7055
165BA-2b	Same	1019	BR	PL	R9	
165BA-3a	Same	1042	C	R	R6	7057
165BA-3b	Same	Same	BR	R	R6	7058
165BA-3i	Same	Same	Z	R	R9	7059
165BA-4a	Same	1047	C	R	R9	
165BA-4d	Same	Same	C-N	R	R10	7060
165BA-5d	Same (H-R 1661)	1069	C-N	R	R10	
165BA-6a	Same (H-R 1662)	1273	C	R	R10	
165BA-1al	Same (H-R 1660)	Same	C	R	R9	

165BAa-1a	BUY YOUR/COAL/FROM/GALWAY SMITH & CO.	GOOD FOR/1/CENT/PAYMENT IN COAL/GALWAY SMITH & CO.	C	PL	R9	
165BB-1a	L.GEILFUS/GROCER,/701 ELM ST.	1247	C	PL	R5	7063
165BB-2a	No comma after Grocer (Listed as Marvin 726c)	1386	C	PL	R9	7062

332

OHIO-Continued

NUMBER　　OBVERSE　　　　　　REVERSE　　　　　　　　METAL　EDGE　RARITY　H&G

CINCINNATI 165-Continued

165BC-1a	J GEISER	1386	C	PL	R7	7065
	(Listed as Marvin 726d — comes with broken obv. die.)					
165BC-2a	Same	1388	C	PL	R7	7066
	(Listed as Marvin 727a)					
165BD-1a	W.GENTSCH/WINE/&/BEER/ SALOON/393 VINE,ST.	1026	C	PL	R6	7073
165BD-2a	Same	1029	C	PL	R9	
165BD-3a	Same	1042	C	R	R7	7068
165BD-3b	Same	Same	BR	R	R7	7069
165BD-3i	Same	Same	Z	R	R9	7070
165BD-4a	Same	1047	C	R	R9	7072
165BD-4d	Same	Same	C-N	R	R10	7071
165BD-5d	Same	1069	C-N	R	R10	
165BE-1a	SEGARS/O.G./TOBACCO	1037	C	R	R9	
	(O.Gufhoj)					
165BE-2a	Same	1030	C	R	R5	7082
165BE-2a1	Same	Same	C	PL	R9	
165BE-3a	Same	1042	C	R	R6	7077
165BE-3b	Same	Same	BR	R	R6	7078
165BE-3i	Same	Same	Z	R	R9	7079
165BE-4a	Same	1047	C	R	R8	7080
165BE-4b	Same	Same	BR	R	R9	7081
165BE-4d	Same (H-R 1664)	Same	C-N	R	R10	

*165BF-1b	R G/5 (incused lettering)		BR	PL	R10	
*165BG-1b	JAS MURDOCK JR./165 RACE ST/CIN'TI (incused lettering)	Same	BR	PL	R8	
	GOOD/FOR 5¢/R/GOHS/ CIN.O (Incused lettering)					
	(NOTE — both of the above may be post-Civil War.)					

333

OHIO-Continued

NUMBER	OBVERSE	REVERSE	METAL	EDGE	RARITY	H&G

CINCINNATI 165-Continued

165BH-1a	J.GROSSIUS,/TINNER./33/ COURT ST./CIN.O.	1056	C	PL	R7	7084
165BI-1a	JACOB GUTH/S.W.COR./ VINE/&/COLUMBIA/STS./ CINCINNATI	1021	C	PL	R9	
165BI-2a	Same	1022	C	PL	R9	
165BI-3a	Same	1026	C	PL	R7	
165BI-4a	Same	1031	C	PL	R9	7090
165BI-5a	Same	1036	C	PL	R5	
165BI-6a	Same	1039	C	PL	R6	
165BI-7a	Same	1042	C	R	R7	7086
165BI-7b	Same	Same	BR	R	R8	7087
165BI-7i	Same	Same	Z	R	R9	7088
165BI-8a	Same	1047	C	R	R9	
165BI-9a	Same	S.&L.SMITH/GROCERS/ CINCINNATI (Obv. Ohio 165FT)	C	PL	R10	

165BJ-1a	CARL HAAS above — CINCINNATI, O. below 493/ VINE/ST. within beaded circle in center.	1019	C	PL	R5	7093
165BJ-2a	Same	1020	C	PL	R6	7094
165BJ-2b	Same	Same	BR	PL	R9	
165BJ-3a	Same	1021	C	PL	R5	7095
165BJ-4a	Same	1036	C	PL	R6	
165BJ-5a	Same (NOTE: Comes with reverse die break.)	1038	C	PL	R3	7096
165BJ-6a	Same	1042	C	R	R6	7097
165BJ-6b	Same	Same	BR	R	R8	7098
165BJ-6i	Same	Same	Z	R	R9	7099
165BJ-7a	Same (H-R 1669)	1047	C	R	R9	
165BJ-7d	Same (H-R 1668)	Same	C-N	R	R10	7100

OHIO-Continued

NUMBER	OBVERSE	REVERSE	METAL	EDGE	RARITY	H&G

CINCINNATI 165-Continued

165BJ-8

165BJ-12

165BJ-8a	Same	CARL HAAS above — 493 VINE, ST below, Rabbit in center (Name in large letters)	C	R	R9	7102
165BJ-8d	Same (H-R 1670)	Same	C-N	R	R10	
165BJ-9a	Same as Rev Ohio 165BJ-8a	1042	C	R	R6	7108
165BJ-9b	Same	Same	BR	R	R6	7109
165BJ-9i	Same	Same	Z	R	R8	7110
165BJ-10a	Same	1045	C	PL	R5	7104
165BJ-11d	Same	1047	C N	R	R10	7111
165BJ-12a	Similar to preceding, but name in smaller letters. All specimens show name recut and shifted to the right.	1020	C	PL	R2	7105
165BJ-12b	Same	Same	BR	PL	R8	
165BJ-13a	Same	1021	C	PL	R6	
165BJ-14a	Same	1022	C	PL	R5	7116
165BJ-14b	Same	Same	BR	PL	R9	7117
165BJ-15a	Same	1023	C	PL	R5	7106
165BJ-16a	Same	1026	C	PL	R2	7112
165BJ-17a	Same	1032	C	PL	R3	7114
165BJ-18a	Same	1033	C	PL	R6	
165BJ-19a	Same	1034	C	PL	R4	7113
165BJ-20a	Same	1035	C	PL	R7	
165BJ-21a	Same	1039	C	PL	R7	
165BJ-22a	Same	1041	C	PL	R6	
165BJ-23a	Same	1044	C	PL	R5	7115
165BJ-24a	Same	1029	C	PL	R9	7107

| 165BK-1e | C.HAHNEMANN'S/BAKERY/ 549 VINE ST | C3 in circle of stars (Same Rev. as Ohio 165AQ) | W-M | PL | R8 | |

335

OHIO-Continued

NUMBER	OBVERSE	REVERSE	METAL	EDGE	RARITY	H&G

CINCINNATI 165-Continued

165BL-1a	W.W.HANLEY/WHOLESALE/ GROCER/25/MAIN ST/ CINCINNATI (NOTE: MAIN clearly reengraved over another name — H and L are distinguishable underneath)	1008	C	PL	R5	7119
165BL-2a	Same	1009	C	PL	R6	7120
165BL-3a	Same	1038	C	PL	R8	7121
165BL-4a	Same	1042	C	R	R7	7122
165BL-4b	Same	Same	BR	R	R8	7123
165BL-4i	Same	Same	Z	R	R8	7124
165BL-5a	Same	1047	C	R	R9	
165BL-5d	Same (H-R 1673)	Same	C-N	R	R9	7125

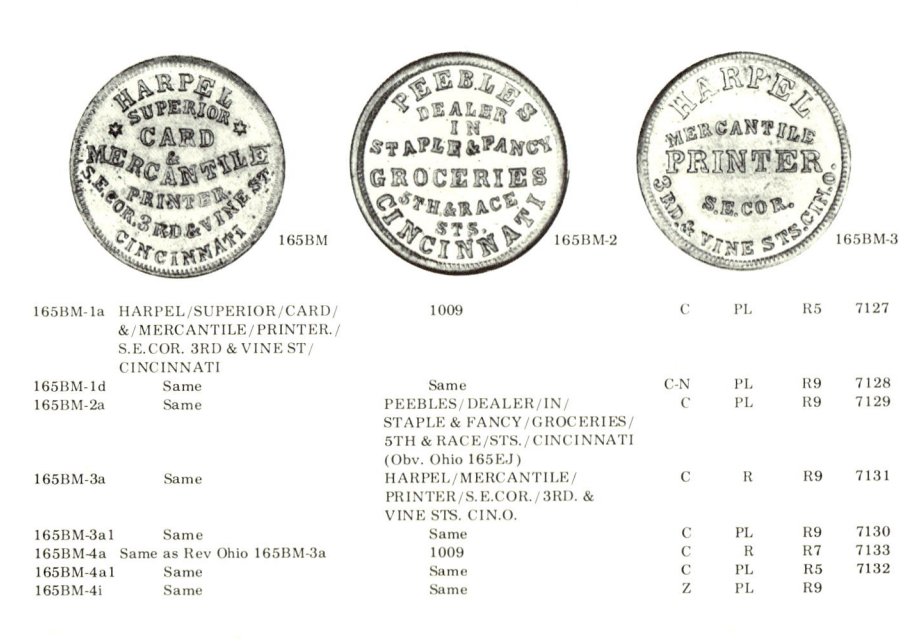

165BM   165BM-2   165BM-3

165BM-1a	HARPEL/SUPERIOR/CARD/ &/MERCANTILE/PRINTER./ S.E.COR. 3RD & VINE ST/ CINCINNATI	1009	C	PL	R5	7127
165BM-1d	Same	Same	C-N	PL	R9	7128
165BM-2a	Same	PEEBLES/DEALER/IN/ STAPLE & FANCY/GROCERIES/ 5TH & RACE/STS./CINCINNATI (Obv. Ohio 165EJ)	C	PL	R9	7129
165BM-3a	Same	HARPEL/MERCANTILE/ PRINTER/S.E.COR./3RD. & VINE STS. CIN.O.	C	R	R9	7131
165BM-3a1	Same	Same	C	PL	R9	7130
165BM-4a	Same as Rev Ohio 165BM-3a	1009	C	R	R7	7133
165BM-4a1	Same	Same	C	PL	R5	7132
165BM-4i	Same	Same	Z	PL	R9	

336

OHIO-Continued

NUMBER	OBVERSE	REVERSE	METAL	EDGE	RARITY	H&G

CINCINNATI 165-Continued

165BN-1a	C.G.HARTMANN,/GROCER/ 140/EVERETT ST./CIN.O.	1248	C	PL	R5	7135
165BO-1a	M.HARTZEL/GROCER/&/ COMMISSION/MERC'T/N.W.COR 3' & ELM/STS./CINCINNATI	1009	C	PL	R3	7138
	(NOTE: The piece listed as 7137 does not exist.)					
165BO-1b	Same (H-R 1676)	Same	BR	R	R9	
165BO-1b1	Same	Same	BR	PL	R9	7139
165BO-1i	Same	Same	Z	R	R9	
165BO-2a	Same	1019	C	PL	R3	7140
165BO-3a	Same	1020	C	PL	R5	
165BO-4a	Same	1042	C	R	R6	7141
165BO-4b	Same	Same	BR	R	R7	7142
165BO-5a	Same	1047	C	R	R8	
165BO-5d	Same	Same	C-N	R	R10	7144
165BO-4i	Same (DBFGB 8/73 LOT 403)	1042	Z	R	R9	

165BP-1a	J.HAYES & BRO. above — 5 in center CENTS below	1169	C	PL	R7	7146
165BP-2a	J.HAYES & BRO. above — 1 in center DRINK. below.	1169	C	PL	R8	7147
165BP-2b	Same	Same	BR	PL	R8	7148
165BP-3a	Same	1181	C	PL	R9	7150
165BP-4a	Same	1295	C	PL	R8	7149
165BP-1d	Same (Kreisberg 10/66 Lot /85)	1169	C-N	PL	R10	

165BQ - HEINMAN'S now listed as MICH. 225AJa.

OHIO-Continued

NUMBER	OBVERSE	REVERSE	METAL	EDGE	RARITY	H&G

CINCINNATI 165-Continued

| 165BR-1a | E.HEINZMANN/NO 12/COURT ST. (Marvin 726e) | 1386 | C | PL | R7 | 7156 |
| 165BR-2a | Same | 1388 | C | PL | R6 | 7158 |

(Marvin 727b — this piece comes with broken reverse die.)
(NOTE: The piece listed as H & G 7157 cannot exist as described.)

165BS-1a	J.HELMIG/GROCER/708/FREEMAN/ST./CINCINNATI	1022	C	PL	R8	
165BS-2a	Same	1029	C	PL	R4	7160
165BS-3a	Same	1042	C	R	R7	7161
165BS-3b	Same	Same	BR	R	R9	7162
165BS-3i	Same	Same	Z	R	R9	
165BS-4a	Same (H-R 1682)	1047	C	R	R9	
165BS-4d	Same (H-R 1681)	Same	C-N	R	R10	7163

165BT 165BT-13

165BT-1a	B.HEMPELMAN/DEALER/IN/GROCERIES/&/FEED N.W.COR./LINN & FINDLAY/STS/CINCINNATI	1019	C	PL	R3	7165
165BT-2a	Same	1020	C	PL	R6	
165BT-3a	Same	1021	C	PL	R4	7166
165BT-4a	Same	1022	C	PL	R7	

338

OHIO-Continued

NUMBER	OBVERSE	REVERSE	METAL	EDGE	RARITY	H&G

CINCINNATI 165-Continued

NUMBER	OBVERSE	REVERSE	METAL	EDGE	RARITY	H&G
165BT-5a	Same	1032	C	PL	R8	
165BT-6a	Same	1034	C	PL	R5	
165BT-7a	Same	1035	C	PL	R6	7173
165BT-8a	Same	1036	C	PL	R5	7172
165BT-9a	Same	1038	C	PL	R6	7168
165BT-10a	Same	1042	C	R	R7	7169
165BT-10b	Same	Same	BR	R	R8	7170
165BT-10i	Same	Same	Z	R	R9	
165BT-11a	Same (H-R 1685)	1047	C	R	R9	
165BT-11d	Same	Same	C-N	R	R10	7171
165BT-12a	Same (H-R 1686)	1273	C	PL	R10	
165BT-13a	Same	JOHN STANTON/STEEL/STAMP/BRAND/& STENCIL CUTTER/139 FIFTH ST./CINCINNATI OHIO (Obv Ohio 165FX-20)	C	PL	R10	7175

165BU

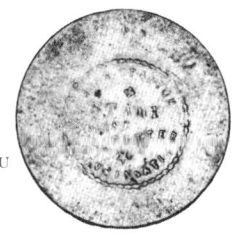

165BV

165BU-1b	DUE THE BEARER/25/CENTS/IN BEER AT/HERANCOURT'S/BREWRY (NOTE: Thin planchet)	JOHN STANTON/STAMP/BRAND/CUTTER/CINCINNATI	BR	PL	R8	
165BV-1a	FARMERS HOTEL/COR./COURT/&/RACE/STS/CINCINNATI/V.HEYL	1018	C	PL	R9	
165BV-2a	Same	1019	C	PL	R9	
165BV-3a	Same	1022	C	PL	R6	
165BV-4a	Same	1026	C	PL	R3	7183
165BV-5a	Same	1029	C	PL	R6	
165BV-6a	Same	1030	C	PL	R8	7177
165BV-7a	Same	1032	C	PL	R5	
165BV-8a	Same	1033	C	PL	R4	7184
165BV-9a	Same	1034	C	PL	R7	
165BV-10a	Same	1038	C	PL	R4	7178
165BV-11a	Same	1039	C	PL	R7	
165BV-12a	Same	1042	C	R	R6	7179
165BV-12b	Same	Same	BR	R	R6	7180
165BV-12i	Same	Same	Z	R	R9	
165BV-13d	Same	1046	C-N	R	R10	7182
165BV-14a	Same	1047	C	R	R9	
165BV-14d	Same	Same	C-N	R	R10	

339

OHIO-Continued

NUMBER	OBVERSE	REVERSE	METAL	EDGE	RARITY	H&G

CINCINNATI 165-Continued

NUMBER	OBVERSE	REVERSE	METAL	EDGE	RARITY	H&G
165BV-15a	FARMERS HOTEL/GOOD FOR/ 5/CENTS/V.HEYL/CINCINNATI (Note: Some pieces have 5 cancelled.)	1008	C	PL	R5	7189
165BV-16a	Same	1019	C	PL	R9	
165BV-17a	Same (NOTE: Some pieces have 5 cancelled.)	1033	C	PL	R3	7190
165BV-18a	Same (H-R 1689)	1047	C	R	R9	
165BV-19a	Same	1192	C	R	R6	7186
165BV-19b	Same	Same	BR	R	R7	7187
165BV-19i	Same	Same	Z	R	R9	7188

165BV-15 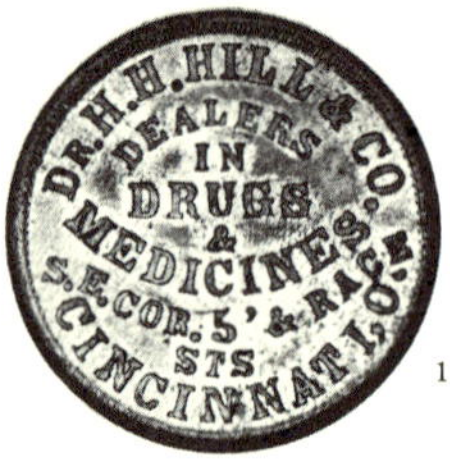   165BW

NUMBER	OBVERSE	REVERSE	METAL	EDGE	RARITY	H&G
165BW-1a	DR.H.H.HILL & CO./DEALERS/ IN/DRUGS/&/MEDICINES/ S.E.COR.5' & RACE/STS/ CINCINNATI,O.	1008	C	PL	R4	7193
165BW-2a	Same	1030	C	PL	R3	7194
165BW-3a	Same	1038	C	PL	R8	7195
165BW-4a	Same	1042	C	R	R6	7196
165BW-4b	Same	Same	BR	R	R8	7197
165BW-4i	Same	Same	Z	R	R9	7198

165BW-7    165BW-8    165BW-9

NUMBER	OBVERSE	REVERSE	METAL	EDGE	RARITY	H&G
165BW-5a	Same	1047	C	R	R9	7199
165BW-5d	Same	Same	C-N	R	R10	7199
165BW-6a	Same	1311	C	PL	R9	
165BW-7a	ONE/SHAVE/HILL	BLANK	C	PL	R8	
165BW-8a	ONE/HAIR CUT/HILL	BLANK	C	PL	R7	
165BW-9a	$5.00/HILL.	BLANK	C	PL	R9	
165BW-10a	Same	F.W. Lutz/Artist (Obv of 165DG-1a)	C	PL	R10	

OHIO-Continued

NUMBER	OBVERSE	REVERSE	METAL	EDGE	RARITY	H&G

CINCINNATI 165-Continued

165BX-1a	B.HINTRICK & C.GLASER/ 636 & 638 ELM ST.	1020	C	PL	R5	7201
	(NOTE: Most combinations with this die have a broken obverse die.)					
165BX-2a	Same	1036	C	PL	R8	7207
165BX-3a	Same	1042	C	R	R6	7202
165BX-3b	Same	Same	BR	R	R6	7203
165BX-3i	Same	Same	Z	R	R8	7204
165BX-4a	Same	1047	C	R	R9	
165BX-4d	Same (H-R 1695)	Same	C-N	R	R10	7205
165BX-5d	Same	1069	C-N	R	R10	7206
165BY-1b	GILBERT B. HOTCHKISS/ 1/PINT/MILK	1362	BR	PL	R8	7074
165BY-1f	Same	Same	S	PL	R9	
165BZ-1a	J.A.HUGHES above CINCINNATI.O. below METALIC CARDS in a wreath (NOTE: METALLIC spelled with one L.)	1131	C	PL	R9	7212
165BZ-1f	Same (Kreisberg 10/66 Lot 786)	Same	S	PL	R10	
165BZ-2a	Same	1172	C	PL	R9	
165BZ-2f	Same (Kreisberg 10/66 Lot 786)	Same	S	PL	R10	
165BZ-3a	Same	TRY ALLEN'S BLACKLEAD/ COMPOUND BABBITT METAL 1863 (Rev. Ohio 175S)	C	PL	R9	7209
165BZ-3f	Same	Same	S	PL	R10	
165CA-1a	GOOD FOR ONE/5/CENT/ LOAF OF BREAD/P. HUGHES	1192	C	R	R9	7214
165CA-2b	Same	1391	BR	R	R9	
165CA-3a	GOOD FOR ONE/10/CENT/ LOAF OF BREAD/P. HUGHES	1393	C	R	R9	7215

OHIO-Continued

NUMBER	OBVERSE	REVERSE	METAL	EDGE	RARITY	H&G

CINCINNATI 165-Continued

165CB-1a	C.C.HYATT/STAPLE/& FANCY/ GROCER/COR./FREEMAN & POPLAR/STS./*CINCINNATI*	1007	C	PL	R4	7217
165CB-2a	Same	1019	C	PL	R9	
165CB-3a	Same	1042	C	R	R6	7218
165CB-3b	Same	Same	BR	R	R7	7219
165CB-3i	Same	Same	Z	R	R9	7220
165CB-4a	Same	1047	C	R	R9	7221
165CB-4d	Same	Same	C-N	R	R10	
165CB-1a1	Same	Same	C	R	R10	
165CC-1d	B.JAHR/549/VINE STR./ CIN'TI.O	1046	C-N	R	R10	7223
165CC-2a	Same	1047	C	R	R9	7224
165CD-1a	B.JAHR & CO/549/VINE ST/ CIN.O. (NOTE: Obv. die cracked on all pieces seen.)	1047	C	R	R9	
165CD-1d	Same	Same	C-N	R	R10	
165CD-2a	Same	1392	C	PL	R9	7226
165CD-3a	Same	1397	C	PL	R9	7227

| 165CE-1a | H.JOHNSTON/DIE/SINKER/ 154/EVERETT ST/CIN.O. (SINKER curved — Marvin 726j) (NOTE: It is assumed this is an error where the H is intended for W. All pieces seen have badly broken reverse die.) | 1388 | C | PL | R8 | 7228 |

342

OHIO-Continued

NUMBER	OBVERSE	REVERSE	METAL	EDGE	RARITY	H&G

CINCINNATI 165-Continued

165CF-1 165CF-3 165CF-5

165CF-1a	W.JOHNSTON,/DIE/SINKER/ 154/EVERETT ST./CIN.O. (SINKER straight)	1056	C	PL	R3	7232
165CF-2a	Same	1248	C	PL	R3	7231
165CF-3a	W.JOHNSTON,/DIE/SINKER/CIN.O.	1247	C	PL	R4	7235
165CF-4a	Same (Marvin 726a)	1386	C	PL	R4	7234
165CF-5a	Similar, SINKER curved	1388	C	PL	R6	7236

(NOTE: All pieces seen have heavy reverse die breaks.)

| 165CG-1a | C.KAHN & CO,/NO.73/ EVERETT ST./MEAT/STORE. | 1056 | C | PL | R7 | 7238 |
| 165CG-2a | Same (Marvin 726f) | 1386 | C | PL | R7 | 7237 |

| 165CH-1a | A.KARMAN/NO./627/CENTRAL/ AVENUE/CIN.O. | 1247 | C | PL | R4 | 7241 |
| 165CH-2a | Same (Marvin 726g) | 1386 | C | PL | R6 | 7240 |

343

OHIO-Continued

NUMBER OBVERSE REVERSE METAL EDGE RARITY H&G

CINCINNATI 165-Continued

Number	Obverse	Reverse	Metal	Edge	Rarity	H&G
165CI-1d	J.KATZENSTEIN/NO: Row of ten dots below.	1047	C-N	R	R10	7244
165CI-2b	Same	1192	BR	R	R9	7243
165CI-3a	Same	1319	C	R	R9	7245

Number	Obverse	Reverse	Metal	Edge	Rarity	H&G
165CJ-1a	WARREN KENNEDY/NEWS/DEPOT/160/VINE,ST.	1022	C	PL	R4	9251
165CJ-2a	Same	1026	C	PL	R4	7250
165CJ-3a	Same	1042	C	R	R7	7247
165CJ-3b	Same	Same	BR	R	R8	7248
165CJ-3i	Same	Same	Z	R	R9	
165CJ-4a	Same	1047	C	R	R9	7249
165CJ-5d	Same	1069	C-N	R	R10	
165CJ-6a	Similar, but NEWS curved	1124	C	PL	R9	
165CJ-6d	Same	Same	C-N	PL	R9	7258
165CJ-7a	Same	1176	C	PL	R2	7253
165CJ-7d	Same	Same	C-N	PL	R9	
165CJ-8a	Same	1290	C	PL	R3	7254
165CJ-8e	Same (thick 3½mm.)	Same	W-M	PL	R9	
165CJ-9a	Same	1295	C	PL	R9	7255
165CJ-9d	Same	Same	C-N	PL	R9	7256
165CJ-9e	Same (Thick 3½mm.)	Same	W-M	PL	R9	
165CJ-10a	Same	1331	C	PL	R8	7257
165CJ-4d	Same (H-R 1698)	Same	C-N	R	R10	
165CK-1d	FRANK KERN/GROCER/692/CEN AVENUE (H-R 1699) (NOTE: CEN is reengraved and moved to the right.)	1018	C-N	R	R10	
165CK-2a	Same	1029	C	PL	R4	7260
165CK-3a	Same	1035	C	PL	R6	
165CK-4a	Same	1042	C	R	R6	7261
165CK-4b	Same	Same	BR	R	R7	7262
165CK-4i	Same	Same	Z	R	R9	7263
165CK-5a	Same	1047	C	R	R9	7264

OHIO-Continued

NUMBER	OBVERSE	REVERSE	METAL	EDGE	RARITY	H&G

CINCINNATI 165-Continued

| 165CL-1a | GOOD FOR/5/CENTS/AT THE/BAR/J.KIRCHENSCHLAGER | 1295 | C | PL | R7 | 7269 |
| 165CL-1b | Same | Same | BR | PL | R8 | 7270 |

165CM-1a	J.KIRKER & CO./GROCERS/AND/PRODUCE/DEALERS/CINCINNATI, O	1225	C	PL	R9	7272
165CM-2a	Same	1227	C	PL	R6	7273
165CM-3a	Same	1352	C	PL	R5	7274
165CM-3d	Same	Same	C-N	PL	R9	

165CN-1a	B.KITTREDGE & CO. 134 MAIN ST.CIN,O. above 1863 below — liberty head to left in center Period after CO.	GUNS,PISTOLS/AND/ SPORTING in wreath in center DEALERS IN MILITARY GOODS above, APPARATUS below	C	PL	R2	7275
165CN-1b	Same	Same	BR	PL	R6	
165CN-1e	Same	Same	W-M	PL	R9	
165CN-2a	Similar — period and comma after CO.,	Same	C	PL	R2	7276
165CN-2b	Same	Same	BR	PL	R6	
165CN-2fp	Same	Same	S-P	PL	R9	

345

OHIO-Continued

NUMBER	OBVERSE	REVERSE	METAL	EDGE	RARITY	H&G

CINCINNATI 165-Continued

165CO   KLARE & FRIEDRICKS - See special non-locals

165CP-1a	J.KLEIN/GROCER/63/ HAMILTON ROAD	1026	C	PL	R7	
165CP-2a	Same	1029	C	PL	R6	7278
165CP-3a	Same	1035	C	PL	R7	
165CP-4a	Same	1042	C	R	R7	7279
165CP-4b	Same	Same	BR	R	R8	7280
165CP-5a	Same	1047	C	R	R9	
165CP-5d	Same	Same	C-N	R	R10	7282
165CQ-1a	JACOB KNAUBER/BUTCHER/ CIN.O.	1007	C	PL	R3	7285
165CQ-2a	Same	1019	C	PL	R8	
165CQ-2b	Same	Same	BR	PL	R9	
165CQ-3a	Same	1038	C	PL	R3	7286
165CQ-4a	Same	1042	C	R	R6	7287
165CQ-4b	Same	Same	BR	R	R7	7288
165CQ-4i	Same	Same	Z	R	R9	
165CQ-5a	Same (H-R 1704)	1047	C	R	R8	
165CQ-5d	Same	Same	C-N	R	R10	7290
165CQ-6a	Same	1192	C	PL	R10	7284

165CR-1a	WM.KNECHT/GROCER/502/ JOHN,ST./CINCINNATI	1026	C	PL	R4	7296
165CR-2a	Same	1030	C	PL	R7	
165CR-3a	Same	1033	C	PL	R8	7298
165CR-4a	Same	1034	C	PL	R3	7297
165CR-5a	Same	1035	C	PL	R7	
165CR-6a	Same	1042	C	R	R6	7292
165CR-6b	Same	Same	BR	R	R7	7293
165CR-6i	Same	Same	Z	R	R8	7294
165CR-7a	Same (H-R 1706)	1047	C	R	R9	
165CR-7d	Same	Same	C-N	R	R10	7295

346

OHIO-Continued

NUMBER	OBVERSE	REVERSE	METAL	EDGE	RARITY	H&G

CINCINNATI 165-Continued

165CS-1a	JOHN KOCH/NO.10/HARRISON ROAD	1026	C	PL	R5	7303
165CS-2a	Same	1042	C	R	R8	7300
165CS-2b	Same	Same	BR	R	R8	7301
165CS-2i	Same	Same	Z	R	R9	
165CS-3a	Same	1047	C	R	R9	
165CS-3d	Same	Same	C-N	R	R10	7302
165CT-1a	BEER CHECK/5/KOOS/ RESTAURANT	1192	C	R	R9	7304
165CT-2a	Same	1391	C	R	R9	7305

165CU-1a	B.KREAGER/GROCER/ COR./HOME & SMITH/STS./ CINCINNATI	1026	C	PL	R4	
165CU-2a	Same	1030	C	PL	R5	
165CU-3a	Same	1031	C	PL	R6	7310
165CU-4a	Same	1032	C	PL	R6	
165CU-5a	Same	1033	C	PL	R5	7311
165CU-6a	Same	1034	C	PL	R7	
165CU-7a	Same	1035	C	PL	R9	
165CU-8a	Same	1042	C	R	R7	7307
165CU-8b	Same	Same	BR	R	R8	7308
165CU-8i	Same	Same	Z	R	R9	
165CU-9d	Same	1047	C-N	R	R10	7309
165CV-1a	H. KREBER/GROCER/ COLUMBIA/BET./ROWE & MILL	1176	C	PL	R4	7314
165CV-1b	Same	Same	BR	PL	R8	
165CV-1d	Same (H-R 1709)	Same	C-N	PL	R9	
165CV-2a	Same	1177	C	PL	R6	7315
165CV-3a	Same	1242	C	PL	R8	7313
165CV-4a	Same	1331	C	PL	R7	7316

347

OHIO-Continued

NUMBER　　OBVERSE　　　　　　REVERSE　　　　　　　METAL　EDGE　RARITY　H&G

CINCINNATI 165-Continued

165CW　　　　　165CX　　　　　　165CY

NUMBER	OBVERSE	REVERSE	METAL	EDGE	RARITY	H&G
165CW-1a	A.KRENGEL'S/UNION/EXCHANGE/218/VINE,ST.	1019	C	PL	R9	
165CW-1b	Same	Same	BR	PL	R9	
165CW-2a	Same	1021	C	PL	R5	7319
165CW-3a	Same	1025	C	PL	R6	
165CW-4a	Same	1026	C	PL	R4	7325
165CW-5a	Same	1028	C	PL	R5	7326
165CW-6a	Same	1029	C	PL	R7	
165CW-7a	Same	1032	C	PL	R7	
165CW-8a	Same	1033	C	PL	R4	7327
165CW-9a	Same	1034	C	PL	R5	7320
165CW-10a	Same	1035	C	PL	R7	
165CW-11a	Same	1038	C	PL	R5	7321
165CW-12a	Same	1039	C	PL	R7	
165CW-13a	Same	1042	C	R	R6	7322
165CW-13b	Same	Same	BR	R	R6	7323
165CW-13i	Same	Same	Z	R	R9	
165CW-14a	Same	1045	C	PL	R8	7318
165CW-15a	Same	1047	C	R	R9	
165CW-15d	Same (H-R 1712)	Same	C-N	R	R10	
165CX-1a	JACOB/KRICK ornaments above below and at sides.	1047	C	R	R8	7329
165CX-1d	Same	Same	C-N	R	R10	7330
165CX-2a	Same	1391	C	R	R9	
165CY-1a	W.K.LANPHEAR above — CINNATI,O. below MAN'FR/OF/METALIC/CARDS in corn wreath in center. (NOTE: Error in spelling METALLIC)	1083	C	PL	R9	
165CY-1b	Same	Same	BR	PL	R9	
165CY-2a	Same	1084	C	PL	R9	7332
165CY-2b	Same (Typkoin 9/69 - Lot 55B)	Same	BR	PL	R9	7333
165CY-3a	Same	1088	C	PL	R3	7334
165CY-3b	Same	Same	BR	PL	R9	7335
1965CY-4a	Same	1089	C	PL	R9	
165CY-4b	Same	Same	BR	PL	R9	
165CY-5a	Same	1122	C	PL	R9	7336
1965CY-5b	Same (Typkoin 9/69 Lot 55A) (Typkoin 1/69 Lot 64)	Same	BR	PL	R8	7337
165CY-5aa	Same	1124	C	PL	R9	
165CY-6a	Same (Typkoin 5/69 Lot 61)	1125	C	PL	R9	7338
165CY-6b	Same	Same	BR	PL	R9	7339
165CY-7a	Same	1127	C	PL	R8	
165CY-7b	Same	Same	BR	PL	R8	
165CY-8a	Same	1166	C	PL	R9	
165CY-8b	Same	Same	BR	PL	R9	

OHIO-Continued

NUMBER	OBVERSE	REVERSE	METAL	EDGE	RARITY	H&G

CINCINNATI 165-Continued

NUMBER	OBVERSE	REVERSE	METAL	EDGE	RARITY	H&G
165CY-9a	Same	1168	C	PL	R9	7354
165CY-9b	Same	Same	BR	PL	R9	7355
165CY-10a	Same	1179	C	PL	R9	7348
165CY-10b	Same	Same	BR	PL	R9	7349
165CY-11a	Same	1180	C	PL	R9	7350
165CY-11b	Same	Same	BR	PL	R9	7351
165CY-12a	Same	1181	C	PL	R9	7352
165CY-12b	Same	Same	BR	PL	R9	7353
165CY-13a	Same	1222	C	PL	R7	7340
165CY-13b	Same	Same	BR	PL	R9	7341
165CY-13d	Same (H-R 1713)	Same	C-N	PL	R9	
165CY-14a	Same	1225	C	PL	R9	7342
165CY-14b	Same	Same	BR	PL	R9	
165CY-15a	Same	1226	C	PL	R3	7344
165CY-15b	Same	Same	BR	PL	R9	7345
165CY-16a	Same	1227	C	PL	R9	7346
165CY-16b	Same	Same	BR	PL	R9	7347
165CY-17a	Same	1280	C	PL	R9	7358
165CY-17b	Same	Same	BR	PL	R9	7359
165CY-18a	Same (Typkoin 3/69 Lot 64)	1295	C	PL	R9	7360
165CY-18b	Same	Same	BR	PL	R9	7361
165CY-19a	Same	1298	C	PL	R9	7362
165CY-19b	Same	Same	BR	PL	R9	7363
165CY-20a	Same	1299	C	PL	R8	7364
165CY-20b	Same	Same	BR	PL	R8	7365
165CY-21a	Same	1300	C	PL	R9	
165CY-22a	Same	1302	C	PL	R9	7367
165CY-22b	Same	Same	BR	PL	R9	7368
165CY-23a	Same (Typkoin 9/69 Lot 55H)	1304	C	PL	R9	7369
165CY-23b	Same	Same	BR	PL	R9	7370
165CY-24a	Same	1310	C	PL	R9	7371
165CY-24b	Same (Typkoin 7/69 Lot 60)	Same	BR	PL	R9	7372
165CY-25a	Same (Typkoin 5/69 Lot 62)	1316	C	PL	R9	7373
165CY-25b	Same (Typkoin 1/69 Lot 61)	Same	BR	PL	R9	7374
165CY-26a	Same (Typkoin 1/69 Lot 57)	1320	C	PL	R8	7375
165CY-26b	Same	Same	BR	PL	R8	7376
165CY-27a	Same	1321	C	PL	R9	7377
165CY-27b	Same	Same	BR	PL	R8	7378
165CY-28a	Same (Typkoin 9/69 Lot 55E)	1323	C	PL	R9	7379
165CY-28b	Same (Typkoin 9/69 Lot 55D)	Same	BR	PL	R9	7380
165CY-29a	Same	1326	C	PL	R9	7381
165CY-29b	Same (Typkoin 9/69 Lot 55J)	Same	BR	PL	R9	7382
165CY-30a	Same	1332	C	PL	R9	
165CY-30b	Same (H-R 1714)	Same	BR	PL	R9	
165CY-31a	Same (Typkoin 1/69 Lot 59)	1336	C	PL	R9	7383
165CY-31b	Same (Typkoin 5/69 Lot 63)	Same	BR	PL	R8	7384
165CY-32a	Same	1337	C	PL	R9	7385
165CY-32b	Same	Same	BR	PL	R9	7386
165CY-33a	Same (Typkoin 5/69 Lot 69)	1340	C	PL	R9	7387
165CY-33b	Same	Same	BR	PL	R8	7388
165CY-34a	Same	1341	C	PL	R9	
165CY-34b	Same	Same	BR	PL	R9	
165CY-35a	Same (Typkoin 3/69 Lot 55, 9/69 Lot 55F)	1342	C	PL	R8	7389
165CY-35b	Same	Same	BR	PL	R9	7390
165CY-36a	Same (Typkoin 1/69 Lot 63)	1344	C	PL	R8	7391
165CY-36b	Same	Same	BR	PL	R8	7392
165CY-37a	Same	1346	C	PL	R9	7393
165CY-37b	Same	Same	BR	PL	R9	7394
165CY-38a	Same	1348	C	PL	R7	7395
165CY-38b	Same	Same	BR	PL	R9	7396
165CY-39a	Same	1351	C	PL	R9	7397
165CY-39b	Same	Same	BR	PL	R9	7398

OHIO-Continued

NUMBER	OBVERSE	REVERSE	METAL	EDGE	RARITY	H&G

CINCINNATI 165-Continued

165CY-40a	Same	1387	C	PL	R9	
165CY-40b	Same	Same	BR	PL	R9	
165CY-41a	Same	1311	C	PL		7399
165CY-41b	Same	Same	BR	PL		7400

(NOTE: The two pieces listed above probably don't exist, and are listed on basis of H&G listing.)

165CY-42a Same (Typkoin 3/69 Lot 56)		ALSO/CUTLERY/NOTIONS/&c in circle of dots — ornaments above and below.	C	PL	R9	7401
165CY-42b Same (Typkoin 5/69 Lot 65)		Same	BR	PL	R9	7402

165CY-43a Same (Typkoin 9/69 Lot 551)		DEALERS/IN/HOOP/SKIRTS/HATS CAPS/AND/NOTIONS	C	PL	R8	7403
165CY-43b Same (Typkoin 3/69 Lot 57)		Same	BR	PL	R8	7404

165CY-44a	Same	BOOTS,/SHOES/AND/YANKEE/NOTIONS	C	PL	R9	
165CY-44b	Same	Same	BR	PL	R9	

350

OHIO-Continued

NUMBER　　OBVERSE　　　　　　REVERSE　　　　　　　　METAL　EDGE　RARITY　H&G

CINCINNATI 165-Continued

165CY-45
165CY-46 

Number	Obverse	Reverse	Metal	Edge	Rarity	H&G
165CY-45a	Same	LEATHER,/AND/SHOE FINDINGS,/WOOL,/SHEEP PELTS,/SHIPPING/FURRS/ &C.&C.	C	PL	R9	
	(NOTE: Spelling error in FURS on reverse.)					
165CY-45b	Same	Same	BR	PL	R9	
165CY-46a	Same	W.K.LANPHEAR/MANUF'R/ OF/METALIC/CARDS/ CINTI/OHIO	C	PL	R9	7417
	(NOTE: spelling error in METALLIC.)					
165CY-46b	Same	Same	BR	PL	R9	7418
165CY-47a	Same as Rev. Ohio 165CY-46a	1083	C	PL	R9	
165CY-47b	Same	Same	BR	PL	R9	
165CY-47aa	Same (Typkoin 9/69 Lot 55G)	1087	C	PL	R9	
165CY-48a	Same (H-R 1716)	1088	C	PL	R9	7422
165CY-48b	Same	Same	BR	PL	R9	7423
165CY-49a	Same (Typkoin 5/69 Lot 66)	1089	C	PL	R9	7424
165CY-49b	Same (Typkoin 5/69 Lot 67)	Same	BR	PL	R9	7425
165CY-50a	Same	1122	C	PL	R6	7426
	(NOTE: Comes with reverse die break)					
165CY-50b	Same (Typkoin 3/69 Lot 58)	Same	BR	PL	R9	7427
165CY-51a	Same	1124	C	PL	R9	
165CY-52a	Same	1125	C	PL	R9	7428
165CY-52b	Same	Same	BR	PL	R9	7429
165CY-53a	Same (Typkoin 1/69 Lot 62)	1127	C	PL	R9	7430
165CY-53b	Same	Same	BR	PL	R8	7431
165CY-54a	Same	1128	C	PL	R9	
165CY-54b	Same	Same	BR	PL	R9	
165CY-55a	Same	1129	C	PL	R9	
165CY-56a	Same	1166	C	PL	R9	
165CY-56b	Same	Same	BR	PL	R9	
165CY-57a	Same (Typkoin 1/69 Lot 56)	1168	C	PL	R9	7444
165CY-57b	Same	Same	BR	PL	R8	
165CY-58a	Same	1169	C	PL	R9	7446
165CY-58b	Same	Same	BR	PL	R9	7447
165CY-59a	Same	1179	C	PL	R9	7440
165CY-59b	Same	Same	BR	PL	R8	7441
165CY-60a	Same (Typkoin 3/69 Lot 59)	1181	C	PL	R9	7442
165CY-60b	Same	Same	BR	PL	R9	7443
165CY-61a	Same	1222	C	PL	R6	7432
165CY-61b	Same	Same	BR	PL	R9	
165CY-62a	Same	1223	C	PL	R9	7434
165CY-62b	Same	Same	BR	PL	R9	7435
165CY-63a	Same	1226	C	PL	R3	7436
165CY-63b	Same	Same	BR	PL	R8	7437
165CY-64a	Same	1227	C	PL	R8	7438
165CY-64b	Same	Same	BR	PL	R8	7439
165CY-65a	Same	1280	C	PL	R8	7448
165CY-65b	Same	Same	BR	PL	R9	7449

OHIO-Continued

NUMBER	OBVERSE	REVERSE	METAL	EDGE	RARITY	H&G

CINCINNATI 165-Continued

NUMBER	OBVERSE	REVERSE	METAL	EDGE	RARITY	H&G
165CY-66a	Same	1295	C	PL	R9	7450
165CY-66b	Same	Same	BR	PL	R9	7451
165CY-67a	Same	1298	C	PL	R9	7452
165CY-67b	Same	Same	BR	PL	R7	7453
165CY-68a	Same (Typkoin 3/69 Lot 60)	1299	C	PL	R8	7454
165CY-68b	Same	Same	BR	PL	R8	7455
165CY-69b	Same	1300	BR	PL	R9	
165CY-70a	Same (Typkoin 5/69 Lot 68)	1302	C	PL	R9	7456
165CY-70b	Same	Same	BR	PL	R9	7457
165CY-71a	Same	1303	C	PL	R9	7458
165CY-71b	Same	Same	BR	PL	R8	
165CY-72a	Same	1310	C	PL	R8	
165CY-72b	Same	Same	BR	PL	R8	
165CY-73a	Same (Typkoin 3/69 Lot 61)	1316	C	PL	R8	7460
165CY-73b	Same	Same	BR	PL	R8	7461
165CY-74a	Same	1320	C	PL	R9	7462
165CY-74b	Same	Same	BR	PL	R9	7463
165CY-75a	Same	1321	C	PL	R8	7464
165CY-75b	Same	Same	BR	PL	R9	7465
165CY-76a	Same	1323	C	PL	R9	7466
165CY-76b	Same (H-R 1717)	Same	BR	PL	R8	7467
165CY-77a	Same	1324	C	PL	R9	7468
165CY-77b	Same	Same	BR	PL	R9	7469
165CY-78a	Same	1326	C	PL	R9	7470
165CY-78b	Same	Same	BR	PL	R8	7471
165CY-79a	Same	1332	C	PL	R9	
165CY-79b	Same	Same	BR	PL	R8	
165CY-80a	Same	1336	C	PL	R9	7472
165CY-80b	Same (Typkoin 1/69 Lot 58)	Same	BR	PL	R9	7473
165CY-81a	Same	1337	C	PL	R9	7474
165CY-81b	Same	Same	BR	PL	R9	7475
165CY-82a	Same (H-R 1718)	1340	C	PL	R9	7476
165CY-82b	Same	Same	BR	PL	R7	7477
165CY-83a	Same	1341	C	PL	R8	7478
165CY-83b	Same	Same	BR	PL	R9	7479
165CY-84a	Same (Typkoin 5/69 Lot 69)	1342	C	PL	R9	7480
165CY-84b	Same (Typkoin 1/69 Lot 54)	Same	BR	PL	R9	7481
165CY-85a	Same (TypKoin 3/69 Lot 62;H-R 1719)	1344	C	PL	R9	7482
165CY-85b	Same (Typkoin 1/69 Lot 59)	Same	BR	PL	R8	7483
165CY-86a	Same (Typkoin 3/69 Lot 63)	1346	C	PL	R9	7484
165CY-86b	Same	Same	BR	PL	R8	7485
165CY-87a	Same	1348	C	PL	R8	7486
	(NOTE: Comes with obverse die break)					
165CY-87b	Same	Same	BR	PL	R8	7487
165CY-88a	Same	1349	C	PL	R9	
165CY-88b	Same	Same	BR	PL	R9	
165CY-89a	Same	1351	C	PL	R8	7488
165CY-89b	Same	Same	BR	PL	R9	7489
165CY-90a	Same	1387	C	PL	R9	7490
165CY-90b	Same	Same	BR	PL	R9	7491
165CY-91a	Same	1311	C	PL		7492
165CY-91b	Same	Same	BR	PL		7493
	(NOTE: The two pieces listed above probably do not exist, but are listed solely on basis of H&G.)					
165CY-92a	Same	1247	C	PL		7420
165CY-92b	Same	Same	BR	PL		7421
	(NOTE: Same comment as above.)					
165CY-93a	Same (Typkoin 9/69 Lot 55C)	Same as Rev Ohio 165CY-42	C	PL	R9	7494
165CY-93b	Same (Typkoin 1/69 Lot 66)	Same	BR	PL	R9	
165CY-94a	Same	Same as Rev Ohio 165CY-43	C	PL	R9	7496
165CY-94b	Same	Same	BR	PL	R9	
165CY-95a	Same	Same as Rev Ohio 165CY-44	C	PL	R9	7498
165CY-95b	Same	Same	BR	PL	R9	7499
165CY-69a	Same	1300	C	PL	R9	

OHIO-Continued

NUMBER	OBVERSE	REVERSE	METAL	EDGE	RARITY	H&G

CINCINNATI 165-Continued

165CY-96a	Same	Same as Rev Ohio 165CY-45	C	PL	R9	
165CY-96b	Same	Same	BR	PL	R9	

165CY-97

165CY-98

165CY-97a	W.K.LANPHEAR above— MANUF'R/OF/METALIC/ CARDS. in corn wreath in center. 134 WEST 4TH.ST.CIN.O. below. (NOTE: spelling error in METALLIC).	SEAL PRESSES/CANCELLING /AND/HAND/STAMPS	C	PL	R2	7504
165CY-97b	Same	Same	BR	PL	R8	7505
165CY-97d	Same (H-R 1721)	Same	C-N	PL	R9	
165CY-98a	Same	W.K.LANPHEAR/SEAL/ PRESSES/CIN.O.	C	PL	R3	7506
	(NOTE: Comes with reverse die breaks.)					
165CY-98b	Same	Same	BR	PL	R9	7507
165CY-98e	Same	Same	N	PL	R9	
165CY-99a	Same as Rev. Ohio 165CY-98	1091	C	PL	R4	7508
165CY-100a	Same	1228	C	PL	R4	7510
165CY-101a	Same	1316	C	PL	R9	7512
165CY-102a	Same	Same as Obv Ohio 165CY-1a	C	PL	R9	7514

165CY-103

165CY-105

165CY-103a	W.K.LANPHEAR/ MANUFACTURER/OF/STORE CARDS/102/WEST FOURTH ST./CINCINNATI O.	1280	C	PL	R9	7516
165CY-104a	Same	1290	C	PL	R3	7518
165CY-104d	Same	Same	C-N	PL	R9	7519
165CY-105a	Same	W.K.LANPHEAR/GENERAL/ ENGRAVER/102/W.4'ST./ CINCINNATI	C	PL	R7	7521
	(NOTE: Comes with heavy reverse die break)					
165CY-103aA	Same	Blank	C	PL	R10	

OHIO-Continued

NUMBER　　OBVERSE　　　　　　　REVERSE　　　　　　METAL　EDGE　RARITY　H&G

CINCINNATI 165-Continued

165CY-107

165CY-105b	Same	Same	BR	PL	R9	7522
165CY-106a	Same	BLANK	C	PL	R9	
165CY-107a	W.K.LANPHEAR/STENCIL/ CUTTER/102 WEST 4' ST. Large star and five small stars between the radiations (Typkoin 5/69 Lot 70?)	1176	C	PL	R9	7524
165CY-107d	Same (H-R 1720)	Same	C-N	PL	R9	
165CY-108a	Same	1331	C	PL	R8	7526
165CY-108d	Same (H-R 1722)	Same	C-N	PL	R9	

NO PHOTO AVAILABLE

165CY-109a	Similar to Obv Ohio 165CY-47, except MANUF'R spelled MANNER	1122	C	PL	R9	7528

165CZ-1　　　　　　165CZ-2

165CZ-1b	GOOD FOR/5/CENTS/IN CIGARS/OR TOBACCO/AT/ LANPHEAR'S/133 VINE ST (NOTE: Struck on a thin planchet)	Blank	BR	PL	R1	7531
165CZ-2b	GOOD FOR/25/CENTS/AT/ LANPHEAR'S/133 VINE ST/ IN/CIGARS OR TOBACCO (NOTE: Struck on a thin planchet.)	BLANK	BR	PL	R2	7532

The Wismer estate had about 400 specimens of these two tokens

OHIO-Continued

NUMBER OBVERSE REVERSE METAL EDGE RARITY H&G

CINCINNATI 165-Continued

165DA-1a	J.F.LARWELL/WATCH/MAKER	1046	C	R	R8	7534
165DA-1b	Same	Same	BR	R	R9	
165DA-1i	Same	Same	Z	R	R9	
165DA-2a	Same	1047	C	R	R9	
165DA-2d	Same	Same	C-N	R	R-	7535
165DA-3d	Same (Kreisberg 10/66 Lot 793)	1319	C-N	R	R10	

165DB-1a	S.LASURS,/DEALER IN/RAGS/ & METALS./26/15 ST. CIN.O. (NOTE: Usually comes with heavy rev. die break, and sometimes with obv. break.)	1057	C	PL	R2	7537
165DB-2a	Same (NOTE: A most unusual mistrike — see photo.)	1057 in incuse	C	PL	R10	
165DB-3a	Same	1247	C	PL	R3	7536

| 165DC-1a | H.LAZARESS,/DEALER/IN/ METALS/26/15 ST. (NOTE: Ohio 165DB and DC obviously allude to the same firm, but we do not know which is the correct spelling.) | 1247 | C | PL | R2 | 7539 |
| 165DC-2a | H.LAZARESS/DEALER/IN/ RAGS &/METALS/26/15TH ST CIN.O. | 1058 | C | PL | R2 | 7540 |

355

OHIO-Continued

NUMBER	OBVERSE	REVERSE	METAL	EDGE	RARITY	H&G

CINCINNATI 165-Continued

165DD-1

165DD-6

165DD-1a	LEAVITT & BEVIS/GENTS/ FURNISHING/GOODS/5TH & VINE/STS./CINCINNATI	1009	C	PL	R3	7542
165DD-2b	Same	1019	BR	PL	R9	
165DD-3a	Same	1042	C	R	R7	7544
165DD-3a1	Same	Same	C	PL	R9	7543
165DD-3b	Same	Same	BR	R	R8	7545
165DD-3i	Same	Same	Z	R	R9	
165DD-4a	Same	1047	C	R	R9	
165DD-4d	Same (H-R 1726)	Same	C-N	R	R10	
165DD-5d	Same	1069	C-N	R	R10	7546
165DD-6d	Same (H-R 1729)	LEAVITT & BEVIS/HOISERY/ &/GLOVES/5TH & VINE/ STS./CINCINNATI	C-N	R	R10	
165DD-7a	Same as Rev Ohio DD-6d (H-R 1727)	1009	C	R	R9	
165DD-7a1	Same	Same	C	PL	R5	7548
165DD-8b	Same	1019	BR	PL	R9	
165DD-9a	Same	1042	C	R	R9	7549
165DD-9b	Same	Same	BR	R	R8	7550
165DD-9i	Same	Same	Z	R	R9	
165DD-10a	Same (H-R 1728)	1047	C	R	R8	7551
165DD-11d	Same	1069	C-N	R	R10	7552
165DD-1b	Same (Dorge 10/73 Lot 342)	Same	BR	PL	R9	

165DE-1a	M.LINDERMANN,/COR./ELM/ & HENRY/CHECK MAKER. (NOTE: Comes with broken reverse die.)	1057	C	PL	R3	7555
165DE-2a	Same (NOTE: Comes with broken reverse die.)	1247	C	PL	R7	7554
165DE-3a	Same	1416	C	PL	R3	7556

356

OHIO-Continued

NUMBER	OBVERSE	REVERSE	METAL	EDGE	RARITY	H&G

CINCINNATI 165-Continued

165DF-1a	H.LOWENSTEIN/BUTCHER/ N.W.COR 9TH & JOHN	1026	C	PL	R8	
165DF-2a	Same	1029	C	PL	R8	
165DF-3a	Same	1032	C	PL	R7	7565
165DF-4a	Same	1033	C	PL	R6	
165DF-5a	Same	1036	C	PL	R4	7564
165DF-6a	Same	1037	C	PL	R8	7558
165DF-7a	Same	1041	C	PL	R7	
165DF-8a	Same	1042	C	R	R7	7559
165DF-8b	Same	Same	BR	R	R7	7560
165DF-8i	Same	Same	Z	R	R9	
165DF-9a	Same	1044	C	PL	R8	
165DF-10a	Same	1047	C	R	R9	7561
165DF-11d	Same	1069	C-N	R	R10	7562
165DF-10d	Same	1047	C-N	R	R10	

| 165DG-1a | F.W. LUTZ/ARTIST | 1298 | C | PL | R7 | 7566 |

| 165DH-1a | GOOD FOR/ONE/LOAF/278/ FIFTH/ST./R.E.MACAULEY (NOTE: Struck on thin planchet.) | JOHN STANTON/STAMP/ BRAND/CUTTER/CINCINNATI. | C | PL | R8 | |

357

OHIO-Continued

| NUMBER | OBVERSE | REVERSE | METAL | EDGE | RARITY | H&G |

CINCINNATI 165-Continued

165DI-1

165DI-2

| 165DI-1a | GOOD FOR 5 CT/DRINK/AT THE/BAR/R.T.MARKHAM. | JOHN'S/5/CENTS/SALOON | C | PL | R8 | |
| 165DI-2a | Similar, but 10 instead of 5. | Similar, but 10 instead of 5. | C | PL | R8 | |

165DJ-1a	MARSH & MINER/VEST/ MANUFACTURERS/207/ WADE,ST./CINCINNATI	1008	C	PL	R3	7567
165DJ-2a	Same (H-R 1732)	1009	C	R	R9	
165DJ-2a1	Same	Same	C	PL	R2	7568
165DJ-2b	Same	Same	BR	PL	R8	7569
165DJ-2i	Same	Same	Z	PL	R9	
165DJ-3a	Same	1019	C	PL	R7	7570
165DJ-3b	Same	Same	BR	PL	R8	
165DJ-4a	Same	1020	C	PL	R3	
165DJ-4b	Same	Same	BR	PL	R9	
165DJ-5a	Same	1021	C	PL	R7	
165DJ-6a	Same	1022	C	PL	R5	
165DJ-7a	Same	1026	C	PL	R3	7574
165DJ-8a	Same	1030	C	PL	R8	
165DJ-9a	Same	1031	C	PL	R8	

358

OHIO-Continued

NUMBER	OBVERSE	REVERSE	METAL	EDGE	RARITY	H&G

CINCINNATI 165-Continued

NUMBER	OBVERSE	REVERSE	METAL	EDGE	RARITY	H&G
165DJ-10a	Same	1035	C	PL	R8	
165DJ-11a	Same	1038	C	PL	R8	
165DJ-12a	Same	1042	C	R	R6	7571
165DJ-12b	Same	Same	BR	R	R8	7572
165DJ-12i	Same	Same	Z	R	R9	
165DJ-13a	Same	1047	C	R	R9	
165DJ-14d	Same	1069	C-N	R	R10	7573

NUMBER	OBVERSE	REVERSE	METAL	EDGE	RARITY	H&G
165DJ-15a	Similar, but MANUFACTURER with no S.	1008	C	PL	R2	7577
165DJ-16a	Same	1009	C	PL	R5	7578
165DJ-16b	Same	1009	BR	PL	R9	
165DJ-17a	Same	1019	C	PL	R4	7579
165DJ-17i	Same	Same	Z	PL	R9	
165DJ-18a	Same	1033	C	PL	R7	7585
165DJ-19a	Same	1038	C	PL	R5	7580
165DJ-20a	Same	1042	C	R	R6	7581
165DJ-20b	Same	Same	BR	R	R7	7582
165DJ-20i	Same	Same	Z	R	R9	7583
165DJ-21a	Same	1047	C	R	R9	
165DJ-21d	Same	Same	C-N	R	R10	7584
165DJ-22d	Same	1069	C-N	R	R10	
165DJ-16b1	Same (H-R 1731)	Same	BR	R	R10	

NUMBER	OBVERSE	REVERSE	METAL	EDGE	RARITY	H&G
165DK-1a	MARTIN'S/GROCERY/23/ WATER, ST./CINCINNATI	1022	C	PL	R3	7592
165DK-2a	Same	1026	C	PL	R3	7591
165DK-3a	Same	1031	C	PL	R8	
165DK-4a	Same	1042	C	R	R6	7587
165DK-4b	Same	Same	BR	R	R6	7588
165DK-4i	Same	Same	Z	R	R8	7589
165DK-5a	Same	1047	C	R	R8	
165DK-5d	Same (H-R 1734)	Same	C-N	R	R10	
165DK-6d	Same	1069	C-N	R	R10	7590

OHIO-Continued

NUMBER　　OBVERSE　　　　　　　　REVERSE　　　　　　　　　　METAL　EDGE　RARITY　H&G

CINCINNATI 165-Continued

165DL

165DM

165DL-1a	W.C.MC.CLENAHAN & CO./ GROCER/N.E.COR./4.&/ SYCAMORE	1089	C	PL	R9	7595
165DL-2a	Same	1123	C	PL	R9	
165DL-3a	Same	1124	C	PL	R6	7594
165DL-4a	Same	1290	C	PL	R6	7596
165DL-4d	Same	Same	C-N	PL	R9	7597
165DM-1a	T.W.MCDONALD/BOOTS/&/ SHOES/299/CEN. AVENUE/ CINCINNATI	1007	C	PL	R4	7599
165DM-2a	Same (H-R 1736)	1008	C	R	R9	
165DM-2a1	Same	Same	C	PL	R3	7600
165DM-3a	Same	1019	C	PL	R9	7601
165DM-3b	Same	Same	BR	PL	R9	
165DM-4a	Same	1042	C	R	R7	7603
165DM-4a1	Same	Same	C	PL	R9	7602
165DM-4b	Same	Same	BR	R	R8	7604
165DM-4i	Same	Same	Z	R	R9	
165DM-5a	Same (H-R 1738)	1047	C	R	R9	
165DM-6d	Same	1069	C-N	R	R10	7605

NO PHOTO AVAILABLE

165DN-1

165DN-2

165DN-1a	L.PHIL.MEREDITH/ &J.N.M'CLUNG/DENTISTS/ AT/M'CLUNG'S/DENTAL ROOMS/152/SIXTH ST./ CINCINNATI,O.	1344	C	PL	R8	7608
165DN-2a	Same	W.K.LANPHEAR above — CINCINNATI below — MANU'FR/METALIC/CARDS in wreath in center. (Obv. Ohio 165CY-1)	C	PL	R9	7607

360

OHIO-Continued

NUMBER	OBVERSE	REVERSE	METAL	EDGE	RARITY	H&G

CINCINNATI 165-Continued

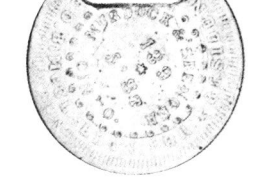

| 165DO-1bo | MERCHANTS HOTEL (Struck over McCllean political token) | MURDOCK & SPENCER/139/ W' FIFTH/STREET/ CINCINNATI (Obv. Ohio 165DZ) | BR | PL | R9 | |

165DP

165DQ

165DP-1a	ADAM METZ/BUTCHER/ 957 CEN. AVENUE	1007	C	PL	R4	7610
165DP-2a	Same	1008	C	PL	R3	7611
165DP-3a	Same	1019	C	PL	R5	7612
165DP-4a	Same	1020	C	PL	R7	
165DP-5a	Same	1038	C	PL	R6	7613
165DP-6a	Same	1042	C	R	R8	7614
165DP-6b	Same	Same	BR	R	R8	7615
165DP-6i	Same	Same	Z	R	R9	
165DP-7a	Same	1047	C	PL	R9	7616
	(NOTE: It is quite unusual for this die combination to be struck with a plain edge.)					
165DP-7a1	Same	Same	C	R	R9	
165DP-8a	Same	1068	C	PL	R4	7617
165DP-9d	Same	1069	C-N	R	R10	
165DP-10a	Same	1102	C	PL	R9	
165DP-8i	Same (Dorge 6/73 Lot 496)	Same	Z	R	R9	
165DQ-1a	J & D. METZ/PORK/PACKERS/ CINCINNATI	1022	C	PL	R5	7623
165DQ-2a	Same	1036	C	PL	R5	7622
165DQ-3a	Same	1042	C	R	R10	7619
165DQ-3b	Same	Same	BR	R	R9	7620
165DQ-4a	Same	1045	C	PL	R5	7618
165DQ-5a	Same	1047	C	R	R8	
165DQ-6a	Same	1069	C	R	R9	
165DQ-6d	Same	Same	C-N	R	R10	7621
165DQ-3i	Same (Dorge 6/73 Lot 497)	Same	Z	R	R9	

OHIO-Continued

NUMBER OBVERSE REVERSE METAL EDGE RARITY H&G

CINCINNATI 165-Continued

165DR 165DS 165DT

165DR-1a	GEO. METZGER/12/MILE/ HOUSE	1029	C	PL	R7	7625
165DR-2a	Same	1042	C	R	R7	7626
165DR-2b	Same	Same	BR	R	R8	7627
165DR-2i	Same	Same	Z	R	R9	
165DR-3a	Same	1047	C	R	R8	7628
165DR-4d	Same (Elder 9/38 Lot 387)	1069	C-N	R	R10	7629
165DR-3d	Same (Kreisberg 10/66 Lot 796)	Same	C-N	R	R10	
165DS-1a	L.MEYER/WEST/END/ SALOON/CINCINNATI	1026	C	PL	R4	7635
165DS-2a	Same	1039	C	PL	R8	
165DS-3a	Same	1042	C	R	R6	7631
165DS-3b	Same	Same	BR	R	R7	7632
165DS-3i	Same	Same	Z	R	R9	7633
165DS-4a	Same	1047	C	R	R9	
165DS-5d	Same	1069	C-N	R	R10	7634
165DT-1a	BUY YOUR/GROCERIES/ FROM/MIEDEKING/ N.E.COR/9'&JOHN STS	1019	C	PL	R7	
165DT-2a	Same	1022	C	PL	R8	7641
165DT-3a	Same	1042	C	R	R7	7637
165DT-3b	Same	Same	BR	R	R7	7638
165DT-3i	Same	Same	Z	R	R9	
165DT-4a	Same	1047	C	R	R8	
165DT-5d	Same	1069	C-N	R	R10	7640
165DT-4d	Same (Kreisberg 10/66 Lot 797)	Same	C-N	R	R10	

165DU-1  165DU-3

165DU-1d	BAR above — S-B-MONARCH below 10 in center.	1047	C-N	R	R10	7642
165DU-2a	Same	1393	C	R	R9	7643
	(NOTE: Also comes with broken reverse die.)					
165DU-3b	Same (Elder 9/38 Lot 361)	MURDOCK & SPENCER/139/ W'FIFTH/STREET/ CINCINNATI (Obv. Ohio 165DY-1)	BR	R	R9	7644

362

OHIO-Continued

NUMBER	OBVERSE	REVERSE	METAL	EDGE	RARITY	H&G

CINCINNATI 165-Continued

165DV-1a	J.T.MOORE/FRUIT/DEALER/ 164/SIXTH ST./CINCINNATI	1007	C	PL	R6	7646
165DV-2a	Same	1019	C	PL	R9	7647
165DV-2b	Same	Same	BR	PL	R9	
165DV-3a	Same	1021	C	PL	R8	7648
165DV-4a	Same	1042	C	R	R7	7649
165DV-4b	Same	Same	BR	R	R7	7650
165DV-4i	Same	Same	Z	R	R9	7651
165DV-5a	Same	1043	C	R	R9	
165DV-6a	Same	1047	C	R	R9	
165DV-6d	Same	Same	C-N	R	R10	
165DV-7d	Same	1069	C-N	R	R10	7652
165DV-8a	Same	1279	C	PL	R9	7653
165DV-8d	Same	Same	C-N	R	R9	

165DW-1a	MORGAN & FERRY/5/ NO 20 E. 5'ST/CINCINNATI	1007	C	PL	R9	7657
165DW-2a	Same	1008	C	PL	R4	7658
165DW-3a	Same	1022	C	PL	R9	
165DW-4a	Same	1047	C	R	R9	7661
165DW-4b	Same	Same	BR	R	R9	7662
165DW-4d	Same (H-R 1743)	Same	C-N	R	R10	
165DW-5a	Same	1192	C	R	R6	7655
165DW-5b	Same	Same	BR	R	R8	7656
165DW-6a	Same	1279	C	PL	R9	7660
165DW-7a	MORGAN & FERRY/10/ NO, 20E. 5'ST/CINCINNATI	1007	C	PL	R9	7664
165DW-8a	Same	1009	C	PL	R4	7665
165DW-9a	Same	1042	C	R	R9	7666
165DW-10a	Same	1047	C	R	R8	
165DW-11d	Same	1069	C-N	R	R10	7667
165DW-12a	Same	1393	C	R	R7	7668
165DW-12b	Same	Same	BR	R	R7	7669
165DW-12i	Same	Same	Z	R	R9	
165DW-6Ad	Same (Obv of 165DW-1)	1069	C-N	R	R10	7659

OHIO-Continued

NUMBER	OBVERSE	REVERSE	METAL	EDGE	RARITY	H&G

CINCINNATI 165-Continued

165DX-1a	H.J. MOSER, WATCHMAKER around, 14 stars in circle in center.	1047	C	R	R9	7671
165DX-1d	Same	Same	C-N	R	R10	7672

*165DY-1b	JAS. MURDOCK, JR/M'F'R' OF/ LEAD SEALS/WIRES/&/ PRESSES/165 RACE ST. CINTI.O.	Around M'F'T'R OF BAGGAGE CHECKS, WAX SEALS & TICKET STAMPS. In center 100/10 IN./WIRES	BR	R	R8	7675
*165DY-1b1	Same	Same	BR	PL	R9	7674

165DY-2a	JAS MURDOCK JR./DIE/ SINKER/139/FIFTH, ST./ CINCINNATI,O.	1018	C	R	R9	
165DY-3a	Same	1047	C	R	R8	
165DY-4a	Same	1069	C	R	R9	
165DY-4b	Same	Same	BR	R	R9	
165DY-4d	Same	Same	C-N	R	R9	7679
165DY-5a	Same	1160	C	R	R9	
165DY-6a	Same	1192	C	R	R9	7677
165DY-4b1	Same	Same	BR	PL	R10	
165DY-6d	Same (Kreisberg 10/66 Lot 800)	Same	C-N	R	R10	

364

OHIO-Continued

NUMBER	OBVERSE	REVERSE	METAL	EDGE	RARITY	H&G

CINCINNATI 165-Continued

165DY-7a	Same	1279	C	R	R9	7678
165DY-8a	Same	1282	C	R	R9	
165DY-8a1	Same	Same	C	PL	R9	
165DY-9a	Same	1283	C	R	R9	7680
165DY-10a	Same	1370	C	R	R9	
165DY-11a	Same	1373	C	R	R9	
165DY-12a	Same	THE/FEDERAL/GOVERNMENT /A/NATIONAL/CURRENCY/ FREE TRADE/AND/HUMAN RIGHTS (Fuld Pat 467, Rev Ohio 165FM-1)	C	R	R9	
165DY-13b	JAS. MURDOCK, JR/ STAMPS/BURNING/BRANDS/ AND/STENCILLS/139/W. 5 ST. CINCINNATI	No	BR	PL	R8	
165DZ-1a	MURDOCK & SPENCER/39/ FIFTH/STREET/CINCINNATI	1393	C	R	R9	7682
165DZ-2b	Same (NOTE: Also occurs with oval hole for suspension.)	ST LAWRENCE	BR	PL	R8	
165DY-8d	Same (Kreisberg 10/66 Lot 800)	Same	C-N	R	R10	
165DY-9d	Same (Kreisberg 10/66 Lot 800)	Same	C-N	R	R10	
165DY-10d	Same (Kreisberg 10/66 Lot 800)	Same	C-N	R	R10	

OHIO-Continued

NUMBER	OBVERSE	REVERSE	METAL	EDGE	RARITY	H&G

CINCINNATI 165-Continued

165DZ-3

165DZ-4

165DZ-3b	MURDOCK & SPENCER/ STAMPS/BRANDS/STENCILS/ BAGGAGE CHECKS/& C & C/ 139/W. 5' ST. CINCINNATI large 30mm.	Obv. incused	BR	PL	R7	
165DZ-3e	Same	Same	W-M	PL	R7	
165DZ-4b	Similar inscription, large 37 mm	Same	BR	PL	R8	
165DZ-4e	Same	Same	W-M	PL	R9	

165EA

165EB-1

165EB-6

165EA-1a	E.MYERS & CO/DEALERS/IN FOREIGN/FRUIT/&/ CONFECTIONERY/52 MAIN, ST.CIN,O.	1019	C	PL	R6	7684
165EA-2a	Same	1020	C	PL	R7	
165EA-3a	Same	1034	C	PL	R8	
165EA-4a	Same	1036	C	PL	R5	7689
165EA-5a	Same	1042	C	R	R6	7685
165EA-5b	Same	Same	BR	R	R7	7686
165EA-5i	Same	Same	Z	R	R9	7687
165EA-6d	Same	1069	C-N	R	R10	7688
165EB-1a	.H.NIEBUHR/WINE/&/BEER/ SALOON/223/CENTRAL AVE'.	1176	C	PL	R7	7691
165EB-2a	Same	1290	C	PL	R9	7692
165EB-3a	Same	1295	C	PL	R4	7693
165EB-3d	Same	Same	C-N	PL	R8	7694
165EB-4a	Same	1384	C	PL	R9	7695
165EB-5a	Same	1416	C	PL	R9	7696
165EB-6a	Same	Obv. incused	C	PL	R10	7697

OHIO-Continued

NUMBER	OBVERSE	REVERSE	METAL	EDGE	RARITY	H&G

CINCINNATI 165-Continued

165EC

165ED

165EC-1a	F.J.NIEMER'S/HOTEL/262/ FRONT, ST./CIN.O.	1124	C	PL	R9	7698
165EC-1d	Same (H-R 1750)	Same	C-N	PL	R9	7699
165EC-2a	Same	1176	C	PL	R3	7700
165EC-3a	Same	1295	C	PL	R9	7701
165EC-3d	Same	Same	C-N	PL	R9	7702
165EC-4a	Same	1331	C	PL	R9	7703
165ED-1a	J.H.NOLWER,/COR./ELM &/ FINDLEY/GROCER.	1388	C	PL	R7	7704

165EF

165EG

165EF-1a	R.D.NORRIS/DRY/GOODS/ 174/FIFTH,ST.	1019	C	PL	R4	7706
165EF-2a	Same	1020	C	PL	R5	7707
165EF-3a	Same	1036	C	PL	R5	7712
165EF-3b	Same	Same	BR	PL	R9	
165EF-4a	Same	1042	C	R	R6	7708
165EF-4b	Same	Same	BR	R	R7	7709
165EF-4i	Same	Same	Z	R	R9	
165EF-5a	Same	1047	C	R	R9	
165EF-6d	Same	1069	C-N	R	R10	7711
165EG-1a	O'DONOGHUE & NAISH/BOOTS/ &/SHOES/164 WEST 5' ST/ CINCINNATI	1007	C	PL	R9	7714
165EG-2a	Same	1008	C	PL	R6	7715
165EG-3a	Same	1009	C	PL	R3	7716
165EG-3b	Same	Same	BR	PL	R9	
165EG-4a	Same	1019	C	PL	R7	7721
165EG-4b	Same	Same	BR	PL	R9	
165EG-5a	Same	1042	C	R	R6	7717
165EG-5b	Same	Same	BR	R	R6	7718
165EG-5i	Same	Same	Z	R	R9	
165EG-6a	Same	1047	C	R	R9	
165EG-6d	Same (H-R 1754)	Same	C-N	R	R10	
165EG-7d	Same	1069	C-N	R	R10	7720

OHIO-Continued

NUMBER	OBVERSE	REVERSE	METAL	EDGE	RARITY	H&G

CINCINNATI 165-Continued

165EH-1

165EH-8

165EH-1a	O'REILLY BROS./DRY/GOODS/ 112/FIFTH,ST./CINCINNATI.	1019	C	PL	R9	
165EH-1b	Same	Same	BR	PL	R9	
165EH-2a	Same	1020	C	PL	R8	
165EH-3a	Same	1023	C	PL	R6	7726
165EH-4a	Same	1025	C	PL	R8	
165EH-5a	Same	1042	C	R	R7	7723
165EH-5b	Same	Same	BR	R	R8	7724
165EH-5i	Same	Same	Z	R	R9	
165EH-6a	Same	1047	C	R	R8	
165EH-6d	Same (H-R 1756)	Same	C-N	R	R10	
165EH-7d	Same	1069	C-N	R	R10	7725
165EH-8a	Same	H.H.ROBINSON/DRY/GOODS/ GROCERIES/&/PRODUCE/ NEW LONDON/B/CO. (Obv. Ohio 620A)	C	PL	R10	7727

165EI

165EI-1

165EI-2

165EI-1a	B. PANZER above, CENTS below. 5 within circle in center (H-R 1758)	JOS. J.SAYRE/DIE/SINKER 4T.H.&/WALNUT CIN.O	C	PL	R8	
165EI-2b	Similar, but 10 instead of 5	Same	BR	PL	R8	7729
165EJ-1a	PEEBLES/DEALER/IN/ STAPLE & FANCY/ GROCERIES/5TH & RACE/ STS./CINCINNATI	1007	C	PL	R4	7732
165EJ-2a	Same	1008	C	PL	R2	7733
165EJ-3a	Same	1009	C	PL	R3	7734
165EJ-4a	Same	1019	C	PL	R3	7735
165EJ-5a	Same	1020	C	PL	R7	7731
165EJ-5aa	Same	1025	C	PL	R8	
165EJ-6a	Same	1026	C	PL	R5	
165EJ-7a	Same	1031	C	PL	R7	7741
165EJ-8a	Same	1036	C	PL	R4	
165EJ-9a	Same	1038	C	PL	R4	7736

OHIO-Continued

NUMBER　OBVERSE　　　　REVERSE　　　　　　METAL　EDGE　RARITY　H&G

CINCINNATI 165-Continued

165EJ

165EK

165EJ-10a	Same	1042	C	R	R6	7738
165EJ-10a1	Same	Same	C	PL	R8	7737
165EJ-10b	Same	Same	BR	R	R7	7739
165EJ-10i	Same	Same	Z	R	R8	
165EJ-11a	Same	1047	C	R	R9	
165EJ-11d	Same (H-R 1760)	Same	C-N	R	R10	
165EJ-12d	Same	1069	C-N	R	R10	7740
165EJ-13a	Same	1279	C	PL	R9	7742
165EK-1a	PHILIP/16/WALNUT/ST./ CINCINNATI	1019	C	PL	R9	
165EK-2a	Same	1036	C	PL	R3	7747
165EK-3a	Same	1042	C	R	R6	7744
165EK-3b	Same	Same	BR	R	R7	7745
165EK-3i	Same	Same	Z	R	R9	
165EK-4a	Same (H-R 1764)	1047	C	R	R9	
165EK-4d	Same (H-R 1763)	Same	C-N	R	R10	
165EK-5d	Same	1069	C-N	R	R10	7746
165EK-6a	Same (Dorge 2/74 Lot 602)	1022	C	PL	R9	

165EL

165EM

165EL-1a	J.G.PLEISTEINER/FANCY/ GOODS/&/NOTIONS/ 555 VINE ST./BT. 15' & LIBERTY/CINCINNATI	1007	C	PL	R7	7749
165EL-2a	Same	1036	C	PL	R9	
165EL-3a	Same	1042	C	R	R8	7750
165EL-3b	Same	Same	BR	R	R8	7751
165EL-3b1	Same	Same	BR	PL	R9	
165EL-3i	Same	Same	Z	R	R9	7752
165EL-4a	Same	1047	C	R	R9	
165EL-5d	Same	1069	C-N	R	R10	7753
165EM-1a	CHAS.PLUMB/HUCKSTER/ MARKET/CINCINNATI	1029	C	PL	R3	7755
165EM-2a	Same	1034	C	PL	R4	7756

369

OHIO-Continued

NUMBER	OBVERSE	REVERSE	METAL	EDGE	RARITY	H&G

CINCINNATI 165-Continued

NUMBER	OBVERSE	REVERSE	METAL	EDGE	RARITY	H&G
165EM-3a	Same	1035	C	PL	R9	7761
165EM-4a	Same	1042	C	R	R6	7757
165EM-4b	Same	Same	BR	R	R7	7758
165EM-4i	Same	Same	Z	R	R9	7759
165EM-5a	Same	1047	C	R	R8	
165EM-5d	Same (H-R 1768)	Same	C-N	R	R10	
165EM-6d	Same	1069	C-N	R	R10	7760

165EN   165EO

NUMBER	OBVERSE	REVERSE	METAL	EDGE	RARITY	H&G
165EN-1a	POGUE & JONES/DRY/GOODS 128/FIFTH,ST./CINCINNATI	1030	C	PL	R4	7763
165EN-2a	Same	1036	C	PL	R3	7768
165EN-3a	Same	1042	C	R	R6	7764
165EN-3b	Same	Same	BR	R	R6	7765
165EN-3i	Same	Same	Z	R	R9	7766
165EN-4a	Same	1047	C	R	R9	
165EN-4d	Same (H-R 1769)	Same	C-N	R	R10	
165EN-5d	Same	1069	C-N	R	R10	7767
165EN-6a	Same	1192	C	PL	R9	
165EO-1a	HENRY PORTER/95/FIFTH/ST./CINCINNATI	1047	C	R	R8	
165EO-1d	Same (H-R 1770)	Same	C-N	R	R10	
165EO-2d	Same (Elder 9/38 Lot 329)	1069	C-N	R	R10	
165EO-3b	Same	1397	BR	R	R8	7769
165EO-4b	Same	1398	BR	R	R9	
165EO-5b	Same	1401A	BR	R	R9	

NUMBER	OBVERSE	REVERSE	METAL	EDGE	RARITY	H&G
165EP-1a	H.RANSICK/GOOD FOR/1/LOAF/	Similar to Rev Ohio 905C, but eagle facing left.	C	PL	R8	

370

OHIO-Continued

NUMBER	OBVERSE	REVERSE	METAL	EDGE	RARITY	H&G

CINCINNATI 165-Continued

165EQ-1a	H.A.RATTERMAN/CINCINNATI	1007	C	PL	R4	7771
	12 stars in circle in center.					
165EQ-2a	Same	1008	C	R	R9	
165EQ-2a1	Same	Same	C	PL	R3	7772
	(NOTE: Comes with broken reverse die.)					
165EQ-2b	Same	Same	BR	PL	R9	
165EQ-3a	Same	1042	C	R	R6	7773
165EQ-3b	Same	Same	BR	R	R7	7774
165EQ-3i	Same	Same	Z	R	R9	7775
165EQ-4a	Same	1047	C	R	R9	
165EQ-4d	Same	Same	C-N	R	R10	
165EQ-5d	Same	1069	C-N	R	R10	7776
165EQ-6a	Same	1192	C	PL	R3	7770
165EQ-6b	Same	Same	BR	PL	R9	
165EQ-7a	Same	BLANK	C	PL	R10	7777
165EQ-1a1	Same (H-R 1772)	Same	C	R	R9	

165ER-1a	JOHN RAVY/CONFECTIONER/	1007	C	PL	R5	7779
	185/RACE/STREET/CINCINNATI					
165ER-2a	Same	1008	C	PL	R2	7780
165ER-3a	Same	1019	C	PL	R9	
165ER-3b	Same	Same	BR	PL	R9	
165ER-3i	Same	Same	Z	PL	R9	
165ER-4a	Same	1021	C	PL	R5	7781
165ER-5a	Same	1022	C	PL	R5	7788
165ER-6a	Same	1038	C	PL	R3	7782
165ER-7a	Same	1042	C	R	R6	7783
165ER-7b	Same	Same	BR	R	R6	7784
165ER-7i	Same	Same	Z	R	R9	
165ER-8a	Same	1047	C	R	R9	
165ER-9a	Same	1068	C	PL	R5	7786
	(NOTE: Comes with broken reverse die.)					
165ER-10a	Same	1069	C-N	R	R10	7787
165ER-11a	Same	BLANK	C	PL	R10	7789
165ER-1a1	Same (H-R 1774)	Same	C	R	R9	

OHIO-Continued

NUMBER	OBVERSE	REVERSE	METAL	EDGE	RARITY	H&G

CINCINNATI 165-Continued

165ES

165ET

165ES-1a	I.REES/401/CENTRAL/AVE./CINCINNATI,O.	1170	C	PL	R1	7792
165ES-1d	Same	Same	C-N	PL	R9	7793
165ES-2a	Same	1176	C	PL	R9	7791
165ET-1a	J.REIS & CO,/COR.7TH&/WALNUT/MEAT STORE. (H-R 1777)	1056	C	PL	R9	
165ET-2a	Same	1386	C	PL	R4	7794

165EU-1

165EU-9

165EV

165EU-1a	J.F.RESTA/3'& SMITH/STS/CINCINNATI/SAUSAGE/MAKER	1022	C	PL	R5	7800
165EU-2a	Same	1026	C	PL	R5	7799
165EU-3a	Same	1029	C	PL	R7	
165EU-4a	Same	1033	C	PL	R6	7801
165EU-5a	Same	1035	C	PL	R7	
165EU-6a	Same	1042	C	R	R7	7796
165EU-6b	Same	Same	BR	R	R7	7797
165EU6i	Same	Same	Z	R	R9	
165EU-7a	Same (H-R 1779)	1047	C	R	R9	
165EU-8d	Same	1069	C-N	R	R10	7802
165EU-9a	Same	CARL HAAS/493 VINE ST. Rabbit in center (Obv. Ohio 165BJ-12)	C	PL	R10	7803
165EV-1a	A.RICKE above — CINCINNATI below square ornament in circle of eleven stars in center.	1022	C	PL	R7	7809
165EV-1d	Same (H-R 1781)	Same	C-N	R	R10	
165EV-2a	Same	1032	C	PL	R8	
165EV-3a	Same	1033	C	PL	R7	
165EV-4a	Same	1034	C	PL	R8	7810
165EV-5a	Same	1036	C	PL	R3	7808
	(NOTE: comes with broken obverse die.)					

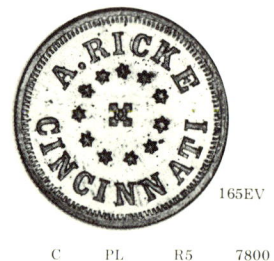

OHIO-Continued

NUMBER　　OBVERSE　　　　　　REVERSE　　　　　　METAL　EDGE　RARITY　H&G

CINCINNATI 165-Continued

165EV-9

165EV-17

165EV-6a	Same	1042	C	R	R6	7805
165EV-6b	Same	Same	BR	R	R10	7806
165EV-7a	Same	1047	C	R	R9	
165EV-8d	Same	1069	C-N	R	R10	7807
165EV-9a	Same inscription, square ornament in center of nine stars surrounded by beaded border.	1007	C	PL	R5	7812
	(NOTE: E of RICKE is double cut — obverse die shows cracks.)					
165EV-10a	Same	1008	C	PL	R8	7813
165EV-11a	Same	1019	C	PL	R0	7815
165EV-11b	Same	Same	BR	PL	R9	
165EV-12a	Same	1036	C	PL	R8	
165EV-13a	Same	1038	C	PL	R7	7816
	(NOTE: All specimens seen have obverse die breaks.)					
165EV-14a	Same	1042	C	R	R6	7817
	(NOTE: All specimens seen have obverse die breaks.)					
165EV-14b	Same	Same	BR	R	R7	7818
165EV-14i	Same	Same	?	R	R9	7819
165EV-15d	Same	1069	C-N	R	R10	7820
165EV-16a	Same	1192	C	PL	R9	7814
165EV-17a	Similar to preceding, but smaller letters.	1036	C	PL	R7	7821
	(NOTE: Most specimens show strong obverse die breaks.)					
165EV-6i	Same (Dorge 10/73 Lot 370)	Same	Z	R	R9	

165EW-1a	B.J.RICKING/GROCER/49/PLUM ST./CINTI.O.	1088	C	PL	R2	7825
165EW-2a	Same	1090	C	PL	R4	7826
165EW-3a	Same	1091	C	PL	R7	7827
165EW-4a	Same	1124	C	PL	R8	7823
165EW-4d	Same (H-R 1782)	Same	C-N	PL	R9	
165EW-5a	Same	1170	C	PL	R8	7834
165EW-5d	Same	Same	C-N	PL	R9	
165EW-6a	Same	1171	C	PL	R8	
165EW-7a	Same	1176	C	PL	R8	7830
165EW-7d	Same	Same	C-N	PL	R9	7831

OHIO-Continued

NUMBER	OBVERSE	REVERSE	METAL	EDGE	RARITY	H&G

CINCINNATI 165-Continued

165EW-8a	Same	1223	C	PL	R3	7828
165EW-9a	Same	1226	C	PL	R6	7829
165EW-10a	Same	1227	C	PL	R9	
165EW-11a	Same	1295	C	PL	R9	7832
165EW-12a	Same	1331	C	PL	R9	7833

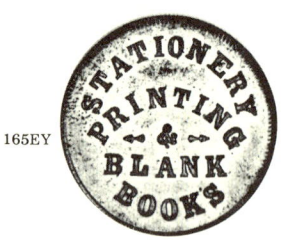

165EX-1a	GEO. W. RITTER'S/MEAT/STORE/241/FOURTH ST.	1290	C	PL	R5	7836
165EX-1d	Same	Same	C-N	PL	R9	7837
165EY-1b	F.H.ROLLINS above, Indian head to left in center. 18, PUBLIC LANDING CIN'TI.O. below (H-R 1783)	STATIONERY/PRINTING/&/BLANK/BOOKS	BR	R	R7	7839

165EZ-1a	YANKEE ROBINSON above THE GREAT COMEDIAN below. Portrait of man in center with gun resting on right shoulder	YANKEE ROBINSON above Triangle enclosing hand in center — pointing to TRIAD — at sides of triangle PAST PRESENT FUTURE	C	PL	R1	7841
165EZ-1a	Same	Same	BR	PL	R9	
165EZ-2m	Same	Obverse incused	TIN	PL	R8	7842
165EZ-3a	Same	Similar to Ohio 165 EZ-1a but hand is shorter and divides date 1863	C	R	R2	7845
165EZ-3b	Same	Same	BR	R	R8	7846
165EZ-4d	Same (H-R 1786)	1018	C-N	R	R10	
165EZ-5a	Same	1028	C	PL	R7	7844
165EZ-6a	Same	1034	C	PL	R7	7843

374

OHIO-Continued

NUMBER	OBVERSE	REVERSE	METAL	EDGE	RARITY	H&G

CINCINNATI 165-Continued

165EZ-3 165EZ-14

165EZ-7b	Same	1069	BR	PL	R10	
	(NOTE: Reverse overstruck over another obv, a flip-over double strike — see photo.)					
165EZ-7d	Same	Same	C-N	R	R10	
165EX-8a	Rev. Ohio 165EZ-1	1023	C	PL	R8	
165EZ-9a	Same	1028	C	PL	R2	
165EZ-10a	Same	1034	C	PL	R2	
165EZ-11a	Same	1045	C	PL	R9	
165EZ-12a	Rev. Ohio 165EZ-3a	1046	C	R	R6	7849
165EZ-13a	Same	1017	C	R	R7	7850
165EZ-13d	Same	Same	C-N	R	R10	
165EZ-14a	Bust facing right, above YANKEE ROBINSON	Similar to Rev. Ohio 165 EZ-3a, but date 1869 and hand points left.	C	R	R4	
165EZ-13a1	Same	Same	C	PL	R9	

165EZ-7 165EZ-16 165FA

165EZ-15d	Same (H-R 1785)	1018	C-N	R	R10	
165EZ-16a	Same	Similar to 165EZ-14a, but hand points right.	C	R	R3	
	(NOTE: The only specimens seen of this type have a broken reverse die.)					
165EZ-17d	Rev. Ohio 165EZ-14a (H-R 1788)	1047	C-N	R	R10	
165FA-1d	ALBERT ROSS, DRUGGIST/ CORNER/ OF CENTRAL/ AVENUE/ &/ 8TH STREET/ CINCINNATI.	1069	C-N	R	R10	
	(NOTE: Listed as Adams Ohio 23 thru 28)					
165FA-2a	Same	1309	C	PL	R3	7852
165FA-2b	Same	Same	BR	PL	R3	7853
165FA-2c	Same	Same	N	PL	R5	
165FA-2d	Same	Same	C-N	PL	R8	7854
165FA-2e	Same	Same	W-M	R	R8	
165FA-2e1	Same	Same	W-M	PL	R5	
165FA-2f	Same	Same	S	PL	R7	7855
165FA-2j	Same	Same	G-S	PL	R7	

375

OHIO-Continued

NUMBER	OBVERSE	REVERSE	METAL	EDGE	RARITY	H&G

CINCINNATI 165-Continued

165FB-1a	ELLIS ROUSE'S/HAIR/ PRESERVATIVE/METROPOLITAN /SHAVING/SALOON	1047	C	R	R8	
165FB-2a	Same	1394	C	R	R9	
165FC-1a	JOHN SACKSTEDER,/MAN'FR/ OF/SEWING/MACHINES/ 419/CEN.AVE./CIN.O.	SEWING/MACHINES/NEATLY/ REPAIRED/1863	C	PL	R3	7857
165FC-1d	Same	Same	C-N	PL	R9	
165FC-2a	Same	1170	C	PL	R2	7858
165FC-3a	Same as Rev. Ohio 165FC-1a	Same	C	PL	R8	

(NOTE: Also to be listed as Patriotic Civil War Token.)

| 165FD-1b | SACKSTEDER & MARTIN/ MANUFACTURERS/ CINCINNATI/OHIO | BLANK | BR | PL | R5 | |

| 165FE-1b | JOS. J. SAYRE/DIE/SINKER/ 4TH &/WALNUT/CIN.O. NOTE: Same as Rev. Ohio 165EI) | BERRY CHECK/GOOD/FOR/ ONE BOX | BR | PL | R9 | |
| 165FE-2e | Same | SODA CHECK/1/GLASS | W-M | PL | R9 | |

376

OHIO-Continued

NUMBER	OBVERSE	REVERSE	METAL	EDGE	RARITY	H&G

CINCINNATI 165-Continued

165FF-1a	CHR.SCHLOENDORN/PAPER HANGINGS/&/FANCY GOODS/492/ MAIN ST./CINCINNATI	1007	C	PL	R5	7860
165FF-2d	Same (H-R 1796)	1018	C-N	R	R10	
165FF-3a	Same	1019	C	PL	R9	
165FF-4a	Same	1042	C	R	R6	7862
165FF-4b	Same	Same	BR	R	R7	7863
165FF-4i	Same	Same	Z	R	R9	7864
165FF-5a	Same	1047	C	R	R9	
165FF-6d	Same	1069	C-N	R	R10	7865
165FG-1a	G.SCH/GROCER/646 VINE ST./ CIN.O.	1056	C	PL	R9	
165FH-1a	H.SCHMIDT'S/AUCTION/&/ COMMISSION/GOODS/27 ELDER,ST./CINCINNATI (H-R 1798)	1026	C	PL	R8	
165FH-2a	Same	1028	C	PL	R8	
165FH-3a	Same	1029	C	PL	R6	
165FH-4a	Same	1031	C	PL	R5	7871
165FH-5a	Same	1033	C	PL	R4	
165FH-6a	Same	1042	C	R	R6	7867
165FH-6b	Same	Same	BR	R	R7	7868
165FH-6i	Same	Same	Z	R	R8	7869
165FH-7a	Same (H-R 1800)	1047	C	R	R9	
165FH-7d	Same	Same	C-N	R	R10	
165FH-8d	Same	1069	C-N	R	R10	7870
165FI-1d	L.SCHNEIDER/557/WALNUT/ ST./CINCINNATI (H-R 1802)	1018	C-N	R	R10	
165FI-2a	Same	1020	C	PL	R6	7873
165FI-3a	Same	1022	C	PL	R5	7880
165FI-4a	Same	1023	C	PL	R7	

OHIO-Continued

NUMBER	OBVERSE	REVERSE	METAL	EDGE	RARITY	H&G

CINCINNATI 165-Continued

165FI-5a	Same	1026	C	PL	R4	
165FI-6a	Same	1029	C	PL	R3	7874
165FI-7a	Same	1036	C	PL	R3	7879
165FI-8a	Same	1042	C	R	R6	7875
165FI-8b	Same	Same	BR	R	R7	7876
165FI-8i	Same	Same	Z	R	R9	
165FI-9a	Same (H-R 1803)	1047	C	R	R8	
165FI-10d	Same	1069	C-N	R	R10	7878

165FJ-1b	H.SCHOTT/248/W.LIBERTY/ ST./CIN'TI.O.	1391	BR	R	R9	
165FJ-2c	Same	1395	N	R	R9	
165FJ-3b	Same	BLANK	BR	R	R9	7882

165FK-1a	I X L/DAIRY/LOT SCOTT	1047	C	R	R8	
165FK-2d	Same	1069	C-N	R	R10	

165FL-1   165FL-3

165FL-1c	SCHULTZ & NEGLEY/ DRUGGISTS/N.E.COR./5' & MAIN ST/CIN'TI.O. (H-R 1804)	1391	N	R	R9	7884
165FL-2b	Same	1395	BR	R	R9	
165FL-3b	S & N	1102	BR	PL	R9	

378

OHIO-Continued

NUMBER	OBVERSE	REVERSE	METAL	EDGE	RARITY	H&G

CINCINNATI 165-Continued

165FM 165FM-6 165FM-7

165FM-1a	WM.SENOUR. in script	1089	C	PL	R8	7899
165FM-2a	Same	1130	C	PL	R7	7903
	(NOTE: The piece listed as H&G 7898 cannot exist as described.)					
165FM-3a	Same	1181	C	PL	R9	7900
165FM-4a	Same	1298	C	PL	R9	7901
165FM-5a	Same	1346	C	PL	R9	7902
165FM-5d	Same (H-R 1808)	Same	C-N	PL	R9	
165FM-6b	Same	CONTINENTAL/HOTEL/MONEY/ CHECK	BR	PL	R9	7897
165FM-7a	Same	W,K,LANPHEAR above CINCINNATI O. below MANU'FR/OF/METALIC/ CARDS in wreath (Obv. Ohio 165CY-1)	C	PL	R9	7407

NOTE: See top of page 380 for additional 165FM listings.

165FN 165FN-1 165FN-11

165FN-1a	M.MEDNDALSHAFER/ ATTORNEY/&/COUNSELOR/ AT/LAW/57/THIRD ST./ CINCINNATI	THE/FEDERAL/GOVERNMENT /A/NATIONAL/CURRENCY/ FREE/TRADE/AND/HUMAN RIGHTS.	C	R	R8	
165FN-1a1	Same	Same	C	PL	R2	7886
165FN-2a	Same	1009	C	PL	R5	7887
165FN-3d	Same (H-R 1806)	1018	C-N	R	R10	
165FN-4a	Same	1019	C	PL	R9	
165FN-5a	Same	1021	C	PL	R3	7888
165FN-6a	Same	1022	C	PL	R7	7893
165FN-7a	Same	1036	C	PL	R6	7892
165FN-8a	Same	1042	C	R	R7	7889
165FN-8b	Same	Same	BR	R	R8	7890
165FN-8i	Same	Same	Z	R	R9	7891
165FN-9a	Same	1017	C	R	R9	
165FN-10d	Same	1069	C-N	R	R10	
165FN-11d	Same (H-R 1807)	MAGI GENI/QUBO/DAIRI/ WHANG (Rev. Ohio 165AD-2a)	C-N	R	R10	
	(NOTE: A very curious muling, which illustrates the absurdity of some Civil War mulings.)					
165FN-4b	Same (Dorge 2/73 Lot 456)	Same	BR	PL	R10	

379

OHIO-Continued

NUMBER　　OBVERSE　　　　　　REVERSE　　　　　　　METAL　EDGE　RARITY　H&G

CINCINNATI 165-Continued

165FM-8 Rev. 　　　　165FM-9 Rev.

Number	Obverse	Reverse	Metal	Edge	Rarity	H&G
165FM-8a	Same	W.K.LAN PHEAR/MANU'FR/OF/METALIC/CARDS/CIN'TI/OHIO (Obv. Ohio 165CY47a)	C	PL	R9	7895
165FM-9a	Same	S.E.HUSTLER/BROWN'S/OLD/CORNER/TROY,O. (Obv. Ohio 880C-1)	C	PL	R9	7904
165FM-10b	Same	BLANK	BR	PL	R9	

NOTE: Varieties 165FM-8a, 9a, and 10b should be listed on previous page under 165FM (Wm. Senour).

165FO 　　　　165FP

Number	Obverse	Reverse	Metal	Edge	Rarity	H&G
165FO-1a	H.E.SHAW,/NEW/AND/SECOND HAND/FURNITURE/18/EAST 4.ST./CIN.O.	1124	C	Pl	R7	7906
165FO-1d	Same (H-R 1809)	Same	C-N	PL	R9	7907
165FO-2a	Same	1176	C	PL	R3	7908
165FO-3a	Same	1295	C	PL	R9	7909
165FO-4a	Same	1331	C	PL	R8	7910
165FP-1d	F.SHEEN/GROCERIES/&/BREAD/STUFFS/70/E.PEARL,ST. (H-R 1811)	1018	C-N	R	R10	
165FP-2a	Same	1020	C	PL	R7	7913
165FP-3a	Same	1023	C	PL	R7	
165FP-4a	Same	1025	C	PL	R7	
165FP-5a	Same	1026	C	PL	R6	
165FP-6a	Same	1029	C	PL	R8	
165FP-7b	Same	1031	BR	PL	R9	
165FP-8a	Same	1033	C	PL	R5	7919
165FP-9a	Same	1034	C	PL	R6	7918
165FP-10a	Same	1036	C	PL	R5	7917
165FP-11a	Same	1042	C	R	R7	7914
165FP-11b	Same	Same	BR	R	R7	7915
165FP-11i	Same	Same	Z	R	R9	7916
165FP-12a	Same	1047	C	R	R9	
165FP-13d	Same	1069	C-N	R	R10	
165FP-5b	Same (Dorge 2/74 Lot 629)	Same	BR	PL	R10	

380

OHIO-Continued

NUMBER　OBVERSE　REVERSE　METAL　EDGE　RARITY　H&G

CINCINNATI 165-Continued

NUMBER	OBVERSE	REVERSE	METAL	EDGE	RARITY	H&G
165FQ-1b	WM. E.SINN/5/CENTS	JOHN STANTON/STAMP/BRAND/CUTTER/CINCINNATI	BR	PL	R7	
165FQ-2b	Similar, but 10 instead of 5.	Same	BR	PL	R8	
165FQ-3b	Similar, but 25 instead of 5 (size 28mm)	Same	BR	PL	R8	
165FR-1a	FRANK SMITH/GROCERY/&/LIQUOR/STORE/119 SYCAMORE, ST./CINCINNATI (H-R 1812)	1018	C-N	R	R10	
165FR-2a	Same	1023	C	PL	R5	7928
165FR-3a	Same	1028	C	PL	R4	7921
						7922
165FR-4a	Same	1042	C	R	R7	7923
165FR-4b	Same	Same	BR	R	R7	7924
165FR-4i	Same	Same	Z	R	R9	7925
165FR-5a	Same	1043	C	PL	R8	
165FR-6a	Same (H-R 1816)	1047	C	R	R8	7926
165FR-7d	Same	1069	C-N	R	R10	7927
165FS-1d	J.SMITH'S/MEAT/STORE/143 LOCK,ST. (H-R 1817)	1018	C-N	R	R10	
165FS-2a	Same	1019	C	PL	R9	
165FS-3a	Same	1022	C	PL	R9	7937
165FS-4a	Same	1026	C	PL	R5	7935
165FS-5a	Same	1034	C	PL	R8	7936
165FS-6a	Same	1036	C	PL	R4	7931
165FS-7a	Same	1042	C	R	R7	7930
165FS-7b	Same	Same	BR	R	R7	7931
165Fs-7i	Same	Same	Z	R	R9	
165FS-8a	Same	1047	C	R	R8	
165FS-9d	Same	1069	C-N	R	R10	7933

OHIO-Continued

NUMBER	OBVERSE	REVERSE	METAL	EDGE	RARITY	H&G

CINCINNATI 165-Continued

165FT

165FT-9

165FT-1d	S.&L.SMITH/GROCERS/ CINCINNATI. (H-R 1819)	1018	C-N	R	R10	
165FT-2a	Same	1026	C	PL	R5	
165FT-3a	Same	1033	C	PL	R4	7946
165FT-4a	Same	1036	C	PL	R3	7945
165FT-5a	Same	1038	C	PL	R4	7940
165FT-6a	Same	1042	C	R	R7	7942
165FT-6a1	Same	Same	C	PL	R8	7941
165FT-6b	Same	Same	BR	R	R8	
165FT-6i	Same	Same	Z	R	R8	
165FT-7a	Same	1047	C	R	R9	
165FT-7b	Same	Same	BR	R	R9	
165FT-8d	Same	1069	C-N	R	R10	7944
165FT-9a	Same	A.B.WILSON/STAPLE/&/ FANCY/GROCER/224/W.6'TH ST./CINCINNATI (Obv. Ohio 165GL-1)	C	PL	R10	7939

NO PHOTO AVAILABLE

165FU

165FV

165FU-1a	F.SNYDER/GROCER/53/ COURT ST./CIN.O.	1247	C	PL	R9	7948
165FV-1a	CHAS. SPREEN/GROCER/&/ PRODUCE/DEALER/COR. COURT & LINN,STS.	1020	C	PL	R8	7950
165FV-2a	Same	1021	C	PL	R4	7951
165FV-3a	Same	1026	C	PL	R6	
165FV-4a	Same	1033	C	PL	R7	7956
165FV-5a	Same	1035	C	PL	R6	
165FV-6a	Same	1042	C	R	R8	7952
165FV-6b	Same	Same	BR	R	R8	7953
165FV-6i	Same	Same	Z	R	R9	7954
165FV-7a	Same	1047	C	R	R8	
165FV-8d	Same	1069	C-N	R	R10	7955

OHIO-Continued

NUMBER　　OBVERSE　　　　　　REVERSE　　　　　　　　METAL　EDGE　RARITY　H&G

CINCINNATI 165-Continued

165FW

165FX

Number	Obverse	Reverse	Metal	Edge	Rarity	H&G
165FW-1a	H.STALKAMP/GROCER/10/ GREEN,ST/CINCINNATI.	1030	C	PL	R6	7959
165FW-2a	Same	1036	C	PL	R3	7964
165FW-3a	Same	1042	C	R	R7	7960
165FW-3b	Same	Same	BR	R	R7	7961
165FW-3i	Same	Same	Z	R	R9	
165FW-4a	Same (H-R 1822)	1047	C	R	R8	
165FW-5d	Same	1069	C-N	R	R10	7963
165FX-1a	JOHN STANTON/ MANUFACTURER/OF/STORE/ CARDS/&/STENCILS/STAMPS & BRANDS/CINCINNATI, OHIO	1009	C	PL	R6	7970
165FX-1b	Same	Same	BR	PL	R9	
165FX-1i	Same (H-R 1823)	Same	Z	PL	R7	7971
165FX-2a	Same	1018	C	R	R9	
165FX-2a1	Same	Same	C	PL	R9	
165FX-3i	Same	1019	Z	PL	R9	
165FX-4a	Same	1033	C	PL	R9	
165FX-5a	Same	1042	C	R	R5	7972
165FX-5b	Same	Same	BR	R	R7	7973
165FX-5i	Same	Same	Z	R	R9	7974
165FX-6a	Same	1045	C	PL	R8	7966
165FX-7a	Same	1046	C	R	R7	7975
165FX-8d	Same	1047	C-N	R	R9	
165FX-9a	Same	1068	C	PL	R9	7977
165FX-10a	Same	1069	C	R	R9	
165FX-10d	Same	Same	C-N	R	R10	7976
165FX-11a	Same	1160	C	R	R6	7978
165FX-11a1	Same	Same	C	PL	R8	
165FX-11b	Same (H-R 1824)	Same	BR	R	R8	7979
165FX-12a	Same	1192	C	R	R9	
165FX-12d	Same (H-R 1825)	Same	C-N	R	R9	
165FX-13a	Same (H-R 1826)	1279	C	R	R8	7967
165FX-13b	Same	Same	BR	R	R9	7968
165FX-13d	Same (H-R 1827)	Same	C-N	R	R9	
165FX-13i	Same	Same	Z	R	R9	7969
165FX-14a	Same	1281	C	R	R9	7980
165FX-14b	Same	Same	BR	R	R9	7981
165FX-14i	Same	Same	Z	R	R9	7982
165FX-15a	Same	1282	C	R	R5	7983
165FX-15b	Same	Same	BR	R	R7	7984
165FX-16a	Same	1283	C	R	R7	7985
165FX-16b	Same	Same	BR	R	R9	7986
165FX-16d	Same (H-R 1828)	Same	C-N	R	R9	
165FX-16i	Same	Same	Z	R	R9	
165FX-7a1	Same	Same	C	R	R	
165FX-9a1	Same	Same	C	R	R10	

OHIO-Continued

NUMBER	OBVERSE	REVERSE	METAL	EDGE	RARITY	H&G

CINCINNATI 165-Continued

165FX-19

165FX-20

165FX-17a	Same	1370	C	R	R9	
165FX-17d	Same (H-R 1829)	Same	C-N	R	R9	
165FX-18a	Same (H-R 1831)	1373	C	R	R9	
165FX-18d	Same (H-R 1830)	Same	C-N	R	R9	
165FX-19a	Same (H-R 1832)	THE/FEDERAL/GOVERNMENT/ A/NATIONAL/CURRENCY/FREE/ TRADE/AND/HUMAN RIGHTS (Rev Ohio 165FN-1a)	C	R	R9	
165FX-20a	JOHN STANTON/STEEL/ STAMP,/BRAND & STENCIL/ CUTTER/139 FIFTH,ST./ CINCINNATI, OHIO	1037	C	R	R9	
165FX-21a	Same	1042	C	R	R8	7991
165FX-21b	Same	Same	BR	R	R9	7992
165FX-21i	Same	Same	Z	R	R9	
165FX-22a	Same	1046	C	R	R5	7994
165FX-22d	Same	Same	C-N	R	R10	7995
165FX-23a	Same	1047	C	R	R9	
165FX-23d	Same (H-R 1833)	Same	C-N	R	R10	

165FY

165FZ

165FY-1a	D.B.S./GROCER,541 MAIN,ST. (D.B. Sterret)	1026	C	PL	R5	6970
165FY-2a	Same	1029	C	PL	R6	6966
165FY-3a	Same	1042	C	R	R7	6967
165FY-3b	Same	Same	BR	R	R7	6968
165FY-3i	Same	Same	Z	R	R9	
165FY-4a	Same	1047	C	R	R8	6969
165FY-4d	Same	Same	C-N	R	R10	
165FZ-1a	C.SUTTON'S/NEW/GROCERY/ STORE/202 FIFTH,ST	1026	C	PL	R3	8002
165FZ-2a	Same	1033	C	PL	R5	
165FZ-3a	Same	1042	C	R	R7	7998
165FZ-3b	Same	Same	BR	R	R8	7999
165FZ-3i	Same	Same	Z	R	R9	8000
165FZ-4a	Same	1047	C	R	R9	
165FZ-5d	Same	1069	C-N	R	R10	8001
165FZ-6d	Same (H-R 1834)	1018	C-N	R	R10	

OHIO-Continued

NUMBER OBVERSE REVERSE METAL EDGE RARITY H&G

CINCINNATI 165-Continued

165GA

165GB

165GA-1a	WM.TELL/HOUSE/225/SIXTH, ST./CINCINNATI	1032	C	PL	R5	8009
165GA-2a	Same	1034	C	PL	R4	8008
165GA-3a	Same	1042	C	R	R8	8004
165GA-3b	Same	Same	BR	R	R8	
165GA-3i	Same	Same	Z	R	R8	8006
165GA-4d	Same	1069	C-N	R	R10	8007
165GB-1a	E.TOWNLEY/HIVES/&/BEES/ MOUNT AUDURN/CINCINNATI	1020	C	PL	R4	8012
165GB-2a	Same	1022	C	PL	R5	8018
165GB-3a	Same	1023	C	PL	R8	
165GB-3aa	Same	1026	C	PL	R8	
165GB-4a	Same	1029	C	PL	R7	
165GB-5a	Same	1030	C	PL	R8	
165GB-6a	Same	1033	C	PL	R5	8020
165GB-7a	Same	1034	C	PL	R4	8013 8019
165GB-8a	Same	1035	C	PL	R7	
165GB-9a	Same	1042	C	R	R6	8014
165GB-9b	Same	Same	BR	R	R7	8015
165GB-9i	Same	Same	Z	R	R9	
165GB-10a	Same	1045	C	PL	R6	8011
165GB-11a	Same	1047	C	R	R9	
165GB-12d	Same	1069	C-N	R	R10	8017

165GC-1a	BUY MEAT/OF/VAN,WUNDER/ IN/MARKET	1007	C	PL	R9	
165GC-2a	Same	1008	C	PL	R8	8023
165GC-3a	Same	1009	C	PL	R0	8024
165GC-4a	Same	1019	C	PL	R9	
165GC-5a	Same	1022	C	PL	R9	
165GC-6a	Same	1042	C	R	R7	8025
165GC-6b	Same	Same	BR	R	R8	8026
165GC-6i	Same	Same	Z	R	R8	8027
165GC-4b	Same (Dorge 10/73 Lot 396)	Same	BR	PL	R9	

385

OHIO-Continued

NUMBER	OBVERSE	REVERSE	METAL	EDGE	RARITY	H&G
165GC-7a	Same	1045	C	PL	R5	8022
165GC-8a	Same	1047	C	R	R9	
165GC-9d	Same	1069	C-N	R	R10	8028
165GC-10a	Same (H-R 1840)	1288	C	R	R9	
165GC-10a1	Same	Same	C	PL	R8	8029
165GC-10i	Same (H-R 1841)	Same	Z	R	R9	
165GC-10i1	Same	Same	Z	PL	R9	

165GD  165GE

165GD-1b	GOOD/FOR 5 CENTS/IN/ BREAD/AT/H.VARWIGS/ 151/WEST COURT ST (NOTE: Struck on thin planchet.)	JOHN STANTON/STAMP/ BRAND/STENCIL/CUTTER/ CINCINNATI	BR	PL	R7	
165GE-1a	JACOB VOGEL/BUTCHER/985/ CEN. AVENUE	1022	C	PL	R9	8039
165GE-2a	Same	1023	C	PL	R4	
165GE-3a	Same	1028	C	PL	R7	8038
165GE-4a	Same	1042	C	R	R6	8033
165GE-4b	Same	Same	BR	R	R6	8034
165GE-4l	Same	Same	Z	R	R9	
165GE-5a	Ssme	1047	C	R	R9	8036
165GE-6d	Same	1069	C-N	R	R10	8037

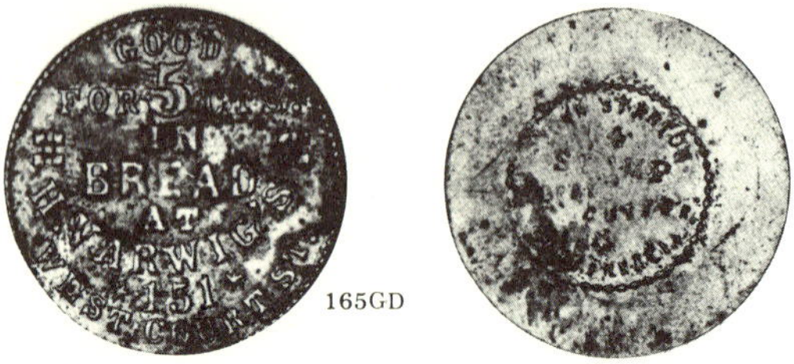

165GF  165GG

165GF-1a	WALDO & BRANDON'S/ EMPORIUM/1863	DRY GOODS/AND/GROCERIES	C	PL	R5	8041
165GF-2a	Same	1168	C	PL	R9	8042
165GF-3d	Same (H-R 1844)	Same as obverse	C-N	PL	R10	
165GG-1a	WETHERBY'S/CHEAP/DRY/ GOODS/EMPORIUM/ CINCINNATI.	1019	C	PL	R5	8046
165GG-2a	Same	1030	C	PL	R5	8047
165GG-3a	Same	1033	C	PL	R6	8051
165GG-4a	Same	1042	C	R	R6	8048
165GG-4b	Same	Same	BR	R	R8	8049
165GG-4i	Same	Same	Z	R	R9	
165GD-1a	Obv of 165GD-1b (NOTE: Struck on thick planchet.)	Rev of 165GD-1b	C	PL	R9	
165GF-4a	Same as 165GF-1a Rev	1168	C	PL	R7	8043

OHIO-Continued

NUMBER	OBVERSE	REVERSE	METAL	EDGE	RARITY	H&G

CINCINNATI 165-Continued

165GG-5a	Same	1045	C	PL	R9	8045
165GG-6a	Same	1047	C	R	R9	
165GG-7d	Same	1069	C-N	R	R10	8050

165GH   165GI

165GH-1a	H.C.WEHRMAN/BAKER/217 EVERETT,ST. Sheaf of wheat in center (H-R 1847)	1022	C	PL	R6	
165GH-2a	Same	1026	C	PL	R2	8058
165GH-3a	Same	1032	C	PL	R9	8059
165CH-4a	Same	1033	C	PL	R3	8060
165GH-5a	Same	1036	C	PL	R4	8057
165GH-6a	Same	1042	C	R	R7	8053
165GH-6b	Same	Same	BR	R	R8	8054
165GH-6i	Same	Same	Z	R	R9	8055
165GH-7a	Same	1047	C	R	R8	
165GI-1a	GOOD FOR/20/*CENTS*/IN/TOBACCO/AT/WEICHELL &/SONS	EXCELSIOR/TABACCO/WORKS/210 & 212/ELM ST. CIN. O./ESTABLISHED/1835 (Obv Ohio 165AMb)	C	PL	R7	
	(NOTE: Part of southern mule series, F 10/11, Adams Ohio 33.)					
165GI-3a	Same (F I/11-King 625)	1418	C	PL	R8	
165GI-4a	Same (F IV/11)	1421	C	PL	R8	
165GI-2a	Same (F III/11)	1158	C	PL	R8	
165GI-5a	Same (H-R 1848)	1425	C	PL	R8	

165GJ-1a	W.W.WERT/AUCTION/&/COMMISSION/BOOTS & SHOES/WHOLESALE/&/RETAIL/154 MAIN,ET	1018	C	PL	R9	
165GJ-2a	Same	1022	C	PL	R4	8067
165GJ-3a	Same	1023	C	PL	R8	
165GJ-4a	Same	1026	C	PL	R4	
165GJ-5a	Same	1029	C	PL	R8	
165GJ-6a	Same	1030	C	PL	R3	8069
165GH-1b	Same (Dorge 2/73 Lot 457)	Same	BR	PL	R9	
165GH-8d	Same	1069	C-N	R	R10	8056
165GH-9d	Same (H-R 1846)	1018	C-N	R	R10	

OHIO-Continued

NUMBER	OBVERSE	REVERSE	METAL	EDGE	RARITY	H&G

CINCINNATI 165-Continued

165GJ-7a	Same	1033	C	PL	R6	
165GJ-8a	Same	1036	C	PL	R4	8066
165GJ-9a	Same	1039	C	PL	R6	8068
165GJ-10a	Same	1042	C	R	R7	8062
165GJ-10b	Same	Same	BR	R	R8	8063
165GJ-10i	Same	Same	Z	R	R9	8064
165GJ-11a	Same (H-R 1849)	1047	C	R	R9	
165GJ-12d	Same	1069	C-N	R	R10	8065

165GK-1b	GOOD FOR/25/CENTS/AT WILKINSON/110 WEST 4TH ST.	REDEEMED/IN/PAR FUNDS/ IN SUMS OF/ONE/DOLLAR (Rev Ohio 165Z-9)	BR	PL	R9	8087

165GL-1a	A.B.WILSON/STAPLE/&/ FANCY/GROCER/224/W 6TH.ST./CINCINNATI (Large letters H-R 1850)	1008	C	R	R9	
165GL-1a1	Same	Same	C	PL	R2	8072
165GL-2a	Same	1019	C	PL	R8	8071
165GL-2b	Same	Same	BR	PL	R9	
165GL-3a	Same	1068	C	PL	R6	8077
165GL-4a	A.B.WILSON/STAPLE/&/ FANCY/GROCER/224/W. 6TH.ST./CINCINNATI, O. (Small letters)	1020	C	PL	R2	8073
165GL-4e	Same	Same	W-M	PL	R10	
165GL-5a	Same	1022	C	PL	R5	
165GL-6a	Same	1026	C	PL	R3	8078
165GL-7a	Same (H-R 1851)	1036	C	PL	R9	
165GL-8a	Same	1042	C	R	R6	8074
165GL-8b	Same	Same	BR	R	R6	8075
165GL-8i	Same	Same	Z	R	R8	
165GL-9a	Same	1047	C	R	R9	
165GL-10d	Same	1069	C-N	R	R10	

OHIO-Continued

NUMBER	OBVERSE	REVERSE	METAL	EDGE	RARITY	H&G

CINCINNATI 165-Continued

165GM-1a	GOOD FOR/5/CENTS/H.WIND	1009	C	R	R9	
165GM-1a1	Same	Same	C	PL	R8	
165GM-2d	Same (H-R 1852)	1018	C-N	R	R10	
165GM-3a	Same	1019	C	PL	R9	8084
165GM-4d	Same	1069	C-N	R	R10	8085
165GM-5a	Same	1192	C	R	R8	8081
165GM-5a1	Same	Same	C	PL	R9	8080
165GM-5b	Same	Same	BR	R	R9	8082
165GM-5i	Same	Same	Z	R	R9	

165GN

165GO

165GN-1a	WINE STEINER/35/EAST/THIRD/ST./CINCINNATI.	1019	C	PL	R9	8090
165GN-1b	Same	Same	BR	PL	R9	8091
165GN-2a	Same	1042	C	R	R8	8092
165GN-2b	Same	Same	BR	R	R8	8093
165GN-2i	Same	Same	Z	R	R9	8094
165GN-3a	Same	1047	C	R	R9	
165GN-4d	Same	1069	C-N	R	R10	8095
165GN-5a	Same	1192	C	R	R4	8089
165GN-5b	Same	Same	BR	PL	R9	
165GO-1a	JOHN WOESSNER'S/JEFFERSON/SALOON/COR./12'& MAIN, STS./CINCINNATI	1007	C	PL	R3	8097
165GO-2d	Same (H-R 1854)	1018	C-N	R	R10	
165GO-3a	Same	1019	C	PL	R9	8098
165GO-3b	Same	Same	BR	PL	R9	
165GO-3i	Same	Same	Z	PL	R9	
165GO-4a	Same	1020	C	PL	R7	8099

OHIO-Continued

NUMBER	OBVERSE	REVERSE	METAL	EDGE	RARITY	H&G

CINCINNATI 165-Continued

165GO-5a	Same	1021	C	PL	R3	8100
165GO-6a	Same	1027	C	PL	R9	
165GO-7a	Same	1038	C	PL	R4	8101
(NOTE: Comes with broken reverse die.)
165GO-8a	Same	1042	C	R	R7	8102
165GO-8b	Same	Same	BR	R	R8	8103
165GO-8i	Same	Same	Z	R	R9	8104
165GO-9a	Same	1047	C	R	R9	
165GO-10d	Same	1069	C-N	R	R10	8105

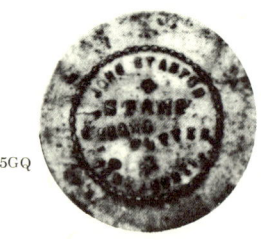

165GP

165GQ

165GP-1a	G.WOLFER/TIN/SHOP/62 FINDLAY, ST/CINCINNATI	1025	C	PL	R8	
165GP-2a	Same	1034	C	PL	R6	8113
165GP-2d	Same	Same	C-N	PL	R10	
165GP-3a	Same	1042	C	R	R7	8109
165GP-3b	Same	Same	BR	R	R7	8110
165GP-3i	Same	Same	Z	R	R9	
165GP-4a	Same	1047	C	R	R8	
165GP-5d	Same	1069	C-N	R	R10	8112
165GQ-1b	WOOD & HARRISON/GOOD FOR/ 10/CENTS	JOHN STANTON/STAMP/BRAND/ STENCIL/CUTTER/CINCINNATI	BR	PL	R9	

165GR

165GS

165GR-1a	WRIGHT/CINCINNATI./1863	1170	C	PL	R2	8107
165GR-2a	Same	1170 struck over obv die	C	PL	R10	
165GS-1a	ROBERT WRIGHT/DRY/GOODS/ 397/CEN.AVENUE. (3½mm between R & C, period after AVENUE.)	1008	C	PL	R7	
165GS-2a	Same	1068	C	PL	R6	8130
(NOTE: Pieces listed as H-R 1857-8 are new types, with Rev 1068 and 1008 respectively with R edge, but obv is either 165GS-1a or 165GS-3a type.)
165GS-2b	Same (Dorge 10/73 Lot 408)	Same	BR	PL	R9	

OHIO-Continued

NUMBER   OBVERSE   REVERSE   METAL EDGE RARITY H&G

CINCINNATI 165-Continued

165GS-3

165GS-12

165GS-3a	Similar. No period after AVENUE — 2½ mm. between R & C.	1007	C	PL	R3	8116
165GS-4a	Same	1008	C	PL	R4	8117
165GS-5a	Same	1018	C	PL	R9	8118
165GS-5d	Same (H-R 1859)	Same	C-N	R	R10	
165GS-6a	Same	1019	C	PL	R3	8119
(NOTE: occurs with both obverse and reverse die breaks.)						
165GS-7a	Same	1020	C	PL	R3	
165GS-8a	Same	1021	C	PL	R2	8120
165GS-9a	Same	1038	C	PL	R2	8122
(NOTE: Comes with reverse die breaks)						
165GS-10a	Same	1068	C	PL	R5	8126
(NOTE: Comes with reverse die breaks.)						
165GS-11a	Same	Rev Ohio 165GY25a	C	PL	R10	
165GS-12a	Similar inscription, but 1½mm between R & C.	1019	C	PL	R7	
165GS-13a	Same	1022	C	PL	R7	
165GS-14a	Same	1023	C	PL	R7	
165GS-15a	Same	1026	C	PL	R4	8129
165GS-16a	Same	1030	C	PL	R6	
165GS-17a	Same	1032	C	PL	R8	
165GS-18a	Same	1033	C	PL	R5	
165GS-19a	Same	1034	C	PL	R3	8121
165GS-20a	Same	1035	C	PL	R7	
165GS-21a	Same	1036	C	PL	R5	8128
165GS-22a	Same	1042	C	R	R7	8123
165GS-22b	Same	Same	BR	R	R8	8124
165GS-22i	Same	Same	Z	R	R9	
165GS-23a	Same	1047	C	R	R9	
165GS-24d	Same	1069	C-N	R	R10	8127
165GS-25a	Same	1192	C	PL	R7	8115

| 165GT-1a | H.B.XELAR/WINE/&/BEER/SALOON.(H-R 1861) | 1033 | C | PL | R9 | |

(NOTE: the piece listed as H&G 8132 does not exist.)

391

OHIO-Continued

NUMBER	OBVERSE	REVERSE	METAL	EDGE	RARITY	H&G

CINCINNATI 165-Continued

165GT-2a	Same (H-R 1860)	1131	C	PL	R9	
165GT-3a	Same	1274	C	PL	R1	8133
165GT-3f	Same (H-R 1862)	Same	S	PL	R9	
165GT-4a	Same (H-R 1864)	ALSO/CUTLERY/&/NOTIONS/ &C.(Rev. Ohio 165CY42)	C	PL	R9	
165GT-5a	Same	Obv of 175S-4	C	PL	R	

165GU-1a	S.Y. surrounded by 13 stars (Stephan Yeatman)	1037	C	R	R9	8135
165GU-1a1	Same	1037	C	PL	R9	
165GU-2a	Same	1042	C	R	R6	8136
165GU-2b	Same	Same	BR	R	R8	8137
165GU-2i	Same	Same	Z	R	R9	8138
165GU-3a	Same	1047	C	R	R9	8139
165GU-3d	Same (H-R 1867)	Same	C-N	R	R9	

165GV-1a	L. YOUNG — scrolls above and below.	1084	C	PL	R9	
165GV-2a	Same	1343	C	PL	R8	8141
165GV-2b	Same	Same	BR	PL	R9	
165GV-2d	(H R 1868)	Same	C-N	PL	R9	

392

OHIO-Continued

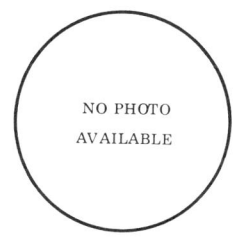

NUMBER	OBVERSE	REVERSE	METAL	EDGE	RARITY	H&G

CINCINNATI 165-Continued

165GW-1a	JOS.ZANDT/ICE/CREAM/ SALOON/285/CENTRAL AV. (NOTE: An obvious error, intended for ZANONE.)	1274	C	PL	R9	8143
165GX-1f	JOS.ZANONE/ICE/CREAM/ SALOON/285/CENTRAL AV. (H.R 1869)	1131	S	PL	R9	
165GX-2a	Same (H-R 1871)	1172	C	PL	R8	8146
165GX-2f	Same (H-R 1870)	Same	S	PL	R9	
165GX-3a	Same	1274	C	PL	R9	8145
165GX-4a	Same (H-R 1872)	Same as obverse	C	PL	R9	

165GX-5  165GX-6  165GX-7

165GX-5f	Same (H-R 1873)	S.A.INGRAM./WATCHES/AND/ CLOCKS/CHICAGO.ILL. (Obv ILL 150AG)	S	PL	R9	
165GX-6e	Same	J.A.HUGHES above, CINCINATI below METALIC/CARDS in a wreath (Obv. Ohio 165BZ)	W-M	PL	R9	8147
165GX-6f	Same (H-R1874)	Same	S	PL	R9	
165GX-7a	Same	S.BACCIOCCO/CONFECTIONARY /AND/ICE/CREAM/SALOON/176 FIFTH ST (Obv Ohio 165H)	C	PL	R9	8148

OHIO-Continued

NUMBER	OBVERSE	REVERSE	METAL	EDGE	RARITY	H&G

CINCINNATI 165-Continued

165GY-1d	JOHN ZELTNER/VINE/ST./HILL (H-R 1880)	1018	C-N	R	R10	
165GY-2a	Same	1030	C	PL	R3	8150
165GY-3a	Same	1032	C	PL	R8	
165GY-4a	Same	1042	C	R	R7	8151
165GY-4b	Same	Same	BR	R	R8	8152
165GY-4i	Same	Same	Z	R	R9	8153
165GY-5a	Same (H-R 1881)	1047	C	R	R9	8154
165GY-5d	Same	Same	C-N	R	R10	
165GY-6d	Same	1069	C-N	R	R10	

165GY-7d	JOHN ZELTNER/NATIONAL/HALL/400/VINE,ST./CINCINNATI, O. (H-R 1878)	1018	C-N	R	R10	
165GY-8a	Same	1019	C	PL	R7	8155
165GY-9a	Same	1022	C	PL	R5	
165GY-10a	Same	1026	C	PL	R6	8162
165GY-11a	Same	1029	C	PL	R7	
165GY-12a	Same	1030	C	PL	R6	
165GY-13a	Same	1031	C	PL	R7	8163
165GY-14a	Same	1033	C	PL	R5	
165GY-15a	Same	1035	C	PL	R7	
165GY-16a	Same	1036	C	PL	R4	8161
165GY-17a	Same	1037	C	PL	R8	8156
165GY-18a	Same	1038	C	PL	R3	8157
165GY-19a	Same	1042	C	R	R7	8158
165GY-19b	Same	Same	BR	R	R8	8159
165GY-19i	Same	Same	Z	R	R9	8160
165GY-20a	Same	1047	C	R	R9	
165GY-21d	Same	1069	C-N	R	R10	
165GY-22a	Same	1283	C	PL	R10	
165GY-23e	Same	1393	W-M	PL	R9	

OHIO-Continued

NUMBER	OBVERSE	REVERSE	METAL	EDGE	RARITY	H&G

CINCINNATI 165-Continued

165GY-24a Same (H-R 1882)   W.K.LAN PHEAR/GENERAL/ENGRAVER/102/W.4'ST./CINCINNATI (Rev. Ohio 165CY-105a)   C   PL   R10

165GY25

165GY32

165GY-25a	Very similar, but JOHN E. ZELTNER	1007	C	PL	R5	8167
165GY-26a	Same	1008	C	PL	R3	8168
	(NOTE: Comes with broken reverse die.)					
165GY-27a	Same	1019	C	PL	R2	8169
165GY-27b	Same	Same	BR	PL	R9	
165GY-27i	Same	Same	Z	PL	R9	
165GY-28a	Same	1020	C	PL	R8	
165GY-29a	Same	1021	C	PL	R4	8170
165GY-30a	Same	1036	C	PL	R4	8172
165GY-31a	Same	1038	C	PL	R2	8171
165GY-32e	JOHN E. ZELTNER/NATIONAL/HALL	Similar to 1393, but 5 and 13 stars around instead of 24	W-M	PL	R10	

395

OHIO-Continued

NUMBER	OBVERSE	REVERSE	METAL	EDGE	RARITY	H&G

CIRCLEVILLE 168

168A-1a	G.H.FICKARDT & CO./ DRUGGISTS/CIRCLEVILLE/OHIO.	1083	C	PL	R8	
168A-2a	Same	1124	C	PL	R9	8175
168A-3a	Same	1130	C	PL	R9	8177
168A-4a	Same	1177	C	PL	R9	
168A-5a	Same	1179	C	PL	R4	8176
168A-6a	Same (Dorge 8/72 Lot 136)	1180	C	PL	R9	

168B

168B-5

168B-1a	J.L.KING/GROCERY/AND PROVISION/STORE/ CIRCLEVILLE,O.	1124	C	PL	R9	8179
168B-2a	Same	1178	C	PL	R8	8180
168B-3a	Same	1179	C	PL	R7	
168B-4a	Same	1331	C	PL	R5	8181
168B-5a	Same	RAILROAD/1863/WAREHOUSE	C	PL	R9	8183
168B-6a	Same	BLANK	C	PL	R9	8182
168B-7a	Same (Dorge 2/74 Lot 455)	1180	C	PL	R9	

168C-1a	MASON & SON/GROCERS/AND/ LIQUOR/DEALERS/ CIRCLEVILLE, O.	1124	C	PL	R3	8184
168C-1d	Same	Same	C-N	PL	R9	8185
168C-2a	Same	1178	C	PL	R9	8186
168C-3a	Same	1179	C	PL	R7	
168C-4a	Same	1331	C	PL	R9	8187
168C-5a	Same	1180	C	PL	R9	

396

OHIO-Continued

NUMBER	OBVERSE	REVERSE	METAL	EDGE	RARITY	H&G

CLARKSBURG 170

| 170A-1a | GROCERIES & NOTIONS/SOLD BY/ONE/FRENCH/ CLARKSBURG, O. | 1059 | C | PL | R5 | 8188 |

| 170B-1a | JAMES & FRENCH/HAVE/IT!/ CLARKSBURG/OHIO. | 1059 | C | PL | R6 | 8189 |

| 170C-1a | GOOD FOR/ONE/CENT/AT/ MAUCK & BRADBURY | 1059 | C | PL | R9 | |

(NOTE: All the above from Clarksburg have an Indian head dated 1873, which is assumed to be an error.)

397

OHIO-Continued

NUMBER	OBVERSE	REVERSE	METAL	EDGE	RARITY	H&G

CLEVELAND 175

175A

175B

| 175A-1a | A & H surrounded by 36 stars Circle at top (for hole) | 1319 | C | R | R9 | |
| 175B-1a | BRATTIN—three stars at top | 1319 | C | R | R9 | |

(NOTE: The above two pieces attributed to Cleveland by J. Barnett.)

| 175C-1a | C. G. BRUCE/AUTHORIZED/ WAR/CLAIM/AGENT/1863/ CLEVELAND, O. A of AGENT between C & L of CLAIM | $100 BOUNTY/PENSIONS/ BACK PAY/&C./COLLECTED/ &/CASHED $ above E of PENSION | C | PL | R2 | 8192 |
| 175C-2a | Same | BLANK | C | PL | R9 | 8193 |

175C-3a	SIMILAR—dash on each side of WAR—A of AGENT under L of CLAIM	Similar, $ opposite to E of PENSION	C	R	R3	8196
175C-3a1	Same	Same	C	PL	R4	8195
175C-3d	Same	Same	C-N	PL	R9	8197
175C-4a	Same	1024	C	PL	R5	
175C-5a	Same	1028	C	PL	R6	

398

OHIO-Continued

NUMBER OBVERSE REVERSE METAL EDGE RARITY H&G

CLEVELAND 175-Continued

175C-6

175C-7

175C-6a	Similar but 1863 spaced differently	Same as Oh 175C-3	C	R	R9	
175C-7a	Similar, A almost directly between C & L	Similar, $ opposite P of PENSION	C	R	R5	8200
175C-7a1	Same	Same	C	PL	R2	8199
175C-7b	Same	Same	BR	R	R7	8201
175C-7i	Same	Same	Z	R	R9	
175C-8a	Same, incused	Same, incused	C	R	R9	8202
175C-9a	Same	BLANK	C	R	R9	
175C-10a	Same	1023	C	PL	R4	8212
175C-11a	Same	1028	C	R	R9	8204
175C-11d	Same	Same	C-N	R	R9	8205
175C-12d	Same	1047	C-N	R	R10	
175C-13a	Same as Rev Ohio 175C-1a	1028	C	PL	R4	8207
175C-14a	Same	BLANK	C	PL	R9	8208
175C-15i	Same as Obv Ohio 175C-3a	Same as Rev. Ohio 175C-7a	Z	R	R9	8210
175C-7d	Same	Same	C-N	R	R10	
175C-16d	Same as Obv Ohio 175C-6a	Same as Rev Ohio 175C-7a	C-N	R	R	

| 175D-1a | C. CHANDLER,/FRUIT/&/SEED/ DEALER/CLEVELAND, O. | 1180 | C | PL | R4 | 8214 |

OHIO-Continued

NUMBER	OBVERSE	REVERSE	METAL	EDGE	RARITY	H&G

CLEVELAND 175-Continued

NUMBER	OBVERSE	REVERSE	METAL	EDGE	RARITY	H&G
175E-1a	DECKAND & ENGELHART/ FASHIONABLE/HATTERS./ CLEVELAND/OHIO.	1098	C	PL	R3	8217
175E-2a	Same	1205	C	PL	R3	8216
175F-1a	DUNN, GOUDY & BRO,/ GROCERIES/ & C./149/ ONTARIO ST./CLEVELAND, O.	1125	C	PL	R3	8219
175G-1a	D. W. GAGE/AUTHORIZED/ WAR/CLAIM/AGENT/1863/ CLEVELAND, O.	$100 BOUNTY/PENSIONS/ BACK PAY/& C/COLLECTED/ & /CASHED (Same as Rev Ohio 165C-7a)	C	R	R3	8222
175G-1a1	Same	Same	C	PL	R9	8221
175G-1b	Same	Same	BR	R	R9	8223
175G-1d	Same	Same	C-N	R	R9	
175G-1i	Same	Same	Z	R	R9	8224
175G-2a	Same	1018	C	R	R8	
175G-3a	Same	1046	C	R	R9	8225
175G-4a	Same	1047	C	R	R9	8226
175G-5d	Same	1069	C-N	R	R10	

400

OHIO-Continued

NUMBER	OBVERSE	REVERSE	METAL	EDGE	RARITY	H&G

CLEVELAND 175-Continued

| 175H-1a | J. H. & A. S. GORHAM/GROCERS/MANUFACTURERS/OF/CRACKERS/AND/CONFECTIONERY/CLEVELAND, O. | 1178 | C | PL | R4 | 8227 |
| 175H-2a | Same | 1180 | C | PL | R4 | 8228 |

175I-1a	JOHN HAWKINS above—THE LADIES MAN below—bust to right.	NEWBURGH HOUSE/226/ONTARIO ST/CLEVELAND/OHIO.	C	PL	R3	8230
175I-1d	Same	Same	C-N	PL	R10	
175I-2a	Same	Obverse incused	C	PL	R9	

175J-1a	J. LANGHORN/MEAT/STORE/BANK, ST./CLEVELAND, O.	1125	C	PL	R8	
175J-2a	Same	1180	C	PL	R3	8232
175K-1a	C. L. MARVIN,/STOVE &/GRATE/DEPOT/50/PUBLIC SQUARE/CLEVELAND, O.	1180	C	PL	R3	8235

OHIO-Continued

NUMBER	OBVERSE	REVERSE	METAL	EDGE	RARITY	H&G

CLEVELAND 175-Continued

175L-1a	T.J. QUINLAN,/BILL/POSTER/AND/DISTRIBUTOR./174/ONTARIO, ST./CLEVELAND, O.	T. J. QUINLAN,/NEWS/PAPERS,/STATIONERY,/SONGS/AND/YANKEE/NOTIONS.	C	PL	R2	8238
175L-2a	Same	Same as obverse	C	PL	R9	8239
175L-3a	Same	1168	C	PL	R4	8240
175L-4a	Same	1346	C	PL	R8	8241

175M

175N

175M-1a	I. P. SHERWOOD/DRY/GOODS/&/MILLINERY/CLEVELAND, O.	1024	C	R	R4	8243
175M-1a1	Same	Same	C	PL	R9	
175M-2a	Same	1037	C	R	R4	8244
175M-3a	Same	1042	C	R	R7	8245
175M-3b	Same	Same	BR	R	R9	8246
175M-3i	Same	Same	Z	R	R9	8247
175M-4a	Same	1047	C	R	R9	
175M-4d	Same	Same	C-N	R	R10	8248

| 175N-1a | J. P. SHERWOOD/DRY/GOODS/&/MILLINERY/CLEVELAND, O. | 1028 | C | R | R5 | 8250 |

(NOTE: Either the 175M or 175N is an error, but we have not been able to determine which is the correct usage.)

175N-2a	Same	1037	C	R	R7	
175N-3a	Same	1042	C	R	R7	8251
175N-3b	Same	Same	BR	R	R8	8252
175N-3i	Same	Same	Z	R	R9	
175N-4a	Same (H-R 1890)	1047	C	R	R8	
175N-5d	Same	1069	C-N	R	R10	8254

OHIO-Continued

NUMBER | OBVERSE | REVERSE | METAL | EDGE | RARITY | H&G

CLEVELAND 175-Continued

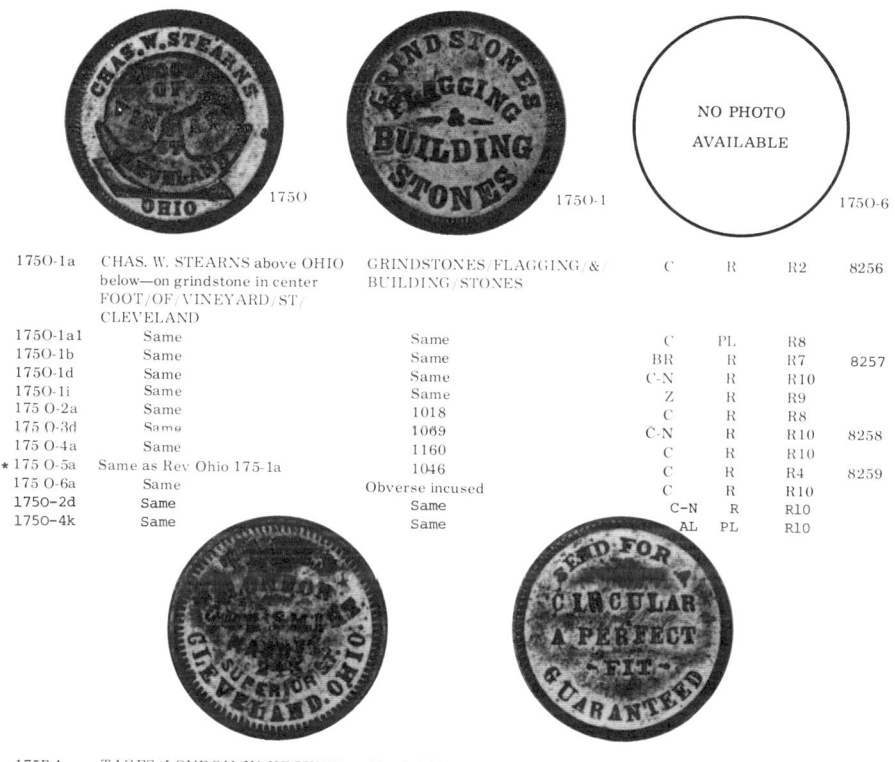

175O-1a	CHAS. W. STEARNS above OHIO below—on grindstone in center FOOT/OF/VINEYARD/ST/CLEVELAND	GRINDSTONES/FLAGGING/&/BUILDING/STONES	C	R	R2	8256
175O-1a1	Same	Same	C	PL	R8	
175O-1b	Same	Same	BR	R	R7	8257
175O-1d	Same	Same	C-N	R	R10	
175O-1i	Same	Same	Z	R	R9	
175 O-2a	Same	1018	C	R	R8	
175 O-3d	Same	1069	C-N	R	R10	8258
175 O-4a	Same	1160	C	R	R10	
*175 O-5a	Same as Rev Ohio 175-1a	1046	C	R	R4	8259
175 O-6a	Same	Obverse incused	C	R	R10	
175O-2d	Same	Same	C-N	R	R10	
175O-4k	Same	Same	AL	PL	R10	

| 175P-1a | TAGES/LONDON/YOKESHIRT./MANUFY/243/SUPERIOR ST./CLEVELAND. OHIO. | SEND FOR A/CIRCULAR/A PERFECT/FIT/GUARANTEED | C | PL | R5 | 8262 |

| 175P-2b | TAGES LONDON/YOKE SHIRS/MANUFY./243/SUPERIOR, ST./CLEVELAND, O. (NOTE: Note error in spelling of SHIRTS.) | Same | BR | PL | R9 | 8263 |

* (NOTE: Also to be listed as Patriotic Civil War Token.)

OHIO-Continued

NUMBER	OBVERSE	REVERSE	METAL	EDGE	RARITY	H&G

CLEVELAND 175-Continued

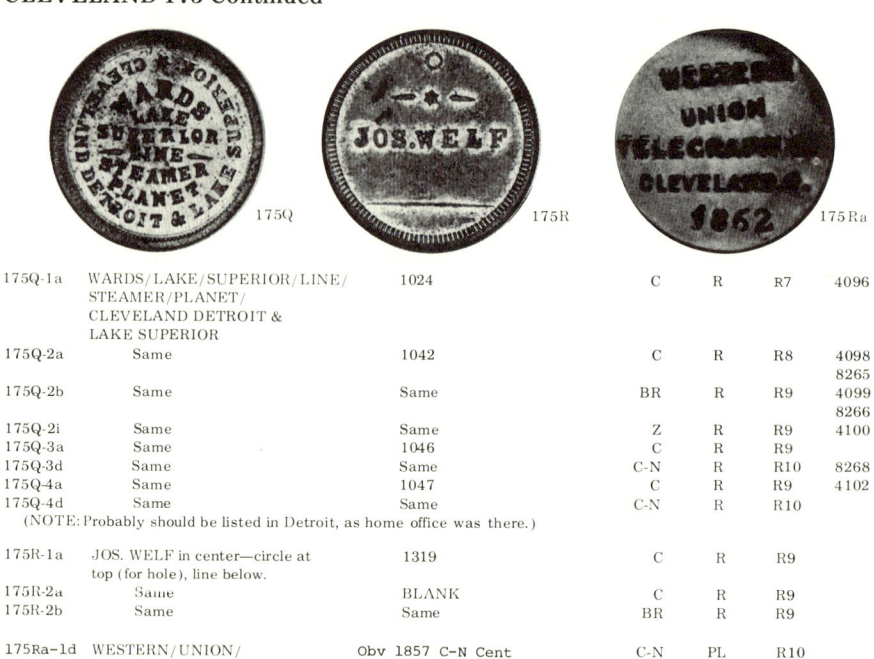

175Q-1a	WARDS/LAKE/SUPERIOR/LINE/ STEAMER/PLANET/ CLEVELAND DETROIT & LAKE SUPERIOR	1024	C	R	R7	4096
175Q-2a	Same	1042	C	R	R8	4098 8265
175Q-2b	Same	Same	BR	R	R9	4099 8266
175Q-2i	Same	Same	Z	R	R9	4100
175Q-3a	Same	1046	C	R	R9	
175Q-3d	Same	Same	C-N	R	R10	8268
175Q-4a	Same	1047	C	R	R9	4102
175Q-4d	Same	Same	C-N	R	R10	

(NOTE: Probably should be listed in Detroit, as home office was there.)

175R-1a	JOS. WELF in center—circle at top (for hole), line below.	1319	C	R	R9	
175R-2a	Same	BLANK	C	R	R9	
175R-2b	Same	Same	BR	R	R9	

| 175Ra-1d | WESTERN/UNION/ TELEGRAPH CO./ CLEVELAND.O./1862 | Obv 1857 C-N Cent | C-N | PL | R10 | |

(NOTE: Incused or planed down reverse of 1857 C-N Cent — was stolen from Dr. H. Aqua collection.)

175S-1a	GEO. WORTHINGTON & CO. above CLEVELAND, O. below-in center a circular saw inscribed HARDWARE/DEALERS.	TRY/ALLEN'S/BLACKLEAD/ COMPOUND/BABBITT/METAL/ 1862	C	PL	R6	8270
175S-1b	Same	Same	BR	PL	R3	8271
175S-1fp	Same	Same	S-P	PL	R9	

404

OHIO-Continued

NUMBER	OBVERSE	REVERSE	METAL	EDGE	RARITY	H&G

CLEVELAND 175-Continued

175S-4 Obv   175S-4 Rev

175S-4a	GEO. WORTHINGTON & CO. above—CLEVELAND, O. below-padlock in center inscribed HARDWARE DEALERS	TRY/ALLEN'S/BLACKLEAD/COMPOUND/BABBITT/METAL/1863	C	PL	R2	8275
175S-4d	Same	Same	C-N	PL	R9	8276
175S-5a	Same	1310	C	PL	R9	8277
175S-5b	Same	Same	BR	PL	R9	8278
175S-6a	Same	1274	C	PL	R9	8279

175S-7   175S-8   175S-9

175S-7a	Same (H-R 1891)		C	PL	R9	8282
175S-8a	Same	J. A. HUGHES above, CINCINNATI below METALIC/CARDS in a wreath (Obv. Ohio 165BZ)	C	PL	R9	
175S-8b	Same	W. K. LANPHEAR above, CINCINNATI, O below MANU'FR/OF/METALIC/CARDS in wreath (Obv. Ohio 165CY-1)				
175S-9a	Same	Same	BR	PL	R9	
175S-9b	Same	W. K. LANPHEAR/MANU'FR/OF/METALIC/CARDS/CINITI/OHIO (Obv. Ohio 165CY-47a)	C	PL	R9	8280
175S-10a	Same as Rev. Ohio 175S-4a (H-R 1903)	Same	BR	PL	R9	8281
175S-11a	Same	1172	C	PL	R8	8273
175S-12a	Same	1180	C	PL	R8	8272
175S-13a	Same	1192	C	PL	R9	8398
	Same	1242	C	PL	R9	

OHIO-Continued

NUMBER	OBVERSE	REVERSE	METAL	EDGE	RARITY	H&G

COLLINSVILLE 185

185A-1a	P. CARLE & SON/GROCCERS/ &/GRAIN/DEALERS/ COLLINSVILLE, O.	1019	C	PL	R3	8286

(NOTE: The second C in GROCERS touches first C and is light, S is also double cut.)

185A-1b	Same	Same	BR	PL	R8	8287
185A-2a	Same	1028	C	PL	R8	
185A-3a	Same	1038	C	PL	R9	
185A-4a	Same	1042	C	R	R7	8288
185A-4b	Same	Same	BR	R	R8	8289
185A-4i	Same	Same	Z	R	R9	
185A-5a	Same	1047	C	R	R9	
185A-5d	Same (Elder 5/39 Lot 556)	Same	C-N	R	R10	
185A-6a	Same	1192	C	PL	R9	8285

COLUMBIANA 190

190A-1a	ICENHOUR & CO/PRODUCE/&/ COMMISSION/MERCHANTS/ COLUMBIANA, O.	1046	C	R	R9	
190A-1d	Same	Same	C-N	R	R10	8351
190A-2a	Same (H-R 1893)	1047	C	R	R9	
190A-2d	Same	Same	C-N	R	R10	
190A-3a	Same	1313	C	R	R5	8346
190A-3b	Same (H-R 1894)	Same	BR	R	R9	8347
190A-3b1	Same	Same	BR	PL	R10	
190A-3c	Same (NOTE: May not exist.)	Same	N	R	R-	8348
190A-3i	Same	Same	Z	R	R9	8349

406

OHIO-Continued

NUMBER	OBVERSE	REVERSE	METAL	EDGE	RARITY	H&G

COLUMBIANA 190 -Continued

190B-1

190B-2

190B-1a	G. KIPP/PRODUCE/DEALER/ COLUMBIANA, O. (R of DEALER under C of PRODUCE.) (NOTE: Comes with obverse die breaks.)	1046	C	R	R3	8353
190B-1a1	Same	Same	C	PL	R8	
190B-1b	Same	Same	BR	R	R9	8354
190B-1d	Same	Same	C-N	R	R10	8355
190B-1i	Same	Same	Z	R	R9	
190B-2a	Similar, but R of DEALER under CE of PRODUCE	1046	C	R	R6	
190B-3a	Same as Ohio 190B-1	1047	C	R	R9	
190B-3d	Same	Same	C-N	R	R9	
190B-4a	Same as Ohio 190B-2 (Dorge 2/74 Lot 461)	Same	C	R	R9	

COLUMBUS 200

200A-1

200A-3

200A-1a	JOHN GRETHER/IMPORTER/ OF/CHINA/& QUEENSWARE/ COLUMBUS, O.	1037	C	R	R7	8294
200A-1b	Same	Same	BR	R	R8	8295
200A-1i	Same	Same	Z	R	R8	8296
200A-2a	Same	1042	C	R	R6	8297
200A-2a1	Same	Same	C	PL	R8	
200A-2b	Same	Same	BR	R	R8	8298
200A-2i	Same	Same	Z	R	R9	
200A-3a	Same (H-R 1895) Error - "IMPORORTER"	1043	C	R	R9	
200A-4d	Same as Ohio 200A-1a	1046	C-N	R	R10	
200A-5a	Same	1047	C	R	R9	
200A-5d	Same	Same	C-N	R	R10	8300
200A-3b	Same	Same	BR	R	R10	
200A-6a	Same (Error: IMPORORTER)	1042	C	R	R9	

OHIO-Continued

NUMBER	OBVERSE	REVERSE	METAL	EDGE	RARITY	H&G

COLUMBUS 200-Continued

200B

200C

200B-1a	HEINTZ & HENKLE/DEALERS/ IN/GROCERIES/136 COR 4TH./ AND/FRIEND/COLUMBUS, O.	1083	C	PL	R6	8302
200B-1d	Same	Same	C-N	PL	R9	
200B-2a	Same	1125	C	PL	R8	8303
200B-3a	Same	1177	C	PL	R3	8304
200C-1a	J.M & V. KOERNER,/GROCERS/ S. E. COR./BROAD/&/FRONT/ COLUMBUS, O.	1082	C	PL	R3	8306
200C-1b	Same	Same	BR	PL	R9	
200C-2a	Same	1087	C	PL	R4	8307
200C-3a	Same	1125	C	PL	R9	8308
200C-4a	Same	1126	C	PL	R9	
200C-5a	Same	1166	C	PL	R9	
200C-6a	Same	1168	C	PL	R9	8310
200C-7a	Same	1178	C	PL	R4	8309

200D-1

200D-6

200D-1a	S. T. MARTIN/EATING/HOUSE/ 160/SOUTH FOURTH ST/ COLUMBUS/OHIO.	1082	C	PL	R2	8312
200D-2a	Same	1089	C	PL	R1	8313
200D-3a	Same	1125	C	PL	R9	
200D-4a	Same	1127	C	PL	R9	8314
200D-5a	Same	1178	C	PL	R9	8315
200D-5b	Same	Same	BR	PL	R9	
200D-6a	S. T. MARTIN/EATING/HOUSE/ 160/SOUTH/FOURTH ST./ COLUMBUS, O.	1123	C	PL	R1	8317
200D-7a	Same	1124	C	PL	R3	
200D-8a	Same	1125	C	PL	R10	8318
200D-9a	Same	1126	C	PL	R8	
200D-10a	Same	1130	C	PL	R5	8320
200D-11a	Same	1166	C	PL	R9	8321
200D-12a	Same	1178	C	PL	R6	8319

OHIO-Continued

COLUMBUS 200-Continued

NUMBER	OBVERSE	REVERSE	METAL	EDGE	RARITY	H&G
200D-13a	Same	W. K. LANPHEAR above, CINNATTI below. MANU'FR/OF/METALIC/CARDS within wreath (Obv. Ohio 165CY-1).	C	PL	R8	8322

200E   MERCHANTS EXCHANGE - See Non-Contemporary NC-1b

NUMBER	OBVERSE	REVERSE	METAL	EDGE	RARITY	H&G
200F-1a	W. M. H. RESTIEAUX,/GROCER/COLUMBUS, O.	1180	C	PL	R5	8325
200F-2a	Same	1222	C	PL	R3	8324
200F-3a	Same	1344	C	PL	R9	8326
200F-4a	Same	W. K. LANPHEAR above, CINNATTI below. MANU'FR/OF/METALIC/CARDS within wreath (Obv. Ohio 165CY-1).	C	PL	R8	
200F-4d	Same (H-R 1896)	Same	C-N	PL	R10	
200G-1a	H. SCHREINER/GROCERIES/AND/PROVISIONS/169/EAST/FRIEND ST./COLUMBUS. O.	1125	C	PL	R3	8328
200G-2a	Same (H-R 1897)	1180	C	PL	R9	8330
200G-3a	Same	1273	C	PL	R9	
200H-1a	MRS. M. A. VAN HOUTEN/MILLINER/68/E. TOWN ST./COLUMBUS/OHIO.	1127	C	PL	R4	8331

409

OHIO-Continued

NUMBER	OBVERSE	REVERSE	METAL	EDGE	RARITY	H&G

COLUMBUS 200-Continued

200I

200J

200I-1a	WAGNER'S/DINING/HALL,/COLUMBUS, O.	1082	C	PL	R4	8335
200I-2a	Same	1124	C	PL	R5	8334
200I-3a	Same	1178	C	PL	R3	8336
200I-4a	Same	1179	C	PL	R8	
200I-5a	Same	1180	C	PL	R6	8337
200I-6a	Same	1342	C	PL	R9	
200J-1a	WIATT & BRO./BAKERS/&/CONFECTIONERS/COLUMBUS, O.	1124	C	PL	R8	8340
200J-2a	Same	1176	C	PL	R5	8341
200J-2d	Same	Same	C-N	PL	R9	8342
200J-3a	Same	1177	C	PL	R9	8343
200J-4a	Same	1295	C	PL	R8	8344

CRESTLINE 215

| 215A-1a | JACOB STUMP/MERCHANT TAILOR/&/READY MADE/CLOTHING,/CRESTLINE, OHIO. | 1342 | C | PL | R5 | 8357 |

410

OHIO-Continued

NUMBER	OBVERSE	REVERSE	METAL	EDGE	RARITY	H&G

DAYTON 230

| 230A-1a | J. C. CAIN/NOTIONS,/305 THIRD ST./DAYTON,/OHIO. | 1083 | C | PL | R5 | 8359 |

230B-1a	J. DURST/GROCER/DAYTON, O.	1018	C	R	R4	8361
230B-2a	Same	1023	C	R	R7	8362
230B-2a1	Same	Same	C	PL	R9	
230B-3a	Same	1042	C	R	R7	8363
230B-3b	Same (H-R 1900)	Same	BR	R	R9	8364
230B-3d	Same	Same	C-N	R	R10	8365
230B-3i	Same	Same	Z	R	R9	
230B-4a	Same	1046	C	R	R7	8366
230B-5a	Same (H-R 1901)	1047	C	R	R9	8367
230B-5d	Same	Same	C-N	R	R10	8369
						8369
230B-6d	Same	1069	C-N	R	R10	

NO PHOTO AVAILABLE

| 230C-1a | HENRY KLINE/CLOCKS/ WATCHES/&/JEWELRY/ DAYTON/O. | BLANK | C | PL | R9 | 8371 |

411

OHIO-Continued

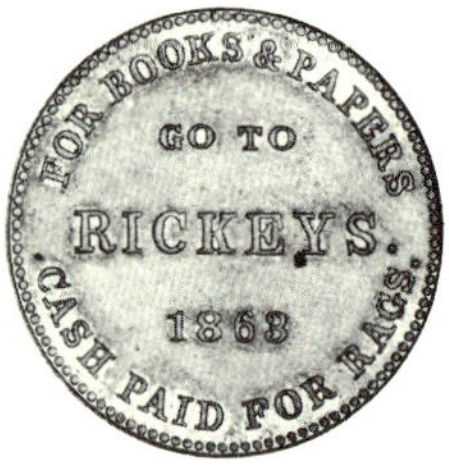

NUMBER	OBVERSE	REVERSE	METAL	EDGE	RARITY	H&G

DAYTON 230-Continued

230D-1a	RICKEYS/BOOKSTORE/326 3RD ST/DAYTON, O. (Adams Ohio 41-29mm.)	FOR BOOKS & PAPERS/GO TO/RICKEYS/1863/CASH/PAID/FOR RAGS	C	R	R5	
230E-1a	S. WILD/COFFEE/HOUSE/DAYTON, O.	1046	C	R	R5	8373
230E-2a	Same	1047	C	R	R9	8374
230E-2d	Same	Same	C-N	R	R10	8375

DEFIANCE 240

240A-1a	RUHL'S/PREMIUM/STEEL/PENS/DEFIANCE, O.	1008	C	PL	R3	8378
240A-2d	Same	1018	C-N	R	R10	
240A-3b	Same	1019	BR	PL	R9	
240A-4a	Same	1042	C	R	R6	8379
240A-4b	Same	Same	BR	R	R7	8380
240A-4i	Same	Same	Z	R	R8	8381
240A-5a	Same	1045	C	PL	R8	8377
240A-6a	Same	1047	C	R	R8	
240A-7d	Same	1069	C-N	R	R10	8382

412

OHIO-Continued

NUMBER	OBVERSE	REVERSE	METAL	EDGE	RARITY	H&G

DELPHOS 250

250A-1a	J. W HUNT/DRUGGIST/ EXPRESS/AGT./DELPHOS, O.	1037	C	R	R4	8385
250A-1a1	Same	Same	C	PL	R9	
250A-1b	Same	Same	BR	R	R9	
250A-1i	Same	Same	Z	R	R9	
250A-2a	Same	1046	C	R	R3	8386
250A-2a1	Same	Same	C	PL	R9	8387
250A-3a	Same	1047	C	R	R9	
250A-3d	Same	Same	C-N	R	R9	

EDGERTON 270

270A-1a	D. FARNHAM & CO./DEALERS/ IN/DRY GOODS,/EDGERTON,/ OHIO.	1088	C	PL	R9	8389
270A-2a	Same	1091	C	PL	R8	
270A-3a	Same	1169	C	PL	R8	8391
270A-4a	Same	1223	C	PL	R5	8390
270A-5a	Same	1229	C	PL	R9	
270A-6a	Same	1337	C	PL	R7	8392
270A-7a	Same	1342	C	PL	R6	8393

OHIO-Continued

NUMBER	OBVERSE	REVERSE	METAL	EDGE	RARITY	H&G

ELYRIA 290

290A-1   290A-1   290A-2

290A-1a	W. B. EAGER ELYRIA O. above. WHOLESALE AGT. below, Indian head to left in center.	TRY/ALLEN'S/BLACKLEAD/ COMPOUND/BABBITT/METAL/ 1862	C	PL	R8	
290A-1b	Same	Same	BR	PL	R2	8395
290A-2a	Similar, star before and after WHOLESALE AGT	Same	C	PL	R8	
290A-2b	Same	Same	BR	PL	R3	8396
290A-3a	Same as Rev 290A-1a	1168	C	PL	R	8397

(NOTE: We doubt that this piece exists. The pieces listed as H&G 8398 and 8399 are listed under Ohio 175S-10a).

FINDLAY 300

300A    300B    300C

300A-1bo	BOGER & KIMMEL/FINDLAY, O. (Struck over a McClellan token)	BLANK	BR	R	R9	
300B-1a	I. BOGER/WATCH MAKER/&/ JEWELER/FINDLAY, O.	1320	C	PL	R8	8401
300B-2b	Same	BLANK	BR	PL	R8	
300C-1a	OSBORNE & BRO/GROCERS/ PRODUCE/DEALERS/ FINDLAY, O.	1024	C	R	R8	
300C-2a	Same (H-R 1904)	1042	C	R	R8	8403
300C-2b	Same	Same	BR	R	R9	8404
300C-2i	Same	Same	Z	R	R9	8405
300C-3a	Same	1046	C	R	R9	8406
300C-4a	Same	1047	C	R	R9	
300C-4d	Same	Same	C-N	R	R10	

414

OHIO-Continued

NUMBER	OBVERSE	REVERSE	METAL	EDGE	RARITY	H&G

FRAZEYBURG 310

310A-1a	E. L. LEMERT/DRY/GOODS/&/ GROCERIES/FRAZEYBURG, O	1037	C	R	R6	8408
310A-1b	Same	Same	BR	R	R9	8409
310A-2a	Same	1046	C	R	R7	8410
310A-3a	Same	1047	C	R	R8	8411
310A-3d	Same	Same	C-N	R	R10	8412

FREDERICKTOWN 320

320A 320B 320C

320A-1a	BARTLETT & RIGBY/DRY/ GOODS/GROCERIES,/& C./ FREDERICKTOWN, O.	1046	C	R	R6	8415
320A-1a1	Same	Same	C	PL	R8	8414
320A-1b	Same	Same	BR	R	R9	8416
320A-1d	Same	Same	C-N	R	R10	8417
320A-li	Same	Same	Z	R	R9	
320A-2a	Same (H-R 1905)	1047	C	R	R9	8418
320A-2d	Same	Same	C-N	R	R10	
320B-1a	MOSURE BRO & LEMON/ CLOTHING /&/ DRY GOODS/ FREDICKTOWN, O.	1346	C	PL	R5	8420
320C-1a	ROGERS & CASSELL/HARDWARE /IRON &/NAILS/FREDERICKTOWN /OHIO	1304	C	PL	R4	8422

415

OHIO-Continued

NUMBER	OBVERSE	REVERSE	METAL	EDGE	RARITY	H&G

FREDERICKTOWN 320-Continued

320D-1a	S. S. TUTTLE/PRODUCE/ COMMISSION/&/FORWARDING /MERCHANT/FREDERICKTOWN, O.	1032	C	PL	R9	
320D-2a	Same	1037	C	R	R6	
320D-3a	Same	1046	C	R	R4	8424
320D-4a	Same	1047	C	R	R8	
320D-4d	Same	Same	C-N	R	R10	

FREMONT 330

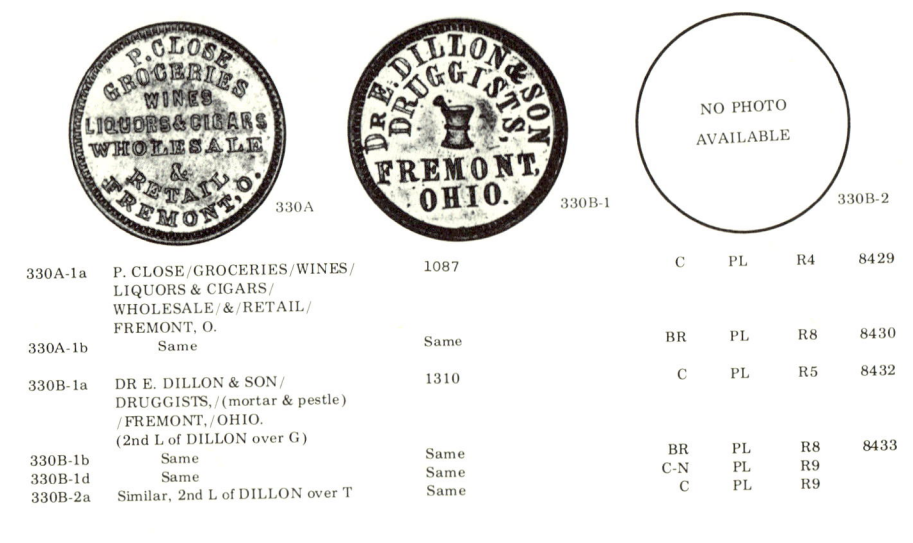

330A   330B-1   330B-2

330A-1a	P. CLOSE/GROCERIES/WINES/ LIQUORS & CIGARS/ WHOLESALE/&/RETAIL/ FREMONT, O.	1087	C	PL	R4	8429
330A-1b	Same	Same	BR	PL	R8	8430
330B-1a	DR E. DILLON & SON/ DRUGGISTS,/(mortar & pestle) /FREMONT,/OHIO. (2nd L of DILLON over G)	1310	C	PL	R5	8432
330B-1b	Same	Same	BR	PL	R8	8433
330B-1d	Same	Same	C-N	PL	R9	
330B-2a	Similar, 2nd L of DILLON over T	Same	C	PL	R9	

416

OHIO-Continued

NUMBER	OBVERSE	REVERSE	METAL	EDGE	RARITY	H&G

FREMONT 330-Continued

330C-1a	M. DRYFOOS/MERCHANT/TAILOR/AND DEALER IN/READY MADE/CLOTHING,/FREMONT, O.	1337	C	PL	R6	8435
330C-1ao	Same, struck over another token	Same	C	PL	R9	
330C-1b	Same	Same	BR	PL	R8	8436
330D-1a	EMRICH & CO./DRY GOODS,/CLOTHING/& C./FREMONT, O.	1087	C	PL	R5	8438
330D-1b	Same	Same	BR	PL	R7	8439
330E-1a	HOOT & MENG/MANUFR'S./AND/DEALERS IN/BOOTS & SHOES,/FREMONT,/OHIO.	1317	C	PL	R4	8441
330E-1b	Same	Same	BR	PL	R6	8442
330E-1d	Same	Same	C-N	PL	R9	
330F-1a	D. W. KREBS & CO./DEALERS/IN/DRY GOODS/CLOTHING/& C./FREMONT, O.	1085	C	PL	R5	8444
330F-1b	Same	Same	BR	PL	R6	8445
330F-2a	Same	1087	C	PL	R9	
330G-1a	ROBERTS & SHELDON,/DEALERS IN/STOVES, TIN,/AND/HARDWARE,/FREMONT, OHIO.	1306	C	PL	R5	8447
330G-1b	Same	Same	BR	PL	R7	8448
330H-1a	THOMPSON & SPICER,/STOVES,/TIN/& HOUSE/FURNISHING/GOODS/FREMONT,/OHIO.	1302	C	PL	R6	8450
330H-1b	Same	Same	BR	PL	R9	8451
330H-1d	Same	Same	C-N	PL	R9	

OHIO-Continued

NUMBER	OBVERSE	REVERSE	METAL	EDGE	RARITY	H&G

GALION 340

340A-1a	D & W. RIBLET, above GALION, OHIO. below. U.S. shield in center.	1333	C	PL	R4	8453
340A-1b	Same	Same	BR	PL	R6	8454
340A-1fp	Same	Same	S-P	PL	R9	

GALLIPOLIS 345

345A-1a	J. D. BAILEY/FANCY/DRY/GOODS/NOTIONS/&/GROCERIES/GALLIPOLIS, O.	1037	C	R	R8	
345A-1a1	Same	Same	C	PL	R9	
345A-2a	Same	1038	C	PL	R9	
345A-3d	Same	1046	C-N	R	R10	
345A-4a	Same (H-R 1909)	1047	C	R	R9	
345A-4d	Same	Same	C-N	R	R10	8455

345B-1a	J.J. CADOT & BRO./GROCERS/GALLIPOLIS/OHIO	1122	C	PL	R5	8458
345B-1b	Same	Same	BR	PL	R8	8459
345B-2a	Same	1181	C	PL	R5	8460

418

OHIO-Continued

NUMBER	OBVERSE	REVERSE	METAL	EDGE	RARITY	H&G

GALLIPOLIS 345-Continued

| 345C-1c | GOOD FOR/5 CTS/AT/S. GOETZ /COR. GRAPE &/3.STS/ GALLIPOLIS, O. | 1391 | N | R | R8 | 8463 |

| 345D-1a | HENKLING, ALLEMONG & CO/ GALLIPOLIS, O. | DRAYAGE/10/CENTS | C | R | R8 | |
| 345D-2a | Same | DRAYAGE/20/CENTS | C | R | R8 | |

GREENVILLE 360

360A-1a	F. H. HAFER & CO./STAPLE/ &/FANCY/GROCERS/ GREENVILLE, O. (NOTE: F and H reengraved over other letters.)	1007	C	R	R9	8466
360A-1a1	Same	Same	C	PL	R4	8465
360A-1b	Same	Same	BR	R	R9	8467
360A-2a	Same	1038	C	PL	R3	8468

OHIO-Continued

NUMBER	OBVERSE	REVERSE	METAL	EDGE	RARITY	H&G

GREENVILLE 360-Continued

NUMBER	OBVERSE	REVERSE	METAL	EDGE	RARITY	H&G
360A-3a	Same	1042	C	R	R7	8469
360A-3b	Same	Same	BR	R	R8	8470
360A-3i	Same	Same	Z	R	R9	
360A-4a	Same (H-R 1910)	1047	C	R	R9	
360A-4al	Same	Same	C	PL	R9	
360A-4d	Same	Same	C-N	R	R9	
360A-5a	Same	1192	C	PL	R9	8472

NUMBER	OBVERSE	REVERSE	METAL	EDGE	RARITY	H&G
360B-1d	T. P. TURPEN/GROCER/&/ TOBACCO/DEALER. GREENVILLE, O.	1018	C-N	R	R10	
360B-2a	Same	1023	C	PL	R8	8478
360B-3a	Same (H-R 1911)	1042	C	R	R7	8474
360B-3b	Same	Same	BR	R	R8	8475
360B-3i	Same	Same	Z	R	R9	8476
360B-4d	Same	1069	C-N	R	R10	8477

HAMILTON 385

NUMBER	OBVERSE	REVERSE	METAL	EDGE	RARITY	H&G
385A-1a	JOHN DEINZER/FAMILY/ GROCERY/NO./19 HIGH, ST./ HAMILTON, O.	1021	C	PL	R5	8480
385A-2a	Same	1042	C	R	R6	8482
385A-2al	Same	Same	C	PL	R9	8481
385A-2b	Same	Same	BR	R	R7	8483
385A-2i	Same	Same	Z	R	R9	
385A-3a	Same (H-R 1913)	1047	C	R	R9	
385A-3d	Same	Same	C-N	R	R10	
385A-4d	Same	1069	C-N	R	R10	

OHIO-Continued

NUMBER	OBVERSE	REVERSE	METAL	EDGE	RARITY	H&G

HAMILTON 385-Continued

385B-1a	H. & W. FRECHTLING/ DEALERS IN/DRY/GOODS/&/ GROCERIES/HAMILTON, O.	1038	C	PL	R9	
385B-2a	Same	1042	C	R	R8	8485
385B-2b	Same (H-R 1914)	Same	BR	R	R8	8486
385B-2i	Same	Same	Z	R	R9	8487
385B-3a	Same	1047	C	R	R8	
385B-3d	Same	Same	C-N	R	R10	
385B-4d	Same	1069	C-N	R	R10	

385C-1b	J. F. GOLLER. GOOD FOR/ 5/CENTS/HAMILTON. O.	JAS. MURDOCK, JR./STAMPS/ BURNINS/BRAND/AND/ STENCILS/139/W'5/ST/ CINCINNATI	BR	PL	R8	
385D-1d	JOHN SCHUBERT/HAMILTON/ SALOON/HIGH/STREET/ HAMILTON, O. (NOTE: L of SALOON cut over another L to the left.)	1018	C-N	R	R10	
385D-2a	Same	1019	C	PL	R5	8489
385D-2b	Same	Same	BR	PL	R9	
385D-3a	Same	1021	C	PL	R4	8490
385D-4a	Same	1036	C	PL	R4	8495
385D-4b	Same	Same	BR	PL	R9	8496
385D-5a	Same	1042	C	R	R7	8491
385D-5a1	Same	Same	C	PL	R9	
385D-5b	Same	Same	BR	R	R8	8492
385D-5i	Same	Same	Z	R	R9	8493
385D-6a	Same (H-R 1916)	1047	C	R	R9	
385D-7d	Same	1069	C-N	R	R10	8494

421

OHIO-Continued

NUMBER	OBVERSE	REVERSE	METAL	EDGE	RARITY	H&G

HILLSBORO 400

400A-1a	BLACK & KIBLER/DEALERS/IN/HARDWARE/IRON/&/NAILS./HILLSBORO. O.	1326	C	PL	R5	8497
400A-2a	Same	1332	C	PL	R4	8498
400A-3a	Same	1334	C	PL	R9	8499
400A-4a	Same	1346	C	PL	R9	8500

| 400B-1a | CHANEY & HARRIS/DEALERS/IN/DRY GOODS/HILLSBORO/OHIO. | 1122 | C | PL | R8 | 8501 |

| 400C-1a | O. J. ECKLEY/DAILY/MEAT/MARKET/HILLSBORO/OHIO. | 1287 | C | PL | R6 | 8503 |

422

OHIO-Continued

NUMBER	OBVERSE	REVERSE	METAL	EDGE	RARITY	H&G

HILLSBORO 400-Continued

| 400D-1a | HERRON & AMEN/DRY GOODS/ &/NOTIONS/HILLSBORO/ OHIO. | 1223 | C | PL | R3 | 8505 |

| 400E-1a | GEO. MARCH/DEALER/IN/ DRY GOODS/HILLSBORO/ OHIO. | 1171 | C | PL | R6 | 8506 |
| 400E-2a | Same (NOTE: Comes with obverse die broken.) | 1223 | C | PL | R4 | 8507 |

JACKSON 415

415A-1d	JOHN CHESNU'S/EXCHANGE/ JACKSON, O	1046	C-N	R	R10	
415A-2a	Same	1047	C	R	R8	
415A-2d	Same (Elder 9/38 Lot 380)	Same	C-N	R	R10	
415A-3b	Same	GOOD FOR/10/CENTS/1862	BR	PL	R9	8511
415A-4d	Same	1069	C-N	R	R10	

(NOTE: The name is undoubtedly meant to be CHESTNUT. On obverse die of all varieties JACKSON is clearly engraved over PORTSMOUTH.)

OHIO-Continued

NUMBER	OBVERSE	REVERSE	METAL	EDGE	RARITY	H&G

KENTON 420

| 420A-1a | J. M. BRUNSON,/DEALER/IN/DRY GOODS,/&C./KENTON OHIO. | Flag on staff in center, FANCY & STAPLE above, DRY GOOD & C. below. | C | PL | R6 | 8513 |

LANCASTER 440

440A-1a	J. AMBRUSTER,/GROCER/LANCASTER, O.	1126	C	PL	R9	
440A-2a	Same	1178	C	PL	R8	8516
440A-3a	Same	1344	C	PL	R9	
440A-4a	J. AMBRUSTER,/GROCER/LANCASTER/OHIO.	1084	C	PL	R4	8517
440A-5a	Same	BLANK	C	PL	R9	
440B-1a	J. BLOCK, AGT./READY/MADE/CLOTHING/TALMADGE/BLOCK/LANCASTER, O.	1337	C	PL	R5	8518

424

OHIO-Continued

NUMBER	OBVERSE	REVERSE	METAL	EDGE	RARITY	H&G

LANCASTER 440-Continued

440C-1a	CHAS. PAIRAN/GROCER/AND/LIQUOR/DEALER/LANCASTER, O.	1126	C	PL	R9	8521
440C-2a	Same	1127	C	PL	R9	8522
440C-3a	Same	1166	C	PL	R5	
440C-4a	Same	1172	C	PL	R9	8524
440C-4d	Same	Same	C-N	PL	R9	8525
440C-5a	Same	1227	C	PL	R8	8523
440D-1a	ANDREW REID,/DRY GOODS/AND/SHOES,/LANCASTER, O.	1273	C	PL	R4	8527
440D-1d	Same	Same	C-N	PL	R9	8528

LAURELVILLE 445

445A-1a	GEO D. RIEGEL/DRY GOODS/AND/GROCERIES/LAURELVILLE/OHIO.	1082	C	PL	R3	8531
445A-1b	Same	Same	BR	PL	R9	8532
445A-2a	Same	1083	C	PL	R6	
445A-2b	Same	Same	BR	PL	R8	
445A-3a	Same	1086	C	PL	R5	8533
445A-4a	Same	1228	C	PL	R5	8534
445A-5a	Same	1229	C	PL	R9	
445A-6a	Same	1280	C	PL	R3	8535

OHIO-Continued

NUMBER	OBVERSE	REVERSE	METAL	EDGE	RARITY	H&G

LIMA 450

450A-1a	R. BOOSE/DEALER/IN/DRY GOODS/LIMA,/OHIO.	1082	C	PL	R8	
450A-1b	Same	Same	BR	PL	R9	
450A-2a	Same	1091	C	PL	R3	8537
450A-2b	Same	Same	BR	PL	R5	8538
450A-3a	Same	1171	C	PL	R8	8540
450A-4a	Same	1223	C	PL	R3	8539

(NOTE: Comes with broken reverse die.)

LONDON 470

JAS. McLAUGHLIN, see listing on non-contemporary - This piece, was struck after 1870.

LOUDENVILLE 485

| 485A-1a | F. SCHUCH,/DEALER/IN/ GROCERIES/LOUDENVILLE/ OHIO. | 1082 | C | PL | R5 | 8544 |
| 485A-1b | Same | Same | BR | PL | R7 | |

OHIO-Continued

NUMBER	OBVERSE	REVERSE	METAL	EDGE	RARITY	H&G

MANSFIELD 505

505A

505B

505A-1a	H. ENDLY,/DEALER/IN/HATS/ AND/CAPS/MANSFIELD, O.	1270	C	PL	R2	8546
505A-1c	Same	Same	N	PL	R9	8547
505B-1a	F. B. ORR./DEALER/ HARDWARE/IRON & NAILS/ MANSFIELD. O.	1006	C	PL	R9	8548
505B-1b	Same	Same	BR	PL	R6	8549
505B-1bo	Same (over Fuld Patriotic 120/256)	Same	BR	PL	R10	
505B-2a	Same (Baker 504)	1137	C	PL	R8	8551
505B-2b	Same	Same	BR	PL	R7	8552
505B-2bo	Same over double-struck N.Y. 95D-5b	Same	BR	PL	R10	
505B-2c	Same	Same	N	PL	R7	8553
505B-2d	Same (Elder 9/38 Lot 1334)	Same	C-N	PL	R9	8554
505B-2e	Same (H-R 1918)	Same	W-M	PL	R7	8555
505B-2f	Same	Same	S	PL	R9	8556
505B-2fo	Same (Struck over a U.S. Dime)	Same	S	R	R9	
505B-3b	Same	1152	BR	PL	R7	8558
505B-3d	Same	Same	C-N	PL	R9	
505B-4b	Same	1214	BR	PL	R8	8570
505B-4c	Same	Same	N	PL	R9	8571
505B-5b	Same (Double struck-H-R 1919)	1243	BR	PL	R8	8561
505B-5c	Same	Same	N	PL	R8	8562
505B-6b	Same	1268	BR	PL	R7	8563
505B-7a	Same	1269	C	PL	R3	8567
505B-2do	Same, over C-N Cent	Same	C-N	PL	R9	

MARION 520

520A-1a	A. E. GRIFFIN/DENTIST above MARION,/OHIO. below—plate of false teeth in center.	1083	C	PL	R5	8574
520A-1d	Same	Same	C-N	PL	R9	
520A-2a	Same	1088	C	PL	R7	8575

427

OHIO-Continued

NUMBER	OBVERSE	REVERSE	METAL	EDGE	RARITY	H&G

MARTINSBURG 530

530A-1a	A. & W. H. BARNES/DRY GOODS, /MARTINSBURG,/OHIO. Eagle in glory in center.	1122	C	PL	R4	8577
530A-1b	Same	Same	BR	PL	R9	8578
530A-1d	Same	Same	C-N	PL	R10	

| 530B-1a | M. N. DAYTON, above, MARTINSBURG/OHIO. below Mortar and pestle in center. | DEALER/IN/DRUGS/MEDICINES/&/GROCERIES | C | PL | R6 | 8579 |

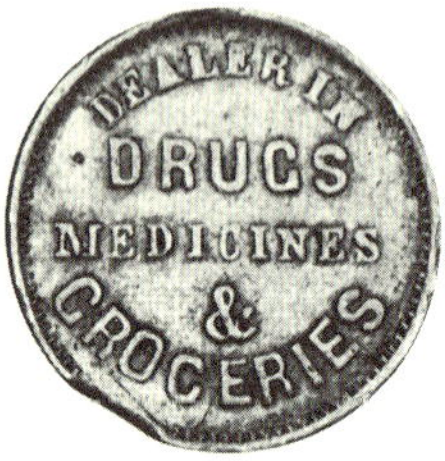

MASSILLON 535

535Ba

| 535A-1a | P. G. ALBRIGHT,/WHOLESALE/AND/RETAIL/GROCER,/MASSILLON, OHIO. (Name in large letters.) | 1087 | C | PL | R4 | 8581 |
| 535A-1b | Same | Same | BR | PL | R8 | 8582 |

428

OHIO-Continued

NUMBER	OBVERSE	REVERSE	METAL	EDGE	RARITY	H&G

MASSILLON 535-Continued

535A-4  535A-7  535A-8

535A-2a	Same	1125	C	PL	R9	8583
535A-3a	Same	1224	C	PL	R2	8584
535A-4a	Similar obv., but & instead of AND—no stars at sides.	1086	C	PL	R4	8586
535A-5a	Same	1127	C	PL	R9	8587
535A-6a	Same (NOTE: Comes with broken reverse die.)	1225	C	PL	R6	8590
535A-7a	Similar to preceding, but no comma after ALBRIGHT	1224	C	PL	R3	8588
535A-7b	Same	Same	BR	PL	R4	8589
535A-8a	Similar, all letters small & four stars at sides.	1084	C	PL	R2	8591
535A-9a	Same	1089	C	PL	R9	8592
535A-10a	Same	1130	C	PL	R3	8593

535B  535C  535D

535B-1a	J. E. DANGLER/DEALER/IN/ DRY GOODS/MASSILLON/ OHIO.	1127	C	PL	R3	8594
535B-2a	Same	1169	C	PL	R2	8595
535C-1a	FRED LOEFFLER,/RETAIL/ GROCER,/MAIN ST./MASSILLON /OHIO	1089	C	PL	R9	8598
535C-2a	Same	1130	C	PL	R2	8599
535C-2b	Same	Same	BR	PL	R9	
535D-1a	H. KNOBLOCH/RETAIL/ GROCER/ERIE ST./MASSILLON, OHIO.	1082	C	PL	R4	8600
535D-2a	Same	1089	C	PL	R3	8601
535D-3a	Same	1128	C	PL	R9	
535D-4a	Same	1224	C	PL	R4	8602
535Ba-1b	G.W. Laughlin/Jeweler/ Massillon, O.	Blank	BR	PL	R10	

OHIO-Continued

NUMBER	OBVERSE	REVERSE	METAL	EDGE	RARITY	H&G

MAUMEE CITY 540

| 540A-1a | H. BURRITT/DRUGS,/MEDICINES,/OILS,/DYE STUFFS & C./MAUMEE CITY,/OHIO. | 1310 | C | PL | R3 | 8605 |
| 540A-1b | Same | Same | BR | PL | R5 | 8606 |

| 540B-1a | MAUMEE/AND/PERRYSBURG/TOLL/BRIDGE, CO. (Atwood Ohio 725A) | 1128 | C | PL | R6 | 8608 |
| 540B-1b | Same (Atwood Ohio 725B) | Same | BR | PL | R7 | 8609 |

McCONNELSVILLE 550

| 550A-1a | H. M. COCHRAN/TOBACCO/MANUFACTURER/McCONNELSVILLE/OHIO/1863 | 1331 | C | PL | R4 | 8611 |
| 550A-1b | Same | Same | BR | PL | R7 | 8612 |

430

OHIO-Continued

NUMBER	OBVERSE	REVERSE	METAL	EDGE	RARITY	H&G

MIDDLETON 555

555A-1a	P. L. POTTER/DEALER/IN/ GROCERIES/&/QUEENSWARE/ MIDDLETOWN, O.	1019	C	PL	R5	8614
555A-1b	Same	Same	BR	PL	R9	
555A-2a	Same	1020	C	PL	R9	
555A-3a	Same	1036	C	PL	R7	
555A-4a	Same	1042	C	R	R6	8615
555A-4b	Same	Same	BR	R	R7	8616
555A-4i	Same	Same	Z	R	R9	
555A-5a	Same	1047	C	R	R9	
555A-5d	Same	Same	C-N	R	R10	8618
555A-6d	Same	1069	C-N	R	R10	
555A-7a	Same	JOHN E. ZELTNER/NATIONAL /HALL/400/VINE, ST./ CINCINNATI, O. (Obv. 165GY-25a)	C	PL	R10	8620

(NOTE: The piece is oddly double struck—see photo. The piece described as H&G 8619 cannot exist.)

MONROEVILLE 560

560A-1a	R. C. MARTIN/MAN'FR /TIN/ SHEET IRON/AND/ COPPERWARE,/MONROEVILLE, /OHIO/	1085	C	PL	R4	8622
560A-1b	Same	Same	BR	PL	R6	8623
560A-1d	Same	Same	C-N	PL	R9	
560A-2a	Same	1128	C	PL	R9	8624
560A-3a	Same	1168	C	PL	R4	8625
560A-4a	Same	1302	C	PL	R9	8626

431

OHIO-Continued

| NUMBER | OBVERSE | REVERSE | METAL | EDGE | RARITY | H&G |

MONROEVILLE 560-Continued

| 560A-5a | R. G. MARTIN/HARDWARE/ STOVES AND/TIN WARE,/ MONROEVILLE/OHIO | 1128 | C | PL | R3 | 8627 |
| 560A-6a | Same | 1302 | C | PL | R4 | 8628 |

| 560A-7a | R. G. MARTIN/HARDWARE STORES/&/TIN WARE/ MONROEVILLE O. | 1085 | C | PL | R6 | 8630 |

(NOTE: An obvious error on the above piece in the word STORES instead of STOVES.)

560B-1a	A. W. PRENTISS/DRY GOODS,/ GROCERIES,/BOOTS & SHOES/ MONROEVILLE, O.	1128	C	PL	R9	
560B-1b	Same	Same	BR	PL	R8	8633
560B-2a	Same	1169	C	PL	R4	8634
560B-2b	Same	Same	BR	PL	R6	8635
560B-3a	Same	1317	C	PL	R5	8636
560B-3b	Same	Same	BR	PL	R8	8637

OHIO-Continued

NUMBER	OBVERSE	REVERSE	METAL	EDGE	RARITY	H&G

MORRISTOWN 565

565A-1a	P. LOCHARY/NEW/STORE/MORRISTOWN, O.	1122	C	PL	R4	8639
565A-2a	Same	1128	C	PL	R3	8640
565A-2b	Same	Same	BR	PL	R7	8641

MORROW 570

| 570A-1a | J. M. DYNES/DRY GOODS/AND/GROCERIES/AT/AUCTION/MORROW, OHIO. | 1303 | C | PL | R3 | 8643 |

| 570B-1a | E. LEVY/DRY GOODS/CLOTHING,/BOOTS/SHOES & C./MORROW, OHIO | 1125 | C | PL | R6 | 8645 |
| 570B-2a | Same | 1178 | C | PL | R5 | 8646 |

433

OHIO-Continued

NUMBER	OBVERSE	REVERSE	METAL	EDGE	RARITY	H&G

MT. EATON 585

| 585A-1a | D. GIAUGE/DEALER/IN/ GROCERIES/AND/PROVISIONS /MT. EATON/O. | 1086 | C | PL | R4 | 8648 |
| 585A-2a | Same | 1087 | C | PL | R5 | |

MUSSEY

(NOTE: E.C. Morse, formerly listed as Mussey, Ohio, is actually Mussey Twp., St. Clair Co., Mich. and is now listed as MICH 680A.)

NAVARRE 597

597A-1a	HALL & FRYMIRE,/DEALERS/ IN/STOVES/AND/TINWARE,/ NAVARRE,/OHIO.	1299	C	PL	R5	8656
597A-1b	Same	Same	BR	PL	R7	8657
597A-2a	Same	1301	C	PL	R9	
597A-3a	Same	1302	C	PL	R5	8658
597A-3b	Same	Same	BR	PL	R9	

OHIO-Continued

NUMBER	OBVERSE	REVERSE	METAL	EDGE	RARITY	H&G

NEWCOMERSTOWN 610

| 610A-1a | A. S. TWIFORD/PHOTOGRAPH/ARTIST/AND/DRUGGIST/NEWCOMERSTOWN/OHIO. | 1310 | C | PL | R4 | 8660 |
| 610A-1b | Same | Same | BR | PL | R7 | 8661 |

NEW LISBON 615

| 615A-1e | A. J. BLOCKSOM/DRUGGIST/NEW LISBON, O. | SODA CHECK/1/GLASS (Same Rev. Ky 370A) | W-M | PL | R9 | |

NEW LONDON 620

620A-1d	H. H. ROBINSON/DRY/GOODS/GROCERIES/&/PRODUCE/NEW LONDON, B. CO. (H-R 1929)	1018	C-N	R	R10	
620A-2a	Same	1023	C	PL	R4	8668
620A-3a	Same	1028	C	PL	R6	8669
620A-4a	Same	1031	C	PL	R9	

435

OHIO-Continued

NUMBER	OBVERSE	REVERSE	METAL	EDGE	RARITY	H&G

NEW LONDON 620-Continued

620A-5a	Same	1039	C	PL	R9	
620A-6a	Same	1042	C	R	R7	8665
620A-6b	Same	Same	BR	R	R7	8666
620A-6i	Same	Same	Z	R	R9	
620A-7a	Same	1045	C	PL	R3	8663
620A-8a	Same	1045 incused	C	PL	R10	8664
620A-9a	Same	1047	C	R	R9	
620A-10d	Same (Elder 9/38 Lot 389)	1069	C-N	R	R10	
620A-11a	Same (H-R 1930)	1274	C	PL	R9	
620A-12a	Same (H-R 1931)	BLANK	C	PL	R6	8670

620B-1a	CHEAP/CASH/STORE/ G. M. SHAW/NEW LONDON/ BUTLER, CO./OHIO.	1124	C	PL	R8	8676
620B-1d	Same	Same	C-N	PL	R9	
620B-2a	Same	1176	C	PL	R7	8672
620B-3a	Same	1177	C	PL	R7	8673
620B-4a	Same	1295	C	PL	R9	8674
620B-5a	Same	1331	C	PL	R9	8675

NORTH HAMPTON 645

645A-1a	M. HARTMAN/DRY/GOODS/ HARDWARE/BOOTS/&/SHOES/ NORTH HAMPTON, O.	1046	C	R	R4	8678
645A-1d	Same	Same	C-N	R	R10	8679
645A-2a	Same	1047	C	R	R9	8680
645A-2d	Same	Same	C-N	R	R10	8681

OHIO-Continued

NUMBER	OBVERSE	REVERSE	METAL	EDGE	RARITY	H&G

NORTH HAMPTON 645-Continued

645B-1a	G. W. McLEAN/PRODUCE/ DEALER/NORTH HAMPTON, O.	1037	C	R	R7	8682
645B-2a	Same	1046	C	R	R7	8683
645B-2b	Same	Same	BR	R	R9	8684
645B-2d	Same	Same	C-N	R	R10	8685
645B-3a	Same	1047	C	R	R9	
645B-3d	Same	Same	C-N	R	R10	

NORTH LIBERTY 650

650A-1a	SAM L. BISHOP,/DEALER/IN/ DRY GOODS,/GROCERIES & C./NORTH LIBERTY/OHIO.	1122	C	PL	R4	8687
650A-1d	Same	Same	C-N	PL	R9	
650A-2a	Same	1225	C	PL	R5	8688
	(NOTE: Comes with broken reverse die.)					

437

OHIO-Continued

NUMBER	OBVERSE	REVERSE	METAL	EDGE	RARITY	H&G

NORWALK 670

670A-1a	P. TIMMENS/GROCERIES &/ PROVISIONS/NORWALK, O.	1082	C	PL	R9	
670A-2a	Same	1084	C	PL	R8	8690
670A-3a	Same	1089	C	PL	R4	8691

OBERLIN 690

| 690A-1a | R H BIRGE/DRUGS/ GROCERIES & C./SIGN BIG MORTAR/MAIN ST./OBERLIN O. (NOTE: R of MORTAR is recut). | 1310 | C | PL | R6 | 8693 |

| 690B-1a | FRANK HENDRY/MAN'FR/OF/ SPECTACLES &/EYE GLASSES/ OBERLIN O. | 1089 | C | PL | R6 | 8695 |
| 690B-2a | Same | 1181 | C | PL | R7 | 8696 |

438

OHIO-Continued

NUMBER	OBVERSE	REVERSE	METAL	EDGE	RARITY	H&G

ORRVILLE 695

695A-1a	J. F. SEAS/DEALER/IN/ HARDWARE/BOOKS/PAINTS, OILS/& C./ORVILLE, O.	1007	C	PL	R7	8698
	(NOTE: The city name should be spelled ORRVILLE—one R is missing.)					
695A-2d	Same	1018	C-N	R	R10	
695A-3a	Same	1019	C	PL	R6	8699
695A-4a	Same (H-R 1934)	1042	C	R	R8	8700
695A-4b	Same	Same	BR	R	R8	8701
695A-4i	Same	Same	Z	R	R9	
695A-5a	Same (H-R 1935)	1047	C	R	R8	
695A-6d	Same	1069	C-N	R	R10	8703

OXFORD 710

710A-1a	McGAW & RICHEY/DEALERS/ IN/DRUGS/BOOKS/AND/ WALL PAPER/OXFORD, O.	1124	C	PL	R6	8705
710A-2a	Same	1180	C	PL	R4	8706
710A-3a	Same	1225	C	PL	R7	
710A-4a	Same	1324	C	PL	R9	
710A-5a	Same	1331	C	PL	R8	
710B-1a	NEWTON & KUMLERS,/ DEALERS/IN/DRY/GOODS/ OXFORD O.	1058	C	PL	R5	8708

OHIO-Continued

NUMBER	OBVERSE	REVERSE	METAL	EDGE	RARITY	H&G

PERRYSBURG 725

725A-1a	G. BEACH, DRY GOODS,/ CLOTHING, BOOTS SHOES & C/ PERRYSBURG,/OHIO.	1177	C	PL	R9	8710
725A-2a	Same	1181	C	PL	R6	8711
725A-2b	Same	Same	BR	PL	R8	8712

725B-1a	D. KREPS/DEALER IN/ AGRICULTURAL/IMPLEMENTS /& FARM TOOLS/PERRYSBURG,/ OHIO.	PORTABLE/STEAM/ENGINES,/ REAPERS &/MOWERS,/CANE/ MILLS/& EVAPORATORS	C	PL	R6	
725B-1b	Same	Same	BR	PL	R7	8714
725B-1g	Same	Same	L	PL	R9	

PIQUA 730

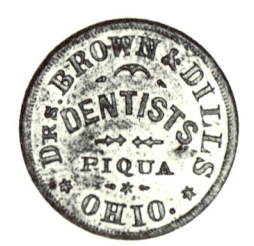

730A-1a	DRS. BROWN & DILLS, DENTISTS/PIQUA/OHIO.	1082	C	PL	R4	8717
730A-2a	Same	1089	C	PL	R9	
730A-3a	Same	1123	C	PL	R5	

440

OHIO-Continued

NUMBER	OBVERSE	REVERSE	METAL	EDGE	RARITY	H&G

PIQUA 730-Continued

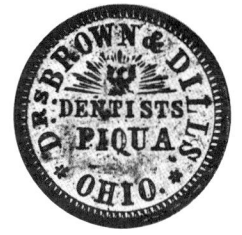

730A-4a	Same	1125	C	PL	R6	8718
730A-5a	Same	1126	C	PL	R4	8719
730A-6a	Same	1127	C	PL	R4	8720
730A-7a	Same	1177	C	PL	R8	8716
730A-8a	DRS. BROWN & DILLS, (Eagle in glory)/DENTISTS/PIQUA/OHIO	BRANCH OFFICE, (False teeth)/TROY,/OHIO.	C	PL	R3	8722
730A-8b	Same	Same	BR	PL	R8	8723
730A-8d	Same	Same	C-N	PL	R9	

730B-1a	FRENCH & SWONGER/DAILY/MEAT/MARKET./PIQUA, O.	1287	C	PL	R4	8725
730C-1a	MARTIN HOEGNER/DAILY/MEAT/MARKET/PIQUA, O.	1287	C	PL	R6	8727

730D-1a	MARROW & PARKER/DEALERS/IN/DRY GOODS/PIQUA, O. (NOTE: Reverse die is broken.)	1223	C	PL	R8	

441

OHIO-Continued

NUMBER	OBVERSE	REVERSE	METAL	EDGE	RARITY	H&G

PIQUA 730-Continued

730E-1a	SMART & CO/GROCERS,/136/ MAIN ST./PIQUA, O.	1122	C	PL	R4	8729
730E-2a	Same	1166	C	PL	R7	
730E-3a	Same	1169	C	PL	R9	8730

POMEROY 735

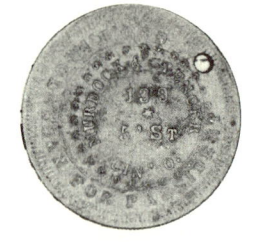

| 735A-1bo | W. A. AICHER/POMEROY, O. (Struck over a McClellan political card.) | MURDOCK & SPENCER/139/5' St/ CIN' O. | BR | PL | R9 | |

735B-1d	J. P. TOU/GROCER/104/ FRONT/ST/POMEROY, O.	1018	C-N	R	R10	
735B-2a	Same	1023	C	PL	R7	
735B-3a	Same	1028	C	PL	R8	8737
735B-4a	Same	1042	C	R	R7	8734
735B-4b	Same	Same	BR	R	R8	8735
735B-4i	Same	Same	Z	R	R9	
735B-5a	Same	1045	C	PL	R5	8733
735B-6d	Same	1047	C-N	R	R10	
735B-7d	Same	1069	C-N	R	R10	8736
735B-6a	Same	1047	C	R	R	

442

OHIO-Continued

NUMBER	OBVERSE	REVERSE	METAL	EDGE	RARITY	H&G

PORTSMOUTH 745

745A-1

745A-2

745A-1a	BURTON'S/EXCHANGE/ PORTSMOUTH, O (H-R 1939)	1047	C	R	R8	
745A-2b	Same	GOOD FOR/10/CENTS/1862 (Same as Ohio 415A-3)	BR	PL	R8	8741
745A-2bp	Same	Same	S-P BR	PL	R8	

NO PHOTO AVAILABLE

| 745A-3a | Same | GOOD FOR/25/CENTS/1862 | C | PL | R9 | |

745B-1a	S. W. CUNNING/WHOLESALE/ LIQUORS/NO. 6/FRONT, ST./ PORTSMOUTH, O.	1009	C	PL	R9	
745B-2a	Same	1038	C	PL	R8	8743
745B-3a	Same	1042	C	R	R0	0744
745B-3b	Same	Same	BR	R	R8	8745
745B-4a	Same (H-R 1942)	1047	C	R	R9	
745B-4d	Same	Same	C-N	R	R10	8746
745B-5d	Same (H-R 1941)	1069	C-N	R	R10	
745B-3i	Same (Dorge 6/73 Lot 589)	Same	Z	R	R9	
745B-6a	Same (Dorge 10/73 Lot 488)	1401	C	PL	R10	

443

OHIO-Continued

NUMBER	OBVERSE	REVERSE	METAL	EDGE	RARITY	H&G

PUTNAM 755

755A-1a	L. WILES/DRY GOODS/& C./PUTNAM, O.	1126	C	PL	R6	8748
755A-1do	Same, over C-N Cent	Same	C-N	PL	R10	
755A-2a	Same	1166	C	PL	R9	8750
755A-3a	Same	1178	C	PL	R8	8749

RAVENNA 765

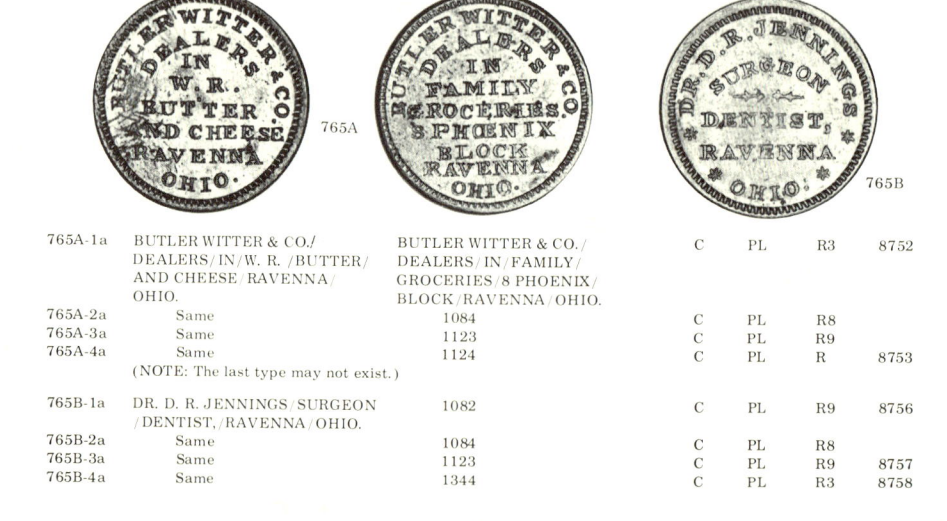

765A-1a	BUTLER WITTER & CO./DEALERS/IN/W. R./BUTTER/AND CHEESE/RAVENNA/OHIO.	BUTLER WITTER & CO./DEALERS/IN/FAMILY/GROCERIES/8 PHOENIX/BLOCK/RAVENNA/OHIO.	C	PL	R3	8752
765A-2a	Same	1084	C	PL	R8	
765A-3a	Same	1123	C	PL	R9	
765A-4a	Same	1124	C	PL	R	8753
	(NOTE: The last type may not exist.)					
765B-1a	DR. D. R. JENNINGS/SURGEON/DENTIST,/RAVENNA/OHIO.	1082	C	PL	R9	8756
765B-2a	Same	1084	C	PL	R8	
765B-3a	Same	1123	C	PL	R9	8757
765B-4a	Same	1344	C	PL	R3	8758

444

OHIO-Continued

NUMBER	OBVERSE	REVERSE	METAL	EDGE	RARITY	H&G

RAVENNA 765-Continued

765C-1a	C. A. PEASE,/DEALER/IN/ GROCERIES/FRUITS & C./ 4 PHOENIX BLOCK/RAVENNA/ OHIO	1082	C	PL	R3	8760
765C-2a	Same	1168	C	PL	R8	8762
765C-3a	Same	1181	C	PL	R8	8761

| 765D-1a | MRS. REED/MILLINERY/AND/ FANCY/GOODS/RAVENNA/ OHIO. | 1273 | C | PL | R4 | 8764 |

765E-1a	BUY/YOUR/DRY GOODS/AND GROCERIES/OF/WM. WARD,/ RAVENNA,/OHIO./1863 (NOTE: The V of RAVENNA is overcut over an A.)	WM. WARD/PAYS/THE/ HIGHEST/MARKET/PRICE FOR /BUTTER/AND/CHEESE.	C	PL	R3	8766
765E-2a	Rev. Ohio 765E-1a	1084	C	PL	R9	
765E-3a	Same	1088	C	PL	R9	
765E-4a	Same	1123	C	PL	R8	

445

OHIO-Continued

NUMBER	OBVERSE	REVERSE	METAL	EDGE	RARITY	H&G

RICHMOND 770

770A-1a	B.L. CREW/DRY/GOODS/&/ GROCERIES/RICHMOND, O.	1028	C	PL	R5	8775
770A-2a	Same	1042	C	R	R6	8771
770A-2b	Same	Same	BR	R	R8	8772
770A-2i	Same	Same	Z	R	R9	
770A-3a	Same	1045	C	PL	R5	8770
770A-4d	Same	1046	C-N	R	R10	8774
770A-5a	Same	1047	C	R	R9	
770A-5d	Same	Same	C-N	R	R10	
770A-6d	Same (H-R 1949)	1069	C-N	R	R10	

RIPLEY 780

| 780A-1bo | DUNBAR & WOLFF/ WATCHMAKERS/RIPLEY O. (Struck over a McClellan political card). | MURDOCK & SPENCER/139/5' ST/ CIN' O. | BR | PL | R9 | |

446

OHIO-Continued

NUMBER	OBVERSE	REVERSE	METAL	EDGE	RARITY	H&G

SHARONVILLE 800

800A-1a	W. K. MCMILLINS/STORE/ SHARONVILLE, O.	1028	C	PL	R6	
800A-2a	Same	1042	C	R	R7	8777
800A-2b	Same	Same	BR	R	R8	8778
800A-2i	Same	Same	Z	R	R9	
800A-3a	Same	1047	C	R	R9	
800A-3d	Same (H-R 1950)	Same	C-N	R	R10	
800A-4d	Same	1069	C-N	R	R10	8780

SHELBY 805

805A

805B

805A-1a	CUMMINS & ANDERSON/DRY/ GOODS/GROCERIES/ MILLINERY/SHELBY, O.	1037	C	R	R7	8782
805A-1b	Same	Same	BR	R	R9	
805A-1i	Same	Same	Z	R	R9	
805A-2a	Same	1042	C	R	R8	
805A-2b	Same	Same	BR	R	R8	
805A-2i	Same	Same	Z	R	R9	
805A-3a	Same	1043	C	R	R7	8783
805A-3al	Same	Same	C	PL	R9	
805A-4a	Same	1046	C	R	R9	
805A-4d	Same	Same	C-N	R	R10	
805A-5a	Same	1047	C	R	R9	
805A-5d	Same (H-R 1952)	Same	C-N	R	R10	
805B-1a	THOS. MICKEY/SHELBY,/ OHIO/DRY GOODS,/ GROCERIES,/HATS, CAPS AND /MILLINERY GOODS.	HIGHEST/CASH/PRICE/PAID/ FOR/COUNTRY PRODUCE.	C	PL	R4	8787
805B-2d	Same (H-R 1953)	Same	C-N	PL	R10	
805A-3b	Same (A.N.S.)	Same	BR	R	R9	8784
805A-3i	Same (Dorge 6/73 Lot 592)	Same	Z	R	R9	

OHIO-Continued

NUMBER	OBVERSE	REVERSE	METAL	EDGE	RARITY	H&G

SIDNEY 815

815A-1a	FRY & JOHNSTON/DRY GOODS/ BOOTS/& SHOES./SIDNEY, O.	1090	C	PL	R9	
815A-2a	Same	1091	C	PL	R9	8789
815A-3a	Same	1122	C	PL	R4	8790
815A-4a	Same	1225	C	PL	R9	8791
815A-5a	Same	1228	C	PL	R7	

| 815B-1a | JASON MCVAY/DRY GOODS/ BOOTS/SHOES & C/SIDNEY, O. | 1337 | C | PL | R3 | 8793 |

| 815C-1a | S. N. TODD & CO./DRUGGISTS/ STATIONERS/SIDNEY, O. | 1316 | C | PL | R7 | 8795 |

448

OHIO-Continued

NUMBER	OBVERSE	REVERSE	METAL	EDGE	RARITY	H&G

SONORA 820

| 820A-1a | WILLIAM LEAS./CALL/AT THE/ CASH/STORE/SONORA. O. | 1091 | C | PL | R5 | 8797 |

SPRINGFIELD 830

830A-1a	W. G. BRAIN/CASH/DRUGGIST/ MARKET/ST./SPRINGFIELD, O	1018	C	R	R8	8800
830A-1a1	Same	Same	C	PL	R9	
830A-2a	Same	1023	C	PL	R7	
830A-3a	Same	1025	C	R	R6	8801
830A-4a	Same	1026	C	PL	R5	
830A-5a	Same	1027	C	R	R7	8802
830A-6a	Same	1028	C	PL	R5	
830A-7a	Same	1030	C	PL	R8	
830A-8a	Same	1033	C	PL	R5	8808
830A-9a	Same	1034	C	PL	R3	8803
830A-10a	Same	1036	C	PL	R8	8807
830A-11a	Same	1042	C	R	R7	8804
830A-11b	Same (H-R 1955)	Same	BR	R	R8	8805
830A-11i	Same	Same	Z	R	R9	8806
830A-12d	Same (H-R 1956)	1069	C-N	R	R10	
830A-13a	Same	1047	C	R	R	
830B-1a	KAUFMANN & CO/CIGARS/&/ LIQUORS/MARKET/ST/ SPRINGFIELD, O.	1028	C	PL	R4	8815
830B-2a	Same	1034	C	PL	R6	8810
830B-3a	Same	1037	C	R	R8	
830B-4a	Same	1042	C	R	R7	8811
830B-4b	Same	Same	BR	R	R8	8812
830B-4i	Same	Same	Z	R	R9	8813
830B-5a	Same	1044	C	PL	R7	

OHIO-Continued

NUMBER	OBVERSE	REVERSE	METAL	EDGE	RARITY	H&G
SPRINGFIELD 830-Continued						
830B-6d	Same	1046	C-N	R	R10	8814
830B-7a	Same	1047	C	R	R9	
830B-7d	Same (H-R 1958)	Same	C-N	R	R9	

830C-1a	J. W. LOW/BOOKS/&/WALL • PAPER/MARKET/ST./ SPRINGFIELD, O.	1022	C	PL	R9	8823
830C-2a	Same	1031	C	PL	R9	
830C-2b	Same	Same	BR	R	R8	
830C-3b	Same	1035	BR	PL	R8	8824
830C-4a	Same	1037	C	R	R8	
830C-4b	Same	Same	BR	R	R4	8817
830C-5a	Same	1042	C	R	R7	8818
830C-5b	Same	Same	BR	R	R8	8819
830C-5i	Same	Same	Z	R	R9	8820
830C-6a	Same	1043	C	R	R9	
830C-6b	Same	Same	BR	R	R7	
830C-7a	Same	1046	C	R	R3	8821
830C-7b	Same	Same	BR	R	R6	8822
830C-8a	Same	1047	C	R	R9	
830C-8d	Same (H-R 1960)	Same	C-N	R	R9	

830D-1a	LUDLOW & BUSHNELL/ DRUGGISTS/85/MAIN, ST./ SPRINGFIELD, O.	1018	C	R	R7	8826
830D-2a	Same	1020	C	PL	R8	8827
830D-3a	Same	1025	C	PL	R7	
830D-4a	Same	1036	C	PL	R5	8833
830D-5a	Same	1042	C	R	R7	8828
830D-5b	Same	Same	BR	R	R8	8829
830D-5i	Same	Same	Z	R	R9	8830
830D-6a	Same	1046	C	R	R8	
830D-7a	Same	1047	C	R	R8	8831
830D-8a	Same (Elder 9/38 Lot 379)	1069	C	R	R9	8832
830D-8d	Same	Same	C-N	R	R10	
830D-6a1	Same (Dorge 10/73 Lot 497)	Same	C	PL	R9	

OHIO-Continued

NUMBER	OBVERSE	REVERSE	METAL	EDGE	RARITY	H&G

SPRINGFIELD 830-Continued

830E-1a	G. W. MCLEAN/PRODUCE/ DEALER/SPRINGFIELD, O.	1042	C	R	R5	8835
830E-1b	Same	Same	BR	R	R7	8836
830E-1i	Same	Same	Z	R	R9	
830E-2a	Same	1043	C	R	R8	
830E-3a	Same	1047	C	R	R9	
830E-3d	Same	Same	C-N	R	R10	8838

830F-1a	MURPHY & BRO./DRY/GOODS/ MARKET/ST/SPRINGFIELD, O.	1026	C	PL	R8	
830F-2a	Same	1037	C	R	R9	8840
830F-3a	Same	1042	C	R	R6	8841
830F-3b	Same (H-R 1964)	Same	BR	R	R8	8842
830F-3i	Same	Same	Z	R	R9	
830F-4a	Same	1047	C	R	R9	
830F-5d	Same	1069	C-N	R	R10	8844

830G-1a	C. RUNYON/GROCERIES/ MARKET ST./SPRINGFIELD, O. (NOTE: SPRINGFIELD spelled SPINGFIELD on this die.)	1037	C	R	R7	8846
830G-1b	Same (H-R 1966)	Same	BR	R	R8	8847
830G-1i	Same	Same	Z	R	R9	8848
830G-2a	Same	1047	C	R	R9	
830G-2d	Same	Same	C-N	R	R10	8849

OHIO-Continued

NUMBER	OBVERSE	REVERSE	METAL	EDGE	RARITY	H&G

STEUBENVILLE 835

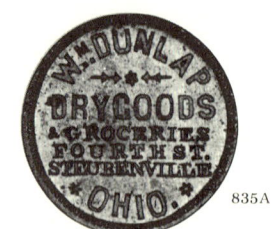

835A-1d	WM. DUNLAP/DRY GOODS/& GROCERIES/FOURTH ST./ STEUBENVILLE/OHIO.	1090	C-N	PL	R9	
835A-2a	Same	1166	C	PL	R3	8851
835A-2d	Same	Same	C-N	PL	R9	8852
835A-3a	Same	W. K. LANPHEAR above, CINCINNATI/O. below.MANU'FR /OF/METALIC/CARDS in wreath (Obv. Ohio 165CY-1)	C	PL	R9	
835B-1a	J. H. BRISTOR/COR./FOURTH/ AND/MARKET/ STEUBENVILLE, O.	1084	C	PL	R9	8854
835B-2a	Same	1326	C	PL	R3	8855
835B-3a	Same	W. K. LANPHEAR above, CINCINNATI/O. below. MANU'FR/OF/METALIC/ CARDS in wreath (Obv. Ohio 165CY-1)	C	PL	R9	8856

835C-1a	J.W. GRAY/GROCERIES/AND/ DRY GOODS/COR. ADAMS/&/ SIXTH/STEUBENVILLE, O.	1127	C	PL	R5	8857
835C-2a	Same	1130	C	PL	R3	8861
835C-3a	Same	1168	C	PL	R9	8860
835C-4a	Same	1181	C	PL	R2	8858
835C-4b	Same	Same	BR	PL	R8	8859

OHIO-Continued

| NUMBER | OBVERSE | REVERSE | METAL | EDGE | RARITY | H&G |

STEUBENVILLE 835-Continued

835D-1a	J. H. HIND'S, NEWS/DEPOT/ COR/4TH. & MARKET/ STEUBENVILLE/OHIO.	1166	C	PL	R5	8865
835D-2a	Same	1322	C	PL	R5	8864
835D-3a	Same	W. K. LANPHEAR above, CINCINNATI/O/below. MANU'FR/OF/METALIC/ CARDS in wreath (Obv. Ohio 165CY-1)	C	PL	R9	8863

| 835E-1a | C. M. MAY/MERCHANT/ TAILOR/AND/CLOTHIER/ STEUBENVILLE/OHIO. | 1337 | C | PL | R5 | 8867 |
| 835E-2a | Same | 1342 | C | PL | R2 | 8868 |

835F-1a	J. McCAULEY/GROCER/ FOURTH ST./STEUBENVILLE/ OHIO.	1227	C	PL	R4	8870
835G-1a	D. McCONVILLE/DRY GOODS/ AND/NOTIONS/ STEUBENVILLE/OHIO.	1166	C	PL	R9	8873
835G-2a	Same	1178	C	PL	R4	8872

453

OHIO-Continued

NUMBER	OBVERSE	REVERSE	METAL	EDGE	RARITY	H&G

STRYKER 840

| 840A-1a | JOHN S. KINGSLAND/& BRO./ (mortar & pestle)/DRUGGISTS. STRYKER/OHIO | 1094 | C | PL | R5 | 8876 |
| 840A-2a | Same | 1390 | C | PL | R9 | 8877 |

| 840B-1a | G.W. HAMBLIN/GENERAL/ GOODS/DEALER/STRYKER, OHIO. | 1106 | C | PL | R9 | 8879 |
| 840B-2a | Same | 1107 | C | PL | R6 | 8880 |

SYRACUSE 845

845A-1a	H. BARTELS/DRY/GOODS/ GROCERIES/BOOTS/&/SHOES/ SYRACUSE, O.	1046	C	R	R5	8881
845A-1d	Same	Same	C-N	R	R10	8882
845A-2a	Same	1047	C	R	R7	8883

454

OHIO-Continued

NUMBER	OBVERSE	REVERSE	METAL	EDGE	RARITY	H&G

TIFFIN 850

850A-1a	M. J. KIRCHNER/GROCERIES/ WASHINGTON/ST./TIFFIN, O.	1037	C	R	R7	8884
850A-2d	Same	1046	C-N	R	R10	8885
850A-3a	Same	1047	C	R	R9	8886

850B-1b	SONDER/&/CARPENTERS/ CARD within a wreath	WHOLESALE/&/RETAIL/DRY GOODS/TIFFIN OHIO	BR	PL	R3	8889
850C-1a	SOUDER/&/CARPENTER'S/ CARD within a wreath	DRY GOODS/DEALERS, TIFFIN,/OHIO	C	PL	R7	
850C-1b	Same	Same	BR	PL	R3	8888

(NOTE: One of the above is an error, but the correct spelling is not known.)

TIPPECANOE 855

855A-1a	E. C. SAYLOR/DAILY/MEAT/ MARKET/TIPPECANOE, O.	1228	C	PL	R5	8891
855A-2a	Same	1287	C	PL	R5	8892
855A-2b	Same	Same	BR	PL	R9	
855A-2d	Same	Same	C-N	PL	R9	8893

OHIO-Continued

NUMBER	OBVERSE	REVERSE	METAL	EDGE	RARITY	H&G

TOLEDO 860

860A-1a	C. P. CURTIS/AUCTION/& COMMISSION/MERCHANT,/157 SUMMIT ST. TOLEDO./OHIO.	1085	C	PL	R3	8895
860A-1b	Same	Same	BR	PL	R7	
860A-2a	Same	1127	C	PL	R5	8896
860A-3a	Same	1169	C	PL	R4	8898
860A-3b	Same	Same	BR	PL	R8	
860A-4a	Same	1181	C	PL	R9	8897
860B-1a	HOUGH & HALL,/DRY GOODS, CARPETS, OIL CLOTH & C/23 SUMMIT ST./TOLEDO,/OHIO.	1168	C	PL	R4	8902
860B-1b	Same	Same	BR	PL	R6	8903
860B-2a	Same	1181	C	PL	R4	8900
860B-2b	Same	Same	BR	PL	R7	8901
860B-3a	HOUGH & HALL/DRY GOODS/ CARPETS/OIL CLOTH & C./ 113 SUMMIT ST./TOLEDO,/ OHIO	1083	C	PL	R4	8904

860C-1a	KETCHAM & BARKER/ DEALERS/IN/HARDWARE/ STOVES&/TINWARE/ TOLEDO OHIO.	1305	C	PL	R3	8906
860C-1b	Same	Same	BR	PL	R3	8907
860D-1a	PLESSNER & SON/(mortar & pestle)/DRUGGISTS,/23/SUMMIT ST./TOLEDO, OHIO.	1310	C	PL	R4	8909
860D-1b	Same	Same	BR	PL	R3	8910

456

OHIO-Continued

NUMBER	OBVERSE	REVERSE	METAL	EDGE	RARITY	H&G

TROY 880

| 880A-1a | J. HALL/GRAIN/DEALER/ TROY, O. | RAILROAD/1863/WAREHOUSE | C | PL | R3 | 8912 |
| 880A-1d | Same | Same | C-N | PL | R9 | |

| 880B-1a | S. K. HARTER/DEALER/IN/ IRON NAILS/HARDWARE/ GUNS & PISTOLS/TROY, O. | 1332 | C | PL | R7 | 8914 |
| 880B-2a | S. K. HARTER/DEALER/IN/ IRON NAILS/HARDWARE/ GUNS &/PISTOLS/TROY, O. (NOTE: D of HARDWARE is backwards.) | 1332 | C | PL | R8 | |

880C-1a	S. E. HUSTLER/BROWN'S/OLD/ CORNER/TROY, O.	1089	C	PL	R9	
880C-2a	Same	1091	C	PL	R7	8917
880C-2d	Same	Same	C-N	PL	R9	
880C-3a	Same	1171	C	PL	R8	8919
880C-4a	Same	1223	C	PL	R3	8918
880C-5a	Same	1318	C	PL	R3	8920
880C-5b	Same	Same	BR	PL	R7	8921
880C-5d	Same (H-R 1973)	Same	C-N	PL	R9	

457

OHIO-Continued

NUMBER	OBVERSE	REVERSE	METAL	EDGE	RARITY	H&G

TROY 880-Continued

880D

880E

880D-1a	JULIAN & CO/WATCHMAKERS/ &/JEWELERS/TROY, O.	1090	C	PL	R8	8924
880D-2a	Same	1320	C	PL	R3	8925
880E-1a	DAVID KELLY/DEALER/IN/ BOOKS,/STATIONERY/& C./ TROY, O.	1083	C	PL	R9	
880E-2a	Same	1122	C	PL	R8	
880E-3a	Same	1124	C	PL	R5	8927
880E-4a	Same	1127	C	PL	R8	
880E-5a	Same	1180	C	PL	R3	8928

880F

880G

880F-1a	PEARSON & BRO./WHOLESALE/ &/RETAIL/GROCERS/TROY, O.	1083	C	PL	R8	
880F-2a	Same	1166	C	PL	R9	8935
880F-3a	Same	1171	C	PL	R3	8933
880F-4a	Same	1222	C	PL	R3	
880F-5a	Same	1223	C	PL	R4	8931
880F-6a	Same	1228	C	PL	R3	8932
880F-7a	Same	1346	C	PL	R5	8934
880G-1a	RINEHART & GRAY/CASH/ DRUGGISTS/SUCCESSORS/TO/ R.WRIGHT/TROY, O.	1126	C	PL	R4	8937
880G-2a	Same	1178	C	PL	R9	8938
880G-3a	Same	1228	C	PL	R9	
880G-4a	Same	1229	C	PL	R9	

OHIO-Continued

NUMBER	OBVERSE	REVERSE	METAL	EDGE	RARITY	H&G

UNIONTOWN 890

| 890A-1a | FAULEY & BRECHBILL/DRY GOODS/CLOTHING/&/ GROCERIES/UNIONTOWN O. | 1091 | C | PL | R5 | 8941 |
| 890A-2a | Same | 1228 | C | PL | R7 | |

URBANA 895

895A-1a	WASHINGTON/HOUSE/ C.MCCARTY/URBANA/O	1047	C	R	R8	
895A-2d	Same	1069	C-N	R	R10	8943
895A-3b	Same	1392	BR	PL	R10	
895A-3e	Same (Elder 9/38 Lot 383)	Same	W-M	PL	R10	
895A-1d	Same (Kreisberg 10/66 Lot 806)	Same	C-N	R	R10	

| 895B-1a | WALKER'S/ALE/DEPOT/ URBANA, O. | 1018 | C | R | R9 | |

459

OHIO-Continued

NUMBER	OBVERSE	REVERSE	METAL	EDGE	RARITY	H&G

VAN WERT 900

| 900A-1a | A.JACOBS/MERCHANT TAILOR/&/READY MADE/CLOTHING,/VAN WERT,/OHIO. | 1342 | C | PL | R7 | 8945 |

WAPPAKONETA 905

905A-1

905A-3

905A-1a	DAVIS & WHITEMAN/GROCERS/AND/COMMISSION/MERCHANTS/WAPPAKONETA/OHIO.	1083	C	PL	R5	8948
905A-2a	Same	1226	C	PL	R8	8949
905A-3a	DAVIS & WHITEMAN/GROCERS/&/COMMISSION/MERCHANTS./WAPPAKONETA,O.	1335	C	PL	R7	8950
905A-4a	Same	1336	C	PL	R4	8951

| 905B-1a | A.C.MILES,GROCERIES/&/STATIONERY./WAPPAKONETA, O. | 1325 | C | PL | R4 | 8953 |

460

OHIO-Continued

NUMBER　　OBVERSE　　REVERSE　　METAL　EDGE　RARITY　H&G

WAPPAKONETA 905-Continued

Number	Obverse	Reverse	Metal	Edge	Rarity	H&G
905C-1a	MOMENTO/OF/THE/SANITARY/FAIR/OF/WAPAKONETA,O. (NOTE: There is only one P in WAPPAKONETA on this piece.)	Trophy of flags & arms with eagle perched on drum.	C	PL	R8	8955
905C-1b	Same	Same	BR	PL	R7	
905D-1a	J.M.TIMMER MEISTER/DRY GOODS/&/GROCERIES/WAPPAKONETA, O.	1181	C	PL	R3	8957

WARREN 910

Number	Obverse	Reverse	Metal	Edge	Rarity	H&G
910A-1a	ROBBINS'/CARD within a wreath	PHOTOGRAPHIC/ALBUMS/15/MARKET ST. WARREN OHIO	C	PL	R3	8959
910A-1b	Same	Same	BR	PL	R5	8960

OHIO-Continued

NUMBER	OBVERSE	REVERSE	METAL	EDGE	RARITY	H&G

WELLSVILLE 915

915A-1a	HOOVER & CAMP/PIANOS/ MELODIANS/AND/MUSICAL/ MDS./WELLSVILLE, O.	1178	C	PL	R9	8962
	(NOTE: N of MELODIANS reengraved over another N to the right.)					
915A-2a	Same	1322	C	PL	R4	8963

| 915B-1a | WM. LAWRENCE/CLOTHIER/ AND/PHOTOGRAPHIC/ARTIST, /WELLSVILLE, O. | 1178 | C | PL | R3 | 8965 |

WEST JEFFERSON 920

920A-1a	WEST JEFFERSON WMS CO. OHIO/JOHN TRESSLER/ GROCERY/STORE/1863	1336	C	PL	R3	8967
	(NOTE: The O of GROCERY is double cut.)					
920A-1b	Same	Same	BR	PL	R6	8968
920A-2a	Same	1346	C	PL	R8	8969
920A-2b	Same	Same	BR	PL	R9	8970

OHIO-Continued

NUMBER	OBVERSE	REVERSE	METAL	EDGE	RARITY	H&G

WEST NEWTON 925

925A-1a	C.M.COFFIN/DEALER/IN/DRY /GOODS/&C./WEST NEWTON, OHIO	1037	C	R	R6	
925A-1b	Same	Same	BR	R	R7	
925A-1i	Same	Same	Z	R	R9	
925A-2a	Same	1046	C	R	R7	8973
925A-2d	Same (Elder 9/39 Lot 380)	Same	C-N	R	R10	
925A-3a	Same	1047	C	R	R9	
925A-3d	Same (H-R 1978)	Same	C-N	R	R10	

WEST UNITY 930

930A-1a	DAVIES & MAXWELL/DEALERS /IN/HARDWARE/AND/ AGRICULTURAL/MACHINERY/ WEST UNITY/OHIO.	1126	C	PL	R4	8980
930A-2a	Same	1178	C	PL	R9	
930B-1a	W. H. McGREW/DRUGGIST, (mortar & pestle) / WEST UNITY/ OHIO.	1089	C	PL	R8	8982
930B-2a	Same	1127	C	PL	R4	8983
930B-3a	Same	1128	C	PL	R9	8984
930B-3b	Same	Same	BR	PL	R8	
930C-1a	S PIERCE & SON/DEALERS/IN/ DRY GOODS/GROCERIES/&C./ WEST UNITY, O.	1083	C	PL	R6	8986
930C-2a	Same	1224	C	PL	R5	8987
930C-2b	Same	Same	BR	PL	R8	8988
930C-2d	Same (H-R 1980)	Same	C-N	PL	R9	

OHIO-Continued

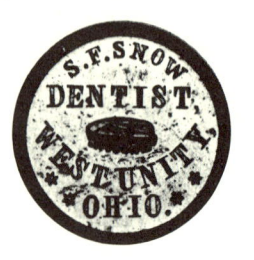

NUMBER	OBVERSE	REVERSE	METAL	EDGE	RARITY	H&G

WEST UNITY 930-Continued

930D-1a	S. F. SNOW/DENTIST, (False teeth)/WEST UNITY,/OHIO.	1127	C	PL	R7	8990
930D-2a	Same	1128	C	PL	R7	
930D-2b	Same	Same	BR	PL	R9	
930D-3a	Same	1130	C	PL	R6	8991

WILMINGTON 935

935A  935B  935C

935A-1a	MRS. OWEN & TAYLOR/MILLERNY/AND/FANCY STORE/SOUTH ST/NEAR DEPOT/WILMINGTON, O.	1127	C	PL	R9	8995
935A-2a	Same	1178	C	PL	R9	8996
935A-3a	Same	1180	C	PL	R8	
935A-4a	Same	1242	C	PL	R9	8993
935A-5a	Same	1278	C	PL	R9	8994
935B-1a	H. PERRIN/HARDWARE,/GROCERIES/&C/WILMINGTON, O.	1178	C	PL	R3	8998
935B-1d	Same	Same	C-N	PL	R9	8999
935C-1a	CHEAP/CASH/STORE/WM PRESTON/WILMINGTON/OHIO	1347	C	PL	R4	9001

OHIO-Continued

NUMBER　　OBVERSE　　REVERSE　　METAL　EDGE　RARITY　H&G

WILMINGTON 935 -Continued

935D-1a	T. R. WRAITH/HARDWARE/ MERCHANT/WILMINGTON. O.	SUGAR/MILLS/AND/ EVAPORATORS.	C	PL	R5	9003
935D-1d	Same	Same	C-N	PL	R9	9004
935D-2a	Same	1178	C	PL	R8	9005

WOODSFIELD 960

960A-1a	J. W. WALTON/GROCER/ WOODSFIELD/OHIO.	J. W. WALTON,/PENSION/ AGENT.	C	PL	R3	9008
960A-1b	Same	Same	BR	PL	R7	9009
960A-2a	Same	1223	C	PL	R3	9010
960A-2b	Same	Same	BR	PL	R7	9011
960A-3a	Same	BLANK	C	PL	R9	

| 960A-4a | Same | WM. SENOUR in script (Obv Ohio 165FM) | C | PL | R9 | |

465

OHIO-Continued

NUMBER	OBVERSE	REVERSE	METAL	EDGE	RARITY	H&G

WOOSTER 975

975A-1a	P. E. BEACH above—silk hat in center WOOSTER. OHIO below. (occurs on both thick and thin planchets.)	DEALER IN/HATS,/CAPS/&/FANCY GOODS	C	PL	R4	9013
975A-1b	Same (occurs on both thick and thin planchets.)	Same	BR	PL	R5	9014
975A-1c	Same	Same	N	PL	R6	9015
975A-1d	Same	Same	C-N	PL	R7	9016
975A-1do	Same, over C-N cent.	Same	C-N	PL	R9	
975A-1e	Same	Same	W-M	PL	R8	9017
975A-1f	Same	Same	S	PL	R9	9018

975B-1a	J. R. BOWMAN/DEALER/IN/WATCHES/CLOCKS/&/JEWELRY/WEST LIBERTY ST./WOOSTER, O.	1026	C	PL	R7	
975B-2a	Same	1031	C	PL	R8	9025
975B-3a	Same	1036	C	PL	R6	9024
975B-4a	Same	1042	C	R	R6	9020
975B-4b	Same	Same	BR	R	R9	9021
975B-4i	Same	Same	Z	R	R9	9022
975B-5d	Same	1046	C-N	R	R10	9023
975B-6a	Same (H-R 1986)	1047	C	R	R7	
975B-7d	Same (H-R 1985)	1069	C-N	R	R10	
975B-6d	Same (A.N.S.)	Same	C-N	R	R10	
975C-1a	G. BRUMTER/DEALER/IN/GROCERIES/W. LIBERTY ST./WOOSTER,/OHIO.	1084	C	PL	R6	9026
975C-2a	Same	1089	C	PL	R7	9027
975C-3a	Same	1178	C	PL	R5	9028
975C-4a	Same	1181	C	PL	R5	9029
975C-4b	Same	Same	BR	PL	R9	

OHIO-Continued

NUMBER	OBVERSE	REVERSE	METAL	EDGE	RARITY	H&G

WOOSTER 975-Continued

975D-1a	JAMES B. CHILDS/CLOTHING/ HATS, CAPS/&/TRUNKS/ WOOSTER/OHIO	1406	C	PL	R3	9030
975D-1b	Same	Same	BR	PL	R5	
975D-2a	Same	1407	C	PL	R3	9031

| 975E-1a | J. S. DUDEN/DEALER/IN/ GROCERIES/AND/PROVISIONS /WOOSTER/OHIO. | 1126 | C | PL | R3 | 9033 |

975F-1a	SAMUEL GEITGEY/DEALER/ IN/STOVES AND/TINWARE/OF/ ALL KINDS/WOOSTER, O.	1169	C	PL	R7	9035
975F-2a	Same	Same, incused	C	PL	R8	9036
975F-3a	Same	1303	C	PL	R4	9037
975F-4a	Same	1304	C	PL	R4	
975F-5d	Same	1309	C-N	PL	R10	
975F-6a	Same	BLANK	C	PL	R10	

467

OHIO-Continued

NUMBER	OBVERSE	REVERSE	METAL	EDGE	RARITY	H&G

WOOSTER 975-Continued

975G-1a	JOHN LEIS above—figure 5 in center—WOOSTER, O.	1343	C	PL	R9	9039
975G-1b	Same	Same	BR	PL	R7	9040
975G-1f	Same	Same	S	PL	R10	
975G-1fp	Same	Same	S-P	PL	R9	

975H S.C. Martin. Listed under Non-Contemporary NC-3b.

975I-1a	MILLER & CO. QUEENSWARE/ AND GLASSWARE/NEAR/ POST OFFICE/WOOSTER, O.	DEALER IN/HOOP/SKIRTS/ HATS CAPS/AND/NOTIONS	C	PL	R3	9042
975I-2a	Same	1124	C	PL	R3	9043
975I-3a	Same	1127	C	PL	R8	9044
975I-4a	Same	1177	C	PL	R6	9045
975I-5a	Same	1178	C	PL	R7	9046
975I-6a	Same	1180	C	PL	R4	
975I-7a	Same	1331	C	PL	R5	9047

468

OHIO-Continued

NUMBER	OBVERSE	REVERSE	METAL	EDGE	RARITY	H&G

WOOSTER 975-Continued

| 975J-1a | NOLD & CO./DEALERS/IN/ PORK/AND/BEEF/WOOSTER/ OHIO. | 1084 | C | PL | R5 | 9049 |
| 975J-2a | Same | 1179 | C | PL | R5 | 9050 |

| 975K-1a | JAMES PATRICK/BUTTER/ PACKER/WOOSTER, OHIO | 1123 | C | PL | R2 | 9052 |
| 975L-1a | C. ROTH/MANUF'R./AND DEALER/IN BOOTS/AND SHOES,/WOOSTER,/OHIO. | 1317 | C | PL | R3 | 9054 |

975M-1a	ROWE & BRO./WATCHES,/ CLOCKS AND/JEWELRY/ S. E. COR. PUB./SQUARE/ WOOSTER, O.	1126	C	PL	R8	9056
975M-2a	Same	1320	C	PL	R2	9057
975M-3a	Same	1343	C	PL	R7	

469

OHIO-Continued

NUMBER	OBVERSE	REVERSE	METAL	EDGE	RARITY	H&G

XENIA 985

985A-1a   F. J. HALLS,/WHOLESALE/&/   1085   C   PL   R7   9059
          RETAIL/GROCERY &/
          CONFECTIONARY/STORE,/
          XENIA, O.

YOUNGSTOWN 990

990A-1a   W. & A. J. PACKARD above—U.S.   WARREN PACKARD/   C   PL   R2   9061
          shield in center—YOUNGSTOWN,   HARDWARE/AND/IRON/
          OHIO. below.   WARREN, OHIO
990A-1b   Same   Same   BR   PL   R3   9062
990A-1c   Same   Same   N   PL   R9
990A-2a   Same   Obv incused   C   PL   R9

470

OHIO-Continued

NUMBER	OBVERSE	REVERSE	METAL	EDGE	RARITY	H&G

ZANESVILLE 995

995A-1a	BARRELL'S/WORM/ CONFECTIONS/H.G.O. CARY/ ZANESVILLE/OHIO	CARY'S/CCC/COUGH/CURE— four stars at each side	C	PL	R2	9063
995A-1b	Same	Same	BR	PL	R8	9064

995B-1  995B-2

995B-1a	ADDRESS/H. G. O. CARY/ DURGGIST/AND/CHEMIST/ ZANESVILLE, O.	Same	C	PL	R9	9065
995B-1d	Same	Same	C-N	PL	R9	9066
995B-2a	Same (comes on both thick and thin planchets.)	Similar, but four stars ommited. & period after cure.	C	PL	R2	9067
995B-2d	Same	Same	C-N	PL	R9	9068
995B-3a	Reverse of Ohio 995A-1a	1349	C	PL	R7	
995B-4a	Same	1350	C	PL	R6	

995C-1a	JOSEPH CROSBY/GROCER/ AND/TEA DEALER/83/MAIN ST./ZANESVILLE. O.	1125	C	PL	R4	9071
995C-2a	Same	1126	C	PL	R4	9072
995C-3a	Same	1166	C	PL	R4	9074
995C-4a	Same	1168	C	PL	R6	

OHIO-Continued

NUMBER	OBVERSE	REVERSE	METAL	EDGE	RARITY	H&G

ZANESVILLE 995-Continued

| 995C-5a | Same | 1178 | C | PL | R4 | 9073 |
| 995C-6a | Same | W. K. LANPHEAR above—CINCINNATI, O. below MANU'FR /OF/METALIC/CARDS in corn wreath. (Obv. Ohio 165CY-1) | C | PL | R9 | 9075 |

| 995D-1a | EVERICH & BARTON/GROCERS /AND/LIQUOR/DEALERS/ ZANESVILLE/OHIO | 1273 | C | PL | R4 | 9077 |

995E-1a	ALEX R GRANT & CO./DRY GOODS/ZANESVILLE OHIO.	1125	C	PL	R3	9079
995E-1d	Same	Same	C-N	PL	R9	9080
995E-2a	Same	W. K. LANPHEAR above CINCINNATI, O below MANU'FR /OF/METALIC/CARDS in wreath (Obv. Ohio 165CY-1)	C	PL	R9	9081

472

OHIO-Continued

NUMBER	OBVERSE	REVERSE	METAL	EDGE	RARITY	H&G

ZANESVILLE 995-Continued

995F-1a	G. W. GRIFFEE, NEWS/DEALER /STATIONER/&C./ ZANESVILLE, O.	1091	C	PL	R4	9083
995F-2a	Same	1322	C	PL	R3	9084
995F-3a	Same	1324	C	PL	R3	9086
995F-3d	Same	Same	C-N	PL	R8	9087

995G-1a	W. B. HARRIS & BRO./DRY GOODS/GROCERIES/ HARDWARE/&C./ZANESVILLE, O.	1082	C	PL	R5	
995G-2a	Same	1083	C	PL	R4	9088
995G-3a	Same	1122	C	PL	R5	9089
995G-4a	Same	1126	C	PL	R6	
995G-5a	Same	1127	C	PL	R5	9090
995G-5b	Same	Same	BR	PL	R9	
995G-6a	Same	1128	C	PL	R4	9091
995G-7a	Same	1168	C	PL	R5	
995G-8a	Same	1178	C	PL	R4	9092
995G-9a	Same	1180	C	PL	R5	9004
995G-10a	Same	W. K. LANPHEAR above CINCINNATI, O below MANU'FR /OF/METALIC/CARDS in wreath (Obv. Ohio 165CY-1)	C	PL	R8	9093

473

OHIO-Continued

NUMBER	OBVERSE	REVERSE	METAL	EDGE	RARITY	H&G

ZANESVILLE 995-Continued

995H-1a	HERENDEEN & WITTER/ SINGERS/SEWING/MACHINES/ ZANESVILLE/OHIO.	1342	C	PL	R3	9097
995I-1a	JOHN IRWIN/WHOLESALE/ DEALER IN/WINES & LIQUORS/ COR. MAIN & SIXTH/ ZANESVILLE/OHIO	1082	C	PL	R6	9099
995I-2a	Same	1089	C	PL	R8	9100
995I-3a	Same	1130	C	PL	R8	9101
995J-1a	C. W. POTWIN & CO. above, padlock in center, ZANESVILLE, O.	AGRICULTURAL IMPLEMENTS/ SADLERY/AND/CARRIAGE/ TRIMINGS (NOTE: only one M in TRIMMINGS)	C	PL	R3	9103
995J-1d	Same	Same	C-N	PL	R9	9104

474

OHIO-Continued

NUMBER	OBVERSE	REVERSE	METAL	EDGE	RARITY	H&G

ZANESVILLE 995-Continued

995J-2a	Same	W. K. LANPHEAR above CINCINNATI O below MANU'FR/ OF/METALIC/CARDS in wreath (Obv. Ohio 165CY-1)	C	PL	R7	9105
995J-2b	Same (H-R 2004)	Same	BR	PL	R7	9106
995J-3a	Same	W. K. LANPHEAR/MANUF'R/ OF/METALIC/CARDS/CIN'TI/ OHIO (Obv. Ohio 165CY-48)	C	PL	R7	9107 7500
995J-3b	Same	Same	BR	PL	R7	9108

| 995K-1a | WEBSTER, DUMM & CO,/ TOBACCONISTS/ZANESVILLE, O. | 1178 | C | PL | R4 | 9110 |
| 995K-2a | Same | 1181 | C | PL | R5 | 9111 |

PENNSYLVANIA

NUMBER	OBVERSE	REVERSE	METAL	EDGE	RARITY	H&G

ALLEGHENY CITY 13

13A

13B

13A-1a	WM.CARSON/LEATHER/ MERCHANT/46/OHIO/ST./ ALLEGHENY CITY	1023	C	PL	R6	9204
13A-2a	Same	1042	C	R	R8	9200
13A-2b	Same	Same	BR	R	R8	9201
13A-2i	Same	Same	Z	R	R9	
13A-3a	Same	1047	C	R	R9	
13A-3d	Same	Same	C-N	R	R10	9203
13B-1a	CITY/TEA/HOUSE/NO. 20/ DIAMOND/ALLEGHENY, PA.	1042	C	R	R8	9218
13B-1b	Same	Same	BR	R	R8	9219
13B-1i	Same	Same	Z	R	R9	
13B-2a	Same (H-R 2011)	1047	C	R	R9	9220
13B-2d	Same	Same	C-N	R	R9	
13B-3d	Same (H-R 2012)	1069	C-N	R	R10	

13C-1

13C-2

13C-1a	GREGG & DALZZEL/ NATIONAL/PLANING/MILL/ ALLEGHENY CITY (NOTE: DALZELL is misspelled on this piece)	1028	C	PL	R5	9207
13C-2a	GREGG & DALZELL/ NATIONAL/PLANING/MILL/ ALLEGHENY CITY (NOTE: This is a corrected die of PA. 13C-1a and the 5th and 6th letters of DALZZEL are overcut to correct the spelling to DALZELL.)	FLOORING/MOULDINGS/ SASH/BLINDS/DOORS/& C.	C	PL	R5	9206
13C-2d	Same	Same	C-N	R	R10	
13C-3a	Same (H-R 2008)	1042	C	R	R9	9208
13C-3b	Same	Same	BR	R	R9	9209
13C-4d	Same	1047	C-N	R	R10	9211
13C-5d	Same (H-R 2009)	1069	C-N	R	R10	

476

PENNSYLVANIA-Continued

NUMBER	OBVERSE	REVERSE	METAL	EDGE	RARITY	H&G

ALLEGHENY CITY 13-Continued

13D

13D-3

13D-1a	HAHN & RIDDLE/GROCERS/ DIAMOND/ALLEGHENY, PA.	1042	C	R	R8	9214
13D-1b	Same (H-R 2010)	Same	BR	R	R8	9215
13D-1i	Same	Same	Z	R	R9	
13D-2a	Same	1047	C	R	R9	9217
13D-2d	Same	Same	C-N	R	R10	
13D-3a	Same	CITY/TEA/HOUSE/NO.20/ DIAMOND/ALLEGHENY,PA. (Obv. PA 13B 1a)	C	PL	R8	9213

13E-1

13E-6

13E-1a	R.&W.JENKINSON,/TOBACCO/ DEALERS/ALLEGHANY PA. (NOTE: spelling error in ALLEGHENY.)	1124	C	PL	R9	9221
13E-2a	Same (H-R 2013)	1176	C	PL	R8	9222
13E-2d	Same	Same	C-N	PL	R9	
13E-3a	Same	1295	C	PL	R8	9223
13E-4a	Same	1331	C	PL	R3	9224
13E-4e	Same, thick 3½mm.	Same	W-M	PL	R9	9225
13E-5a	Same	1352	C	PL	R7	9226
13E-5d	Same (H-R 2015)	Same	C-N	PL	R9	
13E-6a	R & W.JENKINSON/ TOBACONISTS/No. 6/ FEDERAL/St./ALLEGHENY, CITY (NOTE: error in spelling TOBACCONISTS.)	1026	C	PL	R4	9231
13E-7a	Same	1035	C	PL	R4	9232
13E-8a	Same	1042	C	R	R7	9227
13E-8b	Same	Same	BR	R	R8	9228
13E-8i	Same	Same	Z	R	R9	9229
13E-9a	Same	1047	C	R	R9	9230
13E-9d	Same (H-R 2017)	Same	C-N	R	R9	
13E-4d	Same	Same (1331)	C-N	PL	R10	

477

PENNSYLVANIA-Continued

NUMBER	OBVERSE	REVERSE	METAL	EDGE	RARITY	H&G

ALLEGHENY CITY 13-Continued

13F-1a	JOHN SHERER/TOBACCO/ DEALER/75/FEDERAL ST./ ALLEGHANY CITY. (NOTE: spelling error in ALLEGHENY)	1124	C	PL	R8	9234
13F-1b	Same	Same	BR	PL	R9	9235
13F-1d	Same	Same	C-N	PL	R9	9236
13F-2a	Same	1176	C	PL	R9	9237
13F-3a	Same	1177	C	PL	R9	9238
13F-3d	Same	Same	C-N	PL	R9	9239
13F-4a	Same	1180	C	PL	R4	9240
13F-5a	Same	1295	C	PL	R9	9241
13F-6a	Same	1331	C	PL	R5	9242
13F-6d	Same	Same	C-N	PL	R9	
13F-7a	Same	REYMER & BROS./CONFECTIONER/PITTSBURG/PA/ (Obv PA 765T-1a)	C	PL	R10	9243
13F-8a	Same	Blank	C	PL	R10	

BAKERSTOWN 60

| 60A-1a | JAMES MAINES/GALLERY/ MAIN ST./BAKERSTOWN.PA. | 1125 | C | PL | R5 | 9245 |
| 60A-2a | Same | 1178 | C | PL | R9 | 9246 |

PENNSYLVANIA-Continued

NUMBER	OBVERSE	REVERSE	METAL	EDGE	RARITY	H&G

ERIE 360

| 360A-1do | FOR/BARGAINS/IN/DRY GOODS/GO TO/W.BELL'S/S EXCHANGE/ERIE PA (NOTE: the reverse of a regular cent was turned down on a lathe and the legend counterstamped.) | Reverse of this card is the obverse of U.S. cent of 1859 | C-N | PL | R6 | 9248 |

HONESDALE 464

464A-1do	Same (over C-N cent)	Same (1006)	C-N	PL	R9	
464A-1a	PETERSEN'S/HONESDALE./SCRANTON./&PITTSTON./PA/JEWELLERS. (NOTE: Error in spelling JEWELERS.)	1006	C	PL	R4	9250
464A-1b	Same	Same	BR	PL	R6	9252
464A-1c	Same	Same	N	PL	R8	9253
464A-1d	Same	Same	C-N	PL	R8	9254
464A-1e	Same	Same	W-M	PL	R8	
464A-2a	Same (Baker 566)	1137	C	PL	R8	9256
464A-2b	Same	Same	BR	PL	R8	9257
464A-2b1	Same (double struck over itself)	Same	BR	PL	R9	
464A-2c	Same	Same	N	PL	R7	9258
464A-2d	Same	Same	C-N	PL	R8	9259
464A-2do	Same (over C-N cent)	Same	C-N	PL	R9	
464A-2e	Same	Same	W-M	PL	R9	9260
464A-2f	Same	Same	S	PL	R9	9261
464A-3a	Same	1152	C	PL	R9	9262
464A-3b	Same	Same	BR	PL	R8	9263
464A-3c	Same	Same	N	PL	R8	9264
464A-3d	Same	Same	C-N	PL	R8	9265
464A-3e	Same	Same	W-M	PL	R8	9266
464A-4b	Same	1214	BR	PL	R9	9281

PENNSYLVANIA-Continued

NUMBER	OBVERSE	REVERSE	METAL	EDGE	RARITY	H&G

HONESDALE 464-Continued

464A-4c	Same	Same	N	PL	R8	9282
464A-4d	Same	Same	C-N	PL	R8	9283
464A-4e	Same	Same	W-M	PL	R8	9284
464A-5b	Same	1243	BR	PL	R8	9269
464A-5d	Same	Same	C-N	PL	R8	9271
464A-5e	Same	Same	W-M	PL	R7	9272
464A-6b	Same	1268	BR	PL	R8	9275
464A-6c	Same	Same	N	PL	R8	9276
464A-6d	Same	Same	C-N	PL	R8	9277
464A-6e	Same	Same	W-M	PL	R8	9278

JOHNSTOWN-See Non-Contemporary listings

LANCASTER 525

525A-1a	S.H.ZAHM/DEALER/IN/ COINS, TOKENS/MEDALS & C/ LANCASTER,PA.	1148	C	PL	R5	9286
525A-1b	Same	Same	BR	PL	R5	9287
525A-1e	Same	Same	W-M	PL	R5	9288
525A-1f	Same	Same	S	PL	R9	9289
	(NOTE: All W-M pieces seen of this issue have a light silvering, and no authentic silver specimen has been observed — all were the plated W-M pieces.)					
525A-2a	Same	Blank	C	PL	R9	

480

PENNSYLVANIA-Continued

NUMBER	OBVERSE	REVERSE	METAL	EDGE	RARITY	H&G

LAWRENCEVILLE 535

535A-1a	WM SMITH/GROCER/ LAWRENCEVILLE/PA.	1177	C	PL	R9	9290
535A-2a	Same	1180	C	PL	R4	9291
535A-3a	Same	1227	C	PL	R10	
535A-4a	Same	1295	C	PL	R8	9292
535A-5a	Same	1331	C	PL	R9	9293
535A-2d	Same	Same (1180)	C-N	PL	R10	

MEADVILLE 615

| 615A-1a | GO TO G.C.PORTER & CO., above — Indian head in center. FOR YOUR DRY GOODS. below. | G.C.PORTER & CO./CLOTHING &/GENTS FURNISHING/ GOODS,/MEADVILLE,PA. | C | PL | R2 | 9295 |
| 615A-1b | Same | Same | BR | PL | R9 | |

MOUNT WASHINGTON 650

| 650A-1a | J. MCKAIN/GROCER/MOUNT/ WASHINGTON. (NOTE: Formerly listed under Pittsburgh.) | 1389 | C | PL | R2 | 9424 |

481

PENNSYLVANIA-Continued

NUMBER	OBVERSE	REVERSE	METAL	EDGE	RARITY	H&G

PHILADELPHIA 750

| 750A-1a | Small helmented head with ADAMS below in laurel wreath. | TON HALL/457/NORTH 3D. ST./PHILA. | C | PL | R3 | 9297 |
| 750A-1b | Same | Same | BR | PL | R2 | 9298 |

(NOTE: The piece listed as H&G 9299 in bronze cannot be differentiated from the brass specimens.)

750B-1a	M.B.ALLEBACH/WATCH/ MAKER/&JEWELER/126/ N.2.ND..ST./PHILADELPHIA.	1093	C	PL	R9	9301
750B-1b	Same	Same	BR	PL	R9	9302
750B-1c	Same	Same	N	PL	R9	9303
750B-1d	Same	Same	C-N	PL	R6	9304
750B-1e	Same	Same	W-M	PL	R9	9305
750B-1f	Same	Same	S	PL	R9	9306
750B-2e	Same	1154	W-M	PL	R9	
750B-2f	Same	Same	S	PL	R9	

(NOTE: Obviously this piece is post-Civil War, but it is included because it was probably struck at the same time as the other pieces.)

750B-3a	Same	1182	C	PL	R9	
750B-3b	Same (H-R 2028)	Same	BR	PL	R9	
750B-3c	Same	Same	N	PL	R9	9310
750B-3d	Same	Same	C-N	PL	R7	
750B-3e	Same	Same	W-M	PL	R8	9311
750B-3f	Same	Same	S	PL	R9	

PENNSYLVANIA-Continued

NUMBER　　OBVERSE　　　　　　REVERSE　　　　　　　　METAL　EDGE　RARITY　H&G

PHILADELPHIA 750-Continued

750C-1

750C-2

750C-1a	AMON above — sheaf of wheat in center — 1863 below	BAKERY/1011 BEACH ST./PHILA.	C	PL	R3	9314
750C-2a	Same, but denticles show on border	BAKERY/1011 BEACH ST./PHILA.	C	PL	R3	

750D-1 　　　　　　　　　　750D-2

750D-1a	BALTZ & STILZ,/IMPORTERS OF above — WINES/PHILADA.PA. below. Bunch of grapes in center.	1381	C	PL	R3	9316
750D-2a	BALTZ & STILZ,/IMPORTERS OF/333/WINES./NORTH 3. ST./PHILA.	1381	C	PL	R4	9317

PENNSYLVANIA-Continued

NUMBER	OBVERSE	REVERSE	METAL	EDGE	RARITY	H&G

PHILADELPHIA 750-Continued

750E-2 thru 4

750E-1a	M.F.BEIRN/MAGNOLIA/ HOTEL/100 SO. 8TH ST/ AND/416/LIBRARY ST/ PHILADELPHIA.	1093	C	PL	R2	9325
750E-1b	Same	Same	BR	PL	R7	
750E-1d	Same	Same	C-N	PL	R6	
750E-2a	Similar, but different spacing of letters and multiple die cracks	1150	C	PL	R9	9327
750E-2b	Same, obv. die cracks	Same	BR	PL	R9	9328
750E-2d	Same, obv. die cracks	Same, rev. die cracks	C-N	PL	R9	9329
750E-2e	Same, obv. die cracks	Same, rev. die cracks	W-M	PL	R9	9330
750E-2f	Same	Same	S	PL	R9	
750E-3e	Same	1150A	W-M	PL	R9	9332
750E-4a	Same	1182	C	PL	R8	9319
750E-4b	Same	Same	BR	PL	R9	9320
750E-4c	Same	Same	N	PL	R9	9321
750E-4d	Same	Same	C-N	PL	R9	9322
750E-4e	Same (Die cracks - thick flan)	Same	W-M	PL	R9	9323
750E-1a1	Same (Thick planchet, over 2 mm)	Same (1093)	C	PL	R5	
750E-1f	Same	Same	S	PL	R10	
750E-1k	Same	Same	GT	PL	R9	
750E-4a1	Same (Thick planchet, over 2 mm)	Same	C	PL	R9	
750E-4f	Same	Same	S	PL	R10	

| 750F-1a | M.C.CAMPBELL'S DANCING ACADEMY around. COR.8. AND/SP/GARDEN/ST./ PHILA. in center (NOTE: comes with heavy reverse die cracks.) | SKATING/ACADEMY/ WASHINGTON/HALL. | C | PL | R4 | 9334 |
| 750F-1d | Same | Same | C-N | PL | R9 | |

PENNSYLVANIA-Continued

NUMBER	OBVERSE	REVERSE	METAL	EDGE	RARITY	H&G

PHILADELPHIA 750-Continued

750H-1a	CHESTNUT & WALNUT PASSENGER R R CO. around ONE/FARE in center. (Atwood Pa 750I)	1148	C	PL	R9	
750H-1b	Same (Atwood PA 750H)	Same	BR	PL	R9	
750H-1d	Same (Atwood PA 750J)	Same	C-N	PL	R9	
750I-1a	COOMBS/1863 within a wreath.	SECOND ST. EXCHANGE/ 432/N. SECOND/ST./PHILA.	C	PL	R3	9336

485

PENNSYLVANIA-Continued

NUMBER	OBVERSE	REVERSE	METAL	EDGE	RARITY	H&G

PHILADELPHIA 750-Continued

*750J-1a	R.FLANAGAN'S/PUNCH above — goblet in center, 112 156 NORTH 6TH. ST. below (NOTE: This piece is listed in the 1858 Numis. Soc. of Phila. list, and thus must be pre-Civil War. It is left in merely for historical reasons.)	PURE COPPER/PREFERABLE/ TO/PAPER./PHILADA.	C	R	R8	9342
*750J-1a1	Same	Same	C	PL	R2	9341
750J-1a2	Same (Thick planchet, 2½ mm)	Same	C	PL	R8	
750J-2f	Same, C/S on Spanish 2 reals (Adams Pa 165)	Blank	S	PL	R9	

750JA-1a	FOX'S/CASINO	CHESNUT ST./620/PHILA.	C	PL	R5	

750K-1a	J.HENRY GERCKE/ WATCHMAKER/AND/ JEWELER/1206 PINE ST. PHILA. (Baker 536.)	1133	C	PL	R6	
750K-1b	Same (Miller PA 176D)	Same	BR	PL	R6	
750K-1e	Same (NOTE: The same obverse comes with a masonic temple reverse, but the temple was not built until 1873.)	Same	W-M	PL	R6	

486

PENNSYLVANIA-Continued

NUMBER	OBVERSE	REVERSE	METAL	EDGE	RARITY	H&G

PHILADELPHIA 750-Continued

Shown is a coining press used at the Great Central Fair to strike the 750L.

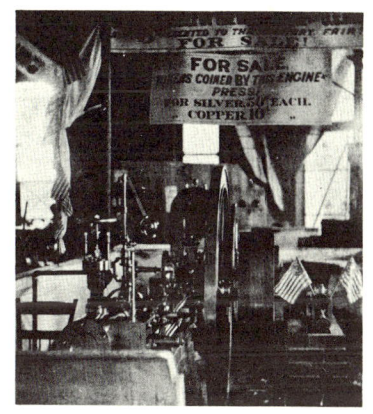

750L-1a	GREAT/CENTRAL/FAIR/ PHILADELPHIA/JUNE 1864 (Baker 363)	1135	C	R	R1	9343
750L-1f	Same	Same	S	R	R5	
750L-1k	Same	Same	Gilt	R	R8	

(NOTE: There are at least 28 different die combinations and metal varieties of these tokens, most of which cannot be distinguished by the naked eye. See detailed list by M. and G. Fuld, **The Numismatist**, Sept., 1959 page 007.)

750M-1a	NORTH MILITARY HALL above — lyre in center — F.&L.LADNER/ 532 N.3.ST. below.	1377	C	PL	R2	9344
750M-2a	Same	1380	C	PL	R5	
750M-3a	Same	1379	C	PL	R2	9345
750M-4e	Similar, but larger	1378	W-M	PL	R10	

(NOTE: This piece might well be a rejected die trial.)

487

PENNSYLVANIA-Continued

NUMBER	OBVERSE	REVERSE	METAL	EDGE	RARITY	H&G

PHILADELPHIA 750-Continued

750N-1a	A.LAMBERT/COR.4TH/AND/ LIBRARY ST./PHILADA.	1092	C	PL	R4	9347
750N-1b	Same	Same	BR	PL	R8	9348
750N-1e	Same	Same	W-M	PL	R9	

750 O-1b	H.MULLIGAN above — watch and chain in center — 444 N. 2ND ST. PHILA.	IMPORTER/OF/WATCHES/ MANUFACTURER OF/ JEWELRY/AGENT/FOR/ EASTERN JEWELRY	BR	PL	R5	9350
750 O-1c	Same	Same	N	PL	R9	9351
750 O-1d	Same	Same	C-N	PL	R8	9352
750 O-1f	Same	Same	S	PL	R9	

750 O-2b	Same inscription as preceding, portrait in center instead of watch.	Same	BR	PL	R6	9353
750 O-2c	Same	Same	N	PL	R9	9354
750 O-2e	Same	Same	W-M	PL	R9	
750 O-2f	Same	Same	S	PL	R9	
750 O-2k	Same	Same	Gilt	PL	R8	
750 O-1k	Same	Same	GT	PL	R8	

PENNSYLVANIA-Continued

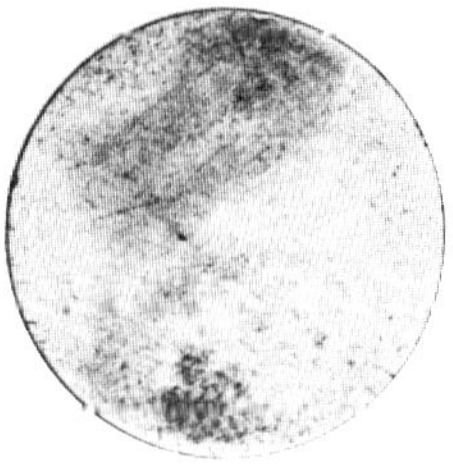

NUMBER	OBVERSE	REVERSE	METAL	EDGE	RARITY	H&G

PHILADELPHIA 750-Continued

750P-1a	F.P.ROGERS.937 STH 10TH ST. PHILADA.. PA.. Milk can dividing date 1863 in center.	MANUFACTURER/OF MILK CANS/DAIRY/FIXTURES /ROOFING & GUTTER TIN	C	PL	R6	9356
750P-1c	Same	Same	N	PL	R9	9357
750P-2a	Same	Obverse incused	C	PL	R8	9361

750P-3a	Similar, but comma instead of period after ROGERS,	Same as Pa 750P-1a	C	PL	R7	9358
750P-3c	Same	Same	N	PL	R5	9359
750P-3d	Same	Same	C-N	PL	R9	
750P-4c	Same	Obverse incused	N	PL	R7	9360

750P-5c	Same as Rev 750P-4a (incused obv) (NOTE: This is a most unusual piece — see photo)	Blank	N	PL	R10	

489

PENNSYLVANIA-Continued

| NUMBER | OBVERSE | REVERSE | METAL | EDGE | RARITY | H&G |

PHILADELPHIA 750-Continued

| 750Q-1a | G.J.RUELIUS/319/NORTH 4. ST./PHILA. | Building with staff and flag in center PHILADA. CITY HOTEL above — 1863 below. | C | PL | R3 | 9363 |
| 750Q-1b | Same | Same | BR | PL | R5 | 9364 |

750R

750S

| 750R-1e | G.A.SCHWARTZ/1006/CHESTNUT/ST./PHILA. (very thick, 4 mm.) | 1250 | W-M | PL | R10 | |
| 750S-1a | STEPPACHER. AGT./ORLEANS/HOUSE/531/CHESNUT ST. PHILA. (NOTE: error in spelling CHESTNUT.) | 1381 | C | PL | R2 | 9366 |

| 750T-1b | GRANVILLE STOKES above — eagle in center 1862/MERCHANT TAILOR/609 CHESNUT ST. PHILADELPHIA below (NOTE: Note spelling error in CHESTNUT. Adams Pa 498 - 31 mm.) | FINE/FASHIONABLE CLOTHING/1862/GRANVILLE STOKES/609/CHESNUT ST./PHILADELPHIA | BR | R | R7 | |

490

PENNSYLVANIA-Continued

NUMBER	OBVERSE	REVERSE	METAL	EDGE	RARITY	H&G

PHILADELPHIA 750-Continued

| 750U-1c | A.B. TAYLOR/1015 CHESTNUT ST. AROUND SODA WATER/ 1861/PHILA. in center | THE BEST PREPARATIONS/FOR THE TEETH/around TAYLOR'S/ ORILOTE/AND/DENTICRETE in center. | N | PL | R7 | |

(NOTE: Other A.B. Taylor pieces listed in Adams are all pre-Civil War — this piece Adams Pa 504A.)

750V-1a	N.&G. TAYLOR CO./1863 above — bust of Washington facing right in center 303/BRANCH ST / PHILADELPHIA (Baker 580)	TIN PLATE,/FILES,/METALS,/ STEEL,/WIRE COPPER & C.	C	PL	R4	9368
750V-1e	Same	Same	W.M	PL	R9	
750V-1f	Same	Same	S	PL	R9	
750V-2a	Similar to preceding, but head of Washington in frame dividing date 18 63	Same	C	PL	R9	

(NOTE: This is probably a rejected die trial.)

491

PENNSYLVANIA-Continued

NUMBER	OBVERSE	REVERSE	METAL	EDGE	RARITY	H&G

PHILADELPHIA 750-Continued

750V-3b	Undraped bust of Washinton left; beneath bust 1862 Legend N&G. TAYLOR CO./303 BRANCH ST./ PHILADELPHIA (Baker 577, Adams Pa. 516 - 37mm)	TIN PLATE/WIRE SHEET IRON/ FILES/METALS/STAMPED/& JAPANNED WARE/COPPER &C.	BR	R	R7	
750V-4b	Similar, but address is in smaller letters. (Baker 578. Adams Pa. 517 - 37mm)	Similar, but differently spaced	BR	R	R7	
750V-5b	Similar inscription, but company name not in gothic letters. (Baker 579, Adams Pa 514 — 37 mm)	TIN PLATE/STAMPED AND/ JAPANNED WARE/METALS/ WIRE SHEET IRON/FILES/ COPPER &C. &C.	BR	R	R8	
750V-5e	Same (Adams pa 515 — 37 mm)	Same	W-M	R	R7	
750V-6b	Same (Adams Pa 513 — 37 mm)	Similar, but different spacing of letters.	BR	R	R7	

492

PENNSYLVANIA-Continued

NUMBER	OBVERSE	REVERSE	METAL	EDGE	RARITY	H&G

PHILADELPHIA 750-Continued

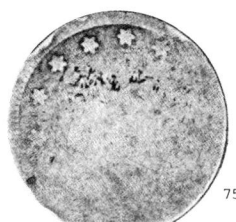

750W-1

750W-2 Rev

750W-1a	UNION/VOLUNTEER/ REFRESHMENT/SALOON/ INSTID./MAY 27, 1861.	SECOND/ANNUAL/FAIR/ HELD/JUNE 15, 1863.	C	PL	R5	
	(NOTE: Comes with heavy obverse die breaks.)					
750W-1b	Same	Same	BR	PL	R9	
750W-1do	Same, over C-N cent	Same	C-N	PL	R10	
750W-2a	Similar, but different spacing of letters	1092	C	PL	R9	

(NOTE: On the only specimen seen of this type, it is quite worn, and all details cannot be ascertained.)

750W-2b	Same	Same	BR	PL	R9	
750W-3a	Same	Rev 750W-1a	C	PL	R3	

(NOTE: Comes with heavy reverse die cuds.)

PITTSBURGH 765

765A-1a	ALLEGHENY VALLEY/ RAILROAD/HOTEL/OPPOSITE/ DEPOT/PITTSBURGH, PA.	1023	C	R	R7	9375
765A-1a1	Same	Same	C	PL	R9	9377
765A-1b	Same	Same	BR	R	R9	9376
765A-2a	Same	1042	C	R	R8	9371
765A-2b	Same	Same	BR	R	R8	9372
765A-3a	Same	1047	C	R	R9	
765A-3d	Same	Same	C-N	R	R9	
765A-4d	Same	1069	C-N	R	R10	
765A-2l	Same	Same (1042)	Z	R	R9	

493

PENNSYLVANIA-Continued

NUMBER	OBVERSE	REVERSE	METAL	EDGE	RARITY	H&G

PITTSBURGH 765-Continued

765B-1a	F.BEILSTEINE/BUTCHER/ 105/DIAMOND/MARKET/ E.SIDE/PITTSBUR.	1124	C	PL	R9	9379
	(NOTE: PITTSBURGH spelled without an H.)					
765B-1e	Same	Same	W-M	PL	R9	
765B-2a	Same	1177	C	PL	R4	9380
765B-2e	Same	Same	W-M	PL	R9	9381
765B-3a	Same	1274	C	PL	R9	9382

765C

765D

765C-1a	BUFFUMS/MINERAL/WATER/ PITTSBURG	Bottle in center within circle of 27 crosses	C	PL	R2	9384
	(NOTE: PITTSBURGH spelled without a H.)					
765D-1a	J.A.ECKERT/BUTCHER/111/ DIAMOND/MARKET/ PITTSBURG.	1124	C	PL	R9	9386
	(NOTE: PITTSBURGH spelled without H.)					
765D-2a	Same	1176	C	PL	R5	9387
765D-3a	Same	1177	C	PL	R8	9388
765D-4a	Same	1295	C	PL	R9	9389
765D-5a	Same	1331	C	PL	R9	9390

PENNSYLVANIA-Continued

NUMBER	OBVERSE	REVERSE	METAL	EDGE	RARITY	H&G

PITTSBURGH 765-Continued

765E

765F

765E-1a	JOS.FLEMING/DRUGGIST/ COR. MARKET, ST/& THE/ DIAMOND/PITTSBURGH	1025	C	PL	R8	
765E-2a	Same	1026	C	PL	R3	9396
765E-3a	Same	1034	C	PL	R5	9397
765E-4a	Same	1042	C	R	R6	9392
765E-4b	Same	Same	BR	R	R7	9393
765E-4i	Same	Same	Z	R	R9	
765E-5d	Same	1016	C-N	R	R10	9395
765E-6a	Same (H-R 2040)	1047	C	R	R8	
765E-7d	Same	1069	C-N	R	R10	
765F-1a	W.A.GILDENFENNEY/BOOKS/ PAPERS/&/STATIONERY/45 FIFTH,ST/PITTSBURGH	1032	C	PL	R4	9404
765F-2a	Same	1042	C	R	R6	9401
765F-2b	Same	Same	BR	R	R9	9402
765F-3a	Same (H-R 2041)	1047	C	R	R8	9403
765F-4d	Same	1069	C-N	R	R10	
765F-5a	Same	1192	C	R	R7	9400
765F-5a1	Same	Same	C	PL	R7	9399
765F-2i	Same	Same (1042)	Z	R	R9	

765G

765H

765G-1a	D.A.HALL & CO./TEA/ DEALERS/27/FIFTH ST./ PITTSBURG (NOTE: PITTSBURG spelled without H.)	1124	C	PL	R2	9406
765G-2a	Same	1274	C	PL	R9	9407
765H-1a	J.W.HANNAH/81/LIBERTY/ ST./PITTSBURG,PA. (NOTE: PITTSBURGH spelled without H.)	1130	C	PL	R9	9410
765H-2a	Same	1177	C	PL	R6	9409

PENNSYLVANIA-Continued

| NUMBER | OBVERSE | REVERSE | METAL | EDGE | RARITY | H&G |

PITTSBURGH 765-Continued

765I-1a	J.C.&W.H.LIPPINCOTT,/GROCERS/NO.19/DIAMOND/PITTSBURG, PA. (NOTE: PITTSBURGH spelled without H.)	1124	C	PL	R9	9412
765I-2a	Same	1176	C	PL	R4	9413
765I-3a	Same	1177	C	PL	R8	9414
765I-4a	Same	Blank	C	PL	R10	

| 765J-1a | A.LUDEWIG,/DEALER IN/TOBACO SNUFF/AND/CIGARS,/310 & 312,/LIBERTY ST,/PITTSBURGH,PA. (NOTE: TOBACCO is spelled with only one C.) | Full sized portrait of man standing in center. Around COPPERS 20 PR CT PREMIUM. | C | PL | R3 | 9416 |
| 765J-1fp | Same | Same | S-P | PL | R9 | |

765K-1a	J.W.MCCARTHY/BILL/POSTER/PITTSBURGH	1026	C	PL	R3	9421
765K-2a	Same	1042	C	R	R6	9418
765K-2b	Same	Same	BR	R	R9	9419
765K-3d	Same (H-R 2045)	1047	C-N	R	R10	

PENNSYLVANIA-Continued

NUMBER	OBVERSE	REVERSE	METAL	EDGE	RARITY	H&G

PITTSBURGH 765-Continued

(NOTE: J.McKain formerly listed as Pittsburgh changed to Mount Washington, Pa)

765M 765M-2 765M-8

765M-1b	HENRY MINER,/NEWS/DEALER/71&73 FIFTH ST./PITTSBURGH	1364	BR	PL	R2	9426
765M-2a	HENRY/MINER/NEWS/DEALER/71&73/FIFTH, ST./PITTSBURG. (NOTE: PITTSBURGH spelled without H.)	1124	C	PL	R3	9428
765M-2d	Same	Same	C-N	PL	R9	9429
765M-3a	Same	1131	C	PL	R9	9430
765M-4a	Same	1176	C	PL	R8	9432
765M-5a	Same	1180	C	PL	R5	9433
765M-6a	Same	1295	C	PL	R9	9434
765M-7a	Same	1331	C	PL	R9	9435
765M-8a	Incuse of obv. Pa 765M-2, with 1124 impression showing (See photo)	1124	C	PL	R10	

765N-1a	PEKIN/TEA/STORE/NO 50/ST. CLAIR,ST./PITTSBURGH	1023	C	PL	R8	9440
765N-2a	Same	1025	C	PL	R7	
765N-3a	Same	1028	C	PL	R3	9437
765N-4a	Same	1029	C	PL	R5	9441
765N-5a	Same	1030	C	PL	R7	
765N-6a	Same	1033	C	PL	R7	9442
765N-7a	Same	1034	C	PL	R4	9438
765N-8a	Same	1039	C	PL	R6	
765N-9a	Same	1041	C	PL	R8	
765N-10a	Same	1042	C	R	R7	9443
765N-10b	Same	Same	BR	R	R8	
765N-10i	Same	Same	Z	R	R9	
765N-11a	Same	1047	C	R	R8	
765N-11d	Same (H-R 2048)	Same	C-N	R	R10	
765N-12d	Same	1069	C-N	R	R10	9439

497

PENNSYLVANIA-Continued

NUMBER	OBVERSE	REVERSE	METAL	EDGE	RARITY	H&G

PITTSBURGH 765-Continued

765O-1a	A.C.PENTZ/TIN COPPER&/ SHEET IRONWARE/STOVES/ 20/PENN.ST./PITTSBURGH	1023	C	PL	R4	9444
765O-2a	Same	1042	C	R	R7	9445
765O-2b	Same	Same	BR	R	R9	
765O-2i	Same	Same	Z	R	R9	
765O-3a	Same	1045	C	PL	R9	
765O-4a	Same (H-R 2052)	1047	C	R	R9	9446
765O-4d	Same (H-R 2051)	Same	C-N	R	R10	
765O-5d	Same	1069	C-N	R	R10	9447

765P-1a	PITTOCK/NEWS/DEALER/ PITTSBURGH	1034	C	PL	R2	9450
	(NOTE: For a discussion of the Pittock tokens, see M. Fuld, *The Numismatist*, Feb., p185 1970)					
765P-2a	Same	1042	C	R	R6	9451
765P-2b	Same	Same	BR	R	R8	9452
765P-2i	Same	Same	Z	R	R9	
765P-3d	Same	1069	C-N	R	R10	9454
765P-4a	Same	1192	C	PL	R4	9449
765P-4b	Same	Same	BR	PL	R9	
765P-5a	PITTOCK'S/NEWS/DEPOT/ OPP./POST/OFFICE/PITTSBURG.	1124	C	PL	R2	9456
	(NOTE: PITTSBURGH spelled without H.)					
765P-5d	Same	Same	C-N	PL	R9	9457
765P-6a	Same	1176	C	PL	R2	9458
765P-6b	Same	Same	BR	PL	R9	
765P-6d	Same	Same	C-N	PL	R9	9459
765P-6e	Same (thick 3½ mm.)	Same	W-M	PL	R9	9460
765P-7a	Same	1180	C	PL	R3	9461
765P-8a	Same	1290	C	PL	R3	9462
765P-8e	Same	Same	W-M	PL	R9	9463

PENNSYLVANIA-Continued

NUMBER	OBVERSE	REVERSE	METAL	EDGE	RARITY	H&G

PITTSBURGH 765-Continued

765P-9a	Same	1295	C	PL	R9	9464
765P-10a	Same (H-R 2057)	1324	C	PL	R9	
765P-11a	Similar to the preceding, but larger lettering	1124	C	PL	R8	
765P-12a	Same	1180	C	PL	R8	

765P-13

765P-14

765P-13a	PITTOCK/NEWS/DEALER/ OPPOSITE P.O./PITTSBURGH PA.	PITTOCK'S/CARD within a wreath	C	PL	R4	9466
765P-13b	Same	Same	BR	PL	R1	9467
765P-14a	PITTOCK'S/NEWS/DEPOT/ OPP./POST OFFICE/ PITTSBURG. (NOTE: PITTSBURGH spelled without an H.)	1124	C	PL	R2	9469
765P-15a	Same	1180	C	PL	R3	9470
765P-16a	Same	1324	C	PL	R3	9471
765P-16d	Same	Same	C-N	PL	R9	

765Q

765Q-12

765Q-1a	JOHN W.PITTOCK/NEWS/ DEALER/OPPOSITE/POST OFFICE/PITTSBURGH	1019	C	PL	R9	
765Q-2a	Same	1020	C	PL	R3	9474
765Q-3a	Same	1022	C	PL	R3	9478
765Q-4a	Same	1031	C	PL	R6	9479
765Q-5a	Same	1033	C	PL	R3	
765Q-6a	Same	1034	C	PL	R8	
765Q-7a	Same	1035	C	PL	R7	
765Q-8a	Same	1036	C	PL	R8	
765Q-9a	Same	1042	C	R	R6	9475
765Q-9b	Same	Same	BR	R	R7	9476
765Q-9i	Same	Same	Z	R	R9	
765Q-10d	Same	1046	C-N	R	R10	

PENNSYLVANIA-Continued

NUMBER	OBVERSE	REVERSE	METAL	EDGE	RARITY	H&G

PITTSBURGH 765-Continued

765Q-11a	Same (H-R 2059)	1047	C	R	R9	9477
765Q-11d	Same	Same	C-N	R	R10	
765Q-12a	Same	M. MENDALL SHAFER/ ATTORNEY/&/COUNSELOR/ AT/LAW/57 THIRD ST./ CINCINNATI (Obv OHIO 165FN)	C	PL	R9	9473

765R-1

765R-3

765R-1a	PITTSBURGH/DRY GOODS/ GROCERIES/HARDWARE/ & NOTIONS	1407	C	PL	R8	
765R-2a	Same	1408	C	PL	R2	9481
765R-2b	Same	Same	BR	PL	R3	
765R-3a	Similar, different spacing of letters	1409	C	PL	R2	9482
765R-3b	Same	Same	BR	PL	R3	
765R-3c	Same	Same	N	PL	R9	

765S

765S-6

765S-1a	PITTSBURGH/GAZETTE/84/ FIFTH,ST.	1172	C	PL	R9	9490
765S-2a	Same	1176	C	PL	R3	9487
765S-3a	Same	1177	C	PL	R3	9488
765S-4a	Same	1180	C	PL	R9	
765S-5a	Same	1331	C	PL	R9	9489
765S-6a	Same	ALSO/CUTLERY,/NOTIONS/ &C	C	PL	R10	

(NOTE: See note with QUEEBY, Peru, Ind 740B-7)

500

PENNSYLVANIA-Continued

NUMBER	OBVERSE	REVERSE	METAL	EDGE	RARITY	H&G

PITTSBURGH 765-Continued

765T-1a	REYMER & BROS./ CONFECTIONERS/PITTSBURG /PA. (NOTE: PITTSBURGH spelled without H.)	1177	C	PL	R3	9492
765T-1d	Same (H-R 2062)	Same	C-N	PL	R9	
765T-2a	Same	1331	C	PL	R9	9493
765T-3a	Same	ALSO/CUTLERY,/NOTIONS/&C	C	PL	R10	9495

NOTE: See note with QUEEBY, Peru, Ind 740B-8)

765U-1a	SINCLAIR & WILSON/ CLOTHING/STORE/120/ MARKET ST./PITTSBURG (NOTE: PITTSBURGH spelled without H.)	1177	C	PL	R4	9497
765V-1a	FRANK SNYDER,/TOBACCO/ AND/SEGARS/43/FOURTH ST./ PITTSBURG. (NOTE: PITTSBURGH spelled without H.)	1124	C	PL	R9	9499
765V-2a	Same	1177	C	PL	R6	9501
765V-3a	Same	1273	C	PL	R9	9500
765V-4a	Same	1331	C	PL	R6	9502

501

PENNSYLVANIA-Continued

| NUMBER | OBVERSE | REVERSE | METAL | EDGE | RARITY | H&G |

WEST GREENVILLE 967

| 967A-1b | PACKARD & CO./HARDWARE/&/IRON/WEST GREENVILLE PA. | D.B.PACKARD & CO./CROCKERY/WEST GREENVILLE PA. | BR | PL | R3 | 9505 |

WILKES BARRE 985

985A-1a	CLARK & CO./NO.	1319	C	R	R9
	(NOTE: The only basis for attribution to Wilkes Barre is the notes of the late Joseph Barnett.)				
985A-2b	Same	Blank	BR	PL	R9

502

RHODE ISLAND

NUMBER	OBVERSE	REVERSE	METAL	EDGE	RARITY	H&G

PROVIDENCE 700

700A-1a	ARCADE/HOUSE/62/BROAD. ST/PROVIDENCE.R.I.	1147	C	PL	R9	9507
700A-1b	Same	Same	BR	PL	R9	9508
700A-1c	Same	Same	N	PL	R9	9509
700A-1d	Same	Same	C-N	PL	R9	
700A-1e	Same	Same	W-M	PL	R9	
700A-1g	Same	Same	L	PL	R9	9510
700A-1j	Same	Same	G-S	PL	R9	9511
700A-2a	Same	1159	C	PL	R9	9513
700A-2b	Same	Same	BR	PL	R9	9514
700A-2c	Same	Same	N	PL	R9	9515
700A-2d	Same	Same	C-N	PL	R9	
700A-2e	Same	Same	W-M	PL	R9	
700A-2g	Same	Same	L	PL	R9	9516
700A-2j	Same	Same	G-S	PL	R9	9517
700A-3a	Same	1374	C	PL	R9	9519
700A-3b	Same	Same	BR	PL	R9	9520
700A-3c	Same	Same	N	PL	R9	9521
700A-3d	Same	Same	C-N	PL	R9	
700A-3e	Same	Same	W-M	PL	R9	
700A-3g	Same	Same	L	PL	R9	9522
700A-3j	Same	Same	G-S	PL	R9	9523
700A-4a	Same	H. DOBSON above UNION/1864 in center, wreath below (OBV RI 700D-1)	C	PL	R3	9525
700A-4b	Same	Same	BR	PL	R5	9526
700A-4c	Same	Same	N	PL	R9	9527
700A-4d	Same	Same	C-N	PL	R9	9528
700A-4e	Same	Same	W-M	PL	R9	
700A-4f	Same	Same	S	PL	R9	
700A-4g	Same	Same	L	PL	R9	9530
700A-4j	Same	Same	G-S	PL	R9	9529
700A-5a	H. DOBSON/ARCADE/HOUSE/ 62/BROAD. ST./PROVIDENCE R.I./1864 (NOTE: This is a recently discovered piece, and is cruder than the preceding and may have been a die trial.)	1147	C	PL	R9	

503

RHODE ISLAND-Continued

NUMBER	OBVERSE	REVERSE	METAL	EDGE	RARITY	H&G

PROVIDENCE 700-Continued

700B

700B-2

700B-1a	BILLIARD ROOM/NO/27-31/ PLEASANT/STREET/ RESTAURANT	1374	C	PL	R8	9662
700B-1b	Same	Same	BR	PL	R8	9663
700B-1c	Same	Same	N	PL	R8	9664
700B-1d	Same	Same	C-N	PL	R8	9665
700B-1e	Same	Same	W-M	PL	R8	
700B-1f	Same	Same	S	PL	R9	9667
700B-1j	Same	Same	G-S	PL	R8	9666
700B-2a	Same	FRANK.L.GAY/BOOKSELLER/ PROV.R.I./& STATIONER/ 140 WESTMINSTER ST. (Obv. RI 700E-1)	C	PL	R8	9582
700B-2b	Same	Same	BR	PL	R8	9583
700B-2c	Same	Same	N	PL	R8	9584
700B-2d	Same	Same	C-N	PL	R8	9585
700B 2e	Same	Same	W-M	PL	R8	
700B-2f	Same	Same	S	PL	R9	9587
700B-2g	Same	Same	L	PL	R8	9588
700B-2j	Same	Same	G-S	PL	R8	9586

700C-1a	Anchor on shield in center, CHARNLEY and 13 stars above — NO. 11 ORANGE ST./ PROVIDENCE	1147	C	PL	R9	9531
700C-1b	Same	Same	BR	PL	R9	9532
700C-1c	Same	Same	N	PL	R9	9533
700C-1d	Same	Same	C-N	PL	R9	
700C-1e	Same	Same	W-M	PL	R9	
700C-1g	Same	Same	L	PL	R9	9534
700C-1j	Same	Same	G-S	PL	R9	9535

RHODE ISLAND-Continued

NUMBER	OBVERSE	REVERSE	METAL	EDGE	RARITY	H&G

PROVIDENCE 700-Continued

NUMBER	OBVERSE	REVERSE	METAL	EDGE	RARITY	H&G
700C-2a	Same	1159	C	PL	R8	9537
700C-2b	Same	Same	BR	PL	R8	9538
700C-2c	Same	Same	N	PL	R8	9539
700C-2d	Same	Same	C-N	PL	R8	9540
700C-2e	Same	Same	W-M	PL	R8	
700C-2g	Same	Same	L	PL	R8	9541
700C-2j	Same	Same	G-S	PL	R8	9542
700C-3a	Same	1374	C	PL	R3	9544
700C-3b	Same	Same	BR	PL	R7	9545
700C-3c	Same	Same	N	PL	R8	9546
700C-3d	Same (H-R 2067)	Same	C-N	PL	R8	9547
700C-3e	Same	Same	W-M	PL	R8	
700C-3f	Same	Same	S	PL	R9	
700C-3fo	Same, over U.S. Dime	Same	S	R	R10	
700C-3g	Same	Same	L	PL	R8	9549
700C-3j	Same	Same	G-S	PL	R8	9548
700C-4a	Same	H. DOBSON reverse (Obv. RI 700D-1)	C	PL	R8	9551
700C-4b	Same	Same	BR	PL	R8	9552
700C-4c	Same	Same	N	PL	R8	9553
700C-4d	Same	Same	C-N	PL	R8	9554
700C-4e	Same	Same	W-M	PL	R8	
700C-4g	Same	Same	L	PL	R8	9556
700C-4j	Same	Same	G-S	PL	R8	9555
700C-5a	Same	FRANK.L.GAY reverse (Obv. RI 700E-1)	C	PL	R7	9558
700C-5b	Same	Same	BR	PL	R8	9559
700C-5c	Same	Same	N	PL	R8	9560
700C-5d	Same	Same	C-N	PL	R8	9561
700C-5e	Same	Same	W-M	PL	R8	
700C-5f	Same	Same	S	PL	R9	9564
700C-5g	Same	Same	L	PL	R8	9563
700C-5j	Same (H-R 2068)	Same	G-S	PL	R8	9562
700C-6a	Same	1429	C	PL	R9	

(NOTE: This mule probably occurs in other metals.)

NUMBER	OBVERSE	REVERSE	METAL	EDGE	RARITY	H&G
700D-1a	H. DOBSON above, UNION/1864 in center, wreath below.	1285	C	PL	R9	9698
700D-1b	Same	Same	BR	PL	R9	9699
700D-1c	Same (Elder, 9/38 Lot 1301)	Same	N	PL	R9	9700
700D-1d	Same	Same	C-N	PL	R9	
700D-1e	Same	Same	W-M	PL	R9	
700D-1g	Same	Same	L	PL	R9	9702
700D-1j	Same	Same	G-S	PL	R9	9701

RHODE ISLAND-Continued

NUMBER	OBVERSE	REVERSE	METAL	EDGE	RARITY	H&G

PROVIDENCE 700-Continued

NUMBER	OBVERSE	REVERSE	METAL	EDGE	RARITY	H&G
700D-2a	Same	1428	C	PL	R9	
700D-2b	Same	Same	BR	PL	R9	
700D-2c	Same	Same	N	PL	R9	
700D-2d	Same (H-R 2069)	Same	C-N	PL	R9	
700D-2e	Same	Same	W-M	PL	R9	
700D-2g	Same	Same	L	PL	R9	
700D-2j	Same	Same	G-S	PL	R9	
700D-3a	Same	1429	C	PL	R9	9704
700D-3b	Same	Same	BR	PL	R9	9705
700D-3c	Same	Same	N	PL	R9	9706
700D-3g	Same	Same	L	PL	R9	9708
700D-3j	Same	Same	G-S	PL	R9	9707
700D-4a	Same	CITY FRUIT STORE/NO4/ WEYBOSSETT/ST. PROV.R.I./ REDEEMED BY/PHILLIPS (Obv RI 700G-1)	C	PL	R9	9611
700D-4b	Same	Same	BR	PL	R9	9612
700D-4c	Same	Same	N	PL	R9	9613
700D-4d	Same	Same	C-N	PL	R9	9614
700D-4e	Same	Same	W-M	PL	R9	
700D-4g	Same (H-R 2071)	Same	L	PL	R9	9616
700D-4j	Same	Same	G-S	PL	R9	9615

700D-4

700E

NUMBER	OBVERSE	REVERSE	METAL	EDGE	RARITY	H&G
700E-1a	FRANK.L.GAY/BOOKSELLER/ PROV./R.I./&STATIONER/140 WESMINSTER ST.	1191	C	PL	R9	
700E-1b	Same	Same	BR	PL	R9	
700E-1c	Same	Same	N	PL	R9	
700E-1d	Same	Same	C-N	PL	R9	
700E-1e	Same	Same	W-M	PL	R9	
700E-1g	Same	Same	L	PL	R9	
700E-1j	Same	Same	G-S	PL	R9	
700E-2a	Same	1264	C	PL	R2	9574
700E-2b	Same	Same	BR	PL	R3	9575
700E-2bp	Same. silver plated	Same	BR-pl	PL	R3	
700E-2c	Same	Same	N	PL	R8	9576
700E-2d	Same	Same	C-N	PL	R8	9577
700E-2e	Same	Same	W-M	PL	R8	
700E-2f	Same	Same	S	PL	R9	9579
700E-2g	Same	Same	L	PL	R8	9580
700E-2j	Same	Same	G-S	PL	R8	9578

RHODE ISLAND-Continued

PROVIDENCE 700-Continued

NUMBER	OBVERSE	REVERSE	METAL	EDGE	RARITY	H&G
700E-3a	Same	1285	C	PL	R9	
700E-3b	Same	Same	BR	PL	R9	
700E-3c	Same	Same	N	PL	R9	
700E-3d	Same	Same	C-N	PL	R9	
700E-3e	Same	Same	W-M	PL	R9	
700E-3f	Same	Same	S	PL	R9	
700E-3g	Same	Same	L	PL	R9	
700E-3j	Same	Same	G-S	PL	R9	

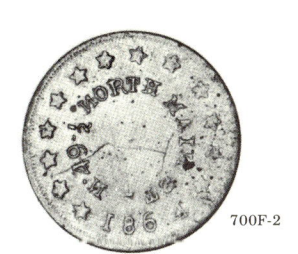

700F   700F-2

700F-1a	H.Y. LE FEVRE, PRO EMPIRE SALOON around — UNION in wreath in center (thick 2½ mm.)	1294	C	PL	R6	9723
700F-2a	Same	N 49½ NORTH MAIN ST in a circle in center — surrounded by 13 large stars, 1864 below.	C	PL	R6	9724
700F-2b	Same	Same	BR	PL	R9	9725
700F-2c	Same	Same	N	PL	R9	9726
700F-2e	Same	Same	W-M	PL	R9	9728
700F-2f	Same	Same	S	PL	R9	
700F-2j	Same	Same	G-S	PL	R9	9727

700G   700G-4

700G-1a	CITY FRUIT STORE/NO 4/WEYBOSSET/ST. PROV.R.I./REDEEMED BY/PHILLIPS	1147	C	PL	R0	9597
700G-1b	Same	Same	BR	PL	R9	9598
700G-1c	Same	Same	N	PL	R9	9599
700G-1e	Same	Same	W-M	PL	R9	
700G-1g	Same	Same	L	PL	R9	9601
700G-1j	Same	Same	G-S	PL	R9	9600

RHODE ISLAND-Continued

NUMBER	OBVERSE	REVERSE	METAL	EDGE	RARITY	H&G

PROVIDENCE 700-Continued

NUMBER	OBVERSE	REVERSE	METAL	EDGE	RARITY	H&G
700G-2a	Same	1159	C	PL	R2	9603
700G-2b	Same	Same	BR	PL	R4	9604
700G-2c	Same	Same	N	PL	R7	9605
700G-2d	Same	Same	C-N	PL	R7	9606
700G-2e	Same	Same	W-M	PL	R7	
700G-2f	Same	Same	S	PL	R8	9608
700G-2g	Same	Same	L	PL	R7	9609
700G-2j	Same (H-R 2075)	Same	G-S	PL	R7	9607
700G-3a	Same	1374	C	PL	R9	9590
700G-3b	Same	Same	BR	PL	R9	9591
700G-3c	Same	Same	N	PL	R9	9592
700G-3d	Same	Same	C-N	PL	R9	9593
700G-3e	Same	Same	W-M	PL	R9	
700G-3g	Same	Same	L	PL	R9	9595
700G-3j	Same	Same	G-S	PL	R9	9594
700G-4a	Same	RHODE ISLAND/IN/THE/FIELD FIRST/1864 surrounded by 13 stars.	C	PL	R6	9618
700G-4f	Same	Same	S	PL	R9	

700H-1a	"POHLE above, 1863 below, bunch of grapes in center"	ELMWOOD VINEYARD around border, anchor in center	C	PL	R9	9626
700H-1b	Same	Same	BR	PL	R9	9627
700H-1g	Same	Same	L	PL	R9	9628

700I-1a	F.W.SHATTUCK/PROV. 1864/R. I./13 WEYBOSSET.ST. with wreath in center.	BURNSIDE above — S in wreath in center — FRUIT STORE below.	C	PL	R7	9620
700I-1b	Same	Same	BR	PL	R9	9621
700I-1c	Same	Same	N	PL	R8	9622
700I-1e	Same	Same	W-M	PL	R9	
700I-1f	Same	Same	S	PL	R9	
700I-1g	Same	Same	L	PL	R9	9624
700I-1j	Same	Same	G-S	PL	R9	9623

TENNESSEE

NUMBER	OBVERSE	REVERSE	METAL	EDGE	RARITY	H&G

CLARKSVILLE 130

130A-1a	ANDREW KING/MERCH'T/ CLARKSVILLE/TENN.	SEE/BEST STOCK/IN CITY AT/ KING'S/FRANKLIN ST.	C	PL	R9	9731
130A-1e	Same	Same	W-M	PL	R9	
130A-2a	Same	1046	C	R	R9	9732
130A-2d	Same	Same	C-N	R	R10	
130A-3a	Same	1047	C	R	R8	
130A-4a	Rev. Tenn 130A-1a	Same	C	R	R9	7267
130A-5d	Same	1069	C-N	R	R10	7266

DEDHAM 180

180A-1b	N. O. UNDERWOOD/GOOD FOR/ 25/CENTS./DEDHAM/TENN	1082	BR	PL	R0	
180A-2b	Same	1085	BR	PL	R7	9735
180A-3a	Same inscription, but 10 substituted for 25	1168	C	PL	R8	5700
180A-4a	Same	1225	C	PL	R8	
180A-5a	Same inscription but 5 substituted for 25	1168	C	PL	R8	9737

TENNESSEE-Continued

NUMBER	OBVERSE	REVERSE	METAL	EDGE	RARITY	H&G

KNOXVILLE 430

430A-1

430A-1a	BARRY & M'DANNEL / PREMIUM CONFECTIONERS / KNOXVILLE, TENN	ARCTIC/SODA WATER around in center GOOD/FOR/1/GLASS (same rev used on OHIO 165V-5a)	C	R	R9	9741
430A-1a1	Same	Same	C	PL	R9	9743
430A-1b	Same	Same	BR	R	R7	9742
430A-2d	Same	1046	C-N	R	R10	
430A-3a	Same	1047	C	R	R8	9740

MEMPHIS 600

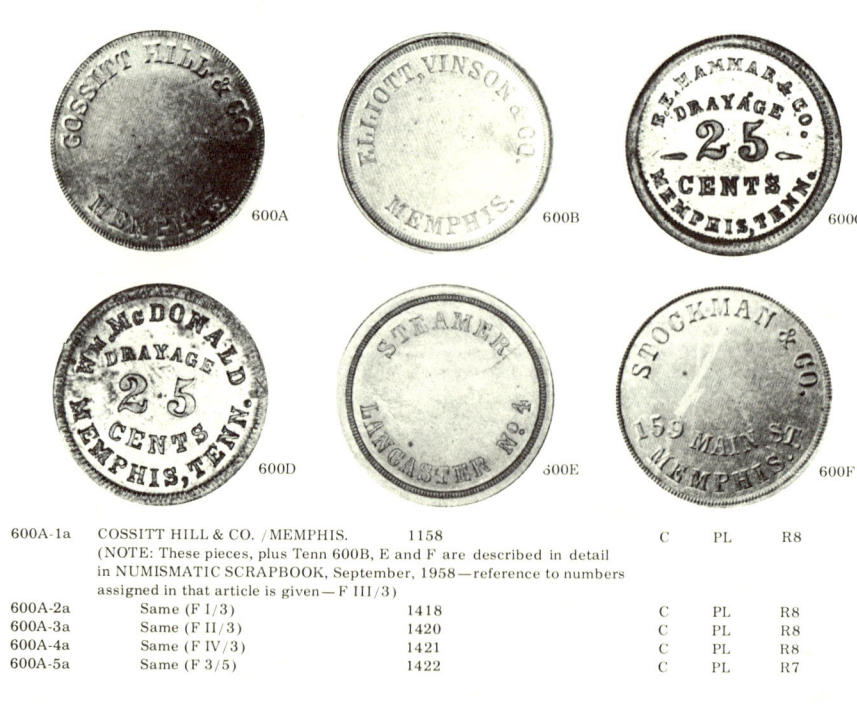

600A   600B   600C
600D   600E   600F

600A-1a	COSSITT HILL & CO. /MEMPHIS. (NOTE: These pieces, plus Tenn 600B, E and F are described in detail in NUMISMATIC SCRAPBOOK, September, 1958—reference to numbers assigned in that article is given—F III/3)	1158	C	PL	R8
600A-2a	Same (F I/3)	1418	C	PL	R8
600A-3a	Same (F II/3)	1420	C	PL	R8
600A-4a	Same (F IV/3)	1421	C	PL	R8
600A-5a	Same (F 3/5)	1422	C	PL	R7

510

TENNESSEE-Continued

NUMBER	OBVERSE	REVERSE	METAL	EDGE	RARITY	H&G

MEMPHIS 600-Continued

NUMBER	OBVERSE	REVERSE	METAL	EDGE	RARITY	H&G
600A-5b	Same (F 3/5)	Same	BR	PL	R7	
600A-6a	Same (F 3/6)	1423	C	PL	R7	
600A-6b	Same (F 3/6)	Same	BR	PL	R7	
600A-7a	Same (F 3/7)	1424	C	PL	R6	
600A-7b	Same (F 3/7)	Same	BR	PL	R6	
600A-8a	Same (F 3/8)	1425	C	PL	R6	
600A-8b	Same (F 3/8)	Same	BR	PL	R6	
600A-9a	Same (F 3/9)	1426	C	PL	R8	
600A-10a	Same (F 3/BL)	1427	C	PL	R6	
600A-10b	Same (F 3/BL)	Same	BR	PL	R6	
600A-11a	Same (F 2/3)	Obverse Tenn 600B-1	C	PL	R6	
600A-12a	Same (F 3/4)	Obverse Tenn 600E-1	C	PL	R6	
600A-13a	Same (F 1/3)	Obverse Tenn 600F-1	C	PL	R6	
600B-1a	ELLIOTT, VINSON & CO./ MEMPHIS. (F III/2)	1158	C	PL	R8	
600B-2a	Same (F I/2, King 626)	1418	C	PL	R8	
600B-3a	Same (F II/2)	1420	C	PL	R8	
600B-4a	Same (F IV/2)	1421	C	PL	R8	
600B-5a	Same (F 2/5)	1422	C	PL	R7	
600B-5b	Same (F 2/5)	Same	BR	PL	R7	
600B-6a	Same (F 2/6)	1423	C	PL	R8	
600B-6b	Same (F 2/6)	Same	BR	PL	R8	
600B-7a	Same (F 2/7)	1424	C	PL	R6	
600B-7b	Same (F 2/7)	Same	BR	PL	R6	
600B-8a	Same (F 2/8)	1425	C	PL	R6	
600B-9a	Same (F 2/9)	1426	C	PL	R8	
600B-10a	Same (F 2/BL)	1427	C	PL	R6	
600B-10b	Same (F 2/BL)	Same	BR	PL	R6	
600B-10bc	Same counterstamped 25 (F 2/BL C/S)	Same	BR	PL	R6	
600B-11a	Same (F 2/4)	Obverse 600E-1	C	PL	R6	
600B-12a	Same (F 1/2)	Obverse 600F-1	C	PL	R6	
600B-3a1	Same	1420 clashed (incused) into 1427	C	PL	R10	
600C-1a	B. E. HAMMAR & CO./ DRAYAGE/25/CENTS/ MEMPHIS,TENN.	1042	C	R	R7	9745
600C-1b	Same	Same	BR	R	R7	9746
600C-2d	Same	1046	C-N	R	R10	
600C-3d	Same	1047	C-N	R	R10	9748
600C-4a	Same	1401	C	R	R8	9749
600D-1a	WM. MCDONALD/DRAYAGE/ 25/CENTS/MEMPHIS,TENN.	1042	C	R	R7	9751
600D-1b	Same	Same	BR	R	R9	9752
600D-2a	Same	1047	C	R	R9	
600D-2d	Same	Same	C-N	R	R10	
600D-3a	Same	1400	C	R	R9	9754
600D-4a	Same	1401	C	R	R8	9753
600D-4a1	Same	Same	C	PL	R10	
600E-1a	STEAMER/LANCASTER NO 4(F III/4)	1158	C	PL	R8	
600E-2a	Same (F I/4, King 623)	1419	C	PL	R8	
600E-3a	Same (F II/4)	1420	C	PL	R8	
600E-4a	Same (F IV/4)	1421	C	PL	R8	
600E-5a	Same (F 4/5)	1422	C	PL	R6	
600E-6a	Same (F 4/6)	1423	C	PL	R7	
600E-7a	Same (F 4/7)	1424	C	PL	R6	
600E-7b	Same (F 4/7)	Same	BR	PL	R6	
600E-8a	Same (F 4/8)	1425	C	PL	R6	
600D-3a1	Same	1420 clashed (incused) into 1427	C	PL	R10	
600B-3b	Same	Same	BR	PL	R10	
600B-8b	Same	Same	BR	PL	R9	

TENNESSEE-Continued

NUMBER	OBVERSE	REVERSE	METAL	EDGE	RARITY	H&G

MEMPHIS 600-Continued

NUMBER	OBVERSE	REVERSE	METAL	EDGE	RARITY	H&G
600E-8b	Same (F 4/8)	Same	BR	PL	R6	
600E-9b	Same (F 4/9)	1426	BR	PL	R8	
600E-10a	Same (F 4/BL)	1427	C	PL	R7	
600E-11a	Same (F 1/4)	Obv. Tenn 600F-1a	C	PL	R6	
600E-9a	Same	1426	C	PL	R9	
600F-1a	STOCKMAN & CO/ 59 MAIN ST./MEMPHIS. (F III/1)	1158	C	PL	R8	
600F-2a	Same (F IA/1, King 622)	1419	C	PL	R8	
600F-3a	Same (F II/1)	1420	C	PL	R8	
600F-4a	Same (F IV/1)	1421	C	PL	R8	
600F-5a	Same (F 1/5)	1422	C	PL	R6	
600F-5b	Same (F 1/5)	Same	BR	PL	R6	
600F-6a	Same (F 1/6)	1423	C	PL	R7	
600F-6b	Same (F 1/6)	Same	BR	PL	R7	
600F-7a	Same (F 1/7)	1424	C	PL	R6	
600F-8a	Same (F 1/8)	1425	C	PL	R6	
600F-9a	Same (F 1/9)	1426	C	PL	R8	
600F-9b	Same (F 1/9)	Same	BR	PL	R8	
600F-10a	Same (F 1/BL)	1427	C	PL	R6	
600F-10b	Same (F 1/BL)	Same	BR	PL	R6	
600F-10bc	Same cstp 25 (F 1/BL C/S)	Same	BR	PL	R6	

NASHVILLE 690

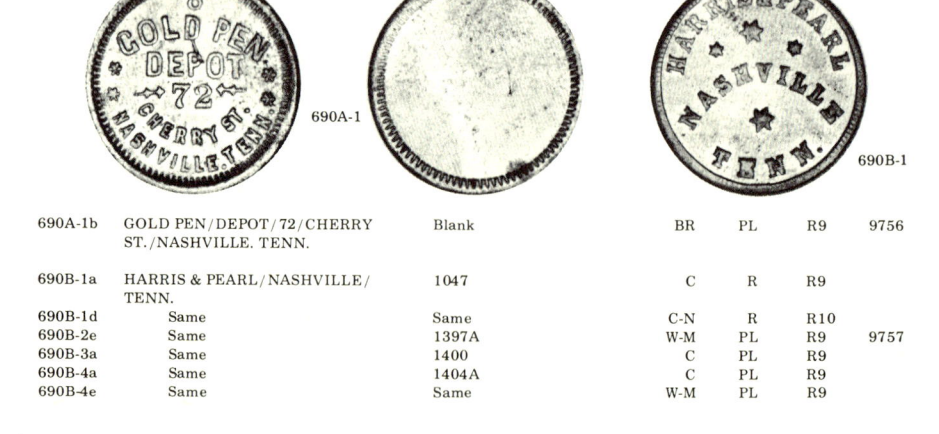

NUMBER	OBVERSE	REVERSE	METAL	EDGE	RARITY	H&G
690A-1b	GOLD PEN/DEPOT/72/CHERRY ST./NASHVILLE. TENN.	Blank	BR	PL	R9	9756
690B-1a	HARRIS & PEARL/NASHVILLE/TENN.	1047	C	R	R9	
690B-1d	Same	Same	C-N	R	R10	
690B-2e	Same	1397A	W-M	PL	R9	9757
690B-3a	Same	1400	C	PL	R9	
690B-4a	Same	1404A	C	PL	R9	
690B-4e	Same	Same	W-M	PL	R9	

TENNESSEE-Continued

NUMBER	OBVERSE	REVERSE	METAL	EDGE	RARITY	H&G

NASHVILLE 690-Continued

690C-1a	D.L. LAPSLEY & CO/NASHVILLE/ TENN.	1047	C	R	R9	
690C-2d	Same	1069	C-N	R	R10	9758
690C-3d	Same (This token was listed in an early article in the Numismatist)	1267	C-N	R	R10	
690C-4a	Same	1394	C	R	R9	9759
690C-5a	Same	1399	C	R	R9	9760
690C-6a	Same	1404	C	R	R9	9761
690C-1d	Same (Kreisberg 10/66 Lot 822)	Same	C-N	R	R10	

690D

690E

690D-1a	MCKAY & LAPSLEY/NASHVILLE/ TENN	1042	C	R	R9	
690D-2a	Same	1047	C	R	R8	9767
690D-3d	Same	1069	C-N	R	R10	9766
690D-4b	Same	1392	BR	R	R9	
690D-5b	Same	1397	BR	R	R9	9762

(NOTE: The only specimen seen of this token was struck over another token, apparently Ohio 165AY)

690D-6b	Same	1397A	BR	R	R9	9763
690D-7a	Same	1399	C	R	R9	
690D-8e	Same	1403	W-M	PL	R9	9764
690D-9a	Same	1405	C	R	R8	9765
690D-9b	Same	Same	BR	R	R9	
690D-10d	Same	1018	C-N	R	R9	
690E-1a	WALKER & NAPIER/ NASHVILLE/TENN.	1047	C	R	R8	9770
690E-2d	Same	1069	C-N	R	R10	9768
690E-3e	Same	1397	W-M	PL	R9	
690E-4e	Same	1404A	W-M	PL	R9	
690E-5a	Same	1405	C	R	R9	9769

VIRGINIA

NUMBER	OBVERSE	REVERSE	METAL	EDGE	RARITY	H&G

NORFOLK 580

580A-1g	PFEIFFER & CO above, VA. in beaded circle in center — NORFOLK below.	1284	L	PL	R8	9772

(NOTE: Possibly non-contemporary.)

WEST VIRGINIA

NUMBER	OBVERSE	REVERSE	METAL	EDGE	RARITY	H&G

GLEN EASTON 220

220A-1a	BASSETT'S/CHEAP/DRY GOODS/GROCERIES/ETC./GLEN EASTON/W.VA.	1084	C	PL	R9	
220A-2a	Same	1126	C	PL	R7	9776
220A-3a	Same	1166	C	PL	R9	9775
220A-4a	Same	1225	C	PL	R8	9777
220A-4b	Same	Same	BR	PL	R9	
220A-5a	Same	BASSETT'E/CHEAP/DRY GOODS/35 MAIN ST/WHEELING/W.VA. (Obv. W.Va. 890A-1)	C	PL	R9	9773
220A-6a	Same	DEALERS/IN HOOP/SKIRTS/HATS/CAPS/AND/NOTIONS (Same as Rev Ohio 165CY-43 H&G 7403, and Rev Ohio 975I-1a.)	C	PL	R9	9774

HARTFORD CITY 260

| 260A-1b | IN MERCHANDISE/KELLY'S/STORE/HARTFORD/CITY/W VA | 1391 | BR | R | R9 | 9779 |
| 260A-2c | Same | 1395 | N | R | R9 | |

WEST VIRGINIA-Continued

NUMBER	OBVERSE	REVERSE	METAL	EDGE	RARITY	H&G

WHEELING 890

890A-1a	BASSETT'S/CHEAP/DRY GOODS/35 MAIN ST/ WHEELING/W.VA.	1084	C	PL	R7	9781
890A-2a	Same	1089	C	PL	R8	9782
890A-2b	Same	Same	BR	PL	R8	9783
890A-3a	Same	1126	C	PL	R9	9784
890A-4a	Same	1127	C	PL	R7	9785
890A-5a	Same	1128	C	PL	R6	9786
890A-6a	Same	1166	C	PL	R8	9780
890A-7a	Same	1168	C	PL	R9	9789
890A-8a	Same	1178	C	PL	R8	9788
890A-9a	Same	1222	C	PL	R9	
890A-10a	Same	1224	C	PL	R9	
890A-11a	Same	1225	C	PL	R7	9787
890A-12a	Same	1226	C	PL	R8	

890B

890B-5

890B-1a	JOHN ECKHART/MANUF'R/ OF/HOISERY & C./187/ MAIN ST/WHEELING/W.VA.	1126	C	PL	R5	9791
890B-2a	Same	1166	C	PL	R9	9790
890B-3a	Same	1169	C	PL	R7	9792
890B-4a	Same	1346	C	PL	R8	9793
890B-5a	Same	W.K.LANPHEAR/MANU'FR/ OF/METALIC/CARDS/ CINCINNATI, O. (corn wreath in center) (Obv. Ohio 165-CY-1)	C	PL	R9	

WEST VIRGINIA-Continued

NUMBER	OBVERSE	REVERSE	METAL	EDGE	RARITY	H&G

WHEELING 890-Continued

890C-1a	JAS.GRAVES & CO./ WALLPAPER/AND/NEWS DEALERS/30 MONROE ST/ WHEELING/W.VA.	1322	C	PL	R6	9795
890D-1a	R.C.GRAVES/PERIODICAL/ AND/NEWS DEALERS/78/ MARKET ST./WHEELING,/ W.VA.	1088	C	PL	R8	9797
890D-2a	Same	1122	C	PL	R6	9798
890D-2b	Same	Same	BR	PL	R9	
890D-3a	Same	1127	C	PL	R9	
890D-3b	Same	Same	BR	PL	R9	
890D-4a	Same	1322	C	PL	R6	9799
890D-5a	Same (Marvin 724C)	1387	C	PL	R7	9800
890E-1a	D.NICOLL & BRO./ VARIETY STORE/109/MAIN ST./WHEELING/W.VA.	1126	C	PL	R7	9801
890E-2a	Same	1166	C	PL	R8	9802
890F-1a	J.W.C.SMITH/DEALER/IN/ LEATHER/AND FINDINGS/ WHEELING,WEST VA	1169	C	PL	R7	9805
890F-2a	Same	1225	C	PL	R7	9804

517

WEST VIRGINIA-Continued

NUMBER	OBVERSE	REVERSE	METAL	EDGE	RARITY	H&G

WHEELING 890-Continued

890G-1

890G-4 Rev

890G-1a	C.E.STIFEL/TIN/AND/SHEET IRON/WARE/WHEELING/W.VA.	1166	C	PL	R9	9808
890G-2a	Same	1178	C	PL	R6	9811
890G-3a	Same	1225	C	PL	R9	9809
890G-4a	Same	1227	C	PL	R9	9810
	(NOTE: The only specimen seen of this, has a trial striking on the reverse — see photo.)					
890G-5a	Same	1299	C	PL	R7	9812
890G-6a	Same	1303	C	PL	R9	9813

518

WISCONSIN

NUMBER	OBVERSE	REVERSE	METAL	EDGE	RARITY	H&G

APPLETON 30

30A-1a	PARSONS & BARLOW/GROCERS/ APPLETON WIS.	1174	C	PL	R8	9825
30A-1b	Same	Same	BR	PL	R9	9826
30A-1d	Same	Same	C-N	PL	R9	9827
30A-1do	Same, struck over CN cent t)	Same	C-N	PL	R10	
30A-1e	Same	Same	W-M	PL	R9	9828
30A-2a	Same	1195	C	PL	R7	9835
30A-3a	Same	1220	C	PL	R9	9830
30A-3b	Same	Same	BR	PL	R9	9831
30A-3d	Same	Same	C-N	PL	R9	9832
30A-3e	Same	Same	W-M	PL	R8	9833

BARABOO 45

45A

45A-7a Rev

45A-1a	PECK & ORVIS/ DRUGGISTS/ &/ GROCERS,/BARABOO,/WIS.	1145	C	PL	R8	9838
45A-1b	Same	Same	BR	PL	R9	9839
45A-1c	Same	Same	N	PL	R9	9840
45A-1d	Same	Same	C-N	PL	R9	9841
45A-1e	Same	Same	W-M	PL	R10	9842
45A-1f	Same	Same	S	PL	R10	9843
45A-2a	Same	1241	C	PL	R9	9845
45A-3a	Same	1244	C	PL	R9	9850
45A-4a	Same	1245	C	PL	R9	9852
45A-5a	Same	1246	C	PL	R5	9847
45A-5d	Same	Same	C-N	PL	R8	9848
45A-6a	Same	1275	C	PL	R9	9854
45A-7a	Same	WASHINGTON MARKET/ (Turkey in center) EXCHANGE	C	PL	R9	9856

519

WISCONSIN-Continued

NUMBER	OBVERSE	REVERSE	METAL	EDGE	RARITY	H&G

BARTON 50

| 50A-1a | JOHN REISSE/DEALER/IN/ DRY GOODS/GROCERIES/ CLOTHING/HATS &/ BARTON. WASH. CO. WIS. | 1194 | C | PL | R7 | 9858 |

BEAVER DAM 55

| 55A-1a | F. KRUEGER/DRY GOODS,/ GROCERIES,/BOOTS & SHOES/ HARDWARE/&C./BEAVER DAM, WIS. | 1194 | C | PL | R5 | 9861 |
| 55A-2a | Same | 1220 | C | PL | R6 | 9862 |

| 55B-1a | A.P. REDFIELD/HARDWARE/ IRON/TIN WARE,/STOVES/ NAILS & C./BEAVER DAM, WIS. | 1194 | C | PL | R5 | 9864 |

WISCONSIN-Continued

NUMBER	OBVERSE	REVERSE	METAL	EDGE	RARITY	H&G

BEAVER DAM 55-Continued

| 55C-1a | O.M. WARREN/HARDWARE/IRON/TINWARE/STOVES/NAILS/&C./BEAVER DAM, WIS. | 1220 | C | PL | R5 | 9866 |
| 55C-2a | Same | 1272 | C | PL | R8 | 9867 |

BELOIT 70

| 70A-1a | PECK & PRATT/DEALERS/IN/WINES/LIQUORS/&SEGARS/BELOIT, WIS. | 1209 | C | PL | R8 | 9869 |

COLUMBUS 120

| 120A-1a | PH. CARPELES & CO./DRY-/GOODS/&/GROCERIES/COLUMBUS, WIS. | 1194 | C | PL | R3 | 9870 |

WISCONSIN-Continued

NUMBER	OBVERSE	REVERSE	METAL	EDGE	RARITY	H&G

COLUMBUS 120-Continued

| 120B-1a | FRANK HUGGINS/DRUGS/ &/MEDICINES/COLUMBUS, WIS. | 1194 | C | PL | R5 | 9872 |

| 120C-1a | D.F. NEWCOMB/DRY GOODS/ GROCERIES/COLUMBUS, WIS. | 1194 | C | PL | R5 | 9874 |

120D-1a	WILLIAMS BRO'S/CHEMISTS/ (Mortar & Pestle)/& DRUGGISTS/ COLUMBUS/WIS.	1105	C	PL	R4	9876
120D-2a	Same	1108	C	PL	R8	9878
120D-3a	Same	1110	C	PL	R8	
120D-4a	Same	1203	C	PL	R8	9879
120D-5a	Same	1205	C	PL	R9	9877

522

WISCONSIN-Continued

NUMBER	OBVERSE	REVERSE	METAL	EDGE	RARITY	H&G

CROSS PLAINS 140

140A-1   140A-2

| 140A-1a | C. DAHMEN & SON/DEALERS/ IN/DRYGOODS/GROCERIES/ & C./CROSS PLAINS/WIS. | 1105 | C | PL | R5 | 9882 |
| 140A-2a | Same, different spacing | Same | C | PL | R5 | 9882 |

EAST TROY 185

185A-1a	C.W. SMITH/DEALER/IN/ DRY GOODS,/GROCERIES,/ HARDWARE &/CROCKERY./ EAST TROY WIS.	1174	C	PL	R8	9884
185A-1b	Same	Same	BR	PL	R9	9885
185A-1d	Same	Same	C-N	PL	R9	9886
185A-1e	Same	Same	W-M	PL	R7	9887
185A-2a	Same	1194	C	PL	R5	9897
185A-3a	Same	1220	C	PL	R9	9889
185A-3b	Same	Same	BR	PL	R9	9890
185A-3d	Same	Same	C-N	PL	R8	9891
185A-3e	Same	Same	W-M	PL	R10	9892
185A-4a	Same	1242	C	PL	R	9894
	(NOTE: It is questionable whether this combination exists)					
185A-5a	Same	1272	C	PL	R9	9896
185A-5b	Same	Same	BR	PL	R9	

523

WISCONSIN-Continued

NUMBER	OBVERSE	REVERSE	METAL	EDGE	RARITY	H&G

EDGERTON 190

| 190A-1a | C.C. ROOT & BRO./DRYGOODS,/ CLOTHING,/BOOTS,/SHOES, CROCKERY,/GROCERIES/ & C./EDGERTON,/WIS. | 1222 | C | PL | R4 | 9898 |

FOND DU LAC 220

220A    220A-3

220A-1a	C.L. ALLING/GROCER,/ FOND DU LAC,/WIS.	1082	C	PL	R6	9900
220A-2a	Same	1168	C	PL	R9	9901
220A-3a	Same	W.K. LANPHEAR/ (wreath encircling MANU'FR/ OF/METALIC/CARDS/) CINCINNATI, O.	C	PL	R9	9902

| 220B-1a | A.R. BRASS/GENERAL/DEALER IN/PRODUCE/FOND DU LAC/ WIS. | 1127 | C | PL | R6 | 9905 |
| 220B-2a | Same | 1168 | C | PL | R6 | 9906 |

524

WISCONSIN-Continued

NUMBER	OBVERSE	REVERSE	METAL	EDGE	RARITY	H&G

FOND DU LAC 220-Continued

| 220C-1a | CARPENTER & PIER./CALL/ AT THE/FARMERS/STORE/ FOND DU LAC/WIS. | 1082 | C | PL | R5 | 9908 |

| 220D-1a | CLARKE & CARPENTER/ DEALERS/IN/DRY GOODS/ AND/GROCERIES/ FOND DU LAC/WIS. | 1181 | C | PL | R6 | 9910 |

220E-1a	F. FRITZ/GROCERIES./ CROCKERY/PROVISI = / ONS & C./FOND DU LAC, WIS	1174	C	PL	R8	9912
220E-1b	Same	Same	BR	PL	R8	9913
220E-1d	Same	Same	C-N	PL	R9	9914
220E-1e	Same	Same	W-M	PL	R8	9915
220E-2a	Same	1194	C	PL	R9	9916
220E-3a	Same	1220	C	PL	R8	9917
220E-3b	Same	Same	BR	PL	R9	9918
220E-3d	Same	Same	C-N	PL	R9	9919
220E-3e	Same	Same	W-M	PL	R10	

525

WISCONSIN-Continued

NUMBER	OBVERSE	REVERSE	METAL	EDGE	RARITY	H&G

FOND DU LAC 220-Continued

220F-1a	J.C. LOWELL/DRUGGIST/ &/GROCER/FONDULAC,/ WIS.	1082	C	PL	R5	9923
	(NOTE: Incorrect spelling of Fond du Lac)					
220F-2a	Same	1089	C	PL	R6	9924
220F-3a	Same	1168	C	PL	R9	9925

| 220G-1a | T. MASON,/GROCER/ FOND DU LAC,/WIS. | T. MASON,/CROCKERY/ AND/GLASSWARE. | C | PL | R6 | 9927 |
| 220H-1a | NYE & YOUMANS/DEALERS/ IN/GROCERIES/& CROCKERY/ FOND DU LAC,/WIS. | 1128 | C | PL | R2 | 9929 |

| 220I-1a | A.T. PERKINS/CITY/BAKERY,/ FOND DU LAC,/WIS. | A.T.PERKINS/MANUFACTURER/ OF/CRACKERS/AND/ CONFECTIONARY. | C | PL | R6 | 9931 |
| 220I-2a | Same | 1082 | C | PL | R6 | 9932 |

WISCONSIN-Continued

NUMBER	OBVERSE	REVERSE	METAL	EDGE	RARITY	H&G

FOND DU LAC 220-Continued

| 220J-1a | PERKINS & SMITH/DEALERS/IN/STOVES/AND/TINWARE/FOND DU LAC/WIS. | 1089 | C | PL | R6 | 9934 |
| 220J-2a | Same | 1303 | C | PL | R6 | 9935 |

| 220K-1a | C.J. PETTIBONE & CO./DRYGOODS/HOUSE,/FOND DU LAC,/WIS. | BOOTS,/SHOES/AND/YANKEE/NOTIONS. | C | PL | R5 | 9938 |
| 220K-2a | Same | 1082 | C | PL | R6 | 9937 |

220L-1a	A. RAYMOND/GROCER,/FOND DU LAC/WIS.	1080	C	PL	R6	9940
220L-2a	Same	1168	C	PL	R5	9941
220M-1a	T.S. WRIGHT/CHEMIST/AND/DRUGGIST,/FONDULAC,/WIS. (NOTE: Incorrect spelling of Fond du Lac)	T.S. WRIGHT/BOOKS/STATIONERY.	C	PL	R4	9943

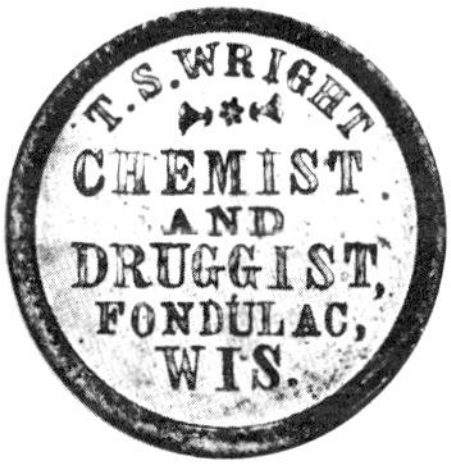

527

WISCONSIN-Continued

NUMBER	OBVERSE	REVERSE	METAL	EDGE	RARITY	H&G

GENESEE STATION 235

| 235A-1a | D.L. EDWARDS/DRY/GOODS &/ GROCERIES/GENESEE/ STATION,/WIS. | 1107 | C | PL | R9 | |

GREEN BAY 250

250A-1a	A. DETRICH/DEALER/IN/ GROCERIES,/PROVISIONS,/ LIQUORS & C./GREEN BAY,/ WIS.	1127	C	PL	R3	9945
250A-2a	Same	1128A	C	PL	R9	
250B-1a	HOFFMAN & LEWIS/ MERCHANT/TAILORS,/ GREEN BAY,/WIS.	1127	C	PL	R6	9947
250B-1b	Same	Same	BR	PL	R9	9948

| 250C-1a | A. KIMBOLL./DEALER/ IN/HARDWARE/ GREENBAY/WIS. | 1084 | C | PL | R5 | 9950 |
| 250C-1b | Same | Same | BR | PL | R9 | |

528

WISCONSIN-Continued

NUMBER	OBVERSE	REVERSE	METAL	EDGE	RARITY	H&G

GREEN BAY 250-Continued

| 250D-1a | PHILIPP KLAUS, / YANKEE NOTIONS / AND / TOYS, / GREEN BAY / WIS. | 1089 | C | PL | R6 | 9952 |

| 250E-1a | DRS RHODE & HICKS / EAGLE / DRUG / STORE, / GREEN BAY/ WIS. | 1316 | C | PL | R7 | 9954 |

250F-1a	F.R. SCHETTLER / DEALER / IN / HARDWARE / GREEN BAY, / WIS.	1004	C	PL	R2	9956
250F-1b	Same	Same	BR	PL	R9	
250F-2a	Same	1085	C	PL	R9	
250F-3a	Same	1171	C	PL	R4	9958
250F-4a	Same	1228	C	PL	R4	9957
250F-5a	Same	1229	C	PL	R8	

WISCONSIN-Continued

NUMBER	OBVERSE	REVERSE	METAL	EDGE	RARITY	H&G

GREEN BAY 250-Continued

| 250G-1a | SAM. STERN/MERCHANT/ TAILOR/& DEALER IN/ CLOTHING,/GREEN BAY,/ WIS. | 1387 | C | PL | R7 | 9960 |
| 250H | Z.Z. ST. LEWIS - See 250I as this is a die-cutting error. | | | | | |

250I-1a	J.J. ST LOUIS/DEALER/ IN/HARDWARE/GREEN BAY/ WIS.	1168	C	PL	R8	9966
250I-2a	Same	1169	C	PL	R10	
250I-3a	Same	1387	C	PL	R7	9967

250I-4a	Z.Z. ST LEWIS,/DEALER/IN/ HARDWARE/GREEN BAY,/ WIS. (NOTE: This is a die cutting error)	1168	C	PL	R5	9962
250I-4b	Same	Same	BR	PL	R9	
250I-5a	Same	1346	C	PL	R6	9963
250I-6a	Same	1387	C	PL	R6	9964
250I-6ao	Same, struck over itself	Same	C	PL	R10	
250I-6b	Same	Same	BR	PL	R9	

WISCONSIN-Continued

NUMBER	OBVERSE	REVERSE	METAL	EDGE	RARITY	H&G

HALES CORNER 270

| 270A-1a | J. SIEGEL/DRY GOODS/ &/GROCERIES./HALES CORNER | 1194 | C | PL | R3 | 9968 |

JANESVILLE 300

300A-1a	E.S. BARROWS./SEEDS/ &/FARMING/TOOLS/ JANESVILLE, WIS	STOVES, HARDWARE, IRON & C. encircling a plow	C	PL	R4	9970
300A-1b	Same	Same	BR	PL	R9	9971
300A-1f	Same	Same	S	PL	R10	
300B-1a	L.R. CARSWELL/ CONFECTIONERY/TOYS &/ GROCERIES/JANESVILLE/ WIS.	1106	C	PL	R6	9973

531

WISCONSIN-Continued

| NUMBER | OBVERSE | REVERSE | METAL | EDGE | RARITY | H&G |

JANESVILLE 300-Continued

300C-1a	CHAPMANS ONE PRICE STORE./ encircling LAPPINS/BL'K/ JANESVILLE WIS.	DRYGOODS. CLOTHING, BOOTS & SHOES encircling HATS/& CAPS/GROCERIES/& C./AT/ LOW PRICES.	C	PL	R5	9975
300C-2a	Same	1111	C	PL	R9	
300C-3a	Same	1205	C	PL	R9	9976
300C-4a	Same	1207	C	PL	R6	9977

| 300D-1a | E. CONNELL & CO / GROCERIES/LIQUORS/ LIME &/ WOOD/ JANESVILLE, WIS. | 1106 | C | PL | R5 | 9979 |

| 300D-2a | E. CONNELL & CO./ GROCERIES/LIQUORS/ LIME & WOOD,/ JANESVILLE,/WIS. (NOTE: | Same | C | PL | R9 | 9980 |
| 300D-3a | Same | Existence doubtful) 1127 | C | PL | R5 | 9981 |

532

WISCONSIN-Continued

NUMBER	OBVERSE	REVERSE	METAL	EDGE	RARITY	H&G

JANESVILLE 300-Continued

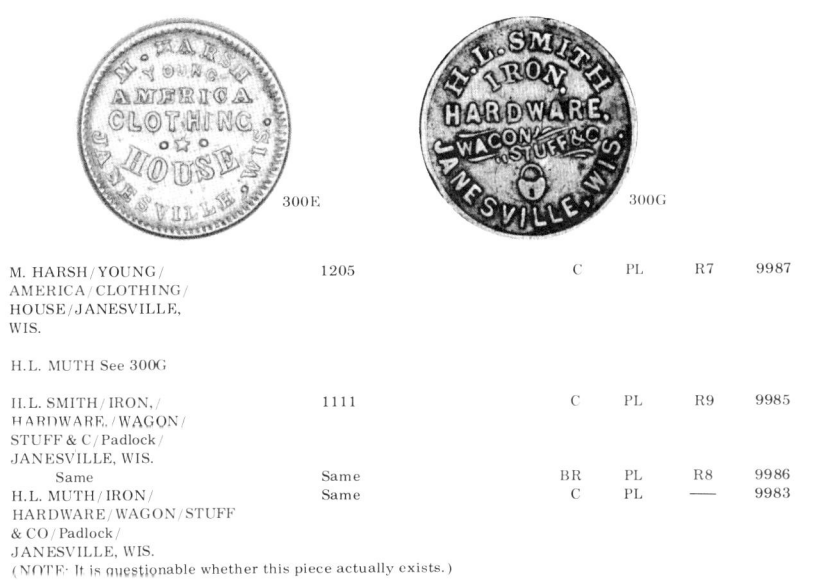

300E-1a	M. HARSH/YOUNG/ AMERICA/CLOTHING/ HOUSE/JANESVILLE, WIS.	1205	C	PL	R7	9987
300F	H.L. MUTH See 300G					
300G-1a	H.L. SMITH/IRON,/ HARDWARE./WAGON/ STUFF & C/Padlock/ JANESVILLE, WIS.	1111	C	PL	R9	9985
300G-1b	Same	Same	BR	PL	R8	9986
300G-2a	H.L. MUTH/IRON/ HARDWARE/WAGON/STUFF & CO/Padlock/ JANESVILLE, WIS.	Same	C	PL	—	9983

(NOTE: It is questionable whether this piece actually exists.)

JEFFERSON 310

310A-1a	PHILIP JOHNSON,/DRUGS/ PAINTS OILS/BOOKS,/ STATIONERY & C./JEFFERSON,/ WIS.	1316	C	PL	R6	9989
310B-1a	JOHN JUNG,/DRY GOODS/ GROCERIES &/HARDWARE/ JEFFERSON,/WIS.	1226	C	PL	R3	9991

533

WISCONSIN-Continued

NUMBER	OBVERSE	REVERSE	METAL	EDGE	RARITY	H&G

JEFFERSON 310-Continued

310C-1a	J.F.W. MEYER/GROCERIES/ PROVISIONS/&/NOTIONS,/ JEFFERSON, WIS.	1088	C	PL	R4	9993
310D-1a	D. OSTRANDER/GROCER/&/ INSURANCE/AGT./ JEFFERSON, WIS.	1298	C	PL	R6	9995
310E-1a	S. STEINHART/DRYGOODS/ &/GROCERIES/JEFFERSON/ WIS.	1337	C	PL	R6	9997

JUNEAU 320

320A-1a	S.H. COLEMAN/DEALER/IN/ DRYGOODS/JUNEAU./WIS.	1122	C	PL	R8	9999
320A-2a	S.H. COLEMAN/DEALER/IN/ DRYGOODS/JUNEAU/MICH.	Same	C	PL	R8	4414
320A-2b	Same	Same	BR	PL	R9	

(NOTE: The Michigan variety is a die-cutting error.)

534

WISCONSIN-Continued

NUMBER	OBVERSE	REVERSE	METAL	EDGE	RARITY	H&G

KENOSHA 330

| 330A-1a | N.A. BROWN'S/CREAM/ALE/STOCK PORTER/&/KENNET/KENOSHA, WIS. | 1105 | C | PL | R8 | 10001 |
| 330A-2a | Same | 1108 | C | PL | R7 | 10002 |

330B-1a	GERKEN & ERNST/DEALERS/IN/GROCERIES/&/PROVISIONS/KENOSHA/WIS.	1095	C	PL	R8	10006
330B-2a	Same	1105	C	PL	R7	10004
330B-3a	Same	1357	C	PL	R8	10005
330B-4a	Same, different spacing	1094	C	PL	R7	10007

330C-1a	HOHN SIMMONS & CO./BOOTS/SHOES &/LEATHER/KENOSHA. WIS.	1106	C	PL	R4	10008-a
330D-1a	LYMAN MOWRY & CO /BOOTS,/SHOES,/LEATHER,/KENOSHA/WIS.	1106	C	PL	R7	10008-c
330D-2a	LYMAN MOWRY & CO./BOOTS/SHOES/ &/LEATHER/KENOSHA/WIS.	1110	C	PL	R7	10008-d

WISCONSIN-Continued

NUMBER	OBVERSE	REVERSE	METAL	EDGE	RARITY	H&G

KILBOURN CITY 340 (WISCONSIN DELLS)

| 340A-1a | J.E. DIXON & SONS/DRY/ GOODS./GROCERIES,/BOOTS/ &SHOES/KILBOURN CITY./ WJS. (NOTE: The mis-spelling of WIS.) | 1205 | C | PL | R7 | 10008-g |

| 340B-1a | T. HOFMANN/barrel in center/ KYLBOURN CITY. WIS. (NOTE: The mis-spelling of KILBOURN) | 1194 | C | PL | R7 | 10008-i |

LA CROSSE 360

| 360A-1a | MONS. ANDERSON/ DEALER/IN/DRY GOODS/ CLOTHING,/BOOTS, SHOES/ &C./LA CROSSE, WIS. | 1280 | C | PL | R6 | 10009 |
| 360A-1b | Same | Same | BR | PL | R8 | 10009-a |

536

WISCONSIN-Continued

NUMBER	OBVERSE	REVERSE	METAL	EDGE	RARITY	H&G

LA CROSSE 360-Continued

360A-2a	MONS. ANDERSON/ DEALER/IN/DRY GOODS/ CLOTHING/BOOTS, SHOES/ & C./LA CROSSE, WIS.	1281	C	PL	R6	10010
360A-3a	Same, different spacing	Same	C	PL	R6	
360B-1a	GEO. E. STANLEY/LA CROSS/ WIS./1863	1321	C	PL	R6	10012
360B-1b	Same (NOTE: Mis-spelling of LA CROSSE)	Same	BR	PL	R8	10013

MADISON 410

| 410A-1a | JAS. FR. BODTKER/ MADISON./WIS./ PHOTOGRAPHER | 1205 | C | PL | R7 | 10016 |
| 410A-2a | Same | 1357 | C | PL | R7 | 10015 |

WISCONSIN-Continued

| NUMBER | OBVERSE | REVERSE | METAL | EDGE | RARITY | H&G |

MADISON 410-Continued

| 410B-1a | EMIGRANTEN/OFFICE/ KING ST./MADISON,/WIS. | THE ONLY/NORWEIGEN/ NEWS PAPER/PUBLISHED/ IN/AMERICA. | C | PL | R3 | 10018 |
| 410B-1d | Same (H-R 2078) | Same | C-N | PL | R10 | |

| 410C-1a | R.K. FINDLAY & CO./ DRUGGISTS/AND/GROCERS,/ MADISON,/WIS. | THE CELEBRATED/TEA/ ESTABLISHMENT. | C | PL | R6 | 10021 |
| 410C-2a | Same | 1310 | C | PL | R6 | 10020 |

| 410D-1a | S. KLAUBER & CO./DRYGOODS/ CLOTHING/&/FURNISHING/ GOODS,/MADISON,/WIS. | 1169 | C | PL | R4 | 10023 |
| 410E-1a | HUNTLEY & STEENSLAND/ GROCERIES/AND/CROCKERY/ MADISON,/WIS. | 1083 | C | PL | R2 | 10025 |

538

WISCONSIN-Continued

NUMBER	OBVERSE	REVERSE	METAL	EDGE	RARITY	H&G

MADISON 410-Continued

| 410F-1a | J.J. LAWRENCE/GROCERIES/ CROCKERY/&/GLASSWARE/ 17/KING ST./MADISON WIS. | 1222 | C | PL | R4 | 10027 |
| 410F-1b | Same | Same | BR | PL | | R10 |

410G-1a	MADISON BREWERY/ MANFR. OF/LAGER BEER/STOCK/&/CREAM ALE	J. RODERMUND/horse pulling wagon with 3 barrels/ MADISON,/WIS. (Obv of 410G-4)	C	PL	R5	10038
410G-2a	Same	J. RODERMUND/horse pulling wagon with 4 barrels/ MADISON,/WIS. (Obv of 410G-5)	C	PL	R7	10039
410G-3a	Same	1390	C	PL	R8	10029

410G-4d	J. RODERMUND/horse pulling wagon with 3 barrels/ MADISON,/WIS.	1105	C-N	PL	R10	
410G-5a	J. RODERMUND/horse pulling wagon with 4 barrels/ MADISON,/WIS.	1357	C	PL	R8	10041
410G-6a	Same	1390	C	PL	R9	10042

WISCONSIN-Continued

NUMBER	OBVERSE	REVERSE	METAL	EDGE	RARITY	H&G

MADISON 410-Continued

410H-1a	BUY/YOUR/MEAT/OF/ E. NEWCOMB/MAIN/ST./ MADISON, WIS.	1169	C	PL	R4	10031
410I-1a	GEORGE V. OTT/MANFR & DEALER/IN/LEATHER/ HIDES & C./TANNERY/ MADISON. WIS.	1205	C	PL	R3	10033
410J-1a	RAMSAY & CAMPBELL/STOVES,/ TIN,/IRON &/FARMING/ TOOLS/MADISON,/WIS.	1332	C	PL	R3	10035
410J-1d	Same (H-R 2079)	Same	C-N	PL	R10	
410K-1a	J. RODERMUND/DEALER/ IN/DRY GOODS/& GROCERIES/ MADISON./WIS.	1105	C	PL	R7	10037

540

WISCONSIN-Continued

NUMBER	OBVERSE	REVERSE	METAL	EDGE	RARITY	H&G

MADISON 410-Continued

410L-1a	CAPITOL STEAM BREWERY/ BY WM. VOIGHT/MNFR. OF/ALE/LAGER/BEER/ MADISON/WIS.	1205	C	PL	R6	10045
410L-2a	Same	1209	C	PL	R6	10046
410L-3a	Same	1357	C	PL	R6	10044

MANITOWOC 420

420A-1

420A-4

420A-1a	W.H. HORN/PRODUCE/ DEALER./MANITOWOC	1174	C	PL	R7	10048
420A-1b	Same	Same	BR	PL	R7	10049
420A-1d	Same	Same	C-N	PL	R9	10050
420A-1e	Same	Same	W-M	PL	R7	10051
420A-2a	Same	1194	C	PL	R4	10057
420A-3a	Same	1272	C	PL	R8	10053
420A-3b	Same	Same	BR	PL	R9	10054
420A-3d	Same	Same	C-N	PL	R9	10055
420A-3e	Same	Same	W-M	PL	R9	10056
420A-4a	W.H. HORN/PRODUCE/ DEALER,/MANITOWOC.	1194	C	PL	R4	10057

WISCONSIN-Continued

NUMBER	OBVERSE	REVERSE	METAL	EDGE	RARITY	H&G

MANITOWOC 420-Continued

420B-1

420B-4

420B-1a	STUCKE & CO./PRODUCE/ DEALERS/MANITOWOC, WIS.	1174	C	PL	R9	10059
420B-1b	Same	Same	BR	PL	R9	10060
420B-1d	Same	Same	C-N	PL	R9	10061
420B-1e	Same	Same	W-M	PL	R9	10062
420B-2a	Same	1194	C	PL	R4	10068
420B-3b	Same	1220	BR	PL	R9	10064
420B-3d	Same	Same	C-N	PL	R10	10065
420B-3e	Same	Same	W-M	PL	R10	10066
420B-4a	STUCKE & CO./PRODUCE/ DEALER/MANITOWOC, WIS.	1194	C	PL	R2	10070

MARSHALL 435

435A-1

435A-1a1

435B

435A-1a	I. LIVINGSTON/DRY GOODS/ GROCERIES/& C./MARSHALL. WIS.	1194	C	PL	R8	10072
435A-1a1	Same	Same (Part of the obverse is incused in reverse design)	C	PL	R10	
435A-2a	Same - (Letter spacing is different also "C" of "& C" has a serif)	Same	C	PL	R9	
435B-1a	G.W. VOSBURGH/HARDWARE,/ STOVES,/ & TIN./MARSHALL, WIS.	1194	C	PL	R5	10074

542

WISCONSIN-Continued

NUMBER	OBVERSE	REVERSE	METAL	EDGE	RARITY	H&G

MAUSTON 450

| 450A-1a | D. CAMPBELL/HARDWARE/ &/GROCERIES/MAUSTON/ WIS. | 1107 | C | PL | R7 | 10076 |

MAYFIELD 460

460A-1a	E. WIRTH/DEALER/IN/DRY GOODS,/GROCERIES,/ CLOTHING,/HATS,/& C./ MAYFIELD. WIS.	1174	C	PL	R8	10078
460A-1b	Same	Same	BR	PL	R8	10079
460A-1d	Same	Same	C-N	PL	R0	10080
460A-1e	Same	Same	W-M	PL	R8	10081
460A-2a	Same	1194	C	PL	R6	10088
460A-3a	Same	1220	C	PL	R8	10083
460A-3b	Same	Same	BR	PL	R8	10084
460A-3c	Same	Same	N	PL	R10	10085
460A-3d	Same	Same	C-N	PL	R8	10086
460A-3e	Same	Same	W-M	PL	R10	10087

WISCONSIN-Continued

NUMBER	OBVERSE	REVERSE	METAL	EDGE	RARITY	H&G

MILWAUKEE 510

510A     510A-2

| 510A-1a | E. ASCHERMANN & CO./ Indian on pony/MILWAUKEE | CIGARS & TOBACCO/ WHOLESALE/&/RETAIL/ 274/WEST WATER ST. | C | PL | R5 | 10090 |

(NOTE: This piece is also struck on an oversized planchet 21½mm)

510A-1a1	Same	Same	C	R	R8	
510A-1b	Same	Same	BR	PL	R9	10091
510A-1d	Same	Same	C-N	PL	R9	10092
510A-2a	Same	Incuse of obverse 510A-1	C	PL	R10	10094

510B-1     510B-2

| 510B-1a | WISCONSIN BREWERY/ beer keg/CH. BAST | MILWAUKEE/six pointed star with beer mug in center/ 18 on the left side of star 63 on right/WISCONSIN | C | PL | R5 | 10096 |
| 510B-2a | Same | Similiar to 510B-1 except an oakleaf appears to the left of 18 and to the right of 63 | C | PL | R10 | 10097 |

| 510C-1a | PHILIP BEST/mug of beer/ 1863/LAGERBEER | EMPIRE BREWERY/beer keg with brewers tools of the trade/ MARR/MILWAUKEE | C | PL | R2 | 10099 |

(NOTE: This piece is also struck on a thin planchet.)

544

WISCONSIN-Continued

NUMBER	OBVERSE	REVERSE	METAL	EDGE	RARITY	H&G

MILWAUKEE 510-Continued

510C-1a1	Same	Same	C	R	R8	
510C-1b	Same	Same	BR	PL	R8	10100
510C-1d	Same	Same	C-N	PL	R9	10101
510C-1do	Same, over cent	Same	C-N	PL	R9	

| 510D-1a | BEST & CO's./beer keg/ BEER HALL | BEER OR CASH/5/MIL./ MARKET STREET | C | PL | R9 | 10103 |

(NOTE: This is a very crude piece and it is doubtful that it is of Civil War origin.)

510E-1a	V. BLATZ/figure of King Gambrinus holding glass of beer/LAGER BEER	CITY BREWERY/&/MALT HOUSE./1863/MILWAUKEE.	C	PL	R2	10105
510E-1b	Same	Same	BR	PL	R9	10107
510E-2a	Incuse of reverse	Same	C	PL	R9	10114

| 510E-3a | Same as 510E-1 | Same inscription but different letter spacing | C | PL | R9 | |

WISCONSIN-Continued

NUMBER	OBVERSE	REVERSE	METAL	EDGE	RARITY	H&G

MILWAUKEE 510-Continued

| 510F-1a | M. BODDEN/MILWAUKEE,/ WISCONSIN. | 1194 | C | PL | R4 | 10110 |
| 510F-2a | Same | 1220 | C | PL | R4 | 10109 |

CITY BREWERY-See Michigan 370F

| 510H-1a | A.J. COOPER/LUMBER/ YARD./EAST WATER ST./ N. OF WALKERS PT/ BRIDGE,/MILWAUKEE. | 1194 | C | PL | R5 | 10116 |
| 510H-2a | Same | Obverse die incused | C | PL | R9 | 10117 |

510I-1a	D. J. DOORNINK/BEEHIVE/ 1863/MILWAUKEE	GROCERIES/&/DRY GOODS./ COR. OF 10TH/&/CHERRY ST.	C	PL	R5	10119
	(NOTE: This piece is also struck on an oversized planchet (21½mm)					
510I-1a1	Same	Same	C	R	R8	
510I-1b	Same	Same	BR	PL	R9	
510I-1d	Same	Same	C-N	PL	R9	
510I-1do	Same, over C-N cent	Same	C-N	PL	R10	
510I-2a	Same	Obverse die incused	C	PL	R9	10120

546

WISCONSIN-Continued

NUMBER	OBVERSE	REVERSE	METAL	EDGE	RARITY	H&G

MILWAUKEE 510-Continued

| 510J-1a | A.H. FILNER,/CORNER/OF 7TH &/SHERMAN/STREET,/MILWAUKEE. | GROCERIES &/KEGELBAHN/PROVISIONS | C | PL | R9 | 10122 |
| 510J-1a1 | Same | Same | C | R | R8 | 10123 |

| 510K-1a | JOSEPH FISCHBEIN/AGT./315./WEST/WATER ST./MILWAUKEE/WIS. | STOVES & HARDWARE./center design consists of axe, shovel, hammer and a saw with the words DON'T DESPAIR on the blade/1863 | C | PL | R9 | 10125 |
| 510K-2a | Same | STOVES, HARDWARE./center design consists of a pick, hammer, shovel and saw with the words DON'T DESPAIR on the blade/1863 | C | PL | R9 | 10128 |

(NOTE: The 3 in the address has been re-cut over a 1.)

| 510K-3a | Same | GROCERIES,/PROVISIONS/DRY GOODS/1863. | C | PL | R5 | 10126 |
| 510K-3a1 | Same | Same | C | R | R6 | |

547

WISCONSIN-Continued

NUMBER	OBVERSE	REVERSE	METAL	EDGE	RARITY	H&G

MILWAUKEE 510-Continued

510L-1a	WM FRANKFURTH./bust of Indian in headdress/ MILWAUKEE, WIS.	Same as reverse of 510K-1	C	PL	R2	10130
510L-1a1	Same	Same	C	R	R5	
510L-2a	Same	Blank	C	PL	R8	10131
510L-2a1	Same	Blank	C	R	R9	
510L-3a	Same	Same as Rev of 510K-2	C	PL	R9	

| 510M-1a | GOES & FALK/three barrels/ 18 on one side and 63 on the other/MILWAUKEE. (NOTE: This piece is also struck on a thin planchet) | WISCONSIN/MALT HOUSE/ &/BAVARIA/BREWERY | C | PL | R2 | 10133 |

| 510N-1a | GOLL & FRANK'S/RETAIL STORE/319/THIRD ST./ MILWAUKEE./J.H. HANTZSCH AGT. | DRY GOODS,/FANCY/GOODS,/ YANKEE/NOTIONS,/FEATHERS/ ETC. | C | PL | R5 | 10135 |

WISCONSIN-Continued

NUMBER	OBVERSE	REVERSE	METAL	EDGE	RARITY	H&G

MILWAUKEE 510-Continued

510O-1a	C.E. GRAFF/DEALER/IN/ ALL KINDS OF/MACHINERY./ MILWAUKEE, WIS	1174	C	PL	R8	10137
510O-1b	Same	Same	BR	PL	R8	10138
510O-1d	Same	Same	C-N	PL	R8	10139
510O-1e	Same	Same	W-M	PL	R8	10140
510O-2a	Same	1194	C	PL	R4	10151
510O-2b	Same	Same	BR	PL	R9	10152
510O-2d	Same	Same	C-N	PL	R9	10153
510O-2e	Same	Same	W-M	PL	R9	10154
510O-3a	Same	1220	C	PL	R8	10142
510O-3b	Same	Same	BR	PL	R8	10143
510O-3d	Same	Same	C-N	PL	R9	10144
510O-3e	Same	Same	W-M	PL	R9	10145
510O-4b	Same	1272	BR	PL	R8	10147
510O-4d	Same	Same	C-N	PL	R8	10148
510O-4f	Same	Same	S	PL	R10	10149
510P-1a	HAMBACH,/MILWAUKEE	1194	C	PL	R5	10156
510P-2a	C. HAMBACH./COR./ HURON &/JEFFERSON/ STS./MILWAUKEE.	Same	C	PL	R6	10158

(NOTE: This piece is also struck on a thin planchet)

510Q-1a	T.W. HART,/SUPT.	M.W.M./PLANK ROAD/ COMPANY.	C	PL	R8	10160

(NOTE: There is no definite proof that this piece is of Civil War vintage or that it was issued in Milwaukee. M.W.M (Milwaukee, Watertown, Madison). (Atwood 511A)

549

WISCONSIN-Continued

NUMBER	OBVERSE	REVERSE	METAL	EDGE	RARITY	H&G

MILWAUKEE 510-Continued

510R-1a	CH. HERMANN & CO./crossed brooms behind a jug/1863/ MILWAUKEE	BROOM &/STONE/WARE/ FACTORY./318/EAST WATER ST.	C	PL	R6	10173
510R-1a1	Same	Same	C	R	R8	
510R-2a	Same	1174	C	PL	R9	10175
510R-2b	Same	Same	BR	PL	R8	10176
510R-2d	Same	Same	C-N	PL	R9	10177
510R-2e	Same	Same	W-M	PL	R8	10178
510R-3a	Same	1220	C	PL	R9	10180
510R-3b	Same	Same	BR	PL	R9	10181
510R-3d	Same	Same	C-N	PL	R9	10182
510R-3e	Same	Same	W-M	PL	R9	10183
510R-4a	Same	1272	C	PL	R8	10185
510R-4b	Same	Same	BR	PL	R8	10186
510R-4d	Same	Same	C-N	PL	R9	10187
510R-4e	Same	Same	W-M	PL	R9	10188
510R-4eo	Same	Same	W-M	PL	R10	

(NOTE: This piece is struck over a 160/417 Patriotic Token.)

| 510R-5a | Same inscription only "&" is smaller. | Same | C | PL | R8 | 10172 |

| 510S-1a | GEO. KANE/DEALER/ IN/FINE FAMILY/ GROCERIES/No 10./ SPRING ST./MILWAUKEE. | 1194 | C | PL | R5 | 10190 |
| 510T-1a | THRESHING/MACHINE/ WORKS/KIRBY/LANGWORTHY/ & CO/MILWAUKEE/WIS. | 1108 | C | PL | R6 | 10192 |

WISCONSIN-Continued

| NUMBER | OBVERSE | REVERSE | METAL | EDGE | RARITY | H&G |

MILWAUKEE 510-Continued

510U-1a	A. KLEINSTEIBER/1863/Lady's hat and flowers/MILWAUKEE	MILLINERY/&/FANCY GOODS/ 5TH/BETW:POPLAR/&/ CHESTNUT ST.	C	PL	R3	10194
	(NOTE: This piece is also struck on thick and thin planchets)					
510U-2a	Same	Blank	C	PL	R9	10195
510U-3a	Same	CARL PAESCHKE./DRY GOODS/STORE FOND DU LAC./ROAD/ MILWAUKEE - Incused	C	PL	R10	

(NOTE: This piece is struck on an oversize planchet - 21½mm.)

510V-1a	CHAS.KLEINSTEUBER/ 18 mans bust 63/MECHANIC.	SMALL MACHINERY,/MODELS,/ ENGRAVING,/STENCIL = / CUTTING./NO. 24/TAMARACK ST./MILWAUKEE.	C	PL	R4	10197
	(NOTE: This piece is also struck on a thin planchet (1½mm) as compared to the regular (2¼mm) and thick 2¾mm.)					
510V-1e	Same	Same	W-M	PL	R9	10199
	(NOTE: It is doubtful whether this piece actually exists with the 1863 date. Miller lists a piece in white metal dated 1867.)					
510V-1f	Same	Same	S	PL	R9	
510V-2a	Same	Obverse die incused	C	PL	R9	10200
510V-3a	Same	Obverse die incused, multiple strike (see photo)	C	PL	R10	

WISCONSIN-Continued

NUMBER	OBVERSE	REVERSE	METAL	EDGE	RARITY	H&G

MILWAUKEE 510-Continued

| 510W-1a | H. KURT/GROCER/COR.OF/ HANOVER & /FLORIDA ST./ MILWAUKEE. | 1194 | C | PL | R4 | 10203 |
| 510W-1b | Same | Same | BR | PL | R8 | 10204 |

| 510X-1a | LOUIS KURZ/PICTORIAL/ LITHOGRAPHER/ MILWAUKEE. | 1194 | C | PL | R6 | 10207 |
| 510X-2a | Same | 1220 | C | PL | R6 | 10206 |

510Y-1

510Y-3

510Y-1a	A. LEDERER & CO./DRY/ GOODS/COR/E. WATER/ &/MICHIGAN/STS./ MILWAUKEE.	1095	C	PL	R7	10211
510Y-2a	Same	1106	C	PL	R7	10209
510Y-3a	A. LEDERER & CO./DRY/ GOODS/COR/E. WATER/ &/MICHIGAN/STS./ MILWAUKEE	1108	C	PL	R5	10210
510Y-4a	Same	1212	C	PL	R7	10212

WISCONSIN-Continued

NUMBER	OBVERSE	REVERSE	METAL	EDGE	RARITY	H&G

MILWAUKEE 510-Continued

| 510Z-1a | M.C. MEYER/M.G.B. PL.ROAD/MILWAUKEE. | 1194 | C | PL | R4 | 10214 |

510AA-1a	A. MILLER & CO./PRODUCE/ &/COMMISSION/MILWAUKEE. WIS.	1174	C	PL	R8	10216
510AA-1b	Same	Same	BR	PL	R9	10217
510AA-1d	Same	Same	C-N	PL	R10	10218
510AA-1e	Same	Same	W-M	PL	R8	10219
510AA-2a	Same	1194	C	PL	R6	10232

510AA-3a Rev

510AA-3a	Same	Obverse die incused	C	PL	R9	10220
510AA-4a	Same	1220	C	PL	R8	10222
510AA-4b	Same	Same	BR	PL	R8	10223
510AA-4d	Same	Same	C-N	PL	R8	10224
510AA-4e	Same	Same	W M	PL	R9	10225
510AA-5a	Same	1272	C	PL	R9	10227
510AA-5b	Same	Same	BR	PL	R9	10228
510AA-5c	Same	Same	N	PL	R10	10229
510AA-5d	Same	Same	C-N	PL	R10	10230

WISCONSIN-Continued

NUMBER	OBVERSE	REVERSE	METAL	EDGE	RARITY	H&G

MILWAUKEE 510-Continued

510AB-1a	FRIEDRICH MILLER/18-Barrel containing tools of the trade and heads of barley-63/LAGERBEER	PLANKROAD/BREWERY,/ MILWAUKEE.	C	PL	R3	10234
510AB-1b	Same	Same	BR	PL	R8	10235
510AB-1e	Same	Same	W-M	PL	R10	
510AB-2a	Same	Blank	C	PL	R9	10236
510AB-3ao	Same	Same	C	PL	R9	
	(Struck over various patriotic tokens, so far 44/350 and 209/414 have been listed.)					
510AB-4b	Same	1/GLAS	BR	PL	R8	10238

| 510AB-5b | FRIEDRICH MILLER/Barrel with various tools of the trade and heads of barley/LAGER BEER/incused Struck on a large (24½mm) thin (1mm) planchet (NOTE: This piece was most likely struck in the 1880's) | 1/QUART | BR | PL | R10 | |

| 510AC-1a | F. MITZLAFF/GROCER./ MILWAUKEE | 1194 | C | PL | R4 | 10240 |
| 510AC-1b | Same | Same | BR | PL | R9 | 10241 |

WISCONSIN-Continued

NUMBER	OBVERSE	REVERSE	METAL	EDGE	RARITY	H&G

MILWAUKEE 510-Continued

| 510AD-1a | MOSSIN & MARR/ENGRAVERS/ MILWAUKEE. | 1220 | C | PL | R4 | 10243 |

510AE-1a	CARL PAESCHKE./DRY GOODS/ STORE/FOND DU LAC/ROAD/ MILWAUKEE.	DRY GOODS,/GROCERIES/ PROVISIONS.	C	PL	R6	10246
510AE-1a1	Same	Same	C	R	R6	10245
510AE-2a	Same	GROCERIES,/PROVISIONS/ DRY GOODS/1863.	C	PL	R5	10248
	(NOTE: This piece is also struck on a thin planchet)					
510AE-2a1	Same	Same	C	R	R8	10247
510AE-3a	Same	1194	C	PL	R7	10250
510AE-3b	Same	Same	BR	PL	R9	
510AE-4a	Same	1220	C	PL	R8	10249

| 510AF-1a | PLANER & KAYSER'S/SEWING/ MACHINE./COR. OF/MAIN & MASON/ST'S./MILWAUKEE WIS. | 1194 | C | PL | R4 | 10252 |

555

WISCONSIN-Continued

NUMBER	OBVERSE	REVERSE	METAL	EDGE	RARITY	H&G

MILWAUKEE 510-Continued

510AG-1a	J. PRITZLAFF & CO. / Stove / NO 303. 3D ST. / MILWAUKEE	HARDWARE, / IRON, / NAILS, GLASS, / & STOVES. / 1863.	C	PL	R7	10255
	(NOTE: This piece is also struck on a thin planchet)					
510AG-1a1	Same	Same	C	R	R4	10254
510AG-1b	Same	Same	BR	PL	R9	10256

510AH   510AI

| 510AH-1a | J. SCHEIDHAUER / MANUFACTURER / OF / SOAP / & / CANDLES. / MILWAUKEE, WIS. | 1194 | C | PL | R5 | 10258 |
| 510AH-1b | Same | Same | BR | PL | R9 | |

| 510AI-1a | J.B. SCHRAM / WHOLESALE / GROCER. / MILWAUKEE | 1194 | C | PL | R3 | 10260 |
| | (NOTE: This piece is also struck on a thin planchet) | | | | | |

510AJ-1   510AJ-3

510AJ-1a	SEVERN & JONES / PRODUCE / & / COMMISSION / MILWAUKEE, WIS.	1194	C	PL	R5	10262
510AJ-2a	Same	1195	C	PL	R9	
510AJ-3a	Same	Obverse die incused	C	PL	R9	10263

WISCONSIN-Continued

NUMBER	OBVERSE	REVERSE	METAL	EDGE	RARITY	H&G

MILWAUKEE 510-Continued

		510AK-1		510AK-2			
510AK-1a	C.T. STAMM & SON / STOVES. / TIN / & HARDWARE / REED / ST. / MILWAUKEE	1108	C	PL	R7	10265
510AK-2a	C.T. STAMM & SON / STOVES / TIN, / & HARDWARE. / REED / ST. / MILWAUKEE Different spacing	1194	C	PL	R5	10266
510AK-2b	Same	Same	BR	PL	R9	10267

| 510AL-1a | A.H. STEINMANN / GROCERIES / DRY GOODS / & / MILLINERY. / CORNER OF 11 & / GALENA ST. / MILWAUKEE. | 1194 | C | PL | R3 | 10269 |

| 510AM-1a | D. STOFFEL / GROCERIES / & / PROVISIONS / 7TH / STREET / MILWAUKEE. | 1194 | C | PL | R4 | 10271 |

WISCONSIN-Continued

NUMBER	OBVERSE	REVERSE	METAL	EDGE	RARITY	H&G

MILWAUKEE 510-Continued

510AN-1a	FRIEDRICH THIELE/MEAT/ MARKET.	1194	C	PL	R6	10274
510AN-2a	Same	1220	C	PL	R6	10273
	(NOTE: This piece is also struck on a thin planchet)					
510AN-2d	Same	Same	C-N	PL	R10	

510AO-1e	I. TELLER,/MILWAUKEE.	1174	W-M	PL	R9	10276
510AO-2a	Same	1194	C	PL	R4	10279
510AO-2b	Same	Same	BR	PL	R9	
510AO-3a	Same	Obverse die incused	C	PL	R9	10277
	(NOTE: The "R" has been re-cut over an "E")					
510AO-4a	I. TELLEE,/MILWAUKEE.	1194	C	PL	R7	10280
	(NOTE: This is a die-cutting error. Neither teller or tellee are listed in the Milwaukee City directories for the war years.)					

510AP-1a	H. UPMEYER/JEWELLER/ MILWAUKEE.	1155	C	PL	R3	10281
	(NOTE: This piece is also struck on a thin planchet)					
510AP-1a1	Same	Same	C	R	R8	
510AP-1b	Same	Same	BR	PL	R9	10282
510AP-2ao	Same	Same	C	PL	R10	
	(NOTE: Struck over 1833 large cent)					
510AP-3a	Same	Obverse incused	C	PL	R9	

558

WISCONSIN-Continued

NUMBER	OBVERSE	REVERSE	METAL	EDGE	RARITY	H&G

MILWAUKEE 510-Continued

NUMBER	OBVERSE	REVERSE	METAL	EDGE	RARITY	H&G
510AP-4a	H. UPMEYER/JEWELLER/ 258/W. WATER ST./MILWAUKEE	1155	C	PL	R5	10284
510AP-4b	Same	Same	BR	PL	R9	10285
510AP-5a	Same	1156	C	PL	R8	10287
510AP-5a1	Same	Same	C	R	R9	

510AQ-1a	HERMANN VOIGHT./1863./ Stove/MILWAUKEE.	STOVES/&/TINWARE/ 329./WEST WATER ST.	C	PL	R4	10291
510AQ-1a1	Same	Same	C	R	R8	
510AQ-1b	Same	Same	BR	PL	R9	
510AQ-1d	Same	Same	C-N	PL	R9	
510AQ-1do	Same, Struck over CN cent	Same	C-N	PL	R9	

WISCONSIN-Continued

NUMBER	OBVERSE	REVERSE	METAL	EDGE	RARITY	H&G

NEENAH 520

520A-1a	JOHN HUNT/GROCERIES/ & PROVISIONS,/NEENAH,/WIS.	McCABE/CORAL/MILLS,/ MANASH,/WIS.	C	PL	R4	10294
520B-1a	C.W. LEAVENS & CO./ GROCERIES/NEENAH,/WIS.	1316	C	PL	R3	10296

NEWBURG 530

530A-1a	FRANCKENBURG & KELLER/ DEALERS/IN/DRY GOODS/ GROCERIES/HARD = / WARE./NEWBURG, WIS.	1194	C	PL	R6	10298

WISCONSIN-Continued

NUMBER	OBVERSE	REVERSE	METAL	EDGE	RARITY	H&G

NEW LISBON 540

540A 540B

| 540A-1a | J. RAMSEY/DRY/GOODS/ GROCERIES/& GENERAL/ MERCHANDIZE/NEW LISBON, WIS. | 1205 | C | PL | R8 | 10300 |
| 540B-1a | L.C. WESCOTT/DEALER/IN/ HARDWARE/STOVES &/ AGRICULTURAL/IMPLEMENTS/ NEW LISBON, WIS. | 1107 | C | PL | R7 | |

NORTH PRAIRIE 550

550A 550B 550C

550A-1a	W.H. BOGARDUS/DEALER/IN/ DRY GOODS,/GROCERIES/ HARD = /WARE/ NORTH PRAIRIE	1194	C	PL	R5	10302
550B-1a	J. REMINGTON/SONS./DRY/ GOODS &/GROCERIES/NORTH/ PRAIRIE/WIS.	1106	C	PL	R8	10304
550C-1a	J. SMART/STEAM/FLOURING &/ PLANING/MILLS/NORTH PRAIRIE. WIS.	1205	C	PL	R7	10306

561

WISCONSIN-Continued

| NUMBER | OBVERSE | REVERSE | METAL | EDGE | RARITY | H&G |

OCONOMOWOC 590

590A-1a   MRS. J. TATE/MILLINER/   1174   C   PL   R9   10308
OCONOMOWOC.
(NOTE: This is a die-cutting error, as newspaper ads of the period list her as Mrs. S.J. Tate.)

OCONTO CO. 600

600A-1   NO PHOTO AVAILABLE   600A-2

600A-1a   STILES GANG MILLS/DEALER/   1194   C   PL   R4   10310
IN/LUMBER,/LATH,/&/
SHINGLES./OCONTO CO. WIS.
600A-2a   Same   Obverse die incused   C   PL   R9   10311
(NOTE: This piece was probably issued in Stiles,
a village in Oconto Co.)

OSHKOSH 620

620A-1a   CITY HOTEL/G. BOCK/   THE NEAREST/HOTEL/TO/   C   PL   R6   10315
PROPRIETOR/OSHKOSH./   THE/STEAM BOAT/LANDING/
WIS.   FERRY ST.

WISCONSIN-Continued

NUMBER	OBVERSE	REVERSE	METAL	EDGE	RARITY	H&G

OSHKOSH 620-Continued

620B-1a	JOS. BOLES,/MERCHANT TAILOR/AND/DEALER IN/CLOTHING,/OSHKOSH,/WIS.	1337	C	PL	R3	10313
620C-1a	FRAKER BRO'S./DEALERS/IN/BOOTS & SHOES/51 FERRY ST./OSHKOSH,/WIS.	FRAKER BRO'S./DEALERS/IN/LEATHER,/HIDES,/WOOL & FURS.	C	PL	R3	10317
620D-1a	ANDREW HABEN & CO./DEALERS/IN/CLOTHING/OSHKOSH,/WIS.	1178	C	PL	R8	10320
620D-2a	Same	1181	C	PL	R8	10321
620D-3a	Same	1222	C	PL	R6	10319
620D-4a	Same	1337	C	PL	R9	10322
620E-1a	HASBROUCK & FANCHER/DEALERS/IN/STOVES &/TIN WARE,/OSHKOSH,/WIS.	1300	C	PL	R3	10324

563

WISCONSIN-Continued

NUMBER	OBVERSE	REVERSE	METAL	EDGE	RARITY	H&G

OSHKOSH 620-Continued

620F-1a	HAY & CLARK/DEALERS/ IN/HARDWARE/OSHKOSH/ WIS.	1178	C	PL	R5	10326
620F-2a	Same	1181	C	PL	R7	10327
620G-1a	JAENICKE & KLOTZSCH/ MANUFACTURERS/&/ DEALERS/IN/LEATHER/ HIDES/& C./OSHKOSH, WIS.	1194	C	PL	R4	10329
620H-1a	KELLOGG & HUGHES/ DRYGOODS/OSHKOSH,/ WIS.	1127	C	PL	R3	10331
620H-1b	Same	Same	BR	PL	R8	10332

564

WISCONSIN-Continued

NUMBER	OBVERSE	REVERSE	METAL	EDGE	RARITY	H&G

OSHKOSH 620-Continued

620I-1a	LEVY & DUNCAN,/DEALERS/ IN/CLOTHING/OSHKOSH,/ WIS.	1082	C	PL	R9	10334
620I-2a	Same	1125	C	PL	R9	10335
620I-3a	Same	1127	C	PL	R8	10336
620I-4a	Same	1128	C	PL	R6	10337
620I-5a	Same	1171	C	PL	R6	
620I 6a	Same	1346	C	PL	R9	10338

| 620J-1a | LINES & RUSSELL/HARNESS/ MAKERS,/OSHKOSH,/WIS. | SADDLERY/HARDWARE | C | PL | R3 | 10340 |

| 620K-1a | A. NEFF/DEALER/IN HARDWARE/GROCERIES & C/OSHKOSH,/WIS. | 1300 | C | PL | R3 | 10342 |

565

WISCONSIN-Continued

NUMBER	OBVERSE	REVERSE	METAL	EDGE	RARITY	H&G

OSHKOSH 620-Continued

620L-1a	S.B & J.A. PAIGE/ GROCERS/OSHKOSH/ WIS.	1084	C	PL	R8	10344
620L-1b	Same	Same	BR	PL	R9	
620L-2a	Same	1087	C	PL	R9	10345
620L-3a	Same	1178	C	PL	R5	10346
620M-1a	H. RANS,/DEALER/IN/ CLOTHING,/OSHKOSH/ WIS.	1082	C	PL	R9	
620M-2a	Same	1084	C	PL	R10	10348
620M-3a	Same	1127	C	PL	R5	10349
620M-4a	Same	1128	C	PL	R7	10350
620M-5a	Same	1130	C	PL	R7	10351
620N-1a	B.H. SOPER,/DEALER/IN/ FURNITURE/OSHKOSH,/ WIS.	1082	C	PL	R4	10353
620N-2a	Same	1127	C	PL	R9	10354
620N-3a	Same	1169	C	PL	R6	10355
620 O-1a	ALLEN VOSBURG & CO./ MUSIC/STORE/OSHKOSH, WIS.	STEINWAY'S/PIANOS,/ SMITH'S/MELODEONS/ &/TREMOLO/HARMONIUMS.	C	PL	R4	10357
620P-1a	WM L. WILLIAMS/CHEMIST/ AND/DRUGGIST/43 FERRY ST/OSHKOSH./WIS.	1123	C	PL	R9	
620P-2a	Same	1127	C	PL	R6	10359
620P-2b	Same	Same	BR	PL	R9	
620P-3a	Same	1130	C	PL	R9	

566

WISCONSIN-Continued

NUMBER	OBVERSE	REVERSE	METAL	EDGE	RARITY	H&G

PORTAGE CITY 660

| 660A-1a | T.M. McMILLAN/GROCERIES/ &/CROCKERY./PORTAGE/ CITY./WIS. | 1205 | C | PL | R7 | 10361 |

PORT WASHINGTON 680

| 680A-1a | J. DRUECKER/DEALER/IN/ DRY GOODS,/GROCERIES,/ CLOTHING,/HATS,/& C./ PORT WASHINGTON WIS. | 1194 | C | PL | R5 | 10362 |

RACINE 700

| 700A-1a | J.I. CASE & CO./THRASHING/ MACHINE/MANUFACTURERS/ RACINE, WIS. | 1205 | C | PL | R9 | 10364 |

WISCONSIN-Continued

NUMBER	OBVERSE	REVERSE	METAL	EDGE	RARITY	H&G

RACINE 700-Continued

700A-2a	J.I. CASE & CO./THRASHING/MACHINE/MANFR'S./RACINE, WIS.	1098	C	PL	R4	10367
700A-3a	Same	1105	C	PL	R8	10366
700A-4a	Same	1203	C	PL	R9	

700B-1a	J. CLOUGH/FINE/FAMILY/GROCERIES./NUTS/&C/RACINE. WIS	1095	C	PL	R7	10371
700B-2a	Same	1105	C	PL	R5	10369
700B-3a	Same	1108	C	PL	R8	10370
700B-3b	Same	Same	BR	PL	R10	

700C-1a	JOHN ELKINS/DEALER/IN/WATCHES./JEWELRY./PIANOS/& C./RACINE,WIS	1101	C	PL	R6	10377
700C-2a	Same	1105	C	PL	R7	10373
700C-3a	Same	1106	C	PL	R6	10374
700C-4a	Same	1110	C	PL	R6	10376
700C-5a	Same	1205	C	PL	R8	10375

568

WISCONSIN-Continued

NUMBER	OBVERSE	REVERSE	METAL	EDGE	RARITY	H&G

RACINE 700-Continued

700D-1   700D-2

| 700D-1a | F. ELMLINGER/MERCHANT/ TAILOR/RACINE, WIS. | 1106 | C | PL | R6 | 10379 |
| 700D-2a | Same, different spacing | Same | C | PL | R6 | 10379 |

700E-1a	J.W. ENGLISH/TRUNK/&/ HARNESS/DEALER/COR. MAIN & 3D ST./RACINE, WIS	1105	C	PL	R5	10381
700E-2a	Same	1206	C	PL	R9	10382
700E-3a	Same	1207	C	PL	R7	10383
700E-3g	Same	Same	L	PL	R10	

| 700F-1a | ERHARDT & RAPS/ AUCTIONEERS/RACINE. WIS. (NOTE: This piece is also struck on a thick planchet) | 1220 | C | PL | R3 | 10385 |
| 700F-1b | Same | Same | BR | PL | R9 | |

569

WISCONSIN-Continued

NUMBER	OBVERSE	REVERSE	METAL	EDGE	RARITY	H&G

RACINE 700-Continued

700G

700H

700G-1a	THOS. FALVEY/MANFR'R/ OF/REAPERS &/MOWERS./ RACINE/WIS.	1101	C	PL	R6	10391
700G-2a	Same	1105	C	PL	R5	10387
700G-3a	Same	1106	C	PL	R7	10388
700G-4a	Same	1110	C	PL	R6	10390
700G-5a	Same	1390	C	PL	R8	10389
700H-1a	D.H.JONES/STAPLE &/FANCY/ DRY GOODS/136/MAIN ST./ RACINE, WIS.	1105	C	PL	R6	10393
700H-2a	Same	1108	C	PL	R7	10395
700H-3a	Same	1110	C	PL	R9	10396
700H-4a	Same	1205	C	PL	R7	10394

700I

700J

700I-1a	J. & H. MILLER/DEALERS/IN/ BOOTS/&/SHOES/RACINE. WIS.	1105	C	PL	R7	10397
700I-2a	Same	1110	C	PL	R8	10399
700I-3a	Same	1203	C	PL	R7	10398
700J-1a	THELEN & DIETERICH/ DEALERS/IN/DRY/GOODS/&/ GROCERIES/RACINE./WIS.	1108	C	PL	R7	10402
700J-2a	Same	1357	C	PL	R7	10401

570

WISCONSIN-Continued

NUMBER	OBVERSE	REVERSE	METAL	EDGE	RARITY	H&G

RIPON 720

720A-1a	GREENWAY & CO'S/ RESTAURANT/&/BILLIARD/ ROOMS/RIPON, WIS.	GREENWAY'S/IMMENSE/ CONCERT/HALL/RIPON,/ WIS./SEATS 1000 PEOPLE	C	R	R8	10404
720A-1b	Same	Same	BR	R	R8	10405
720A-1i	Same	Same	Z	R	R9	10406
720A1il	Same	Same	Z	PL	R9	
720A-2a	Same	1042	C	R	R9	
720A-3a	Same	1046	C	R	R8	10408
720A-4a	Same	1047	C	R	R8	
720A-5d	Same (Kreisberg 10/66 Lot 833)	1069	C-N	R	R10	
720A-6a	GREENWAY'S/IMMENSE/ CONCERT/HALL/RIPON./ WIS./SEATS 1000 PEOPLE (Same as rev of 720A-1)	1046	C	R	R8	10410
720A-6d	Same	Same	C-N	R	R9	

SAUK CITY 770

| 770A-1a | C. NEBEL/STEAM/MILLS/ SAUK CITY, WIS. | 1194 | C | PL | R3 | 10412 |
| 770A-2a | Same | Obverse die incused | C | PL | R9 | |

571

WISCONSIN-Continued

NUMBER	OBVERSE	REVERSE	METAL	EDGE	RARITY	H&G

SHEBOYGAN 790

790A-1a	TROWBRIDGE'S/WATCH/ CLOCK/&/JEWELRY/STORE/ SHEBOYGAN, WIS.	1047	C	R	R9	10414
790A-1d	Same	Same	C-N	R	R10	
790A-2a	Same	1319	C	PL	R10	
790A-2a1	Same	Same	C	R	R8	10416
790A-2b	Same	Same	BR	R	R9	10417
790A-2i	Same	Same	Z	R	R9	10418

SPARTA 830

| 830A-1a | HAMILTON & CO./GROCERS/ SPARTA,/ WIS. | 1107 | C | PL | R5 | 10421 |

| 830B-1a | W.S. NEWTON/DEALER/ IN/ HARDWARE/&/STOVES/ SPARTA, WIS. | 1107 | C | PL | R6 | 10422 |

572

WISCONSIN-Continued

| NUMBER | OBVERSE | REVERSE | METAL | EDGE | RARITY | H&G |

STOUGHTON 860

860A 860B 860C

860A-1a	T.P. CAMP/WATCH/MAKER,/ STOUGHTON/WIS.	1320	C	PL	R7	10423
860A-2b	Same	Blank	BR	PL	R9	10424
860A-2d	Same	Same	C-N	PL	R10	
860B-1a	DEARBOURN/&/ROOT/ GROCERS/STOUGHTON/ WIS.	1222	C	PL	R6	10425
860C-1a	H. PETERSON/DRYGOODS/ CLOTHING/BOOTS SHOES/ & C./STOUGHTON, WIS.	1181	C	PL	R3	10427

TOMAH 890

890A 890B

| 890A-1a | EATON & BARNS/DEALER/ IN/DRY GOODS,/GROCERIES/ & C./TOMAH. WIS. | 1194 | C | PL | R6 | 10429 |
| 890B-1a | WM. RUNKEL/DEALER/IN/ DRY/GOODS/& C./TOMAH & NEW LISBON | 1194 | C | PL | R3 | 10431 |

573

WISCONSIN-Continued

NUMBER	OBVERSE	REVERSE	METAL	EDGE	RARITY	H&G

TWO RIVERS 900

900A-1a   R. SUETTINGER/MANUFACT'R/ & DEALER/IN/STORES, TIN &/ SHEETIRON/WARE./TWO RIVERS, WIS.   1194   C   PL   R4   10433

WATERLOO 915

915A-1a   PH. CARPELES & CO. DRY-/GOODS/&/GROCERIES./ WATERLOO, WIS   1168   C   PL   R10   10435

(NOTE: It's extremely doubtful that this combination even exists. It was first listed by H&G)

915A-2a   Same   1194   C   PL   R4   10436

WATERTOWN 920

920A-1a   H. BELLACK/DRYGOODS/ GROCERIES &/PROVISIONS/ WATERTOWN,/WIS.   1168   C   PL   R3   10438

WISCONSIN-Continued

NUMBER	OBVERSE	REVERSE	METAL	EDGE	RARITY	H&G

WATERTOWN 920-Continued

920B-1a	BERTRAM & CO./BOOTS & SHOES/SIGN/OF THE/MAMMOTH/BOOT,/WATERTOWN, WIS.	1317	C	PL	R4	10440
920C-1a	CORDES & PLATZ/DRY GOODS/GROCERIES &/LIQUORS,/WATERTOWN,/WIS	1084	C	PL	R3	10442
920C-1b	Same	Same	BR	PL	R9	

920D-1a	T. DERVIN/DRY GOODS,/GROCERIES/&/CLOTHING/WATERTOWN WIS.	1174	C	PL	R8	10444
920D-1b	Same	Same	BR	PL	R8	10445
920D-1d	Same	Same	C-N	PL	R8	10446
920D-1do	Same, over CN cent	Same	C-N	PL	R10	
920D-1e	Same	Same	W-M	PL	R8	10447
920D-2a	Same	1194	C	PL	R4	10457
920D-3a	Same	1220	C	PL	R6	10449
920D-3b	Same	Same	BR	PL	R8	10450
920D-3d	Same	Same	C-N	PL	R8	10451
920D-3e	Same	Same	W-M	PL	R10	10452
920D-4b	Same	1272	BR	PL	R8	10454
920D-4d	Same	Same	C-N	PL	R8	10455
920E-1a	PATRICK DUFFY/GROCER /WATERTOWN, WIS.	1194	C	PL	R5	10459

575

WISCONSIN-Continued

NUMBER	OBVERSE	REVERSE	METAL	EDGE	RARITY	H&G

WATERTOWN 920-Continued

| 920F-1a | FISCHER & ROHR / CLOTHIERS / WATERTOWN / WIS. | 1194 | C | PL | R4 | 10461 |

920F-2a	FISCHER & ROHR / READY / MADE / CLOTHING, / 35 MAIN ST. / WATERTOWN, / WIS.	1342	C	PL	R5	10463
920F-2d	Same (H-R 2085)	Same	C-N	PL	R10	
920F-3a	Same	Blank	C	PL	R9	10464

920G-1a	W.C. FOUNTAIN, / DRUGS / PAINTS OILS / BOOKS, / STATIONERY & C. / WATERTOWN, / WIS.	1316	C	PL	R6	10465
920G-1b	Same	Same	BR	PL	R8	10466
920G-2a	Same	1323	C	PL	R7	10468
920G-2b	Same	Same	BR	PL	R8	10469

576

WISCONSIN-Continued

NUMBER　　OBVERSE　　　　　　　REVERSE　　　　　　METAL　EDGE　RARITY　H&G

WATERTOWN 920-Continued

NUMBER	OBVERSE	REVERSE	METAL	EDGE	RARITY	H&G
920H-1a	CHAs GOELDNER,/MUSICAL/ INSTRUMENTS/AND/ NOTIONS,/WATERTOWN/ WIS.	1091	C	PL	R6	10471
920H-2a	Same	1323	C	PL	R6	10472
920H-2b	Same	Same	BR	PL	R8	10473
920H-3a	Same	1341	C	PL	R8	10474
920H-4a	CHAs GOELDNER/MANUFR/ OF/HARNESS/CHILDRENS / CARRIAGES /& C /WATERTOWN, WIS.	Same	C	PL	R5	10476
920H-4b	Same	Same	BR	PL	R9	
920H-4d	Same	Same	C-N	PL	R10	

920I-1a	JOHN HEYMANN/OYSTER/ RESTAURANT/&/BEER HALL./ WATERTOWN, WIS.	1194	C	PL	R4	10478
920J-1a	DANIEL KUSEL/HARDWARE/ WATERTOWN, WIS. (NOTE: This piece is also struck on a thin planchet)	1194	C	PL	R3	10480
920J-1b	Same	Same	BR	PL	R9	
920K-1a	J MOULTON/GROCERIES/ FLOUR & FEED/WATERTOWN/ WIS.	1088	C	PL	R4	10482

577

WISCONSIN-Continued

NUMBER	OBVERSE	REVERSE	METAL	EDGE	RARITY	H&G

WATERTOWN 920-Continued

| | | 920L | | | | |
| | | 920M | | | | |

920L-1a	THEODORE RACEK,/ RESTAURANT/ WATERTOWN,/WIS.	1295	C	PL	R3	10484
920L-1b	Same	Same	BR	PL	R8	10485
920M-1a	GOOD FOR ONE GLASS BEER/ T. RACEK/WATERTOWN/ WIS.	1356	C	PL	R9	10487
920M-1b	Same (NOTE: This piece probably doesn't exist in copper)	Same	BR	PL	R8	

WAUKESHA 930

| | 930A | 930B | 930C | | | |

930A-1a	CHARLES CORK/GROCERIES/ CROCKERY/& NOTIONS/ WAUKESHA,/WIS.	1127	C	PL	R7	10488
930B-1a	J.A. DUNBAR/GROCERIES/ PROVISIONS/FRUITS/& C./WAUKESHA, WIS.	1127	C	PL	R6	10490
930C-1a	H.W. SHERMAN AGT./DRY GOODS/HATS,/CAPS AND/ GROCERIES,/WAUKESHA,/ WIS.	1317	C	PL	R7	10492

WISCONSIN-Continued

| NUMBER | OBVERSE | REVERSE | METAL | EDGE | RARITY | H&G |

WHITEWATER 960

960A-1a	GALLT & COLE / DRY / GOODS. / GROCERIES. / BOOTS & / SHOES & C / WHITEWATER, WIS	1111	C	PL	R5	10494
960A-2a	Same	1115	C	PL	R9	10496
960A-3a	Same - Different Spacing	1128	C	PL	R8	10495
960B-1a	J.S. LATHROP, / GROCERIES / AND / PROVISIONS / WHITEWATER / WIS.	1128	C	PL	R4	10497
960C-1a	J.T. SMITH / JEWELER / WHITEWATER / WIS.	1320	C	PL	R5	10499
960C-1d	Same (H-R 2088)	Same	C-N	PL	R10	
960C-2a	Same	1321	C	PL	R5	10500
960D-1a	DR. VAN VALKENBURGH / DRUGGIST / AND / GROCER, / WHITEWATER, / WIS.	1310	C	PL	R5	10502
960D-2a	Same	1316	C	PL	R6	10503
960E-1a	A. WAHLSTEDT / DRYGOODS / GROCERIES. / AND / LIQUORS, / WHITEWATER / WIS.	1084	C	PL	R6	10505
960E-2a	A. WAHLSTEDT / DRY / GOODS / GROCERIES / & / LIQUORS / WHITEWATER, WIS	1111	C	PL	R4	10506

NON-LOCALS

Sutler Types. **NOTE:** Although there are over 400 varieties of Sutler tokens, we list only those tokens with actual Civil War store card dies, which limits the list considerable. Most of these are rarer than the usual Sutler pieces. For details on the series, see J. I. Curto & M. M. Schwartz, **The Numismatist Volume 59** August, September and December, 1946. Tokens listed are referred to as (C & S.)

NUMBER	OBVERSE	REVERSE	METAL	EDGE	RARITY
NL-1a	J.W.CRUIKSHANK./5/CENTS/ 81ST/REG.O.V.I. (C & S 64)	1290	C	PL	R-7
NL-1b	Same (C & S 64a)	Same	BR	PL	R-9
NL-2a	J.W.CRUIKSHANK/10/CENTS./ 81/REG.O.V.I. (C & S 65)	1295	C	PL	R-7
NL-2b	Same (C & S 65a)	Same	BR	PL	R-8
NL-3a	J.W.CRUIKSHANK/10 CENTS/ 81/REG'T.O.V.I. (C & S 65½) (This description may not be accurate as piece has not been seen.)	1346	C	PL	R-8
NL-4a	Very similar to NL-2, but 25 instead of 10 (C & S 66)	1176	C	PL	R-7
NL-4b	Same (C & S 66a)	Same	BR	PL	R-8
NL-5a	J.W.CRUIKSHANK./5/CENTS/ REG.O.V.I. Note:81st obliterated by cutting into die - (C & S 63)	1295	C	PL	R-7
NL-7b	GOOD/FOR 10 CTS/IN GOODS/ AT/SUTLERS/STORE/A.H. DAVIS.W.L.M. REG.45.ILL.V. (C & S 70) (Size 20.5 mm)	CHILDS MANUFACTURER CHICAGO. Head in center facing left	BR	PL	R-7
NL-8b	Similar, but for 25 cents (Size 25 mm) (C & S 71)	CHILDS MANUFACTURER/ CHICAGO. Eagle in glory, head facing left in center	BR	PL	R-8

(NOTE: The piece listed as C & S 69 might be similar to NL-7b, with reverse 594 in brass, but it has not been seen, and we feel the description as such might be in error. If it exists, it will be listed as NL-6b.)

580

NON-LOCAL-Continued

NUMBER	OBVERSE	REVERSE	METAL	EDGE	RARITY
	NL-9	NL-10			NL-11
NL-9a	G.W.FORBES/SUTLER/5/CENTS 23 D.O.U.S.A. (C & S 87)	1168	C	PL	R-7
NL-10a	Similar, but 10 instead of 5 (C & S 88)	1295	C	PL	R-7
NL-11a	Similar, but 25 instead of 5 (C & S 89)	1084	C	PL	R-7

NL-12b	SUTLER CHECK/REDEEMED/IN/ GOODS TO/SOLDIERS/ONLY/BY/ WM,H.JONES (C & S 143)	1391	BR	R	R-7
NL-12ba	Same (C & S 143a)	Same	BR	PL	R-9
NL-13b	Same (C & S 144)	1394	BR	R	R-8
NL-13ba	Same (C & S 144a)	Same	BR	PL	R-9
NL-14b	Same (C & S 145)	1399	BR	R	R-8
NL-14ba	Same (C & S 145a)	Same	BR	PL	R-9
NL-15b	Same (C & S 146)	1404	BR	R	R-8
NL-15ba	Same (C & S 146a)	Same	BR	PL	R-8

NL-16a	SIMMONDS/BATTERY/ SUTLER/J.M.KERR (C & S 151)	1391	C	R	R-7
NL-16b	Same (C & S 151a)	Same	BR	R	R-8
NL-16i	Same (C & S 151b)	Same	Z	R	R-9
NL-17a	Same (C & S 152)	1394	C	R	R-7

581

NON-LOCAL-Continued

NUMBER	OBVERSE	REVERSE	METAL	EDGE	RARITY
NL-17b	Same (C & S 152a)	Same	BR	R	R-8
NL-17i	Same (C & S 152b)	Same	Z	R	R-9
NL-18a	Same (C & S 153)	1399	C	R	R-7
NL-18b	Same (C & S 153a)	Same	BR	R	R-8
NL-18i	Same (C & S 153b)	Same	Z	R	R-9
NL-19a	Same (C & S 154)	1404	C	R	R-7
NL-19b	Same (C & S 154a)	Same	BR	R	R-8
NL-19i	Same (C & S 154b)	Same	Z	R	R-9

NUMBER	OBVERSE	REVERSE	METAL	EDGE	RARITY
NL-20a	GOOD FOR/5/CENTS/21ST. KY.V.I (C & S 341)	1166	C	PL	R-7
NL-21a	Similar except "10" instead of "5" (C & S 342)	1295	C	PL	R-7
NL-22a	Similar except "25" instead of "5" (C & S 343)	1084	C	PL	R-9

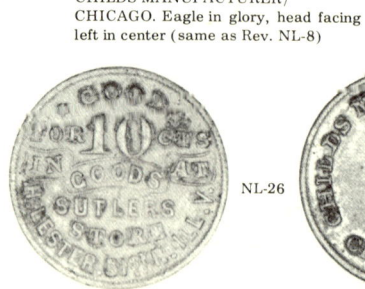

NUMBER	OBVERSE	REVERSE	METAL	EDGE	RARITY
NL-23b	GOOD/FOR 10 CTS/IN GOODS AT/SUTLERS/STORE/R.R. LANDON,1ST R.U.S.M.F. (C & S 163 Size 20.5mm)	CHILDS MANUFACTURER CHICAGO. around head facing left in center (same as Rev. NL-7)	BR	PL	R-8
NL-24b	Similar but "25" instead of "10" (C & S 164 - Size 25mm)	CHILDS MANUFACTURER/ CHICAGO. Eagle in glory, head facing left in center (same as Rev. NL-8)	BR	PL	R-9

582

NON-LOCAL-Continued

NUMBER	OBVERSE	REVERSE	METAL	EDGE	RARITY
NL-25b	GOOD/FOR 5 CTS/IN GOODS AT/SUTLERS/STORE/H.LESTER 51ST R.ILL.V. (C & S 175)	1390	BR	PL	R-8
NL-26b	Similar but "10" instead of "5" (C & S 176 - Size 20.5mm)	CHILDS MANUFACTURER/ CHICAGO. around head facing left in center (same as Rev. NL-7)	BR	PL	R-7

| NL-27b | Similar but "25" instead of "5" (C & S 177) Size 25mm. | CHILDS MANUFACTURER/ CHICAGO. around eagle in glory, head facing left in center (same as Rev. NL-8) | BR | PL | R-8 |

(Note: The piece listed in copper as C & S 177a probably doesn't exist. We examined the specimen used for listing and it was tarnished brass.)

| NL-28a | J.M.LONGWELL/SUTLER/ 119/U.S.C.I. (C & S 182) | 1047 | C | R | R-9 |

(Note: The pieces listed as C & S 183 to 5 do not utilize Civil War dies, and are not listed, but admittedly the exclusion is arbitrary.)

| NL-29b | SUTLER CHECK/REDEEMED/IN/ GOODS TO/SOLDIERS/ONLY/BY/ RICE & BYERS (Not in C & S) | 1391 | BR | R | R-9 |

NON-LOCAL-Continued

NUMBER	OBVERSE	REVERSE	METAL	EDGE	RARITY
NL-30b	Same (C & S 236)	1394	BR	R	R-9
NL-31b	Same (C & S 237)	1399	BR	R	R-9
NL-32b	Same (C & S 238)	1404	BR	R	R-9
NL-33b	Same (C & S 239)	Similar to above but ONE/DOLLAR in circle of stars	BR	R	R-9

NL-34

NL-35

NL-34d	Same	Same	C-N	PL	R10
NL-34a	J.B.SPITZER/SUTLER./ 5/CENTS/550.V.I. (C & S 265)	1346	C	PL	R-7
NL-35a	Similar but "10" instead of "5" (C & S 266)	1226	C	PL	R-8
NL-35d	Same	Same	C-N	PL	R10

NL-36

NL-37

NL-36d	Same	Same	C-N	PL	R10
NL-36a	Similar but "25" instead of "5" (C & S 267)	1168	C	PL	R-8
NL-37a	Similar but "50" instead of "5" (C & S 268)	1122	C	PL	R-8
NL-37d	Same	Same	C-N	PL	R10

NL-38

NL-39

| NL-38b | S.WHITED & CO/SUTLERS/ 97' ILL. VOL/GOOD FOR/5/CTS. IN GOODS (C & S 313) | Shield in headed circle | BR | PL | R-8 |
| NL-39a | S.WHITED & CO/SUTLERS/97' ILLS. VOL/GOOD FOR/10/CTS. IN GOODS (C & S 314) | 1009 | C | PL | R-8 |

NON-LOCAL-Continued

NUMBER	OBVERSE	REVERSE	METAL	EDGE	RARITY
NL-40a	Same (C & S 315)	1042	C	R	R-9
	(Note: The reverse is assumed to be as shown, but the piece has not been seen.)				
NL-40b	Same (C & S 315a)	Same	BR	R	R-9
NL-40i	Same (C & S 315b)	Same	Z	R	R-9
	(Note: The piece described as C & S 316 cannot exist as described.)				
NL-41a	Same (C & S 317)	1069	C	R	R-9
NL-41b	Same (C & S 317a)	Same	BR	R	R-9
NL-41d	Same (C & S 317b)	Same	C-N	R	R-10
NL-41i	Same (C & S 317c)	Same	Z	R	R-9
NL-42a	Same (C & S 318)	1393	C	R	R-8
NL-42b	Same (C & S 318a)	Same	BR	R	R-9
NL-42i	Same (C & S 318b)	Same	Z	R	R-9

NL-43b	GOOD/FOR 10 CTS/IN GOODS/ AT/SUTLERS/STORE/SID. WRIGHT 11 TH R. WIS. V. (C & S 321 - Size 20.5mm)	CHILDS MANUFACTURER/ CHICAGO. around head facing left in center (Same as Rev. NL-7)	BR	PL	R-9

NL-44b	Similar but "25" instead of "10" (C & S 322) Size 25mm.	CHILDS MANUFACTURER/ CHICAGO. around eagle in glory, head facing left in center (Same as Rev. NL-8)	BR	PL	R-8

SPECIAL NON LOCAL

Note: This category includes Civil War Tokens where no definite city can be assigned and several other possible pieces that will be discussed later.

Actually several other tokens should probably be listed in this group, but Joseph Barnett attributed those to several towns in his 1944 supplement and we have followed his list. However, in several cases efforts to verify these listings in directories has failed, but this is not conclusive.

The pieces, with the most questionable city attribution include:
1. TOWN BRANCH STORE (listed as East Sagniaw, Mich 280F)
2. A & H (listed as Cleveland, Ohio 175A)
3. BRATTIN (listed as Cleveland, Ohio 175B)
4. JAS. WELF (listed as Cleveland, Ohio 175R)
5. CLARK & CO. (listed as Wikes Barre, Pennsylvania 985A)

Several pieces are listed below, that were speculatively attributed to cities in our previous **Guide to Civil War Store Cards**. These include S. Wilson Chicago, Ill.) and Klare & Friederick's (Cincinnati, Ohio). The first four pieces listed include these two, plus two other similar tokens — all of extreme rarity and all with the same reverse. Possibly all are from the same city.

NUMBER	OBVERSE	REVERSE	METAL	EDGE	RARITY
SNL-1b	T. ADCOCK'S/BILLARD/SALOON/BAR/CHECK (At this time this piece is unique)	1205	BR	PL	R-9
SNL-2a	KLARE & FRIEDRICK'S/BILLIARD/HALL Crossed pool sticks in center Barnett listed as Non-local under 1336)	1205	C	PL	R-9
SNL-3b	SMITH'S BILLIARD/5 CTS./SALOON (At this time this piece is unique)	1205	BR	PL	R-9
SNL-4a	S. WILSON'S/BILLIARD SALOON/BAR/CHECK	1205	C	PL	R-7

(Barnett listed in his supplementary index as Chicago, but didn't describe it in his Chicago listing supplement.)

SPECIAL NON-LOCAL-Continued

NUMBER	OBVERSE	REVERSE	METAL	EDGE	RARITY

SNL-5

SNL-5b RANKIN & GIBBS/GOOD/FOR 25/ 1192 BR R R-8
CENTS/IN GOODS/SAC & FOX
TRADERS
(Note: This token is listed by Curto as #73 in the 1956 **Numismatist** article "Indian and Post Trader Tokens". This and the following three pieces are listed as Civil War tokens since dies are as on Civil War pieces. They might have been struck as late as 1870.)

SNL-6a Similar but "50" instead of "25" Same as Rev SNL-7b — Ohio 165EP C R R-9
(This piece is listed by Barnett in 1943 **Numismatist** as H & G 4720A and in Curto supplement as #72.)

SNL-7b Similar but ONE/DOLLAR Similar to SNL-8, but eagle facing BR R R-7
instead of "25" left - See Rev Ohio 165EP
(Curto 71 Size 23 MM)

SNL 8

SNL-8b DUNLAP & FLORER OSAGE Eagle in field over drums, flags etc. BR R R-6
TRADERS around GOOD FOR/ Same as Rev Ohio 905C
ONE/DOLLAR/IN GOODS
(Curto 65 - Size 23 MM)

SNL-8Ab Similar to preceeding, but lettering Same BR R R-7
spaced differently
(Curto 65a - Size 23MM)

SNL-9b S.B./TEMPEST Five stars above CAMP SHILOH/APRIL/6TH BR PL R-8
& below & 7TH/1862
18MM. This is listed as a Sutler piece by C & S, but it does not resemble any other Sutlers known. It is listed here as a SNL since no other category appears to fit it and the following.)

587

SPECIAL NON-LOCAL-Continued

NUMBER	OBVERSE	REVERSE	METAL	EDGE	RARITY
SNL-10b	Same as Reverse SNL-9b (C & S 282 - 18 MM)	PITTSBURGH LANDING - cannon and flags in center, below 10	BR	PL	R-8
SNL-11b	Same as Obv SNL-9b (C&S 281)	Same as Rev SNL-10b	BR	PL	R8

NON CONTEMPORARY

This category lists tokens using at least on one side a contemporary Civil War token die but clearly having been struck either before 1860 or after 1864.

Some are definitely post Civil War, as by the date on the pieces, others use die work not as contemporary as with the first four tokens listed.

The following tokens, all with the same reverse dies, have always been assumed to be Civil War pieces, and were listed as such even as early as 1863 in the article by Pliney E. Chase. However, they were also in the list of merchant tokens published by the Antiquarian and Numismatic Society of Pennsylvania published in **1859**. Thus they cannot be legitimately called Civil War tokens, but they have been retained in this catalogs master listing and denoted with an asterik. The reverse die in question is H & G die 575 or new die 1368.

The pieces in this list of tokens, probably struck between 1857 and 1858 are as follows:

Illinois Chicago
  150B Barker & Illsley
  150H J. J. Brown
  150M R. H. Countiss
  150P F. N. Dubois
  150Q Edwards
  150S Flagg
  150T Flagg & McDonald
  150V Freedman & Goodkind

150W Freedman, Goodkind & Co.
150X P. Gaffney
150Z C. E. Gerts & Co.
150AD R. Heilbroner
150AE W. A. Hendrie
150AH Judd & Corthell
150AJ F. A. Leavitt
150AQ Oppenhemer & Metzer
150AU W. R. Prentice

150BE W. Treleaven
Iowa, Lyons
  570A Gage Lyall & Keeler
New York, Binghampton
  80A Evans & Allen
  80B Herschman Bros
New York, Buffalo
  105M Reilly's Bazaar

NUMBER	OBVERSE	REVERSE	METAL	EDGE	RARITY
NC-1b	MERCHANTS EXCHANGE/ COLUMBUS/OHIO	10 in a circle of stars	BR	PL	R-9

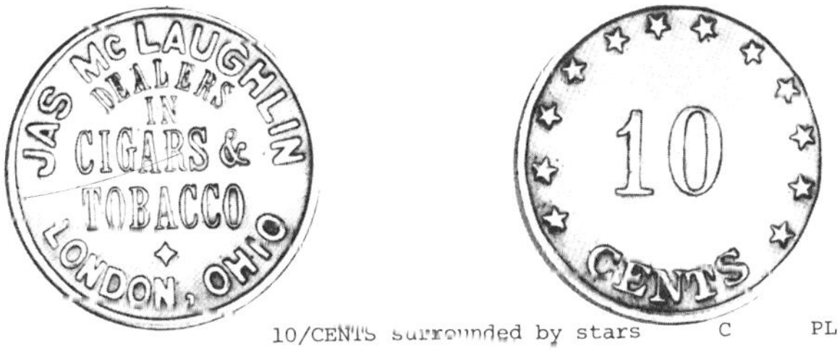

(Formerly H & G 8323, but probably struck about 1870-1875)

| NC-2a | Same | 10/CENTS surrounded by stars | C | PL | R8 |
| NC-2b | JAS McLAUGHLIN/DEALERS/ IN/CIGARS &/TOBACCO/ LONDON,OHIO | 10/CENTS surrounded by stars | BR | PL | R-8 |

(Formerly listed as H & G 8542, but from the die work, this couldn't have been struck before 1875)

| NC-2e | Same | Same | W-M | R | R-8 |
| NC-2f | Same | Same | S | R | R-9 |

589

NON-CONTEMPORARY-Continued

NUMBER	OBVERSE	REVERSE	METAL	EDGE	RARITY
NC-3b	S.C. MARTIN/WOOSTER/OHIO (Formerly listed as H & G 9041, but probably struck well after 1890, and perhaps as late as 1910)	GOOD FOR/5¢/IN TRADE	BR	PL	R-8
NC-4b	COLUMBIA HOTEL/WM/BOCK PROP/JOHNSTOWN PA. (Formerly listed as H & G 9285, but probably struck between 1875 and 1885)	GOOD FOR/5/CENTS/IN TRADE	BR	PL	R-9

Several other pieces are listed in this book that are of questionable vintage but have been left in. Unless evidence as to their contemporary nature is forthcoming, they will be in the next edition.

    ILLINOIS. 290A C VAN DORN, Fairview, Ill.
    INDIANA. 320A MCKEEN & CO, Galveston, Ind.
    INDIANA. 890A FRANK HEINIG, Terre Haute, Ind.
    VIRGINIA. 580A PFEIFFER & CO, Norfolk, Va.

    The latter piece is the subject of some controversy. Certain evidence, presented by David Schenkman in **The Journal of the Civil War Token Society**, Winter, 1970 states that it was not struck until about 1870, but other equally competent writers feel the case is not proven, especially since the spelling of the name in the article referred to by Schenkman is different from that on the token. For the present it will be listed.
    In addition, J. Barnett in his 1943-4 Numismatist supplement listed three pieces, all of which apparently were struck well after 1870, and are not listed in the present work. These are

| NC-5a | C. W. PRESTON/GEN'L./MDSE. DEFIANCE, IOWA. (Barnett listed as H & G 3148a) | GOOD FOR 1¢ IN TRADE | C | PL | R-9 |

590

NON-CONTEMPORARY-Continued

NUMBER	OBVERSE	REVERSE	METAL	EDGE	RARITY
NC-6b	A.E. RYAN/GENERAL MERCHADISE/BARRETT, MINN (Barrett listed as H & G 4635) (The first homestead in Barrett was not until 1868)	GOOD FOR/5/CTS IN TRADE	BR	PL	R-9
NC-7a	ROBT. SMALL/MERCHANT/ COLERAIN (Barrett listed as H & G 4640) NOTE: Colerain wasn't founded until 1905.	PAYABLE AT/ 34 & 35/ CHURCH ST.	C	PL	R-9

| NC-8a | STAMP CUTTER,/DIE SINKER./ AND/MEDALIST./SPRINGFIELD, MASS. (Adams Mass 105) Size 28mm. | Head in center left, above J.A. BOLEN,/1864 | C | PL | R-8 |

This and following have to be assumed to be medals, rather than tokens. Other medals of Bolen probably fell in the 1860-4 category — these are shown as examples.

| NC-9a | Similiar to reverse of NC-8a (Adams Mass. 103) Size 28 mm. | UNITED STATES OF AMERICA/ *LIBERTY* Liberty in rays in center | C | PL | R-9 |
| NC-9f | Same | Same | S | PL | R10 |

| NC-10a | CENTENNIAL ADVERTISING MEDAL CO/1029/CHESTNUT/ST./ PHILADA. (Adams Pa 85, Baker 524) | 1133 | C | PL | R-6 |

This piece, although with Civil War die reverse, was obviously not struck until the middle 1870's, for a company that specialized in tokens & medals in 1876.

NC-10b	Same	Same	BR	PL	R-6
NC-10e	Same (Adams Pa 86)	Same	W-M	PL	R-8
NC-10D1	Same, on trial flan	Same	BR	PL	R8

NON-CONTEMPORARY-Continued

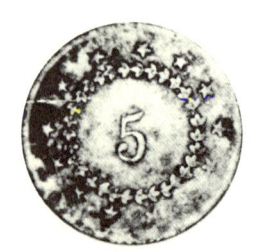

NUMBER	OBVERSE	REVERSE	METAL	EDGE	RARITY
NC-11b	LICENSED/NO(in incused Nos.)/ CINCINNATI, O./18*66	MURDOCK & SPENCER 139/ W FIFTH/STREET/CINCINNATI	BR	PL	R-6

This dog license is listed only to show the date when the reverse die, listed on various Ohio Civil Wars, was still in use, & was used into the '70's.

NC-12b	EUREKA/1867 (Listed as WRIGHT 296)	1391	BR	R	R-8

The actual use of this piece is hypothetical — it may be Eureka, Calif. but this is doubtful. Other denominations probably exist.

NC-13a	EDUARD/FIEDLER	"5" surrounded by wreath	C	PL	R-7

This clearly is related to Ohio 165AP & AQ, although his first name is different. It appears to be of the 1875-1880 vintage.

592

NON-CONTEMPORARY-Continued

NUMBER	OBVERSE	REVERSE	METAL	EDGE	RARITY
NC-14a	J. HENRY GERKE/WATCH MAKER/ AND/JEWELER/1206 PINE ST. PHILA.	NEW MASONIC HALL PHILADELPHIA around building in center	C	PL	R-6

This is obverse of Pa. 750K, but the Masonic temple shown wasn't built until about 1874.

NC-14b	Same	Same	BR	PL	R-6
NC-14e	Same	Same	WM	PL	R-6

NC-15e	FOR/PRESIDENT/GENERAL/ U.S. GRANT/1868 in wreath (DeWitt USG 1868-39)	1151	WM	PL	R-5

This is the original use of die 1151, and undoubtedly all pieces using die 1151 were not struck until 1868. A pure political token.

NC-16a	MASON & CO./1870/COIN & STAMP/DEALERS./1391 NO. 9TH ST PHILA. (Adams Pa 364, Baker 559)	1134	C	PL	R-5

By the date, this piece, using die 1134 was struck in 1870.

NC-16b	Same (Adams Pa 365)	Same	BR	PL	R-6
NC-16e	Same (Adams Pa 363)	Same	WM	PL	R-6

NON-CONTEMPORARY-Continued

NUMBER	OBVERSE	REVERSE	METAL	EDGE	RARITY
NC-17a	MILWAUKEE/1865/SOLDIERS HOME FAIR.	HONOR &/COUNTRY on band	C	PL	R-7

(Soldier's Home Fair was held in June of 1865)

| NC-18a | M.S.C. | Eagle facing left | C | PL | R-4 |

The die resembles dies 1194, and 1195, but was probably struck 1880-1890. See similar die on NC-34.

| NC-19d | C.H. NEEDLES/12 & RACE STS. Gobblet in center (Adams Pa 378) | GOOD FOR ONE/GLASS/OF SODA/WATER | C-N | PL | R-7 |

This piece, although resembling Civil War type, was probably struck during 1858-1860 period.

| NC-19e | Same | Same | WM | PL | R-5 |

594

NON-CONTEMPORARY-Continued

NUMBER	OBVERSE	REVERSE	METAL	EDGE	RARITY

NC-20f   FREE TICKET TO/YANKEE/   S   R   R-8
ROBINSONS/QUADRUPLE-SHOW
Counterstamped on 1854 O half dollar
Probably of the 1869-70 vintage, but if Civil War period, certainly only token (2i) of 50¢ type!!!

NC-21a   GOOD FOR ONE CHANCE/IN/   Fuld Patriotic 113, H&G 94   C   PL   R-3
RAFFLE,/FOR/NUMISMATIC/
BOOKS/AT/A.B. SAGE & CO./
N.Y./NOV. 1859
(Adams NY 762)
Obviously struck in 1859

NC-22e   FOR/PRESIDENT/HORATIO/   1157   WM   PL   R-5
SEYMOUR/1868 in wreath;
(DeWitt HS 1868-11)
A mate to NC-15, and also proof of first use of 1157 die in 1868.

NON-CONTEMPORARY-Continued

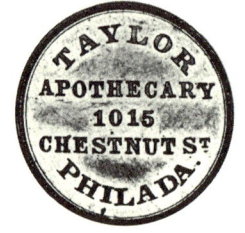

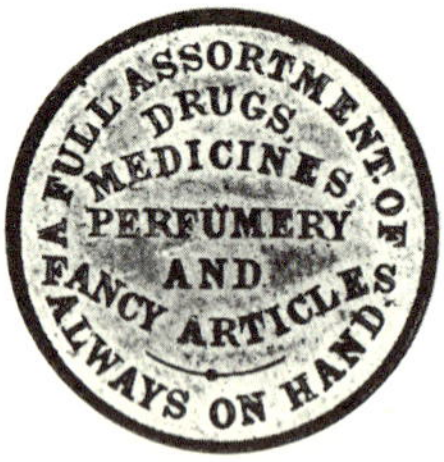

NUMBER	OBVERSE	REVERSE	METAL	EDGE	RARITY
NC-23a	A.B. TAYLOR./SODA WATER/1860/PHILADA./WALNUT & NINTH STS	1182	C	PL	R-9

A mule of 1860 front, and a Civil War die that was often used later - until 1870.
(Adams Pa 506)

NC-23b	Same	Same	BR	PL	R9
NC-23f	Same	Same	S	PL	R10

| NC-24a | TAYLOR/APOTHECARY/1015 CHESTNUT ST/PHILADA. (Adams Pa 512) | A FULL ASSORTMENT OF/DRUGS/MEDICINES/PERFUMERY/AND/FANCY ARTICLES/ALWAYS ON HAND. | C | PL | R-4 |

Another Taylor piece, of non-Civil War type.

| NC-25e | UNION LEAGUE/JULY 4TH/ 1776 1863/PHILADELPHIA. Shield in center inscribed PHILADELPHIA. Size 34mm. | Blank | W-M | PL | R-5 |

An obvious medal of contemporary period, but Barnett called this piece a token.

| NC-25f | Same | Same | S | PL | R-8 |

NOTE: DeWitt lists two other types of this medal: U1861-2 and 1862-3.

596

NON-CONTEMPORARY-Continued

NUMBER	OBVERSE	REVERSE	METAL	EDGE	RARITY
NC-26e	UNION LEAGUE/1863. shield in center (DeWitt U 1862-4) Size 31mm. Same comment as on NC-25.	LANCASTER/PENNA.	W-M	PL	R7

NC-27a	CHAS. K. WARNER./DEALER IN/AMERICAN &./FOREIGN/ COINS/& MEDALS./326 CHESTNUT ST. PHILA. (Adams Pa. 569) Size 25mm. Struck as a mule about 1870.	Fuld Patriotic No. 217	C	PL	R-5
NC-27b	Same	Same	BR	PL	R-5
NC-27e	Same	Same	WM	PL	R-5
NC-28a	Same	Fuld Patriotic No. 479	C	PL	R-5
NC-28b	Same	Same	BR	PL	R-5
NC-28e	Same	Same	WM	PL	R-5
NC-28d	Same	Same	C-N	PL	R9

NC-29a	WHITNEY GLASS WORKS N.J. Jug in center	1182	C	PL	R-9
Another mule, that could not have struck before 1869. (See Adams N.J. 18)					
NC-29e	Same	Same	WM	PL	R-9
NC-29f	Same	Same	S	PL	R-9

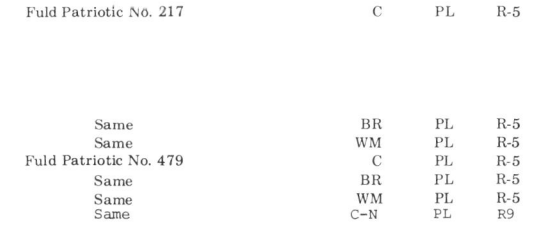

NON-CONTEMPORARY-Continued

NUMBER	OBVERSE	REVERSE	METAL	EDGE	RARITY

NC-30

NC-30ao WOOD CO./BRIDGE/CO. 2½C. C PL R-6
(Atwood Wis 980-A)
These pieces of the 1870 period are generally struck over Civil War tokens, this one being over the Spoot error.
NC-31a Same 10 C. C PL R-8
(Atwood Wis 980B)
NC-32a Same 15 C. C PL R7
(Atwood Wis 980C)
NC-33a Same 25 C. C PL R-8
(Atwood Wis 980D)

NC-34a GOOD/FOR/ONE/GLASS/BEER Eagle head left C PL R-5
Similar reverse to NC-18, but of same period.

NC-35a Y & T struck on 1864 cent C PL R-7
This was called a Civil War token when obtained, but there is no evidence that it is this early.

NON-CONTEMPORARY-Continued

NUMBER	OBVERSE	REVERSE	METAL	EDGE	RARITY
NC-36e	Apparently the gunboat MONITOR in center, inscription below.	Stars in field	W-M or lead	PL	R-9

This piece, obtained in Guttag collection, is too corroded to distinguish whether it is a patriotic or storecard. Illustrated for information only.

NUMBER	OBVERSE	REVERSE	METAL	EDGE	RARITY
NC-37b	NEENAH/S.B.	Target design encircled by a wreath.	BR	PL	R8
NC-38b	ROBT. DODSWORTH/COLD SPRING/KY. (Accurate description of obverse and reverse is not available.)	(?)	BR	(?)	R9
NC-39a	CENTRAL NATIONAL/HOME/FOR/D.V.S. GOOD FOR/5/CENTS/AT STORE (Previously listed as Pa 750G-1a — H&G 9338.)		C	PL	R6
NC-40a	CENTRAL NATIONAL/HOME/FOR/D.V.S. GOOD FOR/10/CENTS/AT STORE (Previously listed as Pa 750G-2a — H&G 9339.)		C	PL	R8
NC-41a	M.B.C./steer(depicted)/1878(below)	1373	C	(?)	R9

ALPHABETICAL INDEX

A

A. & H. ....Cleveland, Ohio
A. B. ....Chicago, Illinois
A. W. E. ....Red Wing, Minnesota
Adam's "Ton Hall" ....Philadelphia, Pennsylvania
Adams, James & Co. ....Buffalo, New York
Adams & Hatch ....La Salle, Illinois
Adderly, W. J. ....Detroit, Michigan
Addocks, T. ....Special Non-local
Adleta, M. ....Cincinnati, Ohio
Agens, J. L. & Co. ....Newark, New Jersey
Aiker, W. A. ....Pomeroy, Ohio
Alberger's Meat Store ....Buffalo, New York
Albright, P. G. ....Massillon, Ohio
Alden & Fink ....Cohoes, New York
Alenburg, W. ....Cincinnati, Ohio
Allebach, M. B. ....Philadelphia, Pennsylvania
Allegheny Valley Railroad Hotel
 ....Pittsburgh, Pennsylvania
Allegre & Wroughton...............................Albany, Indiana
Allen, I. & Son ....Schoolcraft, Michigan
Allen's Blacklead ....See Worthington, Cleveland Ohio
Alling, C. L. ....Fond du Lac, Wisconsin
Alschuler, A. & H. ....Ottawa, Ill.
Alvord, Caldwell & Alvord ....Indianapolis, Indiana
Alward, A. M. ....Dowagiac, Michigan
American Coffee Mills ....Detroit, Michigan
Ames, George B. ....Belvidere, Illinois
Ames, J. ....Hillsdale, Michigan
Amon ....Philadelphia, Pennsylvania
Anderson, C. ....Ft. Wayne, Indiana
Anderson & Evans ....Ft. Wayne, Indiana
Anderson, Mons.................................La Crosse, Wisconsin
Andrew & Cooper ....Dowagiac, Michigan
Andrews, F. W. ....Rochester, Minnesota
Antisdel & Hills......................................Detroit, Michigan
Applegate & Co. ....Bellevue, Ohio
Arbeiter Halle ....Covington, Kentucky
Arcade House.........................Providence, Rhode Island
Arch Saloon......................... Willimantic, Connecticut
Armbruster, J. ....Lancaster, Ohio
Armstrong, B. B. ....Cincinnati, Ohio
Armstrong, T. H. ....Detroit, Michigan
Arnold, F. ....Cincinnati, Ohio
Arnold, O. ....Ligonier, Indiana
Aschermann, E. & Co. ....Milwaukee, Wisconsin
Ash, O. H. P. ....Bowling Green, Indiana
Ash & Black...................................Bowling Green, Indiana
Ashton, F. M. ....Cincinnati, Ohio
Atlantic Garden.................................New York, New York
Atwood, E. W. ....Bridgeport, Connecticut
Austin, J. S. ....Cincinnati, Ohio
Autenrieth Cafe..................................New York, New York
Avermaat, H. ....Cincinnati, Ohio

B

Babcock, Charles .... Troy, New York
Babcock & Cobb ....Kalamazoo, Michigan
Bacciocco's...Cincinnati, Ohio
Bach, Philip ....Ann Arbor, Michigan
Bacher, E...Cincinnati, Ohio

Bahr, C. ....New York, New York
Baierle's Saloon...Chicago, Illinois
Bailey, J. D. .... Gallipolis, Ohio
Baker & Brown..Hudson, Michigan
Baldwin & Sweet................................. Greenboro, Indiana
Baltz & Stilz........................... Philadelphia, Pennsylvania
Bamlet, G. .... Detroit, Michigan
Bang, H. J. ....New York, New York
Barie, L. W. .... Detroit, Michigan
Barker & Illsley......................................Chicago, Illinois
Barnard, Geo. P..........................Grand Rapids, Michigan
Barnes, A. & W. H. .... Martinsburg, Ohio
Barnes, J. P. ....Anderson, Indiana
Barnes, Roswell...................................Brighton, Michigan
Barney Brothers..................................Ligonier, Indiana
Barrell's... Zanesville, Ohio
Barrett, G. B. .... Cadiz, Ohio
Barrows, E. G. .... Buffalo, New York
Barrows, E. S....................................Janesville, Wisconsin
Barry & McDaniel ....Knoxville, Tennessee
Bartels, H. ....Syracuse, New York
Bartholomew & McClelland................Valparaiso, Indiana
Bartlett Goble & Co..................................Chesterville, Ohio
Bartlett & Rigby.............................. Frederickstown, Ohio
Bassett's............................... Glen Easton, West Virginia
Bassett's..Wheeling, West Virginia
Bast, Ch...Milwaukee, Wisconsin
Bathgate, R. ....Cincinnati, Ohio
Bauder & Button ....Lyons, Michigan
Bauer, John...Cincinnati, Ohio
Bauerschmidt, G. ....Chicago, Illinois
Baughman, C. D. and Bro. .... Lisbon, Indiana
Baum, Walter & Co.................................. Avilla, Indiana
Beach, G. .... Perrysburg, Ohio
Beach, P. E. .... Wooster, Ohio
Beane, W. A. .... Goshen, Indiana
Beard, Geo & Son .... Detroit, Michigan
Beck, Sam'l.. Corunna, Indiana
Beer, C. H. ....Cincinnati, Ohio
Beers, Isaac ....Marshall, Michigan
Beeson, H. W. ....Detroit, Michigan
Behr, F...Detroit, Michigan
Beilsteine, F. .... Pittsburgh, Pennsylvania
Beirn, M. F.................................Philadelphia, Pennsylvania
Bell, Wm. .... Erie, Pennsylvania
Belknap, B. P. ....Cincinnati, Ohio
Bellack, H. .... Watertown, Wisconsin
Bellaire Ferry Ticket.................................. Bellaire, Ohio
Bement, W. W. ....South Bend, Indiana
Benjamin & Herrick .... Albany, New York
Benner & Bendinger........................New York, New York
Bennett, Dr. ....Cincinnati, Ohio
Bennett, C. H. ....Cincinnati, Ohio
Bennett, Thos.................................New York, New York
Benson, C. .... Winona, Minnesota
Beresford, Frank ....Cincinnati, Ohio
Bernacki, Charles W.....................East Saginaw, Michigan
Bertram & Co. .... Watertown, Wisconsin
Best, J. C. ....Ligonier, Indiana
Best, Philip ....Milwaukee, Wisconsin
Best & Co. ....Milwaukee, Wisconsin
Betts, O. S. ....Hillsdale, Michigan
Bickel, Wm..Huntington, Ind.

600

ALPHABETICAL INDEX-Continued

Bieler, F. J. .... Buffalo, New York
Bier, Jno F. & Bro. .... Chillicothe, Ohio
Billiard Room & Restaurant .... Providence, Rhode Island
Billiod's, F. .... Cincinnati, Ohio
Binder, Wm. .... Saginaw City, Michigan
Binder & Co. .... Bay City, Michigan
Bingham & Jarvis .... Cooperstown, New York
Bippus & Morgan .... Huntington, Indiana
Birge, R. H. .... Oberlin, Ohio
Bishop, Giles .... Flint, Michigan
Bishop, Sam. .... North Liberty, Ohio
Bittrolff & Geisler .... Evansville, Indiana
Black & Kibler .... Hillsboro, Ohio
Blackman & Dibble .... Adrian, Michigan
Blain, I. W. .... New York, New York
Blaisdell, W. R. .... Lowell, Michigan
Blakeslee, C. C. .... Jonesville, Wisconsin
Blatz, V. .... Milwaukee, Wisconsin
Block, J. .... Lancaster, Ohio
Blockson, A. J. .... New Lisbon, Ohio
Blome, Fred'k C. .... Detroit, Michigan
Blood, Jno. H. .... St. Louis, Missouri
Blowney & Johnson .... South Bend, Indiana
Bock, C. .... Oshkosh, Wisconsin
Bock, Wm. .... See Non-Contemporary
Bodden, M. .... Milwaukee, Wisconsin
Bode, J. L. .... New York, New York
Bodine & Bros. .... Williamstown, New Jersey
Bodtker, Jas. Fr. .... Madison, Wisconsin
Bogar, D. S. .... Freeport, Illinois
Bogardus, W. H. .... North Prairie, Wisconsin
Boger & Kimmel. .... Findlay, Ohio
Boger, J. .... Findlay, Ohio
Bohn, John .... Chillicothe, Ohio
Bolen, J. A. .... See Non-Contemporary
Boles, Jos. .... Oshkosh, Wisconsin
Bollinger, W. J. .... Lena, Illinois
Boman, Lew. .... Cincinnati, Ohio
Bonbright, J. S. .... Bellaire, Ohio
Bond, C. .... Cadiz, Indiana
Boose, R. .... Lima, Ohio
Booth & Sturgis .... Logansport, Indiana
Boston Store .... Indianapolis, Indiana
Bosworth & Witford .... Kendallville, Indiana
Boutwell, Oliver. .... Troy, New York
Bowen, A. N. .... Hudson, Michigan
Bowen, Lisa .... Corunna, Indiana
Bowen, M. M. .... Kendallville, Indiana
Bowman, J. R. .... Wooster, Ohio
Bowne, G. L. .... Cooperstown, New York
Boyd & Bradley .... Cassopolis, Michigan
Brackenridge, T. K. .... Ft. Wayne, Indiana
Brady, P. .... Bellevue, Ohio
Brain, W. G. .... Springfield, Ohio
Brandiff, A. D. & Co. .... Ft. Wayne, Indiana
Brass, A. R. .... Fond du Lac, Wisconsin
Brattin .... Non-local
Braun & Schellworth's .... Brooklyn, New York
Brennan, Jas. .... New York, New York
Brewer, C. M. .... Marshall, Michigan
Brewster, D. S. .... Freeport, Illinois
Bridgen's .... New York, New York
Brimelow, T. .... New York, New York

Bristor, J. H. .... Steubenville, Ohio
Broas Bros. .... New York, New York
Broas Pie Baker .... New York, New York
Broeg & Gerber .... Detroit, Michigan
Brooks, Wm. .... Elkhart, Indiana
Brooks, W. H., Jr. .... Ft. Wayne, Indiana
Brower, H. and Bro. .... Grand Haven, Michigan
Brown, Ira .... Chicago, Illinois
Brown, J. J. .... Chicago, Illinois
Brown, M. S. .... New York, New York
Brown, N. A. .... Kenosha, Wisconsin
Brown, W. S. .... New York, New York
Brown & Dill Drs. .... Piqua, Ohio
Bruce, C. G. .... Cleveland, Ohio
Bruggeman, A. .... Cincinnati, Ohio
Brumter, G. .... Wooster, Ohio
Brunson, J. M. .... Kenton, Ohio
Buchanan, Ella .... Ashland, Ohio
Buchanan, Sam .... Huntington, Indiana
Buck & Farrar .... Adrian, Michigan
Buffums Mineral Water .... Pittsburgh, Pennsylvania
Buhl, C. C. .... Richmond, Indiana
Bunyan, W. & J. R. .... Kendallville, Indiana
Burkhart, F. A. .... Detroit, Michigan
Burkholter, P. .... Beverly, Ohio
Burleson, A. .... Litchfield, Michigan
Burritt, H. .... Maumee City, Ohio
Burton's Exchange .... Portsmouth, Ohio
Busch, Charles .... Detroit, Michigan
Butcher, J. .... Newport, Kentucky
Butler Witter & Co. .... Ravenna, Ohio
Button, A. .... Lyons, Michigan

C

Cadot, J. J. & Bro. .... Gallipolis, Ohio
Cain, J. C. .... Dayton, Ohio
Camp, T. P. .... Stoughton, Wisconsin
Campbell, J. .... Mauston, Wisconsin
Campbell, J. .... Cincinnati, Ohio
Campbell, M. C. .... Philadelphia, Pennsylvania
Campbell & Calnon .... Detroit, Michigan
Campbell Linn & Co. .... Detroit, Michigan
Candler, A. .... Chicago, Illinois
Card Pearce & Co. .... Hillsdale, Michigan
Carland's .... New York, New York
Carle, P. & Son .... Collinsville, Ohio
Carlile, D. .... Warsaw, Indiana
Carpeles, Ph. & Co. .... Waterloo, Wisconsin
Carpeles, Ph. & Co. .... Columbus, Wisconsin
Carpenter & Pier .... Fond du Lac, Wisconsin
Carson, Wm. .... Allegheny City, Pennsylvania
Carswell, L. R. .... Janesville, Wisconsin
Carter, R. K. .... Danville, Indiana
Cary, H. G. O. .... Zanesville, Ohio
Case, J. I. & Co. .... Racine, Wisconsin
Castle, J. A. .... Adrian, Michigan
Castle, M. B. .... Sandwich, Illinois
Castle, W. B. .... Sandwich, Illinois
Cefandorf, G. A. .... New York, New York
Centennial Advertising .... See Non-Contemporary
Central Coal Office .... Cincinnati, Ohio
Central National D. V. S. Home
.... Philadelphia, Pennsylvania

ALPHABETICAL INDEX-Continued

Chadwick, C. .... Camden, Ohio
Chamberlain Bros .... Cincinnati, Ohio
Chandler, C. .... Cleveland, Ohio
Chaney & Harris .... Hillsboro, Ohio
Chapman's One Price Store .... Janesville, Wisconsin
Charnley .... Providence, Rhode Island
Chestnut, John .... Jackson, Ohio
Chestnut & Walnut Passenger R. R. Co.
  .... Philadelphia, Pennsylvania
Childs Die Sinker .... Chicago, Illinois
Childs Manufacturer .... Chicago, Illinois
Childs, James B. .... Wooster, Ohio
Childs, John .... Corunna, Indiana
Chord, S. M. .... South Bend, Indiana
Christiansen, H. A. .... Detroit, Michigan
Cin. & Cov. Ferry Company .... Cincinnati, Ohio
City Brewery .... Chicago, Illinois
City Brewery Malt House .... Milwaukee, Wisconsin
City Hosiery Store .... Cincinnati, Ohio
City of New York .... New York, New York
City Tea House .... Allegheny City, Pennsylvania
Clark & Co. .... Wilkes Barre, Pennsylvania
Clark's Drugs .... Flint, Michigan
Clark, G. & W. .... Detroit, Michigan
Clark, M. H. .... Clarkston, Michigan
Clarke & Carpenter .... Fond du Lac, Wisconsin
Clark, N. W. & Co. .... East Saginaw, Michigan
Clark's C. E. .... Cincinnati, Ohio
Close, P. .... Fremont, Ohio
Clough, J. .... Racine, Wisconsin
Cobb, Wm. R. .... Brighton, Michigan
Cobb & Fisher .... Kalamazoo, Michigan
Cochran, A. C. .... Cambridge, Ohio
Cochran, H. M. .... McConnelsville, Ohio
Coe & Hayden .... Winona, Minn.
Coffin, C. M. .... West Newton, Ohio
Cohen, A. .... Leavenworth, Kansas
Cohen, S. .... Detroit, Michigan
Colby, G. A. & Co. .... Niles, Michigan
Coleman, S. H. .... Juneau, Wisconsin
Coles Bakery .... Cincinnati, Ohio
Collier, V. P. .... Battle Creek, Michigan
Collins Brothers .... Paris, Illinois
Comers Commercial College .... Boston, Massachusetts
Commission Boots & Shoes .... Cincinnati, Ohio
Comstock & Bro. .... Albion, Michigan
Congdon Brothers .... Chelsea, Michigan
Conn. Mutual Life Ins. Co. .... Cincinnati, Ohio
Connell, E. & Co. .... Janesville, Wisconsin
Connely, A. C. .... Paris, Illinois
Connely's New York Store .... Brazil, Indiana
Conroy, Charles .... Cincinnati, Ohio
Conry, T. J. .... Buffalo, New York
Consulere Generi Hominum .... Cincinnati, Ohio
Coombs .... Philadelphia, Pennsylvania
Cooper, A. J. .... Milwaukee, Wisconsin
Copland, A. W. .... Detroit, Michigan
Cordes & Platz .... Watertown, Wisconsin
Cork, Charles .... Waukesha, Wisconsin
Corle, J. F. .... Kendallville, Indiana
Cossitt Hill & Co. .... Memphis, Tennessee
Costello's .... Cincinnati, Ohio
Cotteral, W. W. .... Middletown, Indiana

Countiss, R. H. .... Chicago, Illinois
Courlander & Pressgood .... Grand Rapids, Michigan
Coutts & Bro. .... Perth Amboy, New Jersey
Cov. & Cin. Ferry Co. .... Covington, Kentucky
Cox & Landers .... Brooklyn, Indiana
Craddick & Homan .... Danville, Indiana
Craig & Foy .... Birmingham, Ohio
Crane, H. A. .... Corunna, Michigan
Crew, B. L. .... Richmond, Ohio
Crittenden Shades .... Cincinnati, Ohio
Crooks, C. & Co. .... Granville, Indiana
Crosby, C. L. .... Detroit, Michigan
Crosby, Joseph .... Zanesville, Ohio
Cruikshank, J. W. .... Non-Local
Cullen, J. V. .... Kokomo, Indiana
Cullen, Tom .... New York, New York
Culley, R. C. .... Cairo, Illinois
Cummings, C. .... Charlotte, Michigan
Cummings & Anderson .... Shelby, Ohio
Cunning, S. W. .... Portsmouth, Ohio
Curtis, C. P. .... Toledo, Ohio
Curtis, Geo E. .... Detroit, Michigan

D

D. B. S. (Stessett) .... Cincinnati, Ohio
Daggett, J. M. & Co. .... Cincinnati, Ohio
Dahmen, C. & Son .... Cross Plains, Wisconsin
Dale, J. M. .... Plymouth, Indiana
Danforth, L. .... Buffalo, New York
Dangler, J. B. .... Massillon, Ohio
Darling, W. .... Saranac, Michigan
Dartt, H. .... Almond, New York
Davenport, J. & Son .... Elkhart, Indiana
Davies, Jesse .... Huntington, Indiana
Davies & Maxwell .... West Unity, Ohio
Davis, A. H. .... Non-local
Davis, A. J. .... Rockford, Illinois
Davis, A. M. .... New Paris, Indiana
Davis & Bates .... Kalamazoo, Michigan
Davis & Whiteman .... Wappakoneta, Ohio
Dayton, M. N. .... Martinsburg, Ohio
Dean & Co. .... Ann Arbor, Michigan
Dean & Slade .... Palatine, Illinois
Dean, Godfrey & Co. .... Detroit, Michigan
Dearborn & Root .... Stoughton, Wisconsin
Deckand & Engelhart .... Cleveland, Ohio
Decker, J. .... Ligonier, Indiana
Dehner & Maples .... Pontiac, Illinois
Deinzer, John .... Hamilton, Ohio
Dervin, T. .... Watertown, Wisconsin
Detrich, A. .... Green Bay, Wisconsin
Detroit City Flour Mills .... Detroit, Michigan
Dickinson Comstock & Co. .... Utica, New York
Dickson, A. M & Co .... Dowagiac, Michigan
Dickson, D. .... Detroit, Michigan
Dickson, H. B. & Co. .... Plymouth, Indiana
Diehl, J. J. .... New York, New York
Diem, Carl .... New York, New York
Diffenbaugh, J. D. .... Freeport, Illinois
Dillon, Dr. E. & Son .... Fremont, Ohio
Dixon, Geo R. & Co. .... Cincinnati, Ohio
Dixon, J. E. & Sons .... Kilbourn City, Wisconsin
Dobson, H. .... Providence, Rhode Island

ALPHABETICAL INDEX-Continued

Dodd's Elgin Dairy..................................Chicago, Illinois
Dodsworth, Robert ....See Non-Contemporary
Dolman, J. .... Covington, Kentucky
Doniphan, J. N. ....Cincinnati, Ohio
Doornink, D. J..................................Milwaukee, Wisconsin
Dorland, Garret T. ....Cincinnati, Ohio
Doscher, C. ....New York, New York
Downing, R. ....Cincinnati, Ohio
Driscoll, Jas.. Chillicothe, Ohio
Drovers Hotel..St. Louis, Missouri
Druecker, J...................... Port Washington, Wisconsin
Drury, E. A. .... Detroit, Michigan
Dryer, D. & Co..Chicago, Illinois
Dryfoos, M... Fremont, Ohio
Dubois, F. N. ....Chicago, Illinois
Duburn, A. M.. Buffalo, New York
Duden, J. S. .... Wooster, Ohio
Duffy, Patrick .... Watertown, Wisconsin
Dunbar, J. A. .... Waukesha, Wisconsin
Dunbar & Wolff..Ripley, Ohio
Dunlap, Wm................................... Steubenville, Ohio
Dunlap & Floren.....................................Special Non-local
Dunn & Co. ....Boston, Massachusetts
Dunn, Goudy & Bro. .... Cleveland, Ohio
Durst, J. .... Dayton, Ohio
Dutton, A. C. .... Eaton Rapids, Michigan
Dynes, J. M. .... Morrow, Ohio

E

Eager, W. B. .... Elyria, Ohio
Early, S. S. & Co................................. Brownstown, Indiana
Eastman, H. .... Niles, Michigan
Eastman National Business College
.... Poughkeepsie, New York
Eaton & Barns...Tomah, Wisconsin
Eccard, Francis...................................... Detroit, Michigan
Eckert, J. A. ...., Pittsburgh, Pennsylvania
Eckert, L. ....Cincinnati, Ohio
Eckhart, John....................................Wheeling, West Virginia
Eckley, O. J... Hillsboro, Ohio
Edwards ....Chicago, Illinois
Eisenlord, Wm. .... Detroit, Michigan
Ekstein, David..Lansing, Michigan
Eliel, L. .... La Porte, Indiana
Elkins, John...Racine, Wisconsin
Elliot & Hinshaw ....Lynn, Indiana
Elliot & Swain .... Mechanicsburg, Indiana
Elliot, Vinson & Co. .... Memphis, Tennessee
Ellis, C. W. ....Cincinnati, Ohio
Ellsworth & Halsey ....Lacon, Illinois
Ellwood, I. L. ....DeKalb, Illinois
Elmlinger, F... Racine, Wisconsin
Emigraten Office..................................Madison, Wisconsin
Emmert, W. P. ....Freeport, Illinois
Emrich & Co. .... Fremont, Ohio
Emswiler, G. P. & Co. .... Richmond, Indiana
Endly, H. ....Mansfield, Ohio
Engel, John .... Elizabethport, New Jersey
Engert, V. C .... Covington, Kentucky
English, J. M. ....Racine, Wisconsin
Epting & Eaton..............................Saginaw City, Michigan
Erhardt & Raps..Racine, Wisconsin
Erlenborn, A...Mendota, Illinois

Escherich, A. W. ....Chicago, Illinois
Eureka..See Non-Contemporary
Evans, S. C.......................................Kendallville, Indiana
Evans & Allen .... Binghamton, New York
Even's..Cincinnati, Ohio
Everich & Barton ....Zanesville, Ohio
Eversole, H. C. ....Logansport, Indiana
Excelsior Club................................Boston, Massachusetts
Excelsior Tobacco Works ....Cincinnati, Ohio

F

F. B. ....Chicago, Illinois
F. W. R. ....Chicago, Illinois
Fairbank & Scriver................................Lawton, Michigan
Faller, J. & Son...................................... La Porte, Indiana
Falvey, Thos..Racine, Wisconsin
Farmer's Clothing Store........................ Detroit, Michigan
Farnams Bronchial Tablets..................Hillsdale, Michigan
Farnham, D. & Co. ....Edgertown, Ohio
Fauley & Brechbill...................................Uniontown, Ohio
Felix Dining Saloon ....New York, New York
Fenton & Beck..Cincinnati, Ohio
Ferguson, J...Cincinnati, Ohio
Feuchtwanger.......................................New York, New York
Fickhart, C. H...Circleville, Ohio
Fiedler, E...Cincinnati, Ohio
Fiedler, Edward............................. See Non-Contemporary
Fiedler, Emil..Cincinnati, Ohio
Fifth Street Garden ....Cincinnati, Ohio
Filner, A. H. ....Milwaukee, Wisconsin
Findlay, R. K. & Co. .... Madison, Wisconsin
Fischer, F..Cincinnati, Ohio
Fischbein, Joseph...............................Milwaukee, Wisconsin
Fisher, J. ....New York, New York
Fischer & Hendlyx ....Tecumseh, Michigan
Fisher & Rohr......................................Watertown, Wisconsin
Fisler & Chance ....Cincinnati, Ohio
Fitch, Ira H..Aurora, Illinois
Fithian, W. C. ....Cincinnati, Ohio
Fitzgerald, J. W. ....Cincinnati, Ohio
Fitzsimons, C. & Co. .... Detroit, Michigan
Flach, Chas...Cincinnati, Ohio
Flagg Cheap Store......................................Chicago, Illinois
Flagg & MacDonald...................................Chicago, Illinois
Flanagan, R. ....Philadelphia, Pennsylvania
Fleming, Wm. & Bro. ....Lansing, Iowa
Flemming, Jos.................................Pittsburgh, Pennsylvania
Follett, G. W. ....Fremont, Indiana
Foote, J. R. ....Paw Paw, Michigan
Forbes, G. W. ....Non-Local
Ford, D. ....Cairo, Illinois
Fornshell, J. P. ....Camden, Ohio
Fort, P. V. & Co. .... Albany, New York
Foster, James Jr. & Co. ....Chicago, Illinois
Foster, James Jr. & Co. ....Cincinnati, Ohio
Foster & Metcalf ....Grand Rapids, Michigan
Fountain, W. C..................................Watertown, Wisconsin
Fox, W. G. .... Buffalo, New York
Fox & Smith ....Pontiac, Michigan
Fraker Bros. ....Oshkosh, Wisconsin
Francis, E. P. ....Fall River, Massachusetts
Franckenberg & Keller......................... Newburg, Wisconsin

ALPHABETICAL INDEX-Continued

Frank, John... Cincinnati, Ohio
Frankfurth, Wm. .... Milwaukee, Wisconsin
Frechtling, H. & W... Hamilton, Ohio
Freedman & Goodkind............................... Chicago, Illinois
Freedman, Goodkind & Co. .... Chicago, Illinois
Freeman, L.. Detroit, Michigan
Freise, Fr.. New York, New York
French .... Clarksburg, Ohio
French & Parsons................................. Hillsdale, Michigan
French & Swonger... Piqua, Ohio
Frisbie .... Detroit, Michigan
Fritz, F... Fond du Lac, Wisconsin
Frost's Medicines .... Cincinnati, Ohio
Frost, H. M. .... Eaton Rapids, Michigan
Frost & Daniels .... Eaton Rapids, Michigan
Fry & Johnston.. Sidney, Ohio

G

Gaffney, P.. Chicago, Illinois
Gaffney & McDowell .... Columbia City, Indiana
Gage Lyall & Keller .... Lyons, Iowa
Gage, D. W. .... Cleveland, Ohio
Gage, Geo.. Buffalo, New York
Gale, A. & H. .... Jonesville, Michigan
Gale, A. W. .... Concord, New Hampshire
Gall, F... Chicago, Illinois
Gallagher & Hess..................................... Salina, Michigan
Gallt & Cole................................... Whitewater, Wisconsin
Galvagni, John.. Cincinnati, Ohio
Gardner, H. R. & Co........................... Jonesville, Michigan
Gardner, J. F................................... New York, New York
Gates & Trask.. Aurora, Illinois
Gavron, A.. New York, New York
Gay, Frank L........................... Providence, Rhode Island
Geilfus, L... Cincinnati, Ohio
Geis, F. & Bro's. .... Detroit, Michigan
Geisendorff, C. E. & Co. .... Indianapolis, Indiana
Geisendorff, G. W. & Co................... Indianapolis, Indiana
Geiser, J.. Cincinnati, Ohio
Geiss, F. & Bro's................................... Detroit, Michigan
Geissler, B. .... Evansville, Indiana
Geitgey, Samuel .... Wooster, Ohio
Gentry's... Centerville, Indiana
Gentsch, Charles................................ New York, New York
Gentsch, W. .... Cincinnati, Ohio
Gercke, J. Henry.................... Philadelphia, Pennsylvania
.... Also See Non-Contemporary
Gerdts, H. D. .... New York, New York
Gerken & Ernst .... Kenosha, Wisconsin
Gerts, C. E. & Co..................................... Chicago, Illinois
Giaugue, D. .... Mt. Eaton, Ohio
Gies, F. & Bro's .... Detroit, Michigan
Gildenfenney, W. A.................... Pittsburgh, Pennsylvania
Gillett & Niles.. Hudson, Michigan
Glatte, G, C. .... Kendallville, Indiana
Glacier's Pharmacy..................................... Parma, Michigan
Gleason, A... Hillsdale, Michigan
Goeldner, Chas................................. Watertown, Wisconsin
Goes & Falk..................................... Milwaukee, Wisconsin
Goetz, S. .... Gallipolis, Ohio
O. G. (O. Goffery)...................................... Cincinnati, Ohio
Gohs, R. .... Cincinnati, Ohio
Gold Pen Depot .... Nashville, Tennessee

Goll & Frank..................................... Milwaukee, Wisconsin
Goller, J. E. .... Hamilton, Ohio
Good, M. H. .... Indianapolis, Indiana
Goodell, G. W...................................... Corunna, Michigan
Gooder, Robert...................................... Jonesboro, Indiana
Goodhue, H. & G. .... Waterloo, Iowa
Goodrich, C. B. .... Detroit, Michigan
Goodrich & Gay........................... Grand Rapids, Michigan
Gordon & Thurston................................. Wabash, Indiana
Gorham, J. H. & A. S................................ Cleveland, Ohio
Gotsch, J. H....................................... Kendallville, Indiana
Gottlieb, J... Hillsdale, Michigan
Gould, D. S. .... Rochester, Indiana
Graden, E. .... Kendallville, Indiana
Graff, C. B. .... Milwaukee, Wisconsin
Graham, G.. New York, New York
Grant, Alexr & Co. .... Zanesville, Ohio
Graves, Jas & Co. .... Wheeling, West Virginia
Graves, R. C. .... Wheeling, West Virginia
Gray, J. W. .... Steubenville, Ohio
Great Central Fair .... Philadelphia, Pennsylvania
Great Fair U. S. Sanitary Commission
.... Nantucket, Massachusetts
Green C. T. & Co. .... Elkhart, Indiana
Green & Wardsworth........................... Hudson, Michigan
Greenman, A. G. .... Sandwich, Illinois
Greenleaf, D. G....................................... St. Paul, Minnesota
Greenway & Co. .... Ripon, Wisconsin
Gregg & Dalzel.................. Allegheny City, Pennsylvania
Grether, John.. Columbus, Ohio
Gridley, M. H....................................... Logansport, Indiana
Griffee, G. W. .... Zanesville, Ohio
Griffin, A. E. .... Marion, Ohio
Griffith, J. W....................................... Huntington, Indiana
Grimes & Griner.. Canaan, Ohio
Griswold, H. & Co.................................. Lapeer, Michigan
Grossius, J.. Cincinnati, Ohio
Grout, J. B.. Indianapolis, Indiana
Groyen, Jacob... Como, Indiana
Grube, J. A. C. .... New York, New York
Gruber, John P. .... New York, New York
Guipe, John .... Elkhart, Indiana
Guth, Jacob .... Cincinnati, Ohio

H

Haas, Carl.. Cincinnati, Ohio
Haas & Powell .... Chicago, Illinois
Haben, Andrew & Co......................... Oshkosh, Wisconsin
Hafer, F. H. & Co.................................. Greenville, Ohio
Hagan, W. E. .... Troy, New York
Hahn & Riddle................... Allegheny City, Pennsylvania
Haines, G.. Wolf Creek, Ohio
Haines, D. H. & Bro. .... Swan, Indiana
Hall, E. W. .... Whitehall, New York
Hall, J.. Troy, Ohio
Hall, D. A. & Co.......................... Pittsburgh, Pennsylvania
Hall & Frymire .... Navarre, Ohio
Halls, F. J... Xenia, Ohio
Hambach .... Milwaukee, Wisconsin
Hamblin, G. W. .... Stryker, Ohio
Hamilton & Co....................................... Sparta, Wisconsin
Hamman, F. & Co................................. Detroit, Michigan
Hammar, B. E. & Co. .... Memphis, Tennessee

ALPHABETICAL INDEX-Continued

Hammonds Shoe Store .... South Bend, Indiana
Hammonds Stove Store .... South Bend, Indiana
Hanley, W. W. .... Cincinnati, Ohio
Hanna & Co. .... Detroit, Michigan
Hannah, J. W. .... Pittsburgh, Pennsylvania
Harley & Linville .... Columbia City, Indiana
Harlev, Wm. .... Chicago, Illinois
Harlev & Johnson .... Chicago, Illinois
Harpel .... Cincinnati, Ohio
Harris & Pearl .... Nashville, Tennessee
Harris, W. B. & Bro. .... Zanesville, Ohio
Harsh, M. .... Janesville, Wisconsin
Hart, T. W. .... Milwaukee, Wisconsin
Hart's Arcade Gallery .... Watertown, New York
Harter, S. K. .... Troy, Ohio
Hartmann, C. G. .... Cincinnati, Ohio
Hartman, M. .... North Hampton, Ohio
Hartzel, M. .... Cincinnati, Ohio
Harvey & Co. .... Ft. Edwards, New York
Hasbrouck & Francher .... Oshkosh, Wisconsin
Hascall, Alderman & Brown .... Goshen, Indiana
Haskett & Co. .... Kokomo, Indiana
Hasse, E. E. .... Yonkers, New York
Hastings, William .... New York, New York
Hatch & Craw .... Lowell, Michigan
Hauck, C. J. .... Brooklyn, New York
Hause, Dr. E. .... Tecumseh, Michigan
Hawkins, John .... Cleveland, Ohio
Hawley, D. C. .... Hastings, Michigan
Hay & Clark .... Oshkosh, Wisconsin
Hayes, J. & Bro. .... Cincinnati, Ohio
Heath, L. F. .... Lyons, Michigan
Heilbroner, R. .... Chicago, Illinois
Heinig, F. .... Terre Haute, Indiana
Heinman's .... Detroit, Michigan
Heintz & Henkle .... Columbus, Ohio
Heinzmann, E. .... Cincinnati, Ohio
Helmig, J. .... Cincinnati, Ohio
Hempelman, B. .... Cincinnati, Ohio
Hendrie, W. .... Chicago, Illinois
Hendry, Frank .... Oberlin, Ohio
Henking, Allemony & Co. .... Gallipolis, Ohio
Henning, A. J. .... New York, New York
Herancourt's Brewery .... Cincinnati, Ohio
Herendeen & Witter .... Zanesville, Ohio
Hereth, J. C. .... Indianapolis, Indiana
Herinton's .... Detroit, Michigan
Hermann, Ch. & Co. .... Milwaukee, Wisconsin
Herron & Amen .... Hillsboro, Ohio
Herschman Bros. .... Binghamton, New York
Hertrich, Helena .... Freeport, Illinois
Hetzel, Chr. F. .... New York, New York
Howitt, Isaac .... Maple Rapids, Michigan
Hewitt, E. & Bro. .... Ypsilanti, Michigan
Heyl, V. .... Cincinnati, Ohio
Heymann, John .... Watertown, Wisconsin
Hiatt & Showalter .... Cadiz, Indiana
Higby & Bro. .... Charlotte, Michigan
Higby & Stearns .... Detroit, Michigan
Higgins, H. D. .... Mishawaka, Indiana
Hild, W. .... Chicago, Illinois
Hill, Dr. H. H. & Co. .... Cincinnati, Ohio
Hilterscheid Bro's .... Detroit, Michigan

Hind, J. H. .... Steubenville, Ohio
Hinshaw, J. A. .... Lynn, Indiana
Hintrick, B. & C. Glaser .... Cincinnati, Ohio
Hirst, E. F. .... Richmond, Indiana
Hochstandt, Jacob .... Detroit, Michigan
Hochstetter & Straus .... Buffalo, New York
Hoegner, Martin .... Piqua, Ohio
Hoffman, T. .... Kilbourn City, Wisconsin
Hoffman & Lewis .... Green Bay, Wisconsin
Hohn Simmons & Co. .... Kenosha, Wisconsin
Holcomb, B. .... Mishawaka, Indiana
Holker, J. .... Oldenburg, Indiana
Holland, S. & Son. .... Jackson, Michigan
Holmes, C. L. .... Indianapolis, Indiana
Holmes & Norton .... Rockford, Illinois
Holthofer, C. J. .... Detroit, Michigan
Hoot & Meng .... Fremont, Ohio
Hoover & Camp .... Wellsville, Ohio
Hope & Clow .... Rockford, Illinois
Horn, W. H. .... Manitowoc, Wisconsin
Hotchkiss, Gilbert B. .... Cincinnati, Ohio
Hough & Hall. .... Toledo, Ohio
Howard, R. R. .... Kalamazoo, Michigan
Howe, H. & Co. .... Hudson, Ohio
Howe, Wm. B. .... Detroit, Michigan
Hubbard, Geo E. .... Grand Haven, Michigan
Huggins, Frank .... Columbus, Wisconsin
Hughes, J. A. .... Cincinnati, Ohio
Hughes, P. .... Cincinnati, Ohio
Hulsman & Alexander .... Franklin, Indiana
Humelchouser, H. .... Plymouth, Indiana
Hunt, John. .... Neenah, Wisconsin
Hunt, J. W. .... Delphos, Ohio
Huntley & Steenland .... Madison, Wisconsin
Hussey's .... New York, New York
Hustler, S. E. .... Troy, Ohio
Hyatt, C. C. .... Cincinnati, Ohio
Hyenlein, George .... New York, New York

I

I. B. .... Chicago, Illinois
Ibert, M. .... Brooklyn, New York
Icenhour & Co. .... Columbiana, Ohio
Idler, G. .... Ogdensburg, New York
Ingram, S. A. .... Chicago, Illinois
Insworth, J. H. & Co. .... Huntington, Indiana
Irwin, John .... Zanesville, Ohio
Ismon, H. S. .... Jackson, Michigan
Ivory, T. .... Brooklyn, New York

J

J. S. .... Chicago, Illinois
Jackson, Wm. .... Jackson, Michigan
Jacobs, A. .... Van Wert, Ohio
Jacobs & Co. .... Kendallville, Indiana
Jaonicke & Klotzsch .... Oshkosh, Wisconsin
Jahr, B. .... Cincinnati, Ohio
Jahr, B. & Co. .... Cincinnati, Ohio
James & French .... Clarksburg, Ohio
Jaxon, W. .... Jackson, Michigan
Jenkens, Henry .... St. Louis, Missouri

ALPHABETICAL INDEX-Continued

Jenkinson, R. & W. ....Allegheny City, Pennsylvania
Jenks, A. .... Dublin, Indiana
Jennings, Dr. D. R. ....Ravenna, Ohio
Joergers, John.................................Brooklyn, New York
John's Saloon (See Markham).................Cincinnati, Ohio
Johnson, J. B. ....Indianapolis, Indiana
Johnson, J. F. ....Seymour, Indiana
Johnson, Philip..................................Jefferson, Wisconsin
Johnson, W. S. & Bro.....................Henderson, Kentucky
Johnson & Oursler................................Plainfield, Indiana
Johnston, A. M. ....Buffalo, New York
Johnston, H. ....Cincinnati, Ohio
Johnston, W. ....Cincinnati, Ohio
Jones, D. H...Racine, Wisconsin
Jones, Wm. H. .... Non-Local
Jones Wood Hotel (I. Sommers).......New York, New York
Jones & Mosher................................Kendallville, Indiana
Joyce, J. J. ....Kendallville, Indiana
Judd & Corthell...Chicago, Illinois
Judkins, S. H. .... Mishawaka, Indiana
Julian & Co... Troy, Ohio
Jung, John....................................Jefferson, Wisconsin

K

Kahn, C. & Co. ....Cincinnati, Ohio
Kane, George ....Milwaukee, Wisconsin
Kanter, Edward.....................................Detroit, Michigan
Karl, Christoph ....New York, New York
Karman, A..Cincinnati, Ohio
Katzenstein, J. ....Cincinnati, Ohio
Kaufman & Co..Springfield, Ohio
Kayser, M..New York, New York
Keating, E. C..Hillsdale, Michigan
Keim, H. ....Chillicothe, Ohio
Keiningham, J. N. ....Lexington, Kentucky
Keitteridge, Dr. O. G...................Willimantic, Connecticut
Kellogg & Co. ....Kalamazoo, Michigan
Kellog & Hughes ....Oshkosh, Wisconsin
Kelly, David.. Troy, Ohio
Kelly, R. T. ....New York, New York
Kelly's Store.........................Hartford City, West Virginia
Kendall, A. ....Logansport, Indiana
Kendall, O., Sons & Co................................Chicago, Illinois
Kenmuir, John..............................St. Joseph, Missouri
Kennedy, James...Iona, Michigan
Kennedy, Warren................................Cincinnati, Ohio
Kepner, W. W. & Son ....Columbia City, Indiana
Kern, Frank..Cincinnati, Ohio
Kerr, J. M. .... Non-Local
Ketcham, G. T. ....Tecumseh, Michigan
Ketcham & Barker.. Toledo, Ohio
Killeen, A. ....Greenpoint, New York
Kimboll, A. .... Green Bay, Wisconsin
Kinderman, Dr. C....................... Columbia City, Indiana
Kindig, J. L. ....Goshen, Indiana
King, Andrew .... Clarksville, Tennessee
King, J. L. ....Circleville, Ohio
King & Reed.......................................Logansport, Indiana
Kingsland, John S. & Bro..............................Stryker, Ohio
Kingsley & Whipple........................Waukegan, Illinois
Kipp, G..Columbiana, Ohio
Kirby, Langworthy & Co..................Milwaukee, Wisconsin
Kirchenschlager, J..Cincinnati, Ohio

Kirchner, M. J. ....Tiffin, Ohio
Kirker, J. & Co..Cincinnati, Ohio
Kissek, M.. Chillicothe, Ohio
Kittredge, B. & Co.....................................Cincinnati, Ohio
Klare & Fredericks Billard Hall............Special Non-Local
Klauber, S. & Co.................................. Madison, Wisconsin
Klaus, Philip...................................... Green Bay, Wisconsin
Klein, J...Cincinnati, Ohio
Kleinsteuber, A. ....Milwaukee, Wisconsin
Kleisteuber, Chas...........................Milwaukee, Wisconsin
Kline, Henry... Dayton, Ohio
Knapp, I. J. ....Utica, New York
Knapp, Wm... Rockford, Illinois
Knauber, Jacob..Cincinnati, Ohio
Knecht, Wm. ....Cincinnati, Ohio
Kneeland, P. N. ....Detroit, Michigan
Knoblock, H. .... Massillon, Ohio
Knobloch, J. C....................................South Bend, Indiana
Knoop's Segars ....New York, New York
Koch, John..Cincinnati, Ohio
Koerner, J. M. & V. .... Columbus, Ohio
Kolb, Charles .... Newark, New Jersey
Koos ....Cincinnati, Ohio
Kramer, A. S. ....Chillicothe, Ohio
Kreager, B...Cincinnati, Ohio
Kreber, H..Cincinnati, Ohio
Krebs, D. W. & Co................................. Fremont, Ohio
Krengel, A...Cincinnati, Ohio
Kreps, D. ....Perrysbury, Ohio
Kreutzer, J..Peru, Indiana
Krueger, F. .... Beaver Dam, Wisconsin
Krick, Jacob ....Cincinnati, Ohio
Krug & Reed.......................................Logansport, Indiana
Kruger & Booth...........................Grand Rapids, Michigan
Kuhn, Charles .... Indianapolis, Indiana
Kurt, H. ....Milwaukee, Wisconsin
Kurz, Louis...................................Milwaukee, Wisconsin
Kusel, Daniel................................ Watertown, Wisconsin
Kusterer, C..................................Grand Rapids, Michigan
21st Ky. V. I.. Non-Local

L

Ladner, F. & L. ....Philadelphia, Pennsylvania
Lake, V. A. .... Rockton, Illinois
Lambert, A. ....Philadelphia, Pennsylvania
Landon, R. R. .... Non-Local
Lane, H. M. ....New York, New York
Lane, John... Warsaw, Wisconsin
Lang, Charles........................... Worcester, Massachusetts
Langdons Hardware Store.................. Belmont, New York
Langhorn, J. .... Cleveland, Ohio
Lanphear, W. K. ....Cincinnati, Ohio
Lants, J. ....Kendallville, Indiana
Lapham & Thayer .... Detroit, Michigan
Lapsley, D. L. & Co.........................Nashville, Tennessee
Larwell, J. F. ....Cincinnati, Ohio
Laselere, D. & Co............................. Dowagiac, Michigan
Lash, Wm. H. & Co................................ Goshen, Indiana
Lasurs, S. ....Cincinnati, Ohio
Lathrop, J. S................................. Whitewater, Wisconsin
Lauferty, Joseph .... Goshen, Indiana
Lauferty, I. ....Ft. Wayne, Indiana

606

ALPHABETICAL INDEX-Continued

Lavey, S. S. ....Columbia, City, Indiana
Lawrence, J. J. ....Madison, Wisconsin
Lawrence, Wm. ....Wellsville, Ohio
Lawrence & Noble....................................Goshen, Indiana
Lazaress, H. ....Cincinnati, Ohio
Leas, William...Sonora, Ohio
Leavens, C. W. & Co............................Neenah, Wisconsin
Leavitt, F. A. ....Chicago, Illinois
Leavitt & Bevis ....Cincinnati, Ohio
Lederer, A. & Co. ....Milwaukee, Wisconsin
Lee, John W. ....Lexington, Kentucky
Le Fevre, H. Y. ....Providence, Rhode Island
Leggett, S. T. ....East Saginaw, Michigan
Leis, John.. Wooster, Ohio
Lemert, E. L. ....Frazeysburg, Ohio
Lenour, J. F. ....Indianapolis, Indiana
Leonard, J. B. ....Battle Creek, Michigan
Leonard, P. ....Eaton Rapids, Michigan
Lester, H. ....Non-Local
Levy, E. .... Morrow, Ohio
Levy & Duncan.................................Oshkosh, Wisconsin
Lewis, J. S. ....Jonesville, Michigan
Lewis, James & Co. ....La Porte, Indiana
Lewis & Moses..Detroit, Michigan
Linck, H..Brookville, Indiana
Lindenmueller, Gustavus..................New York, New York
Lindermann, M. ....Cincinnati, Ohio
Lines & Russell.....................................Oshkosh, Wisconsin
Lininger & Bro..Peru, Illinois
Lippincott, J. C. & W. H. ....Pittsburgh, Pennsylvania
Livingston, I. ....Marshall, Wisconsin
Lochary, P. ....Morristown, Ohio
Loeffler, Fred...Massillon, Ohio
Lowenstein, H. ....Cincinnati, Ohio
Longwell, G W. ....Paw Paw, Michigan
Longwell, J. M. ....Non-Local
Loomis, S. J. M. ....Kendallville, Indiana
Lord, D. H. & Co...................................Hillsdale, Michigan
Lott & Warner ....Sycamore, Illinois
Lotz, C. ....Detroit, Michigan
Loveday, J. L. & Co. ....Waukegan, Illinois
Low, J. W. ....Springfield, Ohio
Lowell, J. C. ....Fond du Lac, Wisconsin
Ludewig, A. ....Pittsburgh, Pennsylvania
Ludlow & Bushnell ....Springfield, Ohio
Luhrs, Charles A.................................New York, New York
Luk, F. W. ....Cincinnati, Ohio
Lutes, J. .... Butler, Indiana
Lyman, Mowry & Co..........................Kenosha, Wisconsin
Lyons, James ....Hartford City, Indiana

M

Macauley, R. A. ....Cincinnati, Ohio
Madison Brewery ....Madison, Wisconsin
Magnus, C. ....New York, New York
Mahnken, J. ....New York, New York
Maines, James....................................Bakerstown, Pennsylvania
Maloney, B. ....New York, New York
March, C. G. ....Goshen, Indiana
March, Geo .... Hillsboro, Ohio
Markham, R. T. ....Cincinnati, Ohio
Marsh & Miner..Chicago, Illinois
Marrow & Parker..Piqua, Ohio

Marsh & Miner..Cincinnati, Ohio
Marshall, M. L. ....Oswego, New York
Martin's ....Cincinnati, Ohio
Martin, R. G...Monroeville, Ohio
Martin, S. C. .... Wooster, Ohio
Martin, S. T. ....See Non-Contemporary
Martin Bro's ....Detroit, Michigan
Marvin, C. L. ....Cleveland, Ohio
Marx, M. ....Detroit, Michigan
Mason, T. ....Fond du Lac, Wisconsin
Mason & Co. ....See Non-Contemporary
Mason & Son..Circleville, Ohio
Mather & Shefferly ....Detroit, Michigan
Mathews, John ....New York, New York
Matthews, James ....Centerville, Ohio
Mauck & Bradbury................................Clarksburg, Ohio
Maumee & Perrysburg Bridge Co. ....Maumee City, Ohio
May, C. M. ....Steubenville, Ohio
Mayhew, Ira ....Albion, Michigan
Melville, H. B. ....New York, New York
Merchant's Exchange....................See Non-Contemporary
Merchants Hotel.......................................Cincinnati, Ohio
Meredith, L. Phil & N. M'Clung................Cincinnati, Ohio
Merriam & Co. ....Boston, Massachusetts
Merriam, Jos. A.............................Boston, Massachusetts
Merrill, L. A. ....Grand Rapids, Michigan
Mesing, F. W. ....Kendallville, Indiana
Messmore & Lucking.......................... Detroit, Michigan
Mester, A. & Co ....Eaton Rapids, Michigan
Metcalf, O. C. ....Belmont, Ohio
Metz, Adam...Cincinnati, Ohio
Metz, J. & D. ....Cincinnati, Ohio
Metzger, Geo. ....Cincinnati, Ohio
Meyer, C. E. ....Chicago, Illinois
Meyer, Beyer & Bro ....Kendallville, Indiana
Meyer, A. ....Chicago, Illinois
Meyer, G. R. ....Chicago, Illinois
Meyer, J. A. .... Canton, Ohio
Meyer, L. ....Cincinnati, Ohio
Meyer, J. F. W. ....Jefferson, Wisconsin
Meyer, M. C. ....Milwaukee, Wisconsin
Mickey, Thos. .... Shelby, Ohio
Miedeking..Cincinnati, Ohio
Miehling, Edward ....New York, New York
Mier, S & Co. ....Ligonier, Indiana
Mikesell, J. & Bro.................................Charlotte, Michigan
Miles, A. C. ....Wappakoneta, Ohio
Miles & Sperry.......................................Chesterville, Ohio
Millar, Robert ....Detroit, Michigan
Millen, C. H. .... Ann Arbor, Michigan
Millen, D. P. ....Waukegan, Illinois
Miller, Friedrich...............................Milwaukee, Wisconsin
Miller, James. .... Paris, Illinois
Miller, J. & H. ....Racine, Wisconsin
Miller, Jeff ....Bryan, Ohio
Miller, L. ....New York, New York
Miller & Co. .... Wooster, Ohio
Miller, A. & Co. ....Milwaukee, Wisconsin
Miller, H. & Co..Louisville, Kentucky
Miller & Crow ....Kendallville, Indiana
Miller's Hair Dye...............................New York, New York
Milwaukee Fair ....See Non-Contemporary
Miner, Henry ....Pittsburgh, Pennsylvania

ALPHABETICAL INDEX-Continued

Miner, Henry .... Pittsburgh, Pennsylvania
Minger, J. U. .... Chicago, Illinois
Mitchell, C. T. & Co. .... Hillsdale, Michigan
Mittnacht, G. M. .... New York, New York
Mitzlaff, F. .... Milwaukee, Wisconsin
Moe, Geo. .... Detroit, Michigan
Monarch, S. B. .... Cincinnati, Ohio
Monk's Metal Signs .... New York, New York
Montz, Henry C. .... New York, New York
Moore, J. T. .... Cincinnati, Ohio
Moore, Wm. .... Chemung, Illinois
Morgan & Ferry .... Cincinnati, Ohio
Moritz Bro. & Co. .... Indianapolis, Indiana
Morris & Messinger .... Pontiac, Michigan
Morse, E. C. .... Mussey, Michigan
Mosely, H. L. .... Durand, Illinois
Moser, H. J. .... Cincinnati, Ohio
Mossin & Marr .... Milwaukee, Wisconsin
Mosure Bro. & Lemon .... Fredericktown, Ohio
Mott & Bro. .... Hillsdale, Michigan
Mott, C. E. & Co. .... Hillsdale, Michigan
Motter, Rufus. .... Chillicothe, Ohio
Mt. Vernon Club .... Baltimore, Maryland
Moulton, J. .... Watertown, Wisconsin
M. S. C. .... See Non-Contemporary
Mulligan, H. .... Philadelphia, Pennsylvania
Murdock, A. J. .... Logansport, Indiana
Murdock, Jas. Jr. .... Cincinnati, Ohio
Murdock & Spencer .... Cincinnati, Ohio
Murphy & Bro. .... Springfield, Ohio
Murray & Bro. .... Pierceton, Indiana
Muth, H. L. .... Janesville, Wisconsin
Myers, E. & Co. .... Cincinnati, Ohio
McBurney, Jos. .... Albany, New York
McCarthy, J. W. .... Pittsburgh, Pennsylvania
McCarty, Washington .... Urbana, Ohio
McCauley, J. .... Steubenville, Ohio
McClenahan, W. C & Co. .... Cincinnati, Ohio
McConville, D. .... Steubenville, Ohio
McCreery, Joseph .... Indianapolis, Indiana
McCullough, T. & N. C. .... Anderson, Indiana
McDonald, T. W. .... Cincinnati, Ohio
McDonald, Wm. .... Memphis, Tennessee
McDonald & Co. .... Logansport, Indiana
McGaw & Richey .... Oxford, Ohio
McGrew, W. H. .... West Unity, Ohio
McKain, J. .... Pittsburgh, Pennsylvania
McKay, John .... East Saginaw, Michigan
McKay & Lapsley .... Nashville, Tennessee
McKeen & Co. .... Galveston, Indiana
McLaughlin, Jas. .... See Non-Contemporary
McLean, G. W. .... North Hampton, Ohio
McLean, G. W. .... Springfield, Ohio
McMillan, T. M. .... Portage City, Wisconsin
McMillins, W. K. .... Sharonville, Ohio
McNeil, M. .... Elgin, Illinois
McVay, Jason .... Sidney, Ohio

N

Naper, Robert .... Naperville, Illinois
Nash, G. W. .... Brownsburg, Indiana
Naylor, W. H. .... Brighton, Michigan
Nebel, C. .... Sauk City, Wisconsin

Needles, C. H. .... See Non-Contemporary
Neenah, S. B. .... See Non-Contemporary
Neff, A. .... Oshkosh, Wisconsin
Neuburger & Hamburger .... La Porte, Indiana
Neuburger, J. M. .... La Porte, Indiana
Newcomb, D. F. .... Columbus, Wisconsin
Newcomb, E. .... Madison, Wisconsin
Newton, W. S. .... Sparta, Wisconsin
Newton & Kumlers .... Oxford, Ohio
New York & Albany Steamboat .... New York, New York
N.Y.C.R.R. Express .... Albany, New York
New York Stove .... Cedar Rapids, Iowa
New York Store .... Waterbury, Connecticut
Nicoll, D. & Bro. .... Wheeling, West Virginia
Neibuhr, H. .... Cincinnati, Ohio
Niemer, F. J. .... Cincinnati, Ohio
Nill, George C. .... Ligonier, Indiana
Nold & Co. .... Wooster, Ohio
Nolwer, J. H. .... Cincinnati, Ohio
Norris, R. D. .... Cincinnati, Ohio
N'pt & Cov. Bridge Co. .... Newport, Kentucky
Nye & Youmans .... Fond du Lac, Wisconsin

O

O. G. (O. Goffery) .... Cincinnati, Ohio
Oberly, C. .... Canton, Ohio
Odenwald, D. H. .... Chicago, Illinois
O'Donoghue & Naish .... Cincinnati, Ohio
Oppenheimer & Metzger .... Chicago, Illinois
O'Reilly Bros. .... Cincinnati, Ohio
Orr, F. B. .... Mansfield, Ohio
Osborn, M. .... Plainfield, Indiana
Osborne & Bro. .... Findlay, Ohio
Ostendorf, Wm. .... Chicago, Illinois
Ostrander, D. .... Jefferson, Wisconsin
Ott, George V. .... Madison, Wisconsin
Owen & Taylor, Mrs. .... Wilmington, Ohio

P

Packard, W. & A. J. .... Youngstown, Ohio
Packard & Co. .... West Greenville, Pennsylvania
Paeschke, Carl .... Milwaukee, Wisconsin
Page, J. M. & Co. .... Morenci, Michigan
Paige, S. B. & J. A. .... Oshkosh, Wisconsin
Pairan, Chas. .... Lancaster, Ohio
Palmer, F. J. & F. .... Atlas, Michigan
Palmer & Goodsall .... Hudson, Michigan
Panzer, B. .... Cincinnati, Ohio
Parker, A. .... Pontiac, Michigan
Parker, E. S. .... Niles, Michigan
Parker, Geo. H. .... Detroit, Michigan
Parker, H. S. & Co. .... Kalamazoo, Michigan
Parker, R. R. .... Indianapolis, Indiana
Parsons, G. .... New York, N.Y.
Parson & Barlow .... Appleton, Wisconsin
Patrick, James .... Wooster, Ohio
Passage Certificates from Liverpool to Chicago ....
.... Chicago, Illinois
Patterson. C. S. .... Tecumseh, Michigan
Pattison, I. N. .... Kokomo, Indiana
Pearce, J. .... Ligonier, Indiana
Pearson & Bro. .... Troy, Ohio
Pease, C. A. .... Ravenna, Ohio

608

ALPHABETICAL INDEX-Continued

Peck, W. G. ....Chicago, Illinois
Peck, D. & Co. ....Ironton, Missouri
Peck & Orvis...Baraboo, Wisconsin
Peck & Pratt..Beloit, Wisconsin
Peebles ....Cincinnati, Ohio
Peirce, J. W...Grand Rapids, Michigan
Pekin's Tea Store ....Pittsburgh, Pennsylvania
Penoyer & Larkin ....Paris, Illinois
Pentz, A. C...Pittsburgh, Pennsylvania
Perkins, A. T. ....Fond du Lac, Wisconsin
Perkins Hotel..Detroit, Michigan
Perkins, W. Jr..Detroit, Michigan
Perkins & Smith...Fond du Lac, Wisconsin
Perrin, H...Wilmington, Ohio
Perrin, L. W. ....Kalamazoo, Michigan
Peter, H. & J. T. ....Clarkston, Michigan
Petersen's...Honesdale, Pennsylvania
Peterson, H..Stoughton, Wisconsin
Pettibone, J. & Co. ....Fond du Lac, Wisconsin
Pfaff, Ches. ....New York, New York
Pfeiffer & Co. ....Norfolk, Virginia
Phelps, J, W. & Co. ....Mason, Michigan
Philip ....Cincinnati, Ohio
Phillips..Providence, Rhode Island
Phoenix House..Chillicothe, Ohio
Pierce S. & Son ....West Unity, Ohio
Pierr, P. ....Fort Wayne, Indiana
Piper, C..Charlotte, Michigan
Pittock's News Dealer.................................Pittsburgh, Pennsylvania
Pittock, John W. ....Pittsburgh, Pennsylvania
Pittsburgh Dry Goods ....Pittsburgh, Pennsylvania
Pittsburgh Gazette......................................Pittsburgh, Pennsylvania
Planer & Kayser..Milwaukee, Wisconsin
Platt, G. W. & H. C. ....Niles, Michigan
Pleisteiner, J. G..Cincinnati, Ohio
Plessner & Son..Toledo, Ohio
Plumb, Chas. ....Cincinnati, Ohio
Plum, Fred A. ....Troy, New York
Pogue & Jones...Cincinnati, Ohio
Pohle...Providence, Rhode Island
Pomeroy, Fry & Co......................................Indianapolis, Indiana
Pond, G. C. ....Detroit, Michigan
Pond, D. ....Dowagiac, Michigan
Porter, Henry ....Cincinnati, Ohio
Porter, G. C. & Co. ....Meadville, Pennsylvania
Post, John C. ....Buffalo, New York
Pottenger, D. R. & Co................................Warsaw, Indiana
Potter, P. L. ....Middletown, Ohio
Potwin, C. W. & Co. ....Zanesville, Ohio
Powell, M. L..New Castle, Indiana
Powers, E. K ....Grand Rapids, Michigan
Preissler, H...Louisville, Kentucky
Prentice, W. R. ....Chicago, Illinois
Prentiss, A. W...Monroeville, Ohio
Preston, C. W..See Non Contemporary
Preston, Wm. ....Wilmington, Ohio
Price Brothers ....Sullivan, Indiana
Pritzlaff, J. & Co. ....Milwaukee, Wisconsin
Prouty, F...Detroit, Michigan
Prusel, L. W. & Co.......................................Schoolcraft, Michigan
Pulmonales...Albany, New York
Purdy, A. M. ....South Bend, Indiana

Q

Queeby, J. J. ....Peru, Indiana
Quinlan, T. J..Cleveland, Ohio
Quinn, John ....New York, New York

R

R. G. ....Cincinnati, Ohio
Racek, T. ....Watertown, Wisconsin
Racek, Theodore ....Watertown, Wisconsin
Raker, Charles F..Vincennes, Indiana
Ramsey, J..New Lisbon, Wisconsin
Ramsey & Campbell....................................Madison, Wisconsin
Randal's Gallery ....Detroit, Michigan
Randall, L. H...Grand Rapids, Michigan
Rankin & Gibbs ....Special Non-Local
Rans, H. ....Oshkosh, Wisconsin
Ransick, H...Cincinnati, Ohio
Ratterman, H. A..Cincinnati, Ohio
Rauh, Christian ....New York, New York
Ravy, John ....Cincinnati, Ohio
Raymond, A..Fond du Lac, Wisconsin
Raymond's Gallery......................................Detroit, Michigan
Ream, J. S. ....Huntington, Indiana
Redfield, A. P. ....Beaver Dam, Wisconsin
Reed, Mrs. ....Ravenna, Ohio
Reed & Spayde..Pierceton, Indiana
Rees, I. ....Cincinnati, Ohio
Reeve, E. ....Ligonier, Indiana
Regensburg, H. ....Chicago, Illinois
Reid, Andrew..Lancaster, Ohio
Reilly's Bazaar ....Buffalo, New York
Reinhart, Wm. ....Chicago, Illinois
Reis, J. & Co...Cincinnati, Ohio
Reisse, John..Darien, Wisconsin
Remington, J. & Sons ....North Prairie, Wisconsin
Remington & Bennett.................................Adrian, Michigan
Resta, J. F. ....Cincinnati, Ohio
Restieaux, Wm. H.......................................Columbus, Ohio
Reymer & Bros...Pittsburgh, Pennsylvania
Reynolds & Co..Cedar Rapids, Iowa
Rhode & Hicks, Drs....................................Green Bay, Wisconsin
Riblet, D. & W...Galion, Ohio
Rice & Beyer ....Non-Local
Richards & Co. ....Morenci, Michigan
Richardson, D. W..Almont, Michigan
Richardson & Bro. ....Bellaire, Ohio
Ricke, A. ....Cincinnati, Ohio
Rickeys Book Store ....Dayton, Ohio
Ricking, B. J..Cincinnati, Ohio
Riegel, Geo. D. ....Laurelville, Ohio
Rigby, F. E. ....Chicago, Illinois
Riggs, Joseph ....Detroit, Michigan
Rinehart & Gray..Troy, Ohio
Ritter, Geo. W. ....Cincinnati, Ohio
Roberts, A. & Son.......................................Grand Rapids, Michigan
Roberts & Hillhouse ....Kalamazoo, Michigan
Roberts & Sheldon.....................................Fremont, Ohio
Robbin's Card...Warren, Ohio
Robinson, H. H. ....New London, Ohio
Robinson, J. M..Cadiz, Ohio
Robinson, L. H..Marshall, Michigan
Robinson, Yankee.......................................Cincinnati, Ohio
Robinson & Ball..Buffalo, New York

ALPHABETICAL INDEX-Continued

Robinson & Ballou .... Troy, New York
Rodermund, J. .... Madison, Wisconsin
Rodier, J. A. .... Detroit, Michigan
Rogers, F. P. .... Philadelphia, Pennsylvania
Rogers & Cassell .... Fredericktown, Ohio
Rolfe, Alonzo .... Detroit, Michigan
Roll & Smith .... Indianapolis, Indiana
Rollins, F. H. .... Cincinnati, Ohio
Rollwagen, Frederick Jr. .... New York, New York
Roos & Schmalzried .... Indianapolis, Indiana
Root, C. C. & Bro. .... Edgerton, Wisconsin
Rose, Dr. L. C. .... Detroit, Michigan
Rosenberger, M. .... Detroit, Michigan
Ross, Albert .... Cincinnati, Ohio
Roth, C. .... Wooster, Ohio
Rouse, Ellis .... Cincinnati, Ohio
Rowe, R. .... Hillsdale, Michigan
Rowe, J. L. & G. F. .... Corunna, Indiana
Rowe & Bro. .... Wooster, Ohio
Rowe & Co. .... Buffalo, New York
Rowell, G. S. & Son .... Kendallville, Indiana
Rudd, O. .... Willimantic, Connecticut
Ruelius, G. J. .... Philadelphia, Pennsylvania
Ruhl's .... Defiance, Ohio
Runkel, Wm. .... Tomah, Wisconsin
Runyon, C. .... Springfield, Ohio
Rupel, T. & Co. .... Chillicothe, Ohio
Russell, S. A. .... Danville, Indiana
Ryan, A. E. .... See Non-Contemporary
Ryon, Carr. .... Greenfield, Indiana

S

Stephen Yeatman S. Y. .... Cincinnati, Ohio
Sacksteder, John .... Cincinnati, Ohio
Sacksteder & Martin .... Cincinnati, Ohio
Sage, A. B. .... See Non-Contemporary
Saine & Miller .... Peru, Indiana
Sammons, S. .... Adrian, Michigan
Samm & Kuhlke .... Hillsdale, Michigan
Sam's Inn .... Boston, Massachusetts
Sanitary Commission .... Nantucket, Massachusetts
Sanitary Commission .... New York, New York
Sanitary Fair .... Wappakoneta, Ohio
Saylor, E. C. .... Tippecanoe, Ohio
Sayre, Jos. J. .... Cincinnati, Ohio
Sch, G. .... Cincinnati, Ohio
Schaaf, Ed .... New York, New York
Schafer & Bro. .... Huntington, Indiana
Scheidhauer, J. .... Milwaukee, Wisconsin
Schelven, G. V. .... Grand Haven, Michigan
Schettler, F. R. .... Green Bay, Wisconsin
Schloendorn, Chr. .... Cincinnati, Ohio
Schmidt, Geo. D. .... New York, New York
Schmidt, H. .... Cincinnati, Ohio
Schmidt, J. .... Detroit, Michigan
Schmitz, A. .... East Saginaw, Michigan
Schneider, L. .... Cincinnati, Ohio
Schoerpf, C. & Co. .... Ft. Wayne, Indiana
Schork, J. .... New York, New York
Schott, H. .... Cincinnati, Ohio
Schram, J. B. .... Milwaukee, Wisconsin
Schreiner, H. .... Columbus, Ohio
Schroder, John & Co. .... Detroit, Michigan

Schubert, John .... Hamilton, Ohio
Schuch, F. .... Loudenville, Ohio
Schuh's, John .... New York, New York
Schulze, Edwd. .... New York, New York
Schwartz, G. A. .... Philadelphia, Pennsylvania
Schultz & Negley .... Cincinnati, Ohio
Scott, Lot. .... Cincinnati, Ohio
Scripture, S. H. .... New York, New York
Sealy, H. A. .... Detroit, Michigan
Seas, J. F. .... Orrville, Ohio
Second Annual Fair (Union Saloon)
.... Philadelphia, Pennsylvania
Sedgwick, C. P. & Co. .... Bloomingdale, Illinois
Seeley, John .... Detroit, Michigan
Seiters, PH. J. .... New York, New York
Selby, E. G. .... Bryan, Ohio
Selby's E. G. & Co. .... Bryan, Ohio
Senour, J. F. .... Indianapolis, Indiana
Senour, Wm. .... Cincinnati, Ohio
Severn & Jones .... Milwaukee, Wisconsin
Seward, S. B. .... Buffalo, New York
Shafer, Mendal, M. .... Cincinnati, Ohio
Shagnon, J. B. .... Detroit, Michigan
Shakespeare Club .... Baltimore, Maryland
Shattuck, C. E. .... Owosso, Michigan
Shattuck, F. W. .... Providence, Rhode Island
Shaw, C. M. .... New London, Ohio
Shaw, H. E. .... Cincinnati, Ohio
Sheen, F. .... Cincinnati, Ohio
Sheldon, E. H. .... Constantine, Michigan
Shelvin, C. V. .... Grand Haven, Michigan
Sherer, John .... Allegheny City, Pennsylvania
Sherman, A. & Co. .... Paw Paw, Michigan
Sherman, A. M. .... Ogdenburg, New York
Sherman, H. W. .... Waukesha, Wisconsin
Sherman, J. D. .... Paw Paw, Michigan
Sherwood, I. P. .... Cleveland, Ohio
Sherwood, J. P. .... Cleveland, Ohio
Sherwood & Hopson .... Utica, New York
Shidlers, Isaac M. .... Plainfield, Indiana
Showerman & Bro. .... Ypsilanti, Michigan
Siegel, J. .... Hales Corner, Wisconsin
Siehler, J. F. .... Chicago, Illinois
Sinclair & Wilson .... Pittsburgh, Pennsylvania
Sinn, Wm. E. .... Cincinnati, Ohio
Sisk & Whalen .... Paris, Illinois
Skidmore, D. .... Seneca Falls, New York
Skinner, H. G. .... Marengo, Illinois
Sleight, H. G. .... Niles, Michigan
Sloan, F. .... Ionia, Michigan
Smart, J. .... North Prairie, Wisconsin
Smart & Co. .... Piqua, Ohio
Small, E. & L. .... Hagerstown, Indiana
Small, Robert .... See Non-Contemporary
Smick's .... Atlantic City, New Jersey
Smith, C. W. .... East Troy, Wisconsin
Smith, E. B. .... Detroit, Michigan
Smith, Frank .... Cincinnati, Ohio
Smith, H. L. .... Janesville, Wisconsin
Smith J. .... Cincinnati, Ohio
Smith, J. .... Special Non-Local
Smith, J. T. .... Whitewater, Wisconsin
Smith, J. W. C. .... Wheeling, West Virginia

ALPHABETICAL INDEX-Continued

Smith, S. & L. .... Cincinnati, Ohio
Smith, Seth & Son .... Detroit, Michigan
Smith, Wm. .... Lawrenceville, Pennsylvania
Smith, Wm. B. .... Detroit, Michigan
Smith, Yankee .... Detroit, Michigan
Smith Brothers .... Addison, Michigan
Smith & Taylor .... Indianapolis, Indiana
Snooks, Geo. .... Detroit, Michigan
Snow, S. F. .... West Unity, Ohio
Snow, Wm. .... Detroit, Michigan
Snow Hill .... Snow Hill, Maryland
Snyder, F. .... Cincinnati, Ohio
Snyder, Frank .... Pittsburgh, Pennsylvania
Sohm & Rohmann .... Buffalo, New York
Sommers, I. .... New York, New York
Sonder & Carpenter .... Tiffin, Ohio
Soper, B. H. .... Oshkosh, Wisconsin
Sosman, Wm. M. .... Chillicothe, Ohio
Spencer, M.S. .... Indianapolis, Indiana
Spitzer, J. B. .... Non-Local
Spreen, Chas. .... Cincinnati, Ohio
Squier, J. J. .... Cambridge, Ohio
Stalkamp, H. .... Cincinnati, Ohio
Stamm, C. T. & Son .... Milwaukee, Wisconsin
Standish, J. D. & C. B. .... Detroit, Michigan
Stanley, Geo. E. .... La Crosse, Wisconsin
Stanton, John .... Cincinnati, Ohio
Staples, L. J. .... Detroit, Michigan
Staudinger's .... New York, New York
Steamer Lancaster No. 4 .... Memphis, Tennessee
Stearn, Chas. W. .... Cleveland, Ohio
Stearns, D. E. .... Berea, Ohio
Stebbins & Wilson .... Ann Arbor, Michigan
Steer & Bowen .... Kendallville, Indiana
Stein, C. & S. .... Chicago, Illinois
Steinfield, S. .... New York, New York
Steinhart, S. .... Jefferson, Wisconsin
Steinmann, A. H. .... Milwaukee, Wisconsin
Stenton, Goff. .... Detroit, Michigan
Stephenson, G. W. .... St. Johns, Michigan
Steppacher .... Philadelphia, Pennsylvania
Stern, Sam .... Green Bay, Wisconsin
Stevers, M.D. .... Woodstock, Illinois
Stewart, M. L. .... Owosso, Michigan
Stifel, C. E. .... Wheeling, West Virginia
Stiles Gang Mills .... Oconto County, Wisconsin
Stirling, Wm. F. .... Eaton Rapids, Michigan
St. Charles Billiard Rooms .... New York, New York
St. Lewis, Z. Z. .... Green Bay, Wisconsin
St. Louis, J. J. .... Green Bay, Wisconsin
Stockman & Co. .... Memphis, Tennessee
Stoffel, D. .... Milwaukee, Wisconsin
Stoner & Shroyer .... Adamsville, Ohio
Story & Southworth .... New York, New York
Stokes, Granville .... Philadelphia, Pennsylvania
Straights Elephantine .... Albany, New York
Strasburger & Nuhn .... New York, New York
Straus Brothers .... Ligonier, Indiana
Strauus, Louis & Co. .... Elmira, New York
Stringer, Mrs. A. .... Detroit, Michigan
Strous, D. H. .... Adelphi, Ohio
Stuart, J. & Son .... Battle Creek, Michigan
Stucke & Co. .... Manitowoc, Wisconsin

Stump, Jacob .... Crestline, Ohio
Stumps, Peter .... Chicago, Illinois
Stutz, C. .... Middlebury, Indiana
Suettinger, R. .... Two Rivers, Wisconsin
Sutherland, G. W. .... Detroit, Michigan
Sutton, C. .... Cincinnati, Ohio
Swain, Ezra .... Mechanicsburg, Indiana

T

Tages London Yoke Shirt .... Cleveland, Ohio
Talbot, W. A. & Son .... Barnesville, Ohio
Tamsey & Ballard .... Plainfield, Indiana
Tate, Mrs. J. .... Oconomowoc, Wisconsin
Taylor, A. B. ...... Philadelphia, Pa. and Non-Contemporary
Taylor, C. H. .... Lodi, Illinois
Taylor, I. & C. .... Detroit, Michigan
Taylor, N. & G. Co. .... Philadelphia, Pennsylvania
Tea Store .... Detroit, Michigan
Tell, Wm. .... Cincinnati, Ohio
Teller, I. .... Milwaukee, Wisconsin
Tempest, S. B. .... Special Non-Local
Terhune Brothers .... Jersey City, New Jersey
Thelen & Dietrich .... Racine, Wisconsin
Thew, Joseph .... Kendallville, Indiana
Thiele, Friedrich .... Milwaukee, Wisconsin
Thierbach, Wm. .... New York, New York
Thomas, John .... Albany, New York
Thomas, J. H. .... Fortville, Indiana
Thomas, W. S. .... Kendallville, Indiana
Thompson & Spicer .... Fremont, Ohio
Thompson & Wiley .... Bethel, Indiana
Thompson, Mrs. A. & Son .... Indianapolis, Indiana
Timmerhjelstar, T. H. .... Wappakoneta, Ohio
Timmins, P. .... Norwalk, Ohio
Titus, B. W. .... Trenton, New Jersey
Todd, S. N. & Co. .... Sidney, Ohio
Tollner, C. & H. .... New York, New York
Tompkins Gallery .... Grand Rapids, Michigan
Tompkins, P. H. .... El Paso, Illinois
Torrey, R. S. .... Bangor, Maine
Tou, J. P. .... Pomeroy, Ohio
Town Branch Store .... East Saginaw, Michigan
Townley, E. .... Cincinnati, Ohio
Treleaven, W. .... Chicago, Illinois
Tressler, John .... West Jefferson, Ohio
Trowbridge's Jewelry Store .... Sheboygan, Wisconsin
Tubbs & Spear .... Hudson, Michigan
Tunis, W. E. .... Detroit, Michigan
Turpen, T. P. .... Greenville, Ohio
Turner, Charles .... East Saginaw, Michigan
Turner Hubbell & Co. .... Detroit, Michigan
Tuttle, S. S. .... Fredericktown, Ohio
Tuttles, C. F. .... Boston, Massachusetts
Twiford, A. S. .... Newcomerstown, Ohio
Tyler, C. .... Detroit, Michigan
Tyler, R. G. .... Detroit, Michigan
Tyler's Bee Hive .... Indianapolis, Indiana

U

Underwood, Geo. W. .... Hillsdale, Michigan
Underwood, N. O. .... Dedham, Tennessee
Union League .... See Non-Contemporary
Union Saloon .... Philadelphia, Pennsylvania
Upmeyer, H. .... Milwaukee, Wisconsin

ALPHABETICAL INDEX-Continued

V

Vail, C. G. ....Ligonier, Indiana
Van Cott, A. B. ....Racine, Wisconsin
Van Duyn & Lynch........................ Manchester, Michigan
Van Houten, Mrs. M. A. .... Columbus, Ohio
Van Ness & Turner ....Jonesville, Michigan
Van Wunder's...Cincinnati, Ohio
Van Valkenburgh, Dr. .... Whitewater, Wisconsin
Varwig, H. ....Cincinnati, Ohio
Venn & Wreford .... Detroit, Michigan
Viele, A. J...Lansing, Michigan
Voegtle & Metzger............................ Indianapolis, Indiana
Vogel, Jacob..Cincinnati, Ohio
Voigt, Hermann..................................Milwaukee, Wisconsin
Voight, Wm. .... Madison, Wisconsin
Vosburgh, G. W. ....Marshall, Wisconsin
Vosburg, Allen & Co........................... Oshkosh, Wisconsin

W

Wade, B. A. & Co. .... Chemung, Illinois
Wagner's Dining Hall .... Columbus, Ohio
Wagner, Wm. ....Ann Arbor, Michigan
Wahlstedt, A.................................. Whitewater, Wisconsin
Waldo & Brandon ....Cincinnati, Ohio
Walker, C. R. .... Buffalo, New York
Walker's Ale ....Urbana, Ohio
Walker & Napier............................. Nashville, Tennessee
Wallace, A. ....Chillicothe, Ohio
Wallace, A. W. .... Bridgeport, Connecticut
Wallace, W. W. .... La Porte, Indiana
Walsh, M. & Sons........................ Niagara Falls, New York
Walter & Smith ....Alton, Illinois
Walton, J. W. ....Woodsfield, Ohio
Ward's Lake Superior Line .... Cleveland, Ohio
Ward, William ....Ravenna, Ohio
Warmkessel, Peter ....New York, New York
Warner, C. R................................. See Non-Contemporary
Warner, J. H. ....New York, New York
Warner, Wm. F................................New York, New York
Warren, O. M. .... Beaver Dam, Wisconsin
Washburn, John.........................Columbia City, Indiana
Washington Market ....New York, New York
Washington Restaurant....................New York, New York
Waterman, N. T. .... Coldwater, Michigan
Watson, John.....................................New York, New York
Watson T Store ....New York, New York
Wayland, G. W. ....Jamestown, Indiana
Weatherby's ....Cincinnati, Ohio
Weaver, M. .... Lena, Illinois
Weaver & Fox.....................................Buchanan, Michigan
Weaver & Maguire........................... Indianapolis, Indiana
Webber, L. D. .... La Porte, Indiana
Weber, Henry .... Detroit, Michigan
Webster, R .... Detroit, Michigan
Webster & Co.................................... Buffalo, New York
Webster, Dumm & Co. .... Zanesville, Ohio
Wehrman, H. C. ....Cincinnati, Ohio
Weibezahn, Ed. .... Dixon, Illinois
Weighell & Sons.. Cincinnati, Ohio
Welch, D. S. ....Kendallville, Indiana
Wellers..Norwich, Connecticut
Welles, Henry C................................... Waterloo, New York

Welf, James ....Non-Local
Wentzel, John .... North Vernon, Indiana
Wert, W. W. ....Cincinnati, Ohio
Western Union Telegraph ....Cleveland, Ohio
Wheeler & Wilsons.............................. St. Paul, Minnesota
Wheelock, G. A. .... Dowagiac, Michigan
Wescott, L. C. ....New Lisbon, Wisconsin
White Hatter.....................................New York, New York
White Thomas...................................New York, New York
White & Swann .... Huntsville, Alabama
Whited & Co. ....Non-Local
Whitlark, W. W. .... Detroit, Michigan
Whitney Glass .... See Non-Contemporary
Wiatt & Bro.. Columbus, Ohio
Wightman, J. .... Newark, New Jersey
Wilcox, Wm. S. ....Adrian, Michigan
Wild, S..Dayton, Ohio
Wiles, L...Putnam, Ohio
Wilkins & Martin's................................. Detroit, Michigan
Wilkinson... Cincinnati, Ohio
Willard, C. A. .... Bellevue, Ohio
Willard & Jackson ....New York, New York
Williams, Daniel .... Brooklyn, New York
Williams, Wm. L................................Oshkosh, Wisconsin
Williams Bros .... Columbus, Wisconsin
Williams, J. C. & Co................................. Wheeling, Indiana
Williamsville Express.................. Williamsville, New York
Wilson, A. B. ....Cincinnati, Ohio
Wilson, J. B. .... Indianapolis, Indiana
Wilson, S. ....Special Non-Local
Winans, E. B. & Co. .... Bellaire, Ohio
Winckler, J. W. .... Detroit, Michigan
Wind, H. ....Cincinnati, Ohio
Winesteiner...Cincinnati, Ohio
Wing, F. M. .... Detroit, Michigan
Wing, D. L. & Co. .... Albany, New York
Winsauer, C. ....Chicago, Illinois
Winter, G. .... Detroit, Michigan
Wirth, E. ....Mayfield, Wisconsin
Wisner, D. A. & Son.....................Jonesville, Michigan
Witgen, A. .... Detroit, Michigan
Woessner, John ....Cincinnati, Ohio
Wolfe & Sherman................................ Alexandria, Indiana
Wolfer, C. .... Detroit, Michigan
Wolff, Henry...Detroit, Michigan
Wood Co. Bridge........................... See Non-Contemporary
Wood, A. D. .... Indianapolis, Indiana
Wood & Harrington ....Cincinnati, Ohio
Woodward, W. H. P............................Mooresville, Indiana
Worthington, Geo., & Co............................ Cleveland, Ohio
Wraith, T. R. ....Wilmington, Ohio
Wright...Cincinnati, Ohio
Wright, A. & C. F........................ Harvard, Massachusetts
Wright, Robert..Cincinnati, Ohio
Wright, Sid. .... Non-Local
Wright, T. S. .... Fond du Lac, Wisconsin
Wyman, George.................................South Bend, Indiana

X

Xelar, H. B. ....Cincinnati, Ohio

ALPHABETICAL INDEX-Continued

Y

Yager, J. C. .... Springfield, Illinois
Young, L. .... Cincinnati, Ohio

Z

Zahm, S. H. .... Lancaster, Pennsylvania
Zandt, Joseph .... Cincinnati, Ohio
Zanone, Joseph .... Cincinnati, Ohio
Zeltner, John .... Cincinnati, Ohio
Zimmerman, J. C. .... Ligonier, Indiana

STATES AND TOWNS THAT ISSUED CIVIL WAR CARDS

Alabama
Huntsville................... 32

Connecticut
Bridgeport.................. 7
Norwich..................... 3
Waterbury 3
Willimantic.................. 2
4 towns 15

Illinois
Alton........................ 2
Aurora....................... 2
Belvidere.................... 5
Bloomingdale................ 13
Cairo........................ 8
Chemung..................... 5
Chicago..................... 160
De Kalb...................... 5
Dixon........................ 2
Durand....................... 2
Elgin........................ 1
El Paso...................... 3
Fairview..................... 1
Freeport.................... 14
Lacon........................ 6
La Salle..................... 2
Lena......................... 7
Lodi......................... 3
Marengo...................... 1
Mendota...................... 1
Naperville................... 5
Ottawa....................... 2
Palatine..................... 2
Paris....................... 39
Peru......................... 2
Pontiac...................... 1
Rockford.................... 10
Rockton...................... 4
Sandwich..................... 7
Springfield.................. 5
Sycamore..................... 4
Waukegan..................... 8
Woodstock.................... 1
33 towns 332

Indiana
Albany....................... 1
Alexandria................... 8
Anderson..................... 4
Avilla....................... 6
Bethel....................... 3
Bowling Green............... 16
Brazil....................... 6
Brooklyn..................... 6
Brookville.................. 11
Brownsburg 3
Brownstown 2
Butler....................... 2
Cadiz....................... 13
Centerville.................. 6
Columbia City............... 17
Como......................... 6
Corunna..................... 15

Danville.................... 15
Dublin....................... 6
Elkhart..................... 12
Evansville................... 2
Fortville.................... 4
Fort Wayne.................. 16
Franklin..................... 4
Fremont...................... 7
Galveston.................... 2
Goshen...................... 19
Granville.................... 6
Greenfield................... 6
Greensboro................... 1
Hagerstown.................. 10
Hartford City................ 6
Huntington 12
Indianapolis............... 126
Jamestown 3
Jonesboro.................... 6
Kendallville................ 49
Kokomo....................... 3
La Porte.................... 15
Ligonier.................... 37
Lisbon....................... 2
Logansport.................. 10
Lynn........................ 16
Mechanicsburg 4
Middlebury 5
Middletown 7
Mishawaka 24
Mooresville 3
New Castle 4
New Paris 3
North Vernon 2
Oldenburg.................... 1
Peru........................ 10
Pierceton 2
Plainfield.................. 31
Plymouth 3
Richmond.................... 22
Rochester 6
Seymour 3
South Bend 18
Sullivan..................... 6
Swan......................... 2
Terre Haute................. 1
Valparaiso................... 2
Vincennes.................... 2
Wabash....................... 2
Warsaw...................... 10
Wheeling..................... 4
Wolf Creek................... 5
69 towns 702

Iowa
Cedar Rapids................. 3
Lansing...................... 4
Lyons........................ 1
Waterloo..................... 6
4 towns 14

Kansas
Leavenworth 2

Kentucky
Covington................... 22
Henderson.................... 3
Lexington................... 20
Louisville.................. 20
Newport..................... 14
5 towns 79

Maine
Bangor....................... 3

Maryland
Baltimore.................... 5
Hagerstown................... 1
Snow Hill 5
3 towns 11

Massachusetts
Boston...................... 24
Fall River................... 8
Harvard...................... 1
Nantucket.................... 5
Worcester 2
5 towns 40

Michigan
Addison 3
Adrian 20
Albion 5
Almont 2
Ann Arbor 40
Atlas 7
Battle Creek 5
Bay City 4
Brighton 19
Buchanan 2
Cassopolis 1
Charlotte 10
Chelsea 2
Clarkston 14
Coldwater 2
Constantine 4
Corunna 8
Detroit 709
Dowagiac 17
East Saginaw............... 27
Eaton Rapids............... 13
Flint 4
Grand Haven.................. 8
Grand Rapids 55
Hastings 5
Hillsdale 49
Hudson 17
Ionia 9
Jackson 25
Jonesville 13
Kalamazoo 25
Lansing 11
Lapeer 6
Lawton 4
Litchfield 2
Lowell 7
Lyons 10
Manchester 4

Maple Rapids................. 2
Marshall 18
Mason 6
Morenci 5
Mussey 6
Niles 20
Owosso 5
Parma 2
Paw Paw 9
Pontiac 10
Saginaw City 4
Salina....................... 3
Saranac 2
Schoolcraft 6
St. Johns 3
Tecumseh 12
Ypsilanti 17
55 towns 1292

Minnesota
Red Wing 9
Rochester 7
St. Paul 88
Winona 4
4 towns 108

Missouri
Ironton 4
St. Joseph................... 1
St. Louis 20
3 towns 25

New Hampshire
Concord 1

New Jersey
Atlantic City................ 3
Elizabethport................ 4
Jersey City 1
Newark 79
Perth Amboy 2
Trenton 3
Williamstown 1
7 towns 93

New York
Albany 46
Almond 1
Belmont 3
Binghamton 4
Brooklyn 51
Buffalo 106
Cohoes 8
Cooperstown 41
Elmira 6
Fort Edwards................. 3
Greenpoint 11
New York...................1076
Niagara Falls 6
Ogdensburg 14
Oswego 6
Poughkeepsie 1
Seneca Falls 11
Troy 55

614

STATES AND TOWNS THAT ISSUED CIVIL WAR CARDS

Utica	6
Waterloo	4
Watertown	2
Whitehall	3
Williamsville	1
Yonkers	3
24 towns	**1468**

Ohio

Adamsville	44
Adelphi	2
Ashland	1
Barnesville	8
Bellaire	15
Bellevue	10
Belmont	1
Berea	21
Beverly	1
Birmingham	2
Bryan	9
Cadiz	22
Cambridge	20
Camden	8
Canaan	1
Canton	14
Centerville	4
Chesterville	12
Chillicothe	35
Cincinnati	1973
Circleville	16
Clarksburg	3
Cleveland	104
Collinsville	9
Columbiana	17
Columbus	58
Crestline	1
Dayton	17
Defiance	9
Delphos	8
Edgerton	7
Elyria	5
Findlay	10
Frazeysburg	5
Fredericktown	13
Fremont	21
Galion	2
Gallipolis	12
Greenville	17
Hamilton	28
Hillsboro	9
Jackson	4
Kenton	1
Lancaster	14
Laurelville	8
Lima	6
Loudenville	2
Mansfield	20
Marion	3
Martinsburg	4
Massillon	21
Maumee City	4
McConnelsville	2
Middletown	11
Monroeville	15
Morristown	3
Morrow	3
Mt. Eaton	2
Navarre	5
Newcomerstown	2
New Lisbon	1
New London	20
North Hampton	10
North Liberty	3
Norwalk	3
Oberlin	3
Orrville	8
Oxford	6
Perrysburg	6
Piqua	16
Pomeroy	9
Portsmouth	11
Putnam	4
Ravenna	16
Richmond	9
Ripley	1
Sharonville	7
Shelby	14
Sidney	7
Sonora	1
Springfield	69
Steubenville	20
Stryker	4
Syracuse	3
Tiffin	6
Tippecanoe	4
Toledo	15
Troy	30
Uniontown	2
Urbana	5
Van Wert	1
Wappakoneta	9
Warren	2
Wellsville	7
West Jefferson	1
West Newton	7
West Unity	14
Wilmington	11
Woodsfield	6
Wooster	49
Xenia	1
Youngstown	3
Zanesville	45
102 towns	**3173**

Pennsylvania

Allegheny City	51
Bakerstown	2
Erie	1
Honesdale	29
Lancaster	10
Lawrenceville	5
Meadville	1
Mount Washington	1
Philadelphia	94
Pittsburgh	142
West Greenville	1
Wilkes Barre	2
12 towns	**338**

Rhode Island

Providence	174

Tennessee

Clarksville	7
Dedham	5
Knoxville	5
Memphis	80
Nashville	28
5 towns	**125**

Virginia

Norfolk	1

West Virginia

Glen Easton	7
Hartford City	2
Wheeling	36
3 towns	**45**

Wisconsin

Appleton	9
Baraboo	13
Barton	1
Beaver Dam	5
Beloit	1
Columbus	8
Cross Plains	2
East Troy	12
Edgerton	1
Fond du Lac	30
Genesee Station	1
Green Bay	23
Hales Corner	1
Janesville	15
Jefferson	5
Juneau	3
Kenosha	9
Kilbourn City	2
La Crosse	6
Madison	24
Manitowoc	19
Marshall	4
Mauston	1
Mayfield	10
Milwaukee	161
Neenah	2
Newburg	1
New Lisbon	2
North Prairie	3
Oconomowoc	1
Oconto County	2
Oshkosh	38
Portage City	1
Port Washington	1
Racine	35
Ripon	10
Sauk City	2
Sheboygan	6
Sparta	2
Stoughton	5
Tomah	2
Two Rivers	1
Waterloo	2
Watertown	40
Waukesha	3
Whitewater	11
46 towns	**536**

Total Store Cards	8426
Non-Local	65
Special Non Local	11
Non-Contemporary	53
TOTAL	**8555**

STATES AND TOWNS THAT ISSUED CIVIL WAR CARDS

Utica	6	Kenton	1	Wellsville	7	Beaver Dam	5
Waterloo	4	Lancaster	14	West Jefferson	1	Beloit	1
Watertown	2	Laurelville	8	West Newton	7	Columbus	8
Whitehall	3	Lima	6	West Unity	14	Cross Plains	2
Williamsville	1	Loudenville	2	Wilmington	11	East Troy	12
Yonkers	3	Mansfield	20	Woodsfield	6	Edgerton	1
24 towns	1468	Marion	3	Wooster	49	Fond du Lac	30
		Martinsburg	4	Xenia	1	Genesee Station	1
Ohio		Massillon	21	Youngstown	3	Green Bay	23
Adamsville	44	Maumee City	4	Zanesville	45	Hales Corner	1
Adelphi	2	McConnelsville	2	**102 towns**	**3173**	Janesville	15
Ashland	1	Middletown	11			Jefferson	5
Barnesville	8	Monroeville	15	**Pennsylvania**		Juneau	3
Bellaire	15	Morristown	3	Allegheny City	51	Kenosha	9
Bellevue	10	Morrow	3	Bakerstown	2	Kilbourn City	2
Belmont	1	Mt. Eaton	2	Erie	1	La Crosse	6
Berea	21	Navarre	5	Honesdale	29	Madison	24
Beverly	1	Newcomerstown	2	Lancaster	10	Manitowoc	19
Birmingham	2	New Lisbon	1	Lawrenceville	5	Marshall	4
Bryan	9	New London	20	Meadville	1	Mauston	1
Cadiz	22	North Hampton	10	Mount Washington	1	Mayfield	10
Cambridge	20	North Liberty	3	Philadelphia	94	Milwaukee	161
Camden	8	Norwalk	3	Pittsburgh	142	Neenah	2
Canaan	1	Oberlin	3	West Greenville	1	Newburg	1
Canton	14	Orrville	8	Wilkes Barre	2	New Lisbon	2
Centerville	4	Oxford	6	**12 towns**	**338**	North Prairie	3
Chesterville	12	Perrysburg	6			Oconomowoc	1
Chillicothe	35	Piqua	16	**Rhode Island**		Oconto County	2
Cincinnati	1973	Pomeroy	9	Providence	114	Oshkosh	38
Circleville	16	Portsmouth	11			Portage City	1
Clarksburg	3	Putnam	4	**Tennessee**		Port Washington	1
Cleveland	104	Ravenna	16	Clarksville	7	Racine	35
Collinsville	9	Richmond	9	Dedham	5	Ripon	10
Columbiana	17	Ripley	1	Knoxville	5	Sauk City	2
Columbus	50	Rimersville	7	Memphis	80	Sheboygan	6
Crestline	1	Shelby	14	Nashville	28	Sparta	2
Dayton	17	Sidney	7	**5 towns**	**125**	Stoughton	5
Defiance	9	Sonora	1			Tomah	2
Delphos	8	Springfield	69	**Virginia**		Two Rivers	1
Edgerton	7	Steubenville	20	Norfolk	1	Waterloo	2
Elyria	5	Stryker	4			Watertown	40
Findlay	10	Syracuse	3	**West Virginia**		Waukesha	3
Frazeysburg	5	Tiffin	6	Glen Easton	7	Whitewater	11
Fredericktown	13	Tippecanoe	4	Hartford City	2	**46 towns**	**536**
Fremont	21	Toledo	15	Wheeling	36		
Galion	2	Troy	30	**3 towns**	**45**	Total Store Cards	8426
Gallipolis	12	Uniontown	2			Non-Local	65
Greenville	17	Urbana	5	**Wisconsin**		Special Non-Local	11
Hamilton	28	Van Wert	1	Appleton	9	Non-Contemporary	53
Hillsboro	9	Wappakoneta	0	Baraboo	13	**TOTAL**	**8555**
Jackson	4	Warren	2	Barton	1		

CATALOG OF UNLISTED CIVIL WAR STORECARDS IN THE COLLECTION OF THE AMERICAN NUMISMATIC SOCIETY

Compiled by
Jon Harris

AN INTRODUCTION

The fabulous collection of Civil War Store Cards in the American Numismatic Society numbering approximately 6,000 different pieces, which remained essentially uncatalogued for the entire past century, contains a wealth of new information which further complements this numismatic field. In cataloging this vast collection for the first time many important new discoveries have been made, as expected. The text which follows contains a comprehensive listing of the 181 previously-unknown store cards contained in this collection. This includes, most important of all, several new merchants; new obverse and reverse dies; unlisted overstrikes, brockages, and mulings; and, of course, new metal and edge varieties. Photos of these new merchants and new dies, along with photos of listed pieces for which no photo had been previously available, have been provided in the text in their proper places.

In addition to the listing of new varieties, there follows in this text an extensive group of further corrections and revisions to the second edition of Fulds' *U.S. Civil War Store Cards*. These further corrections and revisions, discovered and verified only through cataloging a collection of this magnitude, will update your store card reference and bring it that much closer to attaining the status of a perfect reference book.

Acknowledgements — A note of appreciation is due the entire curatorial staff of the American Numismatic Society, with whose cooperation this project has been most successfully completed. Special thanks are in order to Dr. Richard G. Doty, Assistant Curator of Modern Coins, whose helpful suggestions and assistance in this cataloging project have been greatly appreciated.

Also, special thanks to Mr. John Francis of Verona, N.J., who devoted a great many hours of his time to this cataloging project along with Mr. Richard Rossa of Brooklyn, N.Y., who ably assisted in the New York section of the cataloging. My sincere gratitude to both of these dedicated specialists of our Civil War Token Society.

Coral Gables, Florida
April 1975

Jon Harris

CATALOGUE of
UNLISTED CIVIL WAR STORECARDS in the COLLECTION of the
AMERICAN NUMISMATIC SOCIETY
NEW YORK CITY, NEW YORK

	Number	Obverse	Reverse	Metal	Edge	Rarity	H&G

CHICAGO, ILL.

(1)	150U-4b	(JAMES FOSTER JR. & CO.) Same (C/S "54" in center of obverse and holed at top)	Blank	BR	R	R10	
(2)	150AI-4b	(O. KENDALL'S SONS) Same	1203	BR	PL	R10	
(3)	150BB-3g	(J.F. SIEHLER) Same	Same (1354)	L	PL	R10	
(4)	150BB-5a	(J.F. SIEHLER) Same	1072	C	PL	R8	

(NOTE: A previously overlooked variety due to the similarity of the two different obverse dies, therefore, probably not rare.)

NAPERVILLE, ILL.

(5)	615A-2d	(ROBERT NAPER) Same	Same (1047)	C-N	R	R10	

DANVILLE, IND.

(6)	230C-2d	(S.A. RUSSELL) Same	Same (1047)	C-N	R	R10	

GRANVILLE, IND.

(7)	355A-1i1	(C. CROOKS & CO.) Same	Same (1037)	Z	PL	R10	

INDIANAPOLIS, IND.

(8)	460F-5a	(J.B. GROUT) Same	1043	C	R	R9	
(9)	460T-1b/a	(M. SPENCER) Same	Same (1037)	BR/C	R	R10	

(NOTE: Obverse is Brass; Reverse is Copper. Struck on a distinctly bi-metallic planchet. Looking at the edge, there is an obvious line between the brass and copper halves of the planchet. Both sides of the piece are bright B.U. thus there is no deceptive toning; the most distinctly obvious bi-metallic C.W. Storecard which I've ever seen.)

(10)	460Y-3e1	(J.B. WILSON'S) Same	Same	W-M	R	R8	
(11)	460Y-4e1	Same	Same	W-M	R	R8	

Number	Obverse	Reverse	Metal	Edge	Rarity	H&G

LOGANSPORT, IND.

(12)
570B-1i (H.C. EVERSOLE)
Same   Same   Z   PL   R10
(C/S "92" in center of obverse and holed at top as probably all are.
Ex-J. Guttag; Acq. - May, 1936.)

PERU, IND.

(13)
740B-6fp (J.S. QUEEBY)
Same   Same (1384)   S-P/C   PL   R?

PLAINFIELD, IND.

(14)
770B-5d (M. OSBORN)
Same   1069   C-N   R   R10

(15)
770C-4d (ISAAC M. SHIDLER)
Same as Rev. of   1069   C-N   R   R10
IND. 770C-1a

RICHMOND, IND.

(16)
800B-5d (G.P. EMSWILER & CO.)
Same   Same (1047)   C-N   R   R10

SULLIVAN, IND.

(17)
870A-5a (PRICE BROTHERS)
Same   1025   C   PL   R9

LANSING, IOWA

(18)
560A-4d (WM. FLEMMING & BRO.)
Same   1046   C-N   R   R10

COVINGTON, KY.

(19)
150B-3d (COV. & CIN. FERRY)
Same   Same (1047)   C-N   R   R10

LEXINGTON, KY.

(20)
480A-2b (J.L. KEININGHAM)
Similar, different die   10/CENTS   BR   R   R10
with different spacing   (New Rev. Die)
(Larger - 22 mm)

480A-2
Obv.

480A-2
Rev.

	Number	Obverse	Reverse	Metal	Edge	Rarity	H&G

LEXINGTON, KY. (Continued)

| (21) | 480B-8d | (JOHN W. LEE)
Same | 1069 | C-N | R | R10 | |

ANN ARBOR, MICH.

| (22) | 40A-1f | (PHILIP BACH)
Same
(NOTE: Not overstruck, both dies heavily clashed.) | Same (1015) | S | PL | R9 | |

BRIGHTON, MICH.

| (23) | 85B-4d | (WM. R. COBB)
Same | 1046 | C-N | R | R10 | |

DETROIT, MICH.

(24)	225D-4d	(BLINDBURY'S HOTEL) Same	Same (1047)	C-N	R	R10	
(25)	225G-1a1	(GEO. BEARD & SON) Same	Same (1025)	C	PL	R9	
(26)	225H-4d	(H.W. BEESON) Same	Same (1046)	C-N	R	R10	
(27)	225J-2d	(FRED'K C. BLOME) Same	Same (1047)	C-N	R	R10	
(28)	225K-4d	(BROEG & GERBER) Same	Same (1046)	C-N	R	R10	
(29)	225L-4d	(F.A. DUIWIART) Same	Same (1046)	C-N	R	R10	
(30)	225MA-5d	(CAMPBELL & CALNON) Same	1046	C-N	R	R10	
(31)	225S-3d	(C.L. CROSBY) Same	1046	C-N	R	R10	
(32)	225V-3a1	(DETROIT CITY FLOUR MILLS) Same	Same (1039)	C	PL	R9	
(33)	225AG-5d	(F. GIES) Same	Same (1047)	C-N	R	R10	
(34)	225AG-6d	(F. GIES & BRO'S) Same as Obv. of MICH. 225AG-1a (NOTE: Multiple die breaks on reverse die.)	1046	C-N	R	R10	
(35)	225AJa-3d	(HEINMAN'S) Same	Same (1047)	C-N	R	R10	
(36)	225AW-2a1	(M. MARX) Same	Same (1039)	C	PL	R9	
(37)	225BM-5a1	(M. ROSENBERGER) Same	1040	C	PL	R10	
(38)	225CJ-4a	(VENN & WREFORD) Same	1039	C	R	R9	

Number	Obverse	Reverse	Metal	Edge	Rarity	H&G

GRAND RAPIDS, MICH.

(39)
370D-4b (GOODRICH & GAY)
Same as Obv. of   1307A   BR   PL   R9
MICH. 370D-1   (New Rev. Die)
(NOTE: Photo of Reverse Die 1307A is located in its proper position in the section of this addendum on further "Corrections & Revisions.")

HILLSDALE, MICH.

(40)
450C-3b (CARD, PEARCE, & CO.)
         Same   Same (1186)   BR   PL   R9
(41)
450G-2g (A. GLEASON)
         Same   Same (1184)   L   PL   R9
(NOTE: Possible cast counterfeit.)

LAPEER, MICH.

(42)
565A-4d (H. GRISWOLD & CO.)
         Same   1046   C-N   R   R10
(NOTE: Reverse die badly cracked.)

NILES, MICH.

(43)
700D-4a (G.W. & H.C. PLATT)
         Same   1099   C   PL   R9

PONTIAC, MICH.

(44)
770C-1c (A. PARKER)
         Same (thick planchet)   Same   N   PL   R10

ST. LOUIS, MO.

(45)
910C-4a (HENRY JENKENS)
         Same   Same as Obv. of   C   PL   R10
                           OHIO 165GX-1
                           Incused
(NOTE: A most curious piece — a bi-state, bi-merchant muling — the reverse of which is incused!)

910C-4
Rev.

	Number	Obverse	Reverse	Metal	Edge	Rarity	H&G

ALBANY, N.Y.

(46)	10A-6e	(BENJAMIN & HERRICK) Same	Same	W-M	PL	R9
(47)	10A-6j	Same	Same	G-S	PL	R9
(48)	10A-9j	Same	Same (1276)	G-S	PL	R9
(49)	10H-6Aa	(D.L. WING & CO.) O-5	Obverse die incused	C	PL	R10

10H-6Aa Rev.

BROOKLYN, N.Y.

(50)	95F-2bl	(DANIEL WILLIAMS) Same, thick planchet	Same (1137)	BR	PL	R9
(51)	95F-2c	Same	Same (1137)	N	PL	R9

COOPERSTOWN, N.Y.

(52)	145B-1e1	(G.L. BOWNE) Same (Lg. Flan — 21.5 mm)	Same	W-M	PL	R9
(53)	145B-1f	Same	Same	S	PL	R9

NEW YORK CITY

(54)	630A-1do	(ATLANTIC GARDEN) Same, over U.S. C-N cent	Same	C-N	PL	R9
(55)	630B-3a1	(CAFE AUTENRIETH) Same, thick planchet	Same (1257)	C	PL	R5
(56)	630H-3bo	(J.L. BODE) Same	1011 struck over Rev. of N.Y. 630H-1	BR	PL	R10
(57)	630K-4fo	(T. BRIMELOW) Same, struck over British Shilling (1846)	Same (1138)	S	R	R10
(58)	630O-2bo	(W.S. BROWN) Same	1011 struck over Rev. of N.Y. 630O-1	BR	PL	R10
(59)	630Q-5bo	(CITY OF NEW YORK) Same, struck over Rev. of 1849-dated California Game Counter	Blank	BR	R	R10

9

Number	Obverse	Reverse	Metal	Edge	Rarity	H&G

NEW YORK CITY (Continued)

(60) 630Q-6bo (CITY OF NEW YORK) Same, struck over Rev. of Temperance Token (Man at well) — Blank — BR — R — R10

(61) 630Q-7a — Same — 1164 — C — PL — R10

(62) 630T-1do (J.J. DIEHL) Same, over U.S. C-N cent — Same (1011) — C-N — PL — R10

(63) 630AE-1f (G. GRAHAM) Same — Same (1263) — S — PL — R9
(NOTE: Not overstruck.)

(64) 630AE-1io Same, Obv. struck over Rev. — Same (1263) struck over Obv. — Z — PL — R10
(NOTE: Flip-over Double-struck.)

(65) 630AG-1fo (JOHN P. GRUBER) Same, struck over Prussian 2½ Groschen (1843) — Same (1197) — Billon — PL — R10

(66) 630AH-1bl (A.J. HENNING) Same — Same — BR — R — R10
(67) 630AH-1el Same, thick planchet — Same — W-M — PL — R9
(68) 630AH-1fo Same, struck over U.S. Quarter of 1862 — Same — S — R — R10
(NOTE: This piece might well be that listed as 630AH-1fl, as the undertype is extremely faint.)

(69) 630AM-1f (CHRISTOPH KARL) Same — Same (1164) — S — PL — R10
(NOTE: Not overstruck.)

(70) 630AP-5do (H.M. LANE) Same, over U.S. C-N cent (1863) — Same (1132) — C-N — PL — R9

(71) 630AP-17do Same, over U.S. C-N cent — Same (1277) — C-N — PL — R9

(72) 630AR-1f (CHARLES A. LUHRS) Same — Same — S — PL — R9
(NOTE: Not overstruck.)

(73) 630AR-3do Same as Rev. of N.Y. 630AR-1 struck over U.S. C-N cent of 1863 — 1293 struck over Obv. of N.Y. 630AR-1 (struck over Rev. of the C-N cent) — C-N — PL — R10
NOTE: This piece might well be that listed as 630AR-2d, in which case the -2d variety is inaccurately described. A most unusual and interesting piece to say the least!)

(74) 630AV-1b (JOHN MATTHEWS) Same — Same — BR — PL — R9

(75) 630BH-1do (CHRISTIAN RAUH) Same, over U.S. C-N cent — Same (1293) — C-N — PL — R9

(76) 630BH-2f Same — Same (1293) — S — PL — R9

(77) 630BK-1bl (ED. SCHAFF) Same, extremely thin planchet — Same (1230) — BR — PL — R9

10

Number	Obverse	Reverse	Metal	Edge	Rarity	H&G

NEW YORK CITY (Continued)

(78) 630BM-4a (JOHN SCHUH'S) Same, struck over Obv. of N.Y. 630H — Same (Obv. of 630Q) — C — PL — R10

630BM-4 Obv.

(79) 630BV-6do (STORY & SOUTHWORTH) Same, over U.S. C-N cent (1863) — Same (1216) — C-N — PL — R9

BELLAIRE, OHIO

(80) 60C-4a (RICHARDSON & BRO.) Same — 1178 — C — PL — R9

BELLEVUE, OHIO

(81) 65B-3do (P. BRADY) Same, over U.S. C-N cent of 1859 — Same (1297) — C-N — PL — R10
(82) 65B-3g Same — Same (1297) — L — PL — R10
(83) 65B-4g Same — Blank — L — PL — R10

CAMBRIDGE, OHIO

(84) 115A-9a (A.C. COCHRAN) Same — 1304 - Incused — C — PL — R10

CINCINNATI, OHIO

(85) 165N-27a (DR. BENNETT'S) Same as Obv. of OHIO 165N-10a — 1030 — C — PL — R9
(86) 165V-3a1 (CHAMBERLAIN BROS) Same — Same (1311) — C — PL — R10
(87) 165X-4d (CITY HOSIERY STORE) Same — Same (1047) — C-N — R — R10
(88) 165AE-3b (COSTELLO'S) Same — Same (1019) — BR — PL — R9

Number	Obverse	Reverse	Metal	Edge	Rarity	H&G

CINCINNATI, OHIO (Continued)

(89)	165AK-2d	(R. DOWNING) Same	Same (1047)	C-N	R	R10	
(90)	165AW-10a	(CHAS. FLACH) Same	1036	C	PL	R8	
(91)	165AX-5d	(JAMES FOSTER JR. & CO.) Same as Obv. of OHIO 165AX-1a	1046	C-N	R	R10	
(92)	165AZ-3d	(FROST'S MEDICINE) Same	Same (1046)	C-N	R	R10	
(93)	165BJ-1b	(CARL HAAS) Same	Same (1019)	BR	PL	R9	
(94)	165BJ-19i	Same	Same (1034)	Z	PL	R9	
(95)	165BJ-25a	Same	1036	C	PL	R8	
(96)	165BT-14a	(B. HEMPELMAN) Same	STANTON/STEEL/STAMPS,/ BRANDS/&/STENCILS/ 139 FIFTH, ST.	C	PL	R10	

NOTE: This is a new reverse die of Stanton. This new variety might very well be the piece listed as 165BT-13a with reverse described as the same as the Obverse of OHIO 165FX-20. The 165BT-13a listing probably does not exist as described as this new Stanton reverse die is probably the correct die intended for the 165BT-13a listing. According to the description in H&G of the reverse Stanton die, this hypothesis is correct.

165BT-14 Rev.

(97)	165CC-2d	(B. JAHR) Same	Same (1047)	C-N	R	R10	
(98)	165CE-2a	(H. JOHNSTON) Same	1386	C	PL	R9	
(99)	165CY-9Aa	(W.K. LANPHEAR) Same	1169	C	PL	R9	
(100)	165CY-9Ab	Same	1169	BR	PL	R9	
(101)	165CY-21b	Same	Same (1300)	BR	PL	R9	
(102)	165CY-66a/b	Same	Same (1295)	C/BR	PL	R9	

(NOTE: Struck on bi-metallic planchet. Obverse is Copper and Reverse is Brass.)

(103)	165CY-71Aa	Same	1304	C	PL	R9	
(104)	165CY-71Ab	Same	1304	BR	PL	R9	
(105)	165EL-6a	(J.G. PLEISTEINER) Same	1019	C	PL	R9	
(106)	165EL-6b	Same	1019	BR	PL	R9	

Number	Obverse	Reverse	Metal	Edge	Rarity	H&G

CINCINNATI, OHIO (Continued)

(107) 165EN-7a	(POGUE & JONES) Same	1028	C	PL	R9	
(108) 165EP-2b	(H. RANSICK) Same	Same as Rev. of OHIO 905C	BR	R	R9	

165EP Obv.

165EP-2 Rev.

(109) 165FB-3d	(ELIS ROUSE'S) Same	1069	C-N	R	R10	
(110) 165FX-24a	(JOHN STANTON) Same	1027	C	PL	R10	
(111) 165GB-13b	(E. TOWNLEY) Same	Same as Obv. of OHIO 165FH (H. SCHMIDT'S)	BR	PL	R10	

(NOTE: An unusual bi-merchant muling.)

(112) 165GT-7fD	(WEIGHELL & SONS) Same	1427	Silvered-BR	PL	R9	
(113) 165GL-2i	(A.B. WILSON) Same	Same (1019)	Z	PL	R9	
(114) 165GS-6b	(ROBERT WRIGHT) Same	Same (1019)	BR	PL	R9	
(115) 165GS-10Aa	Same	1192	C	PL	R8	
(116) 165GX-3f	(JOS. ZANONE) Same	Same (1274)	S	PL	R9	

CLEVELAND, OHIO

(117) 175G-4d	(D.W. GAGE) Same	Same (1047)	C-N	R	R10	
(118) 175N-7a	(J.P. SHERWOOD) Same	1034	C	R	R9	

COLUMBIANA, OHIO

(119) 190A-3i1	(ICENHOUR & CO) Same	Same (1313)	Z	PL	R10	
(120) 190B-4d	(G. KIPP) Same (as Obv. OHIO 190B-2)	Same (1047)	C-N	R	R10	

Number	Obverse	Reverse	Metal	Edge	Rarity	H&G

COLUMBUS, OHIO

(121) 200A-6b — (JOHN GRETHER) Same (Error - "IMPORORTER") — Same (1042) — BR — R — R9

FINDLAY, OHIO

(122) 300A-1bo1 — (BOGER & KIMMEL) Same, Struck over a Lincoln token: DeW. AL 1864-37 — Blank — BR — R — R9

FRAZEYSBURG, OHIO

(123) 310A-2d — (E.L. LEMERT) Same — Same (1046) — C-N — R — R10

LANCASTER, OHIO

(124) 440C-3d — (CHAS. PAIRAN) Same — Same (1166) — C-N — PL — R9

MONROEVILLE, OHIO

(125) 560A-7b — (R.G. MARTIN) Same — Same (1087) — BR — PL — R9

NORTH HAMPTON, OHIO

(126) 645B-2i — (G.W. McLEAN) Same — Same (1046) — Z — R — R9

PUTNAM, OHIO

(127) 755A-1d — (L. WILES) Same, double-struck — Same (1126) — C-N — PL — R10

SHELBY, OHIO

(128) 805A-3b — (CUMMINS & ANDERSON) Same — Same (1043) — BR — R — R9 — 8784

TIFFIN, OHIO

(129) 850A-3d — (M.J. KIRCHNER) Same — Same (1047) — C-N — R — R10

WILMINGTON, OHIO

(130) 935A-6a — (MRS. OWENS & TAYLOR) Same — 1124 — C — PL — R9

Number	Obverse	Reverse	Metal	Edge	Rarity	H&G

WOOSTER, OHIO

(131)	975B-6d	(J.R. BOWMAN) Same	Same (1047)	C-N	R	R10	
(132)	975N-1b	(L. STRAUB) L. STRAUB/5/CENTS/ WOOSTER, O.	***NEW MERCHANT*** JOHN STANTON/ STAMP/& BRAND/ CUTTER/CINCINNATI.	BR	PL	R9	

975N Obv.

975N Rev.

PITTSBURGH, PA.

(133)	765E-6d	(JOS. FLEMING) Same	Same (1047)	C-N	R	R10	
(134)	765F-3d	(W.A. GILDENFENNEY) Same	Same (1047)	C-N	R	R10	
(135)	765F-5i	Same	Same (1192)	Z	PL	R9	
(136)	765Q-13d	(JOHN W. PITTOCK) Same	1069	C-N	R	R10	

PROVIDENCE, R.I.

(137)	700C-3a/b	(CHARNLEY) Same	Same (1374)	C/BR	PL	R10	

(NOTE: Struck on an unusual copper/brass planchet. On the obverse, 50% of the planchet is red copper and 50% is bright yellow brass with a straight line of demarcation down the middle of the planchet dividing the two metals.)

(138)	700C-5e1	Same, thin planchet	Same	W-M	PL	R8	
(139)	700C-6a/b	Same	Same (1429)	C/BR	PL	R10	

(NOTE: Struck on an unusual copper/brass planchet. On the reverse, 60% of the planchet is red copper and 40% is bright yellow brass with a straight line of demarcation dividing the two metals.)

(140)	700D-5a	(H. DOBSON) Same	1191	C	PL	R9	9691
(141)	700D-5b	Same	Same	BR	PL	R9	9692
(142)	700D-5c	Same	Same	N	PL	R9	9693
(143)	700D-5d	Same	Same	C-N	PL	R9	9694
(144)	700D-5e	Same	Same	W-M	PL	R9	
(145)	700D-5g	Same	Same	L	PL	R9	9696
(146)	700D-5j	Same	Same	G-S	PL	R9	9695

Number	Obverse	Reverse	Metal	Edge	Rarity	H&G

PROVIDENCE, R.I. (Continued)

(147) (FRANK L. GAY)
    700E-2b1   Same, thick planchet   Same   BR   PL   R8

(148) (H.Y. LEFEVRE)
    700F-1a1   Same, thin planchet   Same   C   PL   R8
(149)   700F-2g   Same   Same   L   PL   R9

(150) (PHILLIPS CITY FRUIT STORE)
    700G-1d   Same   Same (1147)   C-N   PL   R9
(151)   700G-2fo   Same, over U.S. Bust Dime   Same (1159)   S   PL   R9

(152) (POHLE)
    700H-2b   Same   ELMWOOD VINEYARD around border, Goblet (depicted) in center   BR   PL   R10   9627

(NOTE: This new reverse die was listed by H&G, but was omitted by Fuld as probably non-existent.)

700H-2 Rev.

(153) (F.W. SHATTUCK)
    700I-1d   Same   Same   C-N   PL   R9

CLARKSVILLE, TENN.

(154) (ANDREW KING)
    130A-3d   Same   Same (1047)   C-N   R   R10

MEMPHIS, TENN.

(155) (COSSITT HILL & CO.)
    600A-10bc   Same, C/S "10"   Same (1427)   BR   PL   R8
(156) (STOCKMAN & CO.)
    600F-1b   Same   Same (1158)   BR   PL   R9

| Number | Obverse | Reverse | Metal | Edge | Rarity | H&G |

MEMPHIS, TENN. (Continued)

(157)
600G-1bc   (WESTERN FOUNDRY)   ***NEW MERCHANT***
           WESTERN FOUNDRY/   1427   BR   PL   R9
           MEMPHIS TENNESSEE
           (C/S "25")

600G

690E-6 Obv.

690F Obv.

690F Rev.

NASHVILLE, TENN.

(158)
690E-6a   (WALKER & NAPIER)
           Similar, different spacing 1047   C   R   R9
           and comma after NASHVILLE
           (New Obverse Die)

(159)
690F-1bo   (N.L. TARBOX & CO)   ***NEW MERCHANT***
           N.L. TARBOX & CO/   Blank   BR   R   R9
           CHURCH ST/NASHVILLE TENN.
           (NOTE: Struck over Lincoln Political token DeW. AL 1864-37.)

KENOSHA, WIS.

(160)
330D-1Aa   (LYMAN MOWRY & CO.)
           Same   1110   C   PL   R8

Number	Obverse	Reverse	Metal	Edge	Rarity	H&G

MILWAUKEE, WIS.

(161)   (JOSEPH FISCHBEIN)
       510K-4a   Same   Obverse die incused   C   PL   R9

510K-4 Rev.

(162)   (WM. FRANKFURTH)
      510L-1b   Same   Same   BR   PL   R9
(163)   510L-1do   Same, over U.S.   Same   C-N   PL   R10
                             C-N cent of 1863
(164)   510L-3a1   Same   Same   C   R   R9
(165)   (C.E. GRAFF)
      5100-2a1   Same, Large   Same (1194)   C   PL   R8
                             flan (21.5 mm)
(166)   (CH. HERMANN & CO.)
      510R-5a1   Same   Same as Rev. of   C   R   R9
                                                   WIS. 510R-1a
(167)   (CHAS. KLEINSTEUBER)
      510V-4a   Similar to Rev. of   STALLION rearing   C   PL   R10
                             WIS. 510V-1a, but   (depicted)
                             different spacing   (New Reverse Die)
                             (new Die)

510V-4 Obv.

510V-4 Rev.

Number	Obverse	Reverse	Metal	Edge	Rarity	H&G

MILWAUKEE, WIS. (Continued)

(168) 510Ya-1b (MATSON & LOOMIS) ***NEW MERCHANT***
MATSON & LOOMIS/ N°̲ (in blank field)   BR   PL   R9
MILWAUKEE. WIS.
(NOTE: Reverse die is very similar to Rev. of MINN. 680A-3b.)

510Ya Obv. 510Ya Rev. 510AB-6 Rev.

(169) 510AB-6a (FRIEDRICH MILLER)
Same as Rev. of Obverse die incused   C   PL   R9
WIS. 510AB-1a

(170) 510AP-3Aa (H. UPMEYER)
Same   1156   C   PL   R9   10287
(NOTE: This is the variety listed as H&G 10287, therefore the WIS. 510AP-5a
and -5a1 varieties probably do not exist as described.)

RIPON, WIS.

(171) 720A-4A (GREENWAY & CO'S)
Same   Same (1047)   C-N   R   R10
(172) 720A-7d Same   1047   C-N   R   R10

SAUK CITY, WIS.

(173) 770A-3a (C. NEBEL)
Same   Obverse die incused   C   PL   R10
(double-struck rotated
130°), struck over
normal obverse.

770A-3 Rev.

Number	Obverse	Reverse	Metal	Edge	Rarity	H&G

WATERTOWN, WIS.

(174)
920D-1do1 (T. DERVIN)
           Same, struck over an   Same (1174)   C-N   PL   R10
           unidentified storecard
           (NOTE: This might be the piece described as 920D-1do over C-N cent.)

NON-LOCAL

(175)
NL-19Ad   (SIMMONDS BATTERY SUTLER--J.M. KERR)
           Same (C&S 155)   1069   C-N   R   R10

NON-CONTEMPORARY

(176)
NC-23d   (A.B. TAYLOR)
           Same   Same (1182)   C-N   PL   R9

(177)
NC-40Aa   (CENTRAL NATIONAL HOME FOR D.V.S.)
           Similar to NC-40a,   Similar to NC-40a,   C   PL   R8
           but different die   but "25"

NC-40Aa Obv.

NC-40Aa Rev.

NEW LISTINGS of NEW MERCHANTS under TENTATIVE LOCATIONS

CHICAGO, ILL.

(178)
150Wb-1b   (FWG)
           GOOD FOR/1/   1352A   BR   PL   R9
           CENTS/FWG
           (NOTE: Incused "1" stamped over denomination "4" and "FWG" incused -
           18mm. Tentatively listed under Chicago, ILL. with other pieces of this

| Number | Obverse | Reverse | Metal | Edge | Rarity | H&G |

CHICAGO, ILL. (Continued)

type. Evidence may be forthcoming placing this piece and others of this type under Baltimore, MD.)

150Wb
Obv.

INDIANAPOLIS, IND.

(179)
460AA-1b (JOHN WEILACHER)
JOHN WEILACHER/   C.C. NOYES/MAKER/   BR   PL   R9
5/CENTS/BILLIARDS/   27/S. MERIDIAN ST./
33/N. PENN ST.   INDIANAPOLIS, IND.
(NOTE: The size (22.5 mm), style, and execution of this piece is very similar to the thin brass John Stanton type pieces from Cincinnati, Ohio such as 165Q.)

460AA
Obv.

460AA
Rev.

CINCINNATI, OHIO

(180)
165Sa-1bo (A.A. BUDD)
A.A. BUDD/WATCHMAKER   Blank   BR   R   R9
(C/S "45") Struck over
Lincoln Political token
DeW. AL 1864-37
(NOTE: Tentatively listed under Cincinnati, Ohio with other pieces of this type.)

Number	Obverse	Reverse	Metal	Edge	Rarity	H&G

CINCINNATI, OHIO (Continued)

(181) (E.W. EVANS)
165AMc-1bo E.W. EVANS/WATCHMAKER   Blank   BR   R   R9
Struck over McClellan
political token
DeW. GMcC 1864-27.
(NOTE: Tentatively listed under Cincinnati, Ohio with other pieces of this type.)

165Sa Obv.

165AMc Obv.

CORRECTIONS AND REVISIONS
to the 2nd Edition of the Fuld Civil War Storecard Reference

Page	Line/Listing	Correction/Addition
XXIX	1st Row	Photo of Reverse Die 1146 is incorrect. Present photo is that of Patriotic Die 130. Insert correct photo of Reverse Die 1146. (NOTE: Die 1146 has braided beads around border.)
XXX	1st Row	Photo of Reverse Die 1178 is incorrect. Present photo is that of Storecard Die 1179. Insert correct photo of Reverse Die 1178.
XXX	1st Row	Add photo of <u>NEW</u> Reverse Die "1180A."

1146

1178

1180A

1252

Page	Line/Listing	Correction/Addition
XXXII	2nd Row	Photo of Reverse Die 1252 is incorrect. Present photo is that of Storecard Die 1253. Insert correct photo of Reverse Die 1252.
XXXIII	6th Row	Interchange die numbers 1307 and 1308.
XXXIII	6th Row	Add photo of <u>NEW</u> Reverse Die "1307A."
XXXV	1st Row	Add photo of <u>NEW</u> Reverse Die "1352A."

Page	Line/Listing			Correction/Addition
XXXVI	4th Row			Add photo of NEW Reverse Die "1404a."

      1307A   1352A   1404a

Page		Line/Listing	Correction/Addition
37	ILL.	890A-1a	Change reverse from "1105" to "1106."
37	ILL.	890C-1a	Change reverse from "1105" to "1106."
42	IND.	140A-1a1	Change edge from "PL" to "R."
82	IND.	550D-1a	Change reverse from "1084" to "1085."
84	IND.	550I-1a	Change reverse from "1084" to "1085."
92	IND.	630B-3a	Change reverse from "1077" to "1097."
116	KY.	510B-1ap	Change "510B-1ap" to "510B-1fp." Change metal from "C-pl" to "S-P/C."
153	MICH.	225AS-3d	Change rarity from "R10" to "R9."
153	MICH.	225AT-6d	Change rarity from "R10" to "R9."
155	MICH.	225AZ-3d	Change rarity from "R10" to "R9."
156	MICH.	225BA-4d	Change rarity from "R10" to "R9."
159	MICH.	225BM-4d	Change rarity from "R10" to "R9."
164	MICH.	225CE-3d	Change rarity from "R10" to "R9."
166	MICH.	225CJ-3d	Change rarity from "R10" to "R9."
167	MICH.	225CN-2d	Change rarity from "R10" to "R9."
210	MINN.	680A-3b	Change obverse description from "Same" to "Similar, but different larger die (24 mm)." Change reverse description from "Blank" to "N̲o̲ (in blank field)." Add photos of obverse and reverse dies.

680A-3 Obv.   680A-3 Rev.

24

Page	Line/Listing	Correction/Addition
222	N.Y. 10A-9a	Change obverse from "Obverse of 10A-4a" to "Obverse of 10A-6a (Rusted die)."
222	N.Y. 10A-10b	Change obverse from "Obverse of 10A-4a" to "Same as above."
229	N.Y. 95F-2b	Change rarity from "R10" to "R9."
232	N.Y. 105J-5d	Change rarity from "R10" to "R9."
239	N.Y. 630C-4do	Change rarity from "R10" to "R9."
241	N.Y. 630H-1do	Change rarity from "R10" to "R9."
246	N.Y. 630N-1b	Add "Lg. -25 mm." Add photos of obverse and reverse dies.

630N-1b Obv.

630N-1b Rev.

257	N.Y. 630AM-1h	Change rarity from "R10" to "R9."
260	N.Y. 630AQ-4fob	Change "630AQ-4fob" to "630AQ-4fol." Change rarity from "R10" to "R9."
276	N.Y. 630BV-17a	Change reverse from "1006" to "1000."
283	N.Y. 640A-3d	Change rarity from "R10" to "R9."
283	N.Y. 665A-3d	Change rarity from "R10" to "R9."
283	N.Y. 665B-3d	Change rarity from "R10" to "R9."
300	OHIO 74A-16a	Change rarity from "R9" to "R7."
325	OHIO 165AK-5e	Change reverse from "1270" to "1279."
332	OHIO 165BAa-1a	Add photos of obverse and reverse dies.

165BAa Obv.

165BAa Rev.

333	OHIO 165BF-4d	Change rarity from "R10" to "R9."
339	OHIO 165BT-13a	Add: "(NOTE: Probably does not exist as described.)"

25

Page	Line/Listing		Correction/Addition
352	OHIO	165CY-71a 165CY-71b	Add: "(NOTE: May not exist.)"
365	OHIO	165DY-12a	Change note on reverse description to correctly read: "Rev. Ohio 165FN-1."
371	OHIO	165ER-10a	Change to correctly read "165ER-10d."
374	OHIO	165EZ-1	Change BRASS variety to correctly read "165EZ-1b."
374	OHIO	165EZ-2m	Change obverse description from "Same" to "Similar, but figure divides date 1869." Add: "(NOTE: This variety is obviously Post-Civil War with an 1869 date.)" Add photos of obverse and reverse dies.

165EZ-2m Obv.

165EZ-2m Rev.

Page	Line/Listing		Correction/Addition
374	OHIO	165EZ-3a	Change obverse description from "Same" to "Same as OHIO 165EZ-1."
377	OHIO	165FF-6d	Change edge from "R" to "PL."
377	OHIO	165FH-8d	Change edge from "R" to "PL." Add: "(NOTE: It is extremely unusual to find a C-N variety of the 1069 reverse die with a Plain edge.)"
381	OHIO	165FR-7d	Change edge from "R" to "PL."
384	OHIO	165FX-23d	Change rarity from "R10" to "R9."
390	OHIO	165GO-10d	Change edge from "R" to "PL."
392	OHIO	165GV-1a	Change reverse from "1084" to "1082."
399	OHIO	175D-1a	Change reverse from "1180" to "1180A."
401	OHIO	175H-2a	Change reverse from "1180" to "1180A."
401	OHIO	175J-2a	Change reverse from "1180" to "1180A."
401	OHIO	175K-1a	Change reverse from "1180" to "1180A."
403	OHIO	175O-3d	Change edge from "R" to "PL."
406	OHIO	185A-6a	Change rarity from "R9" to "R7."
408	OHIO	200C-2a	Change reverse from "1087" to "1086."
409	OHIO	200F-1a	Change reverse from "1180" to "1180A."
417	OHIO	330F-1a	Change reverse from "1085" to "1087."
417	OHIO	330F-2a	Delete this listing.
425	OHIO	445A-3a	Change reverse from "1086" to "1085."
429	OHIO	535A-4a	Change reverse from "1086" to "1085."
431	OHIO	560A-1a	Change reverse from "1085" to "1087."
432	OHIO	560A-7a	Change reverse from "1085" to "1087."
434	OHIO	597A-1a	Change reverse from "1299" to "1300."

Page	Line/Listing		Correction/Addition
477	PA.	13E-7a	Change obverse description from "Same" to "Similar, but no comma between ALLEGHENY and CITY, and different spacing of letters. (NOTE: A new obverse die.) Add photo of new obverse die and label "13E-7."

13E-7 Obv.

477	PA.	13E-8a	Change obverse from "Same" to "Same as PA. 13E-6."
498	PA.	765P-8e	Add note: "(thick 3½ mm.)"
516	W.VA.	890A-1a	Change reverse from "1084" to "1085."
518	W.VA.	890G-6a	Change reverse from "1303" to "1304."
527	WIS.	230J-2a	Change reverse from "1303" to "1304."
528	WIS.	250C-1a	Change reverse from "1084" to "1085."
529	WIS.	250F-1a	Change reverse from "1084" to "1085."
529		250F-2a	Delete this listing.
535	WIS.	330B-1a	Change H&G from "10006" to "10007."
535		330B-4a	Change H&G from "10007" to "10006."
544	WIS.	510A-2a	Insert photo of reverse.

510A-2 Rev.

544	WIS.	510B-2a	Change rarity from "R10" to "R9."
550	WIS.	510R-5a	Change reverse description from "Same" to "Same as Rev. of WIS. 510R-1a."

27

Page	Line/Listing	Correction/Addition
551	WIS. 510U-3	Photo of 510U-3 is incorrect. Insert correct photo.
558	WIS. 510AO-3a	Insert photo of reverse.
558	WIS. 510AP-2ao	Add photo of reverse. Label present photo "510AP-2 Obverse."

510U-3
Rev.

510AO-3
Rev.

510AP-2
Rev.

600A-2
Rev.

Page	Line/Listing	Correction/Addition
562	WIS. 600A-2a	Insert photo of reverse.
563	WIS. 620D-1a	Change reverse from "1178" to "1179."
564	WIS. 620F-1a	Change reverse from "1178" to "1179."
566	WIS. 620L-1a	Change reverse from "1084" to "1085."
566	620L-3a	Change reverse from "1178" to "1179."
569	WIS. 700D-1a	Change rarity from "R6" to "R5."
569	700D-2a	Change rarity from "R6" to "R5."
569	WIS. 700E-3g	Add: "(NOTE: This lead piece appears to be a cast counterfeit.)"
570	WIS. 700I	Label present photo "700I-1."

Page	Line/Listing	Correction/Addition
570	WIS. 700I-2a	Change obverse description from "Same" to "Similar, but different spacing. (New obverse die.)" Add photo of new obverse die and label "700I-2."

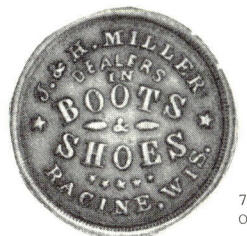

700I-2
Obv.

| 575 | WIS. 920C-1a | Change reverse from "1084" to "1085." |
| 579 | WIS. 960E-1a | Change reverse from "1084" to "1085." |

NON-LOCALS

580	NL-8b	Add photo of obverse die and label "NL-8 Obv."
581	NL-11a	Change reverse from "1084" to "1082."
581	NL-13b	Change reverse from "1394" to "1396."
581	NL-15b	Change reverse from "1404" to "1404a." Add: "(NOTE: This is a new reverse die-photo of which is inserted under Reverse Die Photos.)"
582	NL-24b	Add photo of obverse die and label "NL-24 Obv."

NL-8
Obv.

NL-24
Obv.

| 584 | NL-30b | Change reverse from "1394" to "1396." |
| 584 | NL-32b | Change reverse from "1404" to "1404a." |

Page	Line/Listing	Correction/Addition
584	NL-33b	Change obverse description from "Same" to "Similar, but different spacing and larger die - 26 mm." (New die) Add photos of obverse and reverse dies.

NL-33
Obv.

NL-33
Rev.